MEDIEVAL ENGLISH ANCESTORS OF ROBERT[1] ABELL

WHO DIED IN REHOBOTH, PLYMOUTH COLONY,
20 JUNE 1663,
WITH ENGLISH ANCESTRAL LINES
OF OTHER COLONIAL AMERICANS

COMPILED BY

CARL BOYER, 3RD

CARL BOYER, 3RD
SANTA CLARITA, CALIFORNIA
2001

ISBN 0-936124-22-9

CARL BOYER, 3RD
P.O. BOX 220333
SANTA CLARITA, CALIFORNIA 91322-0333

PRINTED IN THE U.S.A.

TABLE OF CONTENTS

INTRODUCTION

This work was intended to be limited to the ancestors of Robert Abell, but naturally includes the lines of many other colonial Americans, for whom connections will be found in David Faris' *Plantagenet Ancestry of Seventeenth-Century Colonists*, the second edition of which was published by the New England Historic Genealogical Society in 1999, and Frederick Lewis Weis' *Ancestral Roots of Certain American Colonists*, the seventh edition of which was published by the Genealogical Publishing Company, Inc., in 1992.

Indeed, this volume and *Medieval English Ancestors of Certain Americans* (published two days ago after an unanticipated delay of several weeks at the book manufacturer) were prepared as one volume which was simply too large for the market, and thus was split just prior to indexing. The symbol $^+$ indicates that a line is carried on in the other title. This volume does include, for example, Thomas^J Beauchamp and Katherine^J de Mortimer, ancestors of William Bladen, George, Giles and Robert Brent, Elizabeth Bosvile, St. Leger Codd, Edward Digges, Warham Horsmanden, Anne Humphrey, Anne Mauleverer, Philip and Thomas Nelson, Herbert Pelham, Katherine St. Leger, Maria Johanna Somerset and John West, as well as John^G de Sutton and Elizabeth^G de Berkeley, ancestors of Dannett Abney, Agnes Mackworth, Elizabeth Marshall, John and Lawrence Washington and Mary Wolseley. These are two of a number of lines ancestral to dozens of colonial Americans.

Among Robert Abell's ancestors were some of particular notoriety. Sir Bartholomew^L de Badlesmere joined the rebellion led by the Earl of Lancaster after Bartholomew's wife refused Queen Isabel (wife of King Edward II) admission to Leeds Castle on her journey home from France; he was hanged and drawn and quartered. William^L de Beauchamp was renowned for a victory at Maes Madog in 1282 over the Welsh, who were defending their own country, causing "a very great slaughter." Thomas^J Beauchamp was one of several treated herein who were among the original members of the Order of the Garter in 1349; Thomas^J de Beauchamp, William^K de Bohun, Sir Richard^K Fitz Alan, Sir Ralph^K de Stafford, Sir John^K de Stanley, Sir John^J de Stanley, John^G Talbot and John^H Talbot were also K.G.

Elizabeth^D Brereton (wife of Sir Randel^D Mainwaring) was a sister of Sir William Brereton, who was sentenced to die at Tyburn for being too familiar with Queen Anne Boleyn (one of Henry VIII's six wives); Anne was herself executed two days later.

Many were high officials in the English government. Some served as diplomats to the Pope and foreign courts. More than a few spent most of their lives at war. Some were married young, as young as at the age of five or six, even if following these marriages they returned home with their parents. Sir John^J Butler of Lancashire campaigned in Gascony, Aquitaine and Ireland, served in the embassy to Portugal, and was part of an expedition to Barbary in North Africa.

Vivian^N de Davenport was Sergeant of the Peace for Cheshire, and had the power of life and death, without delay or appeal, over thieves, robbers, murderers and cutpurses.

Hugh^N le Despenser, one of the few who supported King Edward II, was tried without being allowed to speak in his own defense, and hanged on the common gallows. His son suffered a worse fate.

Hugh^O Dutton of Dutton was awarded the magistracy of all the letchers and whores of Cheshire; hundreds of years later the family held the right to license the fiddlers who played in the bawdy houses and taverns.

Robert^N de Ferrers was sent to the Tower by Simon de Montfort and was later imprisoned at Windsor Castle by the King. He was not the only one to play both sides.

According to legend Sir John^M Fitz Thomas Fitz Gerald was rescued, as a baby, from a burning castle by a monkey.

Sir John^I Ipstones was a robber, murderer and kidnapper who forced an heiress (Maude^I

de Swynnerton, widow of Humphrey de Peshall) to marry his son. While attending Parliament, John was finally murdered in turn by Roger de Swynnerton, Maude's uncle, who was pardoned by the King for his crime.

Most notorious was Sir Roger[K] de Mortimer, the first Earl of March, who married well, but enjoyed great financial benefit from being the lover of Queen Isabel; it has been said that he murdered Edward II by sticking a hot poker up the King's anus. He took charge of England until Edward III reached adulthood, but was weeks later hanged in the nude at Tyburn. Nonetheless, Edward III's granddaughter, Philippa Plantagenet, married Roger's great-grandson, Edmund Mortimer.

The ancestry of Owain[M] ap Gruffudd ap Gwenwynwyn de la Pole can be traced back as far as one cares to believe.

Sir John[K] de Stanley, who died in 1414, was the most recent ancestor of Robert Abell to be a sovereign, in this case of the Isle of Man. He and a number of his more recent lineage were Knights of the Garter.

Sir John[G] de Sutton was an ancestor of Presidents Washington, Cleveland, Hoover and Ford, as is detailed in *Ancestors of American Presidents*, which is at this time out of print.

Sir John[H] Talbot, K.G., first Earl of Shrewsbury, was called "the great Alcides of the Field" by William Shakespeare, who cast him as the hero of *Henry VI*, part 1. Taken prisoner in 1429 by the French under Joan of Arc, he lived to defeat the French in many battles, and was killed in battle in 1453 at the age of eighty. His death is portrayed in a painting in the Gallery of Battles in the Palace of Versailles.

This compiler welcomes corrections and additions, and criticism, and is publishing a small number of this edition with a view to putting out at least one revision, perhaps several. Citation of sources will be expected, and copies of the sources would be welcomed if they are of a rare nature.

The place index should be used by descendants who are planning to travel to England and Normandy, and may reveal to some readers some connections between families not deduced previously by those of us who have put our work into print.

Perhaps it should be mentioned that while internet research has been treated with the distain it deserves for the most part, much of the work of locating printed sources was done at home on computers.

If this volume is received well it will become possible for the compiler to spend time in the Newberry Library and the British Library, as examples, doing even more research.

Carl Boyer, 3rd

P.O. Box 220333
Santa Clarita, California 91322-0333
cboyer@sosinet.net

8 April 2001

ABELL

By the sixteenth century there were several branches of the Abell family in Derbyshire, England. The brothers John and Richard Abell were the progenitors of the branch at Creighton and Uttoxeter. Richard died before 1536. Henry Abell, who died in 1540, was the earliest known member of the Sommersall branch. Nicholas Abell, the first known member of the Norbury branch, died about 1557. The fourth branch of the family, at Stapenhill, was descended from Robert^C Abell, below [Abell].

The sources have been rechecked and confirmed by Gary Boyd Roberts and others. The registers of Stapenhill and Ticknell, Derbyshire, and Newborough, Staffordshire, date from the 1660s; those of Lockington, Leicestershire, date from 1557.

Although the marriage of Mary^2 Abell to Samuel^2 Luther has been assumed for many years by genealogists (including the renowned Donald Lines Jacobus), Robert Charles Anderson, in the first volume of *The Great Migration Begins* (1995), has called attention to the fact that this marriage has not been documented with reference to original sources.

1. ROBERT^C ABELL, Esquire, of Stapenhill, Derbyshire, England, was of record there about 1533-1538 in a complaint brought by one Walter Blount [see *Chancery Proc. Early 725/38, 738/10*], and in a deed dated 1547.

A Robert Abell, gentleman, was a servant or tenant to Sir William Gryseley and was at Bryslincote, Derbyshire, in 9 Henry VIII (1517-1518) [see *Star Chamber Proc. 19/159*].

Children, listed from family wills:

      i.   Anthony^B, d. 1559; m. (1) Elizabeth, m. (2) Elizabeth; of Ticknall, Derbyshire, gent.

      ii.   George, d. 1597 [*P.C.C. Cobham 43*]; m. Helene; of Newborough, Staffordshire, and Stapenhill.

2.   iii. Robert, d. 1588; m.

      iv.   daughter, m. Royle.

      v.   Anne, d. 1577; unm.

2. ROBERT^B ABELL, of Stapenhill and Ticknell, Derbyshire, England, left a will dated 18 March 1587/8, which was proved in London 17 May 1588 [*P.C.C. Rutland 33*] by Edward Orwell, notary public.

His wife, not mentioned in his will, apparently died before him.

Child, only one mentioned in will:

3.   i.   George^A, d. 1631; m. Wrenbury, Cheshire, 1 May 1599, Frances^A Cotton.

3. GEORGE^A ABELL, Gentleman, born probably in Stapenhill, Derbyshire, about 1561, was buried in Lockington, Leicestershire, England, 13 Sept. 1630.

He married in Wrenbury, Cheshire, 1 May 1599, FRANCES^A COTTON*, who was living in 1630.

Of Stapenhill in Derbyshire, and Hemington in the parish of Lockington, he matriculated at Brasenose College, Oxford, 8 Dec. 1578, aged 17, and was admitted to the Inner Temple in 1581 [Thompson, *TG*, 5:162, cited Joseph Foster's *Alumni Oxoniensis, 1500-1714* (4 vols., London, 1891), 1:2, and supra, note 35, as well as F.A. Inderwick, *et al.*, *A Calendar of the Inner Temple Records* (5 vols., London, 1896-1936), 1:331, 336]. He inherited "all the tithes of Ticknall" belonging to his father in 1588. His will, dated 8 Sept. 1630 and proved 7 Feb. 1630/1 [*P.C.C. St. John 10*], named "my brother Andrew Cotten of Cumbermeer in ye Countie of Chester gent" to invest a bequest of £10 for the benefit of Richard Abell, the third son, who was still an apprentice. Andrew Cotton was also named sole executor of the will, with authority to dispose of the residue of the estate for the benefit of George Abell's widow and eldest son "with ye advise of my brother George Cotton of Cumbermere aforesaid esquier" [Thompson, *TG*, 5:160].

Another item in his will read, "I bequeath unto my second sonne Robert Abell onelie a Twentie shillings peece for his childs parte in regard of ye charges I have beene at in placeing him in a good trade in London wch hee hath made noe use of and since in furnishing him for newe England where I hope he now is."

Thompson [*ibid.*] has built a substantial case for the identification of George Abell's wife Frances Cotton, discussing the known relationships and concluding, "the only possible brotherly relationship between George Abell and George and Andrew Cotton of Combermere must arise from the marriage of their sister Frances to George Abell from Hemington. Moreover, Frances (Cotton) Abell must have been the mother of the children, for otherwise her brothers would have had no particular enthusiasm for the protection of their financial interests."

Children, born in England:

      i.   George[1], eldest son; m. Mary Stanford [Faris, *PA2*]; perhaps moved to Connecticut.

4.   ii.   Robert, d. Rehoboth, Plymouth Colony, 20 June 1663; m. Joannah.

     iii. Richard, third son, an apprentice in 1631.

     iv. Mary, received bequests from her aunt Dorothy Cotton, spinster, by will dated 16 April 1646.

4.   ROBERT[1] ABELL, born in England, perhaps in Hemington, Leicestershire, or Stapenhill, Derbyshire, probably about 1605, died in Rehoboth, Plymouth Colony, 20 June 1663 [1:50].

He married, possibly in England [Abell, 43], but more likely in Weymouth, Massachusetts Bay, by 1639, JOANNAH, who married second, in Rehoboth [1:44], 4 June 1667, William[1] Hyde, and died in Norwich, Connecticut, after 1682, having survived her second husband.

According to his father's will, Robert Abell had been placed "in a good trade in London wch hee hath made noe use of." His father then furnished him for New England, and it is probable he came to America with Governor Winthrop's fleet, arriving at Charlestown, Massachusetts Bay, in June 1630.

His name was mentioned occasionally in the records of the Quarterly Courts at Boston and Weymouth. He requested freeman's status on 19 Oct. 1630 and was admitted 18 May 1631 [*Records of the Governor and Company of the Massachusetts Bay in New England, 1628-1686*, Shurtleff ed. (1853), 1:80, 366, cited by Robert Charles Anderson, *The Great Migration Begins*, 1:3]. He was granted land in Weymouth, but had no holdings there at the time of the inventory of 1643 [R.C. Anderson, 1:4]. From 1631 to 1638 there is no record of Robert Abell in New England. According to Coldham [R.C. Anderson, *Great Migration Begins*, 1:6], on 6 April 1638, "John Arrat, his wife and child, Robert Abell, John Clerke, Edmund Fole and Peter Talbot, sawyer, who were going to New England, say they are willing to go to Providence."

Although he was not among the original proprietors of Rehoboth in the meetings at Weymouth as early as 24 Oct. 1643, he apparently purchased Job Lane's share before the settlement was made. He was among those who drew lots for lands in the new meadow 18 Feb. 1646, and on 26 Feb. 1651/2 he and Richard Bullock were chosen to burn the commons and be paid 20/- out of the first rate. On 1 Feb. 1654 he was ordered to keep the Ordinary, or restaurant, in Rehoboth, and he was a member of the jury at the General Court in Plymouth on 3 June 1657. His name, and the names of his heirs, has been found on lists of lot drawings in 1658 and 1668. The inventory of his estate, taken 9 August 1663, and which included four books, totaled £354.17s.9d, of which £130 was the value of his home and land. His widow was administratrix of his estate.

Through their son Caleb they were ancestors of President Grover Cleveland [Roberts' *Ancestors of American Presidents*].

Children, of record at Weymouth, Rehoboth and Norwich:

  i. Abraham[2], bur. Weymouth, Mass., 14 Nov. 1639 [8:348].

  ii. Mary, b. Weymouth 11 April 1642 [8:348]; m. by 1663 Samuel[2] Luther [original evidence not found by Torrey].

  iii. Preserved, b. Rehoboth say 1644; d. there 18 August 1724; m. (1) Rehoboth 27 Sept. 1667 Martha Redaway [1:45; R.L. Bowen's *Early Rehoboth*, 1:133-135], m. (2) 27 Dec. 1686 Sarah[2] Bowen, m. (3) int. Rehoboth 30 Dec. 1706 Mrs. Anne West of Boston.

  iv. Caleb, b. c. 1647; d. Norwich, Conn., 7 August 1731, in 85th year; m. (1) Norwich July 1669 Margaret Post [18], m. (2) 25 June 1701 Mary (Miller) Loomer.

  v. Joshua, b. say 1649; d. 1 March 1725, bur. Norwich; m. (1) 1 Nov. 1677 Mehitobell Smith [30], who d. there 14 March 1684/5 [30], m. (2) Nov. 1685 Bethiah[3] Gager [30].

  vi. Benjamin, d. Norwich 1699; m. c. 1678 Hannah (?Baldwin), who m. (2) David Caulkins, Sr.

  vii. Experience, d. after 5 June 1705; m. Guilford, Conn. [recorded Norwich VR, 55], 1680, John Baldwin.

  viii. child, name unknown, mentioned in father's will, which enumerated oldest son, dau. Mary and five others.

§ § §

L'ARCEDEKNE

The Maryland Genealogical Society Bulletin, 31 (1989-1990), 137-153, and Cokayne's *Complete Peerage* have been consulted. The family name also appears as Archdeacon.

1. Sir THOMAS[N] L'ARCEDEKNE died after 1274.
He married ALICE.
Child:
 2. i. Otes[M], d. 1289/90; m. Amice.

2. OTES[M] L'ARCEDEKNE died in 1289/90.
He married AMICE.
Child:
 3. i. Thomas[L], m. (1) Alice de la Roche, m. (2) Maud.

3. Sir THOMAS[L] L'ARCEDEKNE, Lord Arcedekne, of Ruan Lanihorne, Cornwall, died shortly before 21 Aug. 1331 [G.W. Watson in *CP*, 1:186-187].
He married first Alice de la Roche, third daughter of Thomas[J] de la Roche of Roch Castle, Pembrokeshire, Wales.
He married second MAUD, who died after 11 June 1362.

He was governor of Tintagel Castle in 1312, and of record as Sheriff of Cornwall at Michaelmas 1313/4. He was summoned to Parliament from 15 May 1321 to 13 Sept. 1324. His arms were Silver with three chevrons sable.

Child, by second wife, from the pedigree:

4.   i.   John[K], aged 25 and more on 15 Sept. 1331; m. 23 Dec. 1327 Cecily[K] Haccombe.

4. Sir John[K] L'ARCHEDEKNE, of Ruan Lanihorne, Cornwall, born about 1306, died between 30 Oct. 1371 [*CP*, 14:32] and 21 Dec. 1377.

He married by papal dispensation (for being within the fourth degree of consanguinity), 23 Dec. 1327, Cecily[K] HACCOMBE of Haccombe, Devonshire, who was living in 1365. Her parents were Jordan[L] Haccombe of Haccombe [*CP*, 1:187], who was living about 1300, and his wife Isabel St. Aubin, daughter of Mauger de St. Aubin.

His will was proved at Clyst in Devon on 27 Jan. 1390/1.

Children, from the *Complete Peerage* and pedigree:

i.   Ralph (or Stephen)[J], d. before 21 Dec. 1377; no issue; was called Ralph in a fine of 1365, but Stephen in his father's *inquisition post mortem*.

5.   ii.   Warine, d. 1400; m. Elizabeth[I] Talbot.

5. Sir Warine[J] L'ARCHEDEKNE of Ruan Lanihorne, Cornwall, died without male issue shortly before 10 Dec. 1400. The name is given as l'Archdeacon in Roberts' *RD500*, 374.

He married Elizabeth[I] TALBOT*, who died 3 Aug. 1407. Her will, dated 12 Dec. 1406, was proved at Crediton 7 Aug. 1407.

Children, listed by Watson in *CP*, 1:186:

*   i.   Eleanor[I], m. (1) Sir Walter[I] Lucy, m. (2) Henry Barrett.
    ii.   Philippe, m. Sir Hugh Courtenay.
    iii.   Margery, m. Thomas Arundell [*cf. CP*, 8:262a].
    iv.   Elizabeth, d. before marriage, but betrothed 12 March 1400/1 to Otes Trevarthian, son and heir of Sir John Trevarthian.

§ § §

DE ARDERNE OF ALDFORD

Aldford is in Edisbury Hundred, Cheshire.

Eustace[P] DE ARDERNE, also called de Watford, of Watford, Northamptonshire, was deceased in 1213.

Sir John[O] DE ARDERNE was grantee of the fee of Aldford after 10 John (1208-1209) and by 13 Hen. III (about 1210-1229). According to a pedigree he married Margaret[O] DE ALDFORD, daughter and heiress of Richard de Aldford, Lord of Aldeford, Cheshire.

Sir Walkelin[N] DE ARDERNE was Lord of Aldeford, in Edisbury Hundred, Cheshire, from 1237 to 1265. He married Agnes[N] DE ORREBY, only daughter and heir of Sir Philip de Orreby, Lord of Alvanley and Elford, Staffordshire.

Sir Peter[M] DE ARDERNE was Lord of Aldford in 1265; his *inquisition post mortem* was dated 20 Edw. I (1291-1292). His wife Margery (or Margaret) was noted as the mother of Sir John.

5. Sir John[L] DE ARDERNE, born about 1266, was aged 26 in 20 Edw. I (1291-1292), according to his father's *inquisition post mortem*, and died about 1308.

He married MARGARET[L] FERCH GRUFFUDD AP MADOG (a daughter of the last Prince of Powys Fadog in Wales), of Bromfield and of the Castle of Dinas Bran near Llangollen. She was a widow in 8 Edw. II [Earwaker's *East Cheshire*, 1:473; Ormerod, 3:566].

Children, listed by Ormerod [2:85, 3:566]:

6. i. Sir John[K], d. 23 Edw. III (c. 1350); m. (1) Alice de Venables, m. (2) Joan (de Stokeport) de Eton, m. (3) Elen[K] de Wastneys.
    ii. Maude (or Matild[a]), d. 1323/4 [Farrer, *VCH Lancs.*, 4:211]; m. (1) John[K] Legh of Bothes, m. (2) John de Warwick [Ormerod, 2:482].
    iii. Margery, l. c. 1318.
    iv. Agnes, m. John de Wetenhall.

6. Sir JOHN[K] DE ARDERNE, of Alford and Elford, was of record 11 Edw. II (1337-1338); his *inquisition post mortem* was dated 23 Edw. III (1349-1350).

He married first, in 1307/8, Alice [see Ellen[K]] de Venables, daughter of Hugh de Venables, Baron of Kinderton [Ormerod, 2:78; Earwaker's *East Cheshire*, 1:474].

He married second Joan (or Jane) de Stokeport, daughter and coheiress of Sir Richard de Stokeport, Baron of Stokeport (Stockport in Cheshire), and the widow of Sir Nicholas de Eton [Ormerod, 2:78]. She had children by her first marriage, but none by her second.

He married third, 1346, ELEN[K] DE WASTNEYS, who had previously been his concubine, daughter of William[L] de Wastneys. She was his cousin and died between 13 July and 23 Dec. 1349. The compiler presumes this was the William de Wastneys who married Cecily[L] de Arderne, above.

As a minor he was ward of Hugh de Venables, Baron of Kinderton [Earwaker, *East Cheshire*, 1:463].

He was Lord of Al[de]ford, son and heir, and Knight of the Shire of Stafford in 1324, when he was summoned to attend the Great Council at Westminster.

Child, by first wife [Ormerod, 2:78]:

    i. John[J], b. before 1330; m. Cecily de Eton (div. 1322); no issue; she m. (2) Sir Edward Warren of Poynton.
    ii. Peter, b. 1327; m. Cicely de Bredbury.
    iii. Margaret, contracted in 4 Edw. III (1330-1331) to Nicholas de Eton; no issue.

Children, perhaps by first wife, mentioned 14 Edw. III (1340-1341):

    iv. Elizabeth.
    v. Aline.
    vi. Cecily.

Children, by third wife [Ormerod, 3:566]:

    vii. Sir Thomas, b. in or before 1328 before m. of his parents; d. 15 Ric. II (1391); m. in or before 1349 Katherine Stafford (l. 1349), dau. of Richard Stafford, Lord of Pipe, Staffs., by his wife Isabel[K] de Vernon [Douglas Richardson of Salt Lake City, Utah, cited as new references Ormerod's *Chester*, 2(1819):42 and 3:301, William Salt Archaeological Society, 13(1892):67, 89, 166, 183, 195, 201 (often cataloged as *Collections for a History of Staffordshire*), *Cal. IPM* 15(1970):145, *Calendar of Patent Rolls, 1334-1338* (393)] (Matilda, dau. of William Campville of Clifton Campville, Staffs., and of Aldford, Alderley and Elford in 19 Edw. III (1345-1346) was called his wife by Earwaker, who said that handsome monuments to this couple are in Elford Church, Staffs. [Earwaker, *East Cheshire*, 1:328]).

    viii.   Walclin, b. before m. of parents; mentioned 19 and 20 Edw. III (1345-1347); d. without issue; m. Cecily de Eton, from whom he was divorced.

    ix.   Katherine, m. Sir John Burdet; apparently no issue.

Children, youngest by third wife, legitimate according to Earwaker:

*   x.   Matild[e], m. Robert^J Legh of Adlyngton; she was coheir with her two sisters of Alice le Grosvenor of Budworth le Frith.

    xi.   Isabel, m. Sir Hugh de Wrottesley; both d. before 9 Hen. IV (1408).

§ § §

ATHERTON OF ATHERTON

This line was originally developed from the work of John C.J. Brown, "The Atherton Family in England," published in 1881 in volume 35 of *The New England Historical and Genealogical Register*, pages 67-72, but has been modified extensively, with citations.

According to John C.J. Brown, Robert de Atherton lived in the time of King John (who ruled from 1199 to 1216), was the Shreave, or High Sheriff, of Lancashire, England, held the Manor of Atherton of the Barons of Warrington, and had a son, William^N, recorded in a pedigree presented to Sir William Dugdale. William^N de Atherton held the manors of Atherton, Lancs., and Pennington in 1251, and had a son William^M, who married Agnes.

Farrer and Brownbill, editors of the *The Victoria History of the County of Lancashire*, wrote [3:436, with notes substituted for footnote numbers]: "Dependent before the Conquest on the chief manor of Warrington, of which it was one of the thirty-four berewicks or dependent manors held by drengs, Atherton was included in the Warrington fee upon the creation of that barony by Henry I, being held by the ancestor of de Atherton as one plough-land by the service of one mark yearly, and by knight's service, where ten ploughlands made the fee of one knight [*Rec. Soc.*, 48:9]. At the taking of the Inquest of Service in 1212, Henry son of William de Atherton held the manor of William le Boteler [*ibid.*]. In 1243 he was succeeded by another William [*Rec. Soc.*, 48:147], supposed to be the son of Henry, who was living in 1259 [Rot. Orig. 23, m. 2], and probably the father of another William, who was amerced before the justices at Lancaster in 1292 with his sons Alexander and Hugh [*Abbrev. Rot. Orig.*, 1:274; *Herald and Gen.*, 4:229] for not appearing to answer a plea [*Plac. de quo War.*, 607b], and with another son William attested a charter of Henry, lord of Tyldesley, about the year 1300 [*Lancs. and Ches. Hist. Notes*, 2:11b; *Chet. Soc.*, 84:120]. In 1298 he was enfeoffed of the manors of Haigh and Blackrod, apparently owing to some connexion by marriage with the Bradshagh family [*Rec. Soc.*, 39:185, 46:106]."

Perhaps inspection of the sources cited will help clarify this presentation. The *Victoria History of Lancashire*, 4:146 and 8:192-193, does not concern this line.

1. WILLIAM^M ATHERTON was of record in 1312, and died about 1315/6, when his son Henry was named Lord of Atherton.

He married before 1305 AGNES, who was living as "late the wife of William Atherton" on 21 June 1332, and was said to be of record in 1339.

Children, listed by Brown:

    2.   i.   Henry^L, m. Agnes.

          ii.   Alexander, m.; issue William, Agnes and Margery [*cf. Herald and Genealogist*, 4(1867):229].

         iii.   Margaret, m. Otho de Halsall, son of Gilbert de Halsall [Dugdale, *Vis. of Lancs.*, 20].

2. HENRY[L] ATHERTON of Atherton in the West Derby Hundred of Lancashire, was of record from 1315/6 to 1352.

He married AGNES, who was mentioned in 1387.

He was summoned in 1324 to attend the Great Council at Westminster on Wednesday after Ascension Day, as he held lands producing £15 annually. He was granted an exemption from knighthood in 1342 as he was very infirm. "In 1352 he settled the manor upon himself for life with remainder to his eldest and other sons successively in tail male" [Farrer, *VCH Lancs.*, 3:436]. In 1352 he was listed as possessing £40 worth of land, but averred that he had only 40/- worth, paid a fine and had another exemption.

Children, from the *Final Concords* [ed. Farrer, *Rec. Soc. Lancs. Cheshire*, 46:87]:

   3.   i.   William[K], m. (1) Jane[K] Mobberly, m. (2) Margerie.

        ii.   Richard [Dugdale].

        iii.   Roger.

3. Sir WILLIAM[K] ATHERTON was a knight in 1351 and died in 1389.

He married first JOAN[K] MOBBERLY* of Mobberley, Cheshire.

His second wife, Margerie, was mentioned as a widow in 1396.

He obtained permission from the Bishop of Lichfield for divine services to be held within his manors. The parish church of Leigh, which stands both in the townships of Pennington and West Leigh, contains private chapels for the family of Tidesley on the north, and for the Athertons on the south. A family vault lies within the Atherton chapel, and some escutcheons hang there. The arms were entered with William Dugdale, Norroy King of Arms, in 1664-65.

He was Knight of the Shire in Parliament in 1373, 1379 and 1381.

Both he and his son were deponents in 1386 in the Scrope and Grosvenor trial [Farrer, *VCH Lancs.*, 3:436].

Children, by first wife:

   4.   i.   William[J], m. Agnes[J] Vernon of Shipbrook.

        ii.   Sir Nicholas, d. 1420 [Roskell, *Hist. Parl.*, 2:82]; m. Joan de Bickerstaff of Ormskirk, Lancs. [Farrer, *VCH Lancs.*, 3:436].

4. Sir WILLIAM[J] ATHERTON of Atherton, Lancashire, England, died 29 Dec. 1414 [Farrer, *VCH Lancs.*, 3:346]

He married AGNES[J] VERNON*, sole daughter and heiress of Raphe Vernon, Baron of Shipbrook.

He had livery of her inheritance in 1397. He died seized of Shipbrook and other manors and lands in Cheshire.

Children:

        i.   Raphe[I], of record 1418; m. Alice.

        ii.   Katherine, m. Robert de Longley, when he was under 15.

   5.   iii.   William, m. (1) 1400 Elizabeth[I] Pilkington, m. (2) Eleanor.

5. Sir WILLIAM[I] ATHERTON was born about 1384, as he was aged 30 when his father died in 1414.

He married first, in 1400, ELIZABETH[I] PILKINGTON, daughter of Sir John[J] Pilkington.

He married second Eleanor, by whom he had no issue [Farrar, *VCH Lancs.*, 3:436].

The Victoria History of the County of Lancaster [3:242; 5:300] has not been helpful.

Children, by first wife, listed by Brown:

   *   i.   Margaret[H], m. John[H] de Dutton of Hatton, Cheshire, who was l. 1461.

   ii.   Sir William, d. 1440; m. Margaret (l. 1479), dau. of Sir John Byron; she m. (2) before 1443 [Farrer, *VCH Lancs.*, 3:436] Sir Robert Harcourt [Dugdale, 20].

        Children: 1. William, d. without issue before 1461, m. Isabella Balderston. 2. Nicholas. 3. John (sheriff of Durham 1461), d. 1488, m., had son George.

§ § §

AUDLEY

This data is from Cokayne's *Complete Peerage*, Weis' *Ancestral Roots* [9:30] and Geo. T. Clark's *The Lands of Morgan: Being a Contribution Towards the History of the Lordship of Glamorgan* (London: Whiting & Co., Lim., 1883). Aleyn Lyell Reade's *Audley Pedigrees* has been checked.

Norr mentioned a Peter Lydulphi, of record as the brother Adam de Stanlegh in 1117.

ADAM[P] DE AUDITHLEY, who died between 1201 and 1211, was son of Liulf[Q], son of Liulf[R]). Liulf[Q] had a grant of Audley, Staffordshire, from Nicholas de Verdun during the reign of King Stephen, which was from 1135 to 1154 [Norr, 9].

HENRY[O] DE AUDITHLEY was born about 1175. He married first Petronella, daughter of Aline, who was sister of Ralph de Derleston. He married second, in 1217, BERTRED[O] MAINWARING, daughter of Sir Ralph[P] le Mesnilwarin, Seneschal of Chester; she was living in 1249. Her marriage portion included Smallwood, Snelson, half of Picmere, and certain rentals in Chester [Croston, 366].

JAMES[N] OF AUDITHLEY, born about 1220, died in Ireland about 11 June 56 Hen. III (1272), of a broken neck. Although Norr stated that he married first Margaret, daughter of Margaret de Plessy, who was the father of his sons; this has been contradicted. He married, in 1244, his only wife ELA[M] LONGESPÉE, daughter and heir of Sir William de Longspée (a grandson of King Henry II) and Idoine de Camville.

4. HUGH[M] DE AUDLEY, a cadet of the Barons Audley of Heleigh Castle, was born about 1267 and died, probably at Wallingford Castle, between Nov. 1325 and March 1325/6, while a prisoner, his title having been forfeited by attainder.

He married before 7 Jan. 1293, and probably in 1288, as her second husband, ISOLDE[K] DE MORTIMER*, who was a daughter of Edmund[L] de Mortimer of Wigmore by a marriage earlier than his to Margaret de Fiennes [*NEHGR*, 116:16-17; Cokayne 1:346, 3:434, 5:736, 11:101-102], and widow of Sir Walter de Balun of Much Marcle in Herefordshire.

He obtained from his mother, soon after her husband's death in the first year of the reign of Edward I (1272-73), a reversionary grant of Stratton Audley, Oxon, which had been her inheritance. He also held Marcle Audley [Norr, 10].

He was in the French wars from 1294, and was a prisoner in France 2 April 1299. He served in the Scottish wars from 1299-1302 and in 1313, was in Gascony in 1304/5, served as Justice of North Wales in 1306, and as Governor of Montgomery Castle in 1309. At one time he was Ambassador to France.

He was summoned to Parliament 15 May 14 Edw. II (1322) [Cokayne, 1:346]. He participated in the rebellion the Earl of Lancaster in 1321/2, but surrendered before the battle of Boroughbridge was fought on 16 March 1321/2, and was confined in Wallingford Castle.

Children, mentioned by Norr:
   i.   Sir James[L], d. 1324.

5.   ii.   Hugh, d. 10 Nov. 1347; m. Windsor 28 April 1317 Margaret[L] de Clare.
*   iii.   Alice, b. c. 1300; d. Greystoke, Northumberland, 12 Jan. 1373/4 (or
           1374/75?), bur. Durham Cathedral; m. (1) Ralph Greystoke, 1st Lord
           of Greystoke, m. (2) c. 14 Jan. 1326/7 Ralph[K] de Neville, 4th Baron
           Neville of Raby.

5. HUGH[L] DE AUDLEY, Lord Audley and 8th Earl of Gloucester 1337, was born about 1289, died 10 Nov. 1347, and was buried in the Priory of Tunbridge.

He married at Windsor, 28 April 1317, MARGARET[L] DE CLARE*, widow of Piers de Gaveston, Earl of Cornwall (whom she had married first 1 Nov. 1307, and who was beheaded 19 June 1312). Piers was born in Béarn, Gascony, probably son of Sir Ernaud de Gavaston. Her parents were Gilbert de Clare, Earl of Gloucester and Hertford, and Joan Plantagenet, second daughter of King Edward I of England. Margaret was aged 22 in the *inquisition post mortem* of her brother 12 Oct. 8 Edw. II (1314), and died before Easter in April 1342.

He was summoned to Parliament from 1317, and participated with his father in the rebellion of 1321/2, but was pardoned. In 1336 he served the King in Scotland, and on 16 March 1336/7 he was created Earl of Gloucester, his wife having become in 1313 coheir to her brother Gilbert, Earl of Gloucester and Hereford.

He served as Ambassador to France in 1341.

His daughter Margaret carried to the Stafford family Thornbury and large estates in Monmouthshire and elsewhere which were passed to those Dukes of Buckingham of the Stafford family [Clark, 161]. However, the title Earl of Gloucester ceased to exist.

Daughter and heir, given by Geo. T. Clark [161], Cokayne and Norr [10]:
*   i.   Margaret[K], heiress, d. after 28 Jan. 1347/8 [d. 7 Sept. 1349 in Weis, *AR*7,
           9:31, or 16 Sept. 1348 in Faris, *PA*2, 6], bur. Tonbridge Castle, Kent;
           m. before 6 July 1336 Sir Ralph[K] de Stafford, K.G., who had abducted
           her and married her against her father's will.

§ § §

DE BADLESMERE

Leeds Castle has been restored heavily into a Victorian-Tudor structure. However, the bath of Edward I (now a boathouse), the vinyard, some of the towers and the village church nearby were familiar to Bartholomew[L] de Badlesmere.

1. BARTHOLOMEW[N] DE BADLESMERE died in 1248.

During the reign of King Henry II he was involved in a lawsuit with William de Cheney concerning property in Kent. He was also fined for trespassing in the royal forests, which was an offence for which a commoner could be put to death [Poole, *Historic Heraldic Families*, 10].

Children:
2.   i.   Guncelin[M], b. Chilham, Kent, c. 1232; d. 1301; m. Joan[M] Fitz Bernard,
          who d. 1310.
     ii. William, taken prisoner at Rochester [Poole, 10].

2. GUNCELIN[M] DE BADLESMERE, born in Chilham Castle, Kent, about 1232, died in 1301. Mention of his alleged wife may be omitted [*CP*, 14:57].

King Henry III had him excommunicated by the Archbishop of Canterbury [Poole, 10], but he fought the Welsh and French with distinction under Edward I.

Also known as Gunselm, he was Justice of Chester [*CP*, 1:371-372].

Children:

3.   i.   Bartholomew[L], b. Chilham Castle, Kent, 1275; hanged Canterbury 14 April 1322; m. by 30 June 1308 Margaret[L] de Clare.

*   ii.   Maud, l. 2 Jan. 1306; m. Robert[N] de Burghersh, who d. 1306.

3. Sir BARTHOLOMEW[L] DE BADLESMERE, born about 1275, was hanged as a traitor at Canterbury, Kent, 14 April 1322.

He was married by 30 June 1308, as her second husband, to MARGARET[L] DE CLARE*, who died in 1333. She had married first Gilbert de Umfraville, son of Gilbert, 8th Earl of Angus.

He attended the siege of Caerlaverock in 1300, and succeeded his father in 1301 at the age of 26. After serving in the Scottish wars in 1303 and 1304, he was Governor of Bristol Castle in 1307, and had a grant of the castle and manor of Chilham, Kent, in 1309, in exchange for the manor of Aldrihleye in Shropshire. He was granted Leeds Castle, Kent, and in 8 Edw. II (1314-1315) was made Governor of Skipton Castle and of all castles in Yorkshire and Westmorland which had been seized of the late Robert de Clifford, to hold during the minority of Clifford's son and heir.

From 26 Oct. 1309 to 15 May 1321 he was summoned to Parliament, although there is no proof he actually sat as a member. He also served as Steward of the King's Household. In the midst of the plot led by Queen Isabel and Roger[K] de Mortimer to overthrow King Edward II in 1321, Bartholomew's wife, "through the mouth of her castellan Walter Colepeper" [Poole, 11], had refused admission to Isabel at Leeds Castle as the Queen was returning from France to England. Edward II then besieged the castle, which fell on 11 Nov. 1321, and Margaret was imprisoned in the Tower of London until she was released on 3 Nov. 1322. She then stayed at the Minorities without Aldgate (at the King's charge) until 1 July 1324, when she was allowed to go to friends. Her husband joined the rebellion of the Earl of Lancaster, whom he joined in defeat at the battle of Boroughbridge on 16 March 1322, was captured at Snow Park and attainted before his execution at Canterbury, where he was hanged and drawn and quartered with about ninety other lords and knights [Poole, 12].

Children, by Margaret de Clare:

*   i.   Margery[K], b. 1306; d. 18 Oct. 1363; m. before 25 Nov. 1326 William[L] de Ros, 2nd Lord Ros, who d. 16 Feb. 1342/3.

   ii.   Maud, second dau. [*CP*, 10:223], m. (1) Robert Fitz Payn, who d. 1322, m. (2) before 27 March 1336 John de Vere, Earl of Oxford, who d. Rheims, France, 23 or 24 Jan. 1359/60.

   iii.   Margaret, d. c. 1344-1347; m. before 24 July 1337 Sir John Tibetot, 2nd Lord Tybotot, who d. 13 April 1367, aged 53, having m. (2) Elizabeth.

*   iv.   Elizabeth, fourth dau., d. 1356; m. (1) 27 June 1316 Edmund Mortimer, who d. 1331, m. (2) c. 1355 Sir William[K] de Bohun, who d. Sept. 1360.

   v.   Giles, b. Hambleton, Rutland, 18 Oct. 1314; d. by 22 June 1338, aged 24; m. after Feb. 1327/8 Elizabeth Montagu [*CP*, 1:373], who d. Ashley, Hampshire, 31 May 1359, bur. Tewksbury Abbey, having m. (2) before 1341 Hugh le Despenser, who d. 8 Feb. 1348/9, and m. (3) before 10 July 1350 Sir Guy de Bryan, who d. 17 Aug. 1390; no issue, but had obtained a reversal of his father's attainder in Nov. 1328.

§ § §

BAGGILEY

This pedigree was developed from George Ormerod's *History of Chester*, 1:550-551, 1:718 and 2:711-718.

1. RAUFE[M] BAGGILEY was the first of this line mentioned by Ormerod.
Child:
2.   i.   William[L], m. Clemence[L] de Chedle of Clifton, who m. (2) John de Molyneux.

2. WILLIAM[L] BAGGILEY was the second of the line.
He married CLEMENCE[L] DE CHEDLE* of Clifton in Cheshire, England, who was daughter and coheiress of Sir Roger[M] de Chedle, alias de Dutton. She married second John de Molyneux.
Child:
*   i.   Isabel[K], m. Sir Thomas[K] Daniell, Jr.

§ § §

DE BALLIOL

This entry was based on the entry for the "Ancient Lords of Galloway" in *The Scots Peerage* [4:135-144], and modified by I.J. Sanders [*English Baronies*, 25], who states the family name is from Bailleul en Vimeu, Hallencourt, arr. Abbeville in France.
A History of Northumberland (Newcastle-upon-Tyne, 1893-1940), volume 6, *passim*, might be of help.

1. BERNARD I[P] DE BALLIOL succeeded his uncle, Guy de Balliol (who was lord of Bywell in Northumberland during the reign of King William II Rufus), some time between 1102 and 1130, and died about 1150.
Child:
2.   i.   Bernard II[O], d. in 1186-1187.

2. BERNARD II[O] DE BALLIOL died in 1186-1187.
Child:
3.   i.   Eustace[N], d. 1200.

3. EUSTACE[N] DE BALLIOL died in 1200.
Child:
4.   i.   Hugh[M], d. 1228.

4. HUGH[M] DE BALLIOL, of Bywell and Barnard Castle, died in 1228.
He married CECILY DE FOUNTAINES.
Children:
5.   i.   John[N], d. 27 Oct. 1268; m. 1233 Devorguilla[N] of Galloway, who d. 28 Jan. 1289/90.
*   ii.   Ada, d. Stokesay 29 July 1251; m. John[O] Fitz Robert (for whom see Fitz Roger).

5. JOHN[N] DE BALLIOL, Lord Galloway of Barnard Castle, was born in Bywell, Northamptonshire, and died 27 Oct. 1268.

He married in 1233 DEVORGUILLA[N] OF GALLOWAY[+], who died 28 Jan. 1289/90 [Weis, *AR*7, 94:28], and was buried in New Abbey with the heart of her husband. She was a daughter of Alan, Lord of Galloway, and his second wife, Margaret of Huntingdon, whom he married in 1209.

He was sometime Regent of Scotland.

She endowed Balliol College at Oxford University, and built a bridge over the Nith at Dumfries. On 10 April 1273 she founded the Sweetheart or New Abbey in Galloway; she also established other religious institutions.

Children, listed by Sir James Balfour Paul [4:142-143]:

    i.   Sir Hugh[M], d. shortly before 10 April 1271; m. Agnes de Valencia, a niece of King Henry III; no issue; named in his mother's charter to Sweetheart (or New) Abbey.

    ii.   Alan, named only in the claim made by John Balliol for the crown of Scotland.

    iii.   Sir Alexander, styled Lord of Balliol, d. shortly before 13 Nov. 1278; m. Alianora de Geneva, who survived him, a kinswoman of Henry III; no issue.

    iv.   John, b. c. 1249; d. France 1313; m. before Feb. 1280/1 Isabella de Warenne; King of Scotland 1292-1296.

    v.   Cecily, b. Bywell, Notts.; d. before 1273; m. Sir John de Burgh, who d. 1279/80, Baron Lanvallei of Walkern.

    vi.   Ada, m. Whitsunday 1266 William Lindsay, son of Walter Lindsay of Lamberton.

*   vii.   Alianore (or Eleanor, Margaret), m. c. 1279-1283 Sir John[M] Comyn, "Black Comyn," who d. c. 1303.

§ § §

DE BAMVILLE

This line is based on George Ormerod's *History of Chester*, the second edition by Thomas Helsby.

1. Sir THOMAS[P] DE BAUMVILLE is the earliest known member of this family.

He married AGNES[P] DE STORETON, daughter and coheir of Alexander Magister (alias de Storeton), who was the tutor of Randle de Blundeville, 6th Earl of Chester, and Annabella de Storeton, sole daughter and heiress of Ralph fitz Alan Sylvester, who was son and heir of Alan Sylvester, the grantee of Storeton, Puddington and the master forestership of Wirral from Randle Meschines, 3rd Earl of Chester, about 1120 [Ormerod, *Chester*, 2:448]. Alexander Magister de Storeton had another daughter, Johanna (or Joan), wife of Richard de Kingsley, but she died young.

    Children:

2.   i.   Sir Philip[O], d. c. 1280; m. (1) de Pulford, m. (2) Letice Venables.

    ii.   Alexander, second son, m. Rose, widow of Robert de Stockport.

    iii.   Alice, m. (1) Sir Philip de Orreby, m. (2) Sir Will. Vernon.

    iv.   Annabel, m. Hugh de Corona (for whom see Legh of Adlington at #3).

2. Sir PHILIP[O] DE BAMVILLE died after 27 Sept. 1282.

He married first in Feb. 1265, probably NICHOLAA[K] DE PULFORD* [Irvine, *Transactions*, 105:52], a daughter of Sir Robert de Pulford.

He married second Letice Venables, daughter and heir of William Venables of Wincham. She married second Richard de Wilbraham, and third, in 1288, Robert Crosslegh [Irvine, 105:52], who had been her attorney.

Children, by first wife, who each had a third of Storeton:

*   i.   Joan[N], m. Astbury 27 Sept. 1282 William[N] de Stanley.
      ii.   Elen, m. William de Lakene.
     iii.   Agnes, m. John de Becheton (or Bechinton).

§ § §

BARDOLF

Cokayne's *Complete Peerage* [1:417-419 and 14:64-65] was the major source for this family.

An Iseulde[P] de Bardolf, otherwise unidentified, married Henry[P] de Grey.

1. THOMAS[R] BARDOLF was born say 1150.
He married ROSE[R] HAUSELYN, daughter of Roger Hauselyn.
Child [*CP*, 1:417b]:
   2.   i.   Doun[Q], m. Beatrice[Q] de Warenne.

2. DOUN[Q] BARDOLF was no doubt born before 1200.
He married BEATRICE[Q] DE WARENNE, daughter and heir of William de Warenne of Wormegay, Norfolk.
Child:
   3.   ii.   William[P], d. 1275.

3. WILLIAM[P] BARDOLF died in 1275.
Child:
   4.   iii.   William[O], d. 1 Dec. 1289; m. Juliana[O] de Gournay, who d. 1295.

4. WILLIAM[O] BARDOLF of Wormegay, Norfolk, died 1 Dec. 1289.
He married JULIANA[O] DE GOURNAY*, who died in 1295.
He was summoned to attend King Edward I at Shrewsbury on 28 June 1283.
Child:
   5.   i.   Hugh[N], b. Shelford, Notts., c. 29 Sept. 1259; d. Sept. 1304; m. Isabel[N] Anguillon, who d. Ruskington, Lincs., shortly before 28 June 1323.

5. Sir HUGH[N] BARDOLF, 1st Lord Bardolf, was born in Shelford, Nottinghamshire, about 29 Sept. 1259, and died in Sept. 1304.
He married before 1282 ISABEL[N] ANGUILLON[+], who died shortly before 28 May 1323.
He was active in the French and Scottish wars, and was a retainer of Hugh de Lucy, Earl of Lincoln, at Caerlaverock. He was summoned to Parliament 6 Feb. 1298/9 to 2 June 1302.
On 15 Feb. 1285/6 she was sole heir of Sir Robert[O] Anguillon and his first wife. On 15 Oct. 1304 she had livery of Ruskington, Lincolnshire; she was of Addington, Surrey, of the manor later known as Bardolf's.
Child:
   6.   i.   Thomas[M], b. Watton at Stone, Herts., 4 Oct. 1282; d. 15 Dec. 1328; m. c. 1310 Agnes, who d. Ruskington, Lincs., 11 Dec. 1357.

6. THOMAS[M] BARDOLPH, 2nd Lord Bardolf, of Wormegay, Norfolk, was born in Watton at Stone, Hertfordshire, 4 Oct. 1282, died 15 Dec. 1329, and was buried in Shelford Priory, Nottinghamshire, aged 47 [*CP*, 14:64].

He married about 1310 AGNES, who was perhaps a Grandson [*CP*, 14:64], and died in Ruskington, Lincolnshire, 11 Dec. 1357. In Aug. 1337 she had a protection as being "by birth of the parts of Almain" [*CP*, 1:418].

Children:

    *   i.   Margaret[L], m. Adam[L] de Welle[s], who d. 1345.

        ii. John, b. 13 Jan. 1312/3 [*CP*, 14:64]; d. Assisi (Italy) July or Aug. 1363; m. before 25 Dec. 1327 Elizabeth Damory (only dau. and heiress of Roger Damory and Elizabeth[L] de Clare), who d. before 1363.

§ § §

BASSET OF DRAYTON

The original presentation of this line was based on Weis, *Ancestral Roots*, with additional sources noted in the text.

RICHARD[R] BASSET of Drayton, Staffordshire, died between 16 Sept. 1144 and 29 May 1147 [*CP*, 14:71]. He married MAUD[R] RIDEL, heiress of Drayton, daughter of Geoffrey Ridel, a powerful feudal baron [*CP*, 2:1], who died as early as 1120.

RALPH[Q] BASSET died in 1160.

RALPH[P] BASSET died in 1211 [*CP*, 2:2b].

RALPH[O] BASSET of Drayton, Staffordshire, and Colston, Nottinghamshire, died between 1254 and 1261.

RALPH[N] BASSET, Lord Basset of Drayton, Staffordshire, was killed at the battle of Evesham, 4 Aug. 1265. He married MARGARET[M] DE SOMERY, who married second, before 26 Jan. 1270/1, Ralph de Cromwell, who died before 18 Sept. 1289; she died after 18 June 1293.

6. RALPH[M] BASSET, Lord Basset of Drayton in Staffordshire, died in Drayton on 31 Dec. 1299.

He married HAWISE.

He was a Member of Parliament from 1295 to 1299.

Child [Weis, *AR*7, 55:31]:

        i.   Sir Ralph[L], d. 25 Feb. 1342/3; m. Joan de Grey, who d. 13 or 16 March 1353 [CP, 14:71].

    *   ii. Margaret, d. 17 March 1336/7; m. by 1298 Edmund[L] Stafford, 1st Baron Stafford.

§ § §

DE BEAUCHAMP

The placement of Alice[I] Beauchamp, below, who died 8 Feb. 1443, having married on or before 18 July 1385 Sir Thomas[J] Boteler, 4th Baron Sudeley, is very tentative. According to Cokayne's *Complete Peerage* [12:1:418k], some have said she was of Powick in Worcestershire and was daughter of Sir John de Beauchamp of Powick, whom Lewis described as Constable of Gloucester Castle, born Alcester, Warwickshire, died before 14 Feb. 1389, who had married Elizabeth[K] Pateshall. Lewis cited Weis, *AR*, 84, but did not mention which edition. Elizabeth[K] Pateshall is not mentioned in the fifth and seventh editions, so the entry was apparently dropped. The seventh edition contains references to Sybil de Pateshull, who was wife of Roger de Beauchamp de Bletsoe in 1337, in lines 84B and 184A.

Dugdale's *Antiq. of Warwickshire* [1:398-400] should be checked for mention of the ten daughters of Thomas[J] Beauchamp, 11th Earl of Warwick, concerning the tomb upon which is engraved the figures of the ten daughters, "curiously drawn and set up in the windows of St. Mary's. These ladies bear their paternal coat on their inner garment, but on the outer mantle their husband's arms."

It is important to note here that Sanders' *English Baronies*, in presenting the barony of Salwarpe in Worcestershire, differs with the material shown below on the ancestry of William[M] Beauchamp. I.J. Sanders began the line with Walter I[Q] (d. 1131), who m. Emmeline d'Abitot, and continues with William I (d. 1170), William II (d. 1197), m. Joane de Mortimer, Walter II (d. 1236), and then William III[M], who married Isabel Mauduit. Sanders is considered a reliable source, but he was dealing with massive amounts of material, and mistakes are possible. Sir Bernard Burke's *A Genealogical History of the Dormant, Abeyant, Forfeited and Extinct Peerages of the British Empire* [Baltimore: Genealogical Publishing Co.] includes a somewhat similar descent, calling Walter "Walcheline" under Beauchamp – Earls of Warwick.

Henry "Hap" Sutliff of Pebble Beach, California (1999), sssbo@earthlink.net, has been very helpful with criticism and additional sources.

GEOFFREY[S] DE MANDEVILLE, born say 1046, was of record at Domesday in 1086 [*CP*, 5:114n]. He married first ATHELAISE. He married second Lasceline.

WILLIAM[R] DE MANDEVILLE, born say 1072, died in or just before 1130. The suggestion that he married Margaret Rie has been termed a probable error by G.W. Watson [*CP*, 5:114].

WILLIAM[Q] DE MANDEVILLE, born about 1104, was brother of the 1st Earl of Essex.

GEOFFREY[P] DE MANDEVILLE was born about 1130. He married MATILDA[P] DE BIDEN de Rochfort, who was born about 1134, daughter of John de Biden by Alice Mauduit and sister of Sarah and Annabel, both of whom married sons of Hugh[P] de Beauchamp (Walter[Q], William[R], Geoffrey[S]).

WILLIAM[O] FITZ GEOFFREY DE BEAUCHAMP, born about 1158, died by 1221. He married OLIVE[O] BEAUCHAMP, sole heiress of Eaton (who was possibly daughter of Oliver Beauchamp [son of Hugh of Eaton], and his wife Agnes), and assumed her family name.

WILLIAM[N] DE BEAUCHAMP (or de Campo Bello), Lord Bedford, was born in Essex and died in 1262. He married first ISABELLA[N] DE MORTUO MARI, or MORTIMER. He married second, by 1220, Ida (or Idonea) de Longespee, widow of Ralph de Somery.

WILLIAM[M] DE BEAUCHAMP, 5th Baron Beauchamp, of Elmley Castle, Worcestershire, left a will dated 7 Jan. 1268, which was proved at Worcester 9 May 1269 [*CP*, 12:2:369a]. He married ISABEL[M] MAUDUIT, who was living when her husband wrote his will, and was buried at the Nunnery of Cokehill. She was the only sister of William Mauduit, 8th Earl of Warwick, and was said to be deceased in the *inquisition post mortem* of her brother, who died 8 Jan. 1267/8. They were parents of Nos. 9 and 10, and according to tradition, of Isabel, who was said to have married first Henry Lovet of Elmley Lovet and Hampton Lovet in Worcestershire (who died underage about 1256), and married second William[L] le Blount, who died apparently in the spring of 1280, but whose wife has also been identified as Isabel (or Ann) de St. Maure (widow of Lovett), which name later evolved into Seymour.

9. WILLIAM[L] DE BEAUCHAMP, 9th Earl of Warwick, of Elmley Castle, Worcestershire, described as aged 26-30 in 1268, died at Elmley 5 or 9 June 1298, and was buried at Friars Manor, Worcs., 22 June 1298.

He married before 1270 MAUD[O] FITZ JOHN FITZ GEOFFREY[+] of Bernard Castle, Warwickshire, who was widow of Sir Gerard de Furnivall of Sheffield, Yorkshire, and Worksop, Nottinghamshire, lord of Hallamshire, who died without issue before 18 Oct. 1261; she died 16 or 18 April 1301 and was buried with him on 7 May 1301 [*CP*, 12:2:370]. Her parents were Sir John[P] FITZ GEOFFREY[+] and Isabel[M] Bigod, who married after 1230.

He inherited the office of Chamberlain of the Exchequer from his uncle, William[M] Mauduit, and did homage for the lands of the Earldom of Warwick on 9 Feb. 1267/8.

He succeeded his father at Elmley, as hereditary Sheriff of Worcestershire, and as Hereditary Pantler (the person responsible for the bread [*BP*, 2:2944]) at the Coronation of King Edward I in 1272. He had been a pledge for the late Earl of Derby in 1269, Keeper of the Forest of Dean in 1270, and was of record 16 Oct. 1270 and 14 April 1274 as a commissioner to treat with Llywelyn ap Gruffudd, Prince of North Wales, concerning problems on the Welsh border. He was present at the Council of Westminster, which gave judgment against Llywelyn on 12 Nov. 1276, and was recorded as Captain of counties Chester and Lancaster four days later. His service continued as he was summoned for service against the Welsh from 1277 to 1294, at the Assembly of Shrewsbury in 1283, against the Scots 1296-1298, and beyond the seas in 1297. He had been present at Westminster when King Alexander of Scotland did homage to King Edward I of England on 29 Sept. 1278.

In Wales he participated in the siege and capture of Dryslwyn, Carmarthenshire, in Aug. and Sept. of 1282, and was credited with winning a "fine victory" over the forces of Madog ap Llywelyn at Maes Moydog in Montgomeryshire on 5 March 1294/5, which was described by Dugdale, as repeated by Sir Bernard Burke, thusly: He "performed a notable exploit; namely, hearing that a great body of the Welsh were got together in a plain, betwixt two woods, and to secure themselves, had fastened their pikes to the ground, sloping towards their assailants, he marched thither with a choice company of cross-bowmen and archers, and in the night time encompassing them about, but betwixt every two horsemen, one cross-bowman, which cross-bowman killing many of them that held the pikes, the horse charged in suddenly, and made a very great slaughter. This was done near Montgomery."

He was a leader of forces under the Earl of Surrey which defeated the Scots at Dunbar on 27 April 1296. From 16 July 1297 until he died he served as Constable of Rockingham Castle and Steward of the forest between Oxford and Stamford. During the absence of King Edward I in Flanders from Aug. 1297 to March 1297/8 he was a member of Prince Edward's Council.

Children, mentioned by Weis and Norr, with no documentation on Sarah and Robert, and the last four daughters mentioned only by Sir Bernard Burke [*Dormant Peerages*]:

*   i.   Isabel[K], b. c. 1268; d. 1306; m. (1) Sir Patrick[M] de Chaworth, who d. by
              7 July 1283, m. (2) by 1286 Sir Hugh[N] le Despencer.
        ii.   Sarah, d. 1306.
        iii. Robert, d. young.
        iv.   John, b. c. 1272; no further data.
11.   v.   Guy, d. Warwick Castle 10 Aug. 1315; m. before 28 Feb. 1309/10 AliceK
              de Tony, widow of Thomas Leyburne (she d. 1 Jan. 1324/5, having m.
              [3] William la Zouche, Lord Zouche of Mortimer).
        vi.   Maud, d. 1360; m. (1) Rithco, m. (2) Gerard Furnival, lord of Hallams.
        vii. Margaret, m. John Sudeley.
        viii. Anne, nun at Shouldham, co. Norfolk.
        ix.   Amy, nun at Shouldham.

10. Sir WALTER[L] DE BEAUCHAMP (brother of William, above) died 16 Feb. 1303.

He married, a papal dispensation dated 1289, ALICE[K] DE TOENI* (or Tony).

They were of Beauchamp's Court, a moiety [part] of the manor of Alcester, Warwickshire, purchased from Reginald Fitzherbert [Burke's *Dormant Peerages*, 34], and Powick, Worcestershire.

According to Burke he was given a legacy of 200 marks by his father for a pilgrimage to the Holy Land. He was Steward of the Household to King Edward I, attending the king in Flanders, and in Scotland, where he shared in the honors of Falkirk on 22 July 1298. He participated in the Parliament at Lincoln, joining the lords signifying to the Pope by their seals that Edward I was the superior of the Kingdom of Scotland.

Children, listed by Norr [22], who cited *The Genealogist*, new ser., 14:251, 16:43 (which did not support the whole list):

    i.   Humphrey[K], b. c. 1281.
    ii.   Eleanor, b. 11 Nov. 1275; m. (1) after 18 July 1284 John[L] Botiller of Wem,
          who d. 1287, m. (2) 1293 John de la Mare.
    iii. Walter of Kinwarden, heir, d. 1328; lord of Alcester, Warks., which he
          gave to his brother Giles; after the death in 1317 [Burke, *Dormant
          Peerages*, 34] of Guy de Beauchamp, Earl of Warwick, Walter had
          custody of Warwick Castle; no issue.
    iv.   William, b. c. 1287; brother of Giles, a celebrated military man who
          succeeded to a part of the estates of his older brother Walter [Burke,
          34]; military officer in Flanders and Scotland, governor of St. Briavel
          Castle; no issue.
12. v.   Giles, d. 12 Oct. 1361; m. c. 1329 Catherine[K] Bures.
    vi.   Margaret, m. 1318 Robert de Lisle.

11. GUY[K] DE BEAUCHAMP, 10th Earl of Warwick, of Elmley, Worcestershire, said to be aged 23-27 in 1298, and over 30 in 1301, died (of poisoning?) at Warwick Castle 12 Aug. 1315, and was buried in Bordesley Abbey, Warwickshire.

It is recorded that he married first, before 11 May 1297, Isabel[L] de Clare, but this marriage was never completed, for she was regarded as unmarried when she married, about 1316 as his second wife, Maurice[J] de Berkeley. She died a childless widow in 1338.

He married between 12 Jan. and 28 Feb. 1309/10, ALICE[K] DE TONY (TOENI*), widow of Thomas de Leyburne, who died before his father and without male issue shortly before 30 May 1307. She had very extensive estates assigned to her in dower, and in 1316 she paid a fine of 500 marks for license to marry third William la Zouche, Lord Zouche de Mortimer, who died 28 Feb. 1336/7. She died 1 Jan. 1324/5, having had children by all three husbands.

He was knighted by King Edward I at Easter, 25 March 1296, and served in the King's division in the battle of Falkirk on 22 July 1298; his distinguished efforts were rewarded with a grant of Scottish lands of the value of 1000 marks annually. He was a commissioner negotiating with the French on 12 May 1299 and 1 March 1300/1. Summoned for service against the Scots, 1299-1314, he participated in the siege of Caerlaverock in July 1300 as a part of the second division under the Earl of Surrey, and was at Perth with the Prince of Wales from Dec. 1303 to April 1304, frequently dining with him. He then served under the Prince at the siege of Stirling Castle from April to July.

On 2 Feb. 1306/7 his service was rewarded with the grant of Barnard Castle in county Durham, and at the Coronation of King Edward II he carried the third sword. However, he became an enemy of the King's friend, Piers de Gavaston, who called him "The Black Dog of Arden," and was prominent in having de Gavaston banished, 18 May 1308; he alone opposed de Gavaston's recall in 1309. On 7 Feb. 1309/10 he and Thomas of Lancaster, with others, defied the King by coming with arms to Parliament at Westminster, and he was sworn as one of the Lords Ordainers on 20 March.

When Piers de Gavaston surrendered on terms set by the Earls of Pembroke and Surrey at Scarborough on 19 May 1312, Piers was escorted by Pembroke to Deddington in Oxfordshire, where he was seized by Guy, Earl of Warwick, on 10 June and taken to Warwick Castle. When the Earls of Lancaster, Hereford and Arundel arrived, Warwick handed over his prisoner, and Piers was beheaded without trial on Blacklow Hill, 19 June 1312. The execution took place outside of Warwick's domain; Warwick refused to attend or take custody of the corpse [*CP*, 12:2:371e].

Although the Earls were pardoned on 16 Oct. 1313, they refused to serve in the Bannockburn campaign of 1314. He was a commissioner to treat with Thomas de Lancaster about the Scottish marches on 28 May 1315.

His will of 25 July 1315 bequeathed his wife Alice a part of his plate, with a crystal cup and half his bedding, as well as the vestments and books belonging to his chapel. To his daughters he gave beds, rings and jewels. His son Thomas was to receive his best coat of mail, helmet and suit of harness, while John was to receive the second set. The rest of his armor, bows and other warlike provisions were to remain in Warwick Castle for his heir.

Child, of Alice[K] de Tony, by first husband, surnamed de Leyburne:

  i.   Julia[J], d. 1367; m. (1) John Hastings, m. (2) Thomas Blount, m. (3) c. 1328 Sir William Clinton.

Children, his by Alice de Tony, with John, Maud, Thomas and Lucy mentioned by Norr [23], and the rest by Sir Bernard Burke:

  ii.   Isabel, m. John Clinton.
  iii. Elizabeth, d. 1359; m. by 1337 Thomas Astley of Astley, Warks., who d. 1385.
  iv.   John, d. 2 Dec. 1360; unm., having had a writ for a marriage which apparently did not take place to Margaret Basset, dau. of Ralph Basset and Joan de Grey.
  v.   Maud, d. 25 July 1369; m. (1) Geoffrey de Say IV, 2nd Lord Say, Admiral of the Fleet, who d. 26 June 1359.
  vi.   Emma, m. Rowland Odingsells.
  vii. Lucy, b. 17 June 1312; m. Sir Robert Napton.
13. viii. Thomas, b. prob. 1313/4; d. Calais 16 Nov. 1369; m. Katherine[J] de Mortimer, who died in 1371.

12. Sir GILES[K] DE BEAUCHAMP of Powick, Worcestershire, died 12 Oct. 1361.

He was alleged by Norr to have married first about 1288, seventy-three years before he died.

He married, about 1329, CATHERINE[K] BURES*, who was living in Oct. 1355 [*CP*, 5:chart between 320-321].

In 14 Edw. III (1340-1341) he had license to fortify Beauchamp's Court, and two years later he had permission to fortify his house at Fresh-Water, on the Isle of Wight.

Children, listed by Norr:

  i.   Roger[J], not documented as son of Giles, but known to be a grandson of Walter [*CP*, 14:75], d. 3 Jan. 1379/80; m. (1) before 1336/7 Sybil de Pateshulle, m. (2) Margaret.
14. ii. John, b. c. 1334; d. by 1401; m. Elizabeth, who d. 1411.

13. Thomas[J] Beauchamp, K.G., 11th Earl of Warwick, born in Warwick Castle, 14 Feb. 1313/4 [*CP*, 12:2:372], died of the plague in Calais (now in France) 16 Nov. 1369, and was buried in St. Mary's, Warwick.

He married, after 22 Feb. 1324/5, his cousin Katherine[J] de Mortimer* of Wigmore, under a dispensation sought by King Edward II and granted by the Pope on 19 April 1319; she died between 4 Aug. and 6 Sept. 1369, and was buried in St. Mary's, Warwick. The marriage was intended to end a feud between the families.

While he was a minor, in 1317, his lands had passed into the care of Hugh[N] le Despenser the elder, but in 1318 he was made a ward of Roger[K] de Mortimer [*CP*, 12:2:372g].

King Edward III knighted him 1 Jan. 1328/9, and on 20 Feb. he was given control of his lands although he was still under age. He also assumed his hereditary titles of Sheriff of Worcestershire and Chamberlain of the Exchequer.

Summoned for service against the Scots from 1333, he was a commissioner negotiating for a truce on 4 May 1336, and for a final peace on 24 July 1337, having been of record as Captain of the army against the Scots on 25 March and Warden of the March of Scotland that year. In 1340 he was in command at Valenciennes, and he served with the king at the siege of Tournai. He was a peace commissioner treating with France on 24 May 1342, and again, in the presence of the Pope, 29 Aug. 1343, having been present at the siege of Vannes.

From 10 Feb. 1343/4 he served as Marshal of England until he died in 1369, and from 26 June 1344 he served as Sheriff of Warwick and Leicester for life.

During the campaign which led to the battle of Crécy, 26 Aug. 1346, he was one of two Marshals of the Army, serving as joint commander in the van under Edward, the Black Prince. He personally took William de Melleun, Archbishop of Sens, prisoner, receiving 8000 marks in ransom. He then took part in the siege of Calais.

He was invested with Knight of the Garter 23 April 1349 as one of the founders of the order. Then he was involved in naval action off Winchelsea, and served before 20 March 1352/3 as Admiral of the fleet from the mouth of the Thames towards the West. In 1355 he was made Constable of the army at Gascony, and he commanded the vanguard at the battle of Poitiers on 19 Sept. 1356.

On 12 July 1356 he had recovered the lands of Gower and Swansea Castle from John de Mowbray, lands which had been taken from the Norman Earls of Warwick in 1203 by King John. On 19 July 1362 he took homage due to the Black Prince as Duke of Aquitaine, and he was in Gascony with the prince in Nov. 1364. In 1366 and 1367 he was engaged in diplomacy in Flanders and Scotland. In 1369, as a prominent member of John of Gaunt's expedition in France, he devastated Caux.

He made his will 4 Aug. 1369.

Children, most listed by Norr [23], who stated that of ten daughters seven are known, with detail added from *Burke's Extinct Peerage* [31], with modification from *CP*, 12:2:375:

    i.   Isabel[I], m. (1) John[I], Lord Strange of Blackmere, Shropshire, who d. 3 Aug. 1375, m. (2) William Ufford, Earl of Suffolk [*CP*, 12:1: 429-434; one source stated there was a dau. Elizabeth, who m. Thomas de Ufford, Earl of Suffolk, in error; the names Isabel and Elizabeth were essentially the same at that time].

    ii. Sir Guy, d. France 28 April 1360, bur. Vendôme; m. c. 1353 Philippe Ferrers, dau. of Henry[L] and Isabel of Groby; Philippe d. 1384.

    iii. Alice, b. c. 1337; m. (1) c. 1355 John Beauchamp, Lord Beauchamp of Hache, Somerset.

    iv. Thomas, K.G. c. Jan. 1372/3, 12th Earl of Warwick, b. before 16 March 1338/9; d. 8 April 1401, bur. St. Mary's, Warwick [mi]; m. before April

1381 Margaret Ferrers, who d. 22 Jan. 1406/7, and was bur. with her husband.

  v.   Reynburn, b. say 1341; d. before 29 July 1361 [*CP*, 12:2:374-375h]; according to Burke he had a daughter Alianore, who m. John Knight of Hanslope.
  vi.   Joan, b. c. 1343; m. Ralph Basset, Lord Basset of Drayton, who d. 1390.
  vii. Philippe, d. before 6 April 1386; m. before 1 March 1350/1 Sir Hugh Stafford, who d. Rhodes 16 Oct. 1386.
  viii. Maud, d. 1403; m. Roger, Lord Clifford, who d. 13 July 1389.
15. ix. William, fourth son [*CP*, 1:24], d. 8 May 1411; m. Joan¹ Fitz Alan.
  x.   Margaret, m. Guy de Montfort; after he died, before 1370 [*CP*, 9:130], she took the veil at Shouldham.
  xi.   Roger, b. before 1356; d. between 29 July and 15 Oct. 1361; unm.
  xii. Agnes, m. (1) Cokesay, m. (2) Bardolf [listed only in Burke].
  xiii. Juliana, d. unm [Burke].
  xiv. John, unm.
  xv.   Hierom [Burke], unm.

14. JOHN^J BEAUCHAMP of Powick, Worcestershire, born Alcester, Warwickshire, died before 14 Feb. 1389, or before 1401.

He married ELIZABETH, who may have been a daughter of Sir John St. John [*MCS*5, 58:7].

He was described by Mr. Marlyn Lewis as Constable of Gloucester Castle. However, Burke [34] stated that little is mentioned of him but that he founded a chantry in the parish church of Alcester during the reign of Edward III, and that he was in the expedition in France during 3 Ric. II (1379-1380).

Children, listed tentatively [*CP*, 12:1:418k], the third listed by Burke:
  i.   Sir William¹, of Powick, Worcs., and Alcester, Warks., who d. before 1431 [*CP*, 2:46-47], m. before March 1414/5 Catherine Ufflete (dau. and coheir of Sir Gerald Ufflete); Sir William¹ was made constable of Gloucester Castle in 16 Ric. II (1392-1393), Sheriff of Worcestershire in 3 Hen. IV (1401-1402), and Sheriff of Gloucestershire upon the beginning of the reign of Henry V (1413).
           Sons: 1. Walter^H. 2. Robert, living 1432. 3. Sir John, K.G., Lord Beauchamp of Powick, who d. April 1475, having m. Margaret Ferrars.
  * ii. Alice, d. 8 Feb. 1443; m. (1) on or before 18 July 1385 Sir Thomas^J Boteler, 4th Baron Sudeley (according to Cokayne [12:1:481k], in 1440 Sir Ralph Boteler, son and successor of Thomas, was described as uncle of Elizabeth, dau. of Sir William Beauchamp, his son and heir, but these "facts cannot be made to tally with the account of Beauchamp of Powick given by Dugdale, Baronage, vol. i, p. 249"), m. (2) Sir John Dalyngrygg.
  iii. Sir Walter.

15. WILLIAM¹ BEAUCHAMP, Baron Abergavenny [*CP*, 10:123-126, 11:705], K.G., died 8 May 1411. His will, proved at Lambeth in 1411 [*CP*, 14:6], directed that he be buried at the Black Friars, Hereford.

He married JOAN¹ FITZ ALAN*, who died 14 Nov. 1435, having held the Castle and Honour of Abergavenny in dower until her death. In her will, dated 10 Jan. 1434/5, proved 19 Nov. 1435, she directed that she be buried next to her husband.

He served "under the gallant Chandos," with great distinction in the wars in France, and was nominated K.G. by King Edward III in 1375 or 1376 [*CP*, 1:24]. He served as Captain of Calais in 1383, and was summoned to Parliament (23 July 1392 to 18 Dec. 1409) as a result of succeeding to the lands of Abergavenny, having been son of a sister of the grandmother of the last owner [*CP*, 1:25c]. In 1399 he was appointed Judiciary of South Wales and Governor of Pembroke.

He fortified Ewyas Castle in 1403.

His *inquisition post mortem* was held at Hereford on 5 June 1411. He directed that he be buried at Black Friars, Hereford.

Children, no doubt an incomplete list:

     i.   Sir Richard[H], Earl of Worcester; b. c. 1397; mortally wounded at the siege of Meaux, France, 18 March 1421/2, bur. Tewkesbury Abbey; m. Tewkesbury, 27 July 1411, Isabel le Despenser, who d. Friars Minoresses, London, 27 Dec. 1439, bur. Tewkesbury Abbey [mi], having m. (2) (by papal dispensation) Hanley Castle, Worcs., 26 Nov. 1423, Richard Beauchamp, 5th Earl of Warwick (her first husband's cousin), who d. 30 April 1439.

*   ii. Joan, d. Shere in Surrey, 3 or 5 Aug. 1430; m. c. 28 Aug. 1413 James[H] Butler, 4th Earl of Ormond.

§ § §

BECK

✓

According to Charles T. Beke's "Observations on the Pedigree of the Family of Beke of Eresby, in the County of Lincoln" [*Collectanea et Genealogica*, 4(1837):338-339], the Beke family was of Flemish origin. Charles Beke mentioned one Nicholas Beke in the pedigree chart, but he lived during the time of King John and King Henry I, as did Anthony Bek, bishop of Durham [Hedley, 1:234].

Marshall's *Genealogist's Guide* suggests (for Beck) additional research in Chetham Society, 84:29 (where this compiler did not find the name, although there were many Staffordshire and Cheshire families mentioned in "Cheshire Plea Roll No. 1"); *Miscellanea Genealogica et Heraldica*, new ser., 2:285; Wotton's *English Baronetage*, 4:154; Burke's *Extinct Baronetcies* (which treats the Barons Beke of Eresby, Lincs., and Nicholas de la Becke of Aldworth, Bucks., who died leaving no issue [38]); W.H.D. Langstaffe's *Pedigrees of the Lords of Alnwick*, 24, and *Burke's Family Records*, 60, which did not help.

Page 139, 140 and 142 were missing from the UCLA copy of *Collections for a History of Staffordshire*, new series, 12 (1909).

1. Sir ROBERT[L] BECK "of Tene" (Tean) in Staffordshire, was listed in the "Pro Savage" and "Savage of Clifton" pedigrees in Rylands' *Visitation of Cheshire, 1580* as the father of Sir Nicholas Beck, named in other records as Nicholas Beke.

The mother of Nicholas[K] was MARY [Wrottesley, *Colls. Hist. Staffs.*, 15 (1894), 114].

He bore arms *Gules, a cross Erm.*

G.W. Watson, in Cokayne's *Complete Peerage* [4:461-462], identified Robert de Bek of Tean and Hopton, Staffordshire, and Orabel, his wife, as parents of Lettice, who died before Oct. 1292. Lettice de Bek married Sir Richard de Draycote of Draycote, Staffordshire (living in May 1324), who was identified further by Watson [*ibid.*], and had a son and heir of Lettice, namely Robert (who assumed the name de Bek).

The *banco roll* of Michaelmas 20 Edw. I (1292) contains record of a suit by the Prior of St. Thomas against Robert de Bek the son of Richard de Draycote concerning a messuage and rent in Tene and Chekkeleye ["Plea Rolls," *Colls. Hist. Staffs.*, pt. 1, 6:208].

Children, listed from the Savage pedigrees and Roskell [3:479]:

2. i. Nicholas[K], m. say 1345 Joan[J] Stafford.
* ii. Elizabeth, m. say 1350 Sir John[J] Ipstones, who d. by 1364.

2. Sir NICHOLAS[K] BEKE was lord of the manors of Hopton and Teanes in Staffordshire, and Dove Repinden, Merthen and Mounstow in Derbyshire and Salop [*Colls. Hist. Staffs.* (1914), 4].

He married say 1345 JOAN[J] STAFFORD* [Rylands, *Vis. Cheshire, 1580* (203)].

The *de Banco* rolls from Easter 31 Edw. III (1358) contain record of a suit against Nicholas for a debt of 46 marks by Richard de Eton of Lychefeld, masoun, and Alice his wife. According to the complaint Nicholas inherited from Sir Robert de Beek, his father, lands and tenements in fee simple in Tene, Chekkeleye, Uttokeshather and elsewhere in Staffordshire [Wrottesley, "Extracts," *Colls. Hist. Staffs.*, 12 (1891), 149].

In 42 Edw. III (1369-1370) he sued Henry[K] de Delves and Katherine his wife over an agreement concerning two messuages and 11s rent in Fulford [*Colls. Hist. Staffs.*, n.s., 9:94]. A suit filed about 1422 by Richard Peshale against Sir John Savage concerned the manors of Tene, Blythewood and Hopton, with twenty marks rent in Draycote, which John de Beck, the parson of the church of Chekeley, had given to Nicholas de Beek and Joan his wife ["Extracts from the Plea Rolls," *Colls. Hist. Staffs.*, 17:96].

Child:
* i. Elizabeth (or Helena)[J] [*Colls. Hist. Staffs.*, n.s., 9:141], m. Sir Robert[J] Swynnerton.

§ § §

BELKNAP

This family is mentioned in Cokayne's *Complete Peerage* [5:320-321].

1. JOHN[K] BELKNAP married ALICE.
Child:
2. i. Thomas[J], m. Juliana Darset, who d. 1414/5.

2. Sir THOMAS[J] BELKNAP was of Hempstead, Kent.
He married JULIANA[J] DARSET of Essex, who died 1414/5, daughter of John Darset of Essex [Watney, *Wallop Family*, 84].
He was Chief Justice of the Common Pleas.
Child:
3. i. Hamon[I], of Seintlynge in St. Mary Cray, Kent.

3. HAMON[I] BE[A]LKNAP, described as being of Seintlynge in St. Mary Cray, Kent, and Knell, Sussex, died without a male heir 9 June 1450 [*CP*, 5:320].
He married JOAN[I] DE BOTELER*, younger daughter and in her issue coheir of Sir Thomas Boteler of Sudeley in Gloucestershire.
Child, mentioned by Cokayne:
* i. Elizabeth[H], d. 28 May 1471; m. Sir William[H] Ferrers.

§ § §

DE LA BERE

George Wrottesley's work on the plea rolls [*The Genealogist*, new series, 8:243 and 15:154] contains what may be helpful clues. At Michaelmas 6 Edw. III (1332-1333), in Essex, Richard de la Bere sued Thomas de Weston, knight, for a messuage and two carucates of land in Reynham near Dagenham in which Thomas had no entry except by an unjust disseisin of Alan de Plukenet his kinsman, whose heir he was. The pedigree showed Richard de la Bere, son of Richard, son of Richard, who was brother of Alan, who was father of Alan de Plukenet, who died during the reign of King Edward III without issue. Thomas claimed by a grant from the king, the tenements in question forming part of the lands of Oliver de Plukenet which had fallen to the king as an eschaet. Oliver was not in the pedigree.

At Michaelmas 8 Hen. IV (1384-1385), in Southampton, a John de la Bere sued William Pershute for the manor of Culmeston, which Alan de Plukenet, the elder, and Joan, his wife, had granted by fine in 23 Edw. I (1294-1295), to Alan de Plukenet, the younger, and Sibil, his wife, and the heirs of their bodies, with reversion to himself and his own right heirs. However, William Pershute denied that Alan Plukenet had a brother Richard, and John afterwards withdrew his suit. The pedigree showed John de la Bere, son of Thomas, son of Richard, son of Richard, son of Richard, who was alleged to be brother of Alan de Plukenet, the elder.

The following presentation is based on the work of G. Andrews Moriarty ["The Family of de la Bere," *The Genealogists' Magazine*, 10 (1947-1950), 412-415]. The account by Vernon Norr is confused.

1. ANDREW[P] DE LA BERE died before 1230.
He married ALICE[P] DE ROCHEFORD, who married second Alan de Plugenet. She apparently died before 20 Nov. 1233, when Richard[O] de la Bere, her son and heir, was made a ward of the Bishop of Winchester. Alice's parents were Thomas de Rocheford and Isabel de Berkeley (daughter of Roger Berkeley of Dursley IV, who died about 1191). Isabel de Berkeley was given Siston and a rent in Cubberley as a *maritagium* by her father, and she carried these to her second husband, William de Walerond, when she married him before Michaelmas of 1206 [*CP*, 10:552a].
Child, hers by first husband, surnamed de la Bere:
    2.   i.   Richard[O].
Child, hers by second husband, surnamed de Plugenet:
         ii.   Sir Alan of Kilpack, d. shortly before 25 Dec. 1298; m. Alice; knighted Oct. 1260, summoned to Parliament 1296.

2. RICHARD[O] DE LA BERE was made a ward of the Bishop of Winchester on 29 Nov. 1233. In 1230 he impleaded (evidently as a minor) Alan de Plugenet, his stepfather, and his wife Alice (Richard's mother) to recover lands in Kilmeston.
Children:
    3.   i.   Sir Robert[N], of record in 1303 and 1316.
         ii.   Richard, m. Cecily Bourne (prob. dau. of James Bourne), who inherited lands in Bishopeston; had children John, Nicholas, William and Cecily [Moriarty, *The Genealogists' Magazine*, 10:413].

3. Sir ROBERT[N] DE LA BERE held a knight's fee in Burleton of the Earl of Hereford in 1303, and the vill of Stratford in 1316 [see *Feudal Aids*, 2:376, 387].

He married, according to Norr, whose presentation on the family was confused, SIBYL[L] HARLEY*, sister of Richard[L] Harley, who was dead in 1316, having married before Dec. 1283 Burga[L] of Willey.

G.T. Clark [*Limbus Patrum*, 2:479] called him Richard, son of Sir Stephen de la Bere (who married Mabel Brian of Brampton-Brian), son of Sir John de la Bere (who married Joan Heven, daughter of Stephen Heven of Heven), son of Sir Richard de la Bere.

Child:

4.   i.   Richard[M], m. Sybel[M] de Chabbenor.

4. RICHARD[M] DE LA BERE was born say 1292, and was serving Herefordshire as an M.P. in 1369.

He married SYBEL[M] DE CHABBENOR of Chabnor, who was born about 1296 [*CP*, 3:149]. Chabnor is called Chadnor in Herefordshire by G. Andrews Moriarty. In a 1412 court action John de Baskerville accused Kinnard[K] de la Bere of illegal distraint in Eardisley, stating that Ingenard de Baskerville gave Chadnor to William de Chabbenor for life, the remainder to Thomas his son and his wife Sibel and the heirs of their bodies, and Richard de la Bere was their heir at law. Indeed, in 1242-1243 William de Chabbenor held three hides in Chadnor; in 1316 Thomas de Chabbenor held Chadnor [see *Feudal Aids*, 2:387], and the rights descended to his son William and then to his daughter Sibel, wife of Richard de la Bere.

In 1327, upon the death of Joan Plugenet, he made a fraudulent but successful claim to Kilmeston, stating that he was descended from a younger son of Andrew de la Bere, whose eldest son and heir was Alan de Plugenet, ancestor of Joan, thus evidently and falsely evading the law of *possessio fratris* [Moriarty, 413].

He was M.P. for Herefordshire in 1353, 1354, 1357-1358, 1360 and 1369 [Moriarty].

According to G.T. Clark [*Limbus Patrum*, 2:479], he married Margaret Gamage, daughter of Sir William Gamage of Rogiad in Monmouthshire.

Child:

5.   i.   John[L], poss. son, d. after 1338; m. Agnes de Turberville.

5. JOHN[L] DE LA BERE, born say in 1308, died after 1338, was given in Norr as before say 1190, or in 1318!

He married AGNES DE TURBERVILLE [Watney, *Wallop Family*, 242, 261, 779], who was identified by G.T. Clark [*Limbus Patrum*, 2:479-480] as daughter of Sir Pain Turberville and granddaughter of Sir Gilbert Turberville of Coyty. However, Clark stated that John de la Bere was of Weobley in Gower, and tested a charter in 1334 [Clark, 2:480].

George T. Clark stated that he was son of Adam, who was son of Sir David, who was son of Sir John de la Bere ap Robert ap Ber.

He was of Talvern and Weobley.

Children, the second and third not listed by Moriarty, and the fourth and fifth only by Moriarty:

*   i.   Sibella[K], b. 19 May 1338; d. 13 May 1382; m. 1370 Thomas[K] Crophull.

    ii.   Elizabeth, b. say 1354, m. Sir John St. John [see George T. Clark's *Genealogies of Morgan and Glamorgan* (1886), 452; Weaver's *Vis. Herefordshire, 1569*].

    iii.   Margaret, b. say 1356; m. (1) Dennis, m. (2) Elias Basset [Clark].

    iv.   Kinnard, d. before 1412; had son Sir Richard, and probably another son William.

    v.   Violette, m. 1363 Sir John Chaundos, lord Chaundos of Snodhill and Fownhope in Herefordshire, who d. Dec. 1428.

§ § §

DE BERKELEY

The following line was based on the work of Jacobus and Weis, but has been expanded with material from Cokayne's *Complete Peerage*, vol. 2, pages 119-130, and other sources.

HARDING[P] was living about 1125.

Sir ROBERT[O] FITZ HARDING, of Bristol, England, born about 1095, died 5 Feb. 1170/1, aged 75, and was apparently buried in the Abbey of St. Augustine, Bristol, which he had founded in 1141, and of which he was later a canon. He married Eve, who died 12 March 1170. She had founded a priory of nuns on St. Michael's Hill, Bristol, and was prioress when she died. She was buried with her husband. She was not sister of Durand or daughter of Sir Estmond by Godiva, his wife.

MAURICE[N] FITZ ROBERT FITZ HARDING, later DE BERKELEY, feudal Lord of Berkeley, called "Maurice the Make Peace," born in Bristol, England, about 1120, died 16 June 1190, and was buried in the church of Brentford, Middlesex. He married about 1153 ALICE[N] DE BERKELEY, the daughter of his dispossessed predecessor, Roger de Berkeley, feudal Lord of Dursley.

THOMAS[M] DE BERKELEY, feudal Lord of Berkeley, called "Thomas the Observer or Temporiser," born about 1170, died 29 Nov. 1243, aged about 73, and was buried at St. Augustine's, Bristol. He married, about 1217, JOAN[M] DE SOMERY of Dudley in Worcestershire, who was still living in 2 Edw. I (1273-1274).

MAURICE[L] DE BERKELEY, 6th Lord Berkeley, called "Maurice the Resolute," born in 1218, died 4 April 1281, aged 63, and was buried at St. Augustine's, Bristol. He married, before 12 July 1247, ISABEL[M] FITZ ROY, who died 7 July, probably in 1276 or 1277, and was buried at St. Augustine's, Bristol, daughter of Richard[N] Fitz Roy (a natural son of John, King of England) and Rose, daughter and heir of Foubert de Douvres [*CP*, 14:87].

6. THOMAS[K] DE BERKELEY, Baron Berkeley, called "Thomas the Wise," born at Berkeley, Gloucestershire, in 1245, died at Berkeley, 31 (24 in *Vis. Leics.* [2]) July 1321, aged 76.

He married in 1267 JOAN[N] DE FERRERS*, who died 19 March 1309/10 and was buried at St. Augustine's, Bristol, daughter of William de Ferrers, Earl of Derby.

He spent much of the last fifty years of his life "employed either against the Welsh, the Scots, or the French." He received summonses to Parliament from 24 June 1295 to 15 May 1321.

He was Vice-Constable of England in 1297, was in the battle of Falkirk in 1298, in the siege of Caerlaverock in July 1300, and was taken prisoner at the battle of Bannockburn, 24 June 1314, which cost him a large ransom. He had also been on an Embassy to France in Jan. 1296, and to Pope Clement V in July 1307.

Children, listed by Fosbroke:

7.   i.   Maurice[J], d. 31 May 1326; m. (1) 1289 Eve[J] la Zouche, m. (2) c. 1316 Isabel de Clare.

   ii. Thomas, ancestor of the Berkeleys of Wymondham, Leics.

   iii. John, d. c. 1317 [*BP*, 1:254]; m. Hawise; no issue.

   iv. James, a bishop.

   v.   Isabel, unm.

   vi. Margaret, m. (1) Thomas Fitz Maurice, m. (2) Reynald Rasel (or Russel) [*BP*, 1:254, 1064].

7. MAURICE[J] DE BERKELEY, Baron Berkeley, called "Maurice the Magnanimous," said to have been born April 1281 (and a father before the age of 14), died in Wallingford Castle 31 May 1326, and was buried at Wallingford, but his remains were removed to St. Augustine's, Bristol.

He married, first, in 1289 (neither being over the age of eight), EVE[J] LA ZOUCHE*, who died 6 Dec. 1314 [CP, 14:87], and was buried in Portbury Church, Somerset.

He married, second, about 1316, Isabel[L] de Clare, daughter of Gilbert[M] de Clare, Earl of Gloucester and Hertford, and his first wife, Alice, daughter of Hugh XI, Count of la Marche and Angoulême, who was the uterine brother of King Henry III. Isabel died childless about 1338 [G.T. Clark, 146].

He served in the Scottish wars from 1295 to 1318 and was at the siege of Caerlaverock in July 1300. He was Warden of Gloucester in 1312, Captain of Berwick in 1315, a commissioner to Scotland in 1316, Chief Justice of South Wales in 1316, and Seneschal of Aquitaine in 1320. Soon after he joined the Earl of Lancaster in the rebellion against King Edward II and the Despenser family, and, within six months of his father's death, he was a prisoner in Wallingford Castle (20 Jan. 1321/2), where he died.

He was styled Lord Berkeley of Berkeley Castle.

Children, listed by Fosbroke and Blore, all by first wife:

8.   i.   Thomas[1], d. 27 Oct. 1361; m. (1) July 1320 Margaret de Mortimer, m. (2) 30 May 1347 Katharine[1] Clivedon.

    ii.   Sir Maurice, ancestor of Berkeleys of Stoke Gifford, Gloucs. [Vis. Shropshire, 1623, 32], d. Berkeley Castle 3 June 1368, bur. St. Augustine's, Bristol; m. Margaret Berkeley of Uley, Gloucestershire [BP, 1:254; cf. Faris, PA2, 22].

    iii.   John, Constable of Bristol Castle.

    iv.   Eudo, a clerk.

    v.   Peter, a clerk.

    vi.   Isabel, d. 25 July 1362; m. (1) Berkeley Castle, June 1328, Robert[K] de Clifford, who d. 20 May 1344, m. (2) 1345 Sir Thomas Musgrave [CP, 3:291].

    vii.   Millicent (Ela), not listed by Fosbroke, d. after 1322; m. (1) 1313 John Maltravers, who b. c. 1290, d. 16 Feb. 1363/4 [Weis, AR7, 59:32].

8. THOMAS[1] DE BERKELEY, Baron Berkeley, called "Thomas the Ritch," was born before 1296, died 27 Oct. 1361, and was buried in Berkeley Church [mi].

He married, first, in July 1320, Margaret de Mortimer, who died 5 May 1337, aged under 30, and was buried at St. Augustine's Bristol, daughter of Roger[K] de Mortimer, Earl of March, and Joan de Geneville, daughter and heir of Sir Piers de Geneville [CP, 14:87]. He received papal dispensation to remain married in Sept. 1329, with past issue legitimized.

He married, second, at Charfield, Gloucestershire, 30 May 1347, KATHARINE[1] CLIVEDON*, who died 13 March 1385 and was buried in Berkeley Church, widow of Sir Piers le Veel of Tortworth.

Knighted before 1322, he was aged 30 or more at the time of his father's death. He fought at Boroughbridge on 16 March 1321/2, was taken prisoner, and was released from Pevensey Castle on 16 Oct. 1326. On 4 April 1327 he was made Joint Custodian of the deposed King Edward II, whom he "curteously received" the next day at Berkeley Castle. However, he had been commanded to deliver his fellow custodians over to the government and left for Bradley "with heavy cheere perceiving what violence was intended" [Cokayne, 2:129]. He was tried by a jury of twelve knights in 4 Edw. III (1330-1331) as an accessory to the murder of Edward II at Berkeley Castle (a deed committed by Sir John Maltravers and Sir Thomas Gurnay), but was acquitted. In 1328 he was in the expedition against Scotland.

From 14 June 1329 to 20 Nov. 1360 he served in the House of Lords. In 1336 he was Chief Warden of the counties of Gloucester, Worcester and Hereford. He was Marshall of the English army in France in 1340, and Captain of the Scottish Marches in 1342. He was Warden and Chief Justice in Eyre south of Trent from 1345 to 1348, and on an Embassy to Pope Innocent VI in 1361.

Children, listed by Fosbroke, by first wife:

    i.   Maurice[H], d. 8 [3 in Weis, *AR*7, 39:32, and *MCS*5, 80:7] June 1368 from wounds received at Poitiers; m. August 1338 (aged 8) Elizabeth[L] Despenser, who d. 13 July 1389, bur. St. Botolph's, London [Faris, *PA*2, 22], dau. of Sir Hugh le Despencer and Alianore de Clare.

    ii.   Roger, no issue.

    iii.   Thomas, no issue.

    iv.   Alphonsus, no issue.

    v.   Joan, m. Sir Reginald Cobham.

Children, listed by Fosbroke, by second wife:

    vi.   Thomas, no issue.

    vii.   Maurice, no issue.

    viii.   Edmund, no issue.

9.   ix.   John, m. (1) Elizabeth Betteshorne; ancestor of Berkeleys of Beverstone.

9. Sir JOHN[H] BERKELEY of Beverstone, county Gloucester, born in 1352, died in 1428.

He married, first, ELIZABETH BETTESHORNE, daughter of Sir John Betteshorne of Betteshorne (or Bisterne [Faris, *PA*2, 123]) in Hampshire [*CP*, 4:480].

He was an M.P. and Sheriff of Gloucestershire [see Sir John Maclean's *The Berkeley Manuscripts*, 3 vols. (Gloucester, 1883-1886), 1:349-351, 3:100, cited in *MCS*5, 80A:7].

Children, the first given by Jacobus, and Weis [*AR*7, 81:36], with the second from Baker [*Northampton*, 1:547]:

  *   i.   Elizabeth[G], d. shortly before 8 Dec. 1478; m. (1) Edward Charlton, Lord Powys, m. (2) after 14 March 1420/1 John[G] de Sutton, who d. 30 Sept. 1487.

    ii.   Eleanor, d. 1455; m. (1) Sir John de Arundel, m. (2) Sir Richard Poynings, m. (3) Sir Walter Hungerford.

§ § §

LE BLOUNT

The Blount family as presented here was originally based on Cokayne's *Complete Peerage*, vol. 9, pages 329-337, under the heading Mountjoy. The sources checked by Vernon M. Norr, in *Some Early English Pedigrees*, 26-28, have been studied with the exception of Sir Alexander Croke's *Croke Family*, 2 vols. (1823), and William Henry Cooke's *History of Herefordshire* (1882), 3:65.

RUDOLPH[S] LE BLOUNT, born say 997, was Count of Guines, grandson of Sigefred, the Dane, first Count, who was grandson of Harold V, King of Denmark [Burke's *Commoners*, 1:355, the line of Sir Alexander Croke of Studley Priory, Oxfordshire]. He married ROSETTA, said by Croke to be a daughter of Hugh, second Count of St. Pol.

Sir ROBERT[R] LE BLOUNT, born say 1029, was the first Baron Ixworth in Suffolk. He married GUNDRED, who was said to be a daughter or sister of Henry, who was identified erroneously as Earl Ferrers.

GILBERT[Q] LE BLOUNT, born say 1055, was second Baron Ixworth. He married ALICE DE COLEKIRKE.

WILLIAM[P] LE BLOUNT, third Baron Ixworth, was born say 1087. He married SARAH[P] DE MUNCHESNE, daughter of Hubert de Munchesne.

GILBERT[O] LE BLOUNT, fourth Baron Ixworth, was born say 1119, and was living in 1173 [Burke's *Commoners*, 3:164]. He married AGNES[O] DE L'ISLE, or de Insúlâ, who was living in 1198.

Sir STEPHEN[N] LE BLOUNT, who was of record 1189-1198, succeeded his nephew William. He married MARIA LE BLOUNT of Saxlington, only daughter and heiress of Sir William le Blound, of Saxlingham (fourth in direct line from Sir William, brother of Sir Robert, according to Burke's *Commoners*, 1:355).

Sir ROBERT[M] BLOUNT, lord of Saxlington, died in 1288. He married ISABEL[M], daughter of [lord of (Burke, 1:355)] Odenselo (or Odinsels). He was a witness to the charter of Hilton Abbey, Staffordshire, in 1223, and acquired Belton, Rutland.

8. WILLIAM[L] LE BLUND (or BLOUNT) apparently died in the spring of 1280 [*CP*, 9:330].

He married first ISABEL, traditionally a member of the Beauchamp family, thought by some to be a daughter of William[M] de Beauchamp of Elmley Castle by Isabel[M] Malduit, sister and ultimately heiress of William Malduit, Earl of Warwick and lord of Hanslope in Buckinghamshire [Cokayne, 9:329d]. Isabel was widow of Henry Lovet of Elmley Lovet and Hampton Lovet in Worcestershire, who died under age about 1256 [Norr, 27]. She has been identified also as Isabel (or Ann) de St. Maure, widow of Lovett [*Visitation of Worcester 1569*, 16-17], but the line given in this pedigree shows him as son of Sir William Blount (who married a daughter of John Meriot), who was in turn son of Sir William Blount and Ellenor, daughter and coheir of John Woodthorpe, Esq.

In addition to property in Worcestershire he held the manor of Belton in Rutland, and there may have been a close connection with a family of the same name in Hanslope, Bucks., which he held in 1268, and which was held by Isabel in 1296.

He was accused in August 1265, before the commissioners appointed under the *Dictum* of Kenilworth, of unlawful violence at Quinton in Northamptonshire, England.

Children, named by Cokayne [9:330-331, 332e], surnamed le Blount:

      i.   son[K], b. say 1262; descendant Alice was heiress of Belton.
9.   ii. Walter, third son, b. say 1264; m. Joan[K] de Sodington.
      iii. Piers, b. say 1266; d. 1294; rector of Hanslope; no issue.

9. Sir WALTER[K] LE BLOUNT of the Rock, Worcestershire, died before May 1324, when his name was absent from the return of the Sheriff of Worcestershire.

According to the *Visitation of Worcester* he married first [20, 51] or second [17] Eleanor de Beauchamp, daughter and heir of John de Beauchamp of Hache, Somerset [*Vis. Worcs.*, 17]. Vernon M. Norr [*Some Early English Pedigrees*, 27] has treated the allegations that he married first, in 1268, Elizabeth Beauchamp.

He married, second according to G.W. Watson [*CP*, 2:196], before Feb. 1294, JOAN[K] DE SODINGTON*.

He was in 1313 a part of the Lancastrian party against Piers de Gaveston. In 1318 and 1321 he was Knight of the Shire for Worcester, and in 1322 he was summoned for personal service against the Scots.

Children, sons named in the return of the Sheriff of Worcestershire, by Joan de Sodington:

i. Sir William[J], d. by 3 Oct. 1337; m. before 20 Feb. 1326/7 Margery[M] de Verdun, who m. (2) before 18 Oct. 1338 Sir Mark Husee (who d. before 21 July 1349), m. (3) before 10 Sept. 1355, as first wife, Sir John[L] Crophull of Bonnington, Notts., who d. 3 July 1383; Sir William was a non resident landholder, M.P. 1327-1335 [*CP*, 2:196]; no issue, according to Watson, but dau. Alice, d. without issue, was listed in *Vis. Worcs.* [17].

10. ii. John, second son, m. Isold; an experienced soldier, but landless; heir to his brother William.

iii. Walter, third son, m. Matilda [*Vis. Shropshire 1623*, 51]; an experienced soldier, but landless.

10. Sir JOHN[J] LE BLOUNT, who was aged 39 in 1337 when he was a knight and found heir to his elder brother, William Blount, Lord Blount, was of Sodington in Worcestershire when he died in 1358.

Norr cited Sir Alexander Croke's *Croke Family* [2:136½] for a first marriage, in 1307, to Elizabeth, by whom no issue was shown.

His often alleged first wife, ISOUDE (or Isolda), has been identified as a Mountjoy [Norr cited the defective *Vis. Worcs.* (Harleian Society), 27:17, 21]. Roskell [2:262] called her daughter and coheir of Sir Thomas de Mountjoy, and stated that she died in 1337.

Some have stated he married second, or third, 1307, Elizabeth Beauchamp, daughter of Sir John Beauchamp of Hache. Norr [27] cited *Burke's Commoners* [1:355, 3:165], and *Croke Family* for the statement she was a widow, daughter of John Beauchamp of Hache, but not the widow of John Meriet, who was the only husband of an Eleanor.

In 1324 he was a practiced soldier of Worcestershire. He was joint commissioner in Worcestershire in 1344, inquiring as to holders of land. He served in Gascony under Henry, Earl of Lancaster, and later, in 1347, under King Edward III at the siege of Calais, until the king returned to England. In Oct. 1350 he was on a pilgrimage to Santiago.

Children, listed by Vernon M. Norr, by wife Isolda [*Vis. Worcs.*, 17:20; 21 is defective (*cf.* Roskell, 2:262), and *BP*, 1:297]:

i. Sir Richard[I], b. 1345; apparently killed in action by 1374, had campaigned in Aquitaine with the Black Prince.

ii. Sir John, d. 4 April 1425; m. Eleanor Beauchamp [*BP*, 1:297]; their second son, John, m. (1) Juliana Foulshurst, m. (2) Isabel Cornwall, dau. and heiress of Sir Bryan Cornwall, of Sodington, Worcs. [*cf.* Bayne, *EG*, 15/16 (1982), 416; Roskell, *Hist. Parl.*, 2:255].

11. iii. Walter, third son, b. c. 1348; d. Shrewbury 21 July 1403; m. c. 1373 Sancha[I] de Ayala.

iv. Thomas, beheaded 1400.

11. Sir WALTER[I] BLOUNT, born about 1348, was slain while fighting for the King against Percy's revolt at Shrewsbury, 21 July 1403. He was buried at St. Mary's, Newark, Leicester, England.

He married, about 1373, Doña SANCHA[I] DE AYALA (daughter of Don Diego de Guzmán, lord of Casarrubios, Malpica and Valdepusa, Governor of the Castle of Toledo in Castilla in Spain, and his wife Inés de Ayala), who had come to England in Dec. 1371 in the service of Constance of Castile, John of Gaunt's second wife. She left a will dated 1415 stating her wish to be buried beside her husband at Newark, Leicester, where her mistress Constance was also interred. Plans by her son's enemies to destroy her manor house at Barton Blount and murder her son Sir John before her eyes did not bear fruit.

He became a noted soldier and apparently acquired a great fortune. Tradition has it that he fought at Najera under John of Gaunt on 3 April 1367. He was apparently in that Duke's service in 1369, and was already a knight in March 1371/2. In Jan. 1372/3 the Duke appointed him Constable of Tutbury Castle for life, and in May he contracted to serve the Duke in peace and war for life.

By 1372 he had joined the household of John of Gaunt, with whom in March 1377/8 he set out for Spain. He had fought in Brittany under Edmund, Earl of Cambridge, in 1375.

In 1380 he was J.P. for Staffordshire, and in 1388 he held the same office in Derbyshire. In 1386 he accompanied John of Gaunt to Spain again. In 1387 he suffered loss of face when Sir John[i] Ipstones forced him to give up a bond for good behavior previously taken from one of Ipstone's servants [Roskell, 2:264]. In 1392 he was a commissioner of array in Staffs., and in 1393 he was to treat with Spain as to peace. He and Sancha his wife obtained papal indults for portable alters in 1394. He was chosen Knight of the Shire for Derby in 1399 after the accession of King Henry IV, whom he had led to Revenspur with a large force of his own. In Feb. 1399/1400 he was receiving instructions for an embassy to Portugal, Spain and Aragon, and in August 1401 he was summoned to a Council. In that year he was a commissioner for *oyer* and *terminer*. Also in 1400 he was sent to Ireland in attendance to the king's son, Thomas of Lancaster. He was a character in Shakespeare's *Henry IV*, although Cokayne did not believe Shakespeare's thesis that Sir Walter le Blount died as a result of being dressed like the King at Shrewsbury.

His will, dated at Liverpool 16 Dec. 1401, was proved 1 Aug. 1403. In it he mentioned "Constance Baroness Dudley."

Children, listed by Vernon M. Norr [*Some Early English Pedigrees*, 28]:

    i.   Walter[H], first son, living 1382.

    ii.   Sir John, second and surviving son, one of the greatest captains of his time, was killed by a cannon shot at the siege of Rouen before 1 Sept. 1418 [1414 in Norr]; m. Alice; no issue.

*   iii.   Constance, d. 1432; m. (1) Hugh Hastings, m. (2) Sir John[H] de Sutton of Dudley Castle, Staffordshire.

    iv.   Sir Thomas, third son, heir in 1418; m. (1) Margaret Gresley, m. (2) Elizabeth; of Elwaston, Derbyshire, treasurer of Normandy.

    v.   Peter, fourth son, no issue.

    vi.   Ann, m. Thomas Griffith of Whichnor, Shropshire.

§ § §

DE BOHUN

This line was developed from Cokayne's treatment of Hereford.

HUMPHREY[R] DE BOHUN III, Baron de Bohun, was also Lord of Hereford. He married MARGARET[O] OF HEREFORD, who died in 1146.

HUMPHREY[Q] DE BOHUN, IV, Baron de Bohun and Lord of Hereford, died in 1182. He married as her second husband MARGARET[P] DE HUNTINGDON, who had married first Conan IV, Duke of Brittany and Earl of Richmond, who died in 1171; she died in 1201.

HENRY[P] DE BOHUN, 5th Earl of Hereford, born in 1176, was said to have died on a pilgrimage to the Holy Land, 1 June 1220, and was buried in the chapter house of Llanthony Priory outside of Gloucester. He married MAUD[P] FITZ GEOFFREY DE MANDEVILLE, who died 27 Aug. 1236, Countess of Essex and daughter of Geoffrey Fitz Piers and Beatrice de Say, daughter of William de Say. She married second Roger de Daunteseye of Dauntsey, Wiltshire, and when her brother, William de Mandeville, Earl of Essex, died on 8 Jan. 1226/7 she became the Countess of Essex. The second marriage was to have ended in divorce, but it was revoked. Roger was still living in Aug. 1238.

HUMPHREY[O] DE BOHUN V, 6th Earl of Hereford and 7th Earl of Essex, born by 1208, died 24 Sept. 1275, and was buried by the high alter at Llanthony by Gloucester. He married first MAUD[O] D'EU DE LUSIGNAN, who died 14 Aug. 1241, and was buried at Llanthony by Gloucester. He married second Maud de Avenbury, who died at Sorges, in Gascony, 8 Oct. 1273, where she was buried until her remains were placed by her husband in 1290.

HUMPHREY[N] DE BOHUN VI, died at Beeston Castle, Cheshire, 27 Oct. 1265, after having been taken prisoner at the battle of Evesham, 4 Aug. 1265 [CP, 6:463], and was buried in Combermere Abbey. He married first, by 15 Feb. 1247/8, ELEANOR[M] DE BRAIOSE of Huntington, Brecon, Wales, who was buried at Llanthony by Gloucester.

HUMPHREY[M] DE BOHUN, VII, Earl of Hereford and Essex, born about 1249, died in Pleshey, Essex, 31 Dec. 1298, and was buried at Walden Priory, Essex. His only marriage was 20 July 1275 to MAUD[M] DE FIENNES*, who predeceased him [CP, 6:466b] and was buried at Walden Abbey, Essex. An entry of her name in 1315 was apparently an error for Maud, Countess of Gloucester and Hertford.

7. HUMPHREY[L] DE BOHUN VIII, Earl of Hereford and Essex, born about 1276, was slain at the battle of Boroughbridge in Yorkshire on 16 March 1321/2, and was buried at the church of the Friars Preachers in Yorkshire.

He married in Westminster, 14 Nov. 1302, ELIZABETH[L] PLANTAGENET*, who died in Quendon, England, 5 May 1316, and was buried at Walden Abbey, Essex. She had married first, in Ipswich, 8 or 18 Jan. 1296/7, John, Count of Holland.

He had livery of his father's lands on 16 Feb. 1298/9, attended the marriage of King Edward I to Queen Margaret at Canterbury on 9 Sept. 1299, and was present at the siege of Caerlaverock in Scotland on 1 July 1300, serving in Scotland several times thereafter. He and the Earl of Lincoln fastened the spurs of Prince Edward when he was knighted on 22 May 1306, but he served as one of the Lords Ordainers in 1310, losing his constableship, which was restored 28 Aug. 1311. Then he was pardoned for his part in the summary execution of Piers de Gavaston in 1312, which was described by Harold F. Hutchinson as "at best judicial murder, and...the beginning of two centuries of baronial slaughter" [Edward II, 1284-1327, 71] which in the next 150 years cost the lives of almost all the ancient baronage and a great many of the royal house.

At the battle of Bannockburn he and the Earl of Gloucester were in dispute as to whom would take precedence in the line of battle; when the Earl of Gloucester dashed forward his horse fell and Gloucester was killed. After the English were defeated Hereford retreated to Bothwell, where he was given up by Governor Sir Walter Gilbertson. The Scots exchanged him for Elizabeth[K] de Burgh (who was wife of King Robert the Bruce of Scotland), and the Bishop of St. Andrews.

On 11 Feb. 1315/6 he was captain of the forces against Llywelyn Bren ap Rhys in Glamorgan, Wales, and on 2 July he was headed for Scotland. On 8 Nov. 1318 he was recorded on a diplomatic mission to the Counts of Flanders, Hainault, Holland and Zealand. Another mission to Robert the Bruce was dated 19 Jan. 1320/1. In May and June 1321 he ravaged the lands of Hugh le Despenser the younger. By 15 Jan. 1321/2 an order for his arrest was issued, he having joined the Earl of Lancaster and assisted in the taking of Gloucester and the burning of Bridgenorth. He was killed while trying to force the bridge at Boroughbridge on 16 March 1321/2.

He was Lord High Constable of England.

Children, no doubt among others:

    i.   son[K], d. young.

    ii.   John, Earl of Hereford and Essex, b. St. Clements 23 Nov. 1306; d. Kirkby-Thore, Westmorland, 20 Jan. 1335/6; m. (1) 1324 Alice Fitz Alan, m. (2) Margaret Basset of Drayton.

    iii.   Humphrey, Earl of Hereford and Essex, d. Pleshey, Essex, 15 Oct. 1361; unm.; succeeded by Humphrey[J] de Bohun, nephew and heir.

    iv.   Edward, Constable of England 26 Oct. 1330 [CP, 6:471].

    v.   Margaret, b. 3 April 1311; d. 16 Dec. 1391, bur. Exeter Cathedral [mi]; m. 11 Aug. 1325 Hugh de Courtenay, K.G., 10th Earl of Devon, who d. 2 May 1377.

8.   vi.   William, b. Fotheringhay, Northants., c. 1312; d. Sept. 1360; m. c. 1335 Elizabeth[K] de Badlesmere, widow of Edmund Mortimer.

*   vii.   Alianore (or Eleanor), second surviving dau., d. 7 Oct. 1363; m. (1) James[K] Butler, Earl of Ormond, who d. c. 17 Feb. 1337/8, m. (2) (lic. 24 Jan. 1343/4 to m. in the chapel of her manor at Vachery in Surrey) Sir Thomas de Dagworth, who was slain 1350 [CP, 4:27-29].

8.   Sir WILLIAM[K] DE BOHUN, K.G., Earl of Northampton, was born in Fotheringhay, Northamptonshire, about 1312, died in Sept. 1360, and was buried at Walden Abbey, Essex.

He married, about 1335, ELIZABETH[K] DE BADLESMERE*, of Sussex, who died in June 1356 and was buried at Black Friars' in London, widow of Edmund Mortimer, who died in 1332, whom she had married first on 27 June 1316. The marriage was probably arranged to make peace between the families of Mortimer and Bohun.

He and his elder brother Humphrey were involved in the seizure of Roger[K] de Mortimer, Earl of March, by King Edward III in 1330, and from that time on he was one of the king's closest councillors until his death. In 1333 and the summer of 1336 he served in Scotland, and was created Earl of Northampton on 16 March 1336/7. On 12 June 1338 he was granted the office of Constable of England for life by his brother Humphrey, Earl of Hereford and Essex [CP, 6:472].

On 24 June 1340 he was a leader in the victory at Sluys, and was with the King at the siege of Tournay, returning to England with him in November. He saw service in Scotland in 1341, and was the King's Lieutenant in Brittany on 20 July 1342.

He fought in the first division, under Prince Edward, at Crécy, and participated in the siege of Calais. Occupied diplomatically 1347-1349, he was made Knight of the Garter at the end of 1349. In August 1350 he took part in the naval victory over Spain off Winchelsea, and in October he was made Warden of the Scottish Marches. In 1351-1353 he was involved in Scotland, and as Admiral of the Fleet in the North. He took part in the expedition to France, 1359-1360, and was a witness to the Treaty of Brétigny on 8 May 1360.

He was actively involved in the wool trade.

Children, mentioned by Cokayne:

    i.   Humphrey[J], Earl of Hereford, Essex and Northampton, Constable of England, b. 25 March 1342; d. 16 Jan. 1372/3, bur. Walden Abbey; m. Joan[J] Fitz Alan, who d. 7 April 1419, bur. Walden Abbey.

          Daughters: 1. Eleanor[I], m. Thomas of Woodstock, youngest son of King Edward III, Earl of Buckingham 1377 and Duke of Gloucester 1385, Constable of England. 2. Mary, m. Henry IV, King of England [Faris, PA2, 35].

*   ii.   Elizabeth, d. 3 April 1385, bur. Lewes, Sussex; m. c. 28 Sept. 1359 Sir Richard[J] Fitz Alan.

§ § §

LE BOTELER of WEM

According to G.W. Watson [*CP*, 2:232a], the family name was assumed by their ancestor, Ralph, who held the office of Butler to Robert, Earl of Leicester, and seated himself at Oversley, Warwickshire. Ralph was the founder of Alcester Priory, Warks., in 1140.

According to Joseph Morris' *Shropshire Genealogies* [1332], Ralph le Boteler held the office of butler to Robert de Beaumont during the reign of King Henry I, and built Oversby (or Oversley?) Castle in Warwick on lands given him by the Earl.

RALPH[N] BOTELER, of Oversley, Warwickshire [*CP*, 2:230], was succeeded by his son shortly before 3 July 1281, the date of his *writ de diem clausit* [Eyton, 7:171]. He married before 1243 MAUD (or Matilda)[N] PANTULF, of Wem, who died shortly before 6 May 1289, having married second, before 9 May 1283, Walter de Hopton of Hopton, Shropshire, who was eminent in the law; she had died before the Assizes were held in 1292.

2. Sir WILLIAM[M] BOTELER of Wem, Shropshire, died shortly before 11 Dec. 1283, the date of a writ by King Edward I, at Leominster, announcing his death [Eyton's *Ant. Shropshire*, 173].

He married (license dated 2 Oct. 1261, at instance of James d'Alditheleg' (Audley), her uncle) ANGHARAD[M] FERCH GRUFFUDD[†] (lord of Dinas Brân, who died 1269, having married Emma[N] de Audley[+], daughter of Henry de Audley [Bartrum, *Welsh Genealogies*, chart Bleddyn ap Cynfyn 4]) AP MADOG AP GRUFFUDD MAELOR (who died in 1191, having married Angharad ferch Owain Gwynedd) AP MADOG of Bromfield, Dinas Bran, and Yale of Lower Powys (now in Denbighshire), Wales; she was born about 1248, and died after 22 June 1308, having held lands in Dodington, and having married second Robert de Neville [Eyton, 7:173].

He was one of three knights, with Ralph le Boteler and John le Brompton, who were summoned 1 July 1277 (to perform military due from his father), when the English army was meeting at Worcester to campaign against Llywelyn [Eyton, 7:173]. He was summoned by King Edward I on 24 May 10 Edw. I (1282) and 14 March 11 Edw. I (1282/3), and to attend the King at Shrewsbury, 28 June 1283 [*CP*, 2:231].

Children, sons listed by G.W. Watson [*CP*, 2:231-232]:

    i.   John[L], b. 17 July 1266 [Eyton, 7:173]; d. shortly before 4 Sept. 1287 seized of his paternal estates in Warwickshire; m. after 18 July 1284 Eleanor (or Alianore)[K] de Beauchamp (who "seems to have completed her twelfth year on November 11th, next after her husband's death" [Eyton, 7:173]), who m. (2) 1293 John de la Mare; no issue.

    ii. Gawain, b. 2 Feb. 1269/70; d. shortly before 3 March 1289/90; m. Alice, who was living 21 Sept. 1334; no issue.

3. iii. William, b. 11 June 1274; d. before 14 Sept. 1334; m. (1) before 1298 Beatrice, m. (2) before Feb. 1315/6 Ela de Herdeburgh.

*   iv. Anne, poss. m. Gilbert[L] Talbot, 1st Lord Talbot of Eccleswall, Herefordshire, who d. 24 Feb. 1345/6 [Weis, *AR*7, 84A:30].

3. WILLIAM[L] LE BOTELER, Lord Boteler, born (probably in Oversley, Warwickshire) 11 June 1274, died before 14 Sept. 1334 [*CP*, 2:232], the date of the writ for his *inquisition post mortem*.

He married first, before 1298, BEATRICE, who died between 1305/6 and Feb. 1316 [Weis, *AR*7, 77:32].

He married second, before Feb. 1315/6, ELA[L] DE HERDEBURGH, who was living 5 July 1343, daughter and coheir of Roger de Herdeburgh.

He had livery of his brother's lands 8 April 1296, was summoned to muster at London 2 Feb. 1298 for service in Flanders, and served in the Scottish wars from 25 March of the same year. He was summoned to Parliament 10 March 1307/8 to 10 Oct. 1325, with the last of more than eighty writs addressed to him being dated 24 Jan. 1326[/7]. He served as a Justice of Assize, a Conservator of the Peace, and Commander of levies, in addition to being an M.P. [Eyton, 7:175].

Child, by first wife:

    4.   i.   William[K], b. 8 Sept. 1298; d. Dec. 1361; m. (1) Margaret Fitz Alan, m. (2) c. 1354 Joan[K] Sudeley, who d. before 1367.

Child, by second wife [Eyton, 7:175]:

*   ii.   Ankaret, d. 8 Oct. 1361; m. John[K] le Strange, 2nd Baron Strange of Blackmere, who d. 21 July 1349.

    iii.   son, d. without issue [Eyton, 7:175-176].

    iv.   son, d. without issue.

4. WILLIAM[K] LE BOTELER, born 8 Sept. 1298, died in Dec. 1361 [*CP*, 2:232].

He married first Margaret[L] Fitz Alan, daughter of Richard, Earl of Arundel.

He married second, about 1354, JOAN[K] SUDELEY*, who died before Aug. 1367 [Walter L. Sheppard, *Gen. Mag.*, 13:173-174; *cf.* Col. F.B. Twemlow, "Manor of Tyrley," *Staffs. Rec. Soc.*, 41-42 (defective citation); *CP*, 14:101].

He was never summoned to Parliament, and died without any lands, having entailed them to his son William prior to 5 July 1343 [Eyton, 7:176].

Child, by first wife:

    i.   William[J], d. 14 Aug. 1369; m. before July 1343 Elizabeth; no sons, dau. Elizabeth[I] (who d. June 1411) m. (1) by 1379 Robert[K] de Ferrers (who d. c. 1380, son of Robert, 2nd Lord Ferrers, and Agnes de Bohun, dau. of Humphrey, Earl of Hereford), m. (2) Sir John Say, m. (3) before Michaelmas 2 Hen. IV (1402-1403) Sir Thomas Molinton, who d. 7 May 1408.

Child, by second wife:

    5.   ii.   Thomas, b. Tyrley, Staffs., 1355; d. 21 Sept. 1398; m. Alice[I] Beauchamp of Powick, Worcs.

Child, mother unknown:

    iii.   Elizabeth, mentioned by Eyton [7:176].

5. Sir THOMAS[J] BOTELER, 4th Baron Sudeley of Sudeley, Gloucestershire, was said to have been christened at Drayton in Halls, Staffordshire, 1 Oct. 1358 (in 1367 he was of record as found to be aged 12 on 1 Nov. 1366), and died 21 Sept. 1398.

He married, on or before 18 July 1385, ALICE[I] BEAUCHAMP* of Powick, Worcestershire, who died 8 Feb. 1442/3, who married second Sir John Dalyngrygg, whom she survived. In Cokayne [12:1:418k] it was observed that her placement as daughter of Sir John[J] Beauchamp cannot be made to tally with Dugdale's treatment of the family [*Baronage*, 1:249].

He was nephew, and ultimately sole heir, of Sir John[K] de Sudeley, who died 11 Aug. 1367 [Sheppard, *Gen. Mag.*, 13:173], his mother's younger brother. On 28 April 1379 he was granted, until he was of lawful age (although in 1367 he was found to have been aged 12 on 1 Nov. then last past), the keeping of a moiety of all the lands in counties Warwick, Gloucester and Worcester of the late John de Sudeley, *chivaler*, and on 30 Nov. 1379 he had a similar grant of lands of his late Aunt Margery. By 23 Nov. 1380 he had proved his age and done homage and fealty.

In 1389/90 he had license to travel to France as a knight, and on 5 Feb. 1397/8 he was exempted "from being made a justice of the peace or other justice, sheriff, escheator, coroner, mayor, bailiff or other minister of the King, and from being put on assizes, juries, attaints, etc." [*CP*, 12:1:418i]; he was never summoned to Parliament.

Children, mentioned in Cokayne:

* i. Joan[I], m. Hamon[I] Belknap, who d. 9 June 1450.
  ii. John, d. before 1410; no issue; prob. unm.
  iii. William, d. on or before 20 Dec. 1417; m. Alice; was in 1412 entitled to a moiety of the castle and manor of Beaudesert, with the town of Henley-in-Arden, Warks.
  iv. Sir Ralph, lord Sudeley [*CP*, 12:1:419-421], d. 2 May 1473; m. (1) Mrs. Elizabeth Hende, who d. 28 Aug. 1462, m. (2) Alice Deincourt (widow of William Lovel), who d. 10 Feb. 1473/4; High Treasurer of England.

§ § §

✓ BRERETON

The following has been adapted largely from Ormerod's *History of Chester* [2:686-688, and 3:81-88]. The compiler has not seen Sir Fortunatus Dwarris' *Memoirs of the Brereton Family* or Robert Maitland Brereton's *The Breretons of Cheshire*, which are mentioned in John Brereton's *Brereton, a Family History* (1919).

WILLIAM[Q] DE BRERETON, possibly a son of Ralph de Brerton, who was witness to a charter by Gilbert Venables at the time of William II or Henry I, is the person with whom the Brereton pedigree begins [Ormerod, 3:88]. WILLIAM[P] DE BRERTON was next in the pedigree. Sir RALPH[O] DE BRERTON was a knight.

Sir WILLIAM[N] DE BRERTON was lord of Brerton, living in the times of King John and Henry I. He married MARGERY DE THORNTON, daughter of Randle de Thornton, according to Ormerod [3:88], but reference to the Thornton lineage makes this subject to question.

Sir RALPH[M] DE BRERTON was Lord of Brerton, and was living, according to Sir Fortunatus Dwarris, in 1275. Some have stated that he agreed to marry Ada, daughter of David, Earl of Huntingdon, and relict of Henry Hastings, who died in 1250. However, Weis [*AR7*, 93:27], does not mention an actual marriage.

Sir WILLIAM[L] DE BRERTON, Lord of Brerton, had been the ward of Sir R. de Sandbach, as named by Ormerod [3:88], in the time of King Henry III. He married a daughter of Sir Richard[M] de Sonbach.

7. Sir WILLIAM[K] DE BRERTON, knighted in 1301, was perhaps Lord of Brereton in 1321. He married ROSE[L] DE VERNON*, daughter of Sir Raulph de Vernon of Shipbrook. She was living 15 Edw. II (1321-1322). It has been alleged that she married second, before 1308, Sir Thomas[L] Davenport.

Children, listed in the pedigree [Ormerod, *Chester*, 3:88]:

  i. Peter[J].
  ii. Richard, living 15 Edw. II (1321-1322).
8. iii. William, d. in his father's lifetime; m. Margery de Bosley; living 15 Edw. III (1341-1342).
  iv. John, rector of Wallasey.
  v. Nicholas, m. Margaret.

    vi.   Margery, m. (contract 1301) John de Davenport, Lord of Davenport, div. 1305.

    vii. Matilda, m. John Dumville.

8. WILLIAM[J] DE BRERTON was living 15 Edw. III (1341-1342).

He married MARGERY[J] DE BOSLEY, daughter of Richard de Bosley. The latter is not mentioned in Ormerod's treatment of the manor of Bosley in Macclesfield Hundred in Cheshire [3:736-738].

Children, listed in the pedigree:

9.   i.   Sir William[I], m. (1?) Ellen[I] de Egerton, m. (2?) Margaret Done, widow of John de Davenport of Henbury.

    ii. John.

    iii. Ralph, rector of Davenham.

    iv. Robert.

    v.   Hugh.

    vi. Margaret, m. Henry[H] Delves, brother of Sir John Delves.

    vii. Jane, m. Adam de Bostock, lord of Bostock.

9. Sir WILLIAM[I] BRERTON, knight, of Brerton, England, was living in 1375.

He married twice, once to ELLEN[I] DE EGERTON*, daughter of Philip de Egerton and sister and finally heiress of David de Egerton, Lord of Egerton and joint Baron of Malpas. She claimed a moiety of a fourth of the barony of Malpas against John Sutton in 1368, and another moiety of a fourth against Sir Walter Cokesay in 1379.

He married probably second MARGARET[I] DONE, daughter of Henry Done of Utkinton, according to Brereton sources. Ormerod's pedigree of Done of Utkinton [2:248] does show a Margaret Done, daughter of Richard Done of Utkinton, who married as her second husband Sir William Brereton and had a nephew who held land in 1402; her first husband had been John Davenport of Davenport (of Henbury, who was living 5 Hen. V [1417-1418]) [Ormerod, 3:88], second brother and heir of Sir Thomas Davenport. This was corrected to show Margaret as daughter of Henry Done in Ormerod's volume 3, page 88 [cf. History of Chester, 3:898].

He had a grant of free warren and market in 42 Edw. III (1368-1369).

Child, by Ellen de Egerton, from the pedigree:

10.   i.   Sir William[H], m. (1) 1386 Anilla[K] Venables, m. (2) Elen Mascy.

Children, by Margaret Done, listed in the pedigree:

11.   ii. Randle, m. Alice[H] Ipstones.

    iii. Elizabeth, m. William de Cholmondeley, who d. before 49 Edw. III (1375-1376).

    iv. daughter, m. the Lord of Spurstow.

10. Sir WILLIAM[H] DE BRERETON, Lord of Brereton, was born in Eggerton in the Feast of St. Valentine, 23 Edw. III (1350-1351), baptized at Malpas, and was dead at the time of an *inquisition post mortem* dated 4 Hen. VI (1425-1426).

He married, perhaps first, at Audley, 1386, ANILLA[K] VENABLES*, daughter of Hugh Venables, Baron of Kinderton.

He married, perhaps second, Elen Mascy (daughter of William Mascy of Tatton, knight), who married next Sir Gilbert de Halsall. Her *inquisition post mortem* was held 23 Hen. VI (1444-1445).

He was a knight in 1385.

Children, by Anilla[K] Venables, listed by Ormerod:
  i.   William[G], d. before his father at Harfleur; m. Alice Corbet, sister and coheir of Richard Corbet of Leghton in the Barony of Caus (she remarried John Streteley, Esq.), her *inquisition post mortem* dated 37 Hen. VI (1458-1459) [A.E. Corbet, 190].
  ii. Nicholas.
  iii. Hugh.
  iv. Matthew.
  v.   John.
  vi. Henry, had son of record Roger 15 Edw. IV (1475-1476).
* vii. Elizabeth, m. Sir John[H] Savage.
Child, by Elen Mascy:
  viii. Thomas, b. c. 1411; rector of Brereton 1433, aged 34 in 23 Hen. VI (1444-1445).

11. Sir RANDLE[H] BRERETON of Malpas, Cheshire, England, was listed in the pedigree Ormerod drew from sources noted as "Cheshire Pedigrees, the Inquisitions and Parochial Registers."

He married ALICE[H] IPSTONES*, daughter and heiress of Sir John Ipstones of Ipstones and his wife Elizabeth Corbet [Paul C. Reed, *TG*, 10:60, note 53]. Ormerod gave her father as William de Ipstones.

Ormerod noted that Sir Randle was the progenitor of Brereton of Malpas Hall, Ipstones and Shocklach.

Children, from Ormerod's pedigree:
12. i.   Randle[G], of Ipstones, m. (1) Joan Holford, dau. of William Holford, m. (2) Katherine Bulkeley, dau. of William Bulkeley of Eaton.
     ii. William, second son, of Burros, m. Katherine, dau. and coheir of Thomas Weild, or Wyld, of Bhyrros, near Wrexham.
     iii. Edward of Burros, or Boresham, m. (1) Elizabeth, dau. of John Roden (or Royden) of Burton, m. (2) Dorothy Hanmer, dau. of Sir Richard Hanmer of Hanmer in Flintshire.
     iv. daughter, m.; lived Spurstow.

12. RANDLE[G] BRERETON was of Ipstones, Cheshire.

He married first, Joan, daughter of William Holford.

He married second, KATHERINE[G] BULKELEY, daughter of William Bulkeley of Eaton in Davenham, a parish in the center of Cheshire. A chronological study might determine whether the William Bulkeley in question was likely the son and heir of John Bulkeley of Ayton, Cheshire, who was aged 21 in 1 Ric. II (1397-1398) and dead in 3 Hen. IV (1401-1402). This William was of record in 6 Hen. IV (1404-1405), and 5 & 6 Hen. V (1417-1419). The next generation William Bulkeley of Ayton, king's sergeant-at-law, was of record 5 Hen. VI (1426-1427), and was deputy justice of Cheshire and Flint in 7, 19 and 26 Hen. VI (1428-1429, 1440-1441 and 1447-1448 respectively), died 1 May 1467, and was buried at Davenham [Ormerod, 3:269]. Ormerod [2:652] contains further data on the family of Bulkylegh or Bulkeley.

Children, from Ormerod's pedigree, illegitimate:
     i.   Randle[F], of Eccleston and Wettenhall.
     ii. Owen, of Barrel, or Bar Hill; ancestor of Brereton of Cuddington.
Children, from Ormerod's pedigree (but deleting Ralph, given in error), by second wife:
13. iii. Randle, d. in Burgundy; m. Emma[F] Carrington.

iv.   Bartholomew, third son, of Grafton.

13. RANDLE^F BRERETON of Ipstones in Cheshire, died in Burgundy.

He married EMMA^F CARRINGTON*, daughter and heiress of John Carrington of Carrington. She had brothers Hamlet and Thomas.

Children, from Ormerod's pedigree, corrected:

    i.   Humphrey^E of Malpas.
    ii.   Ralph, of Iscoyd, m.
    iii. Ellen, m. Nicholas Bruyn of Tarvin.
    iv. Eleanor, m. Philip Egerton, Esq.
14.   v.   Randle, m. Eleanor^E Dutton of Hatton.

14. Sir RANDLE^E BRERETON, was of Ipstones, Shocklach and Malpas, Cheshire, and died 3 or 8 June 1530 [E.W. Ives, ed., *Letters and Accounts of William Brereton of Malpas* (Record Society...Lancashire and Cheshire, 116, Old Woking, Surrey, 1976), pp. 1-65].

He married ELEANOR^E DUTTON* of Hatton, who was buried at Malpas, having survived her husband.

He served as Chamberlain of Chester 21 Hen. VII (1505-1506) to 23 Hen. VIII (1531-1532), was knight banneret, and knight of the body to King Henry VII.

His testament and will (two different documents) were dated 3 June 1530 and proved 30 August 1530, and mentioned his daughter Elizabeth Mainwaring, his son-in-law Richard Cholmondeley, deceased, and grandson Richard Cholmondeley [*P.C.C. Jankyn 26*].

He was made a knight banneret by King Henry VIII "as a reward for his conduct at Terouenne and Tournay" [Brooke, *Proc. Historic Soc. Lancs. & Cheshire*, 2 (1849), 43].

E.W. Ives pointed out that notwithstanding this marriage the Duttons of Hatton were the greatest enemies of the Brereton family in Cheshire.

Children, from Ormerod's pedigree, and *Pedigrees...of Cheshire, 1613* [38-39], and *Cheshire Vis. Pedigrees, 1663* [13-15]:

    i.   Randle^D, knight, m. (1) Eleanor, dau. of Sir Philip Egerton of Egerton and Oulton, m. (2) Isabel Butler, dau. of Thomas Butler of Bewsey [Baines' *Hist. Lancaster*, 3:660; order of marriages reversed in *Cheshire Vis. Pedigrees, 1663*, 13].

    ii.   Sir Richard, m. Jane, dau. of Sir Geoffrey Massey of Tatton.

    iii. John, d. 1542; rector of both moieties of Malpas, and of Astbury, Bebington, and of St. Mary's in Chester.

    iv. Thomas, d. 1511; rector of the high moiety of Malpas.

    v.   Peter, parson of Haswall and vicar of Oswestry.

    vi. Sir Roger, m. Katherine Brereton (dau. of Sir William Brereton of Brereton), widow of Edward Fulleshurst (Foulshurst) of Crewe.

    vii. William, knight, groom of the chamber to King Henry VIII, sentenced to die at Tyburn with Mark Smeaton, the "musician and 'deft dancer' in the King's chamber," Sir Francis Weston and Sir Henry Norris "to be cut down [after hanging] while still alive, disembowelled, castrated and finally to have their limbs quartered" [Antonia Fraser, *The Wives of Henry VIII*, 242-250], but according to John Brereton beheaded Tower Hill, London, 17 May 1536, suspected by King Henry VIII of being too familiar with Queen Anne Boleyn [John Brereton's *Brereton*, 16], who was herself executed two days later [E.W. Ives, ed., *Letters and Accounts of William Brereton of Malpas*, 1]; m. Elizabeth (dau. of Charles, Earl of Worcester [cousin of King Henry VIII and lord chamberlain]), widow

of Sir John Savage; Chamberlain of Chester and Groom of the Privy
Chamber to King Henry VIII.

   viii.   Robert, l. 1566.

    ix.   Sir Urian, of Honford, d. 19 March 1576/7; m. (1) Margaret Honford, dau.
and heiress of William Honford of Honford, m. (2) Alice Trafford (dau.
of Sir Edmund Trafford), who bur. Cheadle 16 June 1578.

     x.   Anne, m. (1) John Harcourt of Ranton, Staffs., m. (2) John Pershall of
Hor[de]sley, Staffs.

*   xi.   Elizabeth, l. 30 Nov. 1545; m. (1) Richard Cholmondeley (Shakerly in
Cheshire Vis. Pedigrees [13]), m. (2) Sir Randel[D] Mainwaring.

    xii.   Jane, m. Sir Thomas Hanmer of Hanmer.

   xiii.   Eleanor, m. Sir William Brereton of Brereton [*Cheshire Vis. Pedigrees*, 13].

§ § §

DE BROMPTON

More local history research in Shropshire and Herefordshire should help with this line.

1. — (John?)[O] DE BROMPTON was mentioned in Eyton's *Antiquities of Shropshire*, 4:244-247].

He married MATILDA[P] DE BRAIOSE[+], daughter of Sir William de Braiose.

Child:

   2.   i.   Sir Brian[N], will dated 27 July 1287; m. Emma Corbet, whose will was dated
1 Aug. 1284.

2. Sir BRIAN[N] DE BROMPTON left a will dated 27 July 1287.

He married EMMA CORBET, whose will was dated 1 Aug. 1284.

Child:

   3.   i.   Sir Walter[M], m. Joan.

3. Sir WALTER[M] DE BROMPTON was next in the pedigree.

He married JOAN.

Child:

   4.   i.   Brian[L], d. 1294.

4. Sir BRIAN[L] DE BROMPTON died in 1294.

Children:

*   i.   Margaret[K], b. Hugford 27 Oct. 1293; d. 24 June 1349, prob. of Black
Death; m. by 2 Nov. 1309 Sir Robert[K] de Harley, who d. 1349.

    ii.   Elizabeth, b. 1294; d. 1354; m. 1313/4 Sir Edmund de Cornwall of Kynlet,
who d. 22 March 1354, Knight of the Shire for London [Weis, *AR*7,
258:29].

§ § §

BROMWICH

Additional sources include Morgan G. Watkins' continuation of John Duncomb's *History
of Herefordshire*; Rev. Charles J. Robinson's *Mansions of Herefordshire* [192 and 202, 216],

and Duncomb [2:306]. *Miscellanea Genealogica et Heraldica*, 4th ser., 5:289 also bears checking. Additional sources include *The Genealogist*, new ser., 23:29 and *Higgs Family History* [CS 439.H54 at the Library of Congress].

1. RALPH[L] BROMWICH was born about 1306.
Norr stated that his listing as John's father was conjecture.
Children, listed by Norr [36-37]:
    2.   i.   John[K], b. c. 1332.
        ii.   Catherine, m. Richard Walwyn.
        iii.   Thomas, possible son, m. Elizabeth (or Eleanor) Harley.

2. JOHN[K] BROMWICH was born about 1332 [Norr, 37].
Children, listed by Norr [37]:
    3.   i.   Thomas[J], b. c. 1361; m. Alice[J] Oldcastle.
        ii.   Robert, m. Margaret Brace (dau. of Richard Brace and Margaret Devereux), widow of Miles Waters; she m. (3) Monington, and in 1511 Thomas Bromwich was heir of the wife of Roger Monington.
        iii.   Elizabeth, m. Walter Hackluyt.

3. THOMAS[J] BROMWICH of Sarnsfield (Sarnesfield, Herefordshire?) was born about 1361. He married ALICE[J] OLDCASTLE* of Almeley, Herefordshire.
Child:
    *   i.   Elizabeth[I], m. Sir Walter[J] Devereux.
        ii.   Thomas, m. (1) Catherine Oldcastle, m. (2) Elizabeth Burghill [Norr, 37].
        iii.   Richard, m. Elizabeth Pryse.

§ § §

DE BURES

Boddington is about three miles west of Cheltenham in Gloucestershire.

1. Sir JOHN[L] DE BURES died at Boddington 21/22 Dec. 1350.
He married HAWISE[M] DE MUSCEGROS* of Charleton, Somerset, and Norton, Staffordshire, who was widow of Sir John[M] de Ferrers.
Child:
    *   i.   Catherine[K], lady of Boddington and Longford, d. 1 Oct. 1355; m. before 21 May 1329 Sir Giles[K] de Beauchamp of Powick [*CP*, 5:chart between 320-321], who d. Oct. 1361.

§ § §

DE BURGH

William[O] de Burgh is the subject of Blake's *William de Burgh, Progenitor of the Burkes in Ireland* (1991), and was probably elder brother of Hubert de Burgh, Earl of Kent, who died 12 May 1243, the most famous Justiciar of England under King Henry III. Their father may have been Walter de Burgh of Burgh-next-Aylsham, Norfolk; William was not identical with William Fitz Aldelm, Justiciar of Ireland under King Henry II.

WILLIAM[O] DE BURGH, Lord of Connaught, Ireland, died about 1205-1206. He married a daughter of Donnell O'Brien, K.T.

RICHARD[N] DE BURGH, Lord of Connaught, born in Connaught, Ireland, about 1200, died in Gascony (now in France), shortly before 17 Feb. 1243. He married, before 21 April 1225, EGIDIA (or Gille)[N] DE LACY of Dublin.

WALTER[M] DE BURGH, Earl of Ulster, Lord Connaught, born in Connaught, Ireland, about 1230, died in Galway, Ireland, 28 July 1271, after a week's illness, and was buried in the monastery at Athassel, on the Suir in Tipperary. He married about 1257 AVELINA[O] FITZ JOHN FITZ GEOFFREY, who died about 20 May 1274, and was buried in Dunmow Priory.

4. Sir RICHARD[L] DE BURGH, Earl of Ulster, 4th Earl of Connaught, "the Red Earl," born about 1259, died in Athassel Monastery, Tipperary, Ireland, 29 July 1326.

He married, by 27 Feb. 1280/1, MARGARET[L] OF GUINES, who died in 1304, perhaps the daughter of Arnoul III, Count of Guines. While it has been alleged that he married second Margaret de Burgh, no evidence has been found [CP, 12:2:176k].

After his mother's death in 1274 he and a brother were raised with the king's children [Parsons, Genealogists' Magazine, 20:336].

He raided the lands of William Fitz Warin in Ulster in 1281, and was with King Edward I in Wales from July to Dec. 1282. He was knighted at Rhuddlan by the king on Edward's birthday in 1283. On 2 July 1283 he was called the Queen's kinsman when she granted him and his wife one of her Irish manors [Parsons, GM, 20 (1981-1982), 335-339]. In 1286 he and other Irish nobles made a mutual aid pact with some of the Scottish nobility, including James Steward, his brother-in-law. From 1286 to 1292 he repeatedly led forces against the O'Neills in Connaught. On 12 Dec. 1294 he was captured, and then imprisoned at Lea Castle in Queen's County. He was released upon royal intervention, surrendering his children as hostages.

On 3 Jan. 1295/6 he was summoned to Whitehaven for an expedition against Scotland, and he was involved there often until 1323. He held negotiations with Sir John Comyn in Feb. 1303/4, and with Robert the Bruce following his appointment as a peace commissioner on 21 Aug. 1309. His forces were defeated during Edward Bruce's invasion of Ireland in May 1315, and he retreated to Connaught, which was in a state of anarchy. On 21 Feb. 1316/7 he and his kinsmen were seized by the Mayor of Dublin on suspicion of complicity with Bruce; he was released on 21 Feb. 1316/7 after King Edward II ordered an enquiry into his arrest. In Aug. 1323 he was ordered to capture Roger[K] de Mortimer, Earl of March who had escaped from the Tower of London.

He was present at the Irish parliament held at Kilkenny on 11 May 1326.

Children, from Cokayne [12:2:177c]:
- i.   Walter[K], first son, d. Ulster c. 1304.
- ii.   John, Earl of Ulster, b. c. 1290; d. Le Ford, Belfast, Ireland, 18 June 1313; m. 30 Sept. 1308 Elizabeth[L] de Clare, who d. 4 Nov. 1360, having m. (2) near Bristol without license 4 Feb. 1315/6 Sir Theobald[N] de Verdun, who d. Alton, Staffs., 27 July 1316, and m. (3) c. April 1317 Roger Damory, who d. "in rebellion" at Tutbury 13/14 March 1321/2.
- iii. Thomas, d. 1316.
- iv.   Sir Edmund, taken prisoner and drowned 1338; widow may have m. (2) Turlough O'Connor, King of Connaught.
- * v. Eleanor, m. St. Peter's Priory, Ipswich, 3 Jan. 1296/7, Sir Thomas[M] de Multon, who d. 1321/2.

    vi. Elizabeth, d. Cullen Castle, Banffshire, Scotland, 26 Oct. 1327, bur. Dunfermline Abbey, Fifeshire, Scotland; m. 1302 Robert the Bruce, Earl of Carrick and later King of Scots, who d. 7 June 1329.

    vii. Aveline, m. John de Birmingham, Earl of Louth.

    viii. Maud (Matilda), d. 1320, bur. Tewkesbury Abbey, Gloucester, England; m. 29 Sept. 1308 Gilbert^L de Clare, Earl of Gloucester and Hereford.

*   ix. Joan, d. 22 April 1359, bur. Kildare, Ireland; m. (1) Greencastle, Ireland, 16 Aug. 1312 Thomas Fitz Gerald, 2nd Earl of Kildare, m. (2) Maynooth, Kildare, 3 July 1329 (as his second wife), Sir John^K Darcy, who d. 30 May 1347.

    x. Katherine, d. Dublin c. 1 Nov. 1331; m. Greencastle 5 Aug. 1312 Maurice Fitz Thomas.

§ § §

DE BURGHERSH

This line was based primarily on Cokayne's *The Complete Peerage*, vol. 2, pages 425-428.

1. REYNOLD^O DE BURGHERSH succeeded his older brother John to Burghersh, Sussex. Son and heir [*CP*, 2:425d]:

  2. i. Robert^N, d. 1306; m. Maud^L de Badlesmere.

2. ROBERT^N DE BURGHERSH, Lord Burghersh, died between 2 July and 8 Oct. 1306. He married MAUD^L DE BADLESMERE*, who was living 2 Jan. 1306.

He held Burghersh (now Burwash, pronounced "Burrish") in Sussex, Chiddingstone in Kent, and other lands. He was Constable of Dover Castle, and Warden of the Cinque Ports from 1299 until his death. His summonses to parliament dated from 12 Nov. 1303 to 13 July 1305.

Children [*CP*, 2:425-426]:

    i. Stephen^M, writ for *inquisition post mortem* dated 22 March 1309/10; had dau. and heir Maud, b. Roydon, Norfolk, 9 Aug. 1304, who m. (1) Walter de Paveley, m. (2) Sir Thomas d'Aldon.

    ii. Henry, Bishop of Lincoln and Lord Treasurer.

  3. iii. Bartholomew, third son, d. 3 Aug. 1355; m. before 11 June 1320 Elizabeth^M de Verdun, who d. 1 May 1360.

3. Sir BARTHOLOMEW^M DE BURGHERSH, Lord Burghersh, died 3 Aug. 1355, and was buried at Grey Friars, London.

He married, before 11 June 1320 (when she became of age), ELIZABETH^M DE VERDUN* of Stoke-upon-Tern, Shropshire, who died 1 May 1360, and was buried at Grey Friars, London.

He served in the Scottish wars of King Edward II's reign, joined the Earl of Lancaster in rebellion, and was defeated with the Earl at Boroughbridge on 16 March 1321/2, but was restored by Isabel, the Queen Consort. He was recorded at Constable of Dover Castle and Warden of the Cinque Ports in 1327, 1343 and 1346-1350. He was summoned to Parliament from 25 Jan. 1329/30 to 15 March 1353/4.

He was justice in eyre South of Trent from 1335 to 1343. In 1340 he was heir to his brother Henry and he was Banneret in 1341. In Aug. 1343 he was part of an important diplomatic mission to the Pope, and he fought at the battle of Crécy on 25 Aug. 1346. He was Chamberlain of the Household, and Constable of the Tower of London from 27 June 1355 until he died.

Children, listed by Norr [128]:

4.   i.   Bartholomew[L], d. 5 April 1369; m. (1) before 11 May 1335 Cecily[L] de Weyland; m. (2) Margaret.

       ii. Jane, m. 1342 John Mohun.

     iii. Elizabeth, m. 1347 Maurice Fitz Thomas, Earl of Kildare.

     iv. Henry, m. 1347 Isabel de St. John; this marriage was not consummated and she m. Luke de Poynings.

      v. Maud, d. 1401; m. Lord John Grey and/or John le Strange.

4. BARTHOLOMEW[L] DE BURGHERSH, K.G., Lord Burghersh of Burghersh, Sussex, died 5 April 1369 and was buried in Walsingham, Norfolk.

He married first, before 11 May 1335, CICELY[L] DE WEYLAND of Blaxhall and Cockfield [*CP*, 4:276], Suffolk, who was living in Aug. 1354 [*CP*, 2:427], daughter of Sir Richard de Weyland of Blaxhall and Cockfield, who died before 10 May 1335.

His second wife was Margaret, widow of Henry Pichard, citizen and vintner of London [*CP*, 14:124], or John de Loveyne [*MCS*5, 13:8]. She married third, as his first wife, William Burcestere. Margaret died 1 July 1393.

He fought at Crécy in 1346 with his father, and was an original Knight of the Garter on 23 April 1349. He accompanied Prince Edward on nearly all his expeditions, fought at Poitiers on 19 Sept. 1356, and was considered to be a distinguished warrior. He made a journey to the Holy Land.

Child, by first wife:

*   i. Elizabeth[K], b. 1342; d. c. 26 July 1409; m. before Dec. 1364 Sir Edward[K] Despenser, K.G., Lord of Glamorgan, who d. 11 Nov. 1375.

§ § §

X   BURNELL

Robert Burnell was granted Acton Burnell and was related to Thomas Corbet. Philip de Burnel succeeded his uncle Robert de Burnel in 1292 under Sir Peter[N] Corbet [A.E. Corbet, 140]. Cokayne [*CP*, 2:434] treated Edward Burnell, son and heir of Sir Philip Burnell of Condover, Holgate and Acton Burnell, Shropshire, as well as Little Rissington, Gloucestershire.

Eyton's treatment of Acton Burnell [*Ant. Shropshire*, 6:121-138] contains mention of Hugh Burnell on page 129, who was apparently a knight (and brother of William and Robert Burnell), who sat as a juror in causes tried by the Grand Assize in Sept. 1272. If this Hugh is identical with "Hugo[N] Burnell of Aston Burnell," his parentage was not known to Eyton. However, he had brothers Robert Burnel, Clerk, of record 8 Nov. 1260, Archdeacon of York 1271, Chancellor of England 1274, Bishop of Bath and Wells 1275, died [*DNB*, 3:388] 25 Oct. 1292, no issue; Philip, occurred 1249 and 1253, died in Wales Nov. 1282, and William, occurred Feb. 1262 and 1264-1279, and died in Wales Nov. 1282, leaving Robert Burnel of Rissington, Gloucestershire, who was of record in 1307. Nonetheless, the *DNB* stated that Robert Burnell, Chancellor, was born at Acton Burnell, his parentage unknown; he was one of at least four brothers, of whom two were slain at Menai Straits in 1282, and Sir Hugh died in 1286 [*DNB*, 3:389].

Hugh Burnell was married to Sibil, was of record about 1258 and 1270-1285, and died about 1287. However, Eyton [6:134] showed only four children: Philip, born 1 Aug. 1264, died 26 June 1294, married Matilda Fitz Alan, sister of Richard Fitz Alan, Earl of Arundel; William, clerk, had lands in Dorset and Somerset 1300; Alice, m. Walter de Beysin, and Petronilla, m. William de Ercalue.

A Joan Burnell married Hugh[O] Bigod.

The Burnell pedigrees in the *Visitation of Shropshire, 1623*, do not provide enough detail to be of use.

1. HUGO[N] BURNELL was of Aston Burnell, Shropshire.

Robert Burnell, Chancellor of King Edward I, held the castle of Acton Burnell [*EB*].

"The Lords of Stowheath Manor," in *The Wolverhampton Antiquary* [2:106] shows that Robert Burnell (who was Bishop of Bath and Wells, and Chancellor of England 1274-1292, was of Acton Burnell, Salop, and died 25 Oct. 1292 without issue) was brother of Hugh Burnell who died in 1287, having married Sybil and had son Philip Burnell, who was born 1 Aug. 1264, died 26 June 1294, and married Maud, sister of Richard Fitz Alan, Earl of Arundel, who was living in 1316.

Child:

*   i.   Helena[M], m. Richard[M] Lacon, who l. 1290 and 1316.

§ § §

BUTLER OF BEWSEY

Much of the material below was taken from a pedigree chart in Latin of Butler of Bewsey, Barons of Warrington, Lancashire, in Edward Baines' *History of the County Palatine and Duchy of Lancaster*, vol. 3 [London: Fisher, Son & Co., 1836], and then developed from the *Victoria History of the County of Lancaster* [3:325-327]. In *Medieval English Ancestors of Certain Americans*, a companion to this volume, there is mention of Christian[S] de Stainton (widow of Michael[S] le Fleming II, who died in 1186), who married second William le Boteler of Workington.

1. WILLIAM[P] LE BOTELER, also called *Pincerna*, Baron of Warrington in Lancashire, born about 1160 [Tildesley, "Sir Thomas Browne," *Biometrika*, 15:68], died 18 Hen. III (1233).

According to M.L. Tildesley he married ADA DE FURNEYS of Lancashire.

Tildesley states that he was son of Richard Pincerna, the fourth Lord of Warrington, who died in 1176 (and Beatrice, Lady of Warrington, who was daughter of Matthew de Vilars, 2nd Baron of Warrington, son of Paganus de Vilars, the 1st Baron, who died about 1160), who was son of Robert Pincerna (who married about 1147 Ivetta Helgot, daughter of William Helgot, lord of Helgot in Salop), who was son of Richard Pincerna, lord paramount of Pulton about 1119.

The family were the "botelers" or butlers of the Earl of Chester before going to Lancashire to become the lords of Warrington [Jessica Lofthouse, *Lancashire's Old Families*, 84].

Burtonwood was perambulated in 1228, and was retained in the King's forest, with pasture and other rights, including timber for the Castle of Warrington and for fuel, was reserved to William le Boteler, but passed in 1229 to the Earl of Chester.

Son and heir:

2.   i.   Almaricus[O] Pincerna, m. Beatrix[O] Villers.

2. ALMARICUS[O] PINCERNA, son and heir 18 Hen. III, died 19 Hen. III (1234-1235).

He married BEATRIX[O] VILLERS, who was daughter and coheir of Mattæus[P] Villers, lord of Warrington, and had brothers Thomas and William.

Children, listed in Baines:

      i.   Gwarin[N], first son; no issue.

3.   ii. William Pincerna, m. Dionysia.

     iii. Richard, m. Alicia de Carleton, dau. of William de Carleton of Inskip.

3. Sir WILLIAM[N] PINCERNA, alias Butler, was raised by William de Ferrers, lord Ferrers.

He married DIONYSIA, who was identified by Hornyold-Strickland [12] as a daughter of Henry de Lostock.

A knight, he was Sheriff of Lancashire in 1258-1259, and Governor of Lancaster Castle [CP, 2: 230]. In 1264 he bought Burtonwood from Robert de Ferrers for 900 marks, to be paid at a rate of £10 every six months.

Child:

4.   i. Henry[M].

4. HENRY[M] LE BOTELER was of record as son and heir 9 Edw. I (1280-1281), and died in 1297 in his father's lifetime.

He married SIBILLA, who was identified by Hornyold-Strickland [12] as Isabel, daughter of Richard le Boteler of Merton, who granted her lands in 1297.

He had protection on going to Wales in July 1277 and July 1287 for the king, and on going to Ireland with William de Vescy 12 Sept. 1290. He was Knight of the Shire for Lancashire 6 Oct. 1297.

Children:

5.   i. William[L], m. Sibilla.

5. WILLIAM[L] BUTLER, lord of Warrington, Lancashire, died about 1328 [CP, 2:230].

He married SIBILLA.

He succeeded his grandfather about 1280, and was summoned 14 June 1294 to attend the king in the French wars in Gascony. From 23 June 1295 to 6 Feb. 1298/9 he was summoned to Parliament. In 34 Edw. I (1305-1306) he was on the expedition to Scotland.

Child:

6.   i. Sir William[K], d. 3 Ric. II (1379-1380); m. Elizabeth.

6. Sir WILLIAM[K] BOTELER, born about 1309, died 3 Ric. II (1379-1380).

He married ELIZABETH, probable daughter of John Argentine. She was identified by Hornyold-Strickland [12] as sister and coheir of Richard de Havering.

He assumed the lordship of Warrington 39 Edw. III (1365-1366), and was active in the wars of King Edward III.

As early as the reign of Edward II the lords of Warrington made their home at Bewsey, originally called "beau site" or "Beausi" [VCH Lancs., 3:325]. The family made grants of their property for lives or for specific terms, thus always regaining cultivated lands at greatly increased values. In Nov. 1356 he entailed most of his barony upon his son John.

Children:

      i. Richard[J], son and heir; m. c. 1340 Johanna, who m. (2) John de Haydock; no issue.

7.   ii. John, b. c. 1328; d. 1399; second son, m. Alicia Plumpton.

     iii. Norman.

7. Sir JOHN[J] BUTLER, born about 1328, died in 1 Hen. IV (1399-1400), before Jan. 1400.

He married 47 Edw. III (1374-1375) ALICIA[J] PLUMPTON (daughter of Sir William Plumpton of Plumpton in Yorkshire), widow of Richard Sherburne (or Sherbirne), who died in 1364, son and heir of Sir John Sherburne of Orington (?) in Lancashire. She was living in 1408.

Knighted by March 1363, he had protection while building a bridge across the Mersey in 1364, served as a commissioner in Lancashire in the period 1365 to 1386, was Sheriff of Lancashire 25 Dec. 1371 to 19 Nov. 1374, and a Member of Parliament for ten terms between 1366 and Sept. 1397.

He campaigned overseas with John of Gaunt five times in Gascony, Aquitaine and Ireland, between 1369 and 1378, and was present at the siege of St. Mâlo in 1378. He was a member of John of Gaunt's embassy to Portugal in 1385, and took part in the expedition to Barbary in 1389, during which he was taken prisoner and ransomed. He served on a jury in Lancaster in 1396.

The barony of Warrington included "appurtenances and franchises in over 20 manors and villages" [Roskell, 2:304].

Children:
- 8.   i.   Sir William[I], d. 3 Hen. V (1415-1416); m. Elizabeth Standish, who m. (2) William Ferrers of Groby.
-       ii.   Alice [Hornyold-Strickland, 14], l. 1408; m. Sir Thomas Gerard [Roskell, 2:305],
-       iii.   John, d. 26 May 1421 [Hornyold-Strickland, 14]; keeper of the jewels to Henry V.

8. Sir WILLIAM[I] BUTLER, K.B., died of dysentery at Harfleur 26 Sept. Hen. V (1415).

He married in March 1403 ELIZABETH[I] STANDISH (elder daughter of Sir Robert Standish of Standish and widow of John de Wrottesley), who married third 19 Hen. VI (1440-1441) William Ferrers de Groby, and died that year.

He had livery of his father's estates 21 March 1400, holding Warrington, Sankey, Penketh, Rixton and twelve more manors and some additional lands, all in Lancashire. He was made Knight of the Bath on 17 March 1400, on the eve of the Coronation of Henry IV.

He served as a commissioner in 1402 and 1403, and as Knight of the Shire for Lancashire in 1406.

Children:
- 9.   i.   John[H], b. Bewsey, Lancs., 3 Hen. IV (1401-1402); m. (1) Margaret de Holand, m. (2) Isabella.
-       ii.   Elizabeth, m. 2 Hen. IV (1423-1424) John Butler, son and heir of Nicholas Butler de Rawcliffe, and m. Sir Piers Dutton of Dutton.

9. Sir JOHN[H] BUTLER, born in Bewsey, Lancashire, 26 Feb. 1403, died 12 Sept. 1430.

He married first Margaret de Holand, daughter of Sir Robert Holand.

He married second, in 1411, ISABELLA (relict of John Butler), who died 19 Hen. VI (1440-1441); she was identified by Hornyold-Strickland [14] as daughter of Sir William Harrington of Hornby. In 1437 she was living with her children at Bewsey when on 22 July William Poole of Wirral entered her home forcibly (with the help of a number of accomplices), violated her and carried her away to Birkenhead, "forcing her by menaces" to marry him the next day. He then took her to Wales, but when he returned with her to Birkenhead she petitioned Parliament for redress. The result of the petition is unknown.

He was probably knighted by the king at Leicester in 1426. He was elected Knight of the Shire for Lancashire on 9 Feb. 1426.

Children, from the pedigree in Baines' *History of Lancaster* [3:660], and Hornyold-Strickland [14]:
- *   i.   Ellen[G], m. 1443 William[G] Mainwaring of Over Peover, Cheshire.

ii. Sir John, Baron of Warrington, Lancs., aged 12 and more in July 1441; d. 26 Feb. 1463; m. (1) 1444 Margaret Gerard, who d. c. 1452, m. (2) 1454 Isabel Dacre (this m. dissolved 1458 on grounds she had contracted to m. Thomas, Lord Clifford), m. (3) 1460 Margaret Stanley, widow of Sir William Troutbeck; a ballad, perhaps contemporary, tells of the surprise of Bewsey by a party of men at the instigation of Sir John Stanley and Sir Piers Legh, who crossed the moat in a boat of a bull's hide and murdered the Chamberlain and then Sir John Butler himself.

iii. Isabella, m. 31 Hen. VI (1452) Sir Galfrid Masey de Tutton (or Tatton?), who d. 14 Hen. VII (1498), having also m. Elizabeth Worseley, dau. and heir of Sir Galfrid Worseley of Worseley.

§ § §

BUTLER OF IRELAND

This line is distinct from the line of le Boteler.

HERVEY^Q WALTER was of West Dereham, Norfolk. He married MAUD^Q DE VALOIGNES, daughter and coheiress of Theobald de Valoignes; her sister, Bertha, was wife of Ranulph de Glanville, the great Justiciar.

THEOBALD^P FITZ WALTER (or le Botiller) died between 4 Aug. 1205 and 14 Feb. 1205/6, and was buried at Wotheny Abbey in county Limerick, Ireland. He married in or shortly before 1200 MAUD^P LE VAVASOUR (daughter and heiress of Robert le Vavasour), with whom he acquired the manors of Edlington, Newborough and others in Yorkshire. She married second, before 1 Oct. 1207, Fulk Fitz Warin.

3. THEOBALD^O BUTLER (or le Botiller), aged 6 in 1206, died in Poitou 19 July 1230, and was buried in the Abbey of Arklow, Ireland.

He married first JOAN^O DU MARAIS, who was sister (and in her issue coheir) of John du Marais, and daughter of Geoffrey du Marais, Justiciar of Ireland. The inheritance followed the death of Sir Stephen de Marreys (or de Marisco), of whom Joan Butler was great-aunt.

He married second, shortly after 4 Sept. 1225 (when the king requested the marriage [Hall, *The Genealogist*, n.s., 15 (1909), 75]), ROHESE^Q DE VERDUN$^+$, heiress of Croxden and foundress of Grace Dieu Monastery in Leicestershire. Her inheritance included Brandon Castle in Warwickshire, Belton in Leics., and Farnham Royal in Buckinghamshire as well as holdings in Ireland [*CP*, 12:2:247a]. She died before 22 Feb. 1246/7.

On 2 July 1221 and 18 July 1222 he had livery of his estates. On 26 Oct. 1229 he was summoned with horse and arms to attend King Henry III in Brittany as *Theobaldus Pincerna*.

Son and heir, by first wife:

4. i. Theobald^N, d. 1248; m. Margery^M de Burgh.

Children, by second wife [*cf.* Weis; *CP*, 2:448d], whose sons retained the maternal surname:

* ii. Maud, d. 27 Nov. 1283; m. (1) John^O Fitz Alan, m. (2) Richard d'Amundville, who was l. 1286/7.

* iii. John^P de Verdun (*q.v.*), b. 1233 (however Hall [*The Genealogist*, n.s., 25 (1909), 76], believes he was born c. 1323, of an earlier husband of Rohese); d. 1274; m. (1) Margaret^P de Lacy, m. (2) Alianore.

iv. Theobald de Verdun, Sr.

v. Theobald de Verdun, Jr. [*CP*, 2:448d].

4. THEOBALD[N] LE BOTILLER was buried in Arklow Abbey in Wicklow, Ireland, before 3 Aug. 1248. The *inquisition post mortem* was held on 6 July 1249.

He married in or before 1242 MARGERY[M] DE BURGH[+], daughter of Richard[N] de Burgh, ancestor of the Earls of Clanricarde, Ireland. She paid a fine to marry whom she chose on 27 April 1250, and was living 1 March 1252/3.

He did homage for his lands, being of full age, on 11 June 1244. During the wars between King Henry III and the barons he sided with the king.

He was Lord Justice in Ireland in 1247 [Cokayne attributed this to his father, who died in 1230].

Child:

    5.   i.   Theobald[M], d. Arklow Castle, Ireland, 26 Sept. 1285, bur. Monastery of Arklow; m. c. 1268 Joan[O] Fitz John Fitz Geoffrey, who d. c. 26 May 1303.

5. THEOBALD[M] BUTLER (or le Botiller) died in the Castle of Arklow in Wicklow, Ireland, 26 Sept. 1285, and was buried in the monastery there [*CP*, 2:449].

He married, in or before 1268, JOAN FITZ JOHN FITZ GEOFFREY (daughter of Sir John[P] Fitz Geoffrey of Fambridge, Essex, who died 23 Nov. 1258, and Isabel Bigod, widow of Gilbert de Lacy of Ewyas Lacy), who died between 25 Feb. and 26 May 1303 [*CP*, 2:449]. His wardship and marriage were granted to John Fitz Geoffrey, Justiciar of Ireland, for 3,000 marks on 21 Jan. 1250/1.

He was the grantee of the prisage of wines in Ireland [Hall, 25:77], and participated in the war with Scotland with King Edward I.

When she died Edmund was named as her heir, while Theobald was his father's heir [Hall, *TG*, n.s., 15:78].

Children, listed by Cokayne:

        i.   Theobald[L], b. 22 Feb. 1268/9; d. at his manor of Turvey, bur. Wotheny Abbey 27 May 1299; M.P. in Ireland 1295, accompanied King Edward I to Scotland in 1296; no issue.

    6.   ii.   Edmund, d. London 13 Sept. 1321, bur. Gowran, Kilkenny, Ireland, 9 Nov. 1321; m. 1302 Joan[L] Fitz John.

6. EDMUND[L] LE BOTILLER died in London 13 Sept. 1321, and was buried in Gowran, Kilkenny, Ireland, 9 Nov. 1321.

He married in 1302 JOAN[L] FITZ JOHN [FITZ THOMAS FITZ GERALD*], daughter of the first Earl of Kildare, who was dead before 2 May 1320 [*CP*, 10:117].

He did homage for his brother's lands on 30 Aug. 1300. He sat in the Irish Parliament in 1302. Then he had livery of his mother's lands on 13 Jan. 1303/4. He was knighted in London by King Edward II in 1309. From 1312 to 1313, and 4 Jan. 1314/5 to 1317 he was Justiciar, Chief Governor of Ireland, and was active in suppressing rebellion. At a feast in Dublin on 20 Sept. 1313 he created thirty knights. On 1 Sept. 1315 he received "the *feodum* of the castle and manors of Karryk Macgriffyn and Roscrea," and was called in some documents the Earl of Carrick [*CP*, 2:449, *cf.* 3:60]; this was for his services against Edward Bruce and the Scots, as well as the rebel Irish. He died while on return from a pilgrimage to Santiago [St. Jago] de Compostella in Spain.

Child:

    7.   i.   James[K], d. c. 6 Feb. 1337/8, bur. Gowran; m. Eleanor[K] de Bohun.

7. JAMES[K] BUTLER, hereditary Chief Butler of Ireland, created 1st Earl of Ormond (the northern part of Tipperary) 2 Nov. 1328, of Gowran and Kilkenny Castle, Ireland, born about

1305, died 6 or 22 Jan. or 1, 16, 18 [according to various documents] or 19 Feb. [*CP*, 4:28] 1337/8, and was buried in Gowran, Tipperary, Ireland.

For two thousand marks he was given a license to marry whom he would on 2 Dec. 1325 (when, although under age, King Edward II took his homage) [*CP*, 10:117], but it was cancelled because he could not provide security for the payment. Apparently, however, it was renewed the following March [*CP*, 10:117e]. He married in 1327 ELEANOR[K] DE BOHUN*, who died 7 Oct. 1363, having married second, in the chapel of La Vacherie in Cranley in Surrey, before 20 April 1344, Sir Thomas Dagworth, who was slain during a time of truce in a skirmish near Aurai in Brittany in July or Aug. 1350 [*CP*, 4:29].

In 1317 he was hostage in Dublin Castle for his father. In 1325 he had protection, being about to accompany King Edward II overseas. In 1326 he was made K.B. In 1326 he received a protection in England on going to Ireland where he supported Mortimer's party. The year he married the king's niece, he obtained a grant of the prisage of wines at Irish ports, which he regarded as a part of his hereditary office of Butler. Apparently he lived and fought primarily in Ireland in spite of the ownership of properties throughout England, and the fact that his wife resided chiefly in England.

Children of James Butler and Eleanor de Bohun:

      i.   John[J] [CP, 10:119e], b. 6 Nov. 1330; d. in infancy.

8.   ii.   James, b. Kilkenny, Ireland, 4 Oct. 1331; d. Knocktopher Castle, Kilkenny, 18 Oct. 1382; m. Anne[J] Darcy, who m. (2) Sir Robert Harford.

*   iii.   Petronilla, l. 28 May 1365, dead in 1368; m. by 8 Sept. 1352 Sir Gilbert[J] Talbot, who d. 24 April 1387.

8. JAMES[J] BUTLER, 2nd Earl of Ormond, born in Kilkenny, Ireland, 4 Oct. 1331, died at Knocktopher Castle, Kilkenny, 18 Oct. (or 6 Nov.) 1382, and was buried at St. Canice Cathedral in Kilkenny (or Gowran [Faris, *PA*, 45]).

He married (the dispensation dated 15 May 1436) ANNE[J] DARCY* (called Elizabeth in *MCS*5, 24:7, and Faris, *PA*2, 59), daughter of his guardian, Sir John Darcy of Knaith, Lincolnshire; she married second, between 28 Dec. 1383 and 30 March 1384, Sir Robert de Hereford (or Harford), who served in Ireland 1386-1389. She died 24 March 1389/90 [*cf.* Watson, *MGH*, 5:8:230[6]].

He had livery of his inheritance and his office of Butler on 16 or 24 Feb. 1346/7, because King Edward III wanted his services overseas. In March 1349/50 he was appointed Constable of Dublin Castle for life, and he attended the English Parliament at Westminster in Nov. 1355. He was Justiciar from 16 Feb. 1358/9 to 16 March 1361, and served several terms as Chief Governor of Ireland.

Child:

9.   i.   James[I], d. 6/7 Sept. 1405; m. before 17 June 1486 Anne[I] Welles.

9. JAMES[I] BUTLER (or le Botiller), 3rd Earl of Ormond, was born after 1361, died in Gowran, Ireland, 6/7 Sept. 1405, and was buried there.

He married before 17 June 1386 ANNE[I] WELLES*, who was living in 1396, and died 13 Nov. (before 1405) [Watson, *MGH*, 5:8:231].

Granted custody of his lands on 2 March 1382/3, he served mostly in Ireland, including several terms as Chief Governor of Ireland. From 1391 to 1393 he was engaged in transactions to purchase Kilkenny Castle from Sir Hugh le Despeneer. In 1400 he was appointed Sheriff of Cork by King Henry IV, and in May 1403 he was made chief commissioner to adjourn and continue the Parliament.

Son and heir:
10.   i.   James[H], d. 23 Aug. 1452; m. (1) c. 28 Aug. 1413 Joan[H] de Beauchamp,
             who d. Aug. 1430, m. (2) Elizabeth Fitz Gerald, who d. 1452.

10. JAMES[H] BUTLER, 4th Earl of Ormond, born probably in 1390 or 1392 [CP, 10:123d],
died in Ardee, Ireland, 23 Aug. 1452, and was buried in St. Mary's Abbey near Dublin.

He married first, on or before 28 Aug. 1413, JOAN[H] DE BEAUCHAMP*, who died in Shere,
England, 3 or 5 Aug. 1430 [CP, 10:123-126, 11:705], and was buried in the chapel of St.
Thomas Acon in London on 8 Aug. 1430.

He married second, Elizabeth Fitz Gerald (daughter of Gerald Fitz Gerald, 5th Earl of
Kildare, and Agnes Darcy), who died 6 Aug. 1452. Elizabeth was the widow of Sir John
Grey, Lord Grey of Codnor [Watson, MGH, 3:8:205]; she had been born about 1398 and
died 6 Aug. 1452, without issue.

On 8 Dec. 1407, when he was about 16, he was appointed Deputy of Stephen le Scrope,
who was Deputy to Prince Thomas (who was created Duke of Clarence in 1412). In 1412
James was granted land in recognition of his great services, and he was involved in the
successful siege of Rouen, which fell in Jan. 1418/9. On 10 Feb. 1419/20 he was appointed
to a two year term as Lieutenant in Ireland, continuing to act as such in 1424, although the
Duke of Bedford had accused him of treason before the English Council in 1423.

He acted as Justiciar 11 Oct. 1426 to 31 July 1427, and was reappointed Lieutenant on
10 Feb. 1428/9. In April 1430 he was taken by ship from Bristol to France, where he joined
King Henry VI in Calais, when the king was going to Rheims for his coronation, which had
to be transferred to Paris. On 27 Feb. 1441/2 he was appointed to a seven year term as
Lieutenant, and in July 1450 he undertook service to Richard, Duke of York (father of King
Edward IV). The last few months of his life were spent in military operations.

Children, by first wife, mentioned by Weis or Cokayne:
        i.   James[G], 5th Earl of Ormond [CP, 10:126-129], beheaded 1 May 1461,
             following his defeat at the battle of Mortimer's Cross on 2 Feb. 1461;
             m. (1) before 4 July 1438 Avice Stafford (dau. and heir of Sir Richard
             Stafford by Maud Lovel), who d. 3 June (or July) 1457, having m. (2)
             Eleanor Beaufort, who d. 16 Aug. 1501, having m. (2) Sir Robert
             Spencer.
        ii. Thomas, K.B., 7th Earl of Ormond, d. 3 Aug. 1515; m. (1) before 11 July
             1445 [Faris, PA2, 60] Anne Hankeford, who d. 13 Nov. 1485, m. (2)
             before Nov. 1496 Lora Berkeley (widow of Thomas Montgomery, K.G.),
             who d. 30 Dec. 1501.
    *   iii. Elizabeth, b. 1420; d. 8 Sept. 1473; m. c. 1444 Sir John[G] Talbot, K.G.,
             2nd Earl of Shrewsbury, who d. Northampton 10 July 1460.

§ § §

DE CALVELEY

The material below has been extracted from Ormerod's History of Chester, 2:281-285,
and 3:898 [corrections].

The Manor of Calveley was among the dependencies of Shipbrook, as shown in the grant
from Richard de Vernon to Hugh[Q] de Calveley, and from the tenure of the manor by the
Davenports under the Vernons and the Savages.

1. HUGH[Q] DE CALVELEY was lord of Calveley, in Edisbury Hundred, Cheshire, in the reign of King John, which was from 1199 to 1216.

He was granted Calveley by Richard de Vernon.

Child, from Ormerod [2:285]:

    2.   i.   Richard[P], m. Leuca de Barnard.

2. RICHARD[P] DE CALVELEY was confirmed in the possession of Calveley by undated deeds from Elena de Vernon (daughter of Matthew de Vernon) and Matthew de Alpraham.

He married LEUCA[P] DE BARNARD, sister and heiress of William de Barnard.

Children, listed by Ormerod:

    3.   i.   Hugh[O], m. Alicia.
        ii.   Robert, had son Richard.
       iii.   William, younger son.

3. HUGH[O] DE CALVELEY was son and heir, as shown by undated deeds of Leuca de Calveley.

He married AMICIA.

An acquittance by his mother of the right which her brother William Barnard had in Calveley by deeds without date, was witnessed by Roger Grey, Justiciar of Chester, and Robert Grosvenor, Sheriff.

Children, listed by Ormerod:

    4.   i.   Kenric[N], d. before 28 Edw. III (1354-1355); m. Matilda.
        ii.   John of Caldey, of record 5 Edw. II to 11 Edw. III (1311-1338).
       iii.   Peter, of record 1 Edw. III (1327-1328), and on the king's service in Brittany 22 Edw. III (1348-1349), in the train of John de Lacy.
       iv.   Richard.
        v.   William.
       vi.   David, held land in Calvilegh 7 Edw. II (1313-1314).
      vii.   Alicia, had grant from her brother John in 3 Edw. III (1329-1330).

4. KENRIC[N] DE CALVELEY, lord of Calveley, son and heir, by deed without date, was living 14-15 Edw. III (1340-1342), but died before 28 Edw. III (1354-1355).

His wife, MATILDA, was recorded as the wife of Kenric de Calvelegh in 3 Edw. III (1329-1330).

The deed was witnessed by Jo. de St. Pierre, Roger Dumville and Patrick de Haselwall, knights, and William Praers, Sheriff.

Children, listed by Ormerod:

        i.   Robert[M], d. by 1350; m. Elizabeth de Haselwall, dau. and coheiress of Ralph de Haselwall, son of David de Haselwall.
    5.   ii.   David, second son, m. (1) Johanna, m. (2) Mabella.
       iii.   Thomas, d. between 21 and 27 Edw. II (1347-1354); m. Isabel de Pennesby, dau. and coheiress of Roger de Pennesby, lord of Thyngwall [Ormerod, 3:898].
       iv.   Henry, held lands in tail in Calvylegh, granted by his father; no issue.

5. DAVID[M] DE CALVELEY, of Lea in the Hundred of Broxton, was the subject of an *inquisition post mortem* dated 35 Edw. III (1361-1362).

He married first JOHANNA, who was identified as mother of Hugh, son of David Calvelegh, in a deed of 29 Edw. III (1355-1356).

He married second Mabella, whose *inquisition post mortem* was held 35 Edw. III (1361-1362).

Children, by first wife:

     i.   Sir Hugh[L], d. seized of the manor of Lea on the feast of St. George, June 1393; m. Agnes Hauberk of Stapleford, Leics. [Roskell, 2:466], who m. (2) Robert Sherard; no issue; founder of the College of Bunbury.

6.   ii.   David, l. 1361, d. before his brother; m. Agnes[L] Mottram.

    iii.   Robert, third son 49 Edw. III (1375-1376).

    iv.   Richard, fourth son 49 Edw. III.

6. DAVID[L] DE CALVELEY died before his brother, who died in 1393.

He married AGNES[L] MOTTRAM, who held one third of Mottram Andrew in dower [*i.p.m.* 17 Ric. II (1393-1394)], and died before 9 Hen. IV (1402-1403), and was possibly a daughter of Thomas de Mottram [Ormerod, *Chester*, 3:693].

He leased lands in Calveley to Thomas Minshull in 1361. He used the Calveley seal (*Argent, a fesse Gules* between three Calves *trippant Sable*) without the *fesse*.

Child, from Ormerod:

7.   i.   Sir Hugh[K], d. 20 April 1394 [Earwaker, 2:348]; m. (poss. Agnes) Handford.

7. Sir HUGH[K] DE CALVELEY of Lea and Mottram, died on Monday after the Feast of Pope St. Leo. His *inquisition post mortem* was dated 17 Ric. II (1393-1394).

He married a daughter (possibly Agnes) and heiress of Handford of Handford.

Children, listed by Ormerod:

     i.   Sir David[J], son and heir, aged 7 in 17 Ric. II (1393-1394); *inq. post mortem* 9 Hen. IV (1407-1408); no issue.

    ii.   Hugh, m. Maude Hubert [*Pedigrees Vis. Cheshire 1613*, 55]; ancestor of the Calveleys of Lea.

    iii.   Alice.

*   iv.   Margaret, m. Sir John[J] Delves of Delves Hall, who d. 1394.

    v.   Sir John, d. before 6 Hen. IV (1404-1405); m. Juliana; he was grantee of the manor of Shotwick.

§ § §

CARRINGTON

The key to developing this line was found in Glover and Flower's *Visitation of Cheshire*, which placed Emma[F] Carrington as the wife of Randle[F] Brereton.

Carrington is located about seven miles southwest of Manchester, on the River Mersey. The family hall was demolished about 1858-1859, to make room for a farmhouse [Ormerod, *Hist. Chester*, 1:542].

1. ADAM[M] DE KARINTON was living about 1191.

Presumed son:

2.   i.   William[L], fl. 1234.

2. WILLIAM[L] DE CARINTON was of record in 1234 as well as 18 and 44 Hen. III (1259-1260).

Presumed son:

3.   i.   William^K, m. Agnes de Toft.

3. Sir WILLIAM^K DE CARYNTON was a knight during the reigns of Edward I and Edward II.

He married AGNES^K DE TOFT*, daughter of William de Toft; her [first?] husband was Walter de Acton (alias Hapesford) of Acton juxtà Weverham, by whom she had an heir Acton of Acton. She had two other husbands as well, of which Ormerod states [*Chester*, 1:502] more could be found under Plumley, but that entry [1:673-699] revealed nothing.

Children, listed as hers by second husband [Ormerod, 1:544]:

4.   i.   John^J, m. Cecily de Hyde.
     ii. Ralph, l. 1389.

4. JOHN^J DE CARYNTON was Lord of Carynton (Carrington), Cheshire, in 1326, and was of record in 10 and 20 Edw. III (1336-1337 and 1346-1347).

He married CICELY^J DE HYDE, daughter of Ralph de Hyde of Urmeston in Lancashire. Ormerod mentions [3:808] a Ralph de Hyde of Urmeston (who had lands in Staveley in 45 Edw. III [1371-1372]) as the ancestor of the family there and likely son of Sir John de Hyde of Hyde in Cheshire (who served under the Black Prince) and Margaret (or Margery) de Davenport, who may have been daughter of Thomas Davenport of Wheltrogh.

Children, mentioned by Ormerod:

5.   i.   William^I, m. Matilda.
     ii. Robert, possible son, l. 1398.

5. Sir WILLIAM^I DE CARYNGTON (son of William according to the *Visitation of Cheshire*, but of John^J according to Ormerod), Lord of Carynton, was of record 32, 46 and 47 Edw. III (1358-1374), and 1381.

He married, 32 Edw. III (1358-1359), MATILDA, who was mentioned as a widow in or before 1384, and was living 15 Ric. II (1391-1392).

Children, listed by Ormerod:

6.   i.   George, d. before 4 Hen. VI (1425-1426); m. (2) Elizabeth, who m. (2) Gilbert de Bexwyk.
     ii. Edward, l. 1389 and 1392; m. Helene de Ines, div. 1396.
    iii. Sir Thomas, possible son, d. by 1387; m. Margaret.

6. Sir GEORGE^H DE CARYNGTON, Lord of Caryngton, was knighted by 1401, and died before 4 Hen. VI (1425-1426).

He married ELIZABETH, mentioned 9 Hen. V (1421-1422), who married second, 4 Hen. VI (1425-1426), Gilbert de Bexwyk.

He was of record in 1397, 3 Hen. IV (1401-1402), 1408 and 9 Hen. V (1421-1422).

An *inquisition post mortem* of Hamon Carrington, held 16 Hen. VII (1500-1501), mentioned George's estate of the manor of Carrington, which passed to his kinsman Hamon, with Owen (or Ewan) and then Andrew Carrington as heirs [Ormerod, 1:543].

Children, listed in the *Visitation of Cheshire* [61], and Ormerod [1:544]:

7.   i.   John^G, m. Isabel de Beeston.
     ii. Nicholas, no issue.
    iii. Ralph, a priest; no issue.
    iv. Peter, no issue.
     v. William, had sons Owen and Andrew.
    vi. Edmund.
   vii. George.

7. Sir JOHN[G] DE CARYNGTON, Lord of Caryngton in Cheshire, son and heir, was of record 8 Hen. V (1420-1421), 4 (1425-1426) & 12 Hen. VI (1434-1435), and died before 31 Hen. VI (1452-1453).

He married ISABEL[G] DE BEESTON, daughter and coheir of Sir John de Beeston, and widow of Sir Robert de Aston. She was of record 8 Hen. V (1420-1421) and 12 Hen. VI (1433-1434). Her *inq. post mortum*, dated 34 Hen. VI (1455-1456), showed that she died aged 40, and held in demesne as of fee the manors of Teverton and Stoke, and lands in Hulgreve in Minshull Vernon, Mayowesee in Leghton, Aldersey [Ormerod, 1:543]. By her first marriage she had a son and heir, Richard de Aston, aged 40 in 34 Hen. VI.

Children, listed by Ormerod [1:544] and the *Visitation of Cheshire* [61]:

    i.   Hamon (or Hamlet[t])[F], son and heir, mentioned 37 Hen. VI (1458-1459) and 1 Ric. III (1483-1484); d. 16 July 3 Ric. III (1485), *inq. post mortem* 16 Hen. VII (1500-1501); m. Katherine, l. a widow 5 Hen. VII (1489-1490); no issue [Ormerod, 1:544].

    ii. Thomas, no issue.

*   iii. Emma, m. Randle[F] Brereton of Ipstones, Cheshire.

§ § §

DE CHAWORTH

Burke's *Dormant Peerages*, from which the earliest generations of this line were taken, is not a particularly reliable source. Burke started this line with Patrick de Cadurcis, called Chaworth, a native of Little Brittany, who said to have made a grant of certain mills in Gloucestershire to the monks of St. Peter's Abbey about the end of the reign of William the Conqueror. He then mentioned Patrick[P] de Chaworth, who was of record a full century later, as his son.

However, Sanders developed the line further, as shown below. Sanders states that the name Chaworth comes from Sourches in Sarthe, in the arrondisement of Le Mans, quoting Loyd's *Anglo-Norman Families*.

1. PATRICK I[S] DE CHAWORTH was of record in 1133.

He married MAUD[S] DE HESDING (daughter of Ernulf I de Hesding), who was also living in 1133, and had taken the honour of Kempsford in Gloucestershire to her husband.

He made gifts to St. Peter's, Gloucester, in 1096 and witnessed a deed in 1100.

Children, mentioned by Sanders [125]:

  2.   i. Patrick II[R], m. Wilburga[R] de Mundubleil.

  +   ii. Sybil, m. Walter[T] Fitz Edward de Salisbury (of the family d'Evereux), who d. 1147.

2. PATRICK II[R] DE CHAWORTH was succeeded by his son before 1155.

He married WILBURGA[R] DE MUNDUBLEIL, daughter of Pain de Mundubleil [Sanders, 125²].

Child:

  3.   i. Pain[Q], took his mother's surname.

3. PAIN[Q] DE MUNDEBLEIL who assumed his mother's surname, died in 1170.

In 1165 scutage was due on forty knights' fees, but while he made some payment in 1166 the debt charged against his property was due from Patrick, Earl of Salisbury and Geoffrey de Ver in 1167, but he regained the lands by 1168, when he was charged on twelve and one-half knights' fees [Sanders, 125[3]]. The lands of the Kempsford barony were not liable to scutage.

4. PATRICK III[P] DE CHAWORTH seems to have died in 1199 [Sanders, 125].

He accounted six pounds for the knight's fees belonging to the honor of Striguil in the collection of the scutage of Galway in 33 Hen. II (1186-1187).

Child, mentioned by Burke:

5. i. Pain[O], of record 2 Hen. III (1217-1218); m. Gundrada de la Ferté.

5. PAIN II[O] DE CHAWORTH was of record 2 Hen. III (1217-1218) as surety, as a marcher baron, for Isabel de Mortimer that she would appear at the King's Exchequer to satisfy her debts owing to King John, and probably died in 1237 [Sanders, 123].

He married GUNDRADA[O] DE LA FERTÉ, daughter and heir of William de la Ferté, of Mereden in Wiltshire (who died in 1216), and his wife Margery[O] de Briwere, daughter of Sir William de Briwere, who died in 1226, and sister of Sir William de Briwere who died in 1233.

Child, mentioned by Burke:

6. i. Patrick[N], d. 1258; m. Hawise[N] de London of Kidwelly in Wales.

6. PATRICK[N] DE CHAWORTH, of Stoke in Northamptonshire, and Kempsford in Gloucestershire, died in 1258.

He married HAWISE[N] DE LONDON, daughter of Thomas[O] de London (or de Londres), lord of Kidwelly, Carmarthen, Wales, who died before 1221.

He paid £500 for his own wardship and marriage while he was a minor in 23 Hen. III (1238-1239), and six years later he was ordered to use his power to annoy the Welsh.

He was excused from paying 200 marks which his father owed for Margery's lands [Sanders, 123].

Children, listed by Sir Bernard Burke [Dormant Peerages, 111]:

i. Pain[M], d. 1278; attended Prince Edward to the Holy Land 54 Hen. III (1269-1270), general of the King's Army in West Wales 5 Edw. I (1276-1277).

ii. Hervey, attended Prince Edward to the Holy Land 1270.

7. iii. Patrick, d. Kidwelly, Carmarthen, 1283; m. (2) Isabel[L] de Beauchamp, who d. 1306.

7. PATRICK[M] DE CHAWORTH, Lord Kidwelly, died in Kidwelly, Carmarthenshire, Wales, about 7 July 1283.

He married second ISABEL[K] DE BEAUCHAMP* of Stoke, Northamptonshire, who died in 1306, having married second Sir Hugh[N] le Despenser, by whom she had more children. She has been called Joan in error, and was in the King's ward.

He was of Kidwelly and Ogmore in county Carmarthen, Wales, and held Hartley Mauduit in Hampshire, England. In 1283 Kempsford was held for the service of one knights' fee [Sanders, 125[7]].

Child:

* i. Maud[L], b. Kidwelly, Carmarthenshire, Wales, 2 Feb. 1282; d. c. 1320; m. before 2 March 1296/7 Henry[L] Plantagenet, Earl of Lancaster, who d. Monastery of Canons, Leics., 22 Sept. 1345, having m. (2) Alix de Joinville.

§ § §

DE CHEDLE

The research on this line has been based on George Ormerod's *History of Chester* [1:718 and 2:711-718]. Clifton, the manor house of this line, was later called Rock-Savage. Ormerod described the house as a "sumptuous building" erected by Sir John Savage in 1565. John, Constable of Cheshire and Baron of Halton, gave Clifton to Galfrid or Geffrey de Dutton, younger son of Hugh Dutton, during the reign of King Henry II (1154-1189). Geffrey's posterity were known as the Lords of Chedle.

1. GEOFFREY[P] DE DUTTON (son of Hugh[Q] de Dutton, for whom see Dutton of Dutton) was during the time of Henry II, who ruled from 1154-1189, grantee in frank-marriage of Clifton (later Rocksavage), Cheshire.

He married first a daughter of John de Lacy, lord of Halton and constable of Cheshire.

He married second, Elen (or Hellen) de Chedle, daughter and coheir of Robert de Chedle.

Child, in Ormerod [3:622]:

2.   i.   Sir Geoffrey[O], m. Agnes[P] de Mascy.

2. Sir GEOFFREY[O] DE DUTTON, alias DE CHEDLE, probably died during the reign of Henry III, who ruled from 1216-1272.

He married AGNES[P] DE MASCY (or MASSY*), daughter of Hamon de Mascy III, lord of Dunham. As a widow she was called Agnes de Nechel (or Etchells) when she gave her son Geoffrey de Chedle her father's gift of Bollinton [Ormerod, 3:622n].

He was lord of Chedle Asshelegh, which was apparently a moiety of Timperlegh. He was seneschal of John de Lacy from 1232-1240.

Children, in Ormerod:

3.   i.   Geoffrey[N], m. Margaret; lord of Chedle, granted half of Bolinton by his mother.

ii.   Hamon de Dutton, alias de Asshelegh; d. before 10 Edw. III (1336-1337); issue.

iii.   Alice, perhaps m. 23 Edw. I (1394-1395) Randle de Clayton of Thelwall; her heirs inherited half of Bolinton in Bucklow.

3. Sir GEOFFREY[N] DE CHEDLE, lord of Chedle, died 22 Edw. I (1293-1294).

His wife MARGARET brought several actions for dower, particularly against Hamon de Dutton for the manor of Asshelegh, a moiety of Timperlegh, and lands in Hale and Apilton.

Children, in Ormerod:

i.   Geoffrey[M], aged 26 in 22 Edw. I (1293-1294); d. in or before 24 Edw. I; no issue.

4.   ii.   Sir Roger, d. before 1323; m. c. 1317 Matild.

4. Sir ROGER[M] DE CHEDLE, alias DE DUTTON, Lord of Chedle and Clifton, Cheshire, died before 16 Edw. II (1322-1323).

He married 11 Edw. II (1317-1318) MATILD[A], who died 20 Edw. II (1326-1327), having perhaps married second a de Sulee.

He was witness to a charter of John Apilton, described by Ormerod as in the Arley collection, in 1295. He and his wife obtained tenements in Chedle, Clifton and Hale by a fine from Robert de Chedle (probably the rector of Chedle).

His two daughters divided the whole inheritance in 1327.

Daughters and coheirs, listed by Ormerod, surnamed de Chedle:

*   i.   Clemence[L], m. (1) William[L] Baggiley, m. (2) John de Molyneux; filed suit
10 Edw. III (1336-1337) [Wrottesley, *The Genealogist*, n.s., 13:102],
inherited Clifton, and lands in Chedle and Hulme in Cheshire from
her father in 1327.

ii.   Agnes, m. Richard de Bulkeley, son of Robert de Bulklegh of Eaton in
Davenham, a parish in the center of Cheshire; inherited the capital
messuage of Chedle, and the moiety of the manor later called Chedle
Bulkeley, and was ancestor of the Lords Bulkeley of Beaumaris
[Ormerod, *Chester*, 3:627].

§ § §

CHERLETON

The entries for Charleton and Cherleton in Cokayne's *Complete Peerage* have been
checked, and Eyton's *Antiquities of Shropshire* has been searched. Remarks in *Notes and
Queries* for Oct. 18, 1902 have little value.

1. WILLIAM[O] DE CHERLETON was named as the father of Robert, next, in the records.
Child, from Eyton [9:31]:
      2.   i.   Robert[N], fl. 1220-1265.

2. ROBERT[N] DE CHERLETON was of record attesting Uppington deeds from about 1220
to 1265.
    He served on juries in 1243, 1246, 1249, 1253, 1259, 1260 and 1262. Records of the
time refer to Robert son of William de Cherlton.
    Children, named by Eyton:
      i.   Richard[M], in 1280 gave his brother Robert certain rents in Aston (under
Wrekin), clearly of Shrewsbury Abbey, and Radulph's meadow in the
field of Cherleton, towards Ukiton; daus. Alicia and Margery of record
in 1294.
      3.   ii.   Robert, fl. 1283-1300.

3. ROBERT[M] DE CHERLETON was of Cherleton in Wrockwardine, Salop (Shropshire),
England.
    He served on juries in 1283, 1285 and 1293, and as a witness of deeds about 1300.
    Children, listed by Eyton [9:32, 319]:
      4.   i.   John[L], m. Hawise Gadarn[L] ferch Owain ap Gwenwynwyn.
      ii.   Alan, of Apley, d. 3 May 1349; m. c. 1317 Elena la Zouch (widow of
Nicholas de St. Maur), who was dead by 1360.
      iii.   Thomas, d. 11 Jan. 1344; Bishop of Hereford in 1327, later Chancellor of
Ireland.

4. Sir JOHN[L] DE CHERLETON of Powys in Wales, Baron of Cherleton, born in Apley near
Wellington in Salop (Shropshire) in 1268 [J. Morris, *Shropshire Genealogies*, 1:544], was
dead by 20 Jan. 1353/4, at age 85, when his son had livery of his lands [*CP*, 3:161]. He
and his wife were buried in the Grey Friars at Shrewsbury, which she had founded.
    He married before 26 Aug. 1309 HAWISE[L] GADARN ["the Hardy"] FERCH OWAIN AP
GWENWYNWYN, who was probably born 25 July 1290 [according to the *inquisition post
mortems* of her grandmother and of her brother (Cokayne, 10: 642g)], sister and heir of

Gruffudd ab Owain (Griffith ap Owen) DE LA POLE*, that is, of Pool in Wales, or Welshpool. She was living in Aug. 1345, but died before her husband.

He was named in a 1306 deed as owner of lands bordering those of William Fraunceys of Cherleton. On 18 Sept. 1308 William Fraunceis of Cherleton sold a messuage next to the land of Sir John de Cherleton, knight. In 1 Edw. II (1307-1308) he had a charter of free warren at Cherleton and Pontisbury in Salop (Shropshire), and the next year had confirmation of Pontisbury, which had belonged to Rhys ap Hywel.

He acquired the feudal barony of Pole, held *in capite* of the English crown, by right of his wife. Her uncles (excepting William ap Gruffudd) disputed her inheritance and besieged Powys Castle, but King Edward II directed Roger de Mortimer, then Justiciar of Wales, to protect John de Cherleton and Hawise Gadarn.

From 26 July 7 Edw. II (1313) to 25 July 27 Edw. III (1353) he was summoned to parliament, having become Lord of Powys by right of his wife, although this right was strongly contested by her uncles, the heirs male; it was confirmed upon John de Cherleton by Royal Charter 7 Edw. II (1313-1314). In and before 1314 he was Lord Chamberlain to King Edward II. In 1313/4 he was constable of Builth Castle in Brecon, Wales. He was summoned to Parliament from 26 July 1313 to 25 July 1353. In 1319 he was required to recruit 500 soldiers from Powys for the wars in France.

Although he joined the rebellion of Thomas, Earl of Lancaster, in 1321/2, he was pardoned 11 Sept. 1322. He was appointed governor (Justiciar), of Ireland, in 1337-1338.

The *Visitation of Shropshire, 1623* [105] interjected Joan[K] de Stafford, daughter of the Earl of Stafford, as the wife of John[K] de Cherlton, with a son John who married Maud de Mortimer, but the pedigree on page 108 showed the correct line.

Children, mentioned by Cokayne, Weis, or Morris:

    i.   John[K], d. 13 July 1374; m. Maud[J] de Mortimer, dau. of Roger[K] de Mortimer, 1st Earl of March.

*   ii. Isabel, d. 1396; m. John[K] de Sutton.

    iii. Owen, d. 42 Edw. III (1368-1369), lord of Lydham [J. Morris, 1:544].

§ § §

DE CLARE

This data is from Cokayne's *Complete Peerage*, vol. 3, pages 242-244, and vol. 6, pages 498-503, as well as the work of George T. Clark. Richard Mortimer made the observation, in *Angevin England*, that the Clares were the only family descended from ancestors important in Normandy before 1066 and represented among the great earls in the 1250s.

RICHARD[W] II, DUKE OF NORMANDY, was listed as the progenitor of this line by Cokayne.

GODFREY[V], COUNT OF BRIONNE, was an illegitimate son of the Duke of Normandy.

GILBERT[U] was COUNT OF BRIONNE in Normandy.

RICHARD[T] FITZ GILBERT possessed Bienfaite and Orbec in Normandy, Clare in Suffolk, and Tonbridge. The mother of Gilbert[S] and Robert was his first wife, ROHESE[T] GIFFARD, daughter of Walter Giffard, the Elder (who died in 1084) [Cokayne, *CP*, 2:387], seigneur de Longeville-sur-Scie in Normandy and son of Osbern de Bolbec, who was seigneur de Longeville 1028-1035, and Duvelina, who was sister of the Duchess Gunnora. Walter Giffard married Agnes, daughter of Girard Flatel [Weis, *AR*7, 184:1, cited *Studies in Medieval History* (1989)].

GILBERT[S] FITZ RICHARD DE CLARE, also de Tonbridge, Lord of Clare, born before 1066, died in 1114 or 1117. He married ADELIZ[S] DE CLERMONT, daughter of Hugh, Count of

Clermont in Beauvaisis, by Marguerite, daughter of Hilduin, Count of Montdidier and Roucy. Adeliz married second (Bouchard?) de Montmorency.

RICHARD[R] FITZ GILBERT DE CLARE, Lord of Clare, was slain, having been surprised by the Welsh, near Abergavenny, 15 April 1136, and was buried at Gloucester. He married ADELIZE[O], daughter of Ranulph[P] le Meschin, Earl OF CHESTER by Lucy, and sister of Ranulph de Gernon (or des Gernons), Earl of Chester; she was rescued from the Welsh by Miles of Gloucester. She married second Robert de Condet.

ROGER[Q] DE CLARE, Earl of Clare or Hertford, died in 1173. He married MAUD[Q] DE ST. HILARY, daughter and heir of James de St. Hilary, Lord of Field Dalling and Great and Little Carbrooke, Norfolk, by his wife Aveline [*CP*, 5:124-125, 6:499-501; Sanders, *English Baronies*, 34-35, 62-63]. She married secondly William[O] d'Aubigny, Earl of Arundel, who died 24 Dec. 1193.

RICHARD[P] DE CLARE, Lord of Clare, styled Earl of Clare, Earl of Hertford, died in November of 1217. He married AMICE[O] who died as Countess of Gloucester, about 1 Jan. 1224/5, daughter (and in her issue heiress) of William Fitz Robert, Earl of Gloucester, by Hawise, daughter of Robert de Beaumont, Earl of Leicester. William Fitz Robert was son of Robert de Caen, created Earl of Gloucester 1122, died 1147, illegitimate son of King Henry I by Sybil Corbet [*CP*, 5:736 chart]; Robert married Mabel, daughter of Robert Fitz Hamon, lord of Creully in Calvados, and his wife Sybil, daughter of Roger de Montgomery, Earl of Shrewsbury. Richard and Amice appear to have been separated before 1200, perhaps pending a dispensation [*CP*, 6:502].

GILBERT[O] DE CLARE, 7th Earl of Clare, 5th Earl of Hertford and 4th Earl of Gloucester, born about 1180, died in Penros, Brittany, 25 Oct. 1230, while returning from an expedition, and was buried at Tewkesbury. He married, 9 Oct. 1217, ISABEL[O] MARSHAL, who died Berkhampstead 17 Jan. 1239/40 after having married second, 30 Mar. 1231, Richard Plantagenet, Earl of Cornwall, second son of King John. She was daughter of William Marshall, Earl of Pembroke, and Isabel de Clare.

10. RICHARD[N] DE CLARE, Lord of Clare, 5th Earl of Gloucester and 6th Earl of Hertford, born 4 August 1222, died at Eschemerfield, Kent, of poison at the table of Peter of Savoy, the Queen's uncle [Geo. T. Clark, 120], 15 July 1262, and was buried at Tewkesbury.

He married, on or before 25 Jan. 1237/8 [*MCS*5, 107:4], MAUD[N] DE LACY (daughter of John de Lacy and Margaret de Quincy), who died before 10 March 1288/9.

Michael Altschul [34] states that there was a secret first marriage in 1232 to Meggotta de Burgh, daughter of Hubert de Burgh, the Justiciar (which produced no issue), and cited *Patent Rolls, 1225-32*, p. 412.

In the struggle between King Henry III of England and the Earl Marshal, Henry summoned his military tenants to Gloucester on 15 August 1533. As Richard, Earl of Gloucester, was absent from this meeting he was proscribed as a traitor, his lands were seized and laid waste, and a date was set for his trial [Geo. T. Clark, 97]. This encounter involved the Earl Marshal's opposition to foreign influence, and was resolved after some warfare.

With the death of the last of the House of Marshal in Dec. 1245, the de Clares were without rival in South Wales [Geo. T. Clark, 109]. In 1256 he founded the house of Black Friars outside the west gate of Cardiff [Clark, 115].

Children, mentioned by Weis, Cokayne, Clark and Altschul [34-36]:

    i.   Isabel[M], b. May 1240 [Geo. T. Clark, 105]; m. Lyons 13 June 1257 Marquis di Monte Ferrato, who m. (2) 1271 a dau. of Alfonso X of Castile.

11.   ii.   Gilbert, b. Christchurch, Hampshire, 2 Sept. 1243; d. 7 Dec. 1295; m. (1) 1257 Alice de Lusignan of Angoulême, m. (2) Joan[L] Plantagenet, dau. of King Edward I.

12.   iii.   Thomas, d. Clare, Ireland, 29 Aug. 1287; m. (2) 1275 Juliane[M] Fitz Maurice of Dublin, who d. 1300.

        iv.   Bevis (or Bogo, a son), b. 21 July 1248, canon of York.

        v.   Margaret, b. Christmas 1250; d. 1312; m. 1272 Edmund, son of Richard, Earl of Cornwall, and Saunchia of Provence, div. 1294.

        vi.   Roesia, b. 17 Oct. 1252; l. 1316; m. Roger de Mowbray of Thirsk in Yorks., who d. 1296.

        vii.   Eglantine, b. 1257; d. infant, bur. Tewkesbury.

11. GILBERT[M] DE CLARE, the Red, Lord of Clare, 6th Earl of Gloucester and Hertford, born Christchurch, Hampshire [Leese, 97], 2 Sept. 1243, died in Monmouth Castle 7 Dec. 1295, and was buried at Tewkesbury Abbey.

He married first, in spring 1253, Alice de Lusignan of Angoulême, daughter of Hugh XI de Lusignan and Yolande de Dreux. The marriage was annulled in 1285 [Altschul, 37]; allegedly she had become a hypochondriac in 1271 [Faris, PA2, 83].

He married second, 30 April 1290, JOAN[L] PLANTAGENET* of Acre, daughter of Edward I, King of England, by Eleanor of Castile; she died in Clare, Suffolk, 28 April 1307, and was buried in the Austin Friars'. Church there. She married second, secretly about 1296, Ralph de Monthermer, a simple squire, who rose to administer the lordship of Glamorgan [Geo. T. Clark, 147-148], and died in 1325, having fought at Bannockburn in 1314, 1st Lord Monthermer, Keeper of Cardiff Castle. Ralph de Monthemer had married second, before 20 Nov. 1318, Isabel le Despenser, widow of John de Hastings.

He led the swearing of fealty to King Edward I at a time when the king was in Sicily, returning from a crusade, and was joint guardian of England while the king was absent.

Clare is now a small parish on the River Stour in Suffolk. It had been a frontier town of the Kingdom of East Anglia, and contains a castle of which considerable remains exist [Brabner, vol. 2].

Children, by first wife, only one according to George T. Clark [160]:

        i.   Isabel[L], b. 10 March 1262/3; d. 1338; m. 1316 Maurice[J] de Berkeley.

        ii.   Joan, m. (1) 1284 Duncan, Earl of Fife, who d. 1288, m. (2) c. 1302 Gervase Avenel.

Children, by second wife, mentioned by Weis:

        iii.   Gilbert, Earl of Gloucester and Hertford, b. 1291; slain at Bannockburn 24 June 1314; m. Maud[K] de Burgh, who d. 1320; no surviving issue, if any.

*   iv.   Alianore, b. Caerphilly Castle, Glams. [CP, 4:267], Oct. 1292; d. 30 June 1337; m. (1) at Westminster, after 14 June 1306, Sir Hugh[M] le Despenser, who was hanged and quartered at Hereford, 24 Nov. 1326, m. (2) c. Jan. 1328/9 Sir William la Zouche de Mortimer, Lord Zouche, who had abducted her from Hanley Castle.

*   v.   Margaret, b. prob. at Caerphilly Castle c. 1292; d. 13 April 1342; m. (1) Barkhamstead 1 Nov. 1307 Piers de Gaveston, Earl of Cornwall, who was beheaded without trial 19 June 1312, m. (2) Windsor, 28 April 1317, Hugh[L] de Audley, who d. 10 Nov. 1347.

        vi.   Elizabeth, b. Tewkesbury 16 Sept. 1295 [MCS5, 13:6]; d. 4 Nov. 1360; m. (1) 30 Sept. 1308 John de Burgh, Earl of Ulster, who d. 1313, m. (2) Bristol, 3 Feb. 1315, having been abducted, Sir Theobald[N] de

Verdun, who d. 27 July 1316 [Clark, 162], m. (3) 1317 Sir Roger Damory, 1st Lord Damory [*NEHGR*, 148:255] of Bletchington, Oxon, who was executed for treason 13/14 March 1321/2.

12. THOMAS[M] DE CLARE, Lord of Inchequin and Youghae, born in 1245/6, died in Clare, Ireland, 29 Aug. 1287.

He married second, in 1275, JULIANE[M] FITZ MAURICE FITZ GERALD of Dublin, who died in 1300, daughter of Sir Maurice[N] Fitz Maurice Fitz Gerald and Emmeline de Longespée. It has been said that Juliane married second Sir Adrian de Creting, but had no more children. Another source stated she married second John Cogan.

Sheppard called him Lord of Thurmond and younger brother of Richard, Earl of Clare, Hertford and Gloucester [*NEHGR*, 116:279].

He was Justiciar of Ireland [Weis, *AR*7, 54:31], and Governor of London.

Children [*NEHGR*, 116:279]:

    i.   Gilbert[L], no issue.

    ii.   Richard, Lord Clare; had son Thomas who d. young.

*   iii.   Maud, d. 1 Feb. 1324/5; m. (1) 13 Nov. 1295 Robert[L] de Clifford, who d. Bannockburn 24 June 1314, m. (2) Robert de Welle, Lord Welles.

*   iv.   Margaret, d. 1333; m. (1) Gilbert de Umfraville, who d. 1303, bur. Hexham Priory [Hedley, 1:211], m. (2) Bartholomew[L] de Badlesmere, who was hanged at Canterbury 14 April 1322.

Child, illegitimate [Altschul, 34]:

    v.   Master Richard, d. 1338.

§ § §

DE CLIFFORD

RICHARD[R] FITZ PONS was born say 1080. He married MAUD[Q] FITZ WALTER.

WALTER[Q] AP RICHARD FITZ PONS DE CLIFFORD was born about 1108. He married MARGARET DE TODENI, a descendant of Ralph de Todeni, son of William Fitz Osbern.

WALTER[P] DE CLIFFORD, born in Clifford's Castle, Herefordshire, about 1150, died 22 Jan. 1222. He married about 1185 AGNES DE CUNDY, daughter of Roger de Cundy, Lord Coventry, and Alice de Cheney, Lady Horncastle, of Cavenby, Lincolnshire.

ROGER[O] DE CLIFFORD, born in Clifford's Castle, Herefordshire, about 1189, died in 1232 and was buried in Dore Abbey, Herefordshire. He married first, before 13 Feb. 1217, SYBIL[N] DE EWYAS (widow of Robert[O] de Tregoz I), who died Ewyas, Herefordshire, in 1236.

ROGER[N] DE CLIFFORD, born say 1226, died in France in 1285, and was buried at Dore Abbey in Herefordshire. He married first HAWISE[N] BOTTERELL, Countess Lorraine, who was born about 1215, daughter of Sir John Botterell of Herefordshire. Possible ties to Tenbury, Worcestershire should be studied. He married second, in St. George, La Rochelle, France, 15 Feb. 1274, the Countess de Lauretania.

ROGER[M] DE CLIFFORD of Herefordshire, born say 1243, drowned in the Menai Straits in Wales, 6 Nov. 1282, and was buried at Shap Abbey, Westmorland. He married ISABEL[M] VIPONT (or Vespont), Lady of Appleby and Brougham, who died 14 May 1292 and was buried at Shap Abbey, Westmorland.

5. ROBERT[L] DE CLIFFORD, 1st Lord Clifford, born at Clifford Castle, Herefordshire, about Easter 1274, was killed in the Battle of Bannockburn, 24 (or 25 [*BP*, 1:784]) June 1314, and buried at Shap Abbey in Westmorland.

He married 13 Nov. 1295 MAUD[L] DE CLARE*, who died 1 Feb. 1324/5, having married second (by force without the King's permission, having been abducted), 13 Nov. 1315, Robert[L] de Welle, Lord Welles, who died Aug. 1320. In 14 Edw. II (1320-1321) she was found to be heiress to her nephew Thomas, only son and heir of Richard de Clare, Lord Clare. The writ for her *inquisition post mortem* was dated 24 May 1327.

His succeeded his grandfather in 1286. On his mother's death he inherited a moiety of the great Vipont family estates, including Brougham Castle, Westmorland, and the Hereditary Shrievalty of that county; thus he was Sheriff of Westmorland in 1291. He had seizin of his inheritance 3 May 1295, and was a coheir of his great-uncle, Richard Fitz John, in 1297.

He served in the Scottish Wars, was Justice in Eyre North of Trent from 1297-1307/8, and Governor of Nottingham Castle in July 1298. He was Captain General of the Marches of Scotland in 1299. His summonses to Parliament dated from 29 Dec. 1299 to 26 Nov. 1313. In 1301 his seal was affixed to a celebrated letter to the Pope.

King Edward I granted him the manor of Skelton, Cumberland, and Skipton Castle in Yorkshire. Edward II made him Marshall of England for a few months in 1307.

Children, from Cokayne:

      i.   Roger[K], b. 21 Jan. (Or 2 Feb.) 1299/1300; executed at York 23 March 1321/2 following his being taken prisoner at the battle of Borough-bridge; he was a Banneret who had supported the Rebellion of Thomas, Earl of Lancaster, against King Edward II.

*   ii.   Idoine, b. Clifford, Herefordshire, c. 1303; d. 24 Aug. 1365, bur. Beresley; m. 1314 Henry[K] de Percy, who d. Warkworth 27 Feb. 1351/2.

   iii.   Robert, b. 5 Nov. 1305; d. 1344; m. Berkeley Castle, June 1328, Isabel[I] Berkeley, who m. (2) Sir Thomas Musgrave.

§ § §

CLIVEDON

This fragment was developed from the section on Berkeley in Cokayne's *Complete Peerage*.

1. Sir JOHN[J] CLIVEDON, of Aller, Somerset, and Charfield, Gloucestershire, born say 1287, died about 1373.

His wife was EMMA [*CP*, 2:129].

A Member of Parliament, he was Keeper of Bristol Castle.

Child:

*   i.   Katharine[I], d. 13 March 1385, bur. Berkeley Church, Gloucs.; m. (1) Charfield, Gloucs., 30 May 1347, Thomas[I] de Berkeley as his second wife, m. (2) Sir Piers le Veel of Tortworth.

§ § §

COMYN

This line has been developed from to James Balfour Paul's *Scots Peerage*.

Paul stated that Comines of Flanders is the probable place of origin of the family.

ROBERT[T] DE COMYN was slain with all of his followers at Durham, England, 28 Jan. 1069/70 [*SP*, 1:503, cited *Chron. de Mailros*, 55].

JOHN^S COMYN was killed in the wars between the forces of the Empress Maud and King Stephen in England after 1135. According to *The Scots Peerage* [1:504], he married a co-heiress of Adam Giffard of Fonthill in Wiltshire.

WILLIAM^R COMYN died before 1140, having held one-third of Fonthill in Wiltshire. He married MAUD^R, daughter of Thurstan Banaster or Basset, who married second in 1140 William de Hastings.

RICHARD^Q COMYN of Northallerton and Badenoch, Scotland, died between 1176 and 1182. He married about 1145 HEXTILDA^Q, daughter of Huctred^R OF TYNDALE, son of Waldef^S; she married second, in 1182, Malcolm, Earl of Atholl.

WILLIAM^P COMYN, Earl of Buchan, died in 1233 [*SP*, 2:253], and was buried, if tradition is correct, before the high alter of the church of the Abbey of Deer, which he had founded. He married first SARAH^P, who was living in 1204, said to perhaps have been a daughter and heiress of Robert Fitz Hugh, who died about 1201 [*SP*, 1:505 note 4]. He married second, no later than 1214, Margaret, daughter and heiress of Fergus, 4th Earl of Buchan, who was dead in 1211. King William the Lion of Scotland confirmed a grant of hers from the church of Turriff to the Abbey of Aberbrothoc. She was dead by August 1244, when her son Alexander was Earl of Buchan.

RICHARD^O COMYN, Lord of Badenoch, Scotland, died about 1244-1249.

7. JOHN^N COMYN, "Red Comyn No. 1," seen in 1242, died after 1273.

He married AMABILIA (or Alicia), who was living in 1280, having married second another Comyn, by whom she had issue. She was named Alicia in a charter of all their demesne lands of Ulseby in Lincolnshire.

He probably succeeded his father by July 1249, and became lord of Badenoch in 1258 (when his uncle Walter died without surviving issue), thus becoming head of the most powerful family in Scotland. He was appointed, before 18 March 1258/9, Justiciar of Galloway, and on 8 Feb. 1261/2 he received a grant from King Henry III of England confirming the grant made of lands in Tynedale to Richard, his great-grandfather, and Hextilda his wife.

Children, listed by Paul [*SP*, 1:507]:

    i. William^M, d. before 2 June 1291; m. Isabella Russell

8.   ii. John, "Black Comyn," m. Alianore^M de Baliol.

    iii. John, "le jeon," younger son of the same name.

    iv. daughter, m. Richard Siward.

    v. daughter, m. Geoffrey Mowbray; had five sons.

    vi. daughter, m. Alexander of Argyll; had son John of Lorne.

    vii. daughter, mother of Sir Andrew Moray of Bothwell who fell at the battle of Stirling Bridge in 1297.

    viii. daughter, m. Sir William Galbrathe, to whom Sir John Comyn granted the barony of Dalserf in Lanarkshire.

8. Sir JOHN^M COMYN, "Black Comyn," Lord of Badenoch, Scotland, died about 1303. He married ALIANORE^M DE BALIOL*, whose brother he supported for the throne of Scotland.

The second son, he succeeded to his father's lands in Tynedale. He was present in 1281 at the Convention of Roxburgh, where the marriage of Margaret, daughter of King Alexander III, was agreed upon. He was one of the Scottish magnates engaged to maintain the title of the Princess of Norway to the throne of Scotland on the death of her grandfather 5 Feb. 1283/4. In 1286 he was appointed one of six guardians of the kingdom. In 1289 he went to Norway as an ambassador to treat with the King concerning the marriage of the

Maid of Norway, his daughter. After the Maid of Norway died he swore fealty, on 10 July 1296, to King Edward I of England.

For a time he was a competitor for the throne of Scotland, basing his claim on descent from Hextilda and Donald Bane, but he withdrew in support of Balliol.

Child:

9.   i.   John[L], "Red Comyn No. 2," murdered at Dumfries 10 Feb. 1306; m. Joan[L] de Valence.

9. JOHN[L] COMYN, "the Red Comyn No. 2," Lord of Badenoch, Scotland, was murdered by Robert the Bruce at the Church of the Minorite [Grey] Friars in Dumfries, 10 Feb. 1306. He married JOAN[L] DE VALENCE*.

One of the leaders of the Scottish army which made a raid into Cumberland in March of 1296, he was taken prisoner by the English at Dunbar on 27 April 1296. On delivering his son as a hostage, he was released on 30 July 1297. In 1299 his wife was given safe conduct to go to him in Scotland; she had been commanded to appear in England in 1298.

On 19 Aug. 1299 he had a meeting with other nobles at Peebles, where he got into a scuffle and seized Robert Bruce, Earl of Carrick, by the throat; they agreed that Comyn should be elected one of the three guardians of the kingdom. On 24 Feb. 1302/3 he inflicted a defeat upon the English at Rosslyn. The next autumn he unsuccessfully defended Stirling Castle against Edward I of England, and he capitulated to Edward at Strathord 9 Feb. 1303/4. He was sentenced to banishment with a disgraceful condition that it would be shortened if he would deliver William de Waleys. He and his knights dined with Prince Edward on Saturday, 22 Feb. 1303/4, and by Oct. 1305 the fines for his rebellion were fixed at three years rental of his estate.

However, in one of the most famous incidents of Scottish history, he was murdered in the Church of the Minorite Friars in Dumfries by Robert Bruce on 10 Feb. 1305/6.

Children, listed in *Scots Peerage* [1:509]L

i.   John[K], only son, fell at Bannockburn fighting for England in 1314; m. Margaret Wake (sister of Thomas Wake, lord of Liddell, and dau. of John Wake, 1st Lord Wake), who m. (2) Edmund of Woodstock, Earl of Kent; hostage in 1297, had one son, who d. by 15 Nov. 1316.

ii.   Joan, b. c. 1295; d. shortly before 24 July 1326; m. David de Strathbogie, Earl of Atholl.

*   iii.   Elizabeth, b. 1 Nov. 1299; d. 20 March 1372; m. 1326 Sir Richard[K] Talbot, who d. 23 Oct. 1356, m. (2) Sir John Bromwich, who d. 1388.

§ § §

CORBET

The presentation following is based largely on Augusta Elizabeth Corbet's *The Family of Corbet*, which was written with the assistance of uncredited professional researchers, and has been studied by the compiler with great care.

The title of the Barons of Caus became extinct when it passed to the Staffords.

In Boyer's *Ancestral Lines*, 3rd ed., in the Owen Ancestor Table, at #2611, there is Cecily, daughter of Peter Corbet of Caus and Anne Cambrey, daughter of Sir Piers Cambrey. Cecily married John Bewprey of Welshpool and had a daughter who married Gwenwys of Cegidfa. Cegidfa is now called Guilsfield, but Cecily has not been found in A.E. Corbet's genealogy, which has not been searched thoroughly, and is not indexed.

A line unresolved is the identity of Sir Ralph Corbet who married Elizabeth[L] de Pulford.

HUGO[U] LE CORBEAU or LE CORBET, Chevalier of Pays de Caux, Normandy [Eyton, *Antiquities of Shropshire*, 7:6], flourished from 1040 and 1076, and was dead before the Domesday survey of 1086.

ROGER[T] FITZ CORBET, Domesday Baron of Caus, formerly Alretone, Shropshire, England, as it was called in Domesday, was born about 1050 to 1056, and died about 1134 [AET, 47], as Pagan Fitz John, sheriff and governor of Shropshire, having succeeded Richard de Belmeis, held Caus in 1134, and would not have dared to take it during Roger's lifetime; the castle was destroyed by the Welsh attacking Pagan Fitz John. It had been one of the strongholds along the Welsh border between the rivers Dee and Wye [AEC, ix]. He married the heiress of Tasley [Horrest, *Trans. Shropshire Arch. Soc.*, 4th ser., 7 (1918-1919), 155].

WILLIAM[S] CORBET, 2nd Baron of Caus, lived in Wattlesborough as the Castle of Caus was destroyed by the Welsh attack on Pagan Fitz John. SIMON[R] CORBET was of Pontesburie, close to the Welsh frontier, and probably died before his father, William Corbet of Wattlesborough.

THOMAS[P] CORBET was called the Pilgrim. He probably spent much time abroad.

Sir RICHARD[O] CORBET of Wattlesborough flourished in 1217 and 1222. Eyton combined this generation with that of Sir Richard[N] Corbet, below.

Sir RICHARD[N] CORBET of Wattlesborough died before 1235. He married, probably by 1196 [Eyton, 10:184], JOANNA[N] TORET, coheir of Bartholomew Toret of Moreton Toret, Salop, who flourished in 1196-1229 and also had lands in Yorkshire.

Sir RICHARD[M] CORBET, knight of Wattlesborough, flourished 1225-1248, and was Lord of Morton at the Inquest of Bradford Hundred taken in 1255. He married Petronilla, lady of Edge Baldenham [Edgebolton] and Booley, who was living in 1272 [Eyton, 9:324-325], made a grant to Buildwas Abbey in 1223 [Eyton, 10:187], succeeded his grandfather Bartholomew Toret (who was dead in 1255), and was Justiciar of Shropshire.

12. Sir ROBERT[L] CORBET, of Wattlesborough and Moreton Toret, Shropshire, died in 1300, and was buried in the chapel at Alberbury which he had built.

It is said that he married first Catherine le Strange, daughter of John le Strange of Knocking, but John le Strange V of Knockin was too young to have been her father. Eyton [10:182] gave his first wife as Ida.

He married second, about 1280, MATILDA DE ARUNDEL of Tiddeshall and Habberley, who died in 1309.

He was of full age in 1255, and apparently served as the Sheriff of Shropshire for the quarter ending Michaelmas 1288 and the year ending Michaelmas 1289. The inquest post mortem was held at Moreton on Sunday, 15 Jan. 1301 [Eyton, 10:188].

Child, by first wife:
*   i.   Joan[K], d. 1348; m. (1) Owain[M] ap Gruffudd ap Gwenwynwyn (for whom see de la Pole), m. (2) c. 1295 Sir Roger Trumwyne.

Children, by second wife:
13.   ii.   Thomas, son and heir, b. 1281; d. 1310; m. Amice.
     iii.   Fulk, a priest, no issue; resigned the rectorship of Ightfield 1323 and was made Canon of Lichfield.
     iv.   John, probable son, of Habberley.
     v.   Roger, of Moreton Corbet c. 1324 [Eyton, 10:182].

13. THOMAS[K] CORBET, born according to Eyton either 25 Dec. 1281 or 25 May 1284, died in 1310, aged 29.

He married Amice.

Child:

14.   i.   Robert[J], b. 25 Dec. 1304; d. 1375; m. by March 1323 Elizabeth[K] le Strange.

14. Sir ROBERT[J] CORBET of Moreton Corbet, born 25 Dec. 1304, died 3 Dec. 1375.

He was married by March 1323 to ELIZABETH[K] LE STRANGE*, daughter of Fulk le Strange, Seneschal of the Duchy of Aquitaine. In the Calendar of Papal Registers, 2:229, for Ides March 1323, is an entry: "To Robert Corbet, lord of the town of Morton in the Diocese of Litchfield and Elizabeth daughter of Fulke le Strange, seneschal of the Duchy of Aquitaine dispensation to remain in marriage which they contracted in ignorance that they were related in the 4th degree, and declaring their present and future offspring legitimate. 1 March, Avignon" [W.L. Sheppard, *TAG*, 35:31].

He was noted as lord of the Vill of Moreton Corbet in 1316, but had not been granted knighthood by 1326. He purchased Shawbury from Giles[J] de Erdington, which property was conveyed to Thomas Gery, vicar of Morton, and Thomas de Lee of Southbache. He went to some lengths to pass his lands to Roger[I] Corbet's heirs [Eyton, 10:190-191].

Children:
15.   i.   Thomas[I], knight, d. c. 1359; m. Elizabeth (or Amice).
       ii.   Sir Fulk, d. 4 Aug. 1382 [Eyton, 10:182]; m. Elizabeth; dau. Elizabeth m. John de la Pole, Lord of Mawddwy ["Descent of Wattlesborough," *Archæologia Cambrensis*, 4th ser., 11 (1880), 6].
16.   iii. Roger, d. prob. 1394; m. Margaret[I] de Erdington (or de Eardiston).
 *   iv.   Joan, l. 20 June 1417; m. (1) c. 1356 Robert[J] de Harley, the idiot, m. (2) c. 1390 John Darras, a Shropshire gentlemen who was Sheriff of Shropshire in 1401.
       v.   Eleanor, m. Sir Brian[J] de Harley, ancestor of the Earls of Oxford.
       vi.   Amice, m. Sir Ed. le Strange, Lord of Mudle.
       vii. Margaret, m. before 24 Jan. 1357/8 Sir Thomas[I] de Erdington, who d. 28 March 1395.

15. Sir THOMAS[I] CORBET died about 1359.
He married Elizabeth (or Amice).
He was of Moreton Corbet and Wattlesborough [Roskell, 3:479].
Child [Paul C. Reed, *TG*, 10:60, note 53]:
 *   i.   Elizabeth[H], m. c. 1375 Sir John[I] Ipstones.

16. Sir ROGER[I] CORBET of Moreton Corbet (by which name Moreton Toret was then called) and Shawbury, died probably in 1394.
He married MARGARET[J] DE ERDINGTON*, who died in 1395.
Children:
17.   i.   Robert[H], b. 8 Dec. 1383; d. 12 Aug. 1420; m. Margaret (——), who m. (2) Sir William Mallory.
       ii.   Roger.

17. Sir ROBERT[H] CORBET, born in Moreton Corbet 8 Dec. 1383 [Roskell, 2:653]; died 12 Aug. 1420 [Roskell, 2:654].

He married MARGARET (who died 26 Jan. 1439), who has been identified erroneously as Margaret Mallory, daughter of Sir William Mallory of Shawbury. The once accepted royal line through her alleged father to Sir Anketil Malory and Alice de Driby, to John de Driby and Amy de Gaveston, to Piers de Gaveston, 1st Earl of Cornwall, and Margaret de Clare, daughter of Gilbert de Clare and Joan Plantagenet, daughter of Edward I, must be discarded. In fact Margaret married second Sir William Mallory [Hoff, *TAG*, 71:187] of Papworth in Cambridgeshire.

As his parents were both dead when he was eleven, his wardship and marriage were granted by King Richard II to Thomas Percy, Earl of Worcester, who was obliged at the beginning of the reign of Henry IV to hand over the wardship to John Burley I of Broncroft. Robert proved his age in 1405 [Roskell, 2:653].

He served as Justice of Shropshire from 14 March 1410 to Feb. 1416, and served the county in Parliament in 1413 and 1419. In May 1413 he and Richard Lacon (who held office on the Fitz Alan estates) joined David Holbache and Urian St. Pierre (both of whom represented Shrewsbury) in acting as sureties for a Matthew ap Maredudd [Roskell, 2:654].

In 1413 problems with tax collections were blamed on the dislike of Robert Corbet and Richard Lacon for their nominees as tax collectors. As a result indictments were brought against Robert[H] and Roger Corbet, Richard Lacon, John Burley II and other esquires of the Earl of Arundel. In 1415 Robert[H] and Roger Corbet served in King Henry V's first expedition to France. Robert was Sheriff of Shropshire in from 23 Nov. 1419 until he died.

Children:

      i.   Sir Thomas[G] of Moreton Corbet, d. 1436; m. Ancareta de Barres, who m. (2) Hanmer; no issue.

18.   ii. Roger, m. Elizabeth[G] Hopton.

     iii. Julianna (or Anna), m. (1) Sir John Sandford of Sandford, Salop, m. (2) Sir Hugh Peshall, who was Sheriff of Staffordshire in 1488.

     iv. Dorothy, m. Philip Kynaston of Walford, Salop.

     v. Mary, m. Sir Robert Charlton of Apley, Salop.

18. Sir ROGER[G] CORBET of Moreton Corbet, born about 1415, died 8 June 1467.

He married ELIZABETH[G] HOPTON*, who died 22 June 1498, having married second John Tiptoft, Earl of Worcester, and married third Sir William Stanley of Holt.

Children:

      i.   Anna[F], m. Thomas Sturry of Rossall.

     ii. Maria, m. Thomas Thornes of Shelvock.

     iii. Elizabeth, m. Sir Richard Cholomley of Chester.

     iv. Jana, m. Thomas Cresset[t] [AEC, 250] of Upton, Salop.

19.   v. Richard, b. 1451; d. 1493; m. Elizabeth[F] Devereux.

     vi. Roger, no issue.

     vii. John, possible son, descendants in Norfolk?

19. Sir RICHARD[F] CORBET of Moreton Corbet, was born in 1451 and died 6 Dec. 1493.

He married before 1478 ELIZABETH[F] DEVEREUX*, who died in 1541, daughter of Sir Walter[G] Devereux, Lord Ferrers of Chartley. She married second Thomas Leighton of Wattlesborough, who was buried in Burford, Salop.

Children:

      i.   Katherine[E], m. Onnslow, knight of Rodington, Salop.

20.   ii. Robert, m. Elizabeth[E] Vernon of Haddon.

     iii. Anne, m. Cornewall, knight of Burford, Salop.

     iv. Maria, m. Sir Thomas Lacon of Willey.

     v. Elizabeth, m. Thomas Trentham of Shrewsbury.

     vi. George, no issue.

     vii. Margaret, m. Sir Richard Clive of Walford.

20. Sir ROBERT[E] CORBET of Moreton Corbet, born in 1477 and died 11 April 1513, was buried in Moreton Corbet.

He married ELIZABETH[E] VERNON* of Haddon, who d. 29 March 1563, and was buried in Moreton Corbet. She survived her husband by fifty years and was called "the old Lady Corbet of Shawbury."

He was Sheriff of Shropshire in 1507.

His will was proved *P.C.C. 27 Fetiplace* [Faris, 103].

Children:

    i.   Jane[D], m. Thomas Lee, knight of Langley.

    ii.   Maria, m. Thomas Powell of Oswaldestre.

   iii. Roger, knight, of Moreton Corbet, bur. Lynceslade, Bucks., 1538; m. Anne (dau. of Andrew, Lord Windsor), who bur. there 1551; Sheriff of Shropshire 1530 [Bridgeman, *Trans. Shropshire*, 4:3:91].

   iv. Richard, bur. Moreton Corbet 1566; m. Margaret Sayville; no issue; Sheriff of Shropshire 1561.

    v.   Reginald, d. 1569; m. Alice Gratewood, who d. 9 April 1603 [AEC, 357 chart], dau. of John Gratewood; issue; of Stoke, Shropshire, Justice of the King's Bench [C.G.O. Bridgeman, "The Devolution of the Manor of Edgmond in the Fourteenth and Following Centuries," *Trans. Shropshire Archæological Society*, 4:4 (1913), 91].

   vi. Joanna, m. Sir Thomas Newport.

* vii. Dorothea, m. Sir Richard[D] Mainwaring of Ightfield.

§ § §

COTTON

Waterman and Jacobus, in *The Granberry Family and Allied Families*, mentioned a line from Charlemagne to Frances[A] Cotton, wife of George[A] Abell. However, the qualification concerning this line was that "further detail is desirable for the three generations immediately preceding Robert Abell." Thus the line was long considered tentative.

However, Neil D. Thompson, F.A.S.G., has since published the results of his research, as well as that by Robert Charles Anderson, Peter Wilson Coldham and David L. Greene, in "Abell-Cotton-Mainwaring: Maternal Ancestry of Robert Abell of Weymouth and Rehoboth, Mass." [*The Genealogist*, 5 (1984), 158-171].

George Ormerod and Thomas Helsby, who treated the family in *The History of the County Palatine and City of Chester* [2nd ed., 1882, 3:414-415], stated that their sources were manuscripts from Sir P. Leycester and Sir F. Leycester, with additions from the College of Arms, Harl. MSS. 2153, Inquisitions and Monuments, collated by Sir George Naylor, York Herald, and brought down by information of the family. However, some of the material in Ormerod has been omitted, below, because of conflicts with more recent research.

Earwaker's *History of Sandbach* [188] described Cotton Township as having been granted to the Cotton family shortly after one Adam Fraser pawned "the whole vill" for eighty marks in silver to Roger de Lacy, constable of Chester (who held the office about 1215), who granted it to Judas Kelly, father of one Gilbert de Cotton.

1. Sir HUGH[J] COTON was of Coton, according to Eyton it has been said, but was not found in a search of the *Antiquities of Shropshire*. Joseph Morris' *Shropshire Genealogies* [2:955, or 2069] showed him as son of Roger Coeton, alias Cotton.

He married ELIZABETH[J] TITLEY, daughter and heiress of Adam Titley (or Tittenlegh) of Cheshire. Ormerod's *History* mentioned a manor of Titley. Joseph Morris called the father Hamon Titley.

Children:

    i.   Alan[I], younger son; m. Matilda le Scot of Acton, dau. of Roger Acton; his son Hugh[I], who m. Jane Hayton [*Visit. Shropshire*, 2:303], has also been mentioned as the father of Sir Nicholas Coton who m. Katherine[I] Hackluyt.

2. ii. Hugh, m. Isabell de Hayton.

   iii. Sir William, Dean of Worcester [J. Morris, 2069].

2. HUGH[I] DE COTON was heir to his brother Alan, who in turn, according to Ormerod [3:414] was heir to their father Sir Alan[K] de Coton, knight, and his wife Margaret, daughter of Roger[L] de Acton. The latter Alan was heir of his brother, Sir Hugh, knight of St. John of Jerusalem, and had another brother, William, dean of Worcester cathedral. Their father was Sir Hugh[L] de Coton, lord of Coton, Shropshire, England, who married Elizabeth[L] de Tittenlegh, daughter of Hamon[M] de Tittenlegh.

He married ISABEL DE HAYTON, daughter and heir to Thomas de Hayton (or Heyton).

Joseph Morris calls him a Knight of Rhodes.

Children, listed by Ormerod:

3. i. Sir Nicholas[H], l. 1356; m. Katherine[I] Hackluyt, sister of Sir Richard Hackluyt of Herefordshire.

   ii. Hugh, second son; Waterman gave him as father of Richard, next, perhaps in error.

4. iii. Richard, given as brother of Hugh by Joseph Morris [2068-2069].

3. Sir NICHOLAS[H] COTON of Coton, Shropshire, was mentioned in George Morris' "Shropshire Genealogies," 2:354, a manuscript in the Shrewsbury Public Library [on microfilm from the Family History Library, Salt Lake City].

He married KATHERINE[I] HACKLUYT*, sister of Sir Richard Hackluyt of Herefordshire.

Children:

* i. Ellen[G], m. Robert[K] Lacon de Lacon as his second wife.

  ii. Hugh, no issue.

4. RICHARD[H] DE COTON was listed as the son and heir of Hugh.

He was of Coton during the reign of Edward III [J. Morris].

Child, given by Waterman and Joseph Morris:

5. i. Roger[G], m. Elen Grymelond.

5. ROGER[G] DE COTON was of Coton and Alkington, county Salop, or Shropshire.

He married ELEN GRYMELOND, daughter and coheiress of John Grymelond (or Gremyton) of Alkington (near Whitchurch), Salop, son of William, son of William, son of Roger Grymeland (or Gremyton) de Alkington [Grazebrook, ed., *Visit. Shropshire*, 154], in Shropshire.

Child, given by Waterman:

6. i. William[F], probable son; m.

6. WILLIAM[F] DE COTON was of Coton and Alkington, county Salop.

He married a daughter of William Hulse of Norbury, Cheshire; she was sister of John Hulse of Cheshire. William Hulse was son of Sir William Hulse and his wife who was the daughter and heir of David Norbury [J. Morris, *Shropshire*, 1769].

Children, given by Waterman and Ormerod:

7.   i.   William[E], m. Agnes Yonge.

       ii.   John, probable son, of Alkington, son of William; m. Katherine, daughter of Thomas Constantine of Dodington.

7. WILLIAM[E] DE COTTON was of Cotton, a township in Wem parish, county Salop, in 9 Henry VI (1430-1431) and 1460 [J. Morris, 2070].

He married in 1460 AGNES[E] YONGE, daughter of Philip Yonge of Cainton, county Salop [George Ormerod's *History of Chester* (2nd ed., Thomas Helsby, 3 vols., London, 1882), 3:414]. Joseph Morris charts [1835] Sir Philip Yonge of Caynton, who married Agnes, cousin and heiress of William Bonarton of Caynton and had son Sir William Yonge of Caynton, who was Sheriff of Shropshire in 1492.

Child, given by Ormerod [3:414]:

8.   i.   John[D], m. Cicely[E] Mainwaring.

8. JOHN[D] COTTON, Esq., of Cotton in Wem, county Salop, born about 1465, was of record 15 Henry VII (about 1500).

He married CECILY[E] MAINWARING* of Ightfield, who has been said to have died before 1516. However, an abstract of the signed will of a Cycelye Cotton widow of Stoke upon Terne, dated 16 Dec. 1549, witnessed by John Robinson and John Stayning, and proved at the Consistory Court of Lichfield 7 May 1550 by the executors (submitted by Thelda Baker of Ventura, California), reads as follows: "To be buried in the high chancel of the Church of Stoke. to John cotton base gotten son of my son Rober Cotton four kine etc. To John Robinson eight sheep, To Alice Robinson my black frock guarded with velvet. To Mistress Maude Cochkins my scarlet peticoat. To my daughter Ann a cow etc. To Margaret Grene my black frock. To Margaret Bats a new sheet. To my daughter Maude my saddle and bridle. To Elizabeth Dod one double winding sheet etc. To little Alice Robinson and Joan Robinson the little mattress. The residue of my goods to be distributed as shall please my executors, namely my son William Cotton and my brother Thomas Mainwaring."

At least some of the death dates given in Harleian MS. 1535, folio 89, are erroneous [*Pedigrees Made at the Visitations of Cheshire, 1613*, 66].

Children, listed by Ormerod and Joseph Morris [2070-2071]:

       i.   William[C], m. Joan Bromley; had six surviving daughters.

       ii.   Sir Richard, of Bedhampton, Hants., and Warbington, Southampton; m. Jane Onley, daughter of John Onley of Catesby, Northants., and thus prob. a sister of Mary Onley.

9.   iii.   George, m. Mary[C] Onley.

      iv.   Rauff, lived in London.

      v.   Thomas.

      vi.   Robert, bur. Richmond, Surrey.

9. Sir GEORGE[C] COTTON, Knight, born in Cotton in Wem, county Salop, about 1505, died at Combermere, county Salop, 25 March 1545.

He married before 11 Nov. 1537 MARY[C] ONLEY*, sister of John Onley of Catesby, county Northampton, whose will, dated 15 Nov. 1537, was proven 16 May 1538. She died at Combermere 14 March 1559/60.

Sir George Cotton served as Sheriff of Denbighshire [Faris' *Plantagenet Ancestry*, 2nd ed., 1], and was esquire to the body of King Henry VIII [Ormerod's *History of Chester*, 2nd ed., 3:404], and knighted by him in or before 1542 [Thompson, *TG*, 5 (1984), 158; W.A. Shaw's *Knights of England*, 2:53].

Sir George Cotton was given a new grant to Combermere, county Salop (Shropshire), by King Henry VIII, 3 Feb. 1541/2, obtaining the site and demesne of the Abbey, and two-thirds of Newhall Manor, upon surrendering a two-year-old grant. They also had grants of the manor of Wilkesley, Cheshire, dated 3 April 1542, and of the manor of Pulton, Cheshire, dated 19 August 1543 [Thompson, *TG*, 5:158].

Children, listed by Ormerod, although Faris [*PA2*, 1] said there were four daughters, but the full list by Joseph Morris [2073] includes Winifred and Elizabeth, who were likely of the next generation, below:

10.   i.   Richard[B], b. c. 1539; d. 14 June 1602; m. (1) 1559 Mary[B] Mainwaring, m. (2) London, 1578, Jane Seyliard, m. (3) Mrs. Philippa (–) Dormer.

       ii.   Mary, d. 16 Nov. 1580; m. (1) before 1 Jan. 1561/2, as his third wife, Edward Stanley, Earl of Derby, m. (2) Henry Grey, Earl of Kent, who d. 31 Jan. 1614/5 [*CP*, 7:172]; she had no issue.

      iii.   Dorothy, living as a widow, 6 June 1608; m. Edward Torbock of Torbock, Lancashire.

10. Sir RICHARD[B] COTTON was born about 1539, and died intestate at Stoke in Warwickshire, England, 14 June 1602.

He married first, in Combermere, Salop, 6 Jan. 1559/60, MARY[B] MAINWARING* of Ightfield, who was dead by 14 June 1578. This marriage was recorded in the register of the parish of Marbury, Cheshire. The will of their daughter, Dorothy, mentioned only full siblings and relations through them.

He married second, at St. Olave, Jewry, London, 14 June 1578, Jane Seyliard (or Silliard, Sulliard) of Chiddingstone, county Kent, youngest daughter of William and Joan (Todd) Seyliard. William Seyliard was of London, citizen and merchant tailor, and member of a well known Kent family. Jane was mentioned in the will of her sister, Isabel Cheke, dated 22 Sept. 1593, but must have died soon after that. Other family wills were also proved at Canterbury [Thompson, *TG*, 5:159]. The will of Jane (Seyliard) Cotton's mother Joan presents conclusive evidence, through its careful list of heirs, that Jane had only one daughter, Jane. "William Seylyard of London, Marchan Taylor," who was later of Stanford le Hope in Essex, gentleman, who married the daughter and heir of Sylvester Todd of Tynwell in Rutland, is found in the pedigree of the Seylyard family published in *Miscellanea Genealogica et Heraldica* [Gower, 4th ser., 1 (1886), 7-11].

He married third, Philippa, widow of John Dormer of Buckinghamshire. She died in the parish of St. Michael, Coventry, and administration was granted in the Consistory Court of Lichfield on 17 June 1631/2 [*sic*]. She had renounced administration of her husband's estate in favor of the eldest son, George Cotton. A letter from Mrs. Philippa Cotton, dated from Stoke, 1 Nov. 1601, addressed to Sir Robert Cecil, later Earl of Shrewsbury, is extant; it asked for help for "me and my children" as his "poor, yet very near kinswoman." She also identified herself as "her Majesty's sworn servant these 20 years." A letter signed "Philipp Cotton" and dated 23 Nov. 1609 thanked the Earl for a gift of £150. Her will, dated 30 May 1625 and proved in the Consistory Court of Lichfield 18 August 1631, mentions sons Sir Thomas Monteith, Kt., John Dormer and Philip Cotton, and daughters Elizabeth Dormer (deceased) and Bridgett Cotton, who served as executrix.

In 1563 he built the Combermere manor house, which incorporated the remains of the Abbey.

According to the Court Rolls at Combermere, a joint manor court was held there by Richard Cotton, armiger, seneschel of the manor. The manor of Newhall was vested in Sir Richard Cotton for two portions, and in the Fitzwarings for one portion.

Sir Richard apparently lived in Stoke, just north of the city of Coventry, for the last few years before his death in 1602.

The research in Wrenbury parish records was commissioned in 1955 by Thelda Baker of 4981 Aurora Drive, Ventura, CA 93003 (2000) and done by W.E.C. Cotton, who was then of 31 Royal Avenue, London SW3.

Children, by first wife, listed by Thompson, with data concerning Wrenbury Parish in Cheshire contributed by Thelda Baker of 4981 Aurora Drive, Ventura, CA 93003 (2000):

 i. Arthur[A], b. c. 1561; d. unm. in his father's lifetime [*Visit. of Cheshire, 1613*].

 ii. Mary, b. c. 1563; m. William (Richard, according to Peter Ellis, British Library Add. Ms. 28034, cited in *TG*, 9:89, or Ralph, according to J. Morris [2078]) Bulkeley (Buckley), son of Rowland Bulckley of Woore, co. Salop [*Vis. London*, 117], and first cousin of the Rev. Peter Bulkeley of Odell, Beds., and Concord, Mass. [*cf.* Brainbridge, *NEHGR*, 23:303].

 iii. George, b. c. 1565; d. 1647 (a George Cotton, gentleman, was bur. Wrenbury in Cheshire 28 April 1646, and George Cotton, Esq., bur. there 1 Dec. 1647); m. Worfield, co. Salop, 25 April 1585, Mary Bromley, dau. of Sir George Bromley of Halton in Shropshire, who was Chief Justice of Cheshire; administrator of his father's estate and listed as an heir at the *inquisition post mortem* held at Sandbach on 6 April 1605, and called "brother" by George Abell "of Hemington in y[e] Countie of Leicester gent" in his will of 8 Sept. 1630 [see *Rec. Soc. Lancs. & Cheshire*, 84:146]; their grandson Sir Robert Cotton was 1st Baronet of Combermere [*BP*, 1:639].

 iv. Elizabeth, m. William (Richard, according to Peter Ellis [*TG*, 9:89] and Joseph Morris [2073]) Francis of Ticknall, Derbyshire.

 v. Andrew, b. c. 1569; bur. Wrenbury parish, Cheshire, 6 Sept. 1640, will proved Chester 21 Oct. 1640 (with inventory 14 Sept. 1640), his sister Mrs. Dorothy Cotton being executrix; unm.

 vi. Winifred, b. c. 1571; m. Thomas Dering of Liss, Hampshire.

* vii. Frances, b. c. 1573; living 8 Sept. 1630 but prob. d. by 16 April 1646; m. Wrenbury, Cheshire, 1 May 1599, George[A] Abell.

 viii. Dorothy, b. c. 1575; prob. that Dorothy Cotton, gentlewoman, bur. Wrenbury, Cheshire, 7 April 1647; unm.

Child, by second wife, given by Thompson:

 ix. Jane, b. c. 1580; living 20 Feb. 1603/4; no further record.

Children, by third wife, listed by Thompson:

 x. Philip, b. c. 1598; prob. d. unm.; said to have been Captain in army of King Charles I and to have been killed in Scotland.

 xi. Bridgett, b. c. 1600; unm. in 1631 when executrix of her mother's will.

§ § §

DE CROPHULL

This pedigree was provided by Mr. Marlyn Lewis.

1. RALPH^M DE CROPHULL of Bonyngton and Sutton, Nottinghamshire, and Hemington, Leicestershire, was born about 1280 and died after 1326/7.

He married MAUD, who married second John de Verdun, son of Thomas de Verdun and Margaret de Knoville.

Child:

2.   i.   John^L, b. c. 1310; d. 1383; m. before 10 Sept. 1355 Margery^L Verdun, widow of William le Blount, who d. 1337, and Sir Mark Husee, who d. 1345/6.

2. Sir JOHN^L DE CROPHULL, of Bonnington, Nottinghamshire [*CP*, 12:2:252], and Sufton, Northamptonshire, born about 1310, died in 1383.

He married after 1346 as her third husband, MARGERY^M VERDUN*, who died in 1377. She had married first William^J le Blount, who was born in 1295 and died in 1337, and second, before 18 Oct. 1339, Sir Mark Husee (or Hussey) [Watney, *Wallop Family*, 2:242]. She was the heir of Weobley.

Child:

3.   i.   Thomas^K, b. c. 1335; d. before 19 May 1382; m. 1370 Sibella^K de la Bere, who d. 13 May 1428.

3. THOMAS^K DE CROPHULL of Newbold Verdun, born about 1335, died before 19 May 1382.

He married in 1370 SIBELLA^K DE LA BERE*, who died 13 May 1428.

Child:

*   i.   Agnes^J, b. 1370; d. Pilleth, Wales, 1402/3; m. (1) 1383/4 Sir Walter^J Devereux, m. (2) John Parr of Kendal, m. (3) John Merbury.

§ § §

DANIELL OR DANYERS

This line was originally developed from the section on Over Tabley in Bucklow Hundred in George Ormerod's *History* [1:470-473]. Lymme and Limme probably refer to Limm, Cheshire. References in *Notes and Queries* [148:320, 354] relate to Cornwall in 1799 and later. J. Paul Rylands gave the father of William^M Danyers as Sir Thomas Danyers of Bradley in Cheshire, of record in 1276, who married a daughter and heir of Robert de Chedle of Chedle and Clifton [*The Genealogist*, n.s., 32:16].

1. WILLIAM^M DANYERS was of record as purchasing lands in Daresbery, Cheshire, from Henry le Norreys in 1291.

His wife was AGNES^M DE LEGH, daughter of Thomas de Legh of High Legh of the West Hall.

Children, given by Ormerod [1:472]:

    i.   Margery^L, m. Henry Horsale of Lymme.

    ii.   Agnes, m. 30 Edw. I (1301-1302) Alexander de Waleton nigh Daresbery.

2.   iii.   Thomas, m. (1) Margaret^L de Tabley, m. (2) Joan Norreys.

    iv.   William, Jr., d. 1306, bur. Limme; m. Agnes; of Daresbury.

2. THOMAS[L] DANYERS made his will in 1354, and was buried at Limme.

He married first MARGARET[L] DE TABLEY, daughter of Adam de Tabley, who was son of William de Tabley [Rylands, *The Genealogist*, n.s., 32:16].

He married second Joan Norreys, who married second William Bostock of Bostock.

His father granted him land in Limme, and in 1301 he purchased Bradley from Peter Dutton, lord of Warburton.

He was Sheriff of Cheshire 25 and 27 Edw. III (1351-1352 and 1353-1354).

Children, by first wife, given by Ormerod:

3.   i.   Sir Thomas, Jr., eldest son, of Bradley, d. 26 Edw. III; m. Isabel[K] Baggiley.

       ii.   Sir John, second son, of Gropenhale; m. (1) Joan Boydell, dau. of William Boydell, m. (2) Alice, who m. (2) Sir Edward Benested [Rylands, *The Genealogist*, n.s., 32:16].

            Children, by first wife: 1. Margaret, l. 1354, affianced to Sir Robert Grosvenor of Houlm (Holme) in Allostock, but d. before m. 2. Nicolaa, m. 1358 Geoffry de Warburton.

      iii.   Augustine, had lands in High Legh.

      iv.   Alice, m. Matthew Mere, son of William Mere of Mere nigh Over Tabley.

       v.   Margaret, m. 1335 John de Derewallshaw (or Thelwallshaw), son of Vivian de Derewallshaw.

      vi.   Joan.

Children, bastards:

      vii.   William.

     viii.   Roger.

      ix.   Robert.

Children, by second wife:

       x.   Sir Thomas of Over Tabley, d. 1383.

      xi.   Henry, was given by his father the marriage of the heir of William Clerke of Over Tabley.

     xii.   Richard, l. 6 Ric. II (1382-1383), m.

3. Sir THOMAS[K] DANIELL [or DANYERS], JR., of Bradley in Appleton, died 26 Edw. III (1352-1353), before his father.

He married ISABEL[K] BAGGILEY*.

At the battle of Crécy he rescued the standard of the Black Prince and took the Earl of Tankerville prisoner [Earwaker, 1:187].

He did not survive his father and left only one daughter "who carried away all her mother's lands, and had Clifton, and other lands in Chedle" [Ormerod, 1:473]. His own lands were settled on the heir males of the Danyers family.

In 28 Edw. III (1354-1355) the family held the manor of Lostock, which Ormerod states [3:684] is extremely difficult to indentify but might be Lostock Graham (Gralam?).

Child:

*   i.   Margaret[J], d. 1428 [Earwaker, 1:188]; m. (1) 1369 John Ratcliffe, who d. without issue; m. (2) c. 1376 John[J] Savage, who d. 1386, m. (3) Nov. 1388 Piers Legh of Maxfield, who was executed at Chester 10 Aug. 1399 by King Henry IV for having been loyal to King Richard II [Rylands, *The Genealogist*, n.s., 32:7].

§ § §

DARCY

This line was developed through careful attention to G.W. Watson's article on the family in Cokayne's *Complete Peerage* [4:50-61].

The arms of Darcy of Nocton were *Argent*, three *sixfoils* or *cinquefoils* [roses] *Gules*. There is a hamlet of Arcie in the parish of St. Aubin de Terregatte, in the Avranchin.

1. NORMAN[S] D'ARECI was of record in 1115 and 1118.

He was Domesday lord of Nocton [Sanders, 67], Coningsby, Dunston, Stallingborough and Cawkwell in Lincolnshire, and other holdings in 1086. The Barony was held of the King in chief by service of two or two and one-half knights' fees.

In 1093 he witnessed a charter of King William II Rufus.

Son, mentioned by G.W. Watson [*CP*, 4:50c]:
2.   i.   Robert[R], of record 1131.

2. ROBERT[R] D'ARCY was of record in the pipe roll of 1131, and died during the period 1148-1160 [Sanders, 67].

Son, mentioned by G.W. Watson:
3.   i.   Thomas[Q], d. 2 July 1180; m. Aline, who d. 1183.

3. THOMAS[Q] D'ARCY, born say 1140 [Sanders, 67[8]], died 2 July 1180.

He married ALINE, who died in 1183. She was identified in *Burke's Peerage* (1999) as Alice, who died 1183, daughter of Ralph d'Eyncourt [*BP*, 1:760].

As Thomas son of Robert he made a gift to Kirkstead Abbey in 1163 [Sanders, 67[8]]. In 1162 and 1165 he answered for twenty knights' fees.

Children, listed in *Burke's Peerage* (1999) [1:760]:
4.   i.   Thomas[P], b. c. 1167; d. 1206; m. Joan.
       ii.   Robert.
      iii.   William.

4. THOMAS[P] D'ARCY, who was aged 18 in 1185 [*CP*, 14:234], died in 1206.

He left a widow, Joan.

He was in Normandy with King Richard I [*BP*, 1:760].

He mentioned his grandfather Robert when he made a gift to Kirkstead Abbey after 1202, witnessed by John, who was abbot of Fountains from 1203 to 1209.

Son, mentioned by G.W. Watson:
5.   i.   Norman[O], d. before 16 Oct. 1254; m. Agnes.

5. NORMAN[O] D'ARCY died before 16 Oct. 1254.

His wife was AGNES.

Son, mentioned by G.W. Watson:
6.   i.   Sir Philip[N], d. shortly before 28 May 1264; m. Isabel[N] Bertram.

6. Sir PHILIP[N] D'ARCY died shortly before 28 May 1264.

He married ISABEL[N] BERTRAM[+] (second daughter of Sir Roger Bertram III of Mitford in Northumberland, who was of record 15 June 1281), and sister and coheir of Sir Roger Bertram of Mitford. She was living 15 June 1281 [*BP*, 1:760].

He was of Nocton, Coningsby, Dunston, Stallingborough and Cawkwell in Lincolnshire.

He had livery of his father's lands on 16 Oct. 1254, after they had been placed in his safekeeping on 6 Feb. 1253/4, when his father was old and infirm.

Children, given by G.W. Watson:

    i. Sir Norman^M, d. shortly before 6 Jan. 1295/6; m. (1) Julian, who d. before 15 June 1261, m. (2) by 20 Jan. 1292/3 Margery (as her third husband), who had m. (1) Barnaby de Stiucele, who d. 1257/8, m. (2) William de Swineford, and m. (4) Relph Rastel.

7.   ii. Sir Roger, d. before 12 May 1284.

    iii. Thomas, left as heir his brother Norman's son, Sir Philip^L d'Arcy.

7. Sir ROGER^L D'ARCY, of Oldcotes and Styrrup, Nottinghamshire [*CP*, 4:54], died before 12 May 1284.

He married ISABEL^L D'ATON$^+$ of West Ayton, Yorkshire [*CP*, 4:54], daughter of William de Aton and Isabel de Vere of Coxhill, Lincolnshire [*CP*, 12:2:285b].

He bought the manor of Sproatley in Holderness from Simon de Vere, and sold it to the king. He bought lands in Oldcotes, Styrrup and Blyth, Nottinghamshire from Ingram d'Ulcotes [*CP*, 4:51h].

    Child:

8.   i. John^K, d. 30 May 1347; m. (1) Emmeline Heron, m. (2) 3 July 1329 Joan^K de Burgh, who had m. (1) 16 Aug. 1312 Thomas Fitz Gerald, 2nd Earl of Kildare.

8. Sir JOHN^K D'ARCY, 1st Baron Darcy, of Knaith, Kexby and Upton, Lincolnshire, died 30 May 1347.

He married first Emmeline Heron, daughter and heiress of Walter Herron of Silkstone, Yorkshire, and granddaughter of William II de Heyron (of Hadstone, Northumberland, and Notton, Yorks., by Alice dau. of Sir Nicholas de Hastings of Allerston, Yorks., and Gissing, Norfolk [Watney, *Wallop Family*, 2:253]), who d. 1296 [Sanders, 119].

He married second at Maynooth, Kildare, Ireland, 3 July 1329 JOAN^K DE BURGH*, who had married first 16 Aug. 1312 Thomas Fitz John, 2nd Earl of Kildare. She died 23 April 1359, and was buried with her first husband in the Church of Friars Minors at Kildare.

Styled *le neveu*, *le cosyn*, and much later *le piere*, he was of Knaith, Kexby and Upton in Lincolnshire. His arms were *Azure*, *crusilly* and three *cinquefoils* [roses], *Argent*.

When he claimed his lands on 15 June 1292 he was underage, and was represented in court by his guardian. He was outlawed for felony in or before 1306, but was pardoned on 19 May 1307 at the instance of Aymer de Valence, who agreed to enfeoff him of twenty marks in land 10 April 3 Edw. II (1310) in return for John taking up knighthood "within the quinzaine of Easter next," and agreeing to serve the Earl in war and peace, at home or abroad, and in going to the Holy Land. He was recorded in the retinue of Aymer de Valence in 1313, 1320 and 1321, and in the expedition to Scotland in 1322. He had been appointed Constable of Norham Castle on 20 Jan. 1316/7, and was Sheriff of Nottinghamshire and Derbyshire 1319-1322. Knight of the Shire for Nottinghamshire in 1320, he was Sheriff of Lancashire from Feb. 1322/3 to July 1323, and served the King against the Scots from 24 Feb. 1322/3 to 4 April 1323. He was banneret on 12 Aug. 1323, Justiciar of Ireland from 18 Nov. 1323 to 12 March 1326/7, and Sheriff of Yorkshire 1327-1328. He was Justiciar of Ireland 21 Aug. 1328 to 27 Feb. 1330/1. He and Guillaume de Seintz (de Sans) were appointed to treat with the nobles of Aquitaine on 27 April 1330, and on 15 July 1331 he was appointed as a special envoy to the King of France concerning the marriage of Prince Edward.

He was summoned to military service in 1332, to Parliament from 27 Jan. 1331/2 to 2 Jan. 1333/4, and to a council on 25 Feb. 1341/2. He served another term as Justiciar of Ireland from 30 Sept. 1332 to 28 July 1337. In the summer of 1335 he took an army to

Scotland, laying waste to Arran and Bute. From March 1336/7 to Dec. 1340 he was Steward of the King's Household, and on 7 Oct. 1337 he was appointed to treat with the King of France, the Emperor, the Count of Flanders and others. On 10 June 1338 he was proxy to sign a treaty with the Flemings. On 3 March 1339/40 he was appointed Justiciar of Ireland for life, but as the king needed his attendance a deputy was appointed a year later, and he resigned the office on 10 Feb. 1343/4. From 1341 to at least Sept. 1346 he was Chamberlain to the King. He went to Brittany with the Earl of Northampton in the expedition of Aug. 1342. Over the years he was granted many lands for his services.

He was then appointed Constable of Nottingham Castle, 2 March 1343/4, and of the Tower of London, 12 March 1345/6, both terms for life. Having participated in the battle of Crécy with eleven knights, 48 esquires and 80 archers, he was sent as a member of the party from Calais, 8 Sept. 1346, to announce the victory in Parliament.

Child, by first wife:

    i.   John[J], aged 30 and more at his father's death; d. Notton, in Royston Parish [CP, 14:234], Yorks., 5 March 1355/6, bur. Guisborough Priory [Watson, MGH, 5:8:230]; m. (1) before 8 July 1332 Alianore Holand, who d. before 21 Nov. 1341, m. (2) Elizabeth de Meinill [CP, 14:234], who d. 9 July 1368, having m. (2) before 18 Nov. 1356 Sir Piers de Mauley of Mulgrave, Yorks., who d. 19 or 20 March 1382/3.

Children, by second wife [BP, 1:761]:

  *   ii.   Anne (or Elizabeth), d. 24 March 1389/90; m. (1) James[J] Butler, 2nd Earl of Ormond, m. (2) Sir Robert Harford (or de Hereford [Faris, PA2, 60].

    iii.   Aymer.

    iv.   Roger.

    v.   Sir William.

§ § §

DAVENPORT

This presentation is based on Ormerod's *History of Chester*, with additions from Robert Ralsey Davenport's genealogy of the family, which included material from the Chetham Society's release, *The Early History of Davenports of Davenport*, by T.P. Highet, as well as other cited materials.

1. ORMUS (or ORME)[P] DE DAVENPORT, born perhaps in the period from 1086 to 1100, was living in 1154, if the Gilbert de Venables in a charter has been properly identified [R.R. Davenport, 1, cited T.P. Highet's *The Early History of the Davenports of Davenport* (Manchester: Chetham Society, 1960)].

He was a witness to a charter of enfranchisement by Gilbert de Venables during the reign of either King William II or King Henry I.

Davenport is about five miles or eight kilometers west of Congleton, Cheshire, about twenty-five miles from the City of Chester. Located on the River Dane, Davenport was well established by 920 A.D. and perhaps was founded by Scandinavian merchants. At the time of the Domesday survey it was held by Gilbert de Venables, Baron of Kinderton.

Child, given in Ormerod's pedigree [3:68], which was based on deeds, Pleas and Recognizance Rolls, *inquisitions post mortem* and other evidence:

  2.   i.   Richard[O], m. Amabilia[P] de Venables.

2. RICHARD[O] DE DAVENPORT was appointed supreme forester of the earl's forests of Leek and Macclesfield, Cheshire, sometime between 1153 and 1181, when Hugh was Earl of Cyfeiliog.

He married AMABILIA[P] DE VENABLES[+], whose brother William Venables, Baron of Kinderton, gave her in marriage after the death of her father. As a dowry she brought with her half of Marton, in Prestbury parish, which her mother had had as her marriage portion. According to Domesday, one-half of Marton was held by Earl Hugh of Cyfeiliog (Hugh[N] of Kevelioc, Earl of Chester), and the other half by Hugh Fitz Norman. From whichever source came the half of Marton which went to the Davenports, it meant a "step up the social ladder [Davenport, 2]." Marton, in the Hundred of Macclesfield, was four miles west of Congleton, and was four miles northeast of Davenport.

During the period 1152-1160 Earl Hugh gave Richard the important post of Master-forester of the Forests of Macclesfield and Leek. A Richard de Davenport, probably a descendant, received a grant at Leek from Earl Ranulf de Blundeville between 1208 and 1211.

Ormerod (and Earwaker [2:385]) inserted Thomas de Davenport as the next generation, followed by another Richard de Davenport, to whom Randle de Blundeville, Earl of Chester and Lincoln 1181-1232, granted acquittance from suit to the shire and hundred court, while Vivian Davenport was called grandson of Richard[O] by Croston [409].

Successor, probable son and heir, listed with his siblings:

3. i.   Vivian[N], living 1254; perhaps m. Beatrix de Hulme.
    ii.   Amicia, m. Randle de Chedleton; lands Abbacy of Dierlacres.
    iii. Walter, lands in Somerford Booths.
    iv.   Peter, living 1263.
    v.   John.

3. VIVIAN[N] DE DAVENPORT, who was probably born before 1190, but certainly before 1205, and was living in 1254 but died in 1260, was Richard's successor as Lord of Davenport and Marton in Cheshire, England. Vivian was apparently buried at Prestbury church, under the pavement of the Tytherington Chantry; in the 1880s fragments of the covering of a stone coffin with the remains of a Norman French inscription were found there.

According to Ormerod [Chester, 3:68], he married BEATRIX DE HULME, daughter of Bertrand de Hulme.

Sometime between 1217 and 1226 the Earl of Chester and Lincoln granted him the hereditary offices of Sergeant of the Peace for the Hundred and Grand Forester of the Forests of Macclesfield in exchange for Vivian's land, called Wilewic (or Wilwhich [Croston, 409], worth about £40 per year), in Macclesfield Park. It has been suggested that this exchange was involuntary on Vivian's part, and that he considered the compensation inadequate. The witnesses to the charter were The Lord Hugh [Grylle], Abbot of Chester, Philip[b] de Orreby, then Justiciary of Cheshire, Henry de Auditheley, Roger de Mannel-wearin, Alured de Sulinur (?), Thomas de Orreby, Herbert de Orreby, Richard de Cagwr' (?), then chamberlain, Master Hugh, and many others [Earwaker, 2:379]. However, the authority to keep the Earl's peace was valuable, with a base income of £12.6s.8d. The Grand Sergeant had the power of life and death, without delay and without appeal. A typical payment for delivering the head of a felon to Chester castle was 1/-. The heads were taken independently of the judicial system. A robber roll in possession of the Davenports at Capesthorne records the execution of 120 thieves, robbers, murderers and cutpurses.

He held rents of the constable of Chester, Edmund de Lacy. This showed a connection to the Lacy family, the Barons of Halton and Earls of Lincoln. He also witnessed a number of charters with leading members of the county society. He witnessed over forty charters.

Children, named in a 1247 grant by Vivian, or listed by R.R. Davenport:

4.   i.   Roger^M, m. Mary Salemon.
        ii.   Edward, living 1272; assumed the name Newton and became the ancestor of the Newtons of Newton, and, through his son Robert, of the Lawtons of Lawton.
       iii.   Richard, father of Roger de Tornock; had lands in Somerford Booths.
       iv.   Robert, but prob. son of Edward, ancestor of the Lawtons of Lawton.
        v.   Peter.
       vi.   Henry.
      vii.   Thomas.
     viii.   Beatrix, m. Bertram de Hulme.

4. ROGER^M DE DAVENPORT, who was probably an adult in the period 1245 to 1249, died between 1291 and 1297 [Ormerod, *Chester*, 3:68; Earwaker, 2:385].

He married MARY SALEMON or SALMON, who died before 1301, daughter of Robert Salmon of Wythington, in Macclesfield Hundred, Cheshire, and received "a moiety of the whole vill of Withington, and 'the services, reliefs and ward of John de Withington and Richard, son of Lawrence, and Roger de Toft, and the moiety of Tunsted, and the moiety of all the wood of Hewode, with aieries of hawks, bees, pannage, &c., and the moiety of Wultroke [Wheltrough] which Henry de Weverham held, and all Butleigh.'"

He exchanged lands in Marton for lands in Bramhall and Hillcroft, and became influential in the northern part of the Hundred of Macclesfield, so that he was able to make extensive grants to other members of his own family.

Children, listed by Ormerod:

        i.   Peter^L, son and heir, d. c. 1280; no issue.
       ii.   Sir Thomas, Lord of Davenport, living c. 1280-1320; m. (1) c. 1280 Agnes de Macclesfield, m. (2?) before 1308 Roesia de Vernon (dau. of Ralph de Vernon, widow of Sir William^K de Brereton), who was living, a widow, 15 Edw. II; ancestor of the Davenports of Wheltrough, Bramall near Stockport, Henbury and Woodford [Croston, 416].
       iii.   John, m. Matilda de Rode, dau. of William de Rode; had lands in Withington; had son Richard.
       iv.   Ellen, m. William de Bulkelegh, ancestor of the Lords Bulkeley.
5.   v.   Henry, fourth son, of Marton, living 1291.

5. HENRY^L DAVENPORT of Marton, Cheshire, had lands in Macclesfield, Cheshire, 20 Edw. I (1294).

Children, listed by Ormerod:

        i.   Roger^K, living 1314.
  *   ii.   Mary, m. William^K Mainwaring de Peover, of Over Peover.
       iii.   Margery, m. Thomas de Swettenham.

§ § §

DE DELVES

This account is based largely on Ormerod's *History of Chester* [3:518-522] and Sir Delves L. Broughton's *Records of an Old Cheshire Family*, the latter published in 1908.

Hugo[N] del Delf was presented by Sir Delves L. Broughton as first in this line, for on 26 July 1281 King Edward I issued a writ to the Sheriff of Staffordshire to inquire whether one messuage and a virgate of land with appurtenances in Delverne, had been in the hands of the king for a year and a day. Twelve jurors swore an oath that they had been since Hugo del Delf was a fugitive on account of felony.

Broughton [1] pointed out that felony was punishable by death, that the "offender's wife and children were cast out, his home demolished, his trees cut down, meadows ploughed up, and his land wasted," while in the case of fugitives "the King took possession of all of his goods, both movable and immovable, and the profits of his Fee-Simple lands for a year and a day, and the profits of his other lands, with all the debts due to the felon, during his life."

However, proof that Hugo was the father of John[M] de Delves was not presented.

1. JOHN[M] DE DELVES was of Delves Hall, near Uttoxeter in Staffordshire, 31 Edw. I (1303-1304).
   Child, from Ormerod [3:522]:
   2.   i.   Richard[L], m. Amicia.

2. RICHARD[L] DE DELVES of Delves Hall, Staffordshire, was an esquire of James Lord Audley in 8 Edw. III (1335-1336), when he was constable of Heleigh Castle. In 1339 he was a witness [Broughton, 7], and was succeeded by his eldest son, John.

His wife AMICIA was of record 16 Edw. II (1323-1324).

In 1305 he gave a mark for a license and sued Ralph de Bromleigh and Agnes over a bovate of land in Dymmesdale.

He was mentioned in deeds between 5 and 16 Edw. II (1311-1323). In 1314 Robert, son of Robert Lord of Cnotton, conveyed to Richard Delves, clerk, all his lands in le Hollerudinge in the fee of Cnotton [Broughton, 3]. In 1317 he was conveyed two plots of land in Knotton by William the Thrower, and in 1323 James, son of Lord Hugo of Audeley, granted Richard de Delves and his wife Amice the whole of James' lands in Burley.

In 1323 he was charged at Tutbury with having taken the forfeited goods of the King's enemies to a value not exceeding £20. On 7 Dec. 1323 he was among the sub-taxers who confessed that they had extorted money from various vills so that the vills might be spared full taxation; the sub-taxers as a group agreed to pay a fine of 340 marks. In 1324 he was of record as an executor of the will of William de Mere.

Children, the first four listed by Ormerod:
   i.   Sir John[K], will dated 16 Aug. 1369, d. of plague, bur. in the Chancel of the Parish Church of Audley, Staffs., 1369; m. (1) Elizabeth, widow of Walter de Bascurvill, m. (2) after 1360 Isabella, dau. and heiress of Philip de Malpas; the purchaser of Doddington and other manors in Cheshire, he was one of the four esquires to James de Audley, who with de Audley were responsible for the famous victory at Poitiers (1356).
   3.   ii.   Sir Henry, d. 19 Ric. II; m. (1) Katherine de Arderne, m. (2) Margaret de Brereton.
         iii.   Thomas, a clergyman 10 Edw. III (1336-1337).
         iv.   Joane, m. — Walton of Bromley.

    v.   Alice, listed by Collins.

    vi.   Hugo, listed by Broughton, received six acres at Haywode, Cheshire, from James d'Audeleie in 1336.

3. Sir HENRY[K] DE DELVES died on Monday after the Feast of St. James the Apostle, 19 Ric. II (1396).

He married first, Katherine de Arderne, daughter of Sir John de Arderne of Alderford [Broughton, 4] and widow of William de Chetilton and Ralph de Wetenal.

He married second, Margaret[I] de Brereton, daughter of William de Brereton. She married second John le Mareschal 21 Ric. II (1399). Collins stated that she was the mother of the children, below.

In 1344 he was conveyed land by his brother Thomas [Broughton, 21], as he conveyed land to Thomas, in deeds sealed at Betteley. In 1358 he sold a third of the manor of Hertwell of Ralph Earl of Stafford for 100 marks of silver.

Children, by first wife according to Ormerod, by second wife according to Collins:

4.   i.   John[J], d. 17 Ric. II; m. Margaret[J] de Calveley.

       ii.   Johanna, m. John Davenport, second son of John Davenport of Davenport.

4. JOHN[J] DE DELVES, of Doddington in Cheshire and Apedale in Staffordshire, died 17 Ric. II (1394), when his inquisition was taken during the lifetime of his father.

He married MARGARET[J] DE CALVELEY*, daughter of "David" de Calveley, of record 49 Edw. III (1375-1376).

On 16 March 1380 he had royal letters of protection on going abroad with Sir Hugh de Calveley, who was in the vanguard of the expedition to assist the Duke of Normandy against the King of France. In 5 and 11 Ric. II (1382-1383 and 1388-1389) he fought in the foreign wars of King Richard II. He was Sheriff of Staffordshire from 7 Nov. 1390 to 21 Oct. 1391, and served as M.P. for Staffordshire in Sept. 1388, Jan. and Nov. 1390, and in 1393 [Roskell, 2:764], and escheator of Shropshire, Staffordshire and the Welsh Marches.

Children, listed by Ormerod [3:522]:

5.   i.   John[I], b. c. 1375; d. 7 Hen. VI (1429-1430); m. (1) Philippa Mainwaring, m. (2) Margaret Norwode.

       ii.   Henry, l. 1429; m. (1) Alicia, m. (2) Joanna, dau. and heiress of Joane, widow of Sir Rustine de Villenoble.

      iii. Hugh, of record 17 Ric. II (1393-1395) and 7 Hen. VI (1428-1429).

      iv. John, l. 1429.

       v.   Matilda, m. Edmund Basset of Blore.

      vi.   Ellen, m. William de Egerton.

     vii. Beatrice, m. Richard de Wybunbury.

5. JOHN[I] DE DELVES was aged 22 in 20 Ric. II (1396-1397), and died 7 Hen. VI (1429), when his inquisition was taken at Stone before John Harpure, the King's Escheator.

He married first, in 20 Ric. II (1396-1397), PHILIPPA MAINWARING of Norwood, who was buried at Wibunbury in 1420. Collins believed she was a daughter of — Harcourt of Ellenhall (probably Staffordshire); this identification was accepted by Broughton.

He married second Margaret Norwode, daughter of John Norwode of Coventry, merchant; she was remarried to Sir John de Gresley by 17 Hen. VI (1438-1439).

In 1399 he was granted a license to lands in Prestatyn and Flint, and bought four messuages, eighty acres of land, twenty acres of meadow and four acres of wood in Bokenhalle for one hundred marks in silver. He had a license to crenelate a tower of

Dodington 4 Hen. IV (1403), was in Picardy guarding the Castle of Hammes in 1404, was fighting against the French in 1410, and was Sheriff of Staffordshire in 1416.

Children, by first wife [Broughton]:

 i.   Thomas[H], called possible son by Ormerod, m. 1412 Anne Holes.
*   ii. Margaret, m. 1411 Sir John[H] Mainwaring.
 iii. Elizabeth, m. Richard Colclough.
 iv. Joan [Anne, m. John Bird of Yowley, listed by Ormerod].

Children, by first wife, listed by Ormerod:

 v.   Ralph.
 vi. Henry, m. (1) Margaret de Brereton, dau. of Sir William[J] Brereton of Brereton, m. (2) Ellen Swinnarton of Steyne, Staffs.

Children, by second wife [Broughton]:

 vii. Richard, b. c. 1416; d. 24 Hen. VI (1445-1446); m. 1439 Elizabeth (or Emma) Wynynton [Collins also had him listed as a son by his father's second wife, which seems to be an error].
 viii. Sir John, of Dodington, b. c. 1423; slain at the battle of Tewkesbury 4 May 1471; m. by dispensation May 1439 Elen Eggerton, dau. of Ralph Eggerton of Wrinehall [Collins listed him as son by second wife, which seems to be correct based on his date of birth].

§ § §

LE DESPENSER

This line is based on the work of G.W. Watson in Cokayne's *Complete Peerage* [4:259-281]. The arms of this family were derived from the Constables of Chester: Quarterly, *Argent*, and *Gules fretty Or*, over all a bend *Sable*.

There is no relationship between this family and that of Spencers of Althorpe, who were descended from wealthy graziers of record at the end of the fifteenth century. J.H. Round has dealt with this issue at length [*Peerage and Family History*, 279-329].

THOMAS[Q] DISPENSATOR died by 1218. He was probably descended from Elyas Dispensator, who was one of three persons enfeoffed in Arnesby by Hugh de Beauchamp. He probably took his name from the Office of Dispenser to the Earls of Chester. This office was that of an under-butler or comptroller who dispensed victuals [BP, 1:1029].

Sir HUGH[P] LE DESPENSER died before 30 May 1238.

Sir HUGH[O] LE DESPENSER, 1st Lord Despenser, born in or before 1223, died at Evesham 4 Aug. 1265. He married (second, according to Vernon Norr [59]) ALINE (or Aliva)[M] BASSETT of Wycombe, Buckinghamshire, who died shortly before 11 April 1281, having married second, before 29 Oct. 1271, Roger Bigod, Earl of Norfolk, who died without issue [*CP*, 14:256] 7 Dec. 1306, and was buried in Thetford Priory. In the inquisitions taken in Nov. 1271 after the death of her father, she was said to be aged 22 and more, 24 and more, 24 and more, 26, or 30 and more.

4. Sir HUGH[N] LE DESPENSER, 2nd Baron Despenser, Earl of Winchester, was born in Wycombe, Buckinghamshire, 1 March 1260/1, and was hanged at Bristol, Gloucestershire, 27 Oct. 1326.

He married 1286, without a license from the king, as her second husband, ISABEL[K] DE BEAUCHAMP*, widow of Sir Patrick[M] Chaworth, who had died without male issue [*CP*, 14:265] in Kidwelly, Carmarthenshire, Wales, about 7 July 1283. She died shortly before 30 May 1306.

He ransomed Loughborough, Arnesby, Parlington, Ryhall and other lands, which had been forfeited by his father [*CP*, 4:262a]. He also had Wycombe, Compton-Bassett and Wootton-Bassett from his mother's family.

He was with King Edward I in Gascony in 1287, and was one of those ordered on 22 Aug. 1288 to abstain from violations of the peace while the king was abroad. He was appointed Constable of Oldham Castle in 1294, and was an envoy to the King of the Romans that year, and to the King of France and the King of the Romans in 1296, the same year he accompanied the king to Scotland. As one of the proxies he swore to the treaty with the Count of Flanders on 5 Feb. 1296/7. In 1297 he was a member of the King's Council, and accompanied the king to Flanders. He was with the king in Scotland in 1300, 1303, 1304 and 1306, served as an envoy to the Pope in 1300, to the King of France in 1302, and again to the Pope in 1305.

At the Coronation of King Edward II he was one of four who carried the table on which the royal robes were laid. In 1307 to 1310 he held the offices of Constable of the Castles of Devizes and Marlborough, Constable of the Castle of Strigoil, and Keeper of the town of Chepstow, as well as Justice of the forests South of Trent. As a deputy to the king he treated with the Magnates after Gavaston's death. In the fight over Gavaston in 1308 he alone had sided with the king against the barons, who pressured the King to dismiss Despenser from the Court.

He was pardoned for all debts and arrears to the King on 25 March 1313, and went with him to Pontoise the next 23 May, but was excluded from the peace between the King and the barons in the autumn.

He was at the battle of Bannockburn on 24 June 1314, and fled with the King to Dunbar and then Berwick. Soon after the Earl of Lancaster obtained Despenser's dismissal from Court and the Council. On 13 July 1315 a commission was appointed to hear complaints about his acts of oppression as Keeper of the forests South of Trent. He was in the Scottish wars in 1317, and in 1318, to avoid the Earl of Lancaster, was said to have gone on pilgrimage to Compostella in Spain. However, on 28 Feb. 1319/20 he was sent to Gascony to straighten out affairs there, followed by missions to the King of France and the Pope. On 2 May 1321 he was appointed Constable of Marlborough Castle. While he was summoned for military service over a period of forty years from 1283 to 1322, and to Parliament from 1295 to 1321/2, in May and June of 1321 the barons of the Welsh Marches ravaged his lands and those of his son throughout the country. Chiefly because of his son's actions he was disinherited and banished with his son on 19 Aug. 1321, and he retired to the Continent. However, a provincial council of the clergy pronounced this punishment to be unlawful about the next Jan., and the following March he accompanied the King against the opposition, and was present for the judgment upon the Earl of Lancaster. His lands were restored 7 May 1322. Three days later Edward II made him Earl of Winchester, and gave him many honors in Wales of the late John Giffard, which passed in 1327 to Roger de Mortimer, Earl of March, and then to William de Montagu. Afterwards Hugh fought in Scotland, treating for peace in August 1324. He was appointed Keeper of the forests South of Trent on 27 June 1324, for life.

When the King fled to Wales in Oct. 1326 Hugh was dispatched to defend Bristol, but surrendered the city to the Queen on her arrival on 26 Oct. The next day he was tried, and, without being allowed to speak in his own defense, was condemned to death as a traitor, and hanged on the common gallows, his honors forfeited.

Children, heir from Cokayne, the remainder undocumented if source not shown:

5.   i.   Hugh^M, hanged at Hereford 24 Nov. 1326; m. 1306 Alianore^L de Clare, who m. (2) William la Zouche de Mortimer.

    ii.   Sir Philip, d. 24 Sept. 1313; m. Margaret de Gousille, who b. 12 May 1294, d. 29 July 1349; of Camoys manor in Essex [MCS5, 9:6].

   iii.   Ada (Elizabeth), m. before 1321 Ralph Camoys.

   iv.   Joan, d. before 15 Feb. 1251; m. John de Saint Amand.

    v.   Aveline (Oliva), d. May 1363; m. Sir Edward Burnel, who d. 1315.

   vi.   Eleanor, d. after 1351; a nun.

  vii.   Isabel, d. 4 Dec. 1334; m. (1) John de Hastings, who was a competitor for the crown of Scotland in 1292 [Norr, 59], m. (2) Richard Meunthermer.

 viii.   Margaret, m. 1310 John St. Amand [MCS5, 10:6].

5. Sir HUGH[M] LE DESPENSER, 3rd Baron Despenser of Loughborough and Arnesby, Leicestershire, was hanged and quartered at Hereford on 24 Nov. 1326; many years later his bones were collected and buried at Tewkesbury Abbey.

He married at Westminster, in 1306, before 14 June, ALIANORE[L] DE CLARE*, who died at Caerphilly Castle, Glamorgan, Wales, 30 June 1337, having married second, about Jan. 1328/9, as his second wife, Sir William la Zouche de Mortimer, who had abducted her from Hanley Castle; he died 28 Feb. 1336/7, and was buried in Tewkesbury Abbey [Faris, PA, 61]. Her lands had been restored to her on 22 April 1328, and she gave homage to the King on 11 May. Soon after her abduction she accompanied Sir William in besieging her castle of Caerphilly, and orders for their arrest were issued. She was imprisoned in the Tower of London, and then Devizes Castle, but was allowed her freedom after 6 Jan. 1329/30.

Hugh was knighted by the Prince of Wales (later King Edward II), at Westminster on 22 May 1306. Having gone overseas without license he lost his lands and goods for a time. He accompanied King Edward II to Pontoise, 23 May 1313, and was appointed Chamberlain by the end of the year. He was summoned to military service and to Parliament from time to time from 1314 to 1325, but was disinherited and exiled on 19 Aug. 1321. He found refuge in the Cinque Ports, engaged in piracy, and did considerable damage with the King's connivance (and for which he received a pardon in 1325). In 1324 he complained to the Pope that he was threatened by magical and secret dealings; the Pope advised him to turn to God and make a good confession. Robert le Mareschal accused thirty inhabitants of Coventry of having employed him and John de Notingham, a necromaner, who then made images of some enemies. It was said that one, a test case, died after his image was pierced by a sharp pin of lead, first in the head and then in the heart. While the accused were acquitted, the necromancer died in prison.

After the battle of Boroughbridge he received large grants of land which had been forfeited by the rebels.

He was a powerful boyfriend of King Edward II, and accompanied him when he fled to Wales in Oct. 1326. He was captured with the king near Llantrisant in Glamorgan on 16 Nov. 1326. He was taken to Hereford and tried for treason. Denied being allowed to speak in his own defence, he was condemned as a traitor and hanged on a gallows fifty feet high 24 Nov. 1326 [CP, 1:243, 4:267-271]. After he was hung his head was displayed on London Bridge, and his quarters were hung at Dover, Bristol, York and Newcastle.

Children, known to the compiler:

    i.   Hugh[L] [CP, 4:271], m. Elizabeth de Montagu [Norr, 59] (widow of Giles[K] de Badlesmere), who m. (3) 1349 Sir Guy de Brian.

6.   ii.   Edward, d. 30 Sept. 1342; m. Groby, Leics., 20 April 1326, Anne[L] de Ferrers.

*   iii.   Isabel, b. c. 1312; m. King's Chapel, Havering-atte-Bower, Essex, 9 Feb. 1320/1, Sir Richard[K] Fitz Alan.
    iv.   Elizabeth, d. 13 July 1389, bur. St. Botolph's, London; m. Aug. 1338 Sir Maurice[H] de Berkeley, who d. Berkeley Castle 3 June 1368.

6. Sir EDWARD[L] DESPENSER died 30 Sept. 1342.

He married in Groby, Leicestershire, 20 April 1335, ANNE[L] DE FERRERS*, who died 8 Aug. 1367 [Faris, *PA*2, 85].

He had lands in Buckland in Buckinghamshire, Eyworth in Bedfordshire, West Winterslow in Wiltshire and Essendine in Rutland, among other properties.

Son and heir, from the pedigree:

  7.   i.   Edward[K], b. Essendine, Rutland, c. 24 March 1335/6; d. Llanbethian, Glamorgan, 11 Nov. 1375, bur. Tewkesbury Abbey; m. before 2 Aug. 1354 Elizabeth[K] de Burghersh.

7. Sir EDWARD[K] DESPENSER, K.G., 4th Lord le Despenser, Lord of Glamorgan, born and baptized in Essendine, Rutland, 24 March 1335/6, died in Llanbethian, Glamorgan, Wales, 11 Nov. 1375, and was buried in Tewkesbury Abbey, in Gloucestershire.

He married before 2 Aug. 1354 ELIZABETH[K] DE BURGHERSH*, who died 26 July 1409, and was buried in Tewkesbury Abbey.

He accompanied the Prince of Wales to Gascony in Sept. 1355, and as a knight was in the skirmish at Romorantin in Sologne and the battle of Poitiers. On 26 March 1357, when he was in Gascony, he had livery of his father's lands. He was summoned to Councils from 1358 to 1361/2, and to Parliament from 1357 to 1372. He was a part of the invasions of France in Oct. 1359 and Sept. 1372, was Constable of the Army in the invasion of 1373-1374, and assisted the Duke of Brittany in his campaign in Brittany in 1375.

He had been nominated K.G. in 1361, went with the Duke of Clarence to Milan in 1368, and was in the war in Lombardy before returning to England in Aug. 1372.

Children, listed by Faris [*Plantagenet Ancestors*, 1st ed., 62]:

  i.   Thomas[J], third but surviving son, 9th Earl of Gloucester (forfeited), b. 22 Sept. 1373; beheaded 13 Jan. 1399/1400; m. by 14 Jan. 1383/4 Constance of York, who d. 29 Nov. 1416, bur. Abbey of Reading, dau. of Edmund of York and Isabella de Castile, and granddau. of King Edward III.
  ii.   Anne, d. testate 30 or 31 Oct. 1426; m. (1) before 1 Nov. 1376 Sir Hugh Hastings, who d. Spain 6 Nov. 1386, m. (2) Sir Thomas de Morley, 4th Lord Morley, who d. 24 Sept. 1416.
  iii.   Elizabeth, d. 11 April 1408, bur. prob. Tewkesbury Abbey, as requested in her will; m. before 1385 Sir John de Arundel, who d. 14 Aug. 1390 [*MSC*5, 121:8].
*   iv.   Margaret, d. 3 Nov. 1415, bur. Merevale Abbey; m. as his second wife Sir Robert[J] de Ferrers of Chartley, who d. 12 or 13 March 1412/3, bur. Merevale Abbey.

§ § §

DEVEREUX

This outline of the family is based on Vernon Norr's *Some Early English Pedigrees*, pages 59-66. As Mr. Norr put it, "Much confusion exists in all printed accounts of the

Devereux family." There was at least three contemporary lines in Herefordshire, and very little is known of two of them. The first few generations follow Norr's work.

ROBERT[W] D'EVEREUX (the third son of Richard I[V] "the Fearless" [sans Peur], Duke of Normandy, who died 20 Nov. 996), Count d'Evreux, was born about 974, and was Archbishop of Rouen. He married first HERLEVA[W]. The name of his second wife is not known. RICHARD[V] D'EVEREUX was the second Count d'Evereux.

ROBERT[V] D'EVEREUX, 3rd Count d'Evereux, born say 1008, was the heir of his half nephew Robert. He married HALEWYSE[V] DE LACY, sister of Walter de Lacy.

WALTER[U] D'EVREUX, born say 1034, was Count of Rosmar. His wife's name is not known. However, in Alveretta Devereux Reed and DeWitt Clinton Reed's *Devereux Family* (1920) he was called son of Richard, son of Robert.

ROBERT[T] D'EVEREUX has been said, mistakenly, to have come with the Conqueror to England in 1066. He married in Cornwall, in 1089, a Miss Longchamp.

REGINALD[S] D'EVREUX, born say 1092, must have lived in Cornwall. It was said he married in Cornwall.

WILLIAM[R] D'EVREUX was born say in 1118. It is said he married Halwyse[R] de Lacy, the de Lacy heiress and niece of Walter de Lacy. The name occurs above as married to Robert[V] and William[T].

EUSTACE[Q] D'EVREUX was born say in 1146. While it has been suggested that he probably married Cicily Longchamp, it should be noted that Robert[T] d'Evreux was also said to have married a Miss Longchamp.

STEPHEN[P] D'EVREUX was born say 1179, was dead by 1245. He married first Constance Picard. He married second ISABEL[P] CANTELUPE, daughter of William, and said by some to be a niece or relative of the de Lacy family; she was a widow in 1245, holding Frome Herbert, and married second Ralph Pembrugge.

Sir WILLIAM[O] D'EVREUX was slain in the battle of Evesham, 1265, while fighting against King Henry III. He married MAUD[O] GIFFORD of Boynton, sister of Walter, Bishop of Bath, and widow of Baron de Freville; she married third Walter de la Bere. As a widow her brother Walter gave her Home Lacy in Frome, Gloucestershire, and Wilby in Norfolk.

11. Sir WILLIAM[N] D'EVEREUX, of Lyonshall in Herefordshire, as well as Home Lacey and Stoke Lacey, was born about 1240 and died about 1314.

He married first ALICE[N] GRANDISON of Herefordshire.

He married second Lucy Burnell, who survived him.

He recovered Lyonshall, which had been forfeited by his father, on payment of a fine of one hundred marks. In 1290 he detained the tithes of Lyonshall and was excommunicated, but was later absolved. He was created Lord Devereux in 1299. In 1300 he granted Home Lacy, Stoke Lacy and Lyonshall (but not Frome) to the Bishop of Coventry for life.

Children, listed by Norr [63], by first wife:

> 12.   i.   William[M], b. c. 1264; m. Margery.
> ii.   Walter, b. c. 1266; m. Margery de Braiose; of Bodenham.

Children, by second wife:

> iii.   Stephen, m. Constance, who m. (2) Henry de Mortimer of Chelmarsh; held Frome Raymonds in 1303; no issue.
> iv.   John, b. 1301; d. 1383.

12. Sir WILLIAM[M] DEVEREUX of Frome in Somerset, was born about 1264.

He married MARGERY[M].

There is confusion in the literature among various people named William Devereux.

Child:

13.   i.   Walter^L, b. c. 1296; m. (1) Margery^L de Braiose.

13. Sir WALTER^L D'EVEREUX of Lenhales in Herefordshire, was born about 1296.

He married first MARGERY DE BRAIOSE of Pipton, Breconshire, who was born about 1306 and died in 1344.

Children, listed by Norr [64], by first wife:

       i.   John^K, b. say 1328; probably fought in Spain 1366.

14.   ii.   William, b. c. 1330; d. 1376; m. Anne^K Barre.

      iii. Walter, b. say 1332; perhaps the M.P. of 1379.

Child, by a second wife:

      iv.   Ann, m. Roger Vaughan.

14. Sir WILLIAM^K DEVEREUX of Hereford Whitechurch in Herefordshire, born about 1330, died in 1376.

He married ANNE^K BARRE* of Herefordshire, who was born about 1340 and died in 1377, daughter of John^L Barre. Watney's *Wallop Family* contains few citations. *The Genealogist*, n.s., 19:59, and 23:29, and C. Platt's *Medieval Southampton* [232] were not helpful.

Children, listed by Norr [64]:

15.   i.   Walter^J, m. 1383/4 Agnes^J Crophull, who m. (2) John Parr of Kendal, m. (3) John Merbury.

      ii.   John, m. Elizabeth de la Bere, dau. of Richard de la Bere of Kinnersley; probable son of William of Bodenham [*CP*, 4:296].

      iii. Thomas, lord of Lyonshall Castle which he deeded in 1426 to grandchildren of his brother John; of Wotton.

15. Sir WALTER^J DEVEREUX of Bodenham, Weobley and Whitchurch in Herefordshire, died 25 June 1402. According to Roskell his parents were Sir Walter Devereux of Bodenham and his wife Maud [Roskell, 2:783].

He married in 1383/4 AGNES^J CROPHULL*, who married second John Parr of Kendal, and married third John^I Merbury, as his third wife. She was sole heiress of Weobley, and received Lyonshall late in life. She died 3 Feb. 1436 [Roskell, 2:783].

He was a commissioner from 1382, and Constable of Builth Castle in Radnorshire from 8 Feb. 1382 for about twelve years. From 9 Nov. 1385 he served many terms as justice of the peace in Herefordshire. He was a king's esquire in the expedition to Scotland in 1385. He received Weobley in 1386 on proof of age of his wife. Apparently he did not support King Richard II during the political crisis of 1387-1388, but he was knighted by 1391 and did go to Ireland with Richard II in Sept. 1394.

He served as Sheriff of Herefordshire in 1401, the year he was a Member of Parliament. He was a member of Sir Edmund Mortimer's expedition to Radnorshire, and was wounded when the English were defeated by the Welsh at the battle of Pilleth on 22 June 1402, and died three days later.

His wife Agnes Crophull was, by her second husband John Parr, the great-great-grandmother of Katherine Parr, the last wife of King Henry VIII [*BP*, 1:1379].

Children, listed by Norr [64]:

16.   i.   Walter^I, b. c. 1387; m. Elizabeth^I Bromwich.

      ii.   Elizabeth.

      iii. Richard.

      iv.   Margaret.

      v.   Thomas.

Children, listed in *Burke's Peerage* (1999) [1:1378], which did not mention Elizabeth, Margaret and Thomas:

    vi.   John.
   vii.   Stephen.
  viii.   Roger.
    ix.   Joan.

16. Sir WALTER[I] DEVEREUX of Salisbury in Wiltshire, was born about 1387, and died in 1436.

He married ELIZABETH[I] BROMWICH* of Herefordshire. She was called Maud in *Burke's Peerage* (1999) [1:1378].

Children, listed by Norr [65]:

17.   i.   Walter[H], d. April 1459; m. Elizabeth[H] Merbury.
      ii.   Elizabeth, m. John Milbourne.
    iii.   Cicily, m. Sir John Baskerville.

17. Sir WALTER[H] DEVEREUX, of Weobley and Bodenham in Herefordshire, Branston, Cottesbach and Newbold Verdon in Leicestershire, and Market Rasen in Lincolnshire, died 22 or 23 April 1459 [*CP*, 5:321].

He married before 26 Nov. 1446 ELIZABETH[H] MERBURY*, daughter of Sir John Merbury.

Children, listed by Norr [65]:

18.   i.   Sir Walter[G], m. (1) Anne[G] de Ferrers.
      ii.   Anne, m. c. 1455 William Herbert, who d. 1469, son of William Herbert and Gwladus Gam (widow of Sir Roger Vaughan of Bredwardine who was slain at Agincourt in 1415 [*cf.* Boyer, *Ancestral Lines*, 3rd ed., 703]), dau. of Sir Dafydd Gam [Norr, 116].
    iii.   Isabel, m. Rowland Lenthal.
    iv.   Sir John, Sheriff in 1489; had Woodhouse.
     v.   Sibilla, m. Sir James Baskerville.

18. Sir WALTER[G] DEVEREUX, K.G., of Weobley and Bodenham (and Lyonshall [Norr, 65]) in Herefordshire, Branston, Cottesbach and Newbold Verdon in Leicestershire, and Market Rasen in Lincolnshire, born about 1433, was slain in the battle of Bosworth, 22 Aug. 1485.

He married first, before 26 Nov. 1446, ANNE[G] DE FERRERS*, who was aged eleven years, eight months in July 1450, daughter and heir of Sir William[H] de Ferrers of Chartley. She died 9 Jan. 1468/9, aged 30.

He married second, Jane Verdun [Norr, 65, but surname not given by Faris, *PA2*, 139], who married second, in 1485, Thomas Vaughn, who was living 18 Nov. 1492. She married third Sir Edward Blount of Sodington in Worcestershire, who died without issue 6 July 1499. She married fourth, before 31 May 1502, Thomas Poyntz; they were both living 9 Nov. 1512.

On 17 March 1452/3 he and Anne had a grant of livery of her father's lands, she being aged 14 and more. By right of his wife he became Lord Ferrers of Chartley.

He was aged about 27 when his father died in April 1459. He was with the Duke of York in the skirmish at Ludford, but surrendered and threw himself on the mercy of King Henry VI; he was allowed to live but had to forfeit his lands, which he redeemed later on payment of a fine of 500 marks.

Nonetheless, he was Knight of the Shire for Herefordshire in 1460. He was with Edward, Duke of York, on the advance from Gloucester to London in Feb. 1460/1, and was present at the council held in Baynard's Castle on 3 March 1460/1, where it was resolved to elevate the Duke of York as King Edward IV. He was knighted after the battle of Towton, 29 March 1461, and then raised to the rank of baron, and on 20 Feb. 1461/2 he was awarded an extensive grant of forfeited lands.

In Nov. 1462 he accompanied King Edward IV in his expedition to the North, and on 18 June 1463 he was appointed Constable of Aberystwyth Castle for life. On 16 Nov. 1469 he was granted the offices of Constable of the castles and Steward of the lordships of Brecknock, Hay and Huntington, as long as Henry, grandson and heir of Humphrey, Duke of Buckingham, was a minor. On 28 July 1470 he was appointed Sheriff of Caernarfon, and master forester of the Snowdon Hills in Wales, for life.

With other lords he swore, in the parliamentary chamber in Westminster on 3 July 1471, to accept Edward, Prince of Wales, as heir to the Crown. He was elevated to K.G. on 24 April 1472. He was among those to be selected on 20 Feb. 1472/3 to be a tutor and councillor to the Prince until he was fourteen years old.

He went to France with King Edward IV in July 1475, and was present at the conference at Saint-Christ in Vermandois when the king agreed, on 13 August 1475, to withdraw his troops to England.

After he was killed in the battle of Bosworth 22 Aug. 1485, which ended the reign of King Richard III, he was attainted of high treason by the Parliament which met 7 Nov. 1 Hen. VII (1485). There he was adjudged to have forfeited lands which he had held fee simple, fee tail, or for life.

Children, by first wife:

*   i.   Elizabeth[F], d. 1541; m. (1) Sir Richard[F] Corbet, m. (2) Sir Thomas Leighton of Wattlesborough.
       ii.   Sir Richard, m.
      iii.   Sir John, b. c. 1464; m. (1) Cecily Bourgchier (or Bourchier), who d. 1493, m. (2) Elizabeth Corbet [Norr, 65]; heir of Weobley.
      iv.   Katherine, b. c. 1468/9; m. her first cousin Sir James Baskerville.

Children, by first wife, added by *BP* [1:1378]:

       v.   Sir Thomas.
      vi.   Isabel (or Sybil), m. Sir James Baskerville.

§ § §

DE DOWNES

In the thirteenth century Robert de Dunes (or Downes) was recorded as holding of Edward I *in capite* the manors of Dounes and Tackeshalch [Earwaker, 2:526].

1. ROBERT[O] DE DOWNES was the subject of an inquisition post mortem dated 23 Feb. 1273.

He was living in 1245, and held the manors of Downes and Taxal by forest service [Earwaker, 2:530].

Children:

       i.   John[N], b. c. 1249; no issue.
   2.   ii.   Robert, l. 1306.

2. ROBERT[N] DE DOWNES was of record in 1306.
Children:

      i.   Edmund^M, l. 1337; m. Margery Throsle, heiress of Roger Throsle of
             Macclesfield.

3.   ii.   Robert, m. Margery^L Fitton.

      iii. William, poss. son, of Shrigley in 1313.

3. ROBERT^M DE DOWNES was of Downes and Taxal in Cheshire.
He married MARGERY^L FITTON*, daughter of Sir Hugh^M Fhyton.
With his wife he held lands in Chorley and elsewhere.
Child, only daughter and heiress:

*   i.   Maud^L, m. (l) William^L Mobberley, who d. 1327, m. (2) John Dumbill (or
            Dumvile) [Ormerod, *Chester*, 3:781].

§ § §

DUTTON OF DUTTON

This line is based on Ormerod's *History of Chester* [1:642-645], with additions from
Peter Leycester's *Leycester's Historical Antiquities* (1673) as copied in Gilbert Cope's
Genealogy of the Dutton Family of Pennsylvania. The Duttons of Hatton were descended
from the Vernons.

HODARD^S (or Odard, Udard or Hudard) came to England with William the Conqueror
and settled at Dutton (now in Budworth parish) in Cheshire, England, which was given to
him by Hugh Lupus, Earl of Chester, as is given in Domesday. HUGH^R, son of Hodard, died
in a place called Kekwick (probably Keckwick in Cheshire, about two miles west of
Hatton).

3. HUGH^Q DE DUTTON had the lands which his father Hugh held of the baron of Halton
confirmed to him by William, son of Nigell, constable to Randle the Second, Earl of
Chester, and by William his son. When William the father and William the son visited
Hugh^R on his deathbed at Kekwick, Hugh^R gave William the father his coat of mail and
charging horse, and Hugh^Q gave William the son a palfrey and a sparrowhawk. Ormerod
thought this happened at the end of the reign of Henry I, the last year of which was 1135.
Children, list by Ormerod:

4.   i.   Hugh^P, m. Isabel^P Massy.

5.   ii. Adam, m. Agnes, dau. of Roger Fitz Alured.

*   iii. Geffrey, ancestor of Duttons of Chedill [for whom see Chedle], m. (1)
           dau. of John de Lacy, lord of Halton, m. (2) Elen de Chedle.

4. HUGH^P DUTTON of Dutton, Cheshire, purchased Little Moldesworth for fifty marks
from Robert, son of Matthew de Moldesworth, about 1250.

He married ISABEL^P MASSY*. From this marriage he received lands in Suttersby, in
Lindsey, Lincolnshire.
Children, listed by Ormerod:

6.   i.   Hugh^O, m. Muriel^O le Despenser.

      ii. Thomas.

      iii. John.

      iv. Adam.

5. ADAM^P DE DUTTON was ancestor of the Warburtons of Arley, and lived during the
reign of King John, which was from 1199 to 1216.

He married AGNES, daughter of co-heir of Roger (or Robert?) Fitz Alured, in the time of King Henry II, who reigned from 1154 to 1189.

Children, listed by Ormerod:

7.   i.   Geoffrey[O], d. c. 1248; m. Alice de Lacy?

        ii.   John, bur. Warburton.

        iii.   Agatha.

6. HUGH[O] DUTTON of Dutton, the alleged son and heir of Hugh[P] de Dutton de Dutton, was of record in 1234 [Ormerod, 1:644].

He married MURIEL[O] LE DESPENSER, daughter of Thomas le Despenser.

He bought Preston nigh Dutton from Henry de Nuers and his wife Julian. This purchase was confirmed by Randle (or Ranulph)[M] de Blundeville, Earl of Chester, about the time of the reign of King John. He also purchased Little Legh from Simon son of Osberne before the time of King John's reign. He also purchased the moiety of Barnton from William, son of Henry, son of Serlo, which Robert de Mesnilwarin held.

John Constable and the barons of Halton granted to him and his heirs the magistracy over all the letchers and whores of all Cheshire. This magistracy had been granted originally to Richard Lacy, Constable of Cheshire, who had raised an army of promiscuous rabble to relieve Randle[M] de Blundevill, Earl of Chester, who was in his castle of Rothelent in Flintshire, under siege by the Welsh. When the Welsh heard the rabble coming they supposed it to be a great army, lifted the siege and fled. That rabble was supposed to have consisted of players, fiddlers and shoemakers. Apparently this led to the Duttons of Dutton having control over licensing minstrels in later years, with the results that those holding such license were exempt from the statute of rogues, 39 Eliz. cap. 4. Each Midsummer Day the Lord of Dutton would hold a court at Chester, and all the licensed minstrels would appear and renew their licenses, although the custom later was to license the fiddlers attendant on the revelers in bawdy houses and taverns.

Children, listed by Ormerod:

        i.   Hugh[N], d. without issue; flourished 1234 and 1236; gave to his brother John the third part of the town of Bolinton in Maxfield Hundred, which Thomas le Dispenser gave in free-marriage *Hugoni Patri meo cum Mariela Matre mea* about 1234 [Cope, *Dutton Family*, 16, quoting Leycester].

8.   ii.   Thomas, m. Philippa de Sandon (or Standon).

        iii.   John.

        iv.   Adam.

        v.   Alice, a dau. of a Hugh de Dutton, Lord of Dutton, m. Sir William de Boydele, Lord of Dodleston, who fl. 1209-1270 [Ormerod, 2:848].

7. Sir GEFFREY[O] DE DUTTON, alias de Buddeworth, a member of the line which became known as the Warburtons of Arley, died about 1248.

He may have married Alice de Lacy, daughter of John de Lacy, Baron of Halton [Ormerod, 1:573].

Of record in 1218, he served in the Holy Land during the Crusades, and had a mansion at Buddeworth [Ormerod, 1:569]. He adopted as his crest the head of a Saracen, in memory of a victory in combat.

Child:

9.   i.   Geffrey[N].

8. Sir THOMAS[N] DUTTON of Dutton, Cheshire, died in battle about the beginning of the reign of King Edward I [Ormerod, 1:644; Cope, 16]. The name of the battle was torn from the copy of Ormerod used by the compiler.

He married Philippa de Sandon, daughter and heir of Vivian de Sandon, or Standon, by whom he had lands in Staffordshire. She was living in 1294, a widow [Ormerod, 1:645].

He was Sheriff of Cheshire in 1268.

He purchased Clatterwigge, a hamlet in Little Legh juxtà Barterton, from Hugh de Clatterwigge in 29 Hen. III (1244-1245). He built a chapel at the manor house of Dutton towards the end of the reign of King Henry III, thus by 1272.

Children, mentioned by Ormerod:
- i. Hugh[M], d. 1294; m. Joan de Sancto Petro (or Sampier), dau. of Sir Vrian de Sancto Petro.
- ii. Thomas, given Great Rownall and Little Rownall in Staffordshire.
- iii. Robert, knight, m. Agnes de Mere, dau. of William de Mere; awarded the two manors of Rownall, apparently after the death of brother Thomas.
- * iv. Margaret (or Margery [Corry, *Lancs.*, 2:663]), m. 1253 Sir William[M] Venables.
- v. Katharine, m. John, son of Sir Vrian de Sancto Petro (Sir Bryan de St. Peter).

9. Sir GEFFREY[N] DE DUTTON, of the line which became known as the Warburtons of Arley, succeeded to his estate about 1248, and was living in 1275.

His second wife was named Isabel.

In addition to Nether Tabley, his daughter brought to her husband the manors of Wethale and Hield, both in Aston nigh Great Budworth, Cheshire.

Children, listed by Ormerod [1:573], by first wife:
- i. Sir Peter[M], alias de Warburton, d. before 8 Edw. II (1314-1315); m.
- ii. Thomas, of Thelwall of 1258.
- * iii. Margaret, m. (1) Robert de Denbigh, m. (2) c. 1276 Sir Nicholas[M] Leycester.

§ § §

DUTTON OF HATTON

The following was extracted from Ormerod's *History of Chester* [2:791-796]. Sir Thomas[K] de Dutton was a son of Sir Ralph[L] de Vernon (for whom see Vernon of Hatton) of Shipbrook and his wife Matilda (or Maud)[L] de Hatton.

1. Sir THOMAS[K] DE DUTTON, knight, Lord of Dutton, died 4 Ric. II (1380-1381), aged 66.

He married ELLEN[K] DE THORNETON*, daughter and coheir of Sir Piers (or Peter[L]) de Thorneton in le Moors, knight; she died before 38 Edw. III (1364-1365).

He was son of Ralph[L] de Vernon of Hatton and his wife Matilda[L] de Hatton.

He was sheriff of Cheshire 30 Edw. III (1356-1357).

Children, from Ormerod's pedigree:
- i. Sir Laurence[J], son and heir.
- 2. ii. Edmund, younger son, m. Joan[J] de Minshull.

2. EDMUND[J] DE DUTTON was a younger son of Sir Thomas de Dutton.

He married JOAN[J] DE MINSHULL*, daughter and coheir of Henry[K] de Minshull, lord of Church Minshull in Nantwich Hundred in Cheshire.

Children, from Ormerod's pedigree:

      i.   Sir Peter[I], first son; heir to his uncle Laurence.

3.   ii.   Hugh, second son, m. Petronilla[I] de Vernon.

3. HUGH[I] DUTTON, Lord of Hatton in right of his wife, was born about 1367, having been recorded as aged 20 in 11 Ric. II (1387-1388) and 26 in 16 Ric. II (1392-1393).

He married first PETRONILLA[I] DE VERNON*, his second cousin of Hatton, who was born 1383, was living 10 Hen. VI (1431-1432), and who was buried with him at the high alter of Waverton.

He married second Emma Warren, daughter of Nicholas Warren of Poynton and widow of Hugh Venables de Golborne.

He was sheriff of Cheshire 10 Hen. V (1422).

About 1432 Robert Aby, vicar of Tarvin, obtained from Hugh de Dutton, sheriff of Cheshire, and Petronilla his wife, the manor of Hatton with twenty-seven messuages, eighteen tofts and 1204 acres of land in Waverton, Chollegh, Little Christleton and Aldersey. This land reverted back to Hugh, according to an *inquisition post mortem* held 18 Hen. VI (1439-1440).

Children, from Ormerod's pedigree:

4.   i.   John[H], heir, b. 1400; m. Margaret[H] de Atherton.

      ii.   Laurence, second son.

      iii.   Hugh.

      iv.   Elizabeth, m. Richard de Manley, Lord of Manley.

      v.   Ralph, bur. by side of his father at Waverton; clerk, rector of Christleton.

4. JOHN[H] DE DUTTON of Hatton, Cheshire, Esquire, born 1400, was living 1461, and was buried near the pulpit in Waverton church.

He married MARGARET[H] DE ATHERTON*, who was living 18 Hen. VI (1439-1440) and was buried by her husband's side.

Apparently he feuded constantly with the Breretons, Whitmores and others [Ormerod, 2:792].

Children, from Ormerod's pedigree:

5.   i.   Peter[G], d. 8 April 18 Henry VII (1502-1503); m. 1464 Elizabeth Grosvenor.

      ii.   Richard, ancestor of the Duttons of Sherborne.

      iii.   Geoffrey, third son, bur. by his father's side.

      iv.   Ellen, bur. Waverton; m. Gillibrand.

5. PETER[G] DE DUTTON [SR.] of Hatton, Cheshire, died 8 April 18 Hen. VII (1502-1503).

He married 1464 ELIZABETH[G] GROSVENOR*, eldest daughter and coheir of Robert Grosvenor of Holme, Esq. She died before her husband, and they were buried together.

He, with Sir John Doune, Sir Thomas Manley, Thomas Leycester of Tabley and others, his sureties, were bound over for three years beginning 6 Edw. IV (1467), eight times in all at 500 marks each, to keep the peace towards Ralph Grosvenor, Esq. of Eaton.

Children, from Ormerod's pedigree:

6.   i.   Peter, Jr.[F], d. before his father; m. Elizabeth[F] Fouleshurst.

      ii.   Ralph, outlawed for felony 21 Edw. IV.

      iii.   Richard.

      iv.   Randle.

6. PETER[F] DUTTON [JR.] of Hatton died before his father, before 18 Hen. VII (1502-1503).

He married ELIZABETH[F] FOULESHURST*, who married second, 22 Henry VII (1506-1507), Thomas Leycester of Tabley, Esq.

He was outlawed for having committed a felony 21 Edw. IV (1482) along with Robert Huxley, yeoman. At the time the proceedings occured before Thomas, Lord Stanley, knight and Chief Justice of Chester, Peter held twelve messuages and 320 acres, of which one-third were arable. The next year he had a general pardon. His brother Ralph had been outlawed the same year.

Children, from Ormerod's pedigree:

   i. Sir Piers[E], d. 1546; m. (1) Eleanor Legh, dau. of Sir Thomas Legh, m. (2) Juliana, dau. of William Poyntz of Worthokiton, Essex.
   ii. Elizabeth, m. Sir George Calveley of Lea.
 * iii. Eleanor, m. Randle[E] Brereton of Malpas.

§ § §

DE EGERTON

The township of Egerton in Broxton Hundred, Cheshire, England, was no doubt within the original limits of the Barony of Malpas, in the pass between England and Wales, according to Ormerod [2:620-629]. It is immediately adjacent to Cholmondeley, about one mile northeast from the thirteenth milestone, on the Whitchurch road from Chester.

JOHN[R] LE BELWARD was living during the reign of William Rufus.

WILLIAM[Q] LE BELWARD of Malpas, Cheshire, lived in 12 Hen. I. He married Mabel (or Mabella [Ormerod, 2:598], Mabilia ["Lettice" in T.C. Banks' *Dormant and Ext. Baronetage*, 1:203]), daughter of Robert Fitz Hugh, Baron of Malpas, who, as a natural son, held many manors under Hugh Lupus, Earl of Chester. Robert Fitz Hugh's other daughter, Letitia, married Richard Patric.

WILLIAM[P] BELWARD was lord of a moiety of the Barony of Malpas, including Egerton. According to some pedigrees he married Tanglust[M] [Tangwystl?], natural daughter of Hugh Kevelioc, Earl of Chester. However the family roll states he married Beatrix, sixth daughter of Randall, Earl of Chester. The Malpas chart in Bartrum's *Welsh Genealogies* shows William le Belward, Baron of Malpas, and Beannan, daughter of Ralph, Baron of Malpas [*cf. Vis. Cheshire*, 159], and Beatrice, daughter of Ranulf and sister of Hugh of Cyfeiliog (Hugh[N] of Kevelioc), Earl of Chester, who died in 1181. The chart showed that Ralph was son of Einion, Baron of Malpas, son of Dafydd, son of Miles of Holt, son of Gruffudd, lord of Maelor a'r Malpas, son of Owain (lord of Bromfield and Holt) ab Iago ab Idwal Foel (d. 942 [Bartrum chart 41]) ab Anarawd ap Rhodri Mawr.

Sir DAVID[O] DE MALPAS, alias Le Clerc, lord of half the Barony of Malpas by descent, and the other half by right of his wife, was dead by 44 Hen. III (1259-1260) [Ormerod, *Chester*, 2:592. Banks stated [1:204] that he married MARGARET, daughter and heir of Ralph ab Einion by his wife Beatrix, sister of Hugh Earl of Chester. Brydges described Ralph ab Einion as a person of great note and large possessions in Wales and Cheshire [171]. In the *Visitation of Cheshire, 1580*, he was called "Radulphus Baro' de Mallpas. ARMS.–*Arg. A cross palance Azure.*" Bartrum's Malpas chart identified Sir David's wife as BEANNAN[O] OF MALPAS. Ormerod [*Chester*, 2:598] identifies the wife of David as Catherine, daughter of Owain Vaghan (Owain Fychan, or Vaughn), lord of Meilor, disputing the relationship to

Ralph ab Einion [2:593], but the editor of the second edition states there may be some relationship.

PHILIP GOCH[N] LE CLERK de Malpas lived during the reign of King Edward I. He married KATHERINE[N] DE HULTON, alias Ancharett, daughter of Jorveth [Iorwerth?], alias Yawrwrit de Hulton, of Hulton in Lancashire.

6. DAVID[M] DE MALPAS, alias DE EG[G]ERTON, Lord of Egerton, Cheshire, died about 1317 [Croston, 121].

He married CECILY[L] DE THORNETON*, daughter of Sir Randle le Roter, lord of Thornton in le Moor.

From his father he received Egerton, Sandhull and other lands in Cheshire [Ormerod, *Chester*, 2:620].

He allegedly received by an undated deed from Amicia, widow of Randle[O] le Roter, alias de Thorneton, all her lands of Crowton, in frank marriage with Cecilia, her daughter. Brydges [173] stated that he married Isabel, daughter of Richard Foulshurst of Crewe, and had sons Philip, Uryan, David and Robert (but see David[K] de Eggerton, below).

Children, listed by Ormerod:

7.   i.   Philip[L], d. c. 10 Edw. II; m. Margaret[L] de Wrenbury.

       ii.   Robert, l. 28-29 Edw. I (1300).

      iii.   Ranulph, presumed son, l. 11 & 18 Edw. II (1317-1325).

      iv.   William, presumed son.

7. PHILIP[L] DE EGGERTON, alias DE MALPAS, died about 10 Edw. II (1316-1317).

He married MARGARET[L] DE WRENBURY, daughter of Richard de Wrenbury and his wife Catherine, daughter of the Lady Matilda de Courtray [Ormerod, *Chester*, 2:691; Croston, 120] (or Coudray [Ormerod, 3:393]). Richard de Wrennebury was of record 13 Edw. I (1284-1285) to 34 Edw. I (1305-1306) concerning the manor of Wrenbury, and had son John who married Matild, who married second Humfrey Tromewyn in or before 17 Edw. III (1343-1344), and a second son Richard, father of Philip [Ormerod, 3:393, 395]. Margaret sued for dower 10 & 11 Edw. II (1316-1318).

He was Sheriff of Cheshire 23 and 24 Edw. I (1295-1297), and 2 Edw. II (1308-1309).

He had lands in Wordhull in frank marriage by an undated deed from Catherine (——) de Wrenbury.

Children, listed by Ormerod:

8.   i.   David[K], m. Isabella de Fulleshurst.

       ii.   Urian, Lord of Caldecote, l. 15 Edw. II; m. Amelia de Caldecote, dau. and heiress of David de Caldecote.

      iii.   Sir Brian de Malpas, a knight of Rhodes (of the Order of St. John of Jerusalem, according to Brydges), l. 8 Edw. III (1334-1335).

      iv.   Richard, killed Robert fitz Madog de Eggerton in 1307.

      v.   Philip.

      vi.   John, l. 1301.

     vii.   daughter, m. David de Malpas of Hampton.

    viii.   William, presumed son, not listed by Brydges.

8. DAVID[K] DE EGGERTON, lord of Eggerton, was Sheriff of Cheshire in 7 Edw. III (1333-1334).

He married ISABELLA[K] DE FULLESHURST, daughter of Richard de Fulleshurst (or Fouleshurst), Lord of Crewe.

He was Sheriff of Cheshire 5 Edw. II (1311-1312) and 7 Edw. III (1333) [Brydges].

Children, listed by Ormerod:

9.　　i.　Philip[J] le Longe, m. (1) c. 9 Edw. II (1315-1316) Elen[J] de St. Pierre, m. (2) 29 Edw. III (1355-1356) Maud Vernon.
　　　ii.　David, l. 1369-1370; d. before 19 Ric. II (1395-1396); no issue.
　　　iii.　Urian, Lord of Egerton, d. before 19 Ric. II; m. Amelia de Warburton.
　　　iv.　Bryan, prob. d. young.
　　　v.　Robert, prob. d. young.
　　　vi.　Margaret, l. unm. 29 Edw. III (1355-1356).
　　　vii.　Alice.
　　　viii.　Isabel.
　　　ix.　Elianor.

9. PHILIP[J] LE LONGE DE EGGERTON, occurred in the plea rolls 23-24 Edw. III (1349-1351), and his *inquisition post mortem* was held 36 Edw. III (1362-1363).

He married first, the contract dated 9 Edw. II (1315-1316), ELEN[J] DE ST. PIERRE*, daughter of John[K] de St. Pierre (also St. Peter, Sancto Pietro or Sampier); the marriage contract, which brought Philip eighty marks, was dated at Egerton the Monday after the Epiphany in 9 Edw. II (1315-1316).

He married second, 29 Edw. III (1355-1356) Maud (or Matilda) Vernon, daughter of Richard Vernon of Shipbrook and widow of William Venables [Croston, 122].

He was Lord of Egerton and Wychehalgh, and obtained by fine lands in Egerton from John fitz William fitz Madoc (or Madog) de Eggerton in 12 Edw. III. In 20 Edw. III he gave to Geoffrey de Denston and John de Wygynton, chaplains, the manor of Egerton and Wychehalgh, with all his lands and tenements in Bykerton, Malpas, Chydelowe, Wygelond, Chester, Hole and Over. The same chaplains released these holdings to Philip's son David and his wife Isabel that same year. In the following year Philip paid David and Isabella £20 rent.

According to the *inquisition post mortem* he died seized of fifteen acres of land in Wordhull which he had bought from Hugh de Wordhull. The other holdings were mentioned, including Wichalgh.

Children, listed by Ormerod [2:598]:

　　　i.　David[I], d. 35 Edw. III (1361-1362); m. before 20 Edw. III (1346-1347) Isabel[K] Venables, dau. of Sir Hugh[L] Venables of Kinderton; no issue.
　*　ii.　Ellen, claimant of two-fourths of a moiety of the barony of Malpas in 1368 and 1369, finally sole heiress; m. Sir William[I] Brereton.
　　　iii.　Isabel[la], coheiress, d. 19 Ric. II (1395-1396); m. (1) Robert de Bulkeley of Eaton, m. (2) John[J] Venables, m. (3) Sir John Delves; no issue; she recovered a moiety of a fourth of the barony of Malpas from John de Brunham, trustee of the Cokesays, in 1363, and another moiety of a fourth from John, son of Sir John Sutton, in 1368.

§ § §

D'ENGAINE

This family was treated by G.W. Watson in Cokayne [5:71-75]. The family arms were *Gules, crusilly* and a *fesse dancette Or.*

1. RICHARD[S] ENGAINE was presented in a chart of the Engaines and their connections in *CP* [5:between 72-73] as the grandfather of Fulk de Lisures.

He married second Matilda Buelot (daughter of Baldwin Buelot [or Bullers] of Bulwick), who was widow of Richard Fitz Urse.

In 11 Stephen (1146) he was forester of Northamptonshire [Baker, *Northampton*, 1:9].

Child:

    2.   i.   Viel[R], lived 1130.

2. VIEL (or Vitalis)[R] ENGAINE was of Laxton and Pitchley, Northamptonshire, and lived in 1130.

He married ALICE[R] LIZURES*, daughter and heiress of William Lizures of Wansford, who was son of Fulk Lizures, who gave tithes to Thorney Abbey during the reign of Henry I. In turn, Fulk was son of William Lizures, son of Fulk Lizures (or Lisoriis), who came to England with William the Conqueror. Alice Lizures held Abington in Spelho Hundred in Northamptonshire in dower, and married second Humphrey Bassingburn.

Children, listed in the register of knights of the Abbey of Peterborough [Baker, *Northampton*, 1:7]:

    3.   i.   Richard[Q], d. 1177; m. Margery, who was l. 21 May 1196, having m. (2) Geoffrey le Breton.

        ii.   Fulk de Lisures, dead 1185, of Benefield and Abington; m. Adelis d'Auberville, who was aged 50 in 1185 and l. Michaelmas 1189.

3. RICHARD[Q] ENGAINE, of Laxton and Pytchley, was dead in 1177.

He married MARGERY[Q] FITZ RICHARD, who was aged 50 in 1185 and was living 21 May 1196. She married second Geoffrey le Breton.

Child:

    4.   i.   Richard[P], d. 23 April 1209; m. Sara[P] de Chesney, who d. 1222.

4. RICHARD[P] ENGAINE, of Laxton and Pytchley, died 23 April 1209.

He married SARA[P] DE CHESNEY (daughter of Richard de Chesney of Horsford and Colne, who died shortly before Michaelmas 1174), lady of Colne, who was dead in April 1222.

Horsford and Colne are in county Norfolk. Colne is a place name in Lancashire, Cambridgeshire and Essex. Richard de Chesney had daughters: Margery, Lady of Horsford, who died shortly before 7 Jan. 1230/1, having married second Robert Fitz Roger of Warkworth and Clavering, who died shortly before 22 Nov. 1214; Clemence, Lady of Hoo, who was living 3 Feb. 1237/8, having married Jordan, seigneur de Sacquenville (no issue), and Sara, Lady of Colne, above.

Children:

    5.   i.   Viel[O], d. 22 Oct. 1248; m. Rohese.

        ii.   Richard, bur. Huntingdon; d. unm.

5. VIEL[O] ENGAINE, of Laxton, Pytchley and Colne, died 22 Oct. 1248.

He married ROHESE, who died before him.

His lands had been restored by writs dated 23 or 24 Sept. 1217. On 5 April 1218 he had livery of the manor of Upminster, Essex, excepting the dower of Ada, widow of William de Curtenay. He recovered a moiety of the manor of Worle, Somerset, from William de Cantelou, and had livery of a moiety of the manor of Badmondisfield, Suffolk, on 11 Dec. 1241, after Hilaire Trussebot (widow of Robert de Boulers) died.

He was a knight of the Abbey of Ramsey, holding ten librates of land in Dillington of the Abbot.

Children:

        i.   Viel[N], d. before Oct. 1248; unm.

  ii. Henry, aged 30 (or more) when his father died [*CP*, 5:71c]; d. 28 Jan.
    1271/2; his father's heir.

  iii. William, d. in or after 1244; no issue; served Army of Scotland in 1244.

6. iv. John, fourth son, d. 5 Jan. 1296/7; m. Joan de Greinville.

  6. JOHN[N] D'ENGAYNE, of Colne Engaine in Essex, and Pytchley and Laxton in
Northamptonshire, died 5 Jan. 1296/7, and was buried in Fineshade Priory by Blatherwycke, Northants.

  He married JOAN[N] DE GREINVILLE of Hallaton (or Halton) in Leicestershire, who died
after 2 Nov. 1305. She was daughter and heir of Gilbert de Greinville of Hallaton, who was
living in 1243, and his wife Joyouse, who married secondly Richard de Muntfichet of
Stansted, Essex, who was dead in Jan. 1267/8. In court during Easter Term 49 Hen. III,
it was stated that she was descended from Eustace de Greville.

  He served the Abbey of Ramsey in the Army of Wales in 1245.

  He was his brother Henry's heir; John was aged 40 and more when his brother died in
Jan. 1271/2. He also had lands in Blatherwycke and Bulwick, Northants., Hunsdon in
Suffolk, and elsewhere. On 5 April 1274 they had livery of the manors of Prested and
Theydon Garnon in Essex, and on 16 Aug. lands in Byfield, Northants., which she had
inherited from her mother.

  He did homage to the Abbot of Burgh in 1275, and was in the Army of Wales in 1287.
Summonses to military service were dated from 12 Dec. 1276 to 16 Dec. 1295. On 26 Jan.
1296/7 he was summoned to attend King Edward I at Salisbury.

  Children, no doubt of several:

    i. Sir John[M], d. 28 Sept. 1322; m. Ellen[L] (who d. shortly before 2 June
      1339), dau. of Sir Robert Fitz Roger of Warkworth, Northumberland
      and Clavering, Essex, and Margery de Zouche.

    ii. Sir Nicholas, m. Anice de Faucomberge.

 * iii. Joan, m. (1) Walter Fitz Robert, who d. 1293, m. (2) Adam[M] de Welle[s],
      who d. 1311.

§ § §

DE ERDINGTON

Further research into the history of Warwickshire might be helpful.

  1. THOMAS[N] DE ERDINGTON of Erdington, in Aston parish, Warwickshire, died at
Wigornia 20 March 1217/8 [*CP*, 5:85d].

  He left a widow, ROHESE de Cocfelde.

  He was granted the manors of Wellington and Shawbury, Shropshire, 3 Nov. 1212, by
King John, and confirmed the honor of Montgomery, with the manor of Badmondisfield,
Suffolk, which Thomas had acquired from Stephen de Stanton and his son Robert on 18
Jan. 1214/5.

  Son and heir, given by Cokayne [5:86]:

  2. i. Giles[M], d. shortly before 10 Jan. 1278/9.

  2. GILES[M] DE ERDINGTON died shortly before 10 Jan. 1268/9 [*CP*, 5:85d].

  Eyton [*Ant. Shropshire*, 2:223] mentioned that on 19 July 1260 Giles de Erdinton was
"commissioned to try an action of *novel disseizin* which John de Pres had brought against
William de Harcourt and others, for a tenement in Thong." On 17 Aug. 1260 he tried a

suit of *novel disseizin* which William le Fraunceys had brought against Robert Beumys concerning a tenement in Stanwey.

Son and heir, given by Cokayne:

    3.   i. Sir Henry[L], d. shortly before 26 March 1282; m. Maud[L] de Somery.

3. Sir HENRY[L] DE ERDINGTON of Erdington, in Aston parish in Warwickshire, Shawbury in Shropshire, Corfe Mullen in Dorset, Barrow-on-Soar in Leicestershire, and Olney in Buckinghamshire, died shortly before 26 March 1282.

He married MAUD[M] DE SOMERY[+] of Dudley in Worcestershire, who married second Sir William de Byfield, who was dead by 24 May 30 Edw. I (1302). He had held a fourth part of the manor of Olney of the King in chief, as well as Barrow-on-Soar, Leics., and Great Tew, Oxon, by right of his wife Maud.

Children, mentioned by Cokayne [5:85]:

        i. Giles[K], d. a minor in the King's ward; no issue.

    4.   ii. Sir Henry, b. say 1274; l. 1341/2; m. before 15 June 1315 Joan[L] de Wolvey.

4. Sir HENRY[K] DE ERDINGTON of Erdington in Warwickshire, and Shawbury, Corfe Mullen, Barrow-on-Soar and Olney, born say 1274, was living in 1341/2.

He married before 15 June 1315 JOAN[L] DE WOLVEY* of Wolvey, Warks.

He gave homage to the King and had livery of his father's lands on 21 July 1295, and had livery of his mother's on 9 July 1302, following the death of his stepfather. He was knighted by the Prince of Wales at Westminster on 22 May 1306, and served as Knight of the Shire for Leicester in 1309. There are records of his being summoned to military service from May 25 Edw. I (1297) to 28 July 11 Edw. II (1317), to a Council in May 17 Edw. II (1324), and to Parliament 22 Jan. 9 Edw. III (1335/6).

He had acquired a fourth of Barrow-on-Soar from Ralph Bassett of Drayton, and one-fourth from John Lestraunge (LeStrange) of Knockin, but afterwards his son Giles entered this manor without livery.

Son and heir [*CP*, 5:86]:

    5.   i. Sir Giles[J], l. 10 June 1359; m. Elizabeth[J] de Tolthorpe.

5. Sir GILES[J] DE ERDINGTON, Lord Shawbury, was living 10 June 1359.

He married ELIZABETH[J] DE TOLTHORPE*.

On 20 June 1343 he was pardoned for having acquired his father's manor of Shawbury without a license. He was pardoned again on 11 June 1345 for not having taken up knighthood by the most recent Feast of St. Lawrence. As a member of the retinue of Sir John de Montgomery he served the King in Flanders in 1346, but returned to England before 20 Jan. 1346/7 due to a severe illness.

On 1 Dec. 1352 he was given an exemption for life from being made to serve on assizes and juries, or being appointed mayor, sheriff or escheator against his will.

He granted the manor of Shawbury, without license, to Robert[J] Corbet of Moreton Corbet, but was on 20 Nov. 1359 he was allowed to complete the transaction upon payment of a fine of £10.

The name was spelled "Eardiston" by Eyton.

Children, the first from Cokayne [5:87]:

        i. Sir Thomas[I], d. 28 Mar. 1395; m. before 24 Jan. 1357/8 Margaret[I] Corbet, who d. 14 Jan. 1404/5.

    *   ii. Margaret, d. June 1395; m. Roger[I] Corbet.

§ § §

DE FERRERS OR DE FERRIÈRES

This account of the line of the Earls of Derby is based on Cokayne's *Complete Peerage* [4:190-199], with additions from Vernon Norr's work.

WALKELIN[U] DE FERRIÈRES sided with Philip Augustus of France [Eyton, 4:208] and was slain in the civil wars which occurred in Normandy during Duke William's youth. His name has also been recorded as Gaulchline.

HENRY[T] DE FERRIÈRES, sire de Ferrières and Chambrais in Normandy, was buried in Tutbury in Staffordshire. His wife was named BERTHA.

ROBERT[S] DE FERRIÈRES, 1st Earl of Derby, died in 1139. He married HAWISE[S] DE VITRÉ, daughter of Andre, seigneur de Vitré in Brittany, by Agnes, daughter of Robert, Count of Mortain.

ROBERT[R] DE FERRIÈRES, 2nd Earl of Derby or Earl of Ferrières, died before 1160, and was buried in Merevale Abbey, Warwickshire, wrapped in an oxhide. He married MARGARET[R] PEVEREL, daughter and heir of William Peverel of Nottingham.

WILLIAM[Q] DE FERRIÈRES, 3rd Earl of Derby, died while on crusade at the siege of Acre, Palestine, before 21 Oct. 1190. He married SYBIL[P] DE BRAIOSE, who was living 5 Feb. 1227/8; she had remarried Adam de Port of Basing [*CP*, 11:319].

WILLIAM[P] DE FERRIÈRES, 4th Earl of Derby, died, after suffering long with the gout, on 22 Sept. 1247. He married in 1192, AGNES[M] OF CHESTER, sister and coheir of Ranulph de Blundeville, Earl of Chester and Lincoln, and third daughter of Hugh de Kevelioc, Earl of Chester, by Bertrade, daughter of Simon de Montfort, Count d'Evreux. They had livery of her share of her brother's lands, including the castle and manor of Chartley, Staffordshire, and the castle and vill of West Derby, Lancashire, on 22 Nov. 1232. She died 2 Nov. 1247, and the King had livery of her inheritance.

7. WILLIAM[O] DE FERRERS, 5th Earl of Derby, born about 1193, died at Evington near Leicester, 24 or 28 March 1254, and was buried at Merevale Abbey on the 31st.

He married first, in her father's lifetime, thus before 14 May 1219, SIBYL[O] LE MARSHAL[+], third daughter of William le Marshal, Earl of Pembroke, and his wife Isabel de Clare, daughter and heir of Richard de Clare, Earl of Pembroke.

He married second, in or before 1238, MARGARET[K] DE QUINCY[+], first daughter and coheir of Roger de Quency, Earl of Winchester, by his first wife, Helen de Galloway, first daughter and coheir of Alan de Galloway, Constable of Scotland.

He accompanied King Henry III to France in April 1230, and was Constable of Bolsover Castle from 28 Feb. 1234/5 to 3 July 1236. He paid homage to the King and had livery of Chartley Castle and the rest of his mother's lands on 10 Nov. 1247. He was invested as Earl 2 Feb. 1247/8, at Westminster, and attended Parliament that month.

He suffered with gout from his youth, and his death was due to the affects of injuries sustained when he was accidently thrown from the litter in which he was carried into a river.

He was described by Norr [100] as an "old widower" whose youngest daughter, by his first wife, Alianor, married Margaret's father Roger when he was an old widower; thus Alianor and Margaret were each other's stepmother, making each of them the stepmother of her own stepmother!

Children, by first wife, from chart by Watson [*CP*, 4:199]:

*   i.   Agnes[N], d. 11 May 1290; m. (1) William[N] de Vescy (or Vesey) of Alnwick and Malton, who d. by 22 Oct. 1253, m. (2) Sir Robert de Muscegros, who d. 1280.

      ii.   Isabel, bur. 11 Nov. 1260; m. (1) Gilbert Basset of Wycombe, who d. by 31 July 1241, m. (2) as his second wife, c. 1243, Reynold de Mohun of Dunster, who d. 20 Jan. 1257/8.

      iii.   Maud, d. 12 March 1298/9; m. (1) Simon de Kyme of Kyme, who d. by 30 July 1248, no issue, m. (2) William le Fort (or le Fortibus) de Vivonne in Poitou, of Chewton, m. (3) Aimery, vicomte de Rochechouart in Poitou, who l. 1284.

      iv.   Sibyl, m. Sir Francis de Bohun of Midhurst, Sussex, who d. 14 Sept. 1273 [*cf.* G.W. Watson, *The Genealogist*, n.s., 28:1].

\+   v.   Joan, dead in Oct. 1267; m. (1) John de Mohun of Dunster, m. (2) Robert[O] Aguillon of Watton and Perching as his first wife [*CP*, 9:21].

      vi.   Agatha, d. 22 May 1306; m. Hugh de Mortimer of Chelmarsh, who was dead in June 1275.

      vii.   Alianore, bur. 26 Oct. 1274; m. (1) William de Vaux of Tharston and Wisset, who bur. 5 Dec. 1252, no issue, m. (2) as his third wife Roger[L] de Quency, Earl of Winchester, who d. 25 April 1264, m. (3) as his second wife Roger de Leyburne of Elham, who was bur. 5 Nov. 1271.

      viii.   John, d. before parents; m. Cicily; no issue [Norr, 68].

Children, by second wife:

8.   ix.   Robert, b. c. 1239; d. 1279; m. (1) Mary de Lusignan, m. (2) 26 June 1269 Alianore[M] de Bohun; Earl of Derby.

9.   x.   William, b. c. 1240; d. 1287; m. (1) Anne, m. (2) before 18 Feb. 1290/1 Eleanor de Lovaine.

*   xi.   Joan, d. 19 March 1309/10, bur. St. Augustine's, Bristol; m. 1267 Thomas[K] de Berkeley [*CP*, 5:320 chart, 14:320].

8.   ROBERT[N] DE FERRERS, 6th Earl of Derby, born about 1239, died in 1279, and was most probably buried in the Priory of St. Thomas at Stafford.

He married first, the contract dated 26 July 1249, in Westminster, Mary de Lusignan, the King's niece, and daughter of Hugh XI le brun, comte de la Marche, sire de Lusignan in Poitou, by Yolande, daughter of Pierre Mauclerc, Duke of Brittany. She died without a male heir.

He married second, 26 (or 27 [*CP*, 5:320 chart]) June 1269, ALIANORE[M] DE BOHUN[+], who died 20 Feb. 1313/4, and was buried in Walden Abbey [*CP*, 4:202]. She was the daughter of Humphrey de Bohun VI and his first wife, Eleanor de Braiose.

The wardship of his lands was granted, 15 April 1254, to Prince Edward, who sold it in 1257 to the Queen and Pierre de Savoie. Robert had livery of his lands in 1260 and then destroyed Tutbury Priory. When the barons went to war in 1263 he seized three of Prince Edward's castles, and on 29 Feb. 1263/4 he captured Worcester, destroying the town and Jewry. However, in April or May Prince Edward retaliated by wasting Robert's lands and demolishing Tutbury Castle. Robert was absent from the battle of Lewes, but in Nov. 1264 he used 20,000 foot and many horsemen to defeat the royal forces near Chester. On 24 Dec. 1264 he was ordered to deliver Peak Castle to Simon de Montfort; the same day he was summoned to Montfort's parliament, where he was accused of trespasses and sent to the Tower by Simon.

On 5 Dec. 1265 he was admitted to the King's grace and had a full pardon for all offenses comitted up to that day on payment of 1500 marks and a certain gold drinking cup.

However, within a few months he rebelled again, joining John d'Eiville, Baldwin Wake and others in devastating the Midlands. They were surprised at Chesterfield on 15 May 1266 and he was sent to prison in Windsor Castle for nearly three years. On 12 July 1266 the honour of Derby was granted to Edmund, the King's son. Under the Dictum of Kenilworth his lands were subject to the penalty of seven year's purchase, and on 1 May 1269 Edmund was ordered to restore his lands to him upon payment of £50,000, which Robert could not make. He lost an action to regain them in 1274, having taken possession of Chartley Castle in 1273 while the King was abroad. Expelled from Chartley, he was allowed to recover the manor of Holbrook in 1274/5, and the manor (but not the castle) of Chartley in 1275, as heir of Thomas de Ferrers of Chartley [*CP*, 4:201c].

Children, by second wife:

10. i.   John^M, b. Cardiff, Wales, 20 June 1271; d. Gascony Aug. 1312; m. Hawise^M de Muscegros, who m. (3) Sir John^L de Bures.

ii.   Alianore, bur. Dunmow Priory; m. 1289 Sir Robert Fitz Walter of Woodham [*CP*, 5:320 chart], who d. 18 Jan. 1325/6, as his second wife.

9. Sir WILLIAM^N FERRERS of Groby, Leicestershire, born about 1240, died shortly before 20 Dec. 1287.

He married first ANNE, who was said to be a daughter of Sir Hugh le Despencer of Ryhall in Rutland, Loughborough in Leicestershire, and Parlington in Yorkshire, by Aline Basset, daughter and heir of Sir Philip Basset [*CP*, 5:322 chart, 340-342; *Scots Peerage*, 3:149].

He married second, by fine 18 Feb. 1290/1, Eleanor de Lovaine, daughter of Sir Matthew de Lovaine of Little Easton, Essex. She married second, a fine levied 18 Feb. 1290/1, Sir William de Douglass, who was committed to the Tower of London 12 Oct. 1297 [*SP*, 3:140], and died before 24 Jan. 1298/9, having abducted her from the manor of Ellen la Zouche at Trenant in Haddington, Scotland, before 28 Jan. 1288/9 [*CP*, 5:341]. She married third, before 6 Oct. 1305, Sir William Bagot of Hide and Patshull, Staffordshire. She was recorded as his widow on 3 May 1326.

He held lands in Groby in Leicestershire; Newbottle in Northamptonshire; Woodham Ferris, Stebbing and Fairsted in Essex, and Bolton-le-Moors in Lancashire.

He was taken prisoner at Northampton on 5 or 6 April 1264, and was committed by Prince Edward to the custody of Roger de Layburne, who demanded an excessive ransom; it was not paid as King Henry III pardoned him 11 July 1266. He was with King Edward I in Wales in 1282. He was summoned to military service from 18 March 1263/4 to 14 March 1282/3, to a military council on 14 June 1283, and to attend the King at Shrewsbury on 28 June 1283.

Child, by first wife:

11. i.   William^M, son and heir, b. Yoxale, Staffs., 30 Jan. 1271/2; d. 20 March 1324/5; m. (1) Ellen^M de Savage, m. (2) Margaret de Segrave.

10. Sir JOHN^M DE FERRERS, 1st Baron Ferrers of Chartley, Staffordshire, was born in Cardiff, Wales, 20 June 1271, and died in Gascony, France, in Aug. 1312, of poisoning, it was said [*CP*, 5:309].

He married, between 2 Feb. 1297/8 and 13 Sept. 1300, as her first husband, HAWISE^M DE MUSCEGROS* of Charleton and Norton, Staffordshire. She had been espoused to William de Mortemer, who died shortly before 30 June 1297, the marriage not having been consummated. She married second Sir John^L de Bures, who died at Boddington on 21 or 22 Dec. 1350. She was of record 24 June 1240, but died before her second husband.

The King took his homage on 21 Nov. 1293, and he had livery of lands inherited from his grandmother Margaret, Countess of Derby. On 6 Aug. 1294 he had livery of Bugbrooke, over the objection of John Bigod [CP, 5:306c], as heir of Cecily de Ferrers, sometime wife of Godfrey de Beaumont. He was the principal supporter of the Earls of Hereford and Norfolk in their quarrel with King Edward I in 1297. He was summoned to military service from May 1297 to 28 May 1311.

About 1298 he petitioned the Pope for a dispensation to permit him to borrow money from prelates and other spiritual persons to redeem his lands, but on 10 Aug. 1301 he was prohibited by the king, under penalty of forfeiting all that he could forfeit, from pursuing the case in Court Christian. On 2 Dec. 1301 he was called into the King's Court to show cause why he had called on Edmund, Earl of Lancaster, to answer in Court Christian.

He was summoned to attend the Coronation of Edward II on 18 Jan. 1307/8, to a Council on 8 Jan. 1308/9, and to Parliament from 6 Feb. 1296/7 to 19 Feb. 1311. He served in Scotland in 1298 and 1303, and was Constable of the Army in Scotland in 1306. On 24 Jan. 1311/2 he was appointed seneschal of Gascony. He then fell into a serious disagreement with Amanieu, sire d'Albret, but before this problem could be resolved in court he died.

In addition to Chartley, he held lands at Southoe and Keyston in Huntingdonshire, and Bugbrooke in Northamptonshire, as the first Baron of Chartley [CP, 5:305].

In 1329 and 1330 she and her second husband dealt with nearly all of her estates.

Children, listed by Watson [CP, 5:310 and chart between 320-321]:

	i.	John[L], of Southoe and Keyston, d. before 23 July 1324; no issue.
12.	ii.	Robert, b. 25 March 1309; d. 28 Aug. 1350; m. (1) before Oct. 1330 Margaret, m. (2) Joan de la Mote.
	iii.	Perronelle, l. 20 April 1331; m. Richard de Monemuthe of Rowley Regis, who was slain in Nottingham Castle 19-20 Oct. 1330.
*	iv.	Eleanor, m. before 21 May 1329 Sir Thomas[L] de Lathom of Lathom and Knowsley in Lancashire, who d. 17 Sept. 1370.

11. Sir WILLIAM[M] FERRERS, 1st Baron Ferrers of Groby in Leicestershire, was born in Yoxale, Staffordshire, 30 Jan. 1271/2, baptized there, and died 20 March 1324/5, aged 53.

He married first ELLEN[M] DE SAVAGE, who died after 9 Feb. 1317, possibly daughter of Sir John Savage.

He married second Margaret de Segrave, who was said to be the daughter of Sir John[I] de Segrave of Chacombe (or Chaucombe, Chalcombe), Northamptonshire, Lord Segrave, by Christine de Plessy, daughter of Sir Hugh de Plessy of Hooknorton and Kidlington, Oxfordshire. Margaret was living 9 Feb. 1316/7 [CP, 5:332 chart, 343-344, 11:605-608].

King Edward I took his homage 17 March 1292/3. He was summoned to military service from 29 June 1294 to 1 May 1325. In Aug. 1295 he was beyond the seas serving the Duke of Brabant. Called to attend the King at Salisbury on 26 Jan. 1296/7, he served in Scotland in the battle of Falkirk 22 July 1298, and at the siege of Caerlaverock in July 1300. He participated in the barons letter to the Pope on 12 Feb. 1300/1, and was serving in Scotland at various times from 1303 to 1311. He attended the Coronation of King Edward II, 18 Jan. 1307/8, and on 1 Nov. 1317 he was appointed joint Constable of Somerton in Lincolnshire. His summonses to Partliament dated from 29 Dec. 1299 to 24 Sept. 1324. On 14 Feb. 1321/2 he was ordered to accompany King Edward II against the contrariants.

Children [Weis, AR7, 58:32]:

	i.	Henry[L], 2nd Baron Ferrers of Groby, b. c. 1294; d. Groby, Leics., 15 Sept. 1343; m. before 20 Feb. 1330/1 Isabel[M] de Verdun.

* ii. Anne, d. 8 Aug. 1347; m. Groby 20 April 1335 Sir Edward[L] Despencer, who d. 30 Sept. 1342.

12. Sir ROBERT[L] DE FERRERS of Chartley, Staffordshire, was born 25 March 1309, and died 28 Aug. 1350 [CP, 5:312].

He married first, by 20 Oct. 1330, MARGARET, who died after Aug. 1333.

He married second Joan de la Mote, Lady of Willisham, Suffolk, and St. Pancras, Middlesex, who died in London 29 June 1375.

He was of record in Sept. 1325 as being about to go overseas with the King, and on 13 Aug. 1327, although he was still a minor, the King took his homage and gave him livery of his brother's lands as a result of his recent good services in northern parts. He was summoned for military service against the Scots in 1335, and in 1338 the King granted him Pirehill Hundred in Staffordshire, at pleasure. He served in Flanders in 1338-1339, and was appointed a justice in 1340, when he was a banneret. Summoned to Council 25 Feb. 1341/2, he was a member of the King's retinue in Brittany in Oct. 1342. On 26 April 1344 he was appointed Vice Admiral of the Fleet, and in Oct. 1345 he was with the Earl of Derby at the battle of Auberoche in Périgord. He served in the battle of Crécy and the siege of Calais in 1346. He attended the tournament at Lichfield 9 April 1347 as one of the eleven knights of the King's Chamber [CP, 14:319-320]. On 13 May 1347 he received a pardon for all homicides, robberies and any consequent outlawries for his good services in France.

Child, by first wife:
13.   i. John[K], b. Southoe, Hunts., on or c. 10 Aug. 1333; d. Najera, Spain, 3 April 1367; m. 1349 Elizabeth[K] de Stafford, widow of Fulk[J] le Strange.

Child, by second wife:
    ii. Sir Robert, of Willisham, b. c. 1350; d. c. 31 Dec. 1380; m. c. 27 Sept. 1369 Elizabeth[l] le Botiller of Wem and Oversley [Weis, AR7, 62:33], who d. 19 June 1411, having m. (2) John Say, m. (3) Thomas Molington [Baker, Northampton, 1:123].

13. Sir JOHN[K] DE FERRERS, 3rd Baron Chartley, born and baptized in Southoe, Huntingdonshire, on or about 10 Aug. 1333, was slain at Najera, Spain, 3 April 1367, according to a poem by Chandos Herald, lines 3443-5 [CP, 5:314b].

He married as her second husband, by license dated 19 Oct. 1349, ELIZABETH[J] DE STAFFORD*, who was born about 1337 and died 7 Aug. 1375; she was the widow of Fulk[J] le Strange, Lord Strange of Blackmere (who died of plague in Aug. 1349 at the age of 18), and married third Sir Reynold de Cobham, Lord Cobham of Sterborough, Surrey, as his first wife. He died 6 July 1403.

On 13 Dec. 1353 the King took his homage and he had livery of his grandmother's lands. He accompanied the King in the invasion of France Oct. 1359 to 1360, and in the invasion of Navarre in 1367. He also petitioned the Duke of Lancaster to restore to him the lands forfeited by Robert, Earl of Derby, and other properties [CP, 5:313].

Son and heir:
14.   i. Robert[J], b. 31 Oct. 1357 or 1359; died 12/13 March 1412/3; m. (1) Elizabeth, m. (2) Margaret[J] le Despencer, who d. 3 Nov. 1415.

14. Sir ROBERT[J] DE FERRERS, 4th Baron Chartley, of Chartley in Staffordshire, was born in Staffordshire 31 Oct. 1357 or 1359 [CP, 5:315d], died 12 or 13 March 1412/3, and was buried at Merevale Abbey, Staffordshire, where there is a brass.

He married first, after 16 Sept. 1376, Elizabeth, who was living 13 Jan. 1378/9.

He married second MARGARET[J] LE DESPENCER*, who died 3 Nov. 1415 and was buried at Merevale Abbey, where there is a brass.

On 13 Jan. 1378/9 the home of Sir Robert and Elizabeth at Southoe in Huntingdonshire was entered by Hanekyn Fauconer of Cardington in Bedfordshire, who mistreated and abducted Elizabeth and stole her clothing and jewelry; a pardon was issued for this crime on 7 Feb. 1381/2 at the instance of Thomas de Holand, the King's brother [CP, 5:316c].

King Richard II took his homage and fealty on 23 July 1381.

Children, charted in CP [between 5:321-322]:

15.   i.   Edmund[I], d. 17 Dec. 1435; m. Ellen[I] de la Roche, who m. (2) Philip Chetwynd.

         ii.   Philippe, bur. Green's Norton [Baker, Northampton, 1:123]; m. by 16 Dec. 1421 Sir Thomas Greene of Boughton, who d. 18 Jan. 1461/2, having m. (2) Marine Bellars [Faris, PA2, 158].

         iii.   Thomas, l. April 1416.

         iv.   Edward, d. unm. at Harfleur, will dated 30 Sept. 1415, proved 6 Feb. 1415/6, to be bur. Church of St. Martin, Harfleur.

15.   Sir EDMUND[I] DE FERRERS, 5th Baron Chartley, was born about 1387, and died 17 Dec. 1435.

He married ELLEN[I] DE LA ROCHE*, who died 4 Nov. 1440, Lady of Castle Bromwich, Worcestershire, having married second Sir Philip Chetwynd [CP, 5:317-319] of Ingestre, Staffordshire (as his first wife), who died without issue on 10 May 1444.

He had livery of his father's lands on 14 April 1413. Soon after he carried on a private war, with the help of his brothers Thomas and Edward, against the Erdeswikes of Sandon, near Chartley. He received a pardon on 24 Jan. 1414/5 for all treasons, murders and other offenses committed up to 8 Dec. 1414, except for any murders committed after 19 Nov. 1414 [CP, 5:317g]. He went to France with King Henry V in Aug. 1415 and was at the siege of Harfleur, and then in the battle of Agincourt on 25 Oct. 1415. He was in the relief for Harfleur with the Duke of Bedford in Aug. 1416. Accompanying Henry V to France again in Aug. 1417, he was at the siege of Rouen from July 1418 to Jan. 1418/9 in the division commanded by the Earl of Huntingdon. He was also in the siege of Melun from July to Nov. 1420, and that of Meaux from Oct. 1421 to May 1422.

Children, listed by Norr [68], with the last by Faris [PA2, 216]:

16.   i.   William[H], d. 9 June 1450; m. Elizabeth[H] Belknap.

         ii.   Joan, m. c. 1431 John de Clinton.

         iii.   Henry [CP, 5:320a].

         iv.   Richard.

         v.   Edmund.

         vi.   Margaret, prob. dau., m. c. 1434 John Beauchamp, K.G., of Powick.

16.   Sir WILLIAM[H] DE FERRERS, 6th Baron Chartley, was born about 1412, and died 9 June 1450.

He married ELIZABETH[H] BE[A]LKNAP*, who died 28 May 1471, having in May 1455 conveyed to feoffees the manors she held for life, in dower or otherwise.

He had livery of his father's lands on 9 Feb. 1435/6 [CP, 5:320], when he was aged 23 and more.

Daughter:

*   i.   Anne[G], b. c. Nov. 1438; d. 9 Jan. 1468/9; m. before 26 Nov. 1446 Sir Walter[G] Devereux, who was killed at Bosworth 22 Aug. 1485, and attainted, having m. (2) Jane Verdun (her surname omitted in Faris

[*PA2*, 139]), who m. (2) Thomas Vaughan, and m. (3) Sir Edward Blount of Sodington, Worcs., who d. 6 July 1499, m. (4) Thomas Poyntz.

§ § §

DE FIENNES

EUSTACHE[S] married ADELLE DE SELVESLE, dame d'Ardes.

CONAN[R], of record in 1059-1207, married ALIX DE BOURNONVILLE.

EUSTACE II[Q] DE FIENNES was Baron of Fiennes. He married MARGARET[Q] DE GUINES, who died in 1187, daughter of Arnulf II, Count of Guines, who died in 1169.

ENGUERRAND[P] DE FIENNES died in 1189. He married SYBIL[P] DE BOULOGNE, heiress of Eaton.

GUILLAUME (or William)[O] DE FIENNES died in 1241. He married first Isabel N. He married second, about 1203, Agnes de Dammartin, daughter of Alberic II, Count of Dammartin, who died in 1200.

4. INGELRAM[N] (or Enguerrand) DE FIENNES, seigneur de Fienes, was of Buckinghamshire, and flourished in 1249 and 1270 [Baker, *Northampton*, 2:273].

He married ISABEL[N] DE CONDÉ, daughter of Jacques, seigneur de Condé, Bailleul and Moriammez in Hainault (now in northern France).

Condé and Bailleul are now in France. Condé is about twenty-five kilometers west of Mons, Belgium, and Bailleul is about thirty kilometers northwest of Lille.

Children:

5. i. William[M], d. in the battle of Courtrain, West Flanders; m. 1269 Blanche[M] de Brienne.

+ ii. Maud, d. 1321, bur. Walden Abbey, Essex; m. (1) 20 July 1275 Humphrey[M] de Bohun VII, who d. 31 Dec. 1298, m. (2) John de Vesey.

5. Sir WILLIAM[M] DE FIENNES, of Wendover, Buckinghamshire, died in the battle of Courtrain in West Flanders, in 1302.

He married in 1269 BLANCHE[M] DE BRIENNE, Lady of Loupland, who died in 1302. She was of Courtrain, Mayenne and Loupland in Maine (now France).

Children:

* i. Margaret[L], of Picardy, d. 7 Feb. 1333/4; m. c. 1280 Sir Edmund[L] de Mortimer, who d. Wigmore Castle, Herefordshire, 17 July 1304.

ii. Joan, possible dau., d. shortly before 26 Oct. 1309; m. before 24 Sept. 1291, John Wake, who d. shortly before 10 April 1300.

§ § §

FITTON

This presentation was assembled from a number of sources. Earwaker's *East Cheshire* cited as authorities a manuscript pedigree compiled by Sir Peter Leycester, Fitton deeds, Dodsworth MSS. (vol. 39), registers at Gawsworth, monuments, wills, and the Fitton Mass Book.

1. Sir RICHARD[O] DE PHYTUN was given Fallybrome by Hugh, second Earl of Chester, in the time of King Henry II, who reigned from 1154 to 1189.
    Child, from Ormerod's *History of Chester* [3:552]:
    2.   i.   Sir Richard[N], d. 30 Hen. III (1245-1246); m. Elen.

2. Sir RICHARD[N] DE PHITON, lord of Bolyn in Cheshire, died 30 Hen. III (1245-1246). His wife ELEN was living during the time of King Edward I, who reigned from 1272. He was Justice of Cheshire from 1233 to 1237 [Earwaker, *East Cheshire*, 1:50].
    Children, from the pedigree in Ormerod [3:552]:
    3.   i.   Sir Hugh, d. before 55 Hen. III (1270-1271).
          ii.   Roger, parson of Wilmeslowe during the reign of Hen. III.

3. Sir HUGH[M] FHYTON died before 55 Hen. III (1270-1271). He was granted the manors of Rushton and Eaton by John Scot, Earl of Chester.
    Children, from Ormerod:
    4.   i.   Sir Edmund[L], d. 26 Edw. I (1297-1298); m. Joyce.
    *   ii.   Margery (or Margaret), m. c. 1280 Robert[M] de Downes; given lands in Chorley by her brother Edmund.

4. Sir EDMUND[L] FITTON of Bollin-Fee in Cheshire was of record from 1268 to 1297. His wife, JOYCE, was living 10 Edw. III (1336-1337).
    Children, mentioned by Ormerod in *History of Chester* [1:522]:
          i.   John[J], m. Cecily de Massy, sister of Sir Hamon Massy, baron of Dunham-Massy, and perhaps widow of Thomas de Orreby of Gawsworth.
    5.   ii.   Thomas, l. 1335; m. Isabel[L] de Orreby.
          iii.   Hugh, rector of Wilmslow Church in 1335.

5. THOMAS[K] FITTON, the second son of Edmund Fitton of Bolyn in Cheshire, was living in 1335.
    He married about 1316 ISABEL[L] DE ORREBY*, who died in 1346, daughter and heiress of Thomas[M] de Orreby of Gawsworth, who died in 1290. She had married first in 1307 Roger de Macclesfield, who died without issue, and second, by 1312 Sir John de Grendon, who died without issue.
    In 10 Edw. II (1316-1317) Thomas Fytoun and Isabel his wife sued Jordan de Macclesfield and Milicent his wife, widow of Thomas de Macclesfield, for dower of 12 messuages and 187 acres in Gowesworth. In 2 Edw. III (1328-1329) Thomas Fyton and Isabel his wife obtained by fine of their son Thomas tenements in Pounale and Chorlegh [Ormerod, 3:548].
    They were the ancestors of the Fittons of Gawsworth. The parish is about three miles southwest of Macclesfield.
    Children, listed by Earwaker in East Cheshire [2:564]:
    6.   i.   Thomas[J], b. c. 1322; d. March 1397; m. (1) Margaret Legh of Bechton, who d. 12 Dec. 1379, m. (2) Elizabeth, who m. (2) William de Honford.
          ii.   Margery, m. (settlement dated 26 Edw. III [1352-1353]) William del Mere, son and heir of Matthew del Mere of Mere in Cheshire.

6. THOMAS[J] FITTON, born about 1322, died 22 [Renaud, 551] March 1397. The *writ de diem* was issued 2 April 20 Ric. II (1397).
    He married first MARGARET[J] LEGH of Bechton, who died 12 Dec. 1379, daughter and

coheiress of Peter Legh of Bechton and his wife Ellen de Bechton, daughter and heiress of Philip de Bechton.

He married second Elizabeth, who married second William de Honford; she and her second husband were living in 1398, when she was granted by her son Thomas an annuity of £10 in lieu of dower [Ormerod, 3:549].

He was of record in land transactions 2 Ric. II (1378-1379) to 15 Ric. II (1391-1392), and was appointed 11 Ric. II (1387-1388) one of the justices for the three hundreds of the eyre at Macclesfield [Ormerod, 3:549]. In 14 and 15 Ric. II (1390-1392) he was a commissioner to inquire into infringements upon the statutes of Edward III regulating the wages of artisans and workmen.

His *inquisition post mortem*, taken at Macclesfield on 7 May 1397, states that he died on Thursday next before the Feast of the Annunciation of the Blessed Virgin Mary seized of his demesne in Gouseworth, and lands in Pounale called Northclyve and in Chorleigh, a forestership within the Forest of Macclesfield, and land at Honbrugge (Handbridge) beyond the Dee, and by his wife half of the manor of Bechton and land in Lostock Gralam called Bancroft. His heir was Laurence, aged 22, and his wife Elizabeth was to receive an annuity of twenty marks for life. This was recorded on the Plea Roll for 21 Ric. II (1398), and it was found that Thomas had already given the forestership to Laurence.

Children, by first wife, the first three listed by Earwaker in *East Cheshire* [2:564]:

7.   i.   Sir Lawrence[J], b. c. 1375; d. 14 Feb. 1456/7; m. (1) Agnes Hesketh, who d. 3 Jan. 1442, m. (2) Clemence, who l. 1459.

    ii.   Philip, l. 1 Hen. V (1413-1414).

    iii. Margaret, m. 1370 Sir John Burdett of Seckington in Warwickshire.

    iv. Thomas, listed by Ormerod [3:552].

    v.   Richard, b. c. 1376; d. 1437; m. by Jan. 1411 Margaret Olton [Roskell, *Hist. Parl.*, 3:77].

7. Sir LAURENCE[l] FITTON, born about 1375, died 14 Feb. 1456/7, aged 82.

He married first AGNES HESKETH of Rufford in Lancashire, who died 3 Jan. 1442 (stained glass formerly in Gawsworth Church, about three miles southwest of Macclesfield). According to Jessica Lofthouse's *Old Lancashire Families*, a William Hesketh was thrust into the class of the landed gentry in 1276 on marrying Maud Fytton, as she and her two sisters had shares in Harwood and Rufford [187]. *Burke's Peerage* (1999) [1:1393] mentions Sir William Hesketh as the ancestor of Heskeths of Rufford, and gives ancestors and a line of descendants, but without detail sufficient to identify the position in the family of Agnes.

The Hesketh line began with Richard Hesketh of Hesketh in Croston in Lancashire, and continued with William Hesketh of Hesketh who married Annabel de Stafford, daughter and heir of Richard de Stafford. He was succeeded by Robert Hesketh of Hesketh, and then William Hesketh of Hesketh, who married Albora, daughter and heir of Richard de Totleworth. The next generation was Sir William Hesketh of Hesketh and Beconsaw, who was living in 1276; he married Maud, daughter and coheir of Richard Fitton of Great Harwood and Martholme in Lancashire, and had Thomas Hesketh of Hesketh, who married Alice Warren of Bispham in Lancashire. His son was Sir John Hesketh of Hesketh and Rufford, who married Alice, daughter and sole heir of Edmond Fitton, lord of half the manor of Rufford in Lancashire. Next was Sir William Hesketh of Rufford, who married Marcella Thweng of Kendal in Westmorland, and had Thomas Hesketh of Rufford, who married Margaret, daughter and coheir of Thomas Banastre of Newton. Next came Nicholas Hesketh of Rufford, whose wife Margaret died in 1418. Margaret was daughter and coheir of the family of Mynshull. Their son was Sir Thomas Hesketh, who married in 1418 Sybil

Lawrance, who died in 1459, daughter and coheir of Sir Robert Lawrance.

In about 1909 manuscripts by antiquarian Roger Dodsworth covering Hesketh of Rufford and Roger Hesketh of Lancashire were in the Bodleian Library in Oxford [Rev. W.G. Procter, *Trans. Historic Soc. Lancs. & Cheshire*, 62:60-61].

Sir Laurence married second Clemence, who was living in 1459.

He served in Ireland under King Richard II in 1399, having been granted protection for his lands on 17 May, shortly after having been commissioned to raise a body of archers for King Richard II. He was knighted in 1401, and granted a general pardon by King Henry IV for all offences committed while he was in "rebellion with Henry Percy, the son, and other rebels." He was appointed in 3 and 4 Hen. IV (1401-1403) as one of the justices for three hundreds of the eyre at Macclesfield, and on 11 Jan. 1402/3 was directed to defend his possessions in the Welsh marches against Owain Glyndŵr. He held a number of offices in Cheshire to the middle of the fifteenth century, and died seized of land in Sutton, near Macclesfield, the manor of Gawsworth (and the advowson of the church there), a forestership in the Forest of Macclesfield, and lands in Bechton as well as in Pownall and Chorley. Those in Pownall and Chorley were settled on his widow Clemence for life.

Children, by first wife, listed by Earwaker in *East Cheshire* [2:564]:

    i.   Thomas[H], d. 16 July 1449, stained glass in Gawsworth Church; m. Ellen Mainwaring, who d. 25 Feb. 1480/1, dau. of Randle Mainwaring of Over Peover, Esq.; twelve children, incl. seven sons [Earwaker, *East Cheshire*, 2:564-565].

    ii.   Hugh, living 1457, had lands in Capesthorne from his father.

    iii.   John, living 1456.

    iv.   Randle, living 1459.

    v.   Richard, slain at Blore Heath 1459; of record 5 Hen. VI (1426-1427).

    vi.   Edward, slain at Blore Heath 1459.

    vii.   Laurence, d. 29 March 1434, brass formerly in Sonning Church; bailiff of Sonning in Berkshire.

    viii.   William, slain at Blore Heath 1459.

    ix.   Ellen, m. John Fitton of Pownall, who d. Sept. 1476, stained glass in Gawsworth Church.

    x.   Elizabeth, m. c. 1412 William Mere of Mere in Cheshire.

*   xi.   Joan, d. a widow in 1480, stained glass in Gawsworth Church; m. 1415 Robert[H] de Grosvenor of Hulme.

    xii.   Alice, m. Robert de Davenport, son and heir-apparent of Robert de Davenport of Bramhall, Esq.

§ § §

FITZ ALAN

The following outline has been taken in part from the material on Arundel in Cokayne's *Complete Peerage* [1:239-243]. The early generations were adapted from the material on Fitz Alan of Oswestry in *CP*, 5:391-392.

The origin and descendants of Alan[S] Fitz Fleald are dealt with in Round's *Peerage and Family History* [120-131]. His younger brother, Walter, became Steward to the King of Scotland, and was ancestor of the royal Stewarts.

ALAN[U] was living in 1045 and was the hereditary steward of the Duke of Brittany.

FLEALD[T], who was living in 1080, was active on the Welsh border in 1101.

ALAN[S] FITZ FLEALD, a Breton, obtained the Castle of Oswaldestre (or Oswestry) in

Shropshire, early in the reign of King Henry I, who ruled England from 1100-1135.

WILLIAM[R] FITZ ALAN of Oswestry, Shropshire, died in 1160. He married second ISABEL[R] DE SAY, who married second Geoffrey de Ver, and third William Boterel. Eyton suggests a second wife, Christiana, daughter of Robert the Consul [7:167].

WILLIAM[Q] FITZ ALAN of Oswestry, Shropshire, died about 1210, having answered for Clun, Shropshire, in 1201.

JOHN[P] FITZ ALAN, lord of Clun and Owestry in Shropshire, died about 1240. He married first ISABEL[M] D'AUBIGNY.

JOHN[O] FITZ ALAN made his will in Oct. 1267 and died before 10 Nov. 1267. He married MAUD[O] LE BOTILLER (or BUTLER), who died 27 Nov. 1283, having married second Richard d'Amundville, who was living in 1286/7.

6. JOHN[N] FITZ ALAN, Lord of Clun, Shropshire, and Earl of Arundel (although he was not known by that title during his lifetime), was born 14 Sept. 1246, died 18 March 1271/2, and was buried in Haughmond Abbey, Shropshire.

He married in 1260 ISABEL[L] DE MORTIMER[+] (daughter of Sir Roger[M] de Mortimer of Wigmore and Maud[M] de Braiose), who was living in 1300, having married second Ralph d'Arderne (who was living about April 1283), and third, in Polling, Essex, 2 Sept. 1285, Robert de Hastang, who was living 1 April 1292. The third marriage was private, and cost a fine of £1000.

At the time of his death he possessed only a quarter of the barony.

Children:

7.   i.   Richard[M], b. 3 Feb. 1266/7; died 9 March 1301/2, bur. Wymondham Priory, Norfolk; m. prob. 1284 Alasia[M] de Saluzzo.

     ii. Matilda, m. Philip Burnell, who d. 26 June 1294 [Eyton, 6:134].

7. Sir RICHARD[M] FITZ ALAN, Earl of Arundel, was born 3 Feb. 1266/7, died 9 March 1301/2, and was buried at Wymondham Priory in Norfolk with his ancestors.

He married, probably in 1284, ALASIA[M] DE SALUZZO, who died 25 Sept. 1292 and was buried in Todingham Priory; she was daughter of Tomasso I, Marquis of Saluzzo in Piedmont (Italy), who died in 1296, and his wife Luisa di Ceva, who died in 1291.

He had seizin of his lands on 8 Dec. 1287, and was recorded as Earl of Arundel in a grant dated 12 Feb. 1290/1. He fought in the Welsh wars in 1288. He was summoned to Parliament 24 June 1295, at a time when he was junior to all other earls. He was in Gascony 1295-1297 and in the Scottish wars 1298-1300; he was present at the siege of Caerlaverock in 1300.

Children:

8.   i.   Edmund[L], b. Marlborough Castle, Wiltshire, 1 May 1285; beheaded Hereford 17 Nov. 1326; m. 1305 Alice[L] de Warenne.

*   ii. Eleanor, presumed by some to be a daughter, b. Arundel, Sussex, c. 1284; d. 1328, bur. Beverley; m. Sir Henry[L] Percy, 9th Baron Percy.

     iii. Alice, m. Stephen de Segrave [Elliott, EG, 9:196].

     iv. Margaret, m. William[K] le Boteler [CP, 2:232].

8. Sir EDMUND[L] FITZ ALAN, 8th Earl of Arundel, born at Marlborough Castle, Wiltshire, 1 May 1285, was beheaded at Hereford 17 Nov. 1326.

He married in 1305 ALICE[L] DE WARENNE* of Arundel, Sussex, who was living in 1330 but died before 23 May 1338 [CP, 1:242]. His wardship had been obtained by John, Earl of Surrey and Sussex, her grandfather.

He was knighted 22 May 1306, with Prince Edward and many others. He was summoned to Parliament in 9 Nov. 1306, and participated in the Scottish wars the same year. On 24 Feb. 1307/8 he officiated as *Pincerna* at the Coronation of King Edward II.

In 1316 he was Captain General north of the Trent, but for a long time opposed the King. He opposed Piers de Gavastan violently, and had been beaten by him in a tournament. However, in 1321 he changed sides, marrying his first son to a daughter of Hugh^M le Despenser, becoming one of the few nobles to support the Edward II. In 1323 he was Chief Justiciar of North and South Wales, and in 1325 he was warden of the Welsh marches.

He was captured in Shropshire by the Quuen's party and beheaded without trial. Subsequently he was attainted, and his estates and honors were forfeited.

Children:

9.   i.   Richard^K, b. c. 1313; d. Arundel, Sussex, 24 Jan. 1375/6, bur. Lewes Priory, Sussex; m. (1) King's Chapel, Havering-atte-Bower, Essex, 9 Feb. 1320/1 Isabel^L Despenser (annulled Dec. 1344), m. (2) Eleanor^L Plantagenet de Lancaster, widow of John de Beaumont, Earl of Buchan.

    ii.   Aline, m. Roger le Strange, 5th Lord Strange, who d. 1382 [Elliott, *EG*, 9:196].

9. Sir RICHARD^K FITZ ALAN, "Copped Hat," K.G., Earl of Arundel and Warenne, born about 1313, died in Arundel, Sussex, 24 Jan. 1375/6, and was buried in Lewes Priory, Sussex.

He married first, when aged about seven, at King's Chapel, Havering-atte-Bower, Essex, 9 Feb. 1320/1, ISABEL^L LE DESPENSER*, who was aged about eight at the time. After her father's execution and attainder, she "ceased to be of any importance" [*CP*, 1:243d], and he was living in adultery with Eleanor (or Alianor) Plantagenet. The first marriage was obligingly annulled 4 Dec. 1344 by a papal mandate on the grounds that he was underage at the time of marriage and had not willingly consented to it.

He married second, at Ditton in the presence of King Edward III, 5 Feb. 1344/5, ELEANOR^K PLANTAGENET* DE LANCASTER, who had married first, before June 1337, John de Beaumont, Earl of Buchan, who died in May 1342. As she was first cousin to his first wife, and his second cousin once removed, a papal dispensation was granted 4 March 1344/5, though he had known Isabel[la] carnally. She died at Arundel on 11 Jan. 1371/2, and was buried at Lewes.

In 1330-1331 he was fully restored "in blood and honours," obtaining restitution of the Castle and Honour of Arundel, thus becoming Earl of Arundel.

He was distinguished in the French wars as Admiral of the West in 1340-41 and 1345-47, and commanded the second division at the battle of Crécy. He was at the fall of Calais in 1347. Upon the death of his mother's brother, John Earl of Surrey and Sussex (without legitimate issue), 30 June 1347, he succeeded to the vast Warenne estates.

He was a Knight of the Garter.

His will was dated 5 Dec. 1375.

Children, by first wife, made bastards by the annulment of their parents' marriage [*CP*, 1:244b, 10:236a]:

    i.   Sir Edmund^J, second son, b. c. 1327; l. 1377; m. before July 1349 Sybil de Montagu, dau. of William de Montagu, Earl of Salisbury.

    ii.   Isabel (or Mary [*CP*, 12:1:344]), d. 29 Aug. 1396; m. John^J le Strange, 4th Baron Strange of Blackmere, who d. 12 May 1361.

Children, by second wife:

10.   iii.   Richard, b. 1346; beheaded Cheapside 21 Sept. 1397, bur. Church of the Austin Friars, Bread Street, London; m. (1) 1359 Elizabeth^J de Bohun, m. (2) 15 Aug. 1390 Philippe Mortimer, widow of John Hastings, 3rd Earl of Pembroke.

        iv.   Sir John, Lord Arundel of Lytchett Mautravers in Dorset [Faris, *PA2*, 49], d. at sea 15 Dec. 1379; m. 17 Feb. 1358/9 Eleanor Maltravers, who d. 12 Jan. 1404/5, having m. (2) 1380 Reynold Cobham of Sterborough, who d. 6 July 1403 [Faris, *PA2*, 50]; Marshall of England, Lord Maltravers.

        v.   Joan, d. 7 April 1419, bur. Walden Abbey; m. Humphrey^J de Bohun, Earl of Hereford.

        vi.   Alice, m. Thomas de Holand, Earl of Kent.

10. Sir RICHARD^J FITZ ALAN, Earl of Arundel and Earl of Surrey, born before 1347, was beheaded at Cheapside 21 Sept. 1397, and was buried in the Church of the Austin Friars in Bread Street, London.

He married first, the contract dated 28 Sept. 1359, ELIZABETH^J DE BOHUN*, who died 3 April 1385 and was buried at Lewes in Sussex.

He married second, 15 Aug. 1390 (without a royal license, for which he was fined £500), Philippe Mortimer, widow of John Hastings, 3rd Earl of Pembroke; she was born at Ludlow 21 Nov. 1375, daughter of Edmund Mortimer, Earl of March, by Philippe, daughter and heiress of Lionel, Duke of Clarence (and third son of King Edward III). She married third, after April 1398, Thomas Poynings, Lord St. John of Basing. She died in Halnaker, Sussex, 24 Sept. 1401, and was buried at Boxgrove.

He was bearer of the crown at the Coronation of King Richard II on 16 July 1377, and was a member of the Council.

He had a distinguished career in the French wars, and on 24 March 1387 won a "brilliant naval victory" against the combined French, Spanish and Flemish fleets off Margate, and was made Governor of Brest in 1388. In that year he joined the Duke of Gloucester in opposition to King Richard II, who was entirely within the Duke's power at that time, and became one of the five Lords Appellant in Parliament. He obtained a pardon in 1394, but was "treacherously seized," tried at Westminster, beheaded at Cheapside 21 Sept. 1397 with "no more shrinking or changing colour than if he were going to a banquet," and attainted, so all his honors were forfeited until the attainder was reversed in Oct. 1400.

Children, all by first wife:

        i.   son^I, did not survive his father.

        ii.   Thomas, Earl of Arundel, b. 13 Oct. 1381; d. Arundel 13 Oct. 1415 (will dated 10 Oct. 1415); m. Lambeth 26 Nov. 1405 Beatrice of Portugal (dau. of King John of Portugal), who d. 23 Oct. 1439, having m. (2) 1433 John Holand, Earl of Huntingdon.

        iii.   Alice, m. John Cherleton, 4th Lord Cherleton of Powys, who d. Castle of Pool, 19 Oct. 1401, no issue; said to have been mother of a daughter, Jane or Joan (who m. Sir Edward Stradling of St. Donat's Castle, Glamorgan), by Henry Beaufort, Cardinal of England and grandson of King Edward III.

  *   iv.   Elizabeth, b. c. 1375; d. 8 July 1425; m. (1) before Dec. 1378 Sir William de Montagu, who d. Windsor 6 Aug. 1382 [*CP*, 11:390-391], son and heir of the Earl of Salisbury, m. (2) July 1384 Thomas de Mowbray, later Duke of Norfolk, who d. of pestilence in Venice (now in Italy), 22

Sept. 1399, m. (3) before 19 Aug. 1401 (as his 2nd wife [*CP*, 9:604])
Robert[J] Goushill of Hoveringham, Notts. [*CP*, 1:253, 4:205, 9:604,
and *DNB*, 54:75], m. (4) before 3 July 1414 Sir Gerard Ufflete, whose
will was proved Feb. 1420/1.

*   v.   Joan, d. 14 Nov. 1435; m. (1) William[I] de Beauchamp, Baron Abergavenny, m. (2) Edward Neville.

Child, by second wife:

     vi.   Richard, m. c. 28 Sept. 1359; m. Elizabeth de Bohun, who d. 3 April 1385
[*MCS*5, 27:7].

§ § §

FITZ GERALD

This account is based largely on Cokayne's *Complete Peerage* [7:200, 10:10-17].

WALTER[S] FITZ OTHER, Castellan of Windsor, was living in or after 1100. He married
BEATRICE.

GERALD[R] OF WINDSOR died presumably before 1136, when his sons were defending their
holdings against the Welsh. He married NEST[R] FERCH RHYS AP TEWDWR MAWR of Wales.

MAURICE[Q] FITZ GERALD, Lord of Llanstephan, Wales, born about 1100, landed in
Wexford 1 Sept. 1176. It has been said that he married ALICE[Q] DE MONTGOMERY.

GERALD[P] FITZ MAURICE, 1st Baron of Offaly, born as late as 1150, died before 15 Jan.
1203/4. He married EVE[P] DE BERMINGHAM, who died before Dec. 1226. She was heiress
of Offaly and daughter of Robert[Q] de Bermingham. She married second Geoffrey Fitz
Robert, who died in 1211, and married third, in or before Feb. 1217/8, Geoffrey de Marsh,
sometime Justiciar of Ireland, who died in exile in 1245.

Sir MAURICE[O] FITZ GERALD, 2nd Baron of Offaly, born in Ireland about 1190, died at
the monastery in Youghal, which he had founded, in 1257, and was buried there. He is
said to have married JULIANE.

6. THOMAS[N] FITZ MAURICE FITZ GERALD, Lord Offaly, died in Ballyloughmask in county
Mayo, Ireland, in 1271.

He married ROHESIA[N] DE ST. MICHAEL of Rheban, Athy and Woodstock.

He was enfeoffed in Banada, County Sligo, by Maurice Fitz Maurice.

It has been alleged that he founded the Trinitarian Abbey Adare in county Limerick
[*BP*, 2:1679].

Child:

7.   i.   John[M] Fitz Thomas, d. Laraghbryan near Maynooth, Kildare, Ireland, 12
Sept. 1316; m. Blanche[M] Roche, who d. after Feb. 1329/30.

7. Sir JOHN[M] FITZ THOMAS FITZ GERALD, 5th Baron of Offaly, 1st Earl of Kildare, died
in Laraghbryan near Maynooth in Kildare, 12 Sept. 1316, and was buried in the Church of
the Friars Minor in Kildare.

He married BLANCHE[M] ROCHE (daughter or sister of Alexander Roche), who died after
Feb. 1329/30.

A legend states that when he was a baby in the Castle of Woodstock near Athy in
Kildare, a fire broke out, and although he was overlooked in the panic he was rescued by
a monkey who held him in his arms and climbed a tower. The Fitz Gerald crest is a
monkey, occasionally used with the motto "*Non immemor beneficii,*" or "Not forgetful of a
helping hand." However, this legend is also part of the Fitz Geralds of Valencia.

In 1288 he was guardian of part of the marches of the English pale in Ireland, and in 1293 he built Sligo Castle to protect his lands in Connaught, which he believed were threatened by Richard[L] de Burgh, Earl of Ulster, whom he took prisoner in 1294. However, he had to release the Earl because of the outcry in Ireland, and for a time he lost Connaught. He had another dispute with William de Vesci of Alnwick, who had to surrender his lands to King Edward I and died 19 July 1297.

Peace between the Geraldines and de Burghs was arranged in 1298, and in Oct. 1309 he, the Earl of Ulster and others were called to provide a force against Scotland. In 1314, however, bickering among the Irish magnates prevented united action against Edward Bruce (brother of King Robert the Bruce of Scotland), who was crowned King of Ireland. Nonetheless, in Feb. 1315/6, he and other magnates did join against the Scots, and on 14 May 1316 he was created Earl of Kildare.

According to Orpen [4:129], he "got all hereditary claims of Juliana de Cogan and Amabil," daughter of Maurice Fitz Maurice and Matilda de Prendergast.

Children, listed by Cokayne [*CP*, 7:221]:

    i.   John[L], d. young.
    ii. Gerald, d. 1303.
    iii. Thomas, d. 5 (or 9 [*BP*, 2:1679]) April 1328; m. Greencastle 16 Aug. 1312 Joan[K] de Burgh, who d. 23 April 1359, having m. (2) Maynooth 3 July 1329 Sir John[K] Darcy, who d. 30 May 1347.
*   iv. Joan, m. 1302 Edmund[L] Butler, who d. London 13 Sept. 1321.
    v. daughter, m. Nicholas Netterville.

§ § §

FITZ ROGER

This account is based on Weis' *Ancestral Roots* and charts ii-iii following *The Complete Peerage*, 9:502, plus lines 44 and 156 in Weis' *Magna Charta Sureties*, 5th edition.

Sanders bears checking. Sir Charles Clay's "Ancestry of the Earls of Warkworth," in *Archæologia Aeliana*, series 4, vol. 32, bears reading.

Alice, daughter of Robert de Warkworth, married in 1203 Piers[P] Fitz Herbert (for whom see Fitz Piers).

1. ROGER[Q] FITZ RICHARD, 1st lord of Warkworth, Northumberland, was son of Richard and Jane (daughter of Roger Bigod), and died in 1178.

He married ALICE[Q] DE VERE[+] (daughter of Aubrey de Vere II and Alice de Clare), who was born before 1141 and was living in 1185. She had married first Robert of Essex, lord of Rayleigh. Weis cited Clay, 53-55.

According to Percy Hedley [*Northumberland Families*, 1:160] he was given lands worth over £58 by King Henry II in 1157-1158. In 1166 he held two knights' fees of Hugh Bigod, Earl of Norfolk. In 1170 he traded Compton in Warwickshire for Aynho in Northamptonshire. His wife's dower included the manor of Clavering in Essex.

Child:

2.   i. Robert[P], d. 1212; m. Margaret de Chesney.

2. ROBERT[P] FITZ ROGER, 2nd Baron Warkworth, lord of Clavering, was born before 1178 and died in 1212.

He married MARGARET DE CHESNEY, daughter of William de Chesney.

A firm friend and counselor of King John, he was given the manor and borough of

Corbridge in Northamptonshire in 1204 to hold at a farm fee rent of £40. In 1205 he was given the royal manors of Newburn and Rothbury, and the forfeited barony of Whalton, the latter *in capite*. He served as Sheriff of Northumberland.

Children:

   3.   i.   John^O, d. 1240; m. (2) Ada^N de Baliol, who d. Stokesley 29 July 1251.

   +   ii. Alice, m. after 28 Nov. 1203 Piers^P Fitz Herbert (for whom see Fitz Piers).

3. JOHN^O FITZ ROBERT, lord of Warkworth, died in 1240.

He married second ADA^N DE BALIOL*, who died in Stokesley on 29 July 1251.

He was a Magna Carta surety in 1215.

Children, listed by Hedley:

   4.   i.   Roger^N, d. Normandy c. 1249; m. Isabel.

         ii. Sir Hugh de Eure, acquired Kirkley in the parish of Ponteland from Roger Bertram, Earl of Mitford.

        iii. Sir Robert de Eure, m. Isabel de Merlay; no issue.

        iv. Stephen de Baillol, rector of Mitford.

        v. Ingram.

        vi. Alicia.

       vii. Annora.

     viii. Margery.

4. ROGER^N FITZ JOHN, 4th Baron Warkworth and Clavering, born in Clavering, Essex, about 1228, died in Normandy about Whitsuntide of 1249.

He married ISABEL.

Child:

   5.   i.   Robert^M Fitz Roger, b. Clavering, Essex, 1247; d. Horsford, Norfolk, before 20 April 1310; m. Margery^J de la Zouche.

5. ROBERT^M FITZ ROGER, 5th Baron Warkworth and Clavering, born in Clavering, Essex, in 1247, died in Horsford, Norfolk, before 20 April 1310.

He married in 1265 MARGERY^J DE LA ZOUCHE* of Winchester, Hampshire, who was born in 1251.

Children, the last four included by Dugdale [*cf. Monasticon*, 3:636]:

        i.   John^L Fitz Robert de Warkworth, d. 18 Jan. 1331/2 [Hedley, 1:161]; m.; M.P., had dau. Eve.

        ii. Edmund de Clavering.

   *   iii. Euphemia, b. after 1265; d. c. 1320; m. Randolph^L de Neville, 1st Baron Neville of Raby, who d. 18 April 1331.

        iv. Ellen, d. 1339; m. Sir John^M d'Engayne, who d. 1322.

        v. Alexander de Clavering.

        vi. Roger de Clavering, m. Beatrice.

       vii. Sir Alan de Clavering of Callaly, aged 28 in 1307.

     viii. Henry de Clavering.

§ § §

FOULESHURST

The following has been taken partly from Ormerod's *History of Chester* [3:302]. *Inquisitions post mortem* mentioned by Ormerod [3:305-309] include those of Robert

Fulleshurst (18 Hen. VI [1439-1440]), his wife Joan (24 Hen. VI [1445-1446]), Thomas Fouleshurst (14 Hen. VII [1498-1499]), Robert Fouleshurst (6 Hen. VIII [1514-1515]) and Joan, his widow (12 Hen. VIII [1520-1521]).

1.   Sir ROBERT^J DE FOULESHURST was the second son of Richard Fouleshurst of Edlaston, who died 13 Ric. II (1320-1321) [inq. p.m. mentioned in Ormerod, 3:302].

He married ELIZABETH^J DE PRAERS, sole daughter and heiress of Thomas de Praers, lord of Bertumlegh, Crue and Landecan in 11 Edw. III (1337-1338), who died 23 Edw. III (1349-1350), and his wife Margery, who was of record 17 Edw. III (1443-1444).

Children [Ormerod, 3:302]:
>   2.   i.   Sir Thomas^I, b. c. 1366; d. 5 Hen. IV (1403-1404); m. Joan de Venables, who d. 3 Hen. V (1415-1416).
>   ii.   Isabel, m. Thomas de Wever; of record 41 Edw. III (1368-1369).

2.   Sir THOMAS^I FOULESHURST was aged 23 in 13 Ric. II (1389-1390), and died in 5 Hen. IV (1403-1404), with his *inquisition post mortem* taken 5 Hen. V (1417-1418), if Ormerod is correct [3:302].

He married JOAN^I DE VENABLES, who was perhaps the same as Eva, daughter of Hugh de Venables; she died 3 Hen. V (1415-1416).

Children, listed in Ormerod [3:302]:
>   3.   i.   Thomas^H, b. Glenfield, Leics., c. 1396; d. c. 1438; m. Cecily^H Mainwaring of Peover, who m. (2) John Curson.
>   ii.   Richard, of record 2 Hen. V (1414-1415).

3.   THOMAS^H FOULESHURST, born in Glenfield, Leicestershire, and aged 21 in 5 Hen. V (1417-1418), was the subject of inquisitions post mortem dated 16, 17 and 18 Hen. VI, and thus died not later than 1438.

He married CECILY^H MAINWARING* of Over Peover, who married second John Curson, who was of record 18 Hen. VI (1439-1440) [cf. Ormerod, 3:119].

Children:
>   4.   i.   Sir Robert^G, b. c. 1419; d. c. 1498; m. Joan Vernon.
>   ii.   Peter of Crue, possible son, gentleman, of record 10 Hen. VII (1494-1495).

4.   Sir ROBERT^G FOULESHURST of Crewe, born in Over Peover, Cheshire, aged 21 in 18 Hen. VI (1439-1440), died 1498; his *inquisition post mortem* was conducted in 14 Hen. VII (1498-1499).

He married JOAN (or JANE) VERNON, daughter and heiress of Sir Robert (Richard in *Vis. Cheshire 1580* [102]). Joan's marriage articles were dated 18 Hen. VI (1439-1440), and she was aged 26 in 24 Hen. VI (1445-1446).

Children, all but Elizabeth found in the Fouleshurst pedigree [Ormerod, 3:302]:
>   i.   Thomas^F, son and heir, d. c. 14 Hen. VII (1498-1499); m. Anne, who d. 22 April 16 Hen. VIII (1525); he was in London 1498.
>   ii.   Hugh.
>   iii.   William.
>   iv.   John.
>   v.   Randul, m. Anne; of record 7 Hen. VIII (1521-1522).
>   vi.   Robert, rector of Barthomley 14 Edw. IV (1474-1475).
>   vii.   Ann, l. 8 Hen. VII (1492-1493).

*   viii.   Elizabeth, identified as a dau. of Sir Robert Fouleshurst of Crewe by Ormerod; m. (1) Peter[F] Dutton [Jr.] of Hatton, who d. 1503, m. (2) 22 Hen. VII (1506-1507) Thomas Leycester of Tabley, Esq.

§ § §

DE FURNIVALL

The article by G.W. Watson in Cokayne's *Complete Peerage* was the basis of this line. The arms of this family were *Argent*, a *bend* between six *marlets Gules*.

Norr suggested that Gerard[P] de Furnivalle, below, was son of Gerard Furnival of Swanland, who married a Margaret Cave, daughter of Robert ap Bryan ap Jordayn, the latter born about 1042 and had a brother who had a grant from William the Conqueror in 1069. Not only does Norr's citation make no sense chronologically, but the names bear scrutiny, being of the Welsh form.

GERARD[P] DE FURNIVALLE was of record as accompanying King Richard I on his Crusade [*CP*, 5:580g]. Norr cited the *Bisshop Family* [CS539.B553] as the source for the statement that he died in Jerusalem in 1219, had married Andele (or Andeluga), and had a second son Galfrid, but offered no other citation.

GERARD[O] DE FURNIVALLE was underage on 12 March 1200/1. He married MAUD[O] DE LUVETOT, who was aged 7 in 1185, underage on 12 March 1200/1, was living 23 June 1247.

Sir THOMAS[N] DE FURNIVALLE was of record 13 April 1238. His wife, BERTA, was living 10 Feb. 1266/7, having married second Ralph le Bigod; she was of record as Ralph's widow on 28 July 1260.

THOMAS[M] DE FURNIVALL, Lord Hallamshire of Sheffield, Yorkshire, was born in 1229, died 12 May 1291, and was buried in the Church of Friars Minor in Doncaster, Yorkshire. His wife's name is not known.

5.   Sir THOMAS[L] DE FURNIVALL, 1st Lord Furnivall, of Sheffield in Yorkshire, Worksop in Nottinghamshire and Grossthorpe, died 3 Feb. 1332, given by Watson as shortly before 18 April 1332.

He married first, as a minor before Jan. 1272/3, JOANE[N] DESPENSER of Ryhall in Rutland, who died before Jan. 1272/3, daughter of Sir Hugh[O] le Despenser, 1st Lord Despenser, and his wife Aline[M] (or Aliva) Bassett.

He married second, the pardon for marrying without a royal license dated 8 June 1322 upon a fine of £200 [*CP*, 5:582], Elizabeth de Mountfort, daughter of Sir Piers de Mountfort (de Montfort) of Beaudesert in Warwickshire, by Maud, daughter of Matthew de la Mare [*CP*, 14:332]. Elizabeth was the widow of Sir William de Mountagu of Shepton Montagu in Somerset, and Aston Clinton in Buckinghamshire, who died 18 Oct. 1319. Elizabeth died in Aug. 1354, and was buried in the Priory of St. Frideswide (now Christ Church), Oxford. Her heir was William, Earl of Salisbury, who was listed as aged 26 and more, 30 and more, or 32 and more.

He was said to have been aged 40 and more when his father died. On 5 June 1291 King Edward I took his homage, and he had livery of his father's lands. He was to attend the king wherever he might be 8 June 1294, obtained the grant of a market and fair at Worksop in Nottinghamshire 24 Edw. I (1295-1296) [R. White, *Worksop*, 14], was to attend the king at Salisbury 26 Jan. 1296/7, was summoned for military service from May 1297 to 5 April 1327, to a military council 16 Sept. 1297, and to the coronation of Edward II on 18 Jan. 1307/8. Further, he was summoned to parliament from 24 June 1295 to 27 Jan. 1331/2, and to councils from 30 Dec. 1324 to 20 Nov. 1331.

He held the castle and manor of Sheffield as his ancestors held these of the King of Scotland [*CP*, 5:582e].

On 6 June 1332 his widow had livery of her dower.

Children, by first wife, mentioned by Watson, Weis [*AR*7, 148A:33, 156:29], or Norr [71]:

    i.   Aline[K], on 16 April 1313 Piers de Manley, who had m. her sister Eleanor, was absolved by the Archbishop of York for incest with her on condition that he paid 100 marks to the fabric of York Minster [*CP*, 8:563].

    ii. Maud, poss. dau., living 1348; m. Sir John Marmion, who d. 30 April 1335 [*CP*, 8:520-521].

6.   iii. Thomas, d. 14 Oct. 1339; m. 24 Feb. 1317/8 Joane[M] de Verdun, widow of John de Montagu.

    iv. Gerard.

    v.   Eleanor, m. before 1299 Piers de Mauley, who d. after 23 May 1348.

    vi. Catherine, m. William de Thweng.

6. THOMAS[K] DE FURNIVALL, 2nd Lord Furnivall, was aged 40 or more when his father died in 1332, and died 14 Oct. 1339.

He married 24 Feb. 1317/8 JOANE[M] DE VERDUN* of Alveton, Staffordshire, who died 2 Oct. 1336. She had married first 21 Sept. 1316 John de Montagu.

On 7 Sept. 1318 he gave fealty to King Edward II, and he and his wife had livery of the castle of Alton with its members, valued at £58.15s.7d per year. On 24 Oct. 1331 the Chancellor of Ireland was ordered to divide the Irish lands of the late Theobald de Verdon into four equal parts, but the matter was finally decided in Chancery on 13 March 1331/2.

Children, listed by Norr:

    i.   Margaret[J], m. Piers de Montfort.

    ii. Sir Thomas, 3rd Lord Furnivall, b. 22 June 1322; d. 21 April 1365; m. (1) Margaret, who was living 20 June 1344, m. (2) Joan Mounteney (dau. and heir of Sir Thomas Mounteney of Cowley and Shirecliffe in Yorks.), widow of Sir John Bret, who had complained on 10 March 1354/5 that Thomas had stolen his wife; no issue.

    iii. Joan, m. Thomas Bosvil of Cavil, Yorks.

7.   iv. William, b. 23 Aug. 1326; d. 12 April 1383; m. 1365 Thomasine, who d. 1409.

    v.   Nicholas, third son.

7. Sir WILLIAM[J] FURNIVALL, 4th Baron Furnivall, born 23 Aug. 1326, died 12 April 1383, aged 56, and was buried in Worksop Priory in Nottinghamshire.

He married between 3 Feb. 1364/5 and 20 Jan. 1365/6 THOMASINE, who had married first, before 12 June 1353, Sir John de Dagworth, who died 16 Aug. 1360 [*cf. Burke's Peerage* (1938), 1057]; she had livery of the manor of Dagworth, Suffolk, and of Dagworths Manor in Elmdon, Essex, and others. She died 20 July 1409.

On 25 May 1365 he paid homage and fealty to King Edward III and had livery of his lands as heir of his brother, and on 28 Oct. 1366 the king took his knights fees and advowsons of his inheritance. He obtained a license on 28 Nov. 1367 to go from Dover to parts of Prussia with five horsemen and £200 in money. He was of record 16 Nov. 1372 as having the park of Worksop, which had been taken into the king's hand because it was enclosed insufficiently, restored to him. On 24 Oct. 1375 he had to be represented by attorneys in the King's Courts because he was infirm.

He was knighted at Kennington on the Tuesday (14 July 1377) before the Coronation of King Richard II. He was summoned to parliament from 20 Jan. 1365/6 to 7 Jan. 1382/3.

Child, by her first husband, surnamed de Dagworth [*CP*, 4:27c]:

    i.   Margaret[I], b. c. 1360.

Child, by her second husband, surnamed de Furnivall:

*   ii.   Joan, aged 14 years, 7 months and more in May 1383; m. before 1 July 1379 Thomas[I] Neville, Baron Furnivall.

§ § §

DE GENEVILLE

Data on this line was taken largely from Cokayne and H.F. Delaborde's *Jean de Joinville et les Seigneurs de Joinville* (1894).

Stargardt's *Europäische Stammtafeln* [vol. 7, charts 6-10] has been consulted.

1. ÈTIENNE[S] DE VAUX-SUR-SAINT-URBAIN, sire de Joinville, was lord of Novi Castelli in 1005.

He married in 1027 a daughter of Engelbert de Brienne, comte de Joigny, and Adélaide.

Child, given by Stargardt:

  2.   i.   Geoffroi I[R], d. 1080; m. Blanche de Reynel.

2. GEOFFROI I[R] DE JOINVILLE, of record in 1050, died in 1080.

He married BLANCHE DE REYNEL, daughter of comte Arnoul.

Children, given by Stargardt:

    i.   Hilduin[Q], seigneur de Nully, of record 1055.

    ii.   Geoffroi II de Joinville, d. 1101; m. before 1080 Hodierne.

    iii.   Ètienne, abbot of Bèze.

    iv.   Renard, comte before 1096.

  3.   v.   Roger, of record 1101-1137; m. Audiarde de Vignory.

3. ROGER[Q] DE JOINVILLE was of record 1101-1137.

He married AUDIARDE DE VIGNORY, who was of record in 1114 and 1140.

Child:

  4.   i.   Geoffroi III[P], d. 1188; m. 1141 Felicité de Brienne.

4. GEOFFROI III[P] DE JOINVILLE, seneschal of Champagne from 1127, of Ecuray in 1145, died in 1188.

He married before 1141 FELICITÉ DE BRIENNE.

Child:

  5.   i.   Geoffroi IV[O], d. Akkon Aug. 1190; m. Helwide de Dampierre.

5. GEOFFROI IV[O] DE JOINVILLE died in Akkon Aug. 1190 [Stargardt, 7:6].

He married HELWIDE DE DAMPIERRE, daughter of Guillaume de Dampierre.

Child:

  6.   i.   Simon[N], d. May 1233; m. (1) before 1209 Ermengarde de Montcler, m. (2) Béatrix d'Auxonne of Burgundy, widow of Aymon II, sire de Faucigny.

6. SIMON[N] DE JOINVILLE, seigneur de Vaucouleurs, France, died in May 1233.

He married first, before 1209 [Stargardt, 7:6], Ermengarde de Montcler, daughter of Jean de Walcourt de Moncler.

He married second, about 1222, Béatrix d'Auxonne of Burgundy, who died 20 March 1261 (or 11 April 1260 [Stargardt, Band 2, Tafel 60]); she had married first Aymon II, sire de Faucigny.

In 1224 he was sénéschal de Champagne.

Children, mentioned by Cokayne:

    i.   eldest son[M], sire de Joinville, b. 1225, before 1 May; biographer of St. Louis.

7.   ii.   Geoffrey, m. 8 Aug. 1252 Maud[M] de Lacy, who had m. (1) Pierre de Geneva.

7. Sir GEOFFREY[M] DE GENEVILLE, seigneur de Vaucouleurs of Maine (France [given as of Champagne in *CP*, 5:785]) in 1241 [Stargardt, 7:9], and Lord of Trim, Meath, Ireland, born in or after 1226, died at the House of the Friars Preachers at Trim, 21 Oct. 1314, and was buried there.

He married as her second husband, at Woodstock 4 Aug. 1252 [*CP*, 14:336], MAUD[M] DE LACY (daughter of Gilbert de Lacy of Ewyas Harold in Herefordshire and Isabel[M] Bigod), who died 11 April 1304; she had married first, before 15 May 1244, Pierre de Geneva [Weis, *MCS5*, 12:4, 17C:4], or Piers de Genevre [*CP*, 5:786], who died in 1249, before 29 June.

He appeared as seigneur de Vaucouleurs in July 1241, and was still in France on 9 March 1250/1, but soon left for England. On 8 Aug. 1252 King Henry III granted him and his wife all the liberties and free customs in Meath, which her grandfather Walter de Lacy had held, and on 18 Sept. 1254 they were allowed to issue their own writs according to the law and custom of Ireland. Three days later they had livery of the Castle of Trim.

In 1255 he was in Gascony with Prince Edward, and a charter dated 10 June 1260 partitioned the barony of Weobley between him and John[P] de Verdun. On 10 Sept. 1267 he was empowered, with Robert Walerand, to treat of peace with Llywelyn ap Gruffudd. In 1272, as a banneret of the King of Navarre (Count of Champagne), he was summoned by the King of France against the Count of Foix. He was in the Holy Land with Edward I, but returned before him and served as Justiciar of Ireland from Sept. 1273 until 17 June 1276. In 1280 he was a member of the Commission sent to France to treat concerning peace between France and Castile. He was with the King in Wales in 1282 and the next year he and his wife gave all lands in England and Wales to their son, Piers.

In 1290 he was sent on a mission to the Pope in an effort to gain aid concerning the Holy Land. In the same decade King Edward I twice took possession of Trim, and Geoffrey was appointed marshal of the army the king took to Flanders in Aug. 1297. His last summons to military service was dated 17 May 1297. He was summoned to Parliament from 6 Feb. 1298/9 to 3 Nov. 1306. He was appointed an envoy to work for peace with France 9 Nov. 1298, and was a representative of the King at the Treaty of Montreuil on 19 June 1299.

On 24 Dec. 1307 he obtained a license to pass his possessions in Ireland on to Roger Mortimer and Joan his wife. He then entered the House of the Friars Preachers at Trim.

Children, the first two mentioned by Cokayne [5:789], the rest by Delaborde:

    i.   Geoffrey[L], d. before 11 Oct. 1283; no issue.

8.   ii.   Piers, d. before 8 June 1292; m. before 11 Oct. 1283 Jeanne[L] de Lusignan, who d. 1322, having m. (1) Bernard-Ezi I, sire d'Albret.

    iii.   Gautier de Vaucouleurs, d. 1304; m. Isabeau de Cirey.

   iv.   Jean, fl. 1315-1319.

   v.   Simon, fl. 1294-1319; m. Joan Fitzlyon.

   vi.   Nicholas, m. Jeanne de Lautrec.

   vii.   Guillaume de Beauregard.

   viii.   Jeanne, m. Johann I von Salm.

   ix.   Catherine.

8. Sir PIERS[L] DE GENEVILLE, Baron de Geneville of Trim and Ludlow Castle, Shropshire, died shortly before 8 June 1292, the date of a writ.

He married as her second husband, before 11 Oct. 1283, JEANNE[L] DE LUSIGNAN[+] of Vienne, France (daughter of Hugh XII de Lusignan and Jeanne[M] de Fougères), who died shortly before 18 April 1323. She had married first Bernard-Ezi I, sire d'Albret in Gascony, whose will was dated 23 Dec. 1280 and who died before 24 May 1281.

The lands which King Edward I had taken in hand because she was living in Germany were restored to her 11 Oct. 1296. The King of France, who was buying up the vast claims of the House of Lusignan, gave to her interests in Couhé in Poitou and Peyrat in Limousin, as well as the towns of Saint-Hilaire and Pontarion.

Stargardt [7:9] describes him as lord of Walterstone, Staunton-Lacy, Ludlow, Malmeshull, Wulverlowe and Ewyas-Lacy in 1283.

Children, mentioned by Cokayne:

  * i.   Joan[K], sole heir, b. Ludlow, Shropshire, 2 Feb. 1285/6; d. 19 Oct. 1356 [i.p.m.]; m. Sir Roger[K] de Mortimer, Earl of March, who was hanged 29 Nov. 1330.

    ii.   Beatrice, b. 1287; nun in the Priory of Aconbury.

    iii.   Maud, b. 4 Aug. 1291; nun in the Priory of Aconbury.

§ § §

GIFFARD

This family also spelled the name Gifford.

OSBERN[V] DE BOLEBEC married WEVIA, who was born say 956.

WALTER[U] GIFFORD was too old to participate in the invasion of 1066.

WALTER[T] GIFFORD died before 1085, having married EMMENGARD[T] FLAITEL.

OSBERT (or Osbern, Bolebec)[S] GIFFORD was lord of Brimsfield, Gloucestershire, in 1086.

ELIAS[R] GIFFARD I, who died by 1211, married ALA, who was probably a daughter of Edward d'Evreux of Boynton in Wiltshire.

ELIAS[Q] GIFFARD II married BERTA[Q] DE CLIFFORD, daughter of Richard Fitz Pons.

ELIAS[P] GIFFARD III died before Michaelmas 1190.

HELIAS[O] GIFFARD IV married first JOAN MALTRAVERS, who died aafter 1221.

HELIAS[N] GIFFARD V, Lord Brimsfield, married second, before 1231, ALICE[N] MALTRAVERS of Litchet Maltravers in Dorset.

12. Sir JOHN[M] GIFFARD of Brim[p]sfield in Gloucestershire, born on the day of St. Wulstan, 19 Jan. [CP, 5:640b], about 1232, died at Boynton in Wiltshire 29 [CP, 5:643] May 1299 [cf. Le Strange Records, 292], and was buried in Malmesbury Abbey 11 June 1299.

He married first, in 1271, MATILDA (or Maud)[N] DE CLIFFORD[+], who was living in 1277 but was dead by 1283, the widow of William de Longespée III, who died by 3 Jan. 1257. She was daughter of Walter de Clifford (III) of Clifford in Herefordshire by Margaret (widow of John de Braiose), daughter of Llywelyn ab Iorwerth, Prince of North Wales, and inherited Corfham in Shropshire, which had been given by King Henry II to Walter de Clifford (I) for the love of fair Rosamond, his daughter.

His first wife had complained to King Henry III that she had been abducted from her manor of Canford in Dorset by John Giffard. John claimed he could prove that he had not abducted her and offered a fine of 300 marks for the marriage he had contracted with her. On 10 March 1270/1 the king ordered commissioners to visit and certify the truth of the matter [CP, 5:642c]. The report has not been found.

He married second, in 1286, Margaret, the widow of Sir John de Neville (who died shortly before 20 May 1282) of Hallingbury in Essex and other properties. She died shortly before 13 Dec. 1338. On 9 May 1285 Richard, Bishop of Hereford, had written from London to the Pope for dispensation for the marriage within the third and fourth degrees of consanguity.

He held lands also in Badgeworth, Stonehouse, Stoke Gifford and Rockhampton in Gloucestershire, and Elston, Orcheston St. George, Sherrington, Ashton and Broughton Gifford in Wiltshire [CP, 5:639].

On 11 June 1263 he and several other barons seized the Bishop of Hereford and took him to Eardisley Castle, and on the following 18 Aug. he was among those who made a treaty with Prince Edward, having been appointed 7 Aug., on the advice of the magnates, keeper of the castle of St. Briavel and the forest of the Dean. On 18 Sept. he was pardoned for failure to observe the Provisions of Oxford. On 24 Dec. of the same year he was appointed keeper of the counties of Gloucester, Worcester and Hereford. As a member of the baronial party he was in command at Kenilworth in April 1264, and surprised and destroyed Warwick Castle, taking the Earl and Countess prisoners.

On 14 May 1264 he was captured early in the battle of Lewes, having already taken William la Zouche prisoner. On 16 Feb. 1264/5 he was among those prohibited from participating in the tournament at Dunstaple, and was ordered to attend Council three days later. He was among those who changed sides with the Earl of Gloucester and was a member of the King's army at Evesham on 4 Aug. 1265. For his services in that battle he was pardoned for having supported Simon de Montfort at Lewes, as well as any other trespasses.

On 24 April 1274 he was a commissioner empowered to make a truce between Llywelyn ap Gruffudd, Prince of Wales, and Humphrey de Bohun of Brecon. On 6 Nov. 1281 he was licensed to hunt wolves with his own hounds throughout the English forests of the King. He joined forces with Sir Edmund[L] de Mortimer in 1282, sharing in the victory over Llywelyn ap Gruffudd. Norr observed that John's wife was thus wife of the victor and stepdaughter of the vanquished. On 9 April 1282 he was appointed keeper of the castle at Llandovery in Carmarthenshire, Wales, and on the following 14 Oct. he was appointed keeper of Builth castle in Brecon as well. On 18 Nov. 1283 he was granted the commote of Iscennen in Carmarthenshire in fee, held by the service of one knight's fee, and on 8 Feb. 1289/90 he was awarded the castle of Dynefor for life; however on 29 July 1297 he was ordered to deliver this castle to Walter de Pederton.

He had been present at the assemblies in Berwick on Oct. and Nov. 1292, which were held to discuss the claims to the Scottish crown. As captain he had surrendered the town of Podensac in Gascony to the French in 1294/5. He had been summoned for military service from 1257 to 1299, to the Council in 1297, and to Parliament from 24 June 1295 to 10 April 1299.

Children, discussed by Watson [CP, 5:647-648], by first wife:

    i.   Catherine[L], b. 1272; m. by 1299 Nicholas de Audley.

    *   ii.   Eleanor, b. 1275; m. by 1307 Fulk[L] le Strange of Blackmere, who was d. by 23 Jan. 1323/4.

          iii.   Maude, b. 1277; d. 1232; m. William Geneville; no issue.

          iv.   Elizabeth.

Child, by second wife:

          v.   Sir John, b. prob. 24 June 1287; hanged at Gloucester for treason 1322; m. before 6 Nov. 1311 Aveline de Courtenay, who d. 27 April 1327.

§ § §

DE GOURNAY

This has been developed from Bardolf sources, namely Weis *AR7*, line 257. Farrer, *Honours and Knight's Fees*, 350, needs to be checked.

1. HUGH[Q] DE GOURNAY died in 1215.

He married JULIANA DE DAMMARTIN, who died in 1238 [Evans, *Genealogists' Magazine*, 15:56, 62[23]], daughter of Aubri II, comte de Dammartin.

He was seigneur de Gournay, in France.

Child:

    2.   i.   Hugh[P], m. Maud.

2. HUGH[P] DE GOURNAY died in 1239.

His wife was MAUD.

He was of Mapledurham, Oxfordshire.

Children:

    *   i.   Juliana[O], d. 1295; m. William[O] Bardolf of Wormegay, Norfolk, who d. 1295 [*CP*, 1:417].

    +   ii.   Melicent, d. 1265; m. (1) Amauri de Montfort, m. (2) William[M] de Cauntelo II, who d. 22 Feb. 1251.

§ § §

GOUSHILL

The details of this line were originally extracted from David Faris' *Plantagenet Ancestry*, 1st ed., 107.

Details of Sir Robert[J] Goushill's first three wives need to be developed. *The Dictionary of National Biography* (1898) [54:75] does not mention them.

1. Sir ROBERT[J] GOUSHILL, of Hoveringham, Nottinghamshire, was slain at the Battle of Shrewsbury on 21 July 1403.

He married fourth, without the king's license, before 19 Aug. 1401, ELIZABETH[I] FITZ ALAN*, sister and coheiress of Thomas Fitz Alan, Earl of Arundel, who died in 1415 without issue. She had married first, before Dec. 1378, Sir William de Montagu, son and heir of the Earl of Salisbury, who died 6 Aug. 1382 without issue. She married second, in July 1384, Thomas de Mowbray, later Duke of Norfolk, with whom she had four children. He died of pestilence in Venice (Italy), 22 Sept. 1399. On 19 Aug. 1401 her dower lands were ordered back into the king's hands, but she was pardoned for marrying third Robert Goushill without the king's license and her lands were restored upon payment of a fine of

2000 marks. She married fourth, before 18 April 1411 [*CP*, 14:503], Sir Gerard Ufflete, whose will was proved in Feb. 1420/1. She died 8 July 1425.

Having received a life interest in the estates of the Duke of Norfolk as dower, at the time of her marriage to Robert Goushill, Esquire, she was one of the richest widows in England, with lands in the counties of York, Lincoln, Warwick, Nottingham, Cambridge, Huntingdon, Salop (Shropshire) and Derby, as well as in the march of Wales.

Subsequent to his fourth marriage he was knighted and received control of Elizabeth's dower land.

Children of Thomas de Mowbray and Elizabeth Fitz Alan, surnamed de Mowbray:

  i.   John[1], Duke of Norfolk.
  ii. Isabel, d. Gloucester Castle, 23 Sept. 1452, bur. Church of the Greyfriars, Gloucester; m. (1) 1416 Sir Henry Ferrers, m. (2) c. 1423 as his third wife James Berkeley, Lord Berkeley of Berkeley, Gloucs., who d. Berkeley Castle Nov. 1463.
  iii. Margaret, d. c. 1440; m. c. 1420 Sir Robert Howard.

Children of Robert Goushill and Elizabeth Fitz Alan, surnamed Goushill:

  * iv. Joan, b. c. 1401; l. 1460; m. Sir Thomas[1] Stanley, K.G.
     v.   Elizabeth, b. c. 1402; l. Oct. 1452; m. Sir Robert Wingfield of Letheringham, Suffolk, who was d. by 21 Nov. 1454; was M.P. for Suffolk 1427/8 and attended the Duke of Norfolk on his embassy to France in 1447 [Hansen, *TAG*, 67 (1992), 100].

§ § §

DE GREY OF RUTHIN

This presentation is based on the work of Miss Burford Butcher (who was assisted by G.W. Watson), which appeared in Cokayne's *Complete Peerage*.

1. HENRY[P] DE GREY was of Grays Thurrock.
He married ISEULDE[P] DE BARDOLF.
Sons, listed in Cokayne's *CP* [6:128 chart]:

     i.   Richard[O], of Codnor, l. 1253; m. Lucy de Humez.
     ii. William, of Sandacre.
2.   iii. John, d. before 18 March 1265/6; m. (1) Emma de Glanville, m. (2) Emma de Cauz, m. (3) Mrs. Joan Peyvre.

2. Sir JOHN[O] DE GREY of Shirland died shortly before 18 March 1265/6.
He married first Emma de Glanville, daughter and coheir of John de Glanville.

He married second EMMA DE CAUZ (apparently the widow of John de Segrave, who died without issue 1230, son of Stephen de Segrave [*CP*, 6:171]), daughter of Roger[P] de Cauz by Nichole[P] de Leigh, daughter of Bartholomew[Q] de Leigh. According to Miss Butcher he was probably a younger son of Roger de Cauz, who succeeded in 1202 as Roger de Duston to the falconer serjeanty held by Roger de Cauz; his grandfather Roger's hawks and falcons were mentioned in Wiltshire in 1155-1156. Bartholomew[Q] de Leigh of Thurleigh, Podinton and Snellson, was son of Hugh[R] de Leigh (of the same lands) presumably by Beatrice de Glanville, for Bartholomew[Q] de Leigh mentioned in his will his "uncle" William de Glanville, whom his father Hugh de Leigh presented to the church of Thurleigh. Bartholomew[Q] de Leigh married Emma (who was living 1242), daughter and coheir of William Ruffus of Armston, Northamptonshire, and Kingsham and Eggele in Sussex.

He married third, in London, without license, after 17 Oct. 1251, Joan, widow of Paul Peyvre or Piper [*CP*, 6:171d] (the king's steward), who died in London, 5 June 1251; they were fined 500 marks for marrying without a license.

He was succeeded as Sheriff of Nottinghamshire and Derbyshire, and Constable of Nottingham Castle, by his son Reynold.

Children, by first wife [*CP*, 6:171e], by first wife:

  i.   Reynold[N], no issue.

  ii. Emma, m. Walter de Huntingfield.

Child, by second wife:

3. iii. Reynold, d. 1308; m. Maud[N] de Longchamp.

3. Sir REYNOLD (or Reginald)[N] DE GREY, lord Grey of Wilton, died in 1308.

He married MAUD[N] DE LONGCHAMP, daughter of Henry de Longchamp of Wilton, Herefordshire; she died before 21 Nov. 1302. Henry's descent from Hugh de Longchamp, grantee in the time of King Richard I, is given in the record of proceedings before the Justices Itinerant at Hereford in Trinity term 20 Edw. I. According to T.C. Banks' *Dormant and Extinct Baronage* [1:120] Hugh Longchamp was given Wilton by King Henry I, and was succeeded by Hugh, his son and heir, who was succeeded by Henry Longchamp, a Sheriff of Herefordshire during the reign of Henry II, and of Worcestershire during the reign of Richard I. Henry married Maud (who was sister of William de Cantelupe [or Cantelou]) and was succeeded by Henry who married Joane, widow of Thomas Birkin. His only daughter Maud married Reginald de Grey, Chief Justice of Cheshire, who thereby acquired Wilton. The last Henry Longchamp was succeeded by his brother William, who became baron in 46 Hen. II.

He had a grant of a weekly market at his manor of Wilton in 1257. He was appointed Sheriff of Nottinghamshire and Derbyshire, and Constable of Nottingham Castle on 18 March 1265/6, succeeding his father. On 28 Dec. 1266 he was ordered to deliver Nottingham Castle to Roger de Leyburne. He then served as constable of Northampton Castle and then, from 1270 to 16 Oct. 1274, as Justice of Chester, Constable of Chester Castle and Sheriff of Cheshire. Summoned for military service from 12 Dec. 1274 to 8 July 1306, he was also called to Parliament from 24 June 1295 to 26 Aug. 1307. He served in Wales with King Edward I in 1277 and 1282, and was appointed on 14 Nov. 1281 as Justice of Chester and Keeper of Cheshire, as well as of the castles in Cheshire and Flint and the cantreds of Englefield and Ros for eight years at a rent of 1000 marks per year. At the conclusion of the term he was reappointed for nine years at 727 marks and 8/- per year. On 15 June 1282 the king granted him Bromfield and Yale in Denbighshire during the king's pleasure, and on 23 Oct. 1282 the castle of Ruthin, the cantred of Dyffryn Clwyd, and those lands which had belonged to Gwenllian de Lascy in the cantreds of Dyffryn Clwyd and Englefield, to hold in fee for the service of three knights' fees.

He was at the battle of Falkirk on 22 July 1298, and on 26 May 1301 he did homage and fealty for Ruthin Castle to Edward, Prince of Wales, at Kenilworth.

His lands included Ruthin in Denbighshire, Wales; Wilton in Herefordshire; Shirland in Derbyshire; Rushton in Cheshire; Purleigh in Essex; Toseland, Hemingford and Yelling in Huntingdonshire; Water Eaton or Waterhall, Snellson and Great Brickhill in Buckinghamshire; Thurleigh, Wrest and Brogborough in Bedfordshire, and Kempley in Gloucestershire, all in England.

Child [*CP*, 6:173]:

4. i. John[M], d. 28 Oct. 1323; m. poss. Anne de Ferrers of Groby, m. (2) Maud (poss. Basset).

4. JOHN[M] DE GREY, lord Grey of Wilton, died 28 Oct. 1323, and was buried about 18 Nov. 1323.

It is said that he married first Anne de Ferrers, daughter of Sir William de Ferrers of Groby, Leicestershire, daughter of Sir William[N] de Ferrers by his first wife Anne Despenser of Ryhall, Rutland.

He married second Maud, who has been identified as a daughter of Sir Ralph[N] Basset by Margaret[M] de Somery.

He sold the manor of Stokesay in Shropshire to Lawrence de Ludlow by 1281 [Eyton, 5:36]. Aged forty or more when he had livery of his father's lands on 5 May 1308, he gave fealty to the escheator South of Trent. By a charter dated 7 April 1310 he founded a collegiate church at Ruthin, and on 18 Nov. 1311 he had license to convey to himself for life Ruthin Castle, the cantred of Dyffryn Clwyd and the manor of Rushton, Cheshire, with the remainder to his son Roger in tail general.

He was at the battle of Bannockburn on 24 June 1314, and on 19 Feb. 1314/5 was appointed Justiciar of North Wales during pleasure; Roger de Mortimer of Chirk was appointed his successor in 1316. Summoned to military service from 21 June 1308 to 3 April 1323, and to Councils in 1308/9 and 1324, he was summoned to Parliament from 4 March 1308/9 to 18 Sept. 1322.

Children [CP, 6:175]:

    i.   Henry[L], b. 28 Oct. 1281 or 1282; d. 10 or 16 Dec. 1342; m. (it is said) Anne de Rockley.

5.   ii.   Sir Roger, younger son, m. Elizabeth[L] Hastings.

5. Sir ROGER[L] DE GREY, 1st Lord Grey of Ruthin, died 6 March 1352/3.

He married by 1311 [CP, 14:354] ELIZABETH[L] DE HASTINGS* of Abergavenny.

On 11 March 1323/4 he gave homage to King Edward II for the castle of Ruthin and the cantred of Dyffryn Clwyd with thirty-one manors, all of which he inherited from his father upon payment of fines. He was of record as about to go to Scotland in June 1327, in the retinue of the Earl of Lancaster. He was summoned for military service from 21 March 1332/3 to 27 March 1335, to Councils from 30 Dec. 1324 to 20 March 1350/1, and to Parliament from 10 Oct. 1325 to 15 Nov. 1351.

He bore arms, Barry of six, *Argent* and *Azure*, in chief three roundlets *Gules*. He held Ruthin in Denbighshire, Wales; Thurleigh, Harrold, Puddington, Wrest and Brogborough in Bedfordshire; Great Brickhill, Bletchley and Snellson in Buckinghamshire; Yelling and Hemingford Turberville in Huntingdonshire, and Holwell in Hertfordshire.

Children, from *CP*:

    i.   John[K], d. between 6 Jan. 1349 [CP, 14:354] and 6 Feb. 1350; m. Anneys de Mountagu; no issue [CP, 6:152].

    ii.   Reynold, lord Grey of Ruthin, d. 1388; m. before 20 Nov. 1360 Alianore[J] Lestrange, who d. 20 April 1396 of Blackmere [CP, 14:354].

*   iii.   Juliane, d. 29 Nov. or 1 Dec. 1361; m. shortly before 14 Feb. 1329/30 Sir John[K] de Talbot, who d. 20 Sept. 1355.

§ § §

GROSVENOR OF HOLME

The surname was said to have been derived from *le Gros Venour*, a hereditary post of chief huntsman to the Dukes of Normandy [Ormerod, 3:149d]. However, Ormerod rejected this theory [3:144].

GILBERT[R] LE GROSVENOR was reputed to be the ancestor of this family, and may have been the same as Gilbert[S] Venables, alias Venator, who was living in Cheshire in 1086. He was said to have been a nephew of Hugh Lupus, Earl of Chester; he came to England with William the Conqueror. James Croston [298] called him a younger son of Eudo, Earl of Blois, and a first cousin of William the Conqueror.

ROBERT[Q] LE GROSVENOR of Over Lostock, Cheshire, has occurred as the father of Henry[P] le Grosvenor in only one document. HENRY[P] GROSVENOR was next in the pedigree presented by Ormerod. RAUFE[O] GROSVENOR was engaged in the battle of Lincoln in 1141, and was living during the reign of King John, who ruled 1199-1216.

RICHARD[N] GROSVENOR, according to the deeds of Randle Grosvenor, according to the abbot of Vale Royal son of Raufe, and according to Sir Peter Leycester, was son of either Raufe or Randle. He was last mentioned in 1269 in an agreement with the prior of Norton concerning the chapel of Nether Peover.

ROBERT[M] GROSVENOR was dead in 21 Edw. I (1292-1293). He married MARGERY, who was living in 1304.

7.   ROBERT[L] LE GROSVENOR, of Hulme, Cheshire, was born after 1272 (for he was underage in 21 Edw. I [1292-1293]), and died in 1342.

He married first Margery, who was likely a Vernon of Shipbrook. They appeared together in trust deeds relating to his manor of Allostock in 34 Edw. I (c. 1306).

He married second Emma[K] de Mobberley, daughter of William[L] de Mobberley and coheiress of her mother Maud[L] Downes, daughter and heiress of Robert Downes of Chorley. She was recorded as a widow in 1342 and 1373.

In right of his wife he had lands in Chorlegh and Werford, and in 1337 he purchased over one-third of Over Alderley from the Heartgreave family.

He served in the wars in Scotland under King Edward II.

Children, mentioned by Ormerod [3:146]:

8.   i.   Ralph[K], d. c. 1357; m. Joan.

8.   RALPH[K] GROSVENOR died in or before 30 Edw. III (1356-1357).

He married JOAN, who was mentioned in a lease concerning Over Alderley in 16 Edw. III (1342).

Child, from Ormerod [3:146]:

9.   i.   Robert[J], d. before 23 April 19 Ric. II; m. (1) Joan Daniell, m. (2) c. 1378 Joan[J] Pulford, m. (3) Anne.

9. Sir ROBERT[J] GROSVENOR died before 23 April 19 Ric. II (1395-1396).

He married first Joan (or Margaret) Daniell, who died without issue.

He married second, about 1378, JOAN[J] PULFORD*, daughter of Sir Robert Pulford and sister and heiress of John Pulford, and widow of Thomas de Belgreave, son of John de Belgreave.

His third wife, Anne, was mentioned in his *inquisition post mortem* 20 Ric. II.

As he was underage when his father died he was made the ward of Sir John Daniell, who married him to his daughter.

He was a party to challenges made by Sir John Daniell and Sir Richard le Scrope to the use of his arms; the latter suit was tried before the Constable and Marshall of England 10-13 Ric. II (1386-1390).

Nearly all the knights and gentlemen of Cheshire and Lancashire were examined concerning the Grosvenor use of arms, along with several abbots and other clergy. All supported Sir Robert Grosvenor, saying they were used by Gilbert le Grosvenor in 1066 and had been used in many battles ever since.

However, Sir Richard Scrope was supported by many from other areas, including Geoffrey Chaucer, then aged 40. Sir Richard was descended from "Richardus Scrobi filius," who was mentioned by Roger Hoveden in 1052 and 1067. Scrope won when it became apparent that both families had used the same arms for centuries, and Scrope had more powerful friends. Grosvenor refused to "beare the other coate with a difference," and adopted new arms.

About 1385-1386 (9 Ric. II) Sir Robert le Grosvenor was commissioned with Sir William de Brereton and others to arrest all disturbers of the peace in Northwich Hundred at a time of rioting.

He was appointed Sheriff of Cheshire on 1 Jan. 1390, and during the next year was made deputy of Roger de Crophull, constable of the castle of Chester. He resigned from office 26 Sept. 1392.

In 16 Ric. II (1392-1393) he was again commissioned, this time with Hugh de Coton, to arrest all disturbers of the peace, and on 31 Oct. 18 Ric. II (1394) he was appointed Sheriff of Cheshire again, but died within the year.

Children, by second wife [James Croston, 306]:

      i.   Cicely[I].

10.   ii.   Thomas, adult c. 1399; m. (1) Joan[I] Phesaunt, m. (2) Joan Venables.

10. Sir THOMAS[I] GROSVENOR was the subject of a *inquisition post mortem* held 8 Hen. VI (1429-1430).

He married first JOAN[I] (or Katherine) PHESAUNT, daughter and heiress of William Phesaunt or Feasant of Hulme [Croston, 309; *cf.* Ormerod, 1st ed., 2:454].

He married second Joan Venables, only daughter of Sir Richard[I] Venables of Kinderton, who was the Baron of Kinderton captured at Shrewsbury 20 July 1403, and executed in the market place of Shrewsbury the following Monday morning [Croston, 307]; she married second, in 1432, Sir Thomas Booth of Barton, Lancashire.

He served in Ireland 23 Ric. II (1399), and was involved in a suit over land on 24 April 1412. He was collector of the subsidy in 3 Hen. IV (1401-1402), and on 11 Jan. 4 Hen. IV (1402/3) was commanded to prepare his possessions at Pulford for defence against Owain Glyndŵr.

At his *inquisition post mortem* the total value of manors and lands, including the manors of Hulme, Pulford, Buyrton, a third of Waverton, a fourth of Chollegh, an eighth of Broxon, and lands in Bancroft, Dunhammasey, Keteleshulme, Claverton, Aldresey, Elton, Sondele-mosse and Nether Peover, was £43.8s.4d.

Children, by first wife [Ormerod, 3:149]:

11.   i.   Robert[H], b. c. 1407; d. c. 1464; m. Joan[H] Fyton.

      ii.   Ralph, of Eaton.

     iii.   Thomas of Bellaport, m. Isabella Peshale [J. Morris, 3498], dau. and coheir of Sir Richard Peshale of Chetwynd and Bellaport in Salop.

     iv.   Randle.

     v.   Margery, m. Hugh Calveley, son of Hugh Caveley of Lea.

     vi.   Joane, m. Randle Poole of Derbyshire.

11. ROBERT[H] GROSVENOR, of Hulme, Cheshire, was the subject of a *writ de diem* on 14 Jan. 4 Edw. IV (1464); on 27 Feb. of that year his widow had her dower.

He married in 1415 JOAN[H] FITTON* of Gawsworth, who died 21 Edw. IV (1481-1482).

His will, dated 8 Jan. 1464, directed that he be buried at Nether Peover, and named his wife executrix.

Children:
*   i.   Elizabeth[G], b. c. 1432; m. Peter[G] de Dutton of Hatton.
   ii.   Emma, b. c. 1434; m. (1) John Legh of Booths, m. (2) 1474 Radulph Egerton.
  iii.   Agnes, b. c. 1438; m. William Stanley of Hooton.
  iv.   Margery, d. 12 Edw. IV (c. 1472); unm.; inherited manor of Allostock.
   v.   Katherine, b. c. 1442; m. Richard Winnington of Wynnington.
  vi.   Margaret, b. c. 1444; m. Thomas Leycester of Tabley.

§ § §

GRUFFUDD AP MADOG

The compiler intends to develop this line in a work on the Welsh ancestors of certain Americans, in which the history will be found.

1. MADOG[Q] (AP MAREDUDD [d. 1132] AP BLEDDYN [d. 1075] AP CYNFYN AP GWERYSTAN AP GWAITHFOED OF POWYS AP GWYNNAN AP GWYNNOG FARFSYCH AP LLES LLAWDDEOG AP CEIDIO AP CORF AP CAENOG AP TEGONWY AP TEON AP GWINEU DEUFREUDDWYD AP BYWYR LEW AP BYWDEG AP RHUN RHUDD BALADR AP LLARY AP CASNAR WLEDIG) died in 1160.
He married first SUSANNA FERCH GRUFFUDD AP CYNAN.
He had children by EFA FERCH EIRIAN [Bertram's chart Idn. B. 5].
He had at least one child by a daughter of Y MAER DU.
He married second ARIANWEN FERCH MORIDDIG WARWYN [chart Drymb. 1].
Children, listed by Bartrum [chart Bl. ap C. 3], by his first wife:
  2.   i.   Gruffudd[P] Maelor, d. 1191; m. Angharad ferch Owain Gwynedd.
      ii.   Elise, of record 1183-1198.
Children, by Efa ferch Eirian:
    iii.   Einion Efell.
    iv.   Cynwrig Efell.
Child, by a daughter of Y Maer Du:
     v.   Owain Brogyntyn, flourished 1060-1088; m. Jonet ferch Hywel [El. G. 33].
Children, mothers not known:
    vi.   Llywelyn, d. 1160.
   vii.   Gwenllian, m. (1) Yr Arglwydd Rhys, m. (2) Maelgwn Hen.
  viii.   Margred, m. Iorwerth Drwyndwn.
    ix.   Efa, m. Cadwallon ap Madog.
     x.   Iorwerth, issue.
    xi.   Owain Fychan of Mechain, d. 1187; issue.
   xii.   Owain, m. Elinor ferch Maelgwn.
  xiii.   daughter, m. Hywel.

2. GRUFFUDD[P] MAELOR AP MADOG AP MAREDUDD AP BLEDDYN died in 1191.
He married ANGHARAD FERCH OWAIN GYWNEDD.
Children, listed by Bartrum:
  3.   i.   Madog[O], d. 1236; m. Gwladus ferch Ithel.
      ii.   Owain, d. 1197.
    iii.   Cristin, m. Meurig ap Robert [for whom see Bartrum chart Wm. of E. 4].

3. MADOG[O] AP GRUFFUDD MAELOR AP MADOG died in 1236.
He married GWLADUS FERCH ITHEL "FRENIN GWENT" AP RHYS AB IFOR of Cantref Selyf

AP HYWEL AP MORGAN FYCHAN of Ewias AP MORGAN HIR OF GWENT.
Children, listed by Bartrum:
4.   i.   Gruffudd[N], d. 1269; m. Emma[N] de Audley, widow of Henry Touchet.
     ii.   Gruffudd Iâl, d. 1238.
    iii.   Madog Fychan, d. 1269.
     iv.   Maredudd, d. 1256; m. Catrin ap Gruffudd.
      v.   Hywel, d. c. 1268.
     vi.   Iorwerth Ddu (for whom see Bartrum chart Bl. ap C. 6).

4. GRUFFUDD[N] AP MADOG AP GRUFFUDD MAELOR AP MADOG, lord of Dinas Brân in Yale, in Denbighshire, Wales, died in 1269.
He married EMMA[N] DE AUDLEY[+], who was born about 1218, and had married first Henry Touchet, who died 8 Jan. 1242 [Norr, 110].
Children, listed by Bartrum:
      i.   Madog[M], d. 1277.
     ii.   Llywelyn.
    iii.   Gruffudd Farwn Gwyn, m. Margred ferch Griffri.
*   iv.   Angharad, m. William[M] Boteler of Wem.
      v.   Gwenllian Deg, mentioned by Bartrum as questionable.

§ § §

HACKLUYT

This line has been adapted from Norr's *Early English Pedigrees* [75], and is highly conjectural insofar as these generations are concerned. The name is spelled Hackluit in Guppy's *Homes of Family Names in Great Britain*.

1. WALTER[J] HAKELUTEL was born say in 1228.
Children, a topic of conjecture:
2.   i.   Sir Walter[I], b. say 1254; m. Alice.
     ii.   Giles, prob. son [Eyton, 5:232], b. say 1256.

2. Sir WALTER[I] HACKLUYT, born say 1254, according to Norr [75], was dead by 17 Aug. 1314 [C. Moor, *Knights of Edward I*].
His wife, ALICE, was living in 1325, when she held one-third of a messuage at Bishop's Frome in Herefordshire of her late son Peter.
Edmund de Mortimer granted him lands of Griffin ab Owen in Elvayl Huchmanyt (Gruffudd ab Owain in Elfael) and he began to build a castle there in 1284. Of record 12 Nov. 1284 as having held an inquisitiion at Buelt, Wales, he was pardoned a debt of £57 to a Jew in Oct. 1285 for his expenses in erecting a new house in the Welsh Marches and crenellating it by license; the Jew was to have £20 from the King.
He was made *custos* of Morgannou 12 April 1292, and in 1293 was to have a messuage and lands at Bishop's Frome in Herefordshire. In 1297 he heard complaints of men of Breconshire, Wales, against the Earl of Hereford, and reinstated them in their lands. In the same year he was to choose 900 Welshmen from Morgannou to go across the sea with the King, and to choose more Welshmen to go to London. He was summoned to Council at Rochester 8 Sept. 1297. From 1292 to 1301 he served as Bailiff of Haverford West. In 1301 he was ordered to send a ship from Haverford against the Scots.
As King's yeoman he was made *custos* of Kynlet Manor, Shropshire, in 1303, to be paid

annually £15. He was knighted with Prince Edward, 22 May 1306, and was going overseas for King Edward II on 11 Dec. 1307. In 1308 he was ordered to levy and lead 600 men against the Scots. On 25 June 1310 he was Sheriff of Herefordshire, and 18 March 1313 he was Knight of the Shire for Hereford.

Children, listed by Norr [75]:

      i. Walter, Jr.[H], son of Alice.

*   ii. Katherine, possible dau., b. say 1288, m. Sir Nicholas[H] Coton (for whom see Cotton).

     iii. Peter, b. say 1290; prob. d. 1325; m. Isabella [Harl. Soc., 81:172]

     iv. Sir Richard, b. say 1292, brother of Katherine.

     v. Sir Edmund, possible son, b. say 1293, of Dynefor [see *Misc. Gen. et Her.*, 5:7:123]; dau. Joan m. (1) Reynold Fitz Herbert, m. (2) Sir Thomas Blount [*Misc. Gen. et Her.*, 5:7:115].

§ § §

DE HARINGTON

This family was developed from an article by James Brownbill in Cokayne's *Complete Peerage* [6:314-321], with some additions from Ian Grimble's *The Harington Family*.

1. OSULF[S] OF FLEMINGBY of Cumberland made a grant of land to the Priory of Carlisle "eighty years after Magnus Barelegs perished in Ireland" [Grimble, 19]. He flourished during the time of Richard I, who reigned from 1189 to 1199.

His name was that of a Northumbrian king who had been murdered 400 years earlier.

Child, mentioned by Grimble [19]:

2.   i. Robert[R], m. Christiana.

2. ROBERT[R] OF HARRINGTON in Cumberland was called Robertus de Hafrinctuna in a grant to the Priory of St. Bee's of a church and two hides of land.

His wife CHRISTIANA was mentioned as his advisor in the grant.

The church at Harrington was rebuilt in 1905.

Child, mentioned by Grimble [19]:

3.   i. Thomas[Q].

3. THOMAS[Q] HARINGTON was said by Grimble to have probably lived at Harrington.

Child:

4.   i. Michael[P].

4. MICHAEL[P] HARINGTON was of Haverington in Cumberland.

Child, mentioned by Grimble [19-20]:

5.   i. Sir Robert[O], d. 1297; m. Agnes[O] Cansfield, who d. 1293.

5. Sir ROBERT[O] DE HAVERINGTON of Havington, Cumberland, died in 1297.

He married AGNES[O] CANSFIELD[+], Lady of Aldingham, who died in 1293, daughter of Sir Richard Cansfield, lord of Cancefield and Farleton in Lancashire, and his wife Eleanor le Fleming, who was also called Alicia and Aline.

According to Grimble [20], the Plea Roll of 1277 contains a pedigree of his descent from Osulf which confirmed the evidence of the Register at St. Bee's [*cf.* Dugdale's *Monasticon*]. This evidence was part of a suit against the Abbot of Holm Culton concerning

Robert's claim to the manor of Flemingby, but Robert had to vacant all but 380 acres of the manor.

When his wife's brother, William Cansfield, drowned in the River Severn, Sir Robert inhertied the manor of Aldingham on the shores of Marecambe Bay in Lancashire. The estate included the manor house, garden and dove-house, 240 acres, an enclosed park and three mills (two water corn mills and a fulling mill). However, most was lost to the encroaching sea.

Children:

      i.   Michael[N], living 1298.

6.   ii. Sir John, heir, b. c. 1281; d. 2 July 1347; m. Joan.

6. Sir JOHN[N] DE HARINGTON, 1st Lord Harington, born about 1281, died 2 July 1347 [*Cal. Inq.p.m.*, 9:30], and was buried in Cartmel Church, with his wife in a tomb where the Dacre escallops alternate with the Harrington fret. On this tomb the chain mail is carved minutely, and its folds at the elbows and other loose places are defined very skillfully.

He married JOAN, who was probably a Dacre [*CP*, 6:315n].

Sir William de Dacre was granted his wardship for five years from Michaelmas 1297 [*CP*, 6:314f].

He was of Aldingham, Lancashire, and Caucefield and Farleton (in the rich valley of the Lune in Lancashire), was knighted in Westminster 22 May 1306 in company with Edward Prince of Wales, and was probably among those going to Scotland with the Prince in an effort to avenge the murder of John[L] Comyn. He was called for military service from 1309 to 1335, to Councils from 30 Dec. 1324 to 25 Feb. 1341/2, and served as a Member of Parliament from 1326 to 1347. He held the manors of Aldingham, Thurnham and Ulverston in Lancashire, Witherslack and Hutton Roof in Westmorland, and Austwick and Harington in Cumberland.

He received a pardon in 1313 for having supported the Earl of Lancaster at the time of the murder of Piers de Gavaston, and another pardon for being the Earl's adherent in Nov. 1318. He obeyed the king's order to stay away from the Earl of Lancaster's meeting of "good peers" at Doncaster in 1321, and was not recorded as having participated in the Earl's uprising in the spring of 1322. He was outlawed in 1323 when the treason of Andrew de Harcla, whom he had assisted in the Scottish Marches, was discovered, but was pardoned on surrender, and was a custodian of the truce with the Scots later in the year.

In 1832, during restoration to its screen, the tomb was opened, and some of his bones and those of his hawk, with a part of his leather doublet, were removed to the possession of the senior descendant.

Children:

7.   i. Sir Robert[M], d. 1334; m. Elizabeth[M] de Multon.

      ii. Sir John, d. 1359; m. Katherine Banastre [Hornyold-Strickland, *Members Parl. Lancs.*, 44].

7. Sir ROBERT[M] DE HARINGTON, of Aldingham, Lancashire, died in Ireland [Grimble, 24] in 1334.

He married in or before 1327 ELIZABETH[M] DE MULTON* of Egremont, who married second, at age 28 in or before Nov. 1334, Walter[L] de Bermingham.

He was a knight in 1331 when he was going to Ireland in the service of King Edward III. By his marriage he brought several manors, including some in Limerick, Ireland, and Suffolk and Lincolnshire, into the hands of the family.

Children [*BP*, 1:1315]:

8.   i. Sir John[L], d. Gleaston Castle 28 May 1363; m. Joan de Bermingham.

ii. Sir Robert.
iii. Simon.

8. Sir JOHN[L] HARINGTON, Lord Harington of Aldingham, died in Gleaston Castle on 28 May 1363.

He married, some have said, JOAN[L] DE BERMINGHAM, daughter of Walter de Bermingham.

Aged 19 or more at the time of his father's death in 1334, he gave fealty to King Edward III on 9 Sept. 1347. He was a Member of Parliament from 13 Nov. 1347 to 10 March 1348/9. From 1351 he served as Commissioner, and in 1353 he confirmed an agreement his grandfather had made with the Abbot of Furness.

As the sea encoached upon Aldingham, leaving only the church at the east end, he built Gleaston Castle rather hurriedly upon a parcel there. The castle, which was probably completed by 1350 [Grimble, 25], consists of four towers and curtain walls enclosing a ward of 240 feet by 120 to 150 feet, although no north curtain wall was ever built. Ruins remain.

Child:
9.   i. Sir Robert[K], b. 1356; d. Aldingham 21 May 1406; m. (2) 1383 Isabel[K] Loring.

9. Sir ROBERT[K] HARINGTON, K.B., born at Gleaston, baptized in Aldingham in Lancashire 28 March 1356, died in Aldingham 21 May 1406.

In 1363 his marriage was granted to Richard de Pembrigg, but the grant was surrendered in 1372. He married first, about 1376, Alice de Greystoke, daughter of William, Lord Greystoke, by his second wife Joan, daughter of Sir Henry Fitz Henry of Ravensworth. She died soon afterwards.

He married second, in 1383, ISABEL[K] LORING*, widow of Sir William Cogan of Huntsfield, or Huntspill, Somerset, who died in 1382. She died 21 Aug. 1400.

He was a ward of the King, who granted custody of his lands in England and Ireland to his daughter Isabel, later the wife of Ingram de Coucy, Earl of Bedford. Once of age in 1377 he had livery of his lands in England, and obtained livery of lands in Ireland in 1380. By his second marriage estates in Somerset, Devon and Cornwall came to the family.

He was knighted on the occasion of the Coronation of Richard II, 16 July 1377, when he was in the king's service at Calais. He was summoned to Parliament from 4 Aug. 1377 to 21 Dec. 1405. As one of the Lords temporal he swore on the alter of the shrine of St. Edward at Westminster, 30 Sept. 1397, to maintained the acts of the previous parliament. In 1398 he was pardoned for adhering to Thomas, Duke of Gloucester, in 1386.

His daughter was of Hornby, Lancashire.

Children, by second wife, mentioned by Brownbill [CP, 6:316-317]:
i. John[J], b. c. 1384; d. 11 Feb. 1417/8 [CP, 6:318]; m. 1411 Elizabeth Courtenay (dau. of Edward Courtenay, 3rd Earl of Devon), who d. 18 Oct. 1471, having m. (2) William, Lord Bonville, who was executed 18 Feb. 1460/1.
* ii. Isabel, m. Sir John[J] Stanley, who d. 1431.
iii. William, b. c. 1389; d. 3/10 March 1457/8; m. Margaret Hill, dau. of Sir John Hill [BP, 1:1315]; he has been confused with his kinsman, Sir William Harington of Hornby, Lancs. [CP, 6:319; cf. Dugdale's Baronage]; had dau. Elizabeth, who m. c. 1442 William Bonville, who was killed at the battle of Wakefield, 31 Dec. 1460 [CP, 6:320].

§ § §

DE HARLEY

This outline was based originally on the work of Vernon Norr and the *Visitations*.

Sir WILLIAM^Q DE HARLEY of Shropshire went to Jerusalem in the company of Godfrey of Bullen, Robert Curteis Duke of Normandy, and Robert Steward of Scotland, where they were made Knight of the Sepulchre. He married CATHERINE^Q CROFTE.

NICHOLAS^P HARLEY DE HARLEY was of Shropshire. He married MARGARET^P BOSTOCK.

WILLIAM^O HARLEY DE HARLEY was of Shropshire. He married JOAN^O DE LA BERE, daughter of Sir John^P de la Bere.

NICHOLAS^N HARLEY DE HARLEY was apparently of Shropshire. He married ALICE^N RANDULPH, daughter of Robert Randulph, alias Prescott, of Westhope in Shropshire.

5. Sir ROBERT^M HARLEY may have lived in Shropshire.

He married ALICE^M PULESTON, daughter and heiress of Sir Robert [Roger in Norr] Puleston.

Children:
6.   i.   Richard^L, dead in 1316; m. before Dec. 1283 Burga^L of Willey.
     ii.   Margaret, m. John Parker.
     iii.   Malcolm.
*   iv.   Sibyl, m. Robert^N de la Bere.

6. RICHARD^L DE HARLEY was dead in 1316.

He married, before Dec. 1283 [Eyton's *Ant. Shropshire*, 2:51], BURGA^L OF WILLEY*, who had married first Philip de Stapleton, son of William de Stapleton. She was the heiress of Willey.

Child:
7.   i.   Sir Robert^K, d. 16 May 1349; m. by 2 Nov. 1309 Margaret^K de Brompton, who d. 24 June 1349.

7. Sir ROBERT^K DE HARLEY of Harley, Shropshire [Eales, 29-30], died, probably of the Black Death, 16 May 1349.

He married, by 2 Nov. 1309, MARGARET^K DE BROMPTON*, who died 24 June 1349, probably of the Black Death.

This was the first generation of Harleys at Brampton Bryan, Herefordshire, about six miles northwest of Wigmore.

He inherited Willey from his mother, and Eylton [Eyton?] in marriage.

Children:
     i.   Walter^J, d. young.
     ii.   Johanna, m. 1344 Gilbert de Lacy of Castle Frome.
8.   iii.   Robert, "fatuus," b. 1320/1; d. 1370; m. c. 1356 Joan^I Corbet, who m.
         (2) by 23 June 1390 John Darras (or d'Aras), and was l. 20 June 1417.
     iv.   Sir Brian, m. Eleanor^J Corbet.

8. ROBERT^J DE HARLEY, called *fatuus* (fool, idiot or simpleton), born in 1320/1, died in 1370.

He married about 1356 JOAN^I CORBET*, who was born about 1330 and was living 20 June 1417 [Paul C. Reed, *TG*, 10:39]. She married second, by 23 June 1390, John Darras (or d'Aras), a Shropshire gentleman who was Sheriff of Shropshire 8 Nov. 1401.

Child:

*   i.   Alesia (or Alice)[l], b. c. 1359; d. by Easter term 1389; m. Sir Hamo[nd][l] de Peshall, who d. by 1399.

§ § §

HASTANG

This outline is based on Cokayne's *Complete Peerage* [6:339-344].

About 1121-1126 Eutrope Hastang gave Robert, Bishop of Coventry, and his successors, a charter granting to St. Oswald Nostell the churches of Chebsey in Staffordshire, Leamington and Newbold, and confirmed a grant by his father, Humphrey, of the mill of Salford. Sir Robert[P] Hastang was Eutrope's descendant [*CP*, 6:340a].

Weis noted [*MCS5*, 28:8] that Ralph de Stafford of Grafton, Broomsgrove, Worcestershire, who died 1 March 1410, married Maud de Hastang, who was baptized 2 Feb. 1358/9, daughter of John Hastang of Leamington House, Warwickshire, citing *CP* [6:343f]. The footnote mentions Humphrey Stafford, son of Humphrey, son of Maud, daughter of John, son of John, son of Sir Thomas Hastang and Elizabeth, and makes reference to *Genealogist*, n.s., 13:30, which might be the source of the additional detail given by Weis.

Sir ROBERT[N] HASTANG was of Chebsey, Staffordshire, and of Leamington Hastang and Budbrook, Warwickshire. He married JOAN[N] DE CURLI, daughter of William de Curli of Budbrook, who was a brother of John de Curli.

Sir ROBERT[M] HASTANG was of Chebsey, Staffordshire, and of Lemington Hastang and Budbrook, Warwickshire, and appears to have died before Michaelmas 1304. He may be the Robert Hastang who married, 2 Sept. 1285, Isabel Fitz Alan. However, she could not have been mother of Lord Hastang or of his elder brother John.

3.   Sir JOHN[L] HASTANG was the brother of Sir Robert[L] Hastang, and father of Sir Thomas[K]. He was apparently dead in or before 1332, when Thomas Hastang was assessed 5s at Chebsey, Staffordshire.

He and his wife EVA were both mentioned in connection with the manor of East Leamington, Warwickshire, in 1311.

He was apparently the Sir John Hastang who had letters of protection while going to the King in Gascony on 8 March 1288/9. He may have been the one in service in Scotland, Ireland and Wales between 1284 and 1287. On 30 July 1307 John de Hastang of Staffordshire was a surety of John, Earl of Atholl, on the earl's release from the Tower of London.

On 31 Aug. 1306 he was steward of the Queen's Household, and he was to accompany the Queen Dowager abroad on 1 Dec. 1307. On 1 Aug. 1309 he was licensed to crenellate his house at Chebsey. On 20 Aug. 1321 he was pardoned for his part against the Despensers. On 9 May 1324 he was summoned to Council from Staffordshire.

Children, the first mentioned by Cokayne [*CP*, 6:341b], the second by Faris in *Plantagenet Ancestry*, 2nd ed. [338]:

         i.   Sir Thomas[K], m. (1) before 28 March 1310 Maud Deiville, m. (2) by July 1325 Elizabeth.

*   ii.   Katherine, m. c. 1326 Sir Ralph[K] Stafford, K.G., who d. 31 Aug. 1372.

§ § §

HASTINGS

This connection was developed by surveying Weis' work and then studying the article on the family by Miss Burford Butcher in Cokayne's *Complete Peerage* [6:345-351], the pedigree chart [*CP*, 6:366] and Vernon Norr's *Some Early English Pedigrees* [36].

WILLIAM[Q] DE HASTINGS was mentioned in Weis' *Magna Charta Sureties*. He married MARGARET[N] BIGOD.

Sir HENRY[P] DE HASTINGS of Ashill, Norfolk [*CP*, 6:345], died shortly before 9 Aug. 1250. He married before 7 June 1237 ADA[O] OF HUNTINGDON, who was living 2 Nov. 1241.

Sir HENRY[O] DE HASTINGS of Ashill, Norfolk, died shortly before 5 March 1268/9. He married JOAN[K] DE CANTELOU, sister and coheir of Sir George de Cantelou, Lord of Abergavenny; she died before June 1271.

4. Sir JOHN[N] HASTINGS, 2nd Baron Hastings, Baron Avergavenny, born in Ashill (or Allesley), Norfolk, 6 May 1262, died 10 Feb. 1312/3; a writ of *diem cl. ext.* was issued 28 Feb. 1312/3 [*CP*, 1:23, 6:348].

He married first, in 1275, ISABEL[N] VALENCE (for whom see DE LUSIGNAN[+]), who died 5 Oct. 1305, and was buried in Coventry Priory. She was a daughter of William[M] de Valence, lord of Valence, Montignac, Bellac, Rancon and Champagnac in France (fourth son of Hugh X "le Brun" de Lusignan and Isabel, the widow of King John of England) and his wife Joan[M] de Munchensi.

He married second, before 1308, Isabel[M] le Despenser, who married second, as his second wife, before 20 Nov. 1318, Sir Ralph de Mounthermer, who died 5 April 1325, and was buried in the Church of the Grey Friars at Salisbury. She had charge of two of the daughters of King Edward II from Michaelmas 1324. She died 4 or 5 Dec. 1334.

Norr referred to him as sixth in descent from William Hastings who held the lordship in 1175 [see *CP*, 1:28].

The King took his homage on 12 July 1283. Of his father and also his share of the Cantelou properties he held the castle and honour of Abergavenny in Monmouthshire, the castle of Kilgerran, Pembrokeshire, one-third of St. Clear in Carmarthenshire, Aston in Warwickshire, and lands in Somerset and Suffolk. In Jan. 1283/4 he was recorded as about to go to Scotland, and in 1287 he served the king in Wales.

In 1292 he claimed a third part of the Kingdom of Scotland as the grandson of Ada, fourth daughter and coheir of David, Earl of Huntingdon; the claim was rejected at Berwick Castle on 17 Nov. 1292.

In Jan. 1296/7 he was about to go to Brabant in attendance on Margaret, Duchess of Brabant, daughter of King Edward I of England. He was at the siege of Caerlaverock in Scotland in July 1300, and took part in the Barons' Letter to the Pope of 12 Feb. 1300/1. He was appointed Lieutenant and Seneschal of Gascony in 1302 and again in 1309. On 15 March 1308/9 he had license to grant lands in Wales in fee to his son John.

Children, by first wife [*CP*, 6:366]:

  i. William[M], b. 4 Oct. 1282; d. shortly before 1 March 1310/1; affianced to Alianore Martin, first dau. of Sir William Martin of Cemais in Pembrokeshire, the contract dated at Ghent 30 Sept. 1297; no issue.

  ii. John, b. 30 Sept. 1286; d. (before?) 5 April 1325; m. Juliane Leybourne (dau. of Sir Thomas Leybourne and stepdau. of Guy de Beauchamp), who m. (2) 1325 Sir Thomas le Blount, m. (3) 1328 William Clynton.

 * iii. Elizabeth, m. Roger[M] Grey, 1st Lord Grey of Ruthin, Denbighshire, who d. 6 March 1352/3.

Children, by second wife:
  iv. Thomas, d. 1333; no issue.
   v. Sir Hugh, m. Margery Foliot.
  vi. Margaret, d. July 1359; m. William Martin, who d. 1326 [Norr, 36].

§ § §

HAWBERKE

This section is from the Hopton pedigree in *The Visitation of Shropshire, 1623* [255].

1. LAWRENCE[L] HAWBERKE was a justice in 1357.
He married MARGARET[L] SIBTON*.
He bore arms of Barry of six *nebulée* [*or* and *vert*].
Child:
  *   i. Isolde[K], m. Thomas[K] Yong of Sibton.

§ § §

DE HELLESBY

This data was based on the pedigree "Aston of Aston," in Ormerod's *Chester* [2:123].

1. Sir JOCERAME[Q] DE HELLESBY died about 1232.
The marriage of AGATHA[P] MASSY to Joceraline de Hellesby is contemporary to this generation. She was the daughter of Hamon Massy III, who founded the priory of Birkenhead in Wirral, in Cheshire.
Children, listed by Ormerod:
        i. Adam[P] de Acton, d. c. 1247.
  2.   ii. John, m. Leuca de Arden vel Mobberley.

2. Sir JOHN[P] DE HELLESBY flourished in the mid thirteenth century.
He married LEUCA DE ARDEN VEL MOBBERLEY.
Children, listed by Ormerod:
  3.   i. Richard[O], d. c. 1263; m. Alice[N] de Thornton.
       ii. Ranulph de Hellesby.
      iii. Henry de Acton.
       iv. Adam de Acton, presumed son.

3. RICHARD[O] DE ACTON, alias DE HELLESBY, paramount lord of Acton in Edisbury Hundred in Cheshire, died about 1263.
He married ALICE[N] DE THORNTON[+] (daughter of Sir Ranulph [or Randle] le Roter, alias de Thornton), who was of record as a widow in 1268.
Children, listed by Ormerod:
        i. Ranulph[N] de Acton.
       ii. Richard de Acton, alias de Hellesby.
  4. iii. Alan, m. c. 1250 Beatrix de Hatton.

4. ALAN[N] DE ACTON, alias DE HELLESBY, died between 17 Edw. I (1288-1289) and 31 Edw. I (1302-1303). He was called "Allen" in *Visitations of Cheshire* by Glover and Flower [111].

He married about 1250 BEATRIX DE HATTON, who was living about 17 Edw. I (1288-1289), and was described as daughter and heir of Adam de Hatton [Corry, 2:663], son of Sir Hugh Hatton (and a daughter of Sir William Boydell [3:661]), son of Sir Hugh Hatton (and a daughter of Sir Edwin Harthull), son of Sir Hugh Hatton (and Isabel), son of Robert Hatton, lord of Hatton, and Margaret Crispin, daughter and heir of Gilbert Crispin.

Children, listed by Ormerod:

      i.   Ranulph[M] de Acton, alias de Hellesby.
5.   ii. William, m. Hawise de Trussell.
     iii. Richard Fitz Alan, l. 1309 and c. 1318; m.
     iv. Adam, m. Maude de Acton, dau. and heir of Ranulph de Acton.

5. Sir WILLIAM[M] DE ACTON, alias DE HELLESBY, was paramount lord of Acton about 1276.

He married HAWISE DE TRUSSEL [*cf.* Corry, 2:663, who gave her name as Avis].

He was apparently granted one third of Acton by his brother Adam.

Children, listed by Ormerod, with the last two from Glover and Flower's *Visitation of Cheshire*:

      i.   Katherine[L], m. Adam de Hatton of Great Aldersey.
     ii. Joan vel Margaret, m. John Griffyn of Bartherton.
*   iii. Lucy, m. Piers (or Peter)[L] de Thornton.
     iv. daughter, Beeston of Beeston.
     v. daughter, m. Trafford of Trafford.

§ § §

DE HOLAND

This line was developed with reference to the article by J. Brownbill in Cokayne [*CP*, 6:528-532] and J.R. Maddicott's "Thomas of Lancaster and Sir Robert Holland," *The English Historical Review*, 86 (1971), 449-472.

According to Bernard Holland, Matthew[P] de Holand was living in the time of King John, and had a son Robert[O] de Holand, of record in 1225 and 1242, who married Cecily, daughter of Alan de Columbers, and had Sir Thurstan[N] de Holand.

1. Sir THURSTAN[N] HOLAND held Upholland, near Wigan in Lancashire, which had been in the family since the reign of King John [Maddicott, *EHR*, 86:450], which ended in 1216, succeeding his father about 1242-1243 [Holland, 3].

He married first the daughter of Adam de Kellet, through whom he acquired Lonsdale, Furness and Cartmel in North Lancashire.

He married second Juliana Gellibrand, a daughter of John Gellibrand.

He married third a daughter of Henry de Hale, who was an illegitimate son of Richard de Meath, Lord of Hale.

He added extensive lands in the southwest Lancashire manors of Hale, Golborne and Cayley in Haydock.

Children, allegedly by first wife:

2.   i.   Sir Robert[M], m. Elizabeth de Samlesbury.
     ii. Sir William, granted by Thurstan all his lands in Cayley in Haydock.

    iii.   Richard, probably inherited land in Hale.

    iv.   Roger.

    v.   Adam.

    vi.   Margaret.

Children, allegedly by second wife:

    vii.   Thurstan, no heirs; witnessed a charter in 1286 [EHR, 86:450[5]].

    viii.   Adam, no heirs; had with brother Thurstan the remainder of an estate in Pemberton and Wigan settled on him by his father.

    ix.   Elias.

    x.   Simon, had lands in Golborne settled on him by his father, and inherited the lands in Pemberton and Wigan from his brothers.

2. Sir ROBERT[M] DE HOLAND, of Upholland, Lancashire, died about 1304.

He married ELIZABETH[M] DE SAMLESBURY, daughter and coheir of William de Samlesbury. She brought with her half the manor of Samlesbury in Blackburn Hundred as well as other lands near Bolton-le-Moors in Salford Hundred.

He was knighted in 1271 and was appointed one of three commissioners in Lancaster to enforce the statute of Winchester [*EHR*, 86:451]. Over the next fifteen years he served as commissioner of oyer and terminer and gaol delivery, and in July 1297 he was appointed collector of the subsidy in Derbyshire. His holdings placed him among the six knights and six esquires who held at least £40 of land in Lancashire in 1300. That year he was commissioner of array and was in May one of three who heard and determined complaints of transgressions against the Charters.

Children:

3.   i.   Sir Robert[L], b. c. 1283; d. 7 Oct. 1328; m. Maud[H] la Zouche, who d. 31 May 1349.

    ii.   William, d. before 1321; no issue; played a brutal part in the suppression of Adam Banaster's uprising in 1315 [*EHR*, 86:464].

    iii.   Alan, ancestor of Hollands of Conway [Holland, chart opposite 1].

    iv.   Joan, m. (1) Sir Edward Talbot of Bashall, m. (2) Sir Hugh de Dutton, m. (3) Sir John de Redcliffe.

    v.   Margery, m. John le Warre.

    vi.   Ameria, m. Adam Ireland, son of Sir John Ireland.

3. Sir ROBERT[L] DE HOLAND, 1st Lord Holland, of Upholland, Lancashire, born about 1283 [*EHR*, 86:452[6]], died 7 Oct. 1328, and was buried at the Franciscan friary in Preston, a Lancastrian manor.

He married, by 1309/10, MAUD[H] LA ZOUCHE*, who died 31 May 1349, and was buried at Brackley. She was of record as preparing to go to Santiago on pilgrimage in 1336.

He became of record first in 1292, when his father settled upon him a tenement in Pemberton and Orrell, Lancs. In 1298 he attended the Earl of Lancaster as *vallettus* on the Falkirk campaign, and he was knighted between May 1302 and Sept. 1305, no doubt by Lancaster, who was about five years older than he.

He became a favorite official of Thomas, Earl of Lancaster, who "raised him from the ranks of the Lancashire gentry, and brought him a baron's daughter in marriage, a summons to parliament, and landed wealth in some sixteen counties" [Maddicott, *EHR*, 86:449], although some of the grants may have simply acted to buffer the Earl of Lancaster from lawsuits, as "chicanery and extortion were characteristic of Lancaster's dealings in land" [*EHR*, 86:455]. A commissioner in 1303, he had charters in 1304 for free warren in his demesne lands of Upholland, Hale, Orrell and Markland in Pemberton, and for a market at Hale. In 1308 he was granted by King Edward II, at Lancaster's request, Melbourne in Derbyshire with all the liberties Thomas of Lancaster had previously enjoyed by charter from Edward I. Sir Robert attended the Dunstable tournament of 1308/9. He served several terms as Justice of Chester from Aug. 1307 to Oct. 1309. Dec. 1311 to Nov. 1312, and about Feb. 1319 to Jan. 1322. The king's trust in Holand was shown in 1312 when he was appointed Governor of Beeston Castle in Cheshire; later that year he was ordered to break Griffin de la Pole's siege of Welshpool Castle. However, his marriage did more than anything else to raise him to baronial status and wealth. The partition of the la Zouche property going to Sir Robert was worth nearly £720 per year, while St. Maur got only £104, mostly in Devonshire [Maddicott, *EHR*, 86:459].

He was a Member of Parliament from 1314 to 1321, and served in the military against the Scots at Newcastle in Aug. 1314 and in 1316.

Having taken the side of the Earl of Lancaster against King Edward II, he was pardoned in 1313 for complicity in the death of Piers de Gavaston. In 1315 he assisted in suppressing the rising of Adam Banastre in Lancashire, and in 1318 he was again pardoned for adhering to the Earl of Lancaster, for whom he served as "companion and friend, estate steward, political agent [as shown by letters to him from king and pope], and general factotum," heading the witness list to twenty-eight of sixty-one charters in which Thomas de Lancaster was grantor or grantee between 1305 and 1321, and controlling the earl's treasure [*EHR*, 86:462-463]. In the Earl's final rising, in Feb. and March 1321/2 he was accused of collecting 500 men in Lancashire for the Earl, but bringing them to the King. It is known that his daughter was on the way to the Tower of London on 26 Feb. He was at Dalbury while the Earl was defeated at Burton-on-Trent. As the Earl was fleeing northward, before the battle of Boroughbridge, Sir Robert surrendered to the King at Derby, and was sent to Dover Castle. However, it appears that he did fight at Boroughbridge, surrendered after the battle, and was treated as a rebel. His lands were taken into the King's hands, and he was imprisoned in Warwick and Northampton, escaping from the latter.

When King Edward III came to the throne he petitioned for restitution of his lands, and was granted this on 23 Dec. 1327. However, on 7 Oct. 1328 he was captured in Boreham Wood, near Elstree in Hertfordshire while on his way to London to see the Queen, by some adherents of his patron, Thomas of Lancaster, who for his treachery cut off his head. They sent his head to Henry, Earl of Lancaster at Waltham Cross in the care of Sir Thomas Wyther, the murderer, and others. Nonetheless, his demise did not hurt the fortunes of his children.

Children [CP, 6:530i]:

    i.   Robert[K], d. Halse or Hawes, Brackley, 16 March 1372/3, bur. St. James Chapel, Brackley; m. Elizabeth; received the bulk of his father's estates.

    ii.   Thomas, founder K.G., Earl of Kent [*CP*, 2:534, 6:530k]; d. Normandy 26 or 28 Dec. 1366; m. c. 1339 Joan Plantagenet of Kent (dau. of Edmund of Woodstock), who d. Wallingford Castle 7/8 Aug. 1385, having m. (2) c. 1361 Edward of England, the Black Prince, who d. Westminster 8 June 1376; ancestor of the Dukes of Exeter.

    iii.   Alan, d. c. 1339; no issue.

    iv.   Sir Otes (or Otho), founder K.G.

*   v.   Maud, m. Sir Thomas[K] Swynnerton, who d. Dec. 1361 [*cf.* NGSQ, 60:25-26].

vi.   Isabel (or Elizabeth), d. 13 July 1387, bur. Chewton Mendip, Somerset; m. by 23 May 1340 Sir Henry Fitz Roger, who d. 29 Jan. 1352 [*MCS*5, 90A:7].

§ § §

HONFORD

Henry de Honefort flourished from 1233-1237, according to the pedigree in Ormerod's *History of Chester* [3:644]. However, the details of a line from Henry to John[F] de Honford were presented by Ormerod sketchily, with several breaks. Sir John de Honford, Lord of Honford and half brother of William[J] Mainwaring of Over Peover, married Elizabeth (who married second Richard le Mascy of Honford), and had son Sir John de Honford, knight, Lord of Honford, who was a distinguished captain in the French wars from 1425 to 1449, and was father of John de Honford of Honford, Esq., who died about 1473, aged about 55, having married Margery, daughter of Sir Laurence Warren of Poynton, knight. The latter two were apparently the parents of John[F] Honford, below, according to Ormerod.

Earwaker presented the line as given below in his *East Cheshire*. He gave Henry de Honford as having the grant of Bosden about 1233. The next Henry was living in 1294 and 1297, and was apparently the father of John de Honford [Trafford deeds, 1317-1335, cited by Earwaker], Henry (next, below), and Roger de Honford, who fought at Poitiers.

Richard Brooke described Handforth in 1849 as a township in the parish of Cheadle, in Cheshire, eleven miles from Manchester and five miles southwest of Stockport.

Earwaker described some of the records as presented in Ormerod as "strangely inaccurate."

1. HENRY[K] DE HONFORD, born say 1325, was named the father of John[J] de Honford in the pedigree "Honford of Honford" by Ormerod, cited by Richard Brooke [*Proc. Historic Soc. of Lancs. & Cheshire*, 2:54].

Child, from the pedigree published by Earwaker in *East Cheshire* [1:250]:

   2.   i.   John[J], d. 1393; m. (1) Margaret[J] de Praers, m. (2) Emma de la Pole.

2. JOHN[J] DE HONFORD, who was called son of Henry[K] de Honford, died in May 1393 [Earwaker, 1:484], or 27 Dec. 1393 [Earwaker, 1:239].

He married first, about 1372, MARGARET[J] DE PRAERS*, coheir of William de Praers of Baddiley, Cheshire, and widow of Hugh del Holt.

He married, probably second, Emma de la Pole, who was probably a sister of John de la Pole.

Children, listed by Earwaker, by first wife:

   3.   i.   John[I], b. 1373 illegitimate, due to having been born before his parents married [Ormerod, 3:456], *natus ante nuptias* [Richard Brooke, *Visits to the Fields of Battle of England*, 282]; d. Dec. 1400; m. Elizabeth.

       ii. William, b. c. 1374; m. Matilda, widow of Robert[H] de Legh of Addington (who d. 1415) [Earwaker, 1:160]; l. 1431, had the lands of Henry de Chorlegh of Chorley, in Wilmslow parish.

3. Sir JOHN[I] HONFORD of Honford, now Handforth, Cheshire, knight, born 1373, died 8 Dec. 1400 [Eakwaker, 1:240]; the *inquisition post mortem* was taken that year.

His wife's name was ELIZABETH.

Children, given by Earwaker [1:251]:
- 4.   i.   John[H], b. 1391; d. c. 1461; said to have m. Joan Hondford.
-       ii.   Joan, mentioned 1404; perhaps m. Hugh Calveley.

4. Sir JOHN[H] HONDFORD of Honford, Cheshire, knight, born in 1391, died about 1461. It is said that he married JOAN HONFORD.

He served in the French wars, and was knighted as a result, probably at the battle of Verneuil in 1424 [Earwaker, 1:240]. In 1434 he was captain of the bridge at Rouen, and in 1444 he was a justice in eyre in Cheshire.

This generation was identified simply as William Honford in the pedigree chart presented by Richard Brooke in *Visits to the Fields of Battle in England* [282].

Children, listed by Earwaker [1:251]:
- 5.   i.   John[G], died Oct. 1473; m. Margaret[G] Warren.
-       ii.   Thomas, of age in 1441.
-       iii.   Robert, of age in 1441; listed with Thomas on the Cheshire Recognizance Rolls.
-       iv.   Elizabeth, m. c. 1439 Thomas de Beeston, who d. 1476.
-       v.   [Margery?], m. c. 1450 Hugh Davenport of Calveley and Haslewood, Cheshire, who d. 1471/2.

5. JOHN[G] HONDFORD of Hondford, Esq., of age in 1441, died in Oct. 1473. No record of an *inquisition post mortem* had been found.

He married MARGARET[G] WARREN, daughter of Sir Lawrence Warren of Poynton, Cheshire, knight. The marriage settlement was dated 10 Hen. V (1422).

He had the manor of Hondford, as well as others, conveyed to him in 1461.

Child, given by Earwaker:
- 6.   i.   John[F], b. c. 1435; d. c. 1485 [Ormerod]; m. Margaret[F] Savage.

6. JOHN[F] HONFORD of Honford, Cheshire, died about the first year of the reign of Henry VII, King of England (1485-1486).

He married MARGARET[F] SAVAGE*, daughter of Sir John Savage of Clifton and niece of the Earl of Derby. She married second Sir Edmund Trafford, K.B., of Trafford, Lancashire, who died 15 Aug. 1514, son of Sir John Trafford and Elizabeth Ashton, daughter of Sir Thomas Ashton of Ashton-under-Lyne, Lancs.

The Honford pedigree in *Proceedings of the Historic Society of Lancashire and Cheshire* [2 (1849-1850), 54], shows this generation to be William[F] Honford of Honford, Esq., who died 9 Sept. 1513, having married Margaret Savage and had a daughter Margaret who married first Sir John Stanley, and second, Sir Urien Brereton.

Children, listed by Earwaker in *East Cheshire*, 1:251:
-       i.   John[E], eldest son and heir, d. young.
-       ii.   William, of Hondford, under age in 1487, when he was styled "son and heir of John Hondford, Esq., deceased"; slain at Flodden Field 9 Sept. 1513, *inquisition post mortem* taken 1516; m. Sibyl Scargell [Ormerod] or Stargell(?) [Earwaker, who cited *Visitation of 1566*] of Norfolk, living 1530; who m. (2) Laurence Warren of Poynton, Esq., as his second wife.
- *   iii.   Katherine, d. 1529; m. Sir John[E] Mainwaring of Over Peover, who d. March 1515/6; next heir in default of her niece Margaret.

§ § §

HOOTON

Hooton is a township which Ormerod described in his history of Cheshire as "one of the most delightful situations which the banks of an estuary can boast, and commanding a particularly beautiful view of the Forest Hills, the bend of the Mersey, and the opposite shore of Hale" [2:410].

Originally granted to Richard de Vernon, the Norman Baron of Shipbrook, at the time of the Conquest, Hooton was obtained in marriage by Randle Walensis during the time of King Richard I or King John.

1. WILLIAM[N] DE HOTON, Lord of Hoton, Cheshire, England, was of record in the time of Henry III and Edward I, the latter half of the thirteenth century.

Children, listed by Ormerod, the first two as probable:

  2.   i.   William[M].

       ii.   Adam, settled lands in Cherleton 23 Edw. I (1294-1295) on Adam fitz William de Stanlegh.

      iii.   Ralph de Hoton, alias Walensis.

2. WILLIAM[M] DE HOTON held lands in Hoton, Cheshire, 15 Edw. II, when he obtained from James de Coghull and Agnes his wife a tenement in Hoton.

Child, listed as probable by Ormerod [2:410]:

  3.   i.   Henry[L], Lord of Hoton.

3. HENRY[L] DE HOTON, Lord of Hoton, was of record in 2, 38 and 40 Edw. III (1328-1367).

Children, listed by Ormerod:

  4.   i.   Sir William[K], m. Katherine Torond.

      ii.   David, second in entail of Hoton.

     iii.   Joan.

     iv.   Isabell.

4. Sir WILLIAM[K] DE HOOTON, Lord of Hooton, son and heir, lived during the time of Edward III; he died 14 Sept. 1396 [Irvine, *Trans. Historic Soc.*, 105:59], and his *inquisition post mortem* was dated 20 Ric. II (1396-1397).

He married KATHERINE[K] TOROND, daughter and heiress of Henry Torond; she was a widow in 6 Hen. VI (1427-1428). The family is not listed in Marshall, Whitmore or Barrow's guides, and was not clearly the owner of the manor of Mollington Torond in Wirral Hundred, Cheshire.

Perhaps he served in the French wars.

He died "seized in demesne as of fee-tail of the manor of Hooton, held from John de Whitemore as heir of Margaret [who was the] wife of Hamo Le Straunge, by fealty," in the value of forty marks.

Sole daughter and heir:

  *   i.   Margaret (or Margery)[J], d. before 6 Hen. VI (1427-1428); m. Sir William[J] de Stanley.

§ § §

HOPTON

Most of the material below was found in Grazebrook's edition of *The Visitation of Shropshire, 1623* [253-256], which has been corrected with reference to Eyton's *Antiquities of Shropshire*.

1. Sir WALTER[R] HOPTON bore arms of [*Gules*], *semée* of cross-crosslets *fitchée*, a lion rampant [*or*]. A Walter de Opton was recorded in the feodary of 1165 as holding two knights' fees in the Barony of Clun in Shropshire under Geoffrey de Vere [Eyton, 11:256].

He married JOANE[R] DE CURES, sister and heir of Robert de Cures (or de Girros, de Gyrros [Eyton, 6:218, 10:156], who died in 1251), who bore arms of *Azure*, a mermaid *argent*.

According to Grazebrook and Eyton [11:256] his father was Henry[S] Hopton, who was son of Walter[T] Hopton.

Child:

    2.   i.   Sir Walter[Q], m. Isabel[Q] Staunton.

          ii. John, mentioned in 1223.

2. Sir WALTER[Q] HOPTON was sued with his brother John in 1223 by Agnes, widow of Brane (Brian?), for the murder of her husband, but on 25 Nov. 1223 Agnes appeared in Westminster and confessed that her challenge against Walter was unjust.

He married ISABEL[Q] STAUNTON, daughter of Henry[R] Staunton and sister and heir of Henry[Q] Staunton of Stanton in Shropshire. The family arms were *Vairé sable* and *argent*, a canton gules.

According to the feodary of 1240 Walter de Hopton held two knights' fees in Hopton of the Barony of Clun [Eyton, 11:257].

Child:

    3.   i.   Sir Walter[O], d. 1305; m. (1) 1283 Maud Pantulf of Wem, m. (2) Jane[O] Longbrughe.

3. Sir WALTER[O] DE HOPTON may have been born about 1220; he died before 10 March 1305, when the King's *writ de diem clausit* announced his death, and his inquest mentioned his son Walter, a minor [Eyton, 3:33-34, 10:149].

He married before 9 May 1283 [Eyton, 7:171-172], as her second husband, Maud (or Matilda)[N] Pantulf of Wem (widow of Ralph[N] Boteler of Oversley, Warwickshire, who died shortly before 3 July 1281), who died shortly before 6 May 1289.

Joseph Morris' *Shropshire Genealogies* [2:552] states that he married JANE LONGBRUGHE, daughter and heir of Robert Longbrughe, who bore *Gules*, a bend between 2 crescents *Or*.

On 4 Aug. 1258 Thomas de Roshall, Richard Tyrel, Robert de Lacy and he were appointed justiciars to inquire about disturbances in Shropshire.

He was Sheriff of Shropshire in the year ending Michaelmas 1268, and sat as a justiciar with Ralph de Hengham at Ludlow in Lent 1277. In about 1286 the Bradford Tenure Roll listed "Walter de Hopton, through his wife Matilda, holds the Manor of Wem with its members, viz. Aston, Stiell, Tilley, Dichelowe [now Lowe and Ditches], Horton, Wolverley, Edistoston (Edstaston), Cotton, Harpecote, Beslow, Dodyngton, Alkyngton, and Edisley. He also holds the Manors of Hinstocke, Upton (Waters Upton), Tibrighton, Dawley (Magna), Eton (Eyton), Brocketon (Bratton), and half the vill of Dawley (read Lawley), and half the vill of Parva Drayton of the King, *in capite sine medio*, freely, as a Barony, by service of three knights'-fees in lieu of all services: and he has at Wem, a Market and Fair, by Charter of King Henry III" [Eyton, 7:172].

At his death he held the "vill of Fittes [manor and parish of Fitz] with the hamlets of Mucton (Mytton) and Grafton, of the said heir and of the Barony of Clun, by service of one-sixth of a knight's-fee" [Eyton 10:149]. When Robert de Gyrros died in 1251 the Dean and Chapter of St. Mary's claimed Mytton, but in a suit at the County Assizes of Jan. 1256, "Thomas de Costantin and Walter de Hopton seek against the Dean and Chapter of St. Mary, Salop, six virgates in Mutton, of which Robert de Gyros, Uncle of Thomas and kinsman of Walter, whose heirs they are, was seized, and of which they say that he died seized. And from the said Robert, because he died without a bodily heir, the fee of the said land descended to a certain Isabella [de Constantine, living in 1253], and a certain Joanna, as to his sisters and heirs.... And from Joanna the fee of her purparty descended to one Walter as her son and heir, and from that Walter to his son and heir, Walter, the present Plaintiff" [Eyton, 10:156-157]. The court held that the Dean and Chapter remained *indefensi* and *in misericordiâ*, and that Thomas and Walter recovered their seizin.

The family held the vill of Stanton in Herefordshire, near Pembridge, under the house of Mortimer [Eyton, 3:34].

Child:
4.   i.   Sir Walter[N], b. c. 1303.

4. Sir WALTER[N] HOPTON was born about 1303, and was listed in the *Nomina Villarum* in 1316 as the sole lord of the vill of Fittes [Eyton, 10:149].

Child:
5.   i.   Sir Walter[M].

5. Sir WALTER[M] HOPTON was the third of the name in three generations.

Child:
6.   i.   Sir John[L], m. Alice[L] le Strange.

6. Sir JOHN[L] HOPTON has been identified only by name in the *Visitation of Shropshire, 1623*.

He married ALICE[L] LE STRANGE, daughter of a Lord Strange.

Child:
7.   i.   Sir John[K], m. Elizabeth[K] Burley.

7. Sir JOHN[K] HOPTON may have been born about 1320.

It has been alleged that he married an ELIZABETH BURLEY, who married second John Trussell, but the chronology seems to be several generations off. Morris stated [*Shropshire Genealogies*, 2:559] mistakenly that her father was Sir John Burley of Broncroft, who was Sheriff of Shropshire in 1409.

Child:
8.   i.   Walter[J], m. Joane[J] Yong.

8. Sir WALTER[J] HOPTON was listed next in the pedigree.
He married JOANE[J] YONG*.

Child:
9.   i.   Thomas[I], m. Joane[I] Mortimer of Shropshire.

9. THOMAS[I] HOPTON was mentioned in *Wallop Family*, 441.
He married JOANE[I] (or Jane) MORTIMER* of Shropshire.

Child:
10.   i.   Thomas[H], b. Stanton, Shropshire; m. Eleanor[H] Lucy.

10. Sir THOMAS[H] HOPTON was born in Stanton, Shropshire, say in 1390.
He married ELEANOR[H] LUCY*, daughter of Sir Walter[I] Lucy.
Children, listed by Morris in *Shropshire Genealogies* [2:552]:
*   i.   Elizabeth[G], d. 22 June 1498; m. (1) Sir Roger[G] Corbet, m. (2) John
           Tiptoft, Earl of Worcester, m. (3) Sir William Stanley of Holt, who was
           Chamberlain to King Henry VII; she was sole heir to her father and
           brother Walter.
    ii.   Walter.

§ § §

HOUGHTON

F.R. Raines' edition of *The Visitation of the County Palatine of Lancaster Made in the
Year 1567, by William Flower, Norroy King of Arms* shows a Richard Houghton of Houghton
of record in 38 Edw. III (1364-1365), son of Adam de Haughton, who was of record 1 Edw.
III (1327-1328). This name is also spelled Hoghton or Halghton.

1. RICHARD[L] DE HOUGHTON was lord of Houghton in Lancashire.
Child:
*   i.   Katherine[K], m. as his second wife Sir Hugh[K] Venables, who d. 1367.

§ § §

IPSTONES

While it has been suggested that Sir John[I] Ipstones and his wife Elizabeth Corbet had
no issue, their daughter Alice was noted by Paul C. Reed [*TG*, 10:60[53]], and son William
was mentioned by Roskell [3:480].
    The father of Sir John[J] Ipstones (who died in or before 1364), "was a violent man, whose
feud with his neighbors, the Brumptons, was kept up by his descendants" [Roskell, 3:479].

1. Sir JOHN[J] IPSTONES of Blymhill in Staffordshire died by 1364.
He married ELIZABETH[K] BECK*, sister of Sir Nicholas Beck of Hopton in Salop and Tean
in Staffordshire [Roskell, 3:479].
He also held Ipstones and Creswell in Staffordshire [Roskell, 3:479].
Child [Roskell, 3:479-489]:
2.   i.   Sir John[I], killed in Feb. 1394; m. c. 1374 Elizabeth[H] Corbet.

2. Sir JOHN[I] IPSTONES, of Ipstones, Staffordshire, was killed by Roger de Swynnerton,
uncle of Maude de Swynnerton, while Sir John was traveling through London to Parliament
in Feb. 1394.
He married by Easter 1374 [Roskell, 3:479] ELIZABETH[H] CORBET*, who was prevented
from inheriting her grandfather's extensive holdings in the Midlands and the March by a
series of entails favoring her uncles Sir Fulk and Sir Roger. Beginning in the Easter term
of 1374, not long after their marriage, they sued for the manor of Braunstone in Leicestershire, which remained in the hands of Sir Robert Corbet's grandson, Thomas Erdington.
    In the early 1370s he was the subject of lawsuits for debt and assault by Thomas
Brumpton. He went to France in the retinue of the Hugh, Earl of Stafford, who sued him
some years later for robbery and violence. In the summer of 1386 he was a member of John

of Gaunt's expedition, who retained him in 1387 at a fee of £10 annually. In Nov. 1387 he received a royal pardon for the murder of a Richard Thornbury. About this time he mobilized "a large following of ruffians" and attacked Sir Walter Blount's manor of Barton Blount, forcing the justice to surrender a bond for good behavior from one of Blount's tenants.

His acquisitions through marriage were limited to property in Shawbury in Shropshire and Bausley in Montgomeryshire. He held land in Northamptonshire by knight service of the Bassets of Weldon. He claimed the manors of Hopton and Tean as nephew and heir of Sir Nicholas Beck, evicting Sir Nicholas' granddaughter, Maude de Swynnerton from the property. When taken to court in Stafford by Maude's father-in-law, Sir Richard Peshall (whose father had been killed in 1346 while resisting arrest by Sir John[J] Ipstones the Elder), in Sept. 1381, he argued unsuccessfully that Maude was illegimate but managed to hold the manors for seven years, during which time Maude's husband, Humphrey de Peshall, died, and Maude had moved to her mother-in-law's home in Chetwynd in Shropshire. In Dec. 1388 he led a large gang of armed men, including his comrade, Sir Philip Okeover of the Spanish campaign, in abducting the heiress Maude, forced her to marry his son William, and to sign over her title to Hopton and Tean. In May 1390 he and Sir Richard Peshall's widow were "bound over in sureties of £500 to keep the peace towards each other. Ipstones and his men were then bound over for trial in Shrewsbury, but the jury was clearly afraid to convict them. Then in Dec. 1390 the Pope condoned the whole affair with a papal mandate allowing William and Maude to marry within the prohibited degrees.

He was commissioner to administer the revenues of Rochester Abbey in Staffordshire in Feb. 1386, of inquiry in Staffordship and Shropshire in April 1388 and July 1389, and of oyer and terminer in Staffordshire in July 1388 regarding disturbances on the estates of the Bishop of Coventry.

He and his wife were members of the Guild of the Holy Trinity at Coventry.

He was a member of the Merciless Parliament in Feb. 1388 and the Parliament of 1394, and was murdered by Maude de Swynnerton's uncle, Roger de Swynnerton, in London, while Sir John was going to parliament unarmed. Roger was pardoned in June 1397 at the behest of Sir Baldwin Raddington in spite of this very serious breach of the royal protection extended to all Members of Parliament [Roskell, 3:480].

Children, noted by Paul C. Reed and Roskell:

*   i.   Alice[H], m. Sir Randle[H] Brereton of Malpas, Cheshire.
       ii. William, d. 1399; forcibly m. c. 1388 Maude[I] de Swynnerton (widow of Humphrey de Peshall), who m. (3) about July 1401 Sir John[I] Savage of Clifton.

§ § §

LACON

Gary Boyd Roberts generously provided a copy of page 37 of Harvey's *The History and Antiquities of the Hundred of Willey in the County of Bedford*, which he obtained while in Salt Lake City at the Family History Library, which was necessary to begin the research suggested by Weis.

Neil D. Thompson of 255 North Second West, Salt Lake City, UT 84105-4545 (1995), was commissioned to research the chronology of this presentation, and provided much helpful material.

Sir ROBERT[Q] DE LAKE was of Lake (now Lacon, about two kilometers northeast of Wem), Shropshire.

RICHARD[P] DE LAKE flourished from 1200 to 1227. He married (first) GILIAN[P] DE SANDFORD, sister of the first Ralph de Sandford [Eyton, *Antiquities of Shropshire*, 9:354], and second Elena, widow of Richard de Bradwall of Bradwall in Cheshire [J. Morris, *Shropshire Genealogies*, 9:254].

RICHARD[O] DE LAKE was living about 1235. He married MATILDA[O] BOTERELL, according to the *Visitation of Shropshire 1623*, but this pedigree said her brother John was of record 3 Edw. II (1329-1330), a century later.

WILLIAM[N] LAKEN of Laken, Shropshire, flourished from 1255 to 1284. He married ELIZABETH[N] ST. OWEN (or Elizabeth St. John) [*Vis. Shropshire*, 302].

5. RICHARD[M] LACON of Lacon sat on a Longslow Inquest in 1290, and served on a jury in 1316.
He married HELENA[M] BURNELL*.
Child:
    6.   i.   John[L], l. 1324 and 1357; m. Elizabeth Stanlowe.

6. JOHN[L] LACON of Lacon, Shropshire, was listed in the return of 1324 as a man-at-arms, and was summoned to attend the Great Council at Westminster; he was living in 1357 [Eyton's *Antiquities of Shropshire*, 9:353].
He married ELIZABETH[L] STANLOWE, daughter of Sir John Stanlowe of Staffordshire.
Child:
    7.   i.   Robert[K], m. (2) Ellen[H] Cotton.

7. ROBERT[K] LACON was of Lacon.
He married first Isabel [*Vis. Shropshire*, 303].
He married second ELLEN[H] COTTON*.
In 1343 he was admitted on the Roll of Guild Merchant of Salop [Morris, 2:954].
Child, perhaps by second wife:
        i.   John[J], m. Ellena.
Child, by second wife:
    8.   ii.   Alan, l. 1375; m. Agnes Pembrugge.

8. ALAN[J] LACON was living in 1375 [Joseph Morris' "Shropshire Genealogies," MS in the Shrewsbury Public Library in Shropshire, available on film from the Family History Library, Salt Lake City, 2:955].
He married AGNES[J] PEMBRUGGE, daughter of Walter Pembrugge.
He was of record in 1357 and 1374.
Child:
    9.   i.   William[I], fl. 1397; m. Margaret[I] Paslowe.

9. WILLIAM[I] LACON of Cotton, who flourished in 20 Ric. II (1397), was murdered that year.
He married MARGARET[I] PASLOWE* of Drayton Parslow in Buckinghamshire.
A retainer of Henry of Bolingbroke, he was murdered in London in 1397 while on his way to Westminster to prosecute a suit against Sir John Hawkstone in the Sept. Parliament.
Child:
    10.   i.   Richard[H], l. 1415, d. by 1446; m. Elizabeth[H] Peshall.

10. Sir RICHARD[H] LACON of Willey, Salop (or Shropshire), was dead by 8 Oct. 1446 [Paul C. Reed, *TG*, 10:46, 66], the date of a deed poll which gave all Richard[G] Lacon's

lands and interests in Altemere, Shropshire, to Agnes, "who was the wife of Richard his father."

He married first, about 1409, ELIZABETH[H] PESHALL*, heiress of Sir Hamon de Peshall and widow of Henry Grendon, whose nuncupative will was dated at the Hospital of St. John of Jerusalem, London, on 7 Dec. 1405. She died on Sunday, the eve of the Nativity of St. John the Baptist, 13 Henry VI (23 June 1435). By Henry Grendon she had one child, a son John, an idiot who died without heirs.

He married second, after 1435, Agnes.

As neither Sir John Hawkstone, his father's murderer, nor his accomplice, Robert Kendale, Esq., were brought to justice, and indeed were pardoned fully by King Richard II, Richard[H] Lacon was no doubt in support of Henry of Bolingbroke and became closely attached to Thomas Fitz Alan, Earl of Arundel.

On 15 Feb. 1404 he was granted lands worth 20 marks per year which had been forfeited by the rebel, John Kynaston. He was Constable of the Earl of Arundel's castle of Oswestry in Shropshire by April 1405. By Jan. 1407 he had developed ties with John Wele, Esq., John Burley I and David Holbache; they were all witnesses of the Earl of Arundel's charter to the borough of Oswestry. As a member of a junior branch of the family he held a lease on "Bulridges," a pasture in Condover manor, and acquired his other lands by marriage, including six manors in Shropshire, of which Willey was one. In 9 Hen. IV (1407-1408) he was admitted on the Roll of Guild Merchant in Shrewsbury [J. Morris, *Shropshire Genealogies*, 9:956].

On 25 Nov. 1409, shortly after the first marriage, Elizabeth's grandmother and uncle Roger de Williley complained that they had been "disseised" of their free tenements in Bold and Cherlcot by Richard de Laken and Elizabeth his wife.

He was Knight of the Shire for county Salop (or Shropshire) in the parliaments which were convened on 14 May 1413 (with Robert Corbet), 19 Nov. 1414, 1 Dec. 1421, 20 Oct. 1423, 12 Jan. 1430/1 and 8 July 1433. His first term in Parliament followed the Earl of Arundel's appointment as treasurer of the Exchequer to King Henry V. In the summer of 1414 he was among those connected to Arundel indicted for numerous offences during the rebellion in Wales. However, he received a royal pardon and was returned to Parliament that November.

In 1415 he took part in the siege of Harfleur, and probably also the battle of Agincourt. On 1 Dec. 1415 he was named to a term as Sheriff of Shropshire, where he served as justice of the peace in 1422-1423. He received a pardon of £40 on 8 May 1417 due to the great expense of serving in office. In Feb. 1419 he was a member of King Henry V's own retinue en route to France. In Parliament in 1422 he was accused by Richard Hankford and his wife Elizabeth of taking Whittington Castle with the support of a band of Welshmen. He was threatened with attainder if he did not make amends, and was elected to the next Parliament as well as two more after an eight year hiatus. He also came to amicable terms with Sir John[H] Talbot, with whom relations had been poor during the Welsh rebellion.

In the Passelewe or Paslowe pedigree published in Harvey's *Hundred of Willey* [37] he was called Sir Richard Lacon of Drayton, Brompton and Buckton.

Children, listed by Paul C. Reed [*TG*, 10:66[131]], from deed poll, with daughter by Joseph Morris [*Shropshire Genealogies*], by his wife:

      i.   Richard[G], eldest son and heir, an adult on 22 July 1439 when he "gave mainprise" for Owain ap Maredudd (Owen Tudor, grandfather of King Henry VII), living 1448/9; will dated 6 Nov. 1446 devised land to brother William "the elder"; no issue.

11.   ii.   William, the younger, m. Magdalene Wisham.

      iii.   Richard, junior.

      iv. Ann, m. Ralph Ottley

Children, illegitimate:

      v. Sir William, the elder, d. 6 Oct. 1475; m. Sibella Siferwast, dau. of John Siferwast of Coleware, Berks., relict of (1) Thomas Rykes, Esq., and (2) John Thorley, Esq.

      vi. Thomas, son of Alice Walcox, an attendant of Lady Elizabeth Lacon; m. Christiana ferch Maredudd Fychan of Deuddwn.

11. WILLIAM[G] LACON of Willey, Shropshire, Esquire, died in 1479 [J. Morris, *Shropshire Genealogies*, 2:957].

He married MAGDALENE WISHAM, daughter of Sir Richard Wisham of Holt in Worcestershire.

He was appointed Sheriff of Shropshire on 8 Nov. 1451.

He was going to Parliament according to a list dated 12 June 1453, but Wedgwood's *History of Parliament* [522-523] apparently confuses him with his brother William.

Children, the first three listed in the Grazebrook and Rylands edition of the *Visitation of Shropshire* [2:307], and the rest by J. Morris [2:957]:

  12.   i. Sir Richard[F] of Willey, m. Margery Horde.

      ii. John, second son.

      iii. Anne, m. Mr. Reade (or Read, Rede, Redd) of co. Surrey.

      iv. William, d. young.

      v. George, d. young.

      vi. John, d. young.

      vii. Ellen.

      viii. Elizabeth.

12. Sir RICHARD[F] LACON, K.B., died 1 July 1503.

He married MARGERY HORDE, daughter of Thomas Horde or Hoord of Horde Park, Bridgnorth, Salop [Paul C. Reed, *TG*, 10:66[131]]; she was called Alicia in the *Visitation of Shropshire* [2:306], and Joan in Burke's *Commoners* [3:199]. Perhaps her father was the Thomas Horde (c. 1420-1498), lawyer, who was the eldest son and heir of Richard Horde (for whom see Roskell's *Hist. of Parliament*, 3:413; a Richard Hord was mentioned as seneschal of Sir William[L] le Boteler of Wem by Eyton [8:21]) and the heiress of John Perell, given as Agnes Perrell in J. Morris' *Shropshire Genealogies* [2:601], whose ancestry is given in several lines by Morris and in *The Visitation of Shropshire 1623* [251-252]. Thomas Horde married Joyce Stapleton, daughter and coheir of Sir John Stapleton. Thomas was an M.P. sometimes between 1442 and 1475, and served frequently as Justice of the Peace between 1453 and 1483, and from 1483 some terms as Sheriff of Shropshire. A Lancastrian, he also served as Sheriff in 1456-1457 and from 6 Nov. 1470 until the Yorkist restoration, when he escaped attainder [Wedgwood's *History of Parliament*, 469].

Sir Richard Lacon was appointed Sheriff of Shropshire 5 Nov. 1476, 5 Nov. 1486 and 5 Nov. 1497.

Richard Lakyn was named Knight of the Bath on 17 Jan. 1477/8 in connection with the marriage on 15 Jan. 1477/8 of Richard, Duke of York, the King Edward IV's second son, to Ann, daughter of John, Duke of Norfolk.

Children, from the sources cited herein:

      i. Sir Thomas[E] of Willey, b. c. 1475; m. Maria Corbet, dau. of Sir Richard Corbet of Moreton Corbet and Elizabeth Devereux [Burke's *Commoners*, 3:199]; Sheriff 1510.

      ii. Edward, m. Elizabeth Acton of Thinglands in Shropshire.

    iii.   Margaret (Mary in J. Morris [2:957]), m. Hugh (or Giles) Harnage of Shenton, Shropshire, and Belswardine.

    iv.   Richard, third son.

*   v.   Joan, d. 13 April 1524; m. (1) Sir John[E] Mainwaring, who d. March 1515/6, m. (2) George Pontesbury, who d. 10 Oct. 1550 (however, J. Morris [2:957] states that Jane, who m. George Pontesbury, d. 30 June 1553 and was bur. St. Alkmund's in Shrewsbury.

    vi.   John, fourth son.

    vii.   daughter, m. Mr. Ponsbury of Shropshire.

    viii.   William of Cotes, Shropshire [*Vis. Shropshire*, 2:307], Justice of the King's Bench [J. Morris, 2:965].

§ § §

DE LATHOM

Work in Lancashire local histories might help with this line.

1. Sir ROBERT[N] DE LATHOM was of Lathom in Lancashire, d. on or just before 2 March 1324/5 [*CP*, 4:205c].
He married KATHERINE[N] DE KNOWSLEY, daughter of Thomas de Knowsley.
Children [*CP*, 4:205c]:

  2.   i.   Sir Thomas[M], b. 1300; d. 17 Sept. 1370; m. before 21 May 1329 Eleanor[L] de Ferrers.

       ii.   Hugh.

      iii.   Philip.

2. Sir THOMAS[M] DE LATHOM of Lathom and Knowsley in Lancashire, born in 1300, died 17 Sept. 1370.
He married, before 21 May 1329, ELEANOR (or Alianore)[L] DE FERRERS*, who survived him.
He had livery of his lands 3 July 1325, having served as commissioner of array in Lancashire 16 May 1322 and 1323, and as commissioner of peace there 2 Nov. 1323 to 1326, and apparently served in the Parliament at Westminster in 1324, as he appears in the enrolment of the *writ de expensis* and in the original docket. He had free warren in his lands at Lathom and elsewhere in 1339. He was involved in levying forces in Lancashire to repel the Scots, and served as knight banneret with the king in the expedition to France of 1344-1347 with a retinue of a knight, eight esquires and 23 archers. In 1355 he had free warren in Knowsley and Roby with permission to enclose a park [Hornyold-Strickland, *Members Parl. Lancs.*, 63-64].
    Child:

  3.   i.   Sir Thomas[L], d. before 20 March 1381/2; m. Joan[J] Venables.

3. Sir THOMAS[L] DE LATHOM of Lathom in Lancashire, died before 20 March 1381/2.
He married JOAN[J] VENABLES* of Kinderton [Weis, *AR7*, 57:33, cited *CP*, 4:205, which does not contain appropriate data]. Cokayne's chart [4:205c] stated that the children below were by a first unknown wife, and that a second wife, Joan (no surname given), married second Roger de Fasacrelegh.
He was the Sir Oskell of the *Stanley* legend [*CP*, 4:205c] given by Bishop Stanley, who died in 1568, which described the lord of Lathom, issueless and aged "fower score,"

adopting an infant "swaddled and clad in a mantle of redd," which an eagle had brought unhurt to her nest in Terlestowe wood. This was Oskell, father of Isabel Stanley.

The other legend was derived from the Stanleys of Irlam, and stated that Thomas[J] Stanley, below, was illegitimate, and Isabel's mother found him under a tree near an eagle's aery, but that he was discarded before the death of Thomas Stanley, after Irlam had been settled upon him. However, as Cokayne pointed out, this was a clumsy fabrication, not uncommon, that the crests were used by the Lathoms, and that Ormerod remarked wisely that the legend might well be traced to the forests of Scandinavia [*CP*, 4:205c, cited Ormerod in *Coll. Top. et Gen.*, 7:4-8].

Children, by first wife [*CP*, 4:205c]:

      i.   Thomas[K], d. 5 Nov. 1383 (the Sir Oskatel of the *Irlam* legend); m. Isabel de Pilkington (dau. of Sir Roger de Pilkington), who m. (2) John de Dalton.

*   ii. Isabel, d. 26 Oct. 1414 [*i.p.m.*]; m. c. 1385 Sir John[K] Stanley, K.G., who d. Ardee, Ireland, 6 Jan. 1413/4 [Earwaker, 2:602].

§ § §

LEGH OF ADLINGTON

This line was extracted from a pedigree chart in George Ormerod's *History of Chester* [3:661], based on Dugdale's *Visitation* and Sir Peter Leycester's work, with additional research by Thomas Robert Wilson France, and data from *The Visitation of Cheshire*, edited by Rylands, and additions from Ormerod's first volume [449-455]. A check of the Harleian Society visitation volumes added nothing.

1. RICHARD[N] DE LEGH was Lord of High Legh and West Hall [Ormerod, *Chester*, 3:113] during the reign of King Edward I [Ormerod, 1:449].

Child and heir:

2.   i.   Agnes[M], m. (1) Richard de Lymme, m. (2) William de Hawarden [Ormerod, 1:499], m. (3) Sir William[L] de Venables.

2. AGNES[M] DE LEGH was the heiress of the Lord of High Legh (Westhall).

He married first Richard de Lymme (younger son of Hugh de Limme [Ormerod, *Chester*, 1:450]).

She married second William de Hawarden [*cf.* Ormerod, 1:450].

She married third Sir WILLIAM[L] DE VENABLES*, knight, of Bradwell, second son of the 5th Baron of Kynderton. After her death Sir William married third Katherine, daughter of Sir Urien de St. Pierre and widow of Sir Randle[M] le Roter of Thornton, according to Ormerod [1:499]; Katherine was living in 1296. However, Frank Renaud states in *Prestbury* that Catherine de Thornton was his first wife [82].

Sir William was the ancestor of the Venables of Bradwell [Earwaker, 2:249], and was living 6 Edw. II (1312-1313) [Ormerod, 1:113].

Earwaker stated, in *East Cheshire* [2:249], that she had children by each of her husbands.

Child, hers by first marriage to Richard de Lymme [Ormerod, 1:451, 499]:

      i.   Thomas de Legh, d. c. 1317; m. Cecily [Ormerod, 1:452], who l. 1305; lord of the moiety of High-Legh.

Child, hers by second marriage [Ormerod, 3:113], surnamed de Hawarden:

     ii. Ralph, of age before 1286.

Child, of Sir William de Venables by Agnes de Legh, from Ormerod [3:661], surnamed de Venables:

    3.   iii.   Sir John[L] de Legh, m. Ellen de Coroun.

Children, of Sir William de Venables by Katherine de St. Pierre (Thornton) [Ormerod, 3:113, 1:450b]:

        iv.   Hugh, of Hope in Bradwall; no issue [Earwaker's *History of Sandbach*, 126].

        v.   William, of Bradwall, *i.p.m.* 36 Edw. III (1362-1363); m. (1) Katherine le Grosvenor, dau. and heiress of Robert le Grosvenor of Little Budworth, m. (2) Joan, who l. 1366.

3. Sir JOHN[L] DE VENABLES, alias DE LEGH, was born in High Legh or High Leigh, and was living in 1338 [Ormerod, *Chester*, 1:499].

He married ELLEN DE COROUN, sister of John de Coroun, Lord of Adelynton in Cheshire, and probably heir-at-law of the Coroun or Corona family; she survived her husband; the *inquisition post mortem* was taken at Chester in July 1352. Earwaker noted that although she was sometimes said to be a daughter of William de Bagulegh [Baggiley], he believed her parents were Hugh de Corona and his wife Lucy, the latter living in 1316, a widow. Frank Renaud states that Lucy, daughter of the first Hugh de Corona, married second William de Baggiley, and had a son who died without issue, and daughters Ellen and Isabel (who married Sir John de Hyde) [*Prestbury*, 78-79]. Hugh de Corona was son of Hugh de Corona, the lord of Adlington in the time of Henry III, and his wife Amabilla (daughter of Sir Thomas[O] de Bamville), who may have married next Simon de Provence and been living in 1307.

He lived at High Legh until his marriage. He was lord of Knottesfordbothes (or Norbury Booths) before 28 Edw. I (1299-1300), by purchase from William de Tabley [Earwaker, 2:249; Ormerod, 1:451]. Thomas de Corona, the last of his line, who died without issue, had given John (de Venables) de Legh and Ellen his wife a moiety of Adlington for life. The manor was seized by Queen Isabella in 9 Edw. II (1315-1316), but in 17 Edw. II (1323-1324) the widow Ellen purchased a pardon from the Queen [Renaud, *Prestbury*, 79].

Children, incompletely listed by Ormerod, surnamed de Legh:

        i.   Sir John[K], eldest son, ancestor of the Leghs of Booths and of Baguley [Earwaker], m. (1) Maude[K] de Arderne, m. (2) Isabel de Baggiley, who d. c. 23 Edw. III (1349-1350).

    4.   ii.   Robert, second son, m. (1) Sybil de Honford, m. (2) Matild de Norley.

        iii.   Sir William, of Isall in Cumberland, l. 1308 and 1316 [Earwaker, 2:249], and 1338 [Ormerod, 1:499].

        iv.   Peter, of Bechton, Cheshire, in right of his wife, living 1316 and 1338; m. Agnes de Bechton, dau. of Philip de Bechton [Renaud, 82].

        v.   Gilbert, chaplain, living 1321, of record as a Townley in 1338.

        vi.   Agnes, said to have m. Hugh Mascy of Timperley [Earwaker].

4. ROBERT[K] DE LEGH died in Macclesfield in Cheshire [Renaud, 83] about 44 Edw. III (1370 [Earwaker, 2:249]).

He married first SYBIL[K] DE HONFORD, who was living in 1336 [Earwaker], daughter of a Henry de Honford.

He married second Matilda (or Maud) de Norley, alias de North Legh, in Pemberton, Lancashire, daughter of Sir Thurston de Norley of Norley [*Vis. Cheshire*, 151-152], by his wife Margery, daughter and heir of John fitz Warin de Waleton, in Leyland Hundred, or of Sir Adam de Norley [Earwaker, 2:249]. Norley was apparently heir to Boydell. In 1375

Matilda and Thomas le Par were indicted for forging a settlement defrauding the rightful heir in favor of his youngest son, John.

He became Lord of Adelynton by settlement of Thomas de Coroun (de Corona) in 9 Edw. II. He was of record in 1308, 1316 and 1353 [Earwaker, 2:249]. In 1353 Thomas de Corona released all his rights in Adlington.

Robert de Legh sat as justice in eyre at Macclesfield, where he resided, and was one of the King's stewards of the manor and forest of Macclesfield.

Children, by first wife:

    5.   i.   Robert^J, d. Nov. 1382; m. Matild^J de Arderne.

          ii.   daughter, m. William de Radcliffe of Lancashire [*cf. Vis. Cheshire 1580*, 151].

         iii.   Margaret, m. Sir John de Ashton under Lyne of Lancashire.

Children, by second wife:

         iv.   Piers (or Peter) of Macclesfeld and later of Hanley, b. c. 1361; m. (1) Nov. 1388 Margaret^J Daniell (or Danyers, widow of Sir John^J Savage), dau. of Sir Thomas Danyers, m. (2) Cicely Hagh, dau. of John Hagh of Hagh, Derbyshire; l. 1382 and 1399, ancestor of the Leghs de Lyme [Newton, *House of Lyme*, 1-2].

         v.   John of Macclesfeld, d. 1407; issue, ancestor of the Leghs de Ridge.

         vi.   Hugh.

         vii.   Matild, m. Ralph Wilberham (or Wilbraham) of Radnor [Ormerod] or Woodhey, Cheshire [Earwaker, 2:249].

        viii.   daughter, m. Jeoffrey Holt [Renaud, 83].

         ix.   daughter, m. Roger Hilton of the Park, Lancs.

5. ROBERT^J DE LEGH, son and heir, died on the feast of St. Martin in Nov. 1382.

He married MATILD^J DE ARDERNE*, who was aged 10 in 1 Ric. II (1386-1387) [Ormerod, 3:566], daughter and coheir of Sir John de Arderne of Aldford and Alvanley, by his third wife, Elen de Wasteneys.

Initially he held his father's offices in Macclesfield. Lord of Adelynton, he served in the French wars, and was in Gascony in 1358. He added lands in Hyde, Cliff, Hattersley, Romiley and Etchells to the family holdings.

His *inquisition post mortem* was held 6 Ric. II (1382-1383).

Children, in the pedigree in Ormerod:

    6.   i.   Sir Robert^l, d. 1408; m. (1) Isabel de Belgrave, m. (2) Margery.

         ii.   Katherine, m. Reginald del Dounes.

6. Sir ROBERT^l DE LEGH, born at Roterlehay and baptized at Aldelym in March of 36 (or 35 [Renaud, 85]) Edw. III (c. 1362), was dead in the Feast of St. Laurence in 1408; his *inquisition post mortem* was held 9 Henry IV (1407-1408).

He married first ISABEL^l (or Anabella [Renaud, 85]) DE BELGRAVE, daughter and heir of Thomas de Belgrave by his wife Joan, sister and heir of John de Pulford. Thomas de Belgrave was of Eccleston, near Chester, as well as of Little Belgrave, Mouldisdale, March and Northwall in Flintshire, and of Kelsall and Tiersworth in Cheshire, and the City of Chester.

His second wife, named Margery, was named co-executor of her husband's will 9 Henry IV, and married second, before 26 Feb. 1409/10, Richard de Clyderhowe (or Clitheroe).

In 10 Ric. II (1386-1387) he was engaged against the French [Renaud, 86-87]. However, he joined Henry IV at Shrewsbury, going with him to Chester and Flint.

Lord of Addelyngton, he was Sheriff of Cheshire in 17, 20 and 22 Ric. II (1393-1394, 1396-1397 and 1398-1399, respectively), served in Scotland in 1385, and in Ireland in 1394. Ormerod states that "he had license for an oratory in Adelynton, 1398." He was justice in Eyre, a retainer of Richard II, constable of the castle of Oswaldestre, and was in 1401 deputy steward and master of the forests of Cheshire. In 6 Hen. IV (1404-1405) he was summoned by Henry, Prince of Wales, to join him with one hundred bowmen at Warrington and to meet the King at Pomfret.

Children, by first wife:

7.   i.   Robert[H], d. 26 Sept. 1415; m. Matild.

      ii.   Robert, living 6 Henry V.

     iii. James of Adlyngton, gent., living 1421 and 1437.

     iv. Reynold, alias Reginold, of Mottrum, living *temp.* Henry V, and perhaps 18 Edw. IV (1478-1479), and perhaps d. 1482 [inscription in Prestbury church]; had dau. Maulde, living 18 Henry VI (1439-1440), who m. Nicholas de Berd of Berd Hall in Derbyshire.

      v.   James, perhaps second son of the name.

     vi. Joan, m. (1) Ralph de Davenport, who d. 1415, m. (2) John de Legh (East-hall).

    vii. Elen, m. David de Calvylegh, son and heir of Sir Hugh de Calvylegh, Jr. of Lea.

7. ROBERT[H] DE LEGH, son and heir, was aged 22 in 9 Henry IV (1407-1408), and died of the plague before Harfleur on 26 Sept. 1415; his *inquisition post mortem* was held in 3 Henry V (1415-1416).

He married MATILD, who married second, in or about 4 Henry V (1416-1417), William[I] de Honford of Chorley; she died 1478, aged about 90, and her *inquisition post mortem* was held 18 Edw. IV (1478-1479).

The executor of his father's will, he was one of the King's retinue abroad in July 1415.

Children, listed by Ormerod:

8.   i.   Robert[G], m. (1) Isabel Savage, m. (2) Isabel[H] Stanley.

      ii.   Elen, m. Roger de Legh of Ridge.

8. ROBERT[G] DE LEGH, Esquire, was born in Adlynton and baptized at Prestbury in Cheshire, in 1410, and died in 1478 [Renaud, *Prestbury*, 90].

He was married first at age five, by 3 May 1415, to Isabel Savage, daughter of Sir John Savage of Clifton, knight. Isabel was of the same age, and probably died in childhood.

He married second ISABEL[H] STANLEY*, daughter of Sir William[I] de Stanley, Lord of Hooton. She was also born about 1410; they were married by dispensation, as she was related to his first wife.

In 1448 he leased Prestbury, which the family had purchased when the monastery was dissolved. In 9 Edw. IV (1469-1470) the King (as Earl of Chester) granted him liberty to enclose and make a park at Whitley Hey and Adlington Wood, and Whitley Hey Green, even though it was within the royal forest of Macclesfield. He was also given free warren in all his desmesnes and woods within Adlington manor and the vills and hamlets of Stockport, Bollington, Hyde and Rainow [Renaud, 89].

Children, by second wife, compiled from Ormerod and Renaud:

      i.   Robert[F], b. c. 1428; d. 8 Dec. 1486; m. Ellen Bothe (or Booth, Boothes), dau. of Sir Robert Bothe of Dunham Mascy.

     ii.   James, rector of Routhesthorne.

    iii. Peter, living 1483.

iv.   Reginold, living 15 Edw. IV.
v.   William.
vi.   Margaret, m. (1) Thomas Mere of Mere.
vii. Margery, m. William Davenport of Bramall, who d. 1483, son of John Davenport.
viii. Elizabeth, m. Robert de Duckenfeld, son of John de Duckenfield of Duckenfield.
ix.   Douce (or Dulce), living 5 Hen. VII.
x.   Isabel, m. (1) Laurence Warren of Poynton, m. (2) 1475 Sir George Holford of Holford.
*   xi.   Maud (or Matild), m. John[F] Mainwaring of Over Peover.
xii. Elen, m. Roger Leigh of Ridge [*Vis. Cheshire 1580*, 151, and Renaud, *Prestbury*, 118]).
xiii. Agnes, m. Sir Andrew Brereton of Brereton, who succeeded his father in 1482.
xiv. A., m. Pigot of Chetwynd in Shropshire.

§ § §

✓

LEYCESTER of NETHER TABLEY

This line is based on Ormerod's *History of Chester*, volume one, pages 617-619.

1. Sir NICHOLAS[M] LEYCESTER was styled knight in 20 Edw. I (1291-1292), and died in 23 Edw. I (1294-1295).

He married about 1276 MARGARET[M] DUTTON*, who had married first Robert de Denbigh, by whom she had had no children.

In addition to Nether Tabley, Margaret brought to her husband the manors of Wethale and Hield, both in Aston nigh Great Budworth in Cheshire.

He was seneschal to Henry Lacy, Earl of Lincoln and constable of Cheshire.

In 1292 he had lands in Adwick, near Doncaster in Yorkshire, and in Wath, near Adwick.

Children, listed by Ormerod:
2.   i.   Roger[L], son and heir, m. Isabel.
     ii. John, vicar of Walleysey in Wirrall, 1312.

2. Sir ROGER[L] LEYCESTER lived constantly at Wethale in Aston, nigh Picmere, in Cheshire, and died about 1349.

He married Isabel.

He bought out all the freeholders and charterers of Nether Tabley, principally William Heart, during the reign of Edward III.

In 1296 he was granted the third part of Over Tabley cum Sudlow by Sir John Grey, son of Sir Reginald Grey. Sir John Grey had obtained the grant from William de Tabley, Lord of Over Tabley and Knotsford.

Children, listed by Ormerod:
3.   i.   Nicholas[K], d. 1349; m. c. 1322 Mary[K] Mobberley.
     ii. Roger.
     iii. Margaret, m. 17 Edw. II (1323-1324) Adam de Molesworth, who was Sheriff of Flint 5 Edw. III.

3. NICHOLAS[K] LEYCESTER died in 1349, about the same time his father died. He married about 1322 MARY[K] MOBBERLEY* of Mobberley.

Children, listed by Ormerod:

   i.   John[J], son and heir, served in the army of John of Gaunt.
   ii. Raufe, ancestor of the Leycesters of Toft, Cheshire.
* iii. Elizabeth, l. 1404; m. William[J] Mainwaring, the Elder, of Over Peover.

§ § §

LINGEN

Additional sources to be checked include Sir Thomas Phillip's *Collections* (5 vols., 1840-1871), vol. 3, in the Library of Congress [CS411.P5]; "HS 1470+6" (cited by Norr), and John Duncumb's *History of Herefordshire*, vol. 2, p. 184. Whitmore and Barrow need to be consulted.

The following material has been adapted from Burke's *Genealogical and Heraldic History of the Landed Gentry, 15th ed.* (London: Shaw Publishing Co., Ltd., 1937), pages 298-299. Burke is not a particularly reliable source, and the early generations need more work; amendments have been made from the work of Vernon Norr [83].

Not included in the presentation below is a John Lingen, who disclaimed arms in 1584, who married Elizabeth Corbet. He was presented by H.E. Forrest [*Trans. Shropshire Arch. Soc.*, 4th series, 5 (1915), 169] as descended from William Lingen, "who belonged to a branch of the family long seated at Lingen," through his son John Lingen, who "married a Welsh wife, the daughter of David ap Griffiths, perhaps of Wollaston," through his son William Lingen, who married Margaret Chetwynd and was the father of John Lingen who married Elizabeth Corbet.

1. RALPH[P] DE LINGEN was born say 1142, and was involved in a fine in 1182.

He was the lord of Lingen and Sutton, was the first to assume the family name, and according to Tom Keelor of RR#2, S29, C7, Peachland, BC, Canada V0H 1X0 (2000), he had a brother William, born about 1145, who married Rose Pendwardine and was a Knight of the Holy Sepulchre.

Children, the first from Norr [83], and the second from Tom Keelor:

2. i.   John[O].
   ii. Brian, b. say 1205; became a secular canon.

2. JOHN[O] DE LINGEN succeeded to property in 1189 and was of record in court in 1196 [Eyton, 5:75-76].

Child, from Norr [83]:

3. i.   John[N], l. 1236.

3. JOHN[N] DE LINGEN, born say 1194 [Norr, 83] or 1200 [Keelor], was in court in 1221 and 1226 [Eyton, 11:333], and had transactions with his suzerein, Ralph de Mortimer [Eyton, 5:77], recorded in 1236.

According to Burke he was son of Ralph de Wigmore, whose ancestor, Turstin de Wigmore, a companion of the Conqueror, held Lingen or Lingham, near Wigmore in Herefordshire, in 1086. However, Ralph de Wigmore was born say 1096, and had a son Brianus born say 1122. Eyton dismissed the allegation that Turstin de Wigmore was ancestral to this family, there being no records of the line between Domesday, in 1086, and 1182.

Children, suggested by Burke:
4.   i.   Sir John[M], his heir, of record 1256.
      ii.   Ralph, living 1292.
     iii.   Maud, m. Walter de Pedwardine.
     iv.   Constance, m. 1253 Grimbald Pauncefort; she cut off her right hand to rescue her husband from captivity in Tunis during the crusade under Prince Edward and St. Louis.

4. Sir JOHN[M] DE LINGEN, born say 1226, had a grant of free warren in 1256.

A Ralph de Lingen was sued in 1283, but Eyton (quoted by Norr [83]) could not "say this Ralph was head of his family" [5:78].

He made a covenant in 1253 regarding the marriage of Constance.

In 1259 a John Lingeyn was paid fifteen marks by the Sheriff of Shropshire [Eyton, 11: 333].

In 44 Hen. III (1259-1260) he served as a dictator of the truce between Henry III and Prince Llywelyn of Wales [J. Morris, *Shropshire Genealogies*, 2:852].

Child:
5.   i.   Sir John[L], b. say 1260; perhaps m. Mawd.

5. Sir JOHN[L] DE LINGEN, born say 1260, was knighted 34 Edw. I (1305-1306) prior to joining King Edward I on his last expedition to Scotland.

A *feodary* dated 1308 gave a John de Lingen as holding Knull for one-fourth of a knight's fee [Eyton, 11:334]; he married Mawd, and in 5 Edw. III (1331) he held a knight's fee at Aymondestre in Herefordshire [J. Morris, 2:852].

Children, listed by Norr [83]:
6.   i.   Sir John[K], b. say 1300.
     ii.   Agnes.

6. Sir JOHN[K] DE LINGEN, born say 1300, was inserted here by Norr because of problems of chronology.

Children, listed by Burke or Norr [83], or Hansen [*TG*, 7:66]:
7.   i.   Ralph[J], b. say 1334; m. perhaps Margery Cheyne.
     ii.   Richard, m. Isabel Holgate, dau. of Philip Holgate; enjoyed power and trust during the reign of King Henry IV.
     iii.   Euphemia, poss. m. William Pembrigge (or Penbrigge, Pembrugge, Pembridge, Penebrigg) [Joseph Morris, 8:852, see "Mytton MSS."].

7. Sir RALPH[J] LINGEN of Lingen, Herefordshire, born say in 1334, probably died in 1399.

George Wrottesley's "Pedigrees from the Plea Rolls" [*The Genealogist*, new ser., 13:34] contained mention of Sir Ralph Lyngeyn who married Margery de Cheyne, daughter of Roger Cheyne (who was son of Roger de Cheyne, who lived 2 Edw. III [1328-1329], and Margery) and Isolda. Margery Cheyne had a sister, according to the suit at Michaelmas term, 3 Ric. II (1379-1380), named Margaret, who married Laurence Hauberk.

While it has been said that he married second Margery Pembrugge [Robinson, *Mansions of Herefordshire*, 179], sister of Sir Robert Pembrugge of Tong Castle, Shropshire, and daughter of Fulk Pembrugge of Tong, this is most unlikely, for the marriage of Isabel[J] Lingen and Sir Fulk de Penbrugge, Robert's son, would have been between first cousins, was undocumented and published for the first time only 400 years later in J.B. Blakeway's *Sheriffs of Shropshire*, which was published in 1831, five years after Blakeway died. Blakeway cited "Blount's MS. Collections for Herefordshire" in the possession of William

Blount, M.D., in 1808, but the extant parts of this work contain no record of a Lingen-Penbrugge/Pembrugge marriage [*cf.* Hansen, *TG*, 7:121[689]]. All sources for a Lingen-Pembrugge marriage were derived from Blakeway.

He was a Member of Parliament during the reigns of Edward III and Richard II. He was of record in 1398-1399 as holding Lingen under Mortimer of Wigmore for half a knight's fee [Eyton, 11:334].

Children, listed by Norr [83-84]:

    i.   Sir Ralph[I], b. 1370; will dated 1452; m. Jane Russell; of Sutton and Lingen in Herefordshire.

*   ii.   Isabel, d. 6 Dec. [*MCS5*, 111:8] 1446; m. (1) cousin Fulke Pembrugge, base son of Robert, m. (2) Sir John[I] Ludlow, who b. say 1360, was of record in 1427, m. (3) Sir Thomas Peytvine; founded a collage at Tong in 1411.

    iii.   Isolda, m. Brian Harley of Brampton, who fought Glyndŵr in 1402; she was mentioned as a daughter of second Ralph by John Burke [*Commoners*, 4:266; see *Collin's Peerage*, 5th ed., 4:238].

    iv.   Richard, of record as having bought cattle in 1406.

§ § §

LORING

This line was originally from Weis [*AR7*, 155A]. Much additional data was found in Elias Ashmole's *The Institution, Laws & Ceremonies of the Most Noble Order of the Garter* [reprint Baltimore, 1971, orig. London, 1672].

1.   ROGER[M] LORING was mentioned by Ashmole [701] as the father of Sir Nele Loring. He married CASSANDRA[M] PEROT, daughter of Reginald Perot.

Child:

2.   i.   Sir Nele[L], K.G., d. 1386, bur. Priory of Dunstable; m. Margaret Beauple.

2.   Sir NELE[L] LORING of Chalgrove in Bedfordshire [*BP*, 14:368], was dubbed Knight of the Garter on 23 April 1349, died in 1386, and was buried in the Priory of Dunstable, to which he had been a great benefactor.

He married MARGARET[L] BEAUPLE, daughter and heir of Sir Ralph Beauple of Knowstone [*CP*, 14:368] or Cnubeston [Ashmole, 701], Devonshire, and his wife Elizabeth Bloyho (daughter and heir of Alan Bloyho), widow of Stephen Tinterne, Esq.

He came to the attention of King Edward I by demonstrating such valor in the naval battle before Sluce that he was knighted and given an immediate grant of £20 per year until Edward I could provide lands of similar annual value. The letters patent were dated 26 June 14 Edw. III (1340). He served in Brittany, and in 18 Edw. III (1344-1345) he and Michael Northburgh, canon of Lichfield and Hereford, were sent to the Pope's Court with a letter from the king requesting a dispensation for the marriage of the Prince of Wales to the daughter of the Duke of Brabant. He then served in Gascoigne, for four years with the Prince of Wales (as Prince of Guyenne), and then in Aquitaine.

He was granted various pensions and the manors of Neuyn and Purchely in North Wales for life.

Children, listed by Ashmole [701]:

  *   i.   Isabel[K], d. 21 Aug. 1400; m. (1) Sir William Cogan of Huntsfield, who d. 1382, m. (2) 1383 Sir Robert[K] Harington, who d. 21 May 1406.

    ii.   Margaret, m. John Peyvre of Tuddington, Bedfordshire.

§ § §

LUCY OF NEWINGTON

This was adapted from Miss Ethel Stokes' work in Cokayne's *Complete Peerage* [8:257-263]. Stokes suggested that the family name probably came from Lucé, a commune in the department of Orne, about six kilometers southeast of Domfront, in the bailiwick of Passeis. A part of Maine, Lucé became connected with Normandy in 1092 when Domfront, the castle of Robert de Bellême, was occupied by Henry Beauclerc, who was then Count of the Côtentin and was later King Henry I of England. In a charter for Séez Cathedral, dated Feb. 1131, Henry mentioned a fief he had bought from Richard de Lucy and his mother Aveline [*CP*, 8:257c].

    Material was added from J.H. Round's article, "The Heirs of Richard de Lucy," *The Genealogist*, n.s., 15(1898-1899):129-133.

    RICHARD[R] DE LUCY, "the Loyal," Justiciar of England, died in 1179. He married ROESIA.

    GEOFFREY[Q] DE LUCY was noted as next in line by Stokes and Round.

    GEOFFREY[P] DE LUCY died in 1234. He married in 1207 JULIANE[P] LE DESPENSER (widow first of William Bardolf and second of Piers de Stokes, steward to King John, dead without issue by Aug. 1206), daughter of Aymer le Despenser by Amabel or Maud, daughter and coheir of Walter de Chesney, by Eve de Broc, daughter and heir of Eustace de Broc [*CP*, 14:457].

    GEOFFREY[O] DE LUCY died before 16 Aug. 1252, when Geoffrey de Lusignan, the King's brother, had wardship of his lands. He married NICHOLE, who was a widow; she had lands at Thornton in dower.

    Sir GEOFFREY[N] LUCY died before 5 June 1284, when writs to the escheators were issued. He was married by about May 1257 [*CP*, 8:260a] to ELENA RAVENINGHAM [Weis], of unknown parentage, who was living in 1316.

    Sir GEOFFREY[M] LUCY, born at Chelmscot, Buckinghamshire, during the first ten days of Aug. 1267, baptized at Soulbury, died before 20 Jan. 1304/5, the date of the writs to the escheators. He married DESIDERATA (or Desiderée), whose parentage is unknown. However, Stokes observed that she was possibly a Leyburn, and later Henry de Leyburn was one of Lucy's trustees [*CP*, 8:260h]. She was living in 1329.

    √   7. Sir GEOFFREY[L] LUCY, born at Cublington in Buckinghamshire, 21 Jan. 1287/8, baptized in St. Nicholas' Church there the next day, died 18 May 1346.

    He married while still a ward, and without the King's license; his widow was KATHERINE, but she may have been a second wife. Katherine apparently died in 1361, having had dower after his death.

    He had a writ for livery of his lands on 6 Oct. 1310, was summoned for service against the Scots in 1319, and again (as a knight) in 1322. In 1335-1336 he was commissioner of array in Bedfordshire with the authority to select archers and send them to Berwick.

    Child:

    8.   i.   Geoffrey[K], b. 1324; d. 1399/1400; m. Margery.

    8. Sir GEOFFREY[K] LUCY, born in 1324, died in 1399/1400.

    In 1355 he obtained a papal indult for himself and his wife, MARGERY, to choose a confessor. Her parentage is not known.

Aged 22 and more at his father's death, he had livery of his lands on 9 June 1346. In 1352 and 1371 he was joint collector of subsidies in Buckinghamshire. In 1353 he was a commissioner under the Statute of Labourers in Bedfordshire, and in 1354 he was joint commissioner to look into malpractice by Sheriffs in the two counties. In 1360 he was among seventeen men-at-arms named to be compelled, if need be, to assemble at Sandwich with 20 armed men and 80 archers from Bucks. for service abroad in the campaign which was concluded by the Peace of Brétigny. At his death he was a knight.

Child:

9.   i.   Reginald (or Reynold)[J], b. 1359; d. 9 Nov. 1427; m. Margaret.

9. Sir REGINALD (or Reynold)[J] LUCY, born in 1359, died 9 Nov. 1427.

By Feb. 1378/9 he had married MARGARET, whose parentage is not known.

He was a knight by 1387.

Child:

10.   i.   Walter[I], d. 1444/5; m. Eleanor[I] l'Archedekne, who d. 20 July 1447, having m. (2) Henry Barrett.

10. Sir WALTER[I] LUCY of Wappenham died 4 Oct. 1444.

He married in or before May 1385 ELEANOR[I] L'ARCHEDEKNE* of Ruan Lanihorne in Cornwall, who married second Henry Barrett [Roberts' *RD500*, 374]. She died 20 July 1447, having made a will dated 1 Jan. 1445/6.

His marriage made him a landowner in the West of England. As early as 1415 he was a commissioner in the Marches of Wales; later he was justice of the peace, and commissioner on occasion in Herefordshire, Shropshire and Worcestershire. In 1416 he was a knight. In 1419/20 he accompanied the Earl of March to the French war as Walter Lucy of Richard's Castle.

His will was dated 18 July 1444.

The Visitation of Shropshire [255] identified him as of Newington Lucy, but stated erroneously that his father was Sir William Lucy, who bore arms *Gules, semée* of cross-crosslets, three *lucies argent.*

Children [*CP*, 8:263]:

    i.   Sir William[H], b. 1404; slain on the royalist side at the battle of Northampton, 10 July 1460; m. (1) Margaret Nevill, kinswoman of the Earl of March [*CP*, 14:457], m. (2) before 1434 Elizabeth Percy, widow of Thomas Burgh, m. (3) Margaret Johan, who m. (2) a Wake, and d. 4 Aug. 1466; he had no issue.

*   ii.   Eleanor, m. Thomas[H] Hopton of Stanton, Shropshire [Paget, 2:445].

    iii.   Maud, m. William Vaux of Harrowden.

§ § §

LUDLOW

The location of Hodnet and Stokesay was determined through the use of the web site http://uk.multimap.com. Eyton and Joseph Morris were major sources.

A royal charter of 1281 showed Laurence de Ludlow in possession of Stokesay in Shropshire [Eyton, *Antiquities of Shropshire*, 5:36]. Reginald de Ballon alienated lands in Much Marcle in Herefordshire to Laurence de Ludlow about 1287 [Sanders, 66]. Laurence was given permission in 19 Edw. I (1290-1291) to fortify and crenellate his house at Stokesay; Laurence was dead by 20 Jan. 1296. He left a widow Agnes and son William.

William de Ludlow was mentioned in March 1316 as lord of Stokesay with his wife Cecilia de Halghton. He had been summoned for military service against the Scots in 1301 [Eyton, 9:333], was assessor and tax collector of the fifteenth in Herefordshire in 3 Hen. IV (1301-1302), and in 1307 was Knight of the Shire for Salop (Shropshire). He also served as collector of taxes in 1307, 1309, 1310 and 1314, and as commissioner of array in 1311 and 1315. In 1313 he was pardoned for being an adherent of the Earl of Lancaster in the matter of Piers de Gavaston. In 1314 and 1316 he was summoned against the Scots. In March 1316 he was of record as joint lord of Stokesay [Eyton, 9:335], and lord of Westbury. He was dead by 11 Nov. 1316. At the inquest estate was valued at £12.17s.6d per year and his widow was named as Matilda de Hodnet [Eyton, 9:333]. His widow Matilda, who died in 1347, married then William Wyn (or de Wynne), who was of record in 1320 and 1322.

Sir Laurence[K] de Ludlow, born 2 March 1301, died 14 Oct. 1353. He married Hawise. He was recorded as a knight in May 1324 when he was summoned to the Great Council at Westminster. His son John de Ludlow was born 6 May 1320 and died 17 Feb. 1382. He married Joanna, and had children Richard de Ludlow, who died 12 Dec. 1390, and John de Ludlow II, who died 20 July 1398, having had a son William, who was born about June 1397.

Francis Jones ["The Dynasty of Powys," *Trans. Hon. Soc. of Cymmrodorion* (1958), 32[31]] states that Elizabeth Grey (daughter of Richard Grey, lord Powys, and Margaret Tuchet [daughter of John, lord Audley], who married before 12 Jan. 1458/9) is said to have married John Ludlow, from whom the Vernons of Stokesay and of Hodnet, and the Curzons (lords Scarsdale) descend. However, this does not seem likely in light of the following.

1. Sir JOHN[J] DE LUDLOW was identified as the father of John, below, in a recognizance in the Exchequer of Shrewsbury dated 1394 [J. Morris, *Shropshire Genealogies*, 2:879].
    Children, listed by Morris:
    i.   Richard[I], d. 1398; a Sir Richard Ludlow, M.P., who d. 12 Dec. 1390 (having been b. c. 1361), with brother John his heir, is given by Roskell [3:650] as son of Sir John Ludlow of Hodnet by his wife Joan, with a note that descent was from Odo de Hodnet, who d. 1201.
2. ii. John, of record 1427; m. Isabel[J] Lingen, widow of Fulke Pembruge.

2. JOHN[I] LUDLOW of Hodnet and Stokesay, both in Shropshire, England, was born 20 July 1398, and was of record in 1427.
    He married ISABEL[J] LINGEN*, widow of Fulke Pembruge; she married third Sir Thomas Prestyvine [J. Morris, 2:879].
    Children, listed by J. Morris [2:879]:
    *   i.   Benedicta[H], l. 1427; m. by 25 Nov. 1410 Sir Richard[H] Vernon of Haddon.
         ii. Margery, m. William Trussell.
         iii. Alice, m. Richard Vernon of Haddon.
         iv. Isabel, m. Nicholas Fitz Herbert of Norbury in Derbyshire.
         v.   William, of Stoke and Hodnet, b. c. June 1397; m. (1) Jane Hussey, dau. of Richard Hussey, m. (2) Elizabeth ferch Thomas ap Sir Rhys ap Gruffudd, lord of Wichnor in Staffs.

§ § §

MAINWARING OF IGHTFIELD IN SHROPSHIRE

The Mainwaring family file at the Society of Genealogists, London, contained page 71 from "Monumental Brasses in Shropshire" dealing with a monumental brass of William[G] Maynwaryng, "the Good," below, died 1497, second son of Hawkyn Maynwaryng by his wife Margaret, daughter and heiress of Gryffin Waren, and Lady of Ightfield. A marginal note in pencil labeled this "Nonsense!"

Neil D. Thompson, FASG, has stated that the Mainwaring family is badly in need of a modern study. In a letter, dated 7 Dec. 1998, addressed to the compiler, he wrote, "The Mainwarings pose a series of difficult problems....

"The best treatment of the earlier generations of the family is still that of Col. Charles M. Hanson, F.A.S.G. as part of his monumental Woodhull article in *TG* 7-8:4-127.... So far as I know, the generations above Ralph Mainwaring, living in 1202, are not yet fully proved. The family study by R. Mainwaring Finley (1890) is virtually worthless and it is unfortunate that it was ever published, much less reprinted.

"For the period where Col. Hansen leaves off and my article begins, the two best available sources are Ormerod's 2nd edition, 1:478-82 and the manuscript by George [*sic*] Morris,... 5:147-48, 154-55, both of which cite numerous original sources. There is also Mainwaring material in an article in the *Journal of the Chester Archeological Society* 57:27-40 and *Cheshire Sheaf* (3rd series) 12:27, 44, 79, 87, neither of which is available to me here [in Salt Lake City]. The 25th Annual Report of the Deputy Keeper of the PRO, p. 49, has a long list of IPMs of Mainwarings, some of which I had abstracted for my article, which others await further examination [all those listed are for 1397 and later].... Ormerod and Helsby (Ormerod's editor) clearly saw some of these IPMs but may not have seen them all. Cheshire fines and other land transactions also need examination...."

The pedigrees of Meinilwarin/Manwaringe of Peever in Rylands' edition of the *Visitation of Cheshire* contain many errors.

E.A. Hilditch has called attention to the following penalties for various crimes committed in the City of Chester:

If a freeman, breaking the kings peace kills a man in a house, his land and all his goods are forfeit, and he becomes an outlaw.

Whoever shed blood between Monday morning and Saturday noon, fined 10s, but from Saturday noon to Monday morning, fine 20s, same on the 12 days of Christmas, first day of Easter, first day of Whitsun, on Ascension day, or on All Saints Day.

Whoever killed a man on these holy days was fined £4, on other days 40s (£2). Similarly whoever committed breaking and entering, or highway robbery on these holidays, or on a Sunday, fined £4, on other days 40s.

Whoever committed robbery, or theft, or did violence to a woman in a house was fined 40s.

If a widow had intercourse with one unlawfully, she was fined 20s, but a girl for such an offense 10s.

1. WILLIAM[G] MAINWARING, "the Good," of Ightfield, Shropshire, England, son of RANDLE[I] MAINWARING* of Over Peover, died 6 March [*cf. CIPM Henry VII* 2:184] 14 Henry VII (1499) [Grazebrook and Rylands's *Visitation of Shropshire 1623*, 348].

He married MARGARET[G] WARREN*.

Children, given by the Abells and other cited sources:

    i.   George[F], son and heir, aged 50 and more at the death of his father [*cf. CIPM Henry VII*, 2:184]; d. 23 June [*cf. IPM Chancery* Ser. 2, 28:9] 5 Henry VIII (1513) [*Visit. Shropshire*, 348].

2. ii. Thomas, b. c. 1450; d. 1508; m. Joan[F] Sutton.
    iii. Anne, m. Richard Charlton, who b. 1450, d. 1522 [Weis, *AR*7, 31:36].
    iv. Margery, bur. Ightfield c. 1495; m. Ph. Egerton of Egerton, Cheshire
         [*Visit. Shropshire*], prob. m. (2) Hugh Calveley of Calveley [Joseph
         Morris' "Shropshire Genealogies," 5:154-155, MS. in Shrewsbury
         Public Library, available on LDS film].

2. THOMAS[F] MAINWARING of Ightfield, Shropshire, was born about 1450 and died in 1508.

He married JANE (JOAN)[F] SUTTON*, who was no doubt considerably older than her husband [a citation to Charles Twamley's *History of Dudley Castle and Priory, Including a Genealogical Account of the Families of Sutton and Ward* (London, 1867), chart bet. 16 and 171 (*sic*), has not been verified].

He was tenant of two copyhold estates in Edstaston and Cotton (in Wem parish), county Salop [see Rev. Samuel Garbet's *History of Wem* (1818), p. 267; the present location of the manorial rolls for this period is not known, but Garbet apparently had access to them].

Children, given by Thompson in the table, "Ancestry of Frances (Cotton) Abell" [*TG*, 5 (1984), 163-171], and *Visit. Shropshire* (348), and by Thompson in letter to the compiler of 28 July 1995:

         i. George[E], m. Margaret Moore of Bankhall, Lancashire [Joseph Morris,
             5:156]; three sons and one daughter.
3. ii. John, b. c. 1483; d. May 1518; m. Joan[E] Lacon.
*   iii. Cicely, of Ightfield, d. before 1516; m. John[D] Cotton.
    iv. Alice, m. Philip Hill of Foord.

3. Sir JOHN[E] MAINWARING, Knight, of Ightfield, Shropshire, died in May of 1518, the date given as "last Ascension tide" in the *Inquisition post mortem* [see PRO C142/33/33].

He married JOAN[E] LACON*, who died 13 April 1524, having married second George Pontesbury, who died 10 Oct. 1550.

He was among those who entered France 16 June 1513; he was a captain in the army of King Henry VIII [see Public Record Office, *Letters and Papers...of the Reign of King Henry VIII* (23 vols. in 38, London, 1862-1932), 1(2):1062], and was knighted at Lille.

He was the heir of his uncle George[F] Mainwaring.

His will, dated 7 July 1516, with a codicil of 28 Jan. 1517/8, was proved in May 1518.

Child, given by Thompson in the table, "Ancestry of Frances (Cotton) Abell" [*TG*, 5 (1984), 163-171], and *Visit. Shropshire*:

4.   i. Richard[D], d. St. Albans, Herts., 30 Sept. 1558; m. Dorothea[D] Corbet.

4. Sir RICHARD[D] MAINWARING, Knight, of Ightfield, Shropshire, was aged 21 and more in the *inquisition post mortem* of his father's estate, taken 22 August 1518), died in St. Albans, Hertfordshire, 30 Sept. 1558 [see PRO, *Calendar of the Patent Rolls... Elizabeth* (London, 1939), 78], and was buried in Ightfield 7 Oct. 1558, according to the parish register.

He married DOROTHY[D] CORBET* [Augusta Elizabeth Corbet's *The Family of Corbet, Its Life and Times*, 2 (London, 1918), 262-263; *Visit. of Shropshire* (Harleian Soc. Visitations Ser., 29, London, 1889), 348; Weis, *AR*7, 56A:40], of Moreton Corbet [dau. of Andrew Corbet in Rylands' *Vis. of Cheshire*, 165].

Sir Richard Mainwaring was knighted by 28 Sept. 1536, when he took a lease from John, late Abbot, and the convent of St. Mary, Combermere, Chester [*cf.* LP Henry VIII, 14(1):43]. He served as Commissioner of Peace in May 1538 [*ibid.*, 13(1):411], was among the knights who welcomed Anne of Cleves to England on 3 Jan. 1539/40 [*ibid.*, 15:6], and served as Sheriff of Shropshire in 1544 and at other times [*ibid.*, 21(2):222, as well as John B. Blakeway's *The Sheriffs of Shropshire* (Shrewsbury, 1831), 18-19].

Children, given by Thompson in the table, "Ancestry of Frances (Cotton) Abell" [*TG*, 5 (1984), 163-171], and other sources cited above [Faris stated they had twelve sons and four daughters, citing *TG*, 5:163-164; one son is missing from this list]:

5.   i.   Arthur[C], b. Ightfield c. 1520; bur. there 4 Sept. 1590; m. Mary[C] Mainwaring of Over Peover, Cheshire.

ii.   Maria, m. to Adam Oteley de Picheford.

iii.   Katherina, m. Tho. Starkey de Wrenbury.

iv.   Cecilia, m. to William Grosvenor de la Port (*i.e.*, Bellaport).

v.   Anna, m. Francis Harnage de Belswardine

vi.   Jasper.

vii.   William.

viii.   Griffith.

ix.   Edward.

x.   Christopher.

xi.   Adam, an apothecary.

xii.   Jacob.

xiii.   Thomas, slain at Berwick.

xiv.   Adam de Hethhouse, m. Dorothy Barker, dau. of John Barker of Couleshurst, Salop.

xv.   Roger.

5. Sir ARTHUR[C] MAINWARING, Knight, born in Ightfield, Shropshire (or county Salop), about 1520, was buried there 4 Sept. 1590 [parish register].

He married, about 1540, MARGARET[C] MAINWARING* of Over Peover, Cheshire, who died before her husband, as she was not mentioned in his will [*P.C.C. Sainberbe 49*].

Knighted at Berwick by John, Earl of Warwick, Lieutenant of the King's Army [Weyman, "Shropshire Members," *Transactions Shropshire Arch. Soc.*, 4th ser., 10:46], in 1547, he was probably engaged in the campaign which led to the battle of Pinkie. He was Member of Parliament for Shropshire in 1558, Commissioner of Peace in 1561/2, and Sheriff in 1563 and 1577. In 1577 he was a member of the Royal Commission of Musters, responsible for seeing that all the men of Shropshire aged between 16 and 60 were "armed, trained and inspected."

His will, dated 2 Sept. 1590, was proved 21 June 1591 [*P.C.C. Sainberbe 49*], and on 29 April 1591 his son was admitted tenant of Edstaston Hall on his father's death.

Children, given by Thompson and *Visit. Shropshire*, ed. Grazebrook:

i.   Elizabeth[B], m. Sir Thomas Aston.

ii.   Margeria (Margery).

iii.   George, m. Anna, dau. of William Moore of Loseley, Surrey; educated at Shrewsbury School, barrister in the Inner Temple 1565, Sheriff of Shropshire 1572, knighted 1595 [Weyman, *Transactions Shropshire*, 4th ser., 10:47].

*   iv.   Mary, b. Ightfield, Shropshire, c. 1541; d. before 14 June 1578; m. Combermere, Shropshire, 6 Jan. 1559/60, Richard[B] Cotton.

§ § §

MAINWARING of OVER PEOVER in CHESHIRE

The following line is based on the work of George Ormerod. Some of the data concerning Sir John[E] Mainwaring was confirmed by additional research presented in *The Genealogist* by Neil D. Thompson, F.S.A.G., as cited below.

In the church of Baddiley is buried Sir Thomas Mainwaring, bart., who was described in the inscription as "the twenty-ninth heir male of the Mainwarings of Over Peover since king William the Conqueror's time" [Ormerod, 3:457].

Henry Sutliff (e-mail address sssbo@earthlink.net) contributed over the internet (1999) an unpublished article by Glenn H. Goodman entitled "The Ancestry of Oliver Manwaring of New London, Ct." It cited an article by J.H. Cavanaugh in *Collections for the History of Staffordshire* (1934), which has not been checked by the compiler.

Goodman stated that Hugh de Waren, Bishop of Coutance, who died about 1020, was believed to be the earliest known ancestor of the family of Mainwaring. His son was allegedly Randolphus de Warenna, who allegedly had held land in Windham, County Norfolk, which had been forfeited to the King about 1075, indicating he may have participated in the rebellion of Ralph Guador that year. Goodman believed that he was the father of Randulphus[T] (below), tenant of Wayborn who was enfeoffed by Earl Hugh of Chester.

RANDULFUS[T] was lord of various towns in Cheshire and Norfolk, England, at the time of the Domesday survey in 1086.

ROGER[S] MESNILWARIN gave Plumley to Chester Abbey, England, before 1119.

WILLIAM[R] MESNILWARIN was a witness to his father's grant of Plumley to Chester Abbey in 1119, with his brother Randle, who was listed in William's place in the pedigree in Rylands' edition of the *Visitation of Cheshire* [164, where William was shown as childless].

ROGER[Q] LE MESNILWARIN gave one third of Nether Tabley to Chester Abbey in the time of Henry II.

Sir RALPH[P] LE MESNILWARIN, knight, was Justiciar of Chester, England, from about 1192-1194 to 1202 [Hansen, *TG*, 7-8:115, cited Geoffrey Barraclough's edition of *Facsimiles of Early Cheshire Charters* (Oxford, 1957), pages 10 and 17]. He married by 1181 AMICIA[M], illegitimate daughter of Hugh Kevelioc, Earl OF CHESTER [Hansen, *TG*, 7-8:61], before her father died. While she was illegitimate, a subsequent suit concerning the use of arms was decided in favor of the Mainwaring family [Burke's *Ext. Baronetcies* (1844), 333], as outlined in The Amicia Tracts, edited by William Beamont in *Cheshire Society Publications*, vols. 78 and 80. Hansen noted that Dugdale believed "nothing can be given in Frank-marriage to a Bastard," but observed that "lands given in frank marriage do not require homage until the third heir of the daughter, insuring their reversion to the father or his heirs should the daughter's line die out before then." Col. Charles M. Hansen commented in "The Barons of Wodhull with Observations on the Ancestry of George Elkinton, Emigrant to New Jersey" [*TG*, 7-8 (1986-87), 115, note 596], "Although the descent of lands and contemporary charters support the conclusion that Ralph de Mainwaring was descended from Ranulf, the Domesday tenant, the exact line of descent cannot be made certain by charter evidence. Farrar [*sic*] 2:227-28. An account of the early Mainwarings is given by J.G. Cavenagh-Mainwaring, 'The Mainwarings of Whitmore and Biddulph in the County of Stafford', Salt 57:47-54, 58-59 (1933)."

Sir ROGER[O] MAINWARING, knight, Lord of Warmincham, Cheshire, England, flourished during the reign of King Henry III, which was from 1216 to 1272.

Sir WILLIAM[N] MAINWARING received Over Peover, Cheshire, by gift from his father during the reign of King Henry III (which was from 1216 to 1272), as appeared by a charter transcribed by Sir Thomas Mainwaring in 1666 [James Croston's *County Families of*

Lancashire and Cheshire, 366], which had a seal, with an escutcheon of six barrulets, attached to it. According to Goodman he died in 1248.

WILLIAM[M] MAINWARING, Lord of Over Peover, was living in 14 Edw. I (1285-1286).

9. ROGER[L] MAINWARING died before his father.

He married CHRISTIAN DE BIRTLES, who married second, John de Byrun, and lastly, Robert de Vernon, who was living in 1334. The Harleian Society's printing of the Cheshire Visitations reveals that the name de Birtles was also sometimes given Birchells of Birchells [22]. She was not found in the Birtles pedigree printed in Ormerod's *History of Chester* [3:710]. Members of the family found in Earwaker's *East Cheshire* [2:357-360] lived in 1397 and later. The earlier records of the family are very poor.

The Visitation record showed this Roger as son of Ralfe, Justiciar of Chester.

Children, the first two mentioned by Ormerod, the third and fourth in *Visit. Cheshire*:

   10.   i.   William[K], son and heir, m. Mary[K] Davenport.

          ii.   Joan, m. Robert de Fallybrome nigh Birtles.

         iii.   Sir Thomas, in a visitation, had son Sir Warren, whose dau. Maud m. (1) Sir William Trussel, and m. (2) Sir Oliver de Burdeaux.

         iv.   Randoll, a priest.

10. WILLIAM[K] MAINWARING of Over Peover died about 12 or 13 Edw. III (1338-1340). He married MARY[K] DAVENPORT*.

Children, listed by Ormerod:

   11.   i.   William[J], son and heir, m. (1) Joan Praers, m. (2) Elizabeth[J] Leycester.

         ii.   Roger, l. 1334.

        iii.   Margery, l. 1334.

        iv.   Millicent, l. 1334.

11. WILLIAM[J] MAINWARING (styled "the Elder" in 33 Edw. III [1359]) of Over Peover died in 1364 [Croston, 369], when the son by his first marriage succeeded as heir.

He married first Joan[J] Praers, daughter and coheir of William[K] Praers of Baddiley, near Nantwich. Margery Praers, her sister and coheir, married first John[l] de Honford of Honford, and had a son, John Honford, who was found to be a bastard in an inquisition taken at Chester 28 Feb. 21 Rich. II (1398), and thus was denied his right to an inheritance of Baddiley. Margery (Praers) Honford married second, 33 Edw. III (1359-1360), Henry (or Hugh) Holt; they had no children and she died in 1380.

William[J] Mainwaring married second, after his first wife's death, ELIZABETH[J] LEYCESTER*, daughter of Nicholas Leycester and sister of John Leycester of Nether Tabley. She was living in 6 Hen. IV (1404-1405).

Child, by first wife:

         i.   William[l], son and heir, lord of Over Peover, d. 1399, bur. Acton Church; m. (1) 1366 Katharine Belgrave, dau. of John Belgrave of Belgrave in Eaton township, near Chester, Cheshire [Burke's *Ext. Baronetcies*, 334], m. (2) Clementia Cotton; illegitimate issue.

Children, by second wife:

         ii.   John, lord of Over Peover, d. 11 Henry IV (1409-1410); m. c. 1390 Margaret Stafford, widow of Sir John Warren of Poynton [Earwaker's *East Cheshire*, 2:286, Roberts' *RD500*, 378], Cheshire, and dau. of Sir John Stafford of Wickham, Norfolk; no lawful issue but had a bastard son, Peter (named in some visitations as base born son of William), by Margery Winnington; Sheriff of Cheshire.

12.   iii. Randle, Lord of Over Peover; d. 1456; m. Margery[I] Venables, widow of Richard Buckley.

      iv. Thomas, l. 38 Edw. III (1364-1365).

      v. Alan, l. 38 Edw. III.

      vi. Richard, l. 38 Edw. III.

      vii. Emme (or Emma, Anne), m. 1357 Richard Wynnington, nigh Northwich, son and heir of Sir Richard Winnington [Burke's *Ext. Baronetcies*, 333].

      viii. Ellen, m. 1359 Raufe (or Ralph) Vernon, grandson of Richard Vernon of Shi[p]bro[o]k, Cheshire, and son of Raulf.

      ix. Joan, m. (aged 5 or 6) 1359 Sir William Legh of Baggiley, who m. (2) Joyce, widow of Sir Ralph Davenport of Davenport [Ormerod, 1:550-551]; no issue.

12. RANDLE[I] MAINWARING died 35 Hen. VI (1456-1457), and was buried in the south chapel of Over Peover, Cheshire, in the stone chapel on the south side of the church, which was erected upon his death by his wife. He was often called Hawkin (or Honkyn) Mainwaring.

He married, 16 Rich. II (1392-1393), with the King's license obtained 14 Sept. 1391 after the marriage, MARGERY[I] VENABLES*; she was the widow of Richard Buckley of Chedill (or Cheadle-Bulkeley) in Cheshire, and daughter of the Baron of Kinderton. Randle had to petition the King to be allowed to enjoy her dower. She died in 1459, aged about 90 [Croston, 374].

In 1399 he was in Ireland in the service of King Richard II [Croston, 372], who had gone there to avenge the death of Roger Mortimer and put down a revolt of Irish chieftains. He succeeded to the family estates after the death of his brother John, entered the service of King Henry IV, and, as a result of an attachment to the court of the Earl of Chester, was in 1405 granted for life the office of Equitator of the Forest of Mara and Mondrem, which then included much of the Hundred of Nantwich and all of Edisbury. Then, when the Earl succeeded as King Henry V, Randle was granted two parts of the serjeanty of Macclesfield during the minority of John Davenport, whose family held the hereditary serjeanty [Croston, *County Families of Lancashire and Cheshire*, 373].

Children, by his wife, listed variously by Ormerod and Croston [373]:

13.   i. John[II], eldest son; m. (1) 1411 Margaret[H] Delves, m. (2) Joan Warren.

 *   ii. William[G], second son, d. 1497; m. Margaret[G] Warren; ancestor of the Mainwarings of Ightfield in Shropshire (see above for this line).

      iii. Ralph [Croston, 373; husband of Margaret Savage is called Randle, who d. 13 Edw. IV (1474), in Weis, *MCS*5, 98A:10A/B], third son, *inquisition post mortem* 1488; m. Margaret Savage, dau. of John[H] Savage of Clifton [Croston, 373] and Margery Brereton, and widow of John Maxfield; ancestor of the Mainwarings of Kermincham or Carincham (Caringham), Cheshire, which he purchased in 1432; shown by Weis to have had possible son Randle of Carincham, *i.p.m.* 3 Hen. VII (1488) naming Randle, aged 18 eldest son and heir, who m. Margaret Davenport, dau. of Hugh Davenport, Esq. of Henbury.

      iv. Elizabeth, m. Raufe Egerton of Wryne-hill in Staffordshire.

 *   v. Cicely, m. (1) Thomas[H] Fouleshurst of Crew in Cheshire, m. (2) John Curson.

      vi. Joan, m. 1411 John (Thomas in one pedigree) Davenport, son and heir of Raufe Davenport of Davenport in Cheshire.

    vii.   Ellen, m. Thomas Fitton of Gawsworth in Cheshire.

    viii.   Agnes, d. young, having been affianced to William Bromley of Badington, Cheshire.

    ix.   Margaret, m. (1) 1426 William Bromley of Badington, Cheshire, m. (2) Sir John Nedham of Crannach, judge of Chester 1 Edw. IV (1461-1462); no issue by second marriage.

Child, illegitimate, by Emma Farington, assumed surname of le Maynwaryng [Croston, 374]:

    x.   Hugh, m. Margaret Croxton, heiress of her brother Ralph Croxton of Croxton; ancestors of the Mainwarings of Croxton.

Children, illegitimate, mentioned only by Croston [374]:

    xi.   Thomas, of North Rode.

    xii.   Randle, m. (not proven [Weis, *MCS5*, 98A:10A/B]) Margaret Davenport (see iii, above).

    xiii.   daughter.

    xiv.   daughter.

    xv.   daughter.

13. Sir JOHN[H] MAINWARING, knight of Over Peover, Cheshire, died about the end of the reign of King Edward IV, the precept to the escheator for his inquisition dated 14 April 20 Edward IV (1481).

He married first, 13 Hen. IV (1411-1412), MARGARET[H] DELVES* of Doddington. While it has been alleged that her mother was born Philippa Mainwaring of the Norwood line, this has not been supported by Delves sources. It has been alleged that he married second Joan Warren, described by Croston [374] as second daughter of John Warren of Poynton by his wife Isabel, daughter of Sir John Stanley, K.G., of Lathom, but this has been held to be unlikely by Earwaker [*East Cheshire*, 2:286].

In 38 Hen. VI (1459-1460), King Henry VI sent him a letter commanding him to deliver to Lord Stanley (his second wife's uncle), persons in custody at the Castle at Chester, including Thomas and John Nevill (sons of the Earl of Salisbury), Sir Thomas Harrington of Hornby, his son James Harrington of Brierly, Raufe Rokeby, Thomas Ashton and Robert Evereus, esquires.

Children, listed by Ormerod or Croston [374], by first wife:

14.   i.   William[G], son and heir; m. 21 Jan. 1443/4 Ellen[G] Butler of Bewsey.

    ii.   John.

    iii.   Elizabeth, m. 1436 Piers Warburton, son and heir of Sir Geffrey de Warburton, Lord of Arley.

    iv.   Margaret, m. 1452 Hamnet Ashley, son and heir of John Ashley of Ashley in Bowdon Parish.

14. WILLIAM[G] MAINWARING died in the lifetime of his father.

He married 22 Hen. VI (1443) ELLEN[G] BUTLER*, sister to John Butler of Bewsey nigh Warrington in Lancashire, and daughter of Sir John Butler [Baines' *History of the County of Lancaster*, 3:660].

Child, mentioned by Ormerod:

15.   i.   John[F], d. 8 July 1495; m. Maud[F] Legh.

15. JOHN[F] MAINWARING of Over Peover, Cheshire, England, Esquire, died 8 July 1495 [Ormerod's *History of Cheshire* (2nd ed.), 1:482].

He married MAUD[F] LEGH*, who was living in 1512, a widow.

Children, by his wife, listed by Ormerod or Croston:
16.   i.   John[E], eldest son, b. c. 1471; d. March 1515/6; m. Katherine[E] Honford, who d. 1529.
    ii.   Robert.
    iii. Maud, m. 1490 Thomas Starkey, Esq. of Wrenbury in Cheshire.
    iv. Joan, m. 1512 Sir Thomas Ashton of Ashton-super-Mersey, Cheshire.
    v.   Agnes, m. Sir Robert Needham of Crannach, then Shenton, Salop.
Child, bastard, mentioned in will of his brother John:
    vi. Charles, living 35 Hen. VIII (1543-1544).

16. Sir JOHN[E] MAINWARING, Knight, of Over Peover, Cheshire, born about 1471, died in March of 1515/6, aged 45, and was buried at Over Peover [mi], beside his father. His alabaster monument is a representation of a knight in plate armor, with his wife by his side, and over their legs and knees is a scroll depicting their fifteen children.

He married KATHERINE[E] HONFORD* (or Handford), who died in 1529 and was buried at Over Peover.

Sir John Mainwaring was knighted 25 Sept. 1513 at Tournai [*LP Henry VIII*, 1(2):1026], and was Sheriff of Flintshire in 23 and 24 Hen. VII (1507-1509) and 6 Hen. VIII (1514-1515). Sir Ralph Egerton was appointed to succeed him as Sheriff [*Ibid.*, 2(1):512].

His will, dated 4 March 1515/6, was proved 18 Nov. 1516 [*P.C.C. Maynwaryng 1*]. Among other bequests, he left his bastard brother, Charles, £1.6s.8d yearly for life. He left his black velvet gown, guarded with cloth of gold, for the use of the priest of the parish church of Over Peover, and £4.13s.4d to an honest priest to pray for his soul for four years in the same church. The £20 he left towards a new stone steeple was not put to use.

Children, only the first given by Thompson in the table, "Ancestry of Frances (Cotton) Abell" [*TG*, 5 (1984), 163-171], all listed by Ormerod, 1:482, and Croston, 377 (although not in the same order):
17.   i.   Randall[D], eldest son, b. c. 1495; d. 6 Sept. 1577; m. (1) [Ormerod, 1:482] Mrs. Elizabeth[D] Brereton, widow of Richard Cholmondeley, m. (2) Elizabeth Leycester (dau. of Raufe Leycester of Toft juxtà Over Peover), who m. (2) Sir Edmund Trafford.
    ii.   Edmund, d. without issue.
    iii. John, d. without issue.
    iv. Piers, d. without issue.
    v.   Philip, succeeded his brother as lord of Over Peover; d. 11 April 1573 (1571 on monument [Brydges' *Stemmata Illustria*, 27]), bur. Over Peover; m. Anne Leycester, who d. 1587, dau. of Raufe Leycester of Toft juxtà Over Peover.
    vi. Edward, m. Alice, granddau. and heir of Humphrey de Boghey (or Bohun); founder of Mainwaring family in Whitmore and Biddulph in Staffordshire, Bromborough in Cheshire, and Oteley in Staffordshire [Burke's *Commoners*, vols. 3-4; Croston, 377].
    vii. Robert, m.; family in Martin-Sands (or Merton Sands), Cheshire.
    viii. Thomas.
    ix. George.
    x.   Henry.
    xi. Nicholas, not listed by Burke [*Ext. Baronetcies*, 335].
    xii. William, d. young; not listed by Burke.
    xiii. William, not listed by Burke.
    xiv. Margaret.

xv.   Katharine, m. c. 1521 William Newton, son of Homfrey (or Humphrey) Newton, Esq. of Pownall.

17. Sir RANDALL[D] MAINWARING, Knight, of Over Peover, Cheshire, was born about 1495 and died 6 Sept. 1557, according to the *inquisition post mortem* [PRO CHES 3/72/13; Croston, 377].

He married, first, in or after 1518, Mrs. ELIZABETH[D] BRERETON*, who was living 30 Nov. 1545, widow of Richard Cholmondeley of Cholmondeley in the parish of Malpas, county Chester (Thompson has noted that Ormerod, in 2:633 and 638, confused Richard Cholmondeley, who died in 1518, with his son Richard, who had no issue).

He married second, 6 Edw. VI (1552), Elizabeth Leycester, daughter of Sir Raufe Leycester of Toft; they had no issue. After his death Elizabeth married Sir Edmund Trafford of Trafford in Lancashire.

Sir Randall's will, now in the John Rylands University Library of Manchester, named his three daughters and their husbands; it set up an entail with the Ightfield and Carincham branches of his family in case his brothers died without issue, but was generous to his daughters.

Another article said to be of interest to descendants is Robert Fawtier's "Handlist of the Mainwaring Manuscripts," *Bulletin of the John Rylands Library*, 7 (1922-23), 143-167, 279-289.

Children, the first given by Thompson in the table, "Ancestry of Frances (Cotton) Abell" [*TG*, 5 (1984), 163-171], the rest by Ormerod, by first wife:

* i.   Margaret[C], b. c. 1521; m. Arthur[C] Mainwaring (for whom see Mainwaring of Ightfield).

ii.   Elizabeth, m. (1) Peter Shakerley, Esq., of Houlm (Holme) in Allostock in Cheshire, m. (2) 1561 Christopher Holford, Esq., of Holford.

iii.   Katharine, m. John Davenport, Esq., of Henbury in Cheshire.

§ § §

MALPAS

According to Ormerod [*History of Chester*, 2:598], Sir William[P] de Malpas was son of Sir David[O] de Malpas, who is treated under Egerton, above, by his alleged wife, Catherine, daughter of Owain Vaghan, lord of Meilor.

1. Sir WILLIAM[P] DE MALPAS died without legitimate issue.

He married Margaret ferch Cadwgon de Linton, who had no children.

His son's control of a fourth of the barony of Malpas was the subject of a suit heard at Chester in 37 Edw. III (1363-1364).

Child, a bastard by Beatrix, daughter of Robert de Montalt, who was seneschal of the Earl of Chester:

2.   i.   Sir David[O] de Mallo Passu, the Bastard, alias le Clerc, m. Constance[O] ferch Owain Cyfeiliog.

2. Sir DAVID[O] DE MALLO PASSU, the Bastard, alias le Clerc, intruded into his father's barony of Malpas.

He married CONSTANCE[O] FERCH OWAIN[P] CYFEILIOG, Prince of Powys, whose descendants were called DE LA POLE*.

He gained control of the Patric share when of his daughter Beatrix married.

Children, named by Ormerod [2:598]:

   *   i.   Beatrix^L, m. (1) Sir William^N Patric (who d. by 1279), m. (2) Roderic ap Gryffin ap Llywelyn (who was l. 17 Edw. I [1288-1289]); she had, on the partition of Malpas, a fourth of the barony in 44 Hen. III [1259-1260], and was l. 17 Edw. I [1288-1289].

   *   ii.   Idonea, m. Urian^L de St. Pierre, who d. c. 1300; she had a fourth of the barony in 44 Hen. III.

§ § §

MASSY OF DUNHAM-MASSY

    The seat of this family was Dunham-Massy, in Bucklow Hundred, Cheshire. According to T.C. Banks' *The Dormant and Extinct Baronage of England* [1:206], Hamon Massey was the first baron made by Hugh Lupus, Earl of Chester. Banks stated that Sir Hamon Massy, the sixth of the name, had children Hamon, who died without issue, and daughters and heirs Cecily, wife of John Fitton; Isabel, wife of Hugh Dittyn or Dutton; a daughter who married Thomas de Latham, and Alice, wife of Thomas de Hilond.

    According to Ormerod, Hamon^S Massy was the 1st Baron of Dunham-Massy. He held the towns of Dunham, Bowdon, Hale, Ashley and half of Owlarton in Bucklow Hundred, Cheshire, under Hugh Lupus, Earl of Chester, during the reign of William the Conqueror; these towns had previously been held by an Edward. He also held Maxfield Hundred, as well as Bromhale and Podinton in Wirrhall (Wirral) Hundred, Cheshire. However, his children were listed as Hamon II^R, d. c. 1216, and Robert, who witnessed the charter of confirmation to the Abbey of St. Werburge in Chester about 1124 [1:119]. Thus more than one generation is missing, and the alleged brothers were of different generations.

1. HAMON^R MASSY II died about 1216.

    He married AGATHA, who called herself Agatha de Theray when she gave the moiety of Bowden to her son Robert; she had bought it from Roger Massy of Hale, son of Geffrey Massy.

Children:

   2.   i.   Hamon III^Q.

        ii.   Robert, ancestor of family of Massy of Sale, Cheshire.

       iii.   John, given Moreton by brother Hamon in exchange for Puddington [Ormerod, 2:365].

2. HAMON^Q MASSY III founded the priory of Birkenhead in Wirral, and died during the reign of King John, or early in that of Henry III (thus about 1216) [Ormerod, 1:521].

    He married AGATHA [Ormerod, 1:521], who called herself Agatha de Theray when she gave the moiety of Bowdon (which she had bought of Roger Massy of Hale, son of Geoffrey Massy) to Robert Massy.

Children, listed by Ormerod:

        i.   Hamon IV^P, issue [Ormerod, 1:521].

       ii.   Robert.

   *   iii.   Agnes, m. Sir Geoffrey^O de Dutton (alias de Chedle) of Chedle (for whom see Chedle).

       iv.   Sibyl.

        v.   John.

      vi.   Cecily.

* vii. daughter (Isabel), m. Hugh[P] de Dutton of Dutton.
* viii. Agatha, m. Jocerame[Q] de Hellesby.

§ § §

MERBURY

John[I] Merbury received incidental mention in Cokayne's *Complete Peerage* [3:322], in the section on Devereux, and the section on Ferrers [5:322]. In Roskell [3:716] he is called a younger brother of Nicholas Merbury (of Braybrooke, Hampshire, who died 1421), who in turn is called a probable son of Sir Thomas Merbury; another brother was Sir Laurence [Roskell, 3:720].

1. JOHN[I] MERBURY of Lyonshall and Weobley in Herefordshire, born about 1361, the subject of writs in 16 Hen. VI (1437-1438), was also the subject of *inquisitions post mortem* in the counties of Nottingham, Lincoln, Hereford, Salop, Leicester, Bedford, Hertford and Gloucester from 9 March to 18 Sept. 1438 [*CP*, 5:322]. He was buried with his second wife at Weobley, where their fine alabaster tomb remains today.

He married first, by 1400 [Roskell, 3:716], ALICE[J] PEMBRIDGE, who died about April 1415, as her third husband. She had married first Edmund Delabere, and second, by license dated 1382, Thomas[J] Oldcastle. She was daughter of Sir John Pembridge of Pembridge, Herefordshire, son of Ralph Pembridge, Esq., who was son of Sir William Pembridge (who lived at the time of King Edward I and was possibly a son of Henry Pembridge of Herefordshire, who was living in 1271).

He married second, by 1417 [Roskell, 3:716], Agnes Crophull (who was born in 1371 and died 3 Feb. 1436), daughter and heir of Thomas Crophull, and widow of Sir Walter Devereux of Weobley and John Parr of Kirkby Kendal, Westmorland.

In Roskell he is called a trusted Lancastrian retainer who became one of the richest and most influential gentlemen in Herefordshire. His arms show a relationship to the family of Marbury of Marbury, which is located on the Cheshire border with Shropshire, who also owned the castle and manor of Lyonshall.

He apparently began his career as an archer for Sir John Stanley in 1389, and then enlisted with John of Gaunt, who granted him an annuity of ten marks in Oct. 1395. From the beginning of the reign of King Henry IV his influence increased rapidly, and by 18 March 1402 his annual income from royal grants and fees was £126, a very large amount.

While the sources for Oldcastle state that he was M.P. for Herefordshire in 1390 and 1393, Roskell lists his service in Parliament as in 1419, May 1421, Dec. 1421, 1425 and 1427. He was Chamberlain and Receiver (chief financial officer) of South Wales from 18 March 1400 to 10 June 1421. Probably due in part to Owain Glyndŵr's rebellion, he served as Tax Collector of Herefordshire in 1404, as justice of the peace of Herefordshire 27 April 1404 until he died, and as Sheriff of Herefordshire for eight one year terms between 22 Nov. 1405 and 7 Nov. 1435.

He was Deputy Justiciar for South Wales from Michaelmas 1411 to 1413, and Justiciar from 10 June 1421 to 17 Nov. 1423. He was also Steward of Brecon (1414-1420) and Kidwelly (1417-1423), escheator of Herefordshire and the adjacent march (1416-1417) and Forester of Cantref Selyf before July 1426. He served as a captain, assuming joint command of a force of 60 men-at-arms and 120 archers in Wales while the king was in France in 1415; his fellow captains were his stepson Richard Oldcastle, Sir Robert Whitney II (husband of his stepdaughter Wintelan Oldcastle) and Thomas Strange.

During the lifetime of his first wife he held by her right the castle and manor of Boughwood near Builth in Radnorshire, Wales, the manor of Eyton by Leominster in Shropshire, and an estate at Burghill in Herefordshire.

After his first wife died he married a rich widow, Agnes Crophull, who brought him her dower from John Parr and the estates of her grandfather, Sir John Crophull, including the castle and manor of Weobley, where he lived near Almeley, the hiding place of the lollard Sir John Oldcastle (his wife's cousin). By 1415 he had become trustee of the late Richard Ruyhale's estate, including the manor of Ryhall in Worcestershire; Ruyhale widow Elizabeth then married Richard Oldcastle, his stepson by his first wife. In 1424 the English tenants of Llanstephan and Penrhyn complained that he John Merbury had amerced them wrongfully, and had employed Welsh jurors who dared not contradict him.

Roskell implied that he had more than one daughter by his first wife, and that a younger daughter Marion survived him; Marion was to have £20 for her marriage.

Child, by first wife, from Cokayne:

*   i.   Elizabeth[H], dau. and heiress, m. Sir Walter[H] Devereux, who was his second wife's grandson and heir.

Child, by second wife, not named by Roskell [3:717]:

      ii.   daughter.

§ § §

MINSHULL

Ormerod's *Cheshire* [3:340] cited Harl. MSS. 2119 and 213, continued from the Visitations and the Minshull Registers. The Rev. Geo. B. Sandford's "An Account of the Parish of Church Minshull, in Cheshire," in *Proceedings of the Historic Society of Lancashire and Cheshire*, 2 (1849), 85-113, concerns later generations.

AUGUSTIN[R] DE MINSHULL was Lord of Minshull, Cheshire, England, in the time of King Henry I, who ruled from 1100 to 1135. It has been stated that he was son of the Saxon Aregrim, who was mentioned in Domesday in 1086.

ADAM[Q] DE MINSHULL was Lord of Minshull in the time of King Stephen, who ruled from 1135 to 1154.

GAMUEL[P] DE MINSULFE was Lord of Minshull in the time of King Henry II, who ruled from 1154 to 1189.

MICHAEL[O] DE MUNSULE lived at the time of King Richard I and King John (about 1189 to 1216).

ADAM[N] DE MUNSULE was of record 28 Hen. III (1243-1244).

RICHARD[M] DE MUNSULE was of record 15 Edw. I (1286-1287). He married ALICE[M] DE HULGREVE, daughter of Matthew[N] de Hulgreve.

7. RICHARD[L] DE MUNISHULL was living 23 and 29 Edw. I (1294-1301), and mentioned in deeds 6 and 22 Edw. III (1332-1349).

He married ALICE[L] DE PRAERS[+], daughter of William[M] de Praers of Bartumley by Sibilla[M] de Crewe, Lady of Aston in Mondrem, daughter of Sir Thomas[N] Crewe of Crewe.

Children:

      i.   Richard[K], *i.p.m.* dated 37 Edw. III (1363-1364); m. Margaret del Holte (dau. of Richard del Holte), who m. (2) John Davenport, who sued for divorce 38 Edw. III (1364-1365).

8.   ii.   Henry, m. Tibota de Pulford.

      iii.   Randle, m. Margaret de Dutton, dau. of Sir Thomas de Dutton.

8. HENRY[K] DE MINSHULL was Lord of Church Minshull in Nantwich Hundred, Cheshire. He married TIBOTA[K] DE PULFORD, daughter of Robert de Pulford; she married second John Barret.

He was of record 16 Edw. III (1342-1343), and had a pardon 34 Edw. III (1360-1361). Their daughter was also the heir of her uncle Richard[K] at age 14 in 37 Edw. III (1363-1364).

Child:

  *   i.   Joan[J], m. (1) Edmund[J] de Dutton, *of Hatton* m. (2) 7 Ric. II (1383-1384) William de Hoton (or Hooton).

§ § §

MOBBERLEY

This line has been adapted from Ormerod's *History of Chester* [1:416].

The arms are *Argent*, two chevrons *Gules*, in a canton of the second, a cross croslet *fitchée, Or*.

Augustine de Brethmete, who was Patrick de Mobberley's older brother, gave half of Mobberley to Patrick for his life. Patrick founded there a priory of the regular canons of the order of St. Augustine about 1206. Patrick's son and heir, John, lived in Mobberley during the reign of King John. Raufe, following, cannot be proved to be the son of John.

1. RAUFE[N] MOBBERLEY of Mobberley, lord of the moiety of Mobberley, in Bucklow Hundred, Cheshire, was living in the reign of King Henry III.

Child:

  2.   i.   William[M], d. c. 1308.

2. WILLIAM[M] MOBBERLEY of Mobberley died about the beginning of the reign of King Edward II (thus 1307 or later).

He bought the moiety of Nether Pever from Richard Bonstable in 1281.

Children, listed by Ormerod [1:416]:

      i.   John[L], d. without issue; had been given Nether Pe[o]ver and Tatton in 1303 by his father.

  3.   ii.   William, m. Maud[L] Downes, who m. (2) John Dumbill.

     iii.   Richard, slain by Richard, son of Richard de Mobberley, in 1320; parson of Mobberley in 1306.

     iv.   Alice, m. William de Tabley; widow in 1300.

3. WILLIAM[L] MOBBERLEY died in 1327.

He married MAUD[L] DOWNES*, daughter and heir of Robert Downes of Chorley juxtà Werford, to whom Edmund Fitton had given "all his lands in Chorley in free marriage with Margery his sister." Maud married second John Dumbill (or Dumvile [Ormerod, *Chester*, 3:781]), Sr.

William Mobberley was Sheriff of Cheshire in 1319.

Children, listed by Ormerod [1:416]:

      i.   Raufe[K], m. Vincentia Pulford, dau. of John Pulford of Pulford, son of Sir Robert Pulford; by his concubine, Alice Rode, he had a dau. Margaret who m. (1) Hugh Toft of Toft, m. (2) Hugh Chaderton.

     ii.   Cecily, m. John Dumbill of Mobberley, son and heir of John Dumbill of Oxton in Wirral.

     iii.   Elizabeth, m. Sir Hugh[K] Venables of Kinderton.

     iv.   Margery, m. Richard Bold of Bold, Lancashire.

X   v.   Emme, m. Robert[M] Grosvenour of Houlme in Allostock, who d. 1342, having purchased the moiety of Nether Pever from William[L] Mobberley.

*   vi.   Mary, m. Nicholas[K] Leycester of Tabley.

*   vii. Joan, m. William[K] Atherton of Atherton, Lancs.

    viii. Ellen, m. Richard Bromhale of Bramhale, Cheshire [Earwaker, 1:423].

    ix.   Agnes, unm.

§ § §

DE MONTFORT OF BEAUDESERT

This line was developed from an article by Miss Ethel Stokes in *The Complete Peerage* [9:120-128].

The only place in Normandy named Montfort is Montfort-sur-Risle in the Department of Eure. About 1054 the seigneur of Montfort was Hugh, who was most likely an ancestor. Roger de Beaumont (father of Henry, 1st Earl of Warwick), was a first cousin of a Thurstan by marriage. Montfort-sur-Risle is about fifteen miles from Beaumont-le-Roger.

Robert[S] de Montfort held Preston in Rutland, in 1130, and that year petitioned that his men there provide him the same services as they had for his father, who was probably Thurstan de Mundford, a baron of Henry, Earl of Warwick. His brother and heir was Thurstan[S] de Montfort, below.

THURSTAN[S] DE MONTFORT appeared in an account by the Sheriff of Berkshire in 1130; his name disappeared from the Pipe Rolls after 1170. He married JULIANE[S] MURDAC, daughter and coheir of Geoffrey Murdac.

HENRY[R] DE MONTFORT was dead in the spring of 1199, when his heir was in the King's hand. His widow was summoned to Westminster in 1199 to answer whether certain disputed land was her marriage portion or not.

Sir THURSTAN[Q] DE MONTFORT, a minor in 1199, died before 21 Nov. (and possibly before 23 July) 1216. Although his wife's name is not known, it is possible that he married a daughter of William de Cauntelo, the elder, steward of the household to King John.

PIERS[P] DE MONTFORT, who was still a minor in Oct. 1231, was slain at the battle of Evesham 4 August 1265. He married ALICE[N] DE AUDLEY, who survived him.

PIERS[O] DE MONTFORT died before 4 March 1286/7, when the writs to the escheators were issued. He married MAUD[O] DE LA MARE, daughter and heir of Matthew de la Mere, son of Henry de la Mere; with her he had Ashtead in Surrey.

6. Sir JOHN[N] MONTFORT, Lord Montfort of Beaudesert in Warwickshire, died before 11 May 1296, the date writs to the escheators were issued [*CP*, 9:128g].

He married ALICE[N] DE LA PLAUNCHE, daughter of William de la Plaunche [*The Genealogist*, n.s., 14:104]. She had dower in Nov. 1296, and in 1303 recovered the manors of Preston and Uppingham.

Apparently of age in 1284/5, when the manors of Preston and Rutland were conveyed to him by Master William de Montfort (who may have been his uncle, and Dean of St. Paul's), presumably in discharge of a trust. In 1291 he was recorded as being given ten oaks fit for timber by the King, and on 13 April 1294 he was going beyond the seas with Eleanor, Countess of Bar, the King's daughter. The following August both William and

John de Montfort were in the company of the Earl of Lincoln in Gascony. He was summoned to Parliament on 24 June 1295.

Children, from Cokayne [12:1:417, 14:600] and Wrottesley [*Gen.*, n.s., 14:104]:

    i.   John[M], b. 1291; slain at Bannockburn 24 June 1314; unm.; had been pardoned for participating in the death of Piers de Gavaston, and being an adherent of Thomas, Earl of Lancaster.

    ii.   Sir Piers, d. before 24 Jan. 1369/70; said to have m. Margaret[J] de Furnivalle, dau. of Thomas de Furnivalle, Lord Furnivalle; had illegitimate children John and Alice by Lora of Ullenhall.

 *   iii.   Maud, of Beaudesert, Warks., d. 1326/7; m. Bartholomew[M] de Sudeley, who d. c. 1326/7.

    iv.   Elizabeth, m. Baldwin Freville.

§ § §

MORTIMER OF BURFORD

This line is based on Cokayne's *The Complete Peerage* [9:257-266].

ROBERT[Q] DE MORTIMER was of Woodham Mortimer, Essex. ROBERT[P] DE MORTIMER died before 5 July 1219. He married in 1210, as her second husband, MARGARET[N] DE SAY, who died before the autumn of 1242. She was the widow of Hugh de Ferrières, and married third William de Stuteville. HUGH[O] DE MORTIMER died 18 Nov. 1274. The name of his wife is not known.

ROBERT[N] DE MORTIMER, aged 22 when his father died in 1274, died 7 April 1287 and was buried the next day in Worcester Cathedral. He married, perhaps second [Eyton, 4:319], Joyce de la Zouche, daughter of William de la Zouche; she was buried near her husband in Nov. 1287. She had Norton in Northamptonshire and other manors.

5. HUGH[M] DE MORTIMER, Lord Mortimer, born in Burford, Shropshire, died without male heirs on 20 July 1304, and was buried in Worcester Cathedral.

He married about 1290 MAUD (or Matilda), who died on or before 15 Feb. 1307/8, when the writ to the escheator was issued. She was a niece of William le Marshal, but her surname is not known. She was believed to be a relation of Queen Eleanor of Castile, as the Prince of Wales referred to her as *nostre chere cosine Dame Maud de Mortimer du Chastel Richard* (of Richard's Castle) in a letter to the Mayor of London on 29 June 1305.

As he was underaged at the time his father died he was given in ward to William de Beauchamp, Earl of Warwick. During his minority his Uncle William had custody of Richard's Castle. In 1295 he had livery of his inheritance. From 1297 he was summoned to military service in Flanders and against the Scots. On 26 Jan. 1296/7 he was summoned to the assembly at Salisbury, and writs directed to *Hugoni de Mortuo Mari* summoned him to Parliament on 6 Feb. and 10 April 1298/9. He was a member of the third division in the siege of Caerlaverock, a castle on the coast south of Dumfries, Scotland, in June 1300.

He died as a result of being poisoned accidentally by his wife, who received a formal pardon in 1305 at the instance of Queen Margaret. She was indicted at Westminster for inciting her chamberlain, William de Billebury, and ten others, to murder Hugh de Kyngeshemede. She received the king's pardon for this as well.

Upon her death wardship of the children was granted to Queen Margaret, who in Oct. 1304 gave custody of Joan's moiety to Thomas de Bykenore, and that of Margaret to Walter de Langton, Bishop of Lichfield.

Children, coheirs listed by Miss Ethel Stokes [*CP*, 9:265-266]:

*   i.   Joan[L], b. Caerphilly Castle, bapt. there 24 Nov. 1291, aged 12 on 25 Nov. 1303 [Eyton, 4:320]; d. before 12 Jan. 14 Edw. III (1340/1); m. (1) by 12 Aug. 1305 Thomas de Bykenore, who d. 1316; m. (2) Sir Richard[L] Talbot, who d. 1340.

     ii.   Margaret, b. 14 Sept. 1295; d. c. Dec. 1345; m. (1) before 12 Jan. 1308/9 Geoffrey de Cornwall, ancestor of John, 1st Baron Fanhope, m. (2) William Deverois [CP, 14:488], who d. shortly before 6 March 11 Edw. III (1337).

§ § §

MORTIMER OF SHROPSHIRE

Perhaps work in Joseph Morris' *Shropshire Genealogies* will help with this line.

1. Sir WALTER[J] MORTIMER has been identified as the father of Joane[I] or Jane Mortimer of the next generation.

According to *The Visitation of Shropshire* [255], his arms were Barry of six *or* and *vert*, sixteen fleur-de-lys, 3, 3, 3, 3, 3, and 1, counter changed.

Child:

*   i.   Joane[I] (or Jane), m. Thomas[I] Hopton.

§ § §

DE MORTIMER OF WIGMORE

This presentation is based on the work of Weis, Cokayne and Eyton. The latter presented a chart in his *Antiquities of Shropshire* [4:196] giving Roger[T] de Mortemer as a son of Hugh, Bishop of Contances in 990, by a daughter of a sister of Richard I, Duke of Normandy.

ROGER[T] DE MORTEMER, seigneur of Mortemer-sur-Eaulne in Normandy, flourished from 1054 to 1078, but was dead by 1086. He married HAWISE, who was, according to Eyton, possibly the daughter of Ranulf de Montdidier.

RALPH[S] DE MORTIMER was granted Wigmore in Herefordshire in 1074, and was living in 1104. He married first Melisande (Milisendis in Eyton's *Antiquities of Shropshire*, 4:196]), who was dead before 30 March 1088 [CP, 9:268]. He married second Mabel.

HUGH[R] DE MORTIMER died about 1148-1150.

HUGH[Q] DE MORTIMER, Lord Mortimer of Wigmore, died about 1148.

HUGH[P] DE MORTIMER, Lord Mortimer of Wigmore, died 26 Feb. 1180/1 [Eyton, 4:205]. Norr stated [89] that he married, before Maud, Felicia de Sancta Sydonio, by whom there was no issue. He married MAUD[O] DE MESCHINES (CHESTER), who had married first, about 1138/9, and was widow of, Philip de Belmeis, lord of Tong, Salop, and Ashby, Leicester-shire. She was living in the reign of Richard I (1189-1199).

ROGER[O] DE MORTIMER, Lord Mortimer of Wigmore, Herefordshire, died before 19 Aug. [CP; Eyton said July in 4:211] 1214, and was buried at Wigmore. He married ISABEL[R] DE FERRIÈRES, daughter of Walkelin de Ferrières, lord of Oakham in Rutland and of Lechlade in Gloucestershire, who died before 29 April 1252, having been granted a life interest in Lechlade, Gloucs., and Oakham, Rutland, which her brother Henry lost at the time of the conquest of Normandy. She had married second Piers[P] Fitz Herbert of Blaen Llyfni, who died 1 June 1235. She was buried in the chapel she had built in the court of the Hospital of St. John of Lechlade.

RALPH[N] DE MORTIMER, Lord Mortimer of Wigmore, died in Wigmore, Herefordshire, 6 Aug. 1246, and was buried there. He married in 1230 GWLADUS DDU[M] FERCH LLYWELYN AB IORWERTH, daughter of the Prince of North Wales and widow of Reginald (or Reynold)[O] de Braiose, who had died 9 June 1228 [Eyton, 4:215]. She died in 1251.

Sir ROGER[M] DE MORTIMER, 6th Baron Mortimer of Wigmore, Lord of Ceri and Cedewain, was born in Cwmaron Castle, Radnorshire, Wales, about 1231, died in Kingsland, Herefordshire, before 30 Oct. 1282, and was buried in Wigmore. He married in 1247 MAUD[M] DE BRAIOSE, who died shortly before 23 March 1300/1, when the writ to the escheator was issued.

9. Sir EDMUND[L] DE MORTIMER, 1st Lord Mortimer, 7th Baron Mortimer of Wigmore, born about 1250 [Evans, NEHGR, 116:17], died in Wigmore Castle in Herefordshire, 17 July 1304, and was buried at Wigmore (but A.W.B. Messenger [Family History, 1:140] states that some say Roger was a son of William de Warenne).

The name of his first wife has not been found. Evans stated that Edmund received the manor of Upper Arley in Staffordshire, in 1282, and granted it to his daughter Isolde.

He married second, about 1285, MARGARET[L] DE FIENNES* of Picardy in Normandy (France), who died 7 Feb. 1333/4.

As the second son "he had been bred to the church," and King Henry III had promised him a benefice in Nov. 1263. The King nominated him to be treasurer of York on 7 Aug. 1265, replacing Amauri de Montfort. Edmund was still treasurer in 1270. In 1271 Philip de Croft was his "guardian and master."

Then on 8 Aug. 1282, while his father was still living, he was given custody of the castle and hundred of Owestry as long as the heir of John Fitz Alan was a minor.

He received his inheritance 24 Nov. 1282, and, by a chance encounter at Builth, where he was in command, Llywelyn ap Gruffudd was killed within three weeks. While Edmund was not present at Builth, he identified the body, and took Llywelyn's head to King Edward I at Rhuddlan. From there the head was set on the Tower of London, crowned with ivy.

Edmund was then summoned to muster against the Welsh at Montgomery on 2 May 1283, and to the meeting at Shrewsbury on 30 Sept. 1282.

In Nov. 1287 he was ordered to reside in his lordship until the rebellion of Rhys ap Maredudd could be put down, and on 5 Dec. 1287 he was made joint keeper of Ystrad-Towy and Cardigan during the pleasure of the King.

On 14 June 1294 he was exempted from military service in Gascony, having been a part of the decision about war with France taken six days before. He was summoned to Parliament from 24 June 1295 to 2 June 1302.

On 7 July 1297 he was called to military service beyond seas, and later that year in Scotland. As Dominus de Wiggemore he joined in the Barons' letter to the Pope on 12 Feb. 1300/1. The next day he had livery of his mother's lands.

The Castle of Radnor, as well as her dower, were restored to widow Margaret after his son's forfeiture, but she was not allowed to stay there. She was lodged in Hampshire, in Skipton-in-Craven and Pontefract Castles, and in the Elstowe nunnery by order of King Edward III.

Child, by the unknown first wife:

+   i.   Isolde[K], b. Thornbury, Herefordshire, c. 1269; m. (1) Walter de Balun [Weis, AR7, 207:31], m. (2) Hugh[M] de Audley, Lord Audley, who d. c. 1325/6.

Children, mentioned by Cokayne and Eyton, by second wife:

10. ii. Roger, 1st Earl of March, b. 25 April 1287; hanged 29 Nov. 1330; m. before 6 Oct. 1306 Joan[K] de Geneville.
     iii. Hugh, rector of Old Radnor.
     iv. Walter, of Kingston.
     v. Edmund, rector of Hudnet.
     vi. William.
  * vii. Maud, d. after childbirth in Alton, Staffs., 17/18 Sept. 1312; m. Wigmore 29 July 1302 Sir Theobald[N] de Verdun, who d. Alton 27 July 1316.
     viii. Alianore, m. Sir William de Kyme, Lord Kyme [Evans, *NEHGR*, 116:16].
     ix. Joan, nun at Lingbrook.
     x. Elizabeth, nun at Lingbrook.

10. Sir ROGER[K] DE MORTIMER, 8th Baron Mortimer of Wigmore, and 1st Earl of March, born 17 or 25 April, or 3 May 1287 [*CP*, 8:433a], was hanged for treason at the Elms, Tyburn, 29 Nov. 1330. He was buried in the Church of the Grey Friars at Shrewsbury.

He married before 6 Oct. 1306 JOAN[K] GENEVILLE*, who died 19 Oct. 1356. In 1347 she was styled Countess of March and Lady of Trim [*CP*, 8:442].

On 29 July 1304 wardship of his lands was awarded to Piers de Gavaston (or de Gaveston), a favorite of Prince Edward, later King Edward II. However, Roger was granted livery of his lands on 9 April 1306, although he was still under age. He was summoned to Parliament from 22 Feb. 1306/7 to 28 Aug. 1328.

On Whitsunday, 22 May 1306, he and many others were made knights by King Edward I at Westminster. He then did service in Scotland, but his lands were seized because he left without permission. He was pardoned in Jan. 1307 and Queen Margaret interceded to have his lands restored.

On 15 Dec. 1307 he received his Irish inheritance of lands. On 24 Dec. Geoffrey de Geneville passed on more lands in Ireland. Thus Roger was a great magnate before he turned 21. At the coronation of Edward II, on 25 Feb. 1307/8, he was one of four bearers of the royal robes.

Edward II married in Boulogne, 13 Jan. 1308, Isabel, daughter of King Philip IV of France. However, Edward seemed to lavish more affection on Piers de Gaveston than Isabel. The furious barons exiled Piers de Gaveston (for a second time), but Piers returned, and following the battle of Blacklow Hill he was beheaded, in 1312. In Nov. 1312 Isabel had the first of five children.

From 1308 Mortimer served often against the Scots, and from 26 Feb. 1309/10 he was custodian of Builth Castle in Wales, at the pleasure of the king. He was active in Ireland during this period, and on 18 March 1315/6 he was one of those to whom Llywelyn Bren surrendered.

Defeated by Edward Bruce in Ireland in 1316, he then helped the Earl of Pembroke suppress an insurrection in Bristol. On 23 Nov. 1316 he was appointed the King's Lieutenant in Ireland, and the following February he assembled a large army at Haverford-west, crossing with them to Youghal on 7 April 1317. It has been said he conducted a parliament in Dublin in May, and he defeated Walter de Lacy and his men twice in early June. He returned to England in 1318.

As disputes arose between King Edward II and the Despensers on one side, and the King and the Earl of Lancaster on the other, he appears to have maintained the middle road with the Earl of Pembroke. On 9 Aug. 1318 he was one of the sureties for the King at the Treaty of Leek between Edward II and Lancaster. He was then nominated to the King's Council. From 15 March 1318/9 to Jan. 1320/1 he served as Justicier of Ireland.

As heir to vast estates in Wales and Ireland, enhanced by his marriage into the wealthy family de Geneville, he was ambitious, and resented the fact that Hugh^M le Despenser was in favor with the king.

In 1320 he and his uncle, Roger^L Mortimer of Chirk, sided with the Earl of Hereford against Despenser over Gower. The next year he and Hereford refused to attend the King because the younger Despenser was influential at court. On 28 June 1321 he and his uncle attended the meetings of the Barons in Sherburn at Elmet and on 29 July he accompanied them to London, lodging at the Hospitallers' House in Clerkenwell. The King yielded, banished the Despensers, and pardoned Roger Mortimer.

On 12 Nov. 1321 he was ordered to abstain from a meeting which Thomas of Lancaster had called of "good peers" for the 29th. As the King's forces laid siege to Leeds Castle in Kent, Hereford and Mortimer moved to Kingston, but made no further move. However, when the King's forces began to move westward, Mortimer burned Bridgnorth, leaving them no way to cross the Severn. Due to a failure to receive any help from Lancaster, they surrendered to the King at Shrewsbury and were sent to the Tower of London.

When Lancaster was defeated at Boroughbridge on 22 March 1321/2, the Despensers returned to power. The Mortimers were tried and in July condemned to death, but the sentences were commuted to perpetual imprisonment on 22 July.

Meanwhile, Mortimer's wife Joan was ordered sent to Southampton on 4 March 1321/2. On 1 April 1324 her daughter Joan was ordered sent to the Priory of Sempringham, Lincolnshire, while Margaret was to go to the Priory of Shouldham, Norfolk, and Isabel to the Priory of Chicksands in Bedfordshire. Joan was in the castle at Skipton-in-Craven with a retinue of five.

On 1 Aug. 1324 Roger^K Mortimer escaped the Tower, his guards having been drugged. His uncle Roger was left behind and died in 1326.

He crossed the Thames, rode to Dover and left on a waiting ship for France, to which King Charles IV welcomed him. In the spring of 1325 Queen Isabel, sister of King Charles IV of France and wife of King Edward II of England, went to France to arrange a peace about Guienne, which was made on 31 May 1325. On 12 Sept. Prince Edward went to France to do homage for Aquitaine and stayed with his mother, with whom Mortimer and other exiles had become close.

Mortimer became the Queen's lover as well as her advisor, and at the end of the year they went to Flanders, where Prince Edward was engaged to Philippe of Hainault, and money and men were raised for an attack on England. On 26 Oct. 1326 Mortimer, the Queen, John of Hainault and their forces landed at Ipswich, where they were joined by Henry, Earl of Lancaster, and other opponents of the Despensers.

On her return from France, Isabella was refused entrance to Leeds Castle, which had been granted to Edward's friend Lord Bartholomew^L de Badlesmere. Later she had the entire de Badlesmere family sent to the Tower of London. Lord Badlesmere was beheaded, and his head exhibited on a pike on the walls of Canterbury. Granting Leeds Castle to herself, Isabel became known as the she-wolf of France.

The King fled to the Despensers in Wales. On 26 Oct. 1326 the senior Despenser was captured at Bristol; he was tried the next day and hanged forthwith. On 16 Nov. Edward II and the younger Despenser were captured at Llantrisant. On the next day Sir Edmund^L Fitz Alan, Earl of Arundel, was ordered executed and beheaded at Hereford, and on the 24th Mortimer, Lancaster and Kent sat in judgment on the younger Despenser; they hanged him from a fifty foot gallows.

Mortimer was present when the great seal was delivered to the Bishop of Norwich at Cirencester on 30 Nov., and on 15 Dec. he was granted custody of Denbigh Castle during pleasure. He spent Christmas of 1326 at Wallingford with the Queen and her son. On 7

Jan. 1326/7 Parliament deposed Edward II and named Edward III king, with Isabel as regent. On 13 Jan. Mortimer visited London and promised at the Guildhall to maintain the liberties of the citizens.

On 1 Feb. 1326/7 he attended the coronation of Edward III, and Mortimer's sons Edmund, Roger and Geoffrey were made knights. Two weeks later he was made Justice of Wales during pleasure, then for life the following year. On 21 Feb. 1326/7 he was formally pardoned for breaking out of the Tower, and his sentences were reversed because he had not been tried by his peers. His lands were restored.

Edward II was imprisoned in Berkeley Castle, where on 21 Sept. 1327, it has been said, Mortimer forced a hot poker up Edward's anus and then tossed Edward's body down a well. Edward was buried by monks in Gloucester near their high alter, and his sarcophagus and effigy are still shown there.

Mortimer was now in charge of England, and he began to enrich himself by taking the lands of Hugh le Despenser and other foes, an act which made him extremely unpopular. In June of 1328 he held a great tournament at Hereford on the occasion of the marriages of two daughters, which the King and his mother attended. Between 25 and 31 Oct. 1328 he was created Earl of March, the first English earldom not created of a county. While he held no office of the government he lived magnificently and gained offices for his friends.

The first person to show resentment was Henry, Earl of Lancaster, in whose charge the young king had been put, but who had lost influence to Mortimer. He and others had refused to attend the Salisbury parliament at which Mortimer's earldom had been created, and on 2 Jan. 1328/9 he formed a coalition in London, with some of the citizens, to destroy Mortimer.

On 4 Jan. 1328/9 Mortimer overran Lancaster's lands, forcing terms. By 20 April 1330 he had acquired more lands, castles and income. However, early in 1330 he had involved Edmund, Earl of Kent, the king's uncle and his former associate, in a plot to restore Edward II, as Edmund had been persuaded that his half-brother was still living. This led to Edmund being tried for treason, and his execution on 19 March 1329/30. This roused Edward III, who resented constraints on his own freedom due to Mortimer.

Then on 18 Oct. 1330 Edward III reached his majority. At a meeting in Nottingham it was decided to capture the Earl of March. The governor of Nottingham Castle revealed to William de Montagu, later the Earl of Salisbury, a secret passage into the castle which bypassed Mortimer's Welsh guards. On the night of the 18th the conspirators burst in on a conference between Mortimer and the Chancellor in Mortimer's apartments. Mortimer killed one of his assailants but was overpowered, arrested by order of the King and sent to London with his sons Edmund and Geoffrey, as well as chief lay assistants Oliver de Ingham and Simon de Barford.

On 28 Oct. 1330 Edward III assumed control of the government. On 26 Nov. Mortimer was tried in parliament in London, impeached on fourteen articles, found guilty of treason and condemned to die, without being allowed to speak in his own defense. Having been attainted, all his honors were forfeited. He was hanged in the nude in the town square of Tyburn, where his body remained on view for two days and two nights. Isabel was imprisoned at Castle Rising in Norfolk, and died 23 Aug. 1358.

In spite of this, Edward III's granddaughter, Lady Philippa Plantagenet, daughter of Lionel, married Edmund Mortimer, a greatgrandson of Roger[K] de Mortimer [Jobe, "Murder in the Family Tree," *The Searcher*, 33 (1996), 201-202].

Children, listed by Cokayne:

      i.   Edmund[J] of Wigmore, d. Dec. 1331; m. 27 June 1316 Elizabeth[K] de Badlesmere, who d. 8 June 1355, having m. (2) Sir William[K] de

Bohun, Earl of Northampton, who d. Sept. 1360; Edmund was summoned to Parliament in Nov. 1331.

ii.   Roger, m. (1) Joan de Botiller, dau. of Edmund de Botiller of Ireland, m. (2) Mary, widow of the Earl of Pembroke.

iii. Geoffrey, arrested in 1330.

iv.   John, granted castles in Ireland in 1328, killed in a tournament at Shrewsbury.

v.   Beatrice, d. 16 Oct. 1383; m. (1) 1328 Edward, who d. before 13 Sept. 1337 [*CP*, 9:599], son of Thomas of Brotherton, Earl of Norfolk and Earl Marshall, who d. before 2 Dec. 1334, m. (2) Thomas de Braiose of Tetbury.

vi.   Agnes, m. Lawrence de Hastings, Earl of Pembroke.

*   vii. Katherine, d. 1371; m. Thomas[J] Beauchamp, 3rd Earl of Warwick.

viii. Joan, m. by 13 June 1330 Sir James de Audley, K.G., who m. (2) by Dec. 1351 Isabel.

ix.   Margaret, d. 5 May 1337; m. 8 July 1320 Thomas[I] de Berkeley.

x.   Maud, m. John[K] de Cherleton.

xi.   Blanche, m. Piers de Grandison.

§ § §

DE MULTON

According to Ethel Stokes, writing in Cokayne, the family name was from Moulton, near Spalding in Lincolnshire.

LAMBERT[S] DE MULTON, held two carucates of land in Revesby of William de Roumare, Earl of Lincoln, by service of one-quarter of a knight's fee, as grandson and heir of an English thegn, Brictive [Brictiva in Latin, or Beorhtigifu in Old English], a woman. He was living in 1166, and, while it is not known when he died, he was buried in Spalding Priory. He married a daughter of Robert (presumed a Norman by Miss Stokes), possibly Robert Briwer. He held an oxgang of land under his wife's father.

THOMAS[R] DE MULTON probably succeeded his father by Mich. 1167, when the King's pardon of his amercement of 60 marks (£40) was recorded, and died in or before 1201. He was married to ELEANOR, who died probably before Oct. 1199; she had property in Boston.

THOMAS[Q] DE MULTON died in 1240. He married first SARAH[Q] DE FLETE, daughter and heiress of Richard de Flete. At Michaelmas 1090 his wife's father owed 100 marks for his daughter to be freed from Ralph de Candos, who said he had married her [*CP*, 9:400j]. He married second, before 10 March 1217/8, Ada[Q] de Morville, widow of Richard[Q] de Lucy, lord of Egremont and Copeland, Cumberland, who had died in 1213. She was living in 1230, the daughter of Hugh de Morville and likely Heloise de Stuteville (or Estuteville). Ada survived her second husband for a short time.

LAMBERT[P] DE MULTON died suddenly before 16 Nov. 1246, the date of his *inquisition post mortem*. He married first, probably in 1213, AMABEL[P] DE LUCY. He married second Ida, who died before 16 Nov. 1246; she had been the widow of Geoffrey d'Oyly (or d'Oyry). Ida married third Godfrey (or Geoffrey) de Millers, lord of the manor of Gedney, Lincs., with whom she was involved in divorce proceedings in 1250.

THOMAS[O] DE MULTON, who was aged 21 on 4 May 1246, died shortly before 29 April 1294. He married first IDA, by whom there was issue surviving in Jan. 1256/7. He married second Elizabeth (or Isabel), widow of John de Munemuth. He married third, before 1288, Margaret, who might have been a Penington, as she was said to have been related to her predecessor Isabel in the 4th degree. She was assigned dower, and was living in Dec. 1313, and likely in March 1322.

Sir THOMAS[N] DE MULTON died before 24 July 1287. He married in Jan. 1274/5 EMOINE[N] (or Edmunda) LE BOTELER (or BUTLER), who was living in 1284 but predeceased him [CP, 9:403].

7. Sir THOMAS[M] DE MULTON, Lord Multon, born 21 Feb. 1276, died in 1321/2, before 8 Feb.

He married in St. Peter's Priory, Ipswich, in the presence of King Edward I [Parsons, Genealogists' Magazine, 20:337], 3 Jan. 1297 ELEANOR[K] DE BURGH*, daughter of Richard de Burgh, Earl of Ulster and Margaret of Guines.

He did homage and had livery of his mother's lands on 12 May 1296, before he became of age. He had livery of his grandfather's lands later. He was probably the Thomas de Moulton who accompanied the Bishop of Ely on a mission to the court of Guelders in Jan. 1295/6, and was summoned to Parliament on 6 Feb. 1298/9, and after 1307 as Thome de Multon of Egremont.

As one of the barons most concerned with the defense against the Scots, he served on the border "with little intermission" from 1297-1315. In 1300 he was in the siege of Caerlaverock. The Barons' letter to the Pope of Feb. 1300/1 bore his seal. In 1305 he went to Ireland with a large retinue; he was in Scotland in 1306 and brought Simon Fraser to London for execution in September. He was summoned, in Jan. 1307/8, to the Coronation of Edward II. He was ordered to defend his demesnes in Ireland against Edward Bruce in Jan. 1316/7, and joined Thomas, Earl of Lancaster, at Pontefract in May 1321, but died before the battle of Boroughbridge, as the writ to the escheator was dated 8 Feb. 1321/2. In 1320 he had given land in Moulton for a chantry in the parish church of Harrington.

Child, mentioned in Cokayne [9:405]:

    i.   Joan[L], aged 30 in 1334, when she was widow of Robert Fitz Water.
*   ii.   Elizabeth, b. c. 1306; m. (1) c. 1327 Sir Robert[L] de Harington, who d. Ireland 1334, m. (2) Walter de Bermingham.
   iii.   John, b. Oct. 1308; d. before 23 Nov. 1334, possibly the Sir John de Multon bur. in the nave of Lincoln Cathedral; m. Alice, who m. (2) Edmund de Ufford and d. before 25 Oct. 1339.
    iv.   Margaret, b. c. 1310; m. Thomas de Lucy, 2nd Lord Lucy.

§ § §

DE MUSCEGROS

Weis' *Ancestral Roots of Certain American Colonists*, 7th edition, line 189:5, the original source of this line, has been checked against other secondary sources.

1. Sir ROBERT[P] DE MUSCEGROS, of Charlton and Brewham [Sanders, 39] in Somerset, died shortly before 29 Jan. 1253/4.

He married, as her second husband, before 11 Feb. 1220/1, HAWISE[P] MALET+ (daughter of Sir William Malet of Curry Malet in Somerset), her father's coheir, who was living 4 May 1287. She had been widow of Sir Hugh Poyntz, who died shortly before 4 April 1220.

Child:

2. i.   John[O], b. 10 Aug. 1232, d. 8 May 1275; m. Cecily Avenal, who d. shortly before 10 Aug. 1301.

2. Sir JOHN[O] DE MUSCEGROS of Charlton [*CP*, 5:chart between 320-321], born 10 Aug. 1232, died 8 May 1275.

He married CECILY[O] AVENAL, who died shortly before 10 Aug. 1301, daughter of Sir William Avenal of Bicknor, Taynton and Longford, who was born about Nov. 1202, and was dead by 21 April 1236.

Child:

    3.   i.   Robert[N], b. c. 1252; d. 27 Dec. 1280; m. (2) Agnes[N] de Ferrers.

3. Sir ROBERT[N] DE MUSCEGROS, born about 1252, died 29 Dec. 1280 [Weis, *AR*7, 189:4].

The name of his first wife is unknown.

He married second, as her second husband, Agnes[N] de Ferrers, who was living 9 May 1281, having married first William[N] de Vesey.

He was of Charlton and Norton, Somersetshire.

Agnes sold her *maritagium* late in life to the Sapy family; this action was typical of a childless widow. Had Hawise been her daughter, Agnes would have passed her *maritagium* to Hawise [Douglas Richardson].

Sir Christopher Hatton's *Book of Seals* in Northants. Rec. Soc. (1950), No. 98, p. 54, answers *CP*, 5:308c completely.

Child, by an unknown first wife (had her mother been Agnes[N] de Ferrers, the dispensation for Hawise's first marriage would have stated that Hawise and Sir John[M] de Ferrers were first cousins [Douglas Richardson]):

    *   i.   Hawise[M], b. 21 Dec. 1276; d. post June 1340, by Dec. 1350; m. (1) William de Mortimer of Bridgewater, m. (2) before 1300 Sir John[M] de Ferrers, who d. Gascony Aug. 1312, m. (3) Sir John[L] de Bures.

§ § §

DE NEVILLE

In addition to Cokayne's section on Furnivall, Miss Ethel Stokes' presentation on Neville of Raby was invaluable [*CP*, 9:491-505].

GILBERT[T] DE NEVILLE held at the time of Domesday, in 1086, carucates at Walcot near Folkingham, Lincolnshire, and at Yawthorpe, of the Abbot of Peterborough, Lincs. He was presumably the same Gilbert who held lands of Peterborough about 1115-1118: two carucates for two hides and one knight's fee. He held, of the Bishop of Lincoln, land in Scothern, Reepham and elsewhere, and of Manasser Arsic land in Middle Rasen.

GEOFFREY[S] DE NEVILLE was, in or before 1146, lord of the fee in which the church of Scothern was located. He also held Walcot and her appendages.

GILBERT[R] DE NEVILLE flourished from 1142, when he witnessed the foundation charter of Revesby Abbey, through the period 1156-1166, during which he and his brother Alan jointly founded Tupholme Abbey.

GEOFFREY[Q] DE NEVILLE was no doubt of age in 1161 when he and his father were pardoned part of the dues on their Arsic fee, and was dead by Michaelmas 1193, when his widow Emma de Humez paid a fine to have her inheritance in peace until King Richard I returned from the Crusades [*CP*, 9:493f]. He married before Michaelmas 1176 EMMA[Q] DE HUMEZ, daughter of Bertram DE BULMER and perhaps Emma, daughter of Robert Fossard. Emma de Humez was widow of Geoffrey de Valoignes, who died in 1169. She was heir of her brother William, and granddaughter of Ansketil de Bulmer, who was in turn steward of Robert Fossard. Ansketil de Bulmer may have been married to the heiress of Piers de Humez of Brancepeth [*CP*, 9:493e].

ISABEL[P] DE NEVILLE, sister and heir of Henry[P] de Neville, was dead in 1254. She married ROBERT[P] FITZ MALDRED, who was lord of Raby and Brancepeth, in county Durham. He died between 25 June 1242, when a fine was levied before him when he was a justice, and 26 May 1248, when his widow had married Gilbert de Brakenberg, a Lincolnshire tenant of the fee Bayeux.

GEOFFREY[O] DE NEVILLE died before Michaelmas 1242, when his son Robert was among the knights fined for not crossing to Gascony with King John, according to the Pipe Roll of 26 Hen. III. JOAN, his widow, was living in Nov. 1247, when she made an agreement with her son Robert.

ROBERT[N] DE NEVILLE died shortly before 20 Aug. 1282. He married second, before 13 April 1273, Ida, who died after 18 May 1315, widow of Sir Roger Bertram of Mitford, Northamptonshire. She married third, before 8 May 1285, John Fitz Marmaduke of Horden and Ravensholm, county Durham; he died shortly before 16 Aug. 1311, while Ida was living 18 May 1315.

ROBERT[M] DE NEVILLE died before his parents in 1271. He married about 1260 MARY[M] FITZ RALPH, who died shortly before 11 April 1320, and was buried at Coverham Abbey. She was elder daughter and coheir of Ralph Fitz Randolph of Middleham, Durham; her pedigree was written during her lifetime in the history of the foundation of Coverham Abbey.

9. RANDOLPH[L] DE NEVILLE, 1st Baron Neville of Raby, born 18 Oct. 1262, died shortly after 18 April 1331.

He married first EUPHEMIA[L] DE CLAVERING (for whom see FITZ ROGER*) of Clavering, Essex, who was buried at Staindrop. She inherited from her brother John Fitz Robert de Clavering the manors of Clavering in Essex, Aynho in Northamptonshire, Iver in Buckinghamshire and Blythburgh in Suffolk, all held by her son the 2nd Lord Neville by 1345.

He married second Margery de Thweng (by whom he had no issue), daughter of John de Thweng.

He was of Raby and Middleham, Durham, and had livery of his grandfather's estates on 11 Jan. 1282/3. He was summoned with horses and arms to a military council at Gloucester before Edmund, Earl of Cornwall, 15 July 1287, and to attend the King at Westminster in June 1294. He was summoned to Parliament from 24 June 1295 to 18 Feb. 1330/1. Summonses to military service in Scotland dated from 1291, to Gascony in 1294, 1297 and 1324, and against the forces of the Earl of Lancaster in 1322.

In 1313 he was convicted of incest with his daughter Anastase, wife of Sir Walter de Faucomberge. In 1319 his sons Ralph, Alexander and John were taken prisoner at Berwick, where Robert was killed, and their ransom strained their father's resources to the utmost.

Children, by first wife:

      i.   Robert[K], slain at Berwick in June 1319 [*CP*, 9:499], purportedly in revenge for the death of Richard Fitz Marmaduke at his hands and those of his brothers; m. Ellen.

10.   ii.   Ralph, d. 5 Aug. 1367, bur. Durham Cathedral; m. Alice[L] de Audley, who d. 12 Jan. 1374/5.

     iii. Sir Alexander, d. 15 March 1366/7.

    iv.   John, imprisoned at York 1322 (probably as a supporter of the Earl of Lancaster), and was later pardoned for complicity in the death of Richard Fitz Marmaduke.

    v.   Thomas, Prebendary of St. Patrick's, Dublin, Archdeacon of Durham in 1340.

    vi.   Anastase, m. Sir Walter de Faucomberge.

    vii.   Mary.

    viii.   Ida.

    ix.   Eupheme.

10. RALPH[K] DE NEVILLE, 2nd Baron Neville of Raby, died 5 Aug. 1367, and was buried in Durham Cathedral, the "first layman that ever had lycense to be buried [there]...for the great battayle they wonne at Durham."

He married as her second husband (license 14 Jan. 1326/7) ALICE[L] DE AUDLEY*, who died 12 Jan. 1374/5, and was buried in Durham Cathedral with her husband. She was the widow of Ralph de Greystoke, 1st Baron Greystoke, who had died in 1323. She had a son William de Greystoke.

He was educated at Oxford [*Burke's Peerage* (1999), 1:14]. Taken prisoner at Berwick in 1319, and ransomed by his father, he was Constable of Warkworth Castle in 1322, the year he served the Earl of Carlisle. Two years later he was appointed with the Earl of Angus to escort envoys of Robert the Bruce to York, where they negotiated peace; he was a commissioner to keep the truce in Northumberland in 1325. By the time his father died, about 1331, he was already steward of the King's household. In Jan. 1331/2 he was indented to Sir Henry Percy, and during the next five years was very active in the Scottish Marches. In 1335 he was made keeper of Bamburgh Castle for life, and by March 1336/7 he was banneret. In 1338 and 1340 he served the council of Prince Edward as Keeper of the Realm. He commanded the first division in the victory at Durham (or Nevill's Cross), 17 Oct. 1346, where King David of Scotland was taken prisoner.

He founded the hospital at Wells, Yorkshire, and was a benefactor of many institutions. Children [CP, d9:501b; *BP*, 1:14]:

11.   i.   John[J], m. (1) 1364 Maud[J] Percy, who d. before 18 Feb. 1378/9, m. (2) before 9 Oct. 1381 Elizabeth de Latimer, who d. 5 Nov. 1395, having m. (2) Robert de Willoughby of Eresby.

    ii.   Alexander, d. Louvain 16 May 1392; Archbishop of York 1374-1388.

    iii.   Robert, d. after 1345.

    iv.   Ralph, took the name and arms of Greystoke 1345, of Cundall, North Yorks., ancestor of Nevilles of Thornton Bridge [*BP*, 1:14].

    v.   Sir William, d. after 1388; m. Elizabeth; took the name and arms of Greystoke 1345, friend of John Wyclif and the Lollard movement [*BP*, 1:14].

    vi.   Eupheme, d. 1393; m. (1) April 1343 Robert de Clifford, 4th Lord Clifford [*CP*, 14:498], m. (2) Reynold de Lucy, son of Thomas, Lord Lucy, m. (3) Sir Walter de Heselarton.

    vii.   Katherine, m. 2nd Baron Dacre.

    viii.   Margaret, d. May 1372; m. (1) William de Ros [*cf.* Hedley, 1:227], who d. before 3 Dec. 1352, m. (2) 12 July 1358 Henry de Percy, K.G., who was slain 19 Feb. 1407/8.

    ix.   Isabel, m. Hugh Fitz Henry.

    x.   Eleanor, m. Sir Geoffrey le Scrope, who was killed during the siege of the
Castle of Piskre in Lithuania in 1362; became Abbess of the Minories
in London as a widow.

   xi.   Elizabeth, nun of the Minories, London.

11.   Sir JOHN^J DE NEVILLE, K.G., 3rd Baron Neville of Raby, Durham, died at
Newcastle-upon-Tyne, 17 Oct. 1388.

He married first, in 1364, MAUD^J DE PERCY*, who died before 18 Feb. 1378/9 and was
buried in Durham Cathedral.

He married second, before 9 Oct. 1381, Elizabeth le Latimer, daughter and heir of
William le Latimer. She married second, as his third wife, Robert de Willoughby of
Eresby. She died 5 Nov. 1395, and was buried at Guisborough.

He did homage for his father's lands in England and Scotland in Oct. 1367. He had
been captain under his father at the battle of Nevill's Cross in 1346, was knighted about
April 1360 after a skirmish near Paris. In 1361 with thirteen lances he defeated fifty men-
at-arms near Étampes. He served in Aquitaine in 1366 and following, and was issued
numerous commissions from Dec. 1367 onwards. In Sept. and Oct. 1368 he was joint
ambassador to France. Made Knight of the Garter in 1369, he was Admiral of the North in
1370, was indented to John de Lancaster, and treated with Genoa. In 1372 he became
steward of King Henry II's household. In the mid-1370s he was engaged in Scotland and
the Scottish Marches, was keeper of Bamburgh Castle and had a license to castellate Raby.
In 1376 he was the subject of a bill of impeachment because he lost fortresses in Brittany.

He was keeper of Fronsac Castle on the Dordogne on 3 June 1378, and seneschal of
Gascony the next week. On his return to England he was warden of the Marches, where he
was still active in 1387. In Nov. 1384 he had a license to dig for coal for the men of
Bamburgh Castle, where he completed the fortifications.

Children, by first wife:

    i.   Ralph^l, K.G., Earl of Westmorland, b. c. 1364; d. Raby Castle 21 Oct.
1425; m. (1) Margaret de Stafford, who d. 9 June 1396, m. (2) before
29 Nov. 1396 Joan de Beaufort (widow of Sir Robert Ferrers), who d.
Howden 13 Nov. 1440, dau. of John of Gaunt [*CP*, 12:2:544-547], who
was son of King Edward III.

12.   ii.   Thomas, Lord Furnivalle, d. 14 March 1406/7, bur. Worksop Priory; m.
(1) 1379 Jane^l Furnivall, m. (2) 1401 Ankarette le Strange.

Child, by second wife:

   iii.   John, Lord Latimer, slain at Towton 29 March 1461, m. Anne Holand
(widow of his nephew John Neville), who d. 26 Dec. 1486, having m.
(3) as his 2nd wife, James Douglas, Earl of Douglas, who d. 1491; he
was attainted, but this was reversed in 1472, and the barony succeeded to his son Ralph, who became later the 3rd Earl of Westmorland.

12. Sir THOMAS^l NEVILLE [apparently mentioned in *CP*, 11:698-704 and 731 chart, and
Banks' *Baronia Anglica Concentrata*, 1:428] died 14 March 1406/7, and was buried with
his first wife in Worksop Priory.

He married first, before 1 July 1379, JOAN^l FURNIVALL*, who had been born about Oct.
1368.

He married second, with a pardon for marrying without a royal license dated 4 July
1401, Ankarette Lestraunge [le Strange], daughter and eventual heiress of Sir John
Lestraunge of Whitchurch in Shropshire by Mary de Arundel, daughter of Richard, Earl of

Arundel, and widow of Sir Richard Talbot of Goodrich, Herefordshire, who died in London 8 or 9 Sept. 1396. She died 1 June 1413 [*CP*, 5:591].

On 22 June 1383 they had livery of her father's lands, John de Neville of Raby having been ordered to take his son's fealty, and on 12 Feb. 1384/5 they had delivery of the knights' fees and advowsons of her inheritance [*CP*, 5:589]. Thomas was summoned to military service against the Scots on 13 June 1385, and to parliament from 20 Aug. 1383 to 9 Feb. 1405/6. On 9 Feb. 1393/4 he was appointed a commissioner to work for peace with the Scots. On 30 Sept. 1397 he swore to maintain the acts of the preceding session of Parliament, and in Parliament on 23 Oct. 1399 he assented to the secret imprisonment of King Richard II.

On that day he was appointed for life Keeper of Annandale and Constable of Lochmaben Castle in the Western Marches of Scotland. On 3 Dec. 1403 he was appointed Keeper of the castles of Berwick-on-Tweed, Alnwick and Warkworth until he had further orders. On 12 Nov. 1404 he and Sir John Pelham were appointed by Parliament as Treasurers of War, holding office until 19 June 1406. He was one of the Lords temporal who sealed the exemplifications of the Acts settling the issue of succession to the Crown on 7 June and 22 Dec. 1406. He was Treasurer of England from July to Nov. 1406, and probably until his death.

Child, by first wife:
*   i.   Maude[H], Baroness Furnivall, d. 13 Dec. 1421; m. before 12 March 1406/7 (as his first wife) Sir John[H] Talbot, K.G., 1st Earl of Shrewsbury.

Child, by second wife:
     ii.   daughter[s].

§ § §

OLDCASTLE

This outline is based on the work of Vernon Norr in *Some Early English Pedigrees*. The family name is probably from the hamlet of Oldcastle in Almeley [*CP*, 10:46a].

1. PETER[M] OLDCASTLE of Almeley, Herefordshire, was born say 1284 [Norr, 92].
Child:
   2.   i.   John[M], b. c. 1310; d. 1377; m. (1) Isabel, m. (2) Maud.

2. JOHN[L] OLDCASTLE of Almeley, Herefordshire, born about 1310, died about 1377.
His first wife, ISABEL, was born say 1314.
His second wife was Maud.
He held during the reign of Edward III the manor and advowson of Almeley. During the period 1363-1370 he and his wife Maud settled tenements in King's Caple, Baysham and Brockhampton on their son John and his brother Thomas.
He was a Member of Parliament in 1367 and 1372.
Children, by first wife:
   3.   i.   Richard[K], b. say 1336.
     ii.   Thomas, b. say 1338; prob. d. young.
Children, by second wife:
     iii.   Thomas, b. say 1342; M.P. 1393.
     iv.   John, b. say 1344.

3. Sir RICHARD[K] OLDCASTLE, of Almeley, Herefordshire, was born say 1336.

In Harl. MSS. 1041, fo. 24 [*Vis. Gloucs.*, 29], Thomas[J] Bromwich was shown as having married a daughter of John Oldcastle.

He was shown as his father's son and heir in the *De Banco* Roll, East. 1 Hen. IV (1399-1400), m. 199. He was escheator in Gloucestershire and Herefordshire 1388-1399, was summoned before the Privy Council in April 1398, and was dead in Sept. 1400 [Oldcastle chart in *CP*, note 4].

Children, listed by Norr [92]:

    i.   Sir John[J], Lord Cobham in right of his last wife, b. say 1360 [see Robinson's *Castles of Herefordshire*, 4] or 1370 [*CP*, 10:46c]; hanged or burned alive as a heretic 25 Dec. 1417; m. (1) Catherine ferch Richard ab Ieuan by Isabel, m. (2 or 3) as her fourth husband, Joan (ferch John ap John, lord Cobham), who m. again after 1417.

    ii. Thomas, second son, b. say 1364; m. (lic. 1382) Alice Pembridge (or Penbrugge, d. 1415, dau. of John), widow of Edmund de la Bere, who m. (3) John[l] Merbury of Woebley, who was Sheriff of Herefordshire, 1405, had Eyton in right of his wife 1418; M.P. for Herefordshire in 1390, 1393.

    iii. Catherine, b. say 1366; m. Richard Cliderow (*cf.* Cooke's *Vis. Herefordshire*, which states she m. Thomas Bromwich).

*   iv. Alice, m. Thomas[J] Bromwich of Sarnsfield [Norr's *Some Early English Pedigrees*, 92].

§ § §

ONLEY

This family is the subject of pedigrees in Walter C. Metcalfe's edition of *The Visitations of Northamptonshire Made in 1564 and 1618-19, with Northamptonshire Pedigrees* (London: Mitchell and Hughes, 1887), pages 38-39 and 121.

1. JOHN[D] ONLEY of Shropshire (or Salop), England, was found under Onley of Onley Catesby in the Northamptonshire visitations of 1564. While Ormerod provided no details in calling him John, the identification was accepted in Cokayne [4:211].

He married JANE[D] PONTESBURY ("Ponsperye" and "Ponspery" in the visitations) of Shropshire. She was from Albrighton, and was alive 11 Nov. 1537, having married second Robert Pigot of Chetwynd, Shropshire. She was daughter of Thomas[E] Pontesbury of Albrighton, Shropshire, who died 25 March 1514 and was buried in St. Alkmund, and his wife Elizabeth Grafton, who died 9 Sept. 1514 and was also buried at St. Alkmund, daughter of Richard Grafton of London. A Richard Grafton of London is mentioned in *The Visitation of Buckinghamshire* [168] as having written a chronicle during the reign of King Henry VIII, but only sons are listed. Either Thomas[E] Pontesbury, or his father Thomas, served as Bailiff of Shrewsbury several times.

Catesby is a parish sixteen miles due west of Northampton, on the Warwickshire border, with registers dating from 1705. Onley is not marked on the maps reproduced in Gardner, Harland and Smith's *Genealogical Atlas of England*.

Children, found in the pedigrees, with Jane added as a likely daughter:

    i.   John[C], son and heir, of Catesby, Northants., will dated 15 Nov. 1537, proved 16 May 1538; m. (1) Jane Smith, dau. of Henry Smith of Sherwood, Warwickshire, m. (2) Elizabeth, who l. 1536 [Baker, *Northamptonshire*, 287].

     ii.   Robert, second son.

    iii.   Adam, third son.

    iv.   Elizabeth, m. Thomas Pigott of Chetwynd, Shropshire.

*   v.   Mary, d. Combermere 14 March 1559/60; m. before 11 Nov. 1537 Sir George[C] Cotton of "Combermore" or "Combe Mole," Shropshire.

    vi.   Jane, likely dau., m. Sir Richard[C] Cotton.

§ § §

DE ORREBY OF GAWSWORTH

According to Earwaker's *East Cheshire* [2:564], Richard[N] de Orreby was perhaps a grandson of Herbert de Orreby who was married to Lucy and had a grant of Gawsworth in 1130.

1. RICHARD[N] DE ORREBY of Gawsworth in Cheshire was of record in 1255 and died in 1276.

He married ALICE, who was living in 1290.

He was descended from Herbert of Orreby.

Child:

  2.   i.   Thomas[M], b. c. 1262; d. 1290; m. Cicely[L] de Macsy.

2. THOMAS[M] DE ORREBY, of Gawsworth in Cheshire, was born about 1262 and died in 1290.

He married CICELY[M] DE MACSY, daughter and heiress of Hamo de Macsy, baron of Dunham; she may have remarried John Fitton of Bolyn.

Children, mentioned by Earwaker [*East Cheshire*, 2:564]:

    i.   Richard[L], son and heir, b. c. 1284; no issue.

*   ii.   Isabel, d. 1346; m. (1) 1307 Roger de Macclesfield, son and heir of Thomas de Macclesfield, m. (2) c. 1311 Sir John de Grendon, m. (3) Thomas[L] Fitton.

§ § §

PASLOWE

This line was originally based on Harleian manuscript 1396.

1. HAMON[Q] DE PASLOWE was of record in Drayton Paslew, Buckinghamshire, in 1192.

Child:

  2.   i.   Ralph[P], flourished during the reign of King John (1199-1216); m. Lucy.

2. RALPH[P] PASLOWE "had lands given him in Ireland as appeareth by his charter by King John."

He married LUCY.

Child:

  3.   i.   John[O], m, Margaret.

3. Sir JOHN[O] PASHLOW was of record in 1298 and 1308, almost a century after his alleged father had a charter from King John.

He married MARGARETT.
Child:
    4.   i.   John^N, of record in 1295 and 1327.

4. JOHN^N PASHLOW was of Drayton Pashlow, Buckinghamshire, in 1295 [Harl. 1241] and 1327 [Harl. 1396].
Child:
    5.   i.   Nicholas^M, m. Margarett Burghe of Wattlesborough in Shropshire.

5. NICHOLAS^M PASHLOW DE DRAYTON was of record in 1377.
He married MARGARETT^M BURGHE of Wattlesborough, Shropshire, who was daughter of Thomas Burghe of Wattlesborough [Harl. 1396].
Child:
    6.   i.   Nicholas^L.

6. NICHOLAS^L PASLOWE was mentioned in Harleian manuscript 1241.
Child:
    7.   i.   Richard^K, m. Isabella.

7. RICHARD^K PASLOWE was next in the Harleian pedigree 1396.
He married ISABELLA.
Child:
    8.   i.   Raphe^J, m. Amye^J Kynaston.

8. RAPHE^J PASLOWE, of Drayton Parslow in Buckinghamshire, had his arms listed in Harleian manuscript 1396.
He married AMYE (or Amicia)^J KYNASTON, who was given as a daughter of Sir Roger Kynaston, a descendant of King Henry IV. However, this is chronologically impossible.
Child, daughter and heiress:
    *   i.   Margaret^I, m. William^I Lacon, who was murdered in 1397.

§ § §

PATRIC

The highly tentative early pedigree of the family presented by Ormerod [2:598] began with Robert Fitz Hugh, baron of Malpas at Domesday in 1086 and witness to the foundation charter of the Abbey of St. Werbergh in 1093. He was father of Leticia, who married Richard Patric (and of Mabella, wife of William le Belward of the Egerton line), whose possible son William was lord of a moiety of Malpas. A William Patric witnessed a charter in 1178 and was perhaps the father of Robert Patric, a witness in 1200, possible father of William Patric, of record in 1230, who may have been the father of Robert^O Patric.

1. ROBERT^O PATRIC, lord of a moiety of Malpas, was a witness to Richard de Aldford's grant of Thornton.
He granted about the 1230s a moiety of Malpas to David de Malpas.
His seal was three pheons.
Child:
    2.   i.   William^N, m. Beatrix^L de Malpas.

2. WILLIAM[N] PATRIC was lord of a moiety of Malpas.

He married BEATRIX[L] DE MALPAS*, who was living 17 Edw. I (1288-1289), having had a fourth of the barony of Malpas on its partition in 44 Hen. III (1259-1260).

She was said to have married second "Roderic ap Gryffin ap Llywellyn," who was living 17 Edw. I (1288-1289) [Ormerod, *Chester*, 2:598].

Child, shown by Ormerod [2:598]:

*   i.   Isabella[M], sole dau. and heiress, m. (1) Philip Burnel, m. (2) Richard[M] de Sutton; had three-fourths of the Barony of Malpas and claimed the manors of Saighton, Huntinton, Cheveley and Boughton, releasing them to the Abbot of St. Werbergh in 1281 before King Edward I at Westminster.

§ § §

DE PEMBRIDGE OR DE PEMBRUGGE

This line was originally based on Weis' *Ancestral Roots*, line 7, and was expanded substantially with material from Eyton's *Antiquities of Shropshire*.

According to Norr [95] the line may begin with Henry Pembridge, who had a charter from King Henry I, and who had a daughter Sybil, who married Simon de la Bere, and son Walter, who was born in 1108. In turn Walter had a daughter Eleanor, who married Eustace Cecil, and a son Sir Richard, who settled at Welsh Newton early in the thirteenth century and had sons Sir Henry[P] (born about 1192), Sir John (born about 1196) and Sir Fulk (born about 1200).

The family distinguished itself for anti-Royalist sentiment.

Sir HENRY[P] DE PEMBRIDGE, of Pembridge, Herefordshire, was of record in 1235 and 1254.

2. HENRY[O] DE PEMBRUGE was of record in 1254 and 1267, and died before 20 Jan. 1272.

He married before 20 April 1254 [Eyton, 4:149] ELIZABETH[O] DE GAMAGE, daughter and coheir of Godfrey de Gamage, of Mansell Gamage and Burghill, Herefordshire, who was of record in 1263 [see Eyton's treatment of the manor of Stottesden, Shropshire], by Alda [*Colls. Hist. Staffs.* (1914), 193-194]. According to Norr [95], William de Gamage, who was born about 1170, died about 1200 (son of Geoffrey), having married Elizabeth (or Isabella) Myners, who probably was also married to Galfrid de Longchamp. Their son, Godfrey, born about 1196, died in 1253, lord of Mansel Gamage in 1231, had daughters Elizabeth[O], Euphemia (married William[O] Pembridge), and Lucy, who was dead by 1263.

On 1 July 1263 Henry and his brother William, and their wives, were suing William de Plessetis at Westminster for the manor of Stottesden, Shropshire, which was seized into the King's hand when the plaintiff did not appear [Eyton, 2:227]. In 1265 he was a strong supporter of Simon de Montfort against the King. After the Battle of Evesham (4 Aug. 1265) and the Council of Westminster (Sept. 1265), he insulted Prince Edmund at Warwick, set fire to the town, and was taken prisoner. He was committed to Sir Roger[M] de Mortimer, who placed his captive in the dungeon at Wigmore and took the estate of Pembridge for himself, forcing a conveyance from his prisoner [Eyton, 2:228].

He worked to redeem his estates in accordance with the *Dictum of Kenilworth*, but could not regain title to Pembridge.

Children, listed by Eyton:

3.   i.   Sir Henry[N], d. c. Jan. 1279/80; m. (1) Orabella[N] de Harcourt, m. (2) Alice.

    ii.   Godfrey, of record 1267.

    iii. Edward.

    iv. William, m. Euphemia Lingen, dau. of Sir Ralph Lingen.

    v.   Simon, accused of homicide in 1281.

    vi. John, had bastard son Edward.

3. Sir HENRY[N] DE PEMBRUGGE, of Tong, Shropshire, died 16 Jan. 1279/80 [Norr cited Eyton, 2:232], or before 25 Jan. 1279/80.

He married first ORABELLA (or Arabel)[N] DE HARCOURT[+], daughter of William de Harcourt and Alice de la Zouche of Aylestone (Elstow) in Leicestershire, and Tong in Shropshire; Orabella was of record in 1267 and 1272.

His second wife, Alice, was living in 1300.

On 20 Jan. 1272 Sir Henry appeared with the Archbishop of York (Walter Giffard), Matthew de Gamages, and Hugh de Mortimer. In 1273 it was decided that Henry would relinquish the Manor of Weston super Egge (Weston sub Edge) to the Archbishop in exchange for one thousand marks and the manor of Ullingwyke in Herefordshire, which he would hold from the Archbishop under a penny rent. Henry did regain the manors of Gillock in Herefordshire, and Leye in Worcestershire.

In July 1272 they went to court in an apparently friendly suit to divide the undivided lands left to Orabella and her sister Margery by Alan[J] la Zouche. On 3 Feb. 1274 they received Tong by fine.

On 20 Jan. 1274 Henry had the temerity to sue Roger[M] de Mortimer, accusing Roger of using duress against Henry's father, but Henry's claim was dismissed as false on 3 Feb. 1274.

Children:

   4.   i.   Fulke[M], b. c. 1270; d. by 20 Feb. 1296; m. Isabel.

        ii. Henry, was granted by Charter of King Henry III, 26 Dec. 1271, a weekly market in Tong on Thursdays, and a three day fair on the vigil, the day and the morrow of St. Bartholomew the Apostle.

4. FULKE[M] DE PEMBRUGGE of Aylestone in Leicestershire, and Tong in Shropshire, was born in 1271 and died by 20 Feb. 1296.

He married ISABEL of Tong, Shropshire, who was living 17 Feb. 1297, having married second John de Dene of Huntingdonshire.

Child:

   5.   i.   Sir Fulke[L], b. 27 Aug. 1291 [Eyton, *Ant. Shropshire*, 2:209]; d. 8 Jan. 1325/6; m. Maud.

5. Sir FULKE[L] DE PEMBRUGGE, born in Tong, Shropshire, 27 Aug. 1291, died 8 (or 21 [*MCS*5, 111:7]) Jan. 1325/6.

He married MAUD, or Matilda, who was living 17 March 1326, was perhaps a member of the de Bermingham family, and remarried, before 1333, Robert Corbet of Hadley, who recovered Aylestone, Leicestershire, as her dowry [Eyton, 2:240].

On 16 Oct. 1313 he was included among the adherents of Thomas Earl of Lancaster who were pardoned for their part in the death of Piers de Gaveston.

He was a Knight of the Shire of Salop at Parliament in York in May and Nov. 1322.

Children:

        i.   Fulk[K], b. 30 Nov. 1310; d. c. 1334; in Hillary term 6-7 Edw. III (1333) he sued Matilda de Pennebrugge for a moiety of the manor of Tong [*The Genealogist*, n.s., 8:243].

6.   ii.   Robert, d. by 1 Aug. 1364; m. Juliana[K] la Zouche.
      iii.   Margery (did not m. Sir Ralph Lingen [*MCS5*, 111:7]).

6.   ROBERT[K] DE PEMBRUGGE of Ayleston was living in 1350 and was dead by 1 Aug.
1364 [Weis, *AR7*, 56A:33].
He married JULIANA[K] LA ZOUCHE, who was living in 1345.
Children, listed by Eyton [2:226, who credited Shaw's *Hist. Staffordshire*]:
      i.   Fulk[J], called base son of Robert by Norr [84], d. 24 May 1409; m. (1)
            before Aug. 1363 Margaret Trussel, who d. 10 June 1399, m. (2)
            before Oct. 1405 Isabel Lingen, alias Elizabeth[J] Lingen, who d. Dec.
            1446, having m. (2) Sir John[J] Ludlow, and m. (3) Sir Thomas Petvine.
*   ii.   Juliana, aged 60 in 1409; m. Sir Richard[J] Vernon, of Haddon and Harles-
            ton, who d. 1376.

§ § §

DE PERCY

This line was based on Cokayne's *Complete Peerage* [10:435-463].
The name is derived from Percy-en-Auge, arr. Lisieux, cant. Mézidon [*CP*, 10:435b].
WILLIAM[S] DE PERCY died and was buried at Mount Joy, near Jerusalem, in the Holy
Land, having joined the First Crusade in 1096. He married EMMA[S] DE PORT, who was
related closely to Hugh de Port of Basing [*CP*, 10:438a].
ALAN[R] DE PERCY died probably before Dec. 1135 [*CP*, 10:440b]. He married EMMA[R]
DE GANT, who as a widow gave land in Wold Newton, of her *maritagium*, to Bridlington
Priory, and probably died shortly after her husband, also by Dec. 1135.
WILLIAM[Q] DE PERCY (who was living in the year ending Michaelmas [Sept. 29] 1170,
and probably in the year ending Mich. 1174) died before Easter 1175, and was buried at
Fountains Abbey. He married first, before 1136, ALICE[Q] DE TONBRIDGE. He married
second, about 1166, Sibyl[R] de Valonges, widow of Robert[R] de Ros of Helmsley. She
married third, having dower in Leconfield and Nafferton, about 1182, Ralph d'Aubigny,
who died before Mich. 1192. She was living in 1212, and was buried at Nun Appleton
Priory.
AGNES[P] DE PERCY was living in the year ending Michaelmas 1202, and was dead before
13 Oct. 1204. She married after 1154 JOCELIN[P] DE LOUVAIN, brother of Queen Adeliz (the
second wife of King Henry I of England, she married second William d'Aubigny, Earl of
Arundel), and son of Godfrey, Duke of Lower Lorraine and Count of Brabant. It is
presumed that Joscelin died in the year ending Michaelmas 1180, when the honor of
Petworth passed into the King's hand.
HENRY[O] DE PERCY died before Michaelmas 1198. He married ISABEL[O] DE BRUS,
daughter of Adam de Brus II of Skelton in Cleveland, in frank-marriage of the vill of Kirk
Levington except his freeholders there and their holdings. She married second Sir Roger
Mauduit, and was apparently living in 1230.
WILLIAM[N] DE PERCY, 6th Baron Percy, born Alnwick, Northumberland, about 1193, died
shortly before 28 July 1245. He married first Joan[O] de Briwere, who died before 12 June
1233, possibly in Feb. 1232/3 [*CP*, 10:454e] and was buried at Sandown Hospital, Surrey.
He married second, about 1233, ELLEN DE BALIOL of Alnwick, Northumberland, who was
born about 1200, daughter of Ingram de Baliol by his wife, the daughter and heir of Walter
de Berkeley of Red Castle, county Forfar, Scotland, Chamberlain of Scotland. Ellen

brought in marriage Dalton (Percy), Durham. Her dower was ordered to be assigned 19 Aug. and 29 Oct. 1245, and she died shortly before 22 Nov. 1281.

Sir HENRY[M] DE PERCY, 7th Baron Percy, was born in Alnwick about 1235, died 29 Aug. 1272, and was buried in Salley Abbey. He married in York, 8 Sept. 1268, ELEANOR[M] WARENNE of Warren, Sussex, who died after 1282 and was buried at Sallay Abbey. Her mother was a half-sister of Henry III.

8. Sir HENRY[L] PERCY, 9th Baron Percy and 1st Lord Percy of Alnwick, was born posthumously in Petworth, Sussex, about 25 March 1273, died between 2 and 10 Oct. 1314, and was buried in Fountains Abbey.

He married after June 1294 ELEANOR[L] FITZ ALAN* (sister of Richard de Arundel), who died in July or Aug. 1328 and was buried in Beverley. Her parentage has not been established clearly [MCS5, 152:6].

He succeeded his brother before 20 July 1293 and in June 1294 was summoned to military service in Gascony, but instead went with King Edward I to Wales. In Oct. 1295 he was in Scotland with his grandfather, the Earl of Surrey. He was knighted by the King at the capture of Berwick on 30 March 1296, and fought at Dunbar 27 April 1296. In Sept. of that year he was warden of Galloway and Ayrshire, and the next June he was serving as Justiciar in Dumfries and joint Justiciar in Lancashire, Cumberland and Westmorland. His seal was affixed to a treaty with the Count of Flanders in court at Ipswich on 7 Jan. 1296/7. Although he had been summoned for service in person overseas in May 1297, in July he was in Scotland to receive submissions of Scottish prelates and nobles, including Robert de Brus. That year he served as Justiciar of Dumfries, and joint justiciar of Cumberland, Lancashire and Westmorland. In 1297-1298 he was a member of the Council of the King's son and Regent during the King's absence abroad. In Jan. 1297/8 he was among the magnates summoned to a convention at York, which the Scottish magnates were ordered to attend.

In July 1300 he served with his maternal grandfather at the siege of Caerlaverock. He was summoned to Parliament from 6 Feb. 1298/9 to 29 July 1314. He spent much of the remainder of his life either fighting in Scotland or preparing for new campaigns there, including the siege of Stirling in 1304 and service as King's lieutenant and captain over all men-of-arms of the West Borders in 1306. In Nov. 1309 he purchased Alnwick from Anthony Beck (or Bek), the Bishop of Durham, and in 1310 he joined the barons in opposition to Edward II; he was one of the Lords in Council present at the proclamation of the Ordinances at the cross in St. Paul's Churchyard in Oct. 1311, but was among those who declared that the Lords Ordainers should not be precedent setting. He was with the Earl of Lancaster in May 1312, nearly capturing the King at Newcastle; he was with the Earls of Pembroke and Surrey when Piers de Gavaston surrendered to them. As he was a surety for Gavaston's safe conduct, his arrest was ordered and his lands were seized when Piers was executed. On 24 March 1313/4 he was again summoned against the Scots.

Children:

9.   i.   Henry[K], b. Leconfield 6 Feb. 1300/1; d. Warkworth 27 Feb. 1351/2; m. 1314 Idoine[K] de Clifford, who d. 24 Aug. 1365.

        ii.   William, d. 1535 [BP (1999). 2:2119]; mentioned in the will of Henry[K] de Percy [CP, 10:459b].

        iii. Joan, d. in infancy [Hedley, 2:13].

9. Sir HENRY[K] DE PERCY, 2nd Lord Percy, born in Leconfield, Northumberland, 6 Feb. 1300/1 [CP, 10:459e], died after a slight illness in Warkworth 27 Feb. 1351/2, and was buried at Alnwick Abbey.

He married in 1314 IDOINE[K] DE CLIFFORD*, who died 24 Aug. 1365 and was buried in Beverley Minster under the "Percy shrine."

Although very young he was summoned by Archbishop Greenfield in April 1315 as one of fifty knights to attend a council of war concerning Scotland at Doncaster. Given custody of Alnwick Castle in 1318, in May 1321 he attended the meeting of northern magnates at Pontefract called by the Earl of Lancaster, but by Nov. 1321 he was warned to stay away from the Earl's meeting at Doncaster and on 25 Dec. 1321 he was given custody of Scarborough Castle. The next day he did homage and had livery of his inheritance, though he had not proved his age.

Knighted by the King at York in 1322, he was summoned to military service in Scotland, where he spent most of his life when he was not in the Marches. In April 1323 he served as a hostage in Scotland for the Earl of Moray, the Scottish ambassador for peace in England. He joined the Queen against the Despensers in Oct. 1326. In Feb. 1326/7 he was chief commissioner to see the Scottish truce observed, and then he served as chief plenipotentiary to make peace. In the subsequent treaty it was agreed that the English (except Percy and three others) should lose their inheritances in Scotland. In May 1327 the Scots raided the borders and beseiged Alnwick Castle, but Percy defended his stronghold well.

He was with the King at Durham in Aug. 1327, at York in Aug. 1328 and in May 1329 sailed with the King from Dover to do homage for Guienne. He was keeper of Bambrough Castle in April 1330, and the following January was an envoy to France. In Jan. 1330/1 he was Justiciar of the English (or Eastern) March. In Aug. 1332 he was appointed Warden of the March. In Oct. 1333 he was chief commissioner to attend Edward Balliol's parliament in Perth, to obtain confirmation of Balliol's agreement with Edward III. With Lord Neville he defeated raiding Scots at Redesdale in Jan. 1334/5. In 1340 he was a member of the council of regency during the king's absence in Flanders. In 1341, as the leader of seven famous English captains disguised as pilgrims to St. Andrews, he temporarily raised the siege of Stirling. In 1343 he was given the power to receive the Scots in peace, and in 1344 to take Newcastle-upon-Tyne into the king's hand. He commanded the third division at the victory of Neville's Cross on 17 Oct. 1346, after which King David of Scotland was taken as prisoner to Bamburgh Castle. He then participated in the invasion of 1347. In Oct. 1350 he was a commissioner to treat with the Scots for a conclusive peace.

Children, listed by Hedley [2:15]:

i.   Henry[J], d. c. 18 May 1368, bur. Alnwick; m. (1) Tutbury Castle, in or before Sept. 1314, Mary[K] (who d. 1 Sept. 1362, bur. Alnwick), dau. of Henry, Earl of Lancaster (for whom see Plantagenet), and Maud[L] Chaworth [CP, 10:463], m. (2) in or before May 1365, Joan Orreby, who m. (2) Sir Constantine Clifton, who d. end of July 1369 [CP, 10:462-463]; he was father of Henry Percy who deposed King Richard II, and grandfather of Henry "Hotspur" Percy.

ii.   Richard, of Semar, Yorks., 1335; no issue.

iii.   Thomas, b. 1333 [BP (1999), 2:2119]; d. 1369; Bishop of Norwich.

iv.   Roger, no issue.

v.   Sir William, of Kirk Levington, d. 1355; no issue.

vi.   Robert, no issue.

vii.   Margaret, d. 1375; m. (1) (royal license 20 Jan. 1339/40) Robert Umfraville, m. (2) by 25 May 1368 William de Ferrers, who d. 1372 (or Sept. 1375 [BP (1999), 2:2119]), lord of Groby.

* viii. Maud, b. Alnwick c. 1345; d. before 18 Feb. 1378/9, bur. Durham Cathedral, Durham [Roberts' *RD500*, 354]; m. 1364 John[J] de Neville, 3rd Baron Neville of Raby, who d. Newcastle 17 Oct. 1388.
   ix. Maud, d. by 18 Feb. 1378/9 [*BP* (1999), 2:2119]; m. Ralph Nevill of Raby.
    x. Isabel, d. by 25 May 1368; m. by Jan. 1326/7 Sir William de Aton, who d. by March 1388/9 [Weis, *MCS5*, 11:8].
   xi. Alianore (or Eleanor), m. (2) Lord Fitzwalter [*BP* (1999), 2:2119].

§ § §

DE PESHALL

While Joseph Morris [*Shropshire Genealogies*, 3745] states that Sir Hamo[I] de Peshall (who married Alice de Harley) was son of Sir Richard de Peshall and Aliva de Braiose, daughter and heiress of William de Braiose, lord of Gower, and that Sir Richard de Peshall was brother of Adam de Peshall, Sheriff of Salop and Stafford in 1341, the research by Roskell is more recent.

1. Sir ADAM[J] DE PESHALL was of Horsley and Bishops Offley, Staffordshire, and died in 1346.

He married JOAN[J] DE EYTON, daughter and heiress of John Eyton of The Wildmoors in Salop, or Shropshire.

He served as Member of Parliament in 1341 [Roskell, 4:61-64], but was ordered arrested in 1345 for homicide and other crimes, and was either captured at Cainton, Shropshire, and beheaded, or, in the view of Sir Richard[I] de Peshall, was slain by Sir John Ipstones on Caynton Heath early in 1346, allegedly while resisting arrest.

Child, found in Roskell [4:61-64]:
   i. Sir Richard[I].
  ii. Sir Adam, d. 1419; m. (1) c. 1362 Elizabeth Weston, widow of Sir John Whiston, m. (2) 1369 Elizabeth ferch Sir Philip ap Rhys of Talgarth, widow of Sir Henry Mortimer of Chelmarsh, m. (3) Joyce de Botetourt, widow of Sir Baldwin Freville.
2. iii. Hamo[nd], d. by 1399; m. (1) by 1380 Alesia[I] de Harley, m. (2) Thomasine de Wastneys of Colton, Staffs.

2. Sir HAMO[ND][I] DE PESHALL, of Staffordshire, died by 1399.

He married first, by 1380 (probably in 1375), ALESIA[I] DE HARLEY*, who had died by Easter term 1389.

He married second Thomasine de Wastneys of Colton in Staffordshire, daughter and heiress of Sir Thomas Wastneys of Colton and widow of Sir Nicholas Gresley of Drakelow in Derbyshire.

He was probably a retainer of Hugh, Earl of Stafford, and campaigned with him, possibly from 1373. He joined forces with Admiral Richard, Earl of Arundel, in 1386.

He was executor for his wife's uncle, Sir Fulk Corbet, who died in 1382.

Child:
* i. Elizabeth[H], d. 23 June 1435; m. (1) Henry Grendon, whose will was proved 8 Feb. 1405/6; m. (2) 1409 Sir Richard[H] Lacon.

§ § §

DE PIPE

This line was originally based on an ancestor table by Mr. Marlyn Lewis.

1. ROBERT^M DE PIPE was seneschal (steward or major domo), of Tutterbury.
Child:
   2.   i.   Thomas^L, d. after 1326; m. Johanna^L de Jarpenville.

2. THOMAS^L DE PIPE, Lord Draycote, died after 1326.
He married JOHANNA^L DE JARPENVILLE, daughter of Andrew de Jarpenvill and Matilda de Suydenham.
Children [*Wallop Family*, 625]:
   3.   i.   Robert^K, d. after 1342; m. Emma Stafford.
        ii. Margaret, m. Sir Philip Somerville, who d. 23 Jan. 1355/6.

3. ROBERT^K DE PIPE, Lord Draycote, Parva and Rydware, died after 1342.
He married EMMA^K STAFFORD of Sandon, Bramshall and Amblecote in Staffordshire.
Child:
   4.   i.   William^J, d. after 1358; m. Johanna^J Ridware.

4. WILLIAM^J DE PIPE, Lord Chirche Sheile and Pipe Rydeware, died after 1358.
He married JOHANNA^J RIDWARE*, heiress of Sheile.
Child:
   *   i.   Joan^I, m. Robert^I Swynfen.

§ § §

PLANTAGENET

Further material on this Plantagenet line is available in *Medieval English Ancestors of Certain Americans.*

1. HENRY III^N, King of England, son of John Lackland, King of England, and Isabelle d'Angoulême, born at Winchester Castle in Hampshire, 1 Oct. 1207, died in at Bury St. Edmunds in Suffolk on 16 June 1272, and was buried at Westminster Abbey.
    He married in Canterbury, 14 Jan. 1236/7, ELEANOR^N OF PROVENCE, who was born at Aix-en-Provence in 1217, died in Amesbury, Wiltshire, 24/25 June 1291, and was buried in the Priory of Amesbury. She was the second daughter and coheir of Raymond Berenger V, comte de Provence, by Béatrix, daughter of Thomas I, comte de Savoie.
    Crowned at age nine on 28 Oct. 1216, he declared himself to be of full age in Jan. 1227 and assumed personal rule. Due to disastrous attempts to regain the French lands lost by his father, his attempts to take control of royal finances without the participation of the barons, and the influence of the Queen's kinsmen, he was forced in 1258 to agree to formation of a Privy Council of barons. In 1259 he made peace with King Louis IX of France, giving up claims to Normandy, Anjou, Maine, Touraine and Poitou, and agreed to hold the Duchy of Gascony as a vassal to the French kings.
    The ensuing civil war with forces led by his brother-in-law, Simon de Montfort, Earl of Leicester, resulted in the capture of Henry III and his eldest son, Edward, at the battle of Lewes on 14 May 1264. Montfort then ruled England in Henry's name until he was in turn

killed at the battle of Evesham on 4 Aug. 1265 by Prince Edward's forces. Edward then assumed effective control of the government.

Children, after a list by Faris [PA1, 226]:

2.   i.   Edward I[M], King of England, b. Westminster 16/17 June 1239; d. Burgh-on-Sands, Cumberland, near Carlisle, 7/8 July 1307; m. (1) Burgos, Kingdom of León (now in Spain), 18 Oct. 1254, Eleanor[M] of Castile, who d. 28 Nov. 1290, m. (2) Canterbury, 8 Sept. 1299, Marguerite de France, who d. Marlborough Castle 14 Feb. 1317.

ii.   Margaret, b. Windsor Castle 5 Oct. 1240; m. Alexander III, King of Scots.

iii.   Beatrice, b. Bordeaux 25 June 1242; m. Jean II de Dreux.

3.   iv.   Edmund "Crouchback," b. London 16 Jan. 1244/5; d. in Bayonne 5 June 1296, bur. Westminster Abbey; m. (1) Westminster 8 April 1270 Avelina de Fort, m. (2) Paris by 18 Jan. 1275/6 Blanche[M] d'Artois of Arras, who d. Paris 2 May 1302.

v.   Richard, b. c. 1247; d. before 1256, bur. Westminster Abbey.

vi.   John, b. c. 1250; d. before 1256, bur. Westminster Abbey.

vii.   Katherine, b. Westminster 25 Nov. 1253; d. Windsor Castle 3 May 1257.

viii.   Henry, d. young, bur. Westminster Abbey.

2. EDWARD I[M] Longshanks, King of England from 1272 to 1307, born in Westminster 16 or 17 June 1239, died in Burgh-on-Sands, Cumberland, near Carlisle, 7/8 July 1309, and was buried in Westminster Abbey 28 Oct. 1307.

He married first, in the monastery of Los Heulgas, Burgos, León (now in Spain), 18 Oct. 1254, ELEANOR[M] OF CASTILE, who was born about 1244, and died in Herdeby, Grantham, Nottinghamshire, 28 Nov. 1290, and was buried in Westminster Abbey 16 Dec. 1290. She was daughter of Fernando III, King of Castilla y Léon, and his second wife Jeanne de Dammartin, daughter of Simon de Dammartin, comte d'Aumale et de Ponthieu.

He married second, in Canterbury Cathedral in Kent, 8 Sept. 1299, Marguerite de France (daughter of Philippe III, King of France, and his second wife, Maria von Brabant), who had been born in 1279 and died in Marlborough Castle 14 Feb. 1317.

He was granted Gascony, and was created Earl of Chester on 14 Feb. 1254. His first marriage was arranged (when he was 15 and his wife was 10) to prevent Gascon rebels from getting help from Castille. He took the cross in 1268 and was on crusade in the Holy Land from May 1271 to Sept. 1272. While in Sicily on returning to England he learned of his father's death; he then paid homage to King Philippe III of France for his French lands. He landed at Dover 2 Aug. 1274 and was crowned at Westminster 19 Aug. 1274. He worked to regain royal authority by looking into the jurisdictions of landowners and over-hauling the civil and criminal law, and from 1275 to 1307 calling representatives of the counties and boroughs to Parliament, as Simon de Montfort had.

Then he pushed to assert his claims to sovereignty over all of Britain. In 1277 he defeated Llywelyn ap Gruffudd, Prince of North Wales, later annexing Wales to the Crown. In 1296 he invaded Scotland and deposed John Balliol (who had been his choice for King of Scots). He defeated William Wallace at Falkirk in 1298, but died without conquering that land, as Robert Bruce was crowned King of Scotland in 1306.

In 1294 he went to war against his French overlord, King Philippe IV, over control of Gascony, leading to a great need for financing which cost him much support.

Children, by Eleanor of Castile, listed by T. Anna Leese, with some detail from Faris:

i.   Joan[L] of England, b. 1260; d. 1260 [Leese] or young before 7 Sept. 1265.

ii.   Eleanor of England, b. c. 17 June 1264; m. Henry III, comte de Bar.

iii.   Katherine, d. 1264.

iv. John of England, b. 10 June 1266; d. Westminster 3 Aug. 1271.

v. Henry of England, b. Windsor 13 July 1267; d. 14 Oct. 1274, bur. Westminster Abbey.

vi. Julian (or Catherine) of England, b. Holy Land 1271; d. there 5 Sept. year unknown (possibly 1271).

* vii. Joan of Acre, b. Acre, Palestine, spring 1272; d. Clare, Suffolk, 28 April 1307, bur. Friary Church there; m. (1) 30 April or "the beginning of May" 1290 Gilbert^M de Clare as his second wife, m. (2) 1296 (secretly) Ralph de Monthemer, a simple squire who later rose to administer the Lordship of Glamorgan.

viii. Alphonso of England, b. Bayonne 24 Nov. 1273; d. 19 Aug. 1284; Earl of Chester.

ix. Margaret of England, b. Windsor Castle 11 Sept. 1275; d. 1318; m. Westminster Abbey, 8 July 1290, John II, Duke of Brabant.

x. Berengaria of England, b. Kennington 1276; d. c. 1279, bur. Westminster.

xi. Mary of England, Windsor b. 11 March 1278; d. Amesbury before 8 July 1332; nun.

xii. Alice of England, b. Woodstock 12 March 1279; d. 1291.

xiii. Isabella, b. 1279; d. 1279.

* xiv. Elizabeth, b. Rhuddlan Castle, Caernarfon, Wales, 7 Aug. 1282; d. Quendon, England, 5 May 1316, bur. Walden Priory, Essex; m. (1) Ipswich, 7/8 or 18 Jan. 1296/7, John, Count of Holland, who d. Haarlem 10 Nov. 1299, m. (2) Westminster 14 Nov. 1302 Humphrey^L de Bohun VIII, who was slain at the battle of Boroughbridge, Yorks., 16 March 1321/2.

xv. Edward II, King of England, b. Caernarfon Castle, Wales, 25 April 1284; murdered Berkeley Castle 21 Sept. 1327; m. Boulogne 25 Jan. 1308 Isabelle de France (dau. of Philippe IV, King of France), who d. Hertford Castle 22 Aug. 1358.

xvi. Beatrice of England, b. Aquitaine c. 1286; d. young.

xvii. Blanche of England, b. 1290; d. young.

Children, by Marguerite de France:

xviii. Thomas of Norfolk (of Brotherton), b. Brotherton, Yorks., 1 June 1300; d. Aug. 1338, bur. Bury St. Edmunds; m. (1) c. 1316 Alice de Hales, who d. after 8 May 1326, m. (2) c. 1328 Mary de Brewes, widow of Ralph de Cobham, Lord Cobham, who d. Feb. 1326; no surviving issue.

xix. Edmund of Kent (of Woodstock), b. Woodstock, Oxfordshire, 5 Aug. 1301; beheaded 19 March 1330 for alleged treason; m. c. 25 Dec. 1325 Margaret Wake (widow of John Comyn of Badenoch), b. c. 1299, d. 29 Sept. 1349, dau. of John Wake, 1st Lord Wake, by Joan, dau. of William de Fiennes.

3. EDMUND^M "CROUCHBACK" PLANTAGENET, born in London, England, 16 Jan. 1244/5, died in Bayonne, France, 5 June 1296, and was buried in Westminster Abbey.

He married first, in Westminster Abbey, 8 or 9 April 1270, Avelina de Fort (or de Forz, de Fortibus, daughter of William de Fort, comte d'Aumale and lord of Holderness, by Isabel, daughter and heiress of Baldwin de Redvers, 7th Earl of Devon), who died at Stockwell 10 Nov. 1274, without issue, and was buried at Westminster Abbey.

He married second, in Paris, by 18 Jan. 1275/6, BLANCHE[M] D'ARTOIS of Arras, Pas de Calais, widow of King Henry I of Navarre, who died 22 July 1276; she died in Paris 2 May 1302, and was buried in Minoress Convent, Aldgate, Leicestershire. She was daughter of Robert I d'Artois, comte d'Artois and son of King Louis VIII of France, and his wife Matilda of Brabant, daughter of Henry II, Duke of Brabant, and his wife Marie von Hohenstauffen of Swabia.

There was an old tradition that he was older than his brother Edward, but that because of his deformity he was held back. However, Edward was six and one-half years older.

On 7 March 1253/4 he was offered the Kingdom of Sicily by Pope Innocent IV through the Papal legate, Albert. On 25 May 1254 a great seal was ordered and four days later Edmund and his mother sailed from Portsmouth for Bordeaux, but when peace was made between the Pope and Manfred, son of King Frederick of Apulia, a renunciation of the title was in order.

He was Earl of Leicester (succeeding Simon de Montfort), Derby (which was forfeited by Robert de Ferrers, who sued him unsuccessfully later) and Lancaster. In 1266 he participated in the siege of Kenilworth with his father and Prince Edward, and was granted that castle three days after it surrendered. In the spring of 1267 he was authorized to negotiate peace with Llywelyn ap Gruffudd, and on 30 June 1267 he was awarded the honor, county, castle and town of Lancaster as well as other castles, manors, forests and rents.

He was appointed Steward of England for life in 1269 (a position which he renounced in 1274), and after lengthy preparations was in the Holy Land in July 1272. He was summoned for military service a number of times from 1276 to 1291, was named commander in Wales on 8 Aug. 1277, and began building a castle in Aberystwyth. In 1282 he captured Llywelyn ap Gruffudd and beheaded him, and on 28 June 1283 he was summoned to Shrewsbury for the trial of Dafydd ap Gruffudd.

At various times he served in Ponthieu, Gascony and Aquitaine; he was appointed Lieutenant of Aquitaine weeks before he died while besieging Bordeaux. As a result of his second marriage he was styled comte de Champagne et Brie in France. He was summoned to Parliament 24 June 1295.

Children, from Cokayne [7:387-401] and Faris [PA2, 202], by second wife:

    i. Thomas[L], Earl of Lancaster and Derby (or Ferrers), b. c. 1278; beheaded 22 March 1321/2, bur. Priory of St. John at Pontefract; m. on or before 28 Oct. 1294 Alice de Lacy (dau. of Henry de Lacy, Earl of Lincoln), who d. 2 Oct. 1348, having m. (2) Sir Ebles Lestraunge, who d. 8 Sept. 1335, m. (3) before 23 March 1335/6 Sir Hugh de Frene, who d. c. Dec. 1336; no issue.

4.   ii. Henry, b. Grismond Castle, Monmouthshire, Wales, 1281; d. Monastery of Canons, Leics., 22 Sept. 1345, bur. Newark Abbey, Leics.; m. (1) before 2 March 1296/7 Maud[L] de Chaworth, m. (2) Alice de Joinville.

    iii. John, b. before May 1286; d. France before 1327; unm.

    iv. Mary, d. young.

4. HENRY[L] PLANTAGENET, created Earl of Lancaster 10 May 1324, was born at Grosmont Castle, Monmouthshire, Wales, in 1281, died at the Monastery of Canons, Leicestershire, 22 Sept. 1345, aged 64, and was buried on the north side of the high alter of Newark Abbey, Leicester.

He married first, before 2 March 1296/7, MAUD[L] DE CHAWORTH*, who was living on 19 Feb. 1317 and was dead by 3 Dec. 1322, and was buried at Mottisfont Priory as heir of William de Briwere, who was one of the founders.

He married second Alice de Joinville (widow of Jean, seigneur d'Arcies-sur-Aube et de Chacenay), daughter of Jean de Joinville, *sénéchal de* Champagne, by Alix, daughter and heir of Gautier, seigneur de Risnel. Alice died in Leicester 22 Sept. 1435, and was buried at Newark Abbey.

He had livery of Monmouth and his father's lands beyomd the Severn on 20 March 1296/7. He served with King Edward I in Flanders in 1297-1298, and in Scotland every year afterwards until 1323, providing men from his Welsh lordship from 1310 onwards. He was summoned to Parliament on 6 Feb. 1298/9 and took part in the siege of Caerlaverock in July 1300. As Lord of Monmouth he joined in the Barons' letter to the Pope of 12 Feb. 1300/1. On 16 Oct. 1313 he was pardoned for his part in the execution of Piers de Gavaston. As a lord marcher he fought in South Wales, Jan. 1315 to March 1315, against the rebellion of Llywelyn Bren. In 1320 he joined the Marchers against the Despensers, but he did not join his brother's rebellion in 1322. He was created Earl of Leicester on 29 March 1324, and also succeeded his older brother Thomas as Earl of Lancaster upon the restoration, which was made between 1324 and 1326.

When Queen Isabel returned to England with Roger de Mortimer in 1326 he joined her party against Edward II; this led to general desertion of the King. He was appointed keeper of the castles of Abergavenny and Kenilworth. He captured the King at Neath, taking him to Llantrisant in Glamorgan on 16 Nov. 1326, and was responsible for his custody at Kenilworth until 4 April 1327.

He attended the Coronation of Edward III on 1 Feb. 1326/7, whom he knighted, and of whom he was appointed guardian. Upon his brother's rehabilitation he received estates and honors. In 1327 he served as Captain General of the King's armies against the Scots. However, Queen Isabel and Roger de Mortimer usurped his authority, and he was forced to submit at Bedford. About 1330 he became blind, but he enjoyed close relations with Edward III after the fall of Mortimer. In 1335 he was with the King at Newcastle, where the invasion of Scotland by Edward III from Newcastle and Balliol from Carlisle was planned. He was summoned to attend a great council at Northhampton in 1338, and in June 1339 he led the Earls who were sureties for the treaty at Brussels between England and Brabant. In 1345 he was appointed to the Council of Prince Lionel, who was keeper of England during the absence of the King.

Children, listed in Cokayne [7:401b]:

   i. Henry "of Grosmont"[K], Earl of Derby 1336/7, Earl of Lancaster and of Leicester, Steward of England in 1345, Earl of Lincoln, Duke of Lancaster, Earl of Moray, K.G., b. Grosmont Castle c. 1300; d. of the plague at Leicester, 24 March 1360/1; m. c. 1337 Isabel de Beaumont; no surviving male issue, but left daughters Maud (who m. [1] 1 Nov. 1344 Ralph[J] Stafford, m. [2] William, Duke of Bavaria) and Blanche (who m. John of Gaunt).

   ii. Blanche, m. Thomas Wake, 2nd Lord Wake.

   iii. Mary, b. 1320; d. 1 Sept. 1362, bur. Alnwick; m. Tutbury Castle 1334 Henry[J] de Percy, Lord Percy, who d. May 1368, bur. Alnwick, having m. (2) 1365 Joan Orreby.

   iv. Isabel, d. 5 May 1377; m. Henry de la Dale.

   v. Maud, m. (1) William de Burgh 4th, Earl of Ulster, who was murdered at Le Ford (now Belfast) 6 June 1333, m. (2) Ralph de Ufford, who d. Kilmainham, Ireland, 9 April 1346.

*   vi. Eleanor (or Alianore), b. Grismond Castle, Wales, c. 1311/2; d. Arundel, Sussex, 11 Jan. 1371/2; m. (1) before June 1337 John de Beaumont, Earl of Buchan, who d. May 1342, m. (2) Ditton 5 Feb. 1344/5 Sir

Richard[K] Fitz Alan, Earl of Arundel and Warenne, who d. Arundel 24 Jan. 1375/6.

vii.   Joan, d. 7 July 1349, bur. Byland; m. c. 28 Feb. 1326/7 John de Mowbray, Lord Mowbray, who d. of pestilence at York 4 Oct. 1361, having m. (2) Elizabeth de Vere, widow of Hugh de Courteney.

§ § §

DE LA POLE OR POWYS

This family line, based originally on Peter C. Bartrum's *Welsh Genealogies, AD 300-1400*, has been developed in part by reference to Cokayne's *Complete Peerage*, but Welsh spellings have been given precedence in this treatment.

GWAITHFOED[V] of Powys AP GWYNNAN[W] AP GWYNNOG FARFSYCH[X] AP LLES LLAWDDEOG[Y] AP CEIDIO[Z] AP CORF AP CAENOG AP TEGONWY AP TEON AP GWINEU DEUFREUDDWYD AP BYWYR LEW AP BYWDEG AP RHUN RHUDD BALADR AP LLARY AP CASNAR WLEDIG, who was said to be perhaps the same as Casanauth Wledig. The ancestry of Gwaithfoed of Powys is given in a straight line pedigree with no additional details, and is regarded by many to be legendary at some point.

GWERYSTAN[U] AP GWAITHFOED was of Powys. He married NEST[U] FERCH CADELL AP BROCHWEL, who was not identified further in Bartrum's chart 47.

CYNFYN[T] AP GWERYSTAN AP GWAITHFOED was of Powys. He married ANGHARAD[T] FERCH MAREDUDD AB OWAIN AP HYWEL DDA [Bartrum's chart 42]; Angharad was widow of Llywelyn ap Seisyll (who died in 1023 [Bartrum chart 41]) ap Prawst ab Elise (who died in 942) ab Anarawd (Prince of Gwynedd, who died in 916) ap Rhodri Mawr, who died in 878. Angharad's father Maredudd died in 999. His father was Owain ap Hywel Dda ap Cadell ap Rhodri Mawr, while his mother was Angharad ferch Llywelyn ap Merfyn ap Rhodri Mawr.

BLEDDYN[S] AP CYNFYN AP GWERYSTAN of Powys died in 1075. He married second HAER[S] FERCH CILLIN AP Y BLAIDD RHYDD o'r Gest yn Eifionydd, who is not identified further in chart Bleddyn ap Cynfyn 1. He married third a daughter of Brochwel ap Bledrus y Moelwyn ab Aelan ap Greddyf ap Cwnws Ddu ap Cillin Ynfyd. The names of his first and fourth wives have not been recorded.

MAREDUDD[R] AP BLEDDYN AP CYNFYN died in 1132. He married first HUNYDD[R] FERCH EINUDD [Bartrum's chart Einudd] of Dyffryn Clwyd (sometimes called Eunydd Gwerngwy) AP MORIEN AP MORGENEU AB ELYSTAN AP GWAITHFOED of Powys [chart 47]. He married second Cristin ferch Bledrus ab Ednywain Bendew I ap Neiniad ap Gwaithfoed of Powys.

GRUFFUDD[Q] AP MAREDUDD AP BLEDDYN AP CYNFYN, Lord of Cyfeiliog, was of record in 1116 and died in 1128. He married GWERFUL[Q] FERCH GWRGENEU [Bartrum's chart El. G. 31] AP HYWEL AB IEUAF AP CADWGON AB ELYSTAN GLODRYDD, the latter descended fifteen generations from Casnar Wledig, according to the Welsh pedigrees. He had a mistress, Iwera ferch Iago ap Gruffudd ap Cynan [Gr. ap C. 1].

OWAIN[P] CYFEILIOG, the Prince-Bard, was living in 1149 and died in 1197 [Bartrum's *Welsh Genealogies 300-1400*, chart Bleddyn ap Cynfyn 29]. He married first GWENLLIAN[P] FERCH OWAIN GWYNEDD (who died in 1170 [Bartrum's chart Gr. ap C. 3]) AP GRUFFUDD AP CYNAN AB IAGO (died 1039) AB IDWAL (died 996) AP MEURIG (died 986) AB IDWAL FOEL (died 942) AB ANARAWD AP RHODRI MAWR, who died in 818.

Owain[P] Cyfeiliog married second Gwenllian ferch Ednywain ab Eginir ap Gollwyn ap Tangno ap Cadfael ap Lludd ap Llew ap Llyminod Angel ap Pasgen ab Urien Rheged ap

Cynfarch Oer ap Meirchion Gul ap Gwrwst Ledlum ap Ceneu ap Coel Hen ("Old King Cole") [Gollwyn 3]. The mother of his daughter Constance, who married David[O] de Malpas, has not been identified.

GWENWYNWYN[O] AB OWAIN CYFEILIOG flourished in 1187, and died in Cheshire in 1216. He married first Margred ferch Yr Arglwydd Rhys [Bartrum's chart Rs. ap T. 4]. She was living in Derbyshire by 1231.

He married second, MARGARET (or Margred)[O] CORBET [Bartrum's chart Bl. ap C. 29], daughter of Robert Corbet of Caus and his wife Emma Pantulf of Wem. He held the manor of Buttington, Shropshire, for one knight's fee [Eyton's *Antiquities of Shropshire*, 11:177].

GRUFFUDD[N] AP GWENWYNWYN died in 1286 [Bartrum chart Bleddyn ap Cynfyn 30]. He married HAWYSE[M] LE STRANGE, daughter of John[N] le Strange III, the rebellious baron of Knockin [Bartrum's chart Bl. ap C. 30], identified by Eyton [*Ant. Shropshire*, 11:177] as of Ness and Cheswardine. She "long survived her son Owen," and died in 1310 [Eyton, 11:177]. The Prince of Powys, he was loyal to England until 1255, but then joined the Welsh rebels. He made a deed, dated Wednesday before the Feast of St. Martin 24 Hen. III (1240), which mentioned his parents Gwenwynwyn and Margaret daughter of Robert Corbet and niece of Thomas Corbet [A.E. Corbet, 114, 118-119].

10.   OWAIN[M] AP GRUFFUDD AP GWENWYNWYN (in English, Owen ap Griffith ap Gwenwynwyn), or Owen of Arwystli [*Jones, Feudal Barons of Powys*, 7], otherwise called DE LA POLE because he was from Pool in Wales, or Welshpool, died shortly before 15 Oct. 1293.

He married JOAN[K] CORBET*, who according to the *Montgomeryshire Collections* [1:54] and Bartrum [Bl. ap C. 2, 30] was a daughter of Sir Robert Corbet of Wattlesburgh and Moreton Corbet and his wife, who was a daughter of John[N] le Strange III of Ness and Cheswardine, Salop (Shropshire, England), baron of Knockyn; John[N] le Strange III was also the father of Hawise, Owain's mother. Owain's widow Joan had an order for assignment of dower on 20 Jan. 1293/4, and married second, between 18 Aug. 1295 and 22 Nov. 1298, Sir Roger Trumwyne, Sheriff of Salop and Staffordshire 1307-08 and 1316-18, and knight of the shire for Staffordshire in 1312 and 1313; he died about 1333 [*Colls. Hist. Staffs.*, 11:56]. She died before Michaelmas 1348. Cyfeiliog and other manors were assigned for her dowery.

He was called Lord de la Pole by the English, and was seated at Powys Castle in Welshpool in Montgomeryshire, Wales. He succeeded to the comots of Cyfeiliog, Arwystli, Llannerchdol and half of Caereinion.

According to Eyton's *Antiquities of Shropshire* [11:176], Dafydd, brother of Llywelyn, had promised Owain ap Gruffudd that he would have Dafydd's eldest daughter in marriage, and with her the lands of Cedewein and Ceri, which lands were granted by King Edward I to Roger Mortimer of Wigmore in 1281.

He stayed out of the fighting in 1255 [A.E. Corbet]. With his father he conspired with Dafydd (David), the brother of Llywelyn, Prince of North Wales, in 1276; Llywelyn released him in 1277 as provided by the Treaty of Conway.

Children, hers by first marriage, surnamed de la Pole:

   *   i.   Hawise "Gadarn," the Hardy, b. prob. 25 July 1290; m. 1309 John[L] de Cherleton.

         ii.   Gruffudd (Griffith)[L] ap Owain, b. c. 1291; d. shortly before 25 June 1309; m. Ela de Audley of Brimpsfield (dau. of Nicholas de Audley and his wife Catherine Giffard, dau. of John Giffard), who m. (2) 1309 Sir James de Perrers, m. (3) Piers Corbet; she d. 1325.

Child, hers by second marriage, surnamed Trumwyne:

  iii. Roger, as mother's executor sued for a debt on Michaelmas 1348.

Child, listed by Bartrum, mother not given:

  iv. daughter, m. Gwen ap Gronwy [Seisyll 4].

§ § §

DE PRAERS

Ormerod's treatment of the Praers pedigree [3:299-301] was based on Harleian manuscript No. 2119, with, as stated, a few corrections and additions, collated and revised from the *inquisitions post mortem* as well as the Plea and Recognizance Rolls.

RICHARD^Q DE PRAERS was living in 1119, when he gave Knoctirum to Chester Abbey. He married GALTHA.

ADAM^P DE PRAERS was a witness to Earl Randle's charter to Chester Abbey in 1119.

ROGER^O DE PRAERS was of record in the time of King John, which was from 1199 to 1216.

Sir ADAM^N DE PRAERS was of record 17 Hen. III (1232-1233). He married ANELLA^N DE LANCELYN, daughter of Robert de Lancelyn. He was the ancestor of Praers of Baddiley.

Sir ROBERT^M DE PRAERS was also of record 17 Hen. III. He married ELLEN^M DE RODE, daughter of Thomas de Rode.

WILLIAM^L DE PRAERS, lord of Badileigh, Cheshire, was Sheriff of Cheshire of record 5, 7, 8 and 20 Edw. I (1276-1292). His wife was ELEN^L.

9. WILLIAM^K DE PRAERS, lord of Badylegh (Baddiley), Cheshire, 22 Edw. III (1348-1349), was Sheriff of Cheshire in 23 Edw. III (1349-1350).

Children, listed by Ormerod:

  i. Joan^J, m. William^J Mainwaring of Over Peover, who d. 1364, having m. (2) Elizabeth^J Leycester.

 * ii. Margery, m. (1) Hugh del Holt, m. (2) John^J de Honford.

§ § §

PULFORD

This presentation is based on Ormerod's treatment of Pulford in Broxton Hundred, Cheshire [2:854-858]. It should be noted that almost every link between generations can be questioned.

Pulford is located on the old turnpike road from Chester to Wrexham, five miles southwest of Chester, on flat land on a brook which divides Cheshire from Wales. The site of the old castle is between the church and the boundary, along side the brook; the defences were probably last used during the rebellion of Owain Glyndŵr, when Sir Thomas le Grosvenor was mandated by Henry, Prince of Wales, on 11 Jan. 4 Hen. IV (1404), to "hasten to his possesssions at Pulford, Churchenheth, and elsewhere on the marches of Wales, on the occasion of war against the king and kingdom of England."

Pulford, which contained the townships of Pulford and Pulton, was divided, at the time of the Domesday survey in 1086, unequally between the secular canons of St. Werburgh, the former possessors, and Hugh Fitz Osberne, the Norman grantee, who had ejected the Saxon proprietors. Pulford was then divided between the Ormesbees, the probable successors to the seculars, and the Pulfords, who may have been descendants of Hugh Fitz

Osberne, who was possibly a son of Osberne Fitz Tezzon, the ancestor of the Boydells. Both the Pulfords and the Eatons (descendants of the Pulfords), adopted the Boydell coat with variations in the colors [Ormerod, 2:854].

RICHARD[P] DE PULFORD, possibly alias de Orreby, lived in the time of King Henry II.

Sir ROBERT[O] DE PULFORD was of record as witness to a charter of Richard de Aldford during the reign of King John, and granted lands in Pulford to Pulton Abbey.

ROBERT[N] DE PULFORD, lord of Pulford, was the grantee of Pulford Castle from Ralph, son of Simon de Orreby, at the time John le Strange was justiciar of Chester, 28 and 29 Hen. III (1243-1245).

HUGH[M] DE PULFORD, son of a Robert de Pulford [Wrottesley, *The Genealogist*, new ser., 13:100], was lord of Pulford and held lands in Neuton juxtà Frodesham in francmarriage; he died between 10 and 17 Edward I (about 1281-1289). He married first MARGERY[M] LE CHAUMBLENG, daughter of Robert le Chaumbleng (also alias de Frodesham in 1260), who was probably Robert de Frodesham, chamberlain of Frodesham. He married second Matilda, who was his widow in 17 Edw. I (1288-1289).

5. Sir ROBERT[L] DE PULFORD, probably lord of Pulford, son and heir of Hugh, was a minor in the wardship of Richard de Stokeport, by demise of the king, 17 Edw. I (1288-1289), and died in or before 8 Edw. II (1314-1315).

He married first Elizabeth de Corbet, daughter of Sir Ralph Corbet.

His second wife, Joan, was a widow 8 Edw. II (1314-1315), and held the advowson of Pulford in 1315; perhaps married second Richard de Botley or Walter de Verdon 13 Edw. II (1319-1320). According to the Mascy chart described below, Robert[K] de Pulford, if he married Joan, was son of a de Pulford who married Katherine, daughter of Hugh Dutton of Dutton, who was born in 1276, and his first wife Isabella, daughter of Sir Hamon de Mascy, last Baron of Dunham (who was under age in 1275 and died about 1334), by Mary de Beauchamp, who was living in 1309.

In 17 Edw. I (1288-1289) Roger de Monte Alto (Mohaut), Peter de Ardern, Rotheric fitz Griffin and Beatrice his wife (widow of William Patric who was coheir of the barony of Malpas) also held parts of the estates of Hugh de Pulford, as mentioned in a suit. In 1295 "Robert son and heir of Hugh de Pulford" granted land in Pulford to Richard Ingeniator (or Lenginour) and Agnes his wife, who at the same time received a grant there, according to the Eaton charters, from Richard son of Radulf de Pulford.

He confirmed his great-grandfather Robert's charter to Pulford Abbey 25 Edw. I (1296-1297). He was executor of his father's will in 2 Edw. II, when he acquired by fine sixty acres in Broxton and Chowley, and he acquired more land two years later.

In 8 Edw. II (1314-1315) his widow Joan sued Almaric Lengenour (who was perhaps a son of Richard and Agnes Lengenour of Belgrave) for dower of a bovate of land in Pulford. She also sued William, son of William Boydel of Wallefeld, for dower of a messuage, a carucate and six acres in Wallefeld.

Children [Ormerod, 2:858], by which wife unknown:

 i. John[K] [not shown in the Massy chart in *The Genealogist*, new ser., 16:23].
6. ii. Robert, possible son, heir of John[K], possibly son of Philip[L], perhaps d. 1349.
 iii. Nicholaa, m. Sir Philip[O] de Bamville, who d. after 27 Sept. 1282, having m. (2) Lettice de Venables.

6. ROBERT[K] DE PULFORD, lord of Pulford and rector of Chele, was of record in 1321 and 1337, and may have died in 1349.

His wife was named LEUCA in a suit brought by Joan de Pulford in 7 Edw. II (1313-1314) [Ormerod, 2:855]. Leuca had sisters Margaret de Caurthon and Elen. In the chart of descendants of Sir Hamon de Mascy by W.H.B.B. in *The Genealogist* [new ser., 13:23], Joan[J] was daughter of Robert de Pulford and his wife Joan, which Robert was son of a de Pulford and his wife Katherine de Dutton of Dutton, daughter of Hugh de Dutton of Dutton (born 1276), who married first about 1297 Isabella de Macsy (de Massy), daughter of Sir Hamon de Macsy, last baron of Dunham (who was underage about 1275 and dead in 1334), by his second wife Mary de Beauchamp, who was living in 1309.

Children, tentatively listed by Ormerod:

    i.   John[J], son and heir of Robert, *i.p.m.* 36 Edw. III (1362-1363), said to have had a son Robert, who died young, leaving a widow Isabel with no issue; he held in demesne as of fee, the manor of Pulford, land called Clareton, the manor of Buyrton, a third of a moiety of Warton, a fourth of Chollegh, and lands in Dunham Mascy juxtà Boudon and Aldreshey.

*   ii.   Joan, lady of Pulford, daughter of Robert and sole sister and heir of John, aged 14 in 36 Edw. III (1362-1363); d. before 20 Ric. II (1396-1397); m. (1) Thomas de Belgreave (of record 36 and 40 Edw. III and 1 or 2 Ric. II (1362-1379) [Ormerod, 2:826] (and had daus. Maud, Elizabeth and Joan), m. (2) c. 1378 Sir Robert[J] le Grosvenor of Holme, who was of record 12 Ric. II (1388-1389), ancestor of Grosvenor of Holme and Eaton.

§ § §

DE RIDWARE

This line needs to be researched in the local histories of Staffordshire.

1. WALTER[M] DE RIDWARE of Hempstale Ridware, Staffordshire, died after 1240 [Watney, *Wallop Family*, 660].

He married MATILDA[M] PECHE of Boylestone, Derbyshire, who died after 25 Nov. 1283, daughter of Sir Nicholas Peche.

Child:

  2.   i.   Walter[L], d. after 1282; m. Ellen[L] Fitz Herbert, who d. after 1269.

2. WALTER[L] DE RIDWARE of Staffordshire died after 1282.

He married ELLEN[L] FITZ HERBERT of Rossington, Derbyshire, who died after 1269. Watney [*Wallop Family*, 2:324] shows her parents as Sir William Fitz Herbert, 6th Lord of Norbury, who was granted free warren in his manors of Norbury and Rossington in Derbyshire in 1252, was Sheriff of Derby and Notts. 1272-1274, granted Norbury to his son Henry in 1267, son of John Fitz Herbert, 5th Lord Norbury, who married Emmeline de Grendon, daughter of William de Grendon, lord of Ockbrook, Derbyshire, a founder of Dale Abbey in 1204 and living 24 June 1228. However, for an internal inconsistency in Watney's work, see Sir Walter[J] de Ridware.

Child:

  3.   i.   Thomas[K], d. after 1325/6; m. (1) Margaret, m. (2) Isabella.

3. Sir THOMAS[K] DE RIDWARE died after 1325/6.

He married first Margaret.

He married second ISABELLA, joint heiress of Sheile Manor.

Child, by first wife:
> i. Sir Walter[J], m. Ellen, dau. of Walter Fitz Herbert of Norbury [Watney, *Wallop Family*, 660].

Child, by second wife:
> * ii. Johanna, m. William[J] de Pipe.

§ § §

ROCHE OF CASTLE BROMWICH

The family's castle was built upon a "rocky eminence," from which the family name was taken, overlooking St. Bride's Bay in Pembrokeshire, Wales. Roche, as a barony, included the adjoining parishes of Roch, Nolton, Camrose and Treffgarne. It was presumed that the family was descended from Godebert the Fleming of Ros, one of the Flemings who settled in Pembroke during the reign of King Henry I.

This line was taken from Cokayne [*CP*, 1:186-187, 11:41-45] and Faris' *Plantagenet Ancestry*, 2nd ed. [138], but Cokayne's treatment required corrections [*CP*, 14:550], and is still not clear to the compiler.

According to the confused treatment the earliest generation named was that of Sir David[M] de la Roche of Langwm, who had by Joan[M] de la Roche, a son Sir Robert[L] de la Roche, who was father of Sir John[K] de la Roche, who died in 1376, having married Isabel[K] de Bromwich, and they in turn were parents of Thomas[J], following. However, William de la Roche was at one point called the maternal grandfather of Margaret Fleming, who was daughter of John Fleming and Mary de la Roche, while Mary was sister of John de la Roche who was son of William de la Roche.

Douglas Richardson of Salt Lake City, Utah, has mentioned that Ellen[I] Roche has an illegitimate descent from the Marmion family, and thus has Carolingian ancestry. He recalled that it might be found in the *Victoria County History of Staffordshire*.

1. THOMAS[J] DE LA ROCHE was aged 11 in 1383, and died 4 Nov. 1440.

He married ELIZABETH[J] BERMINGHAM, dau. and heir of Sir Thomas de Birmingham, and niece and heir of Sir John de Birmingham of Birmingham, Warwickshire [*CP*, 5:318] and Kingston Bagpuze, Berkshire.

He was of Roch Castle in Pembrokeshire, Wales, and Castle Bromwich in Worcestershire.

Children, listed in Cokayne [11:44, corrected in 14:550, with Alice named as a dau. of Thomas by G.W. Watson in *CP*, 1:186-187]:
> i. Elizabeth[I], m. Sir George Longueville of Wolverton, Bucks.
> * ii. Ellen, m. (1) Sir Edmund[I] de Ferrers of Chartley, m. (2) Sir Philip Chetwynd of Ingestrie in Staffordshire, by whom no issue.
> iii. Lucy, had, perhaps by William Levelance, a dau. Eleanor who m. Robert Verney and had dau. and heir Isabel Verney who m. John Perrot.
> iv. Alice, m. Thomas[L] Arcedekne, Lord Arcedekne, who d. 1331, having m. (2) Maud, who d. after 11 June 1362.
> v. Margaret, m. Simon Fleming.

§ § §

DE ROS

Cokayne's *Complete Peerage* [11:90-101] and the *Dictionary of National Biography* (1949-1950 ed.) were the basis for this presentation. Additional data was entered as a result of searches in the work of Frederick Lewis Weis.

While the origin of the family is unknown, it is likely that the name came from Ros in Holderness in the East Riding of Yorkshire. There is apparently no connection with anyone named Ros from Kent or Essex, where the name derived from Rots, which is eight kilometers from Caen in Normandy, France.

PIERS[S] DE ROS was presumably dead by 1130, having died before his father-in-law. He married ADELINE[S] ESPEC, youngest of three sisters and coheirs of Walter[T] Espec, Lord of Helmsley (or Hamlake) in the North Riding of Yorkshire, and Ware, Northumberland. She died before her brother.

ROBERT[R] DE ROS died in 1162 or 1163. He married SYBIL[R] DE VALOGNES, who married second, about 1166, William de Percy, who gave 400 marks for the marriage and died in 1174 or 1175; she married third, in 1181 or 1182, Ralph d'Aubigny, who died before Michaelmas 1192, brother of William[Q] d'Albini of Belvoir. She was living in 1212, and possibly in 1218, and was buried at Nun Appleton Priory.

EVERARD[Q] DE ROS, who was still a minor in 1166, when his "pedagogue" William witnessed his father's confirmation to Rievaulx, died before Michaelmas, in 1183. He married ROESE[Q] DE WARTER, first sister and in her issue sole heir of Robert, and daughter of William Trussebut, Lord of Warter in the East Riding of Yorkshire, by Aubreye de Harcourt. Concerning the Trussbut inheritance one should consult the *Rolls of the King's Court*, 1194-95 [Pipe Roll Society], p. 12. Roese was said to be aged 34 in 1185, and to have two sons, the elder aged 13. She was living in the summer of 1194 and died before Michaelmas 1196.

ROBERT[P] DE ROS, "Furfan" or "Furson" (which nickname is unexplained), a minor in 1185, retired from secular life before 23 Dec. 1226, when his son did homage for his lands, died in 1227, and was buried in the Temple Church in London. He married early in 1191 ISABEL[O] OF SCOTLAND, widow of Robert de Brus, son of Robert de Brus II; she was the illegitimate daughter of William the Lion, King of Scotland, by a daughter of Richard Avenal.

Sir WILLIAM[O] DE ROS died probably in 1264, and was buried at Kirkham. He married LUCY[O] FITZ PIERS, who was said in Dugdale's *Baronage* [1:547], citing Glover, Somerset Herald, to have been a daughter of "Reginald Fitz-piers of Blewlebeny in Wales." However, said Cokayne [*CP*, 11:94h], if she was a member of this family she was presumably a sister of Herbert Fitz Piers and of his brother and heir Reynold Fitz Piers, and daughter of Piers Fitz Herbert, lords of the honor of Brecknock, whose castle was at Blaenllyfni. Piers Fitz Herbert married in 1203, and his son Reynold did not marry until 1249. Lucy was living during Michaelmas term in 1266.

ROBERT[N] DE ROOS, born in Helmsley, Leicestershire, about 1223, died 16 June 1285, and was buried at Kirkham, with his bowels buried at Belvoir and his heart at Croxton Abbey. His *inquisition post mortem* was dated 27 June 1285. He married between 5 June 1243 and 17 May 1244 ISABEL[N] D'ALBINI of Belvoir Castle, Leicester, who died 15 June 1301, and was buried at Newstead, near Stamford. In 1285 her age was given both as 50 and 52; she had been raised at Windsor with the other wards of the king.

Sir WILLIAM[M] DE ROOS, 1st Lord Ros, of Helmsley, born say 1255, died 15 Aug. 1316, and was buried at Kirkham. He married in 1287 MAUD[M] DE VAUX of Preston, Lincolnshire, younger daughter, and in 1287 coheir, of John de Vaux (and his wife Sybil) of Preston in Lincolnshire and Walton in Norfolk, son of Sir Oliver de Vaux, who married Petronell de

Creon [Watney, *Wallop Family*, 790]. She probably died before her husband and was buried in Pentney Priory, Norfolk, with her bowels buried in the wall at Belvoir.

8. WILLIAM[L] DE ROOS, 2nd Lord Ros, died 3 [Cokayne, *CP*, 11:99] Feb. 1342/3 (not in Brittany about 1 Aug. 1359, as shown by Weis [*MCS5*, 1:5]), and was buried at Kirkham.

He married before 25 Nov. 1326 MARGERY[K] DE BADLESMERE*, who died shortly before 22 [*CP*, 11:99] Oct. 1363, eldest of the four daughters of Bartholomew de Badlesmere, having been called aged 32 in 1338. This marriage brought him considerable estates in England and Ireland. Her marriage as widow was granted in March 1342/3 to Robert de Ferrers, and dower was assigned to her in April, but she married second (under a royal license dated 6 March 1350/1 allowing her to marry whomever she wished as long as he was in allegiance to the king) Sir Thomas de Arundel, who was killed apparently in a disturbance at Cockfield, Suffolk. She married third, probably as his third wife, Sir John Avenel, the king's lieutenant in Brittany, who died in Brittany about 1 Aug. 1359; she was suing for divorce in April 1355.

Of Hamelake Castle, Yorkshire, William had writ for the livery of his inheritance on 20 Aug. 1316, having occupied Wark Castle in Aug. 1310 and been summoned to the Archbishop's councils in 1314 and 1315 with his father. He had also been admitted a banneret of the King's household on 2 Nov. 1315. Summoned for service in Scotland from 1316-1319, in 1322, 1323, 1327 and 1335, he had also undertaken to defend Wark in Dec. 1316 (selling it to the Crown in 1317), and to join the Warden of the March with more men. In Jan. 1317/8, as joint commander, he received the surrender of Knarlsborough. He remained loyal during the Earl of Lancaster's rebellion against King Edward II in 1321-1322. He was among the magnates who guaranteed in person the terms of the surrender of Berwick in 1333.

He was summoned to Parliament from 20 Nov. 1317 until 21 Feb. 1339/40. In July 1324 he served as Joint Warden of the Yorkshire coast, and in Dec. he served in Gascony. He was appointed by Prince Edward's government as Sheriff of Yorkshire in Nov. 1326, and was one of two representing the barons who went to Kenilworth in Jan. 1326/7 to announce to King Edward II that he was being deposed. He then served as a member of the Council of Regency in Feb. In Nov. 1327 he was commissioned to negotiate peace with the Scots, and he served in the same capacity with France in Feb. 1329/30. During King Edward III's absence in Flanders, in 1337-1338, he was one of the commissioners to preserve the peace of England.

In Sept. 1340 he was appointed one to keep Edward Balliol informed of the intentions of the English parliament. In Nov. 1341 he was part of the defense of Newcastle against the Scots, and in Dec. 1342 he was ordered to Brittany.

The Patent Rolls show he was appointed to many local offices in Yorkshire, Lincolnshire, Norfolk and Northamptonshire.

Children, all but Maud and Alice mentioned by Cokayne [11:99c], Maud and Alice by Weis [*AR7*, 54:35]:

     i.   Margaret[K], m. Edward de Bohun, younger son of Humphrey de Bohun, Earl of Hereford.

    ii.   Sir William, b. Frieston, Lincs., 19 May 1329; d. overseas before 8 May 1352; m. before 8 May 1341 Margaret de Neville, dau. of Ralph de Neville, 2nd Lord Neville of Raby (no issue); she m. (2) Henry de Percy, K.G., who d. 19 Feb. 1407/8 (mother of "Harry Hotspur" Percy).

  iii. Elizabeth, m. William la Zouche, 1st Lord Zouche of Haryngworth, who
    d. 23 April 1382
  iv. Alice, d. before 4 July 1344; m. Nicholas de Meinell, 1st Baron Meinell
    of Whorlton, who d. before 20 Nov. 1341.
* v. Maud, b. c. 1331; d. 9 Dec. 1388; m. John[K] de Welles, who d. 1361.
  vi. Sir Thomas, b. Stoke Albany, Northants., 13 Jan. 1336/7; Uffington,
    Lincs., 8 June 1384; m. (royal license 1 Jan. 1358/9) Beatrice[J] de
    Stafford (dau. of Ralph de Stafford, Earl of Stafford, and Margaret de
    Audley, dau. of Hugh de Audley, Earl of Gloucester), widow of
    Maurice Fitz Maurice, Earl of Desmond, who d. 1358; she d. April
    1415, having m. (3) by 20 Aug. 1385 Sir Richard de Burley, who d. 23
    May 1387.

§ § §

DE SAINT PIERRE

This name was also commonly Saint Peter or Sancto Pietro, as well as Sampier, in the
records. Descendants used the name Bunbury [*Burke's Peerage* (1939), 434].

1. URIAN[L] DE ST. PIERRE (or SEYNPERE), called son of John, son of William (who
entered England with King Richard I), was the subject of an inquisition post mortem of 28
Edw. I (1299-1300).

  He married first IDONEA[N] DE MALPAS[+], who had a fourth of the barony of Malpas when
it was partitioned in 44 Hen. III (1259-1260).

  His second wife may have been Margaret, who married second, 24 Edw. I (1295-1296),
Ralph Basset.

  According to Ormerod [2:596], he was the first to set up the standard of Prince Edward
in the Earldom of Chester after the prince's escape from Simon de Montfort, and seized
Beeston Castle on the prince's behalf in 1265.

  Children [*Vis. Shropshire 1623*, 424]:
 2. i. John[K], m. Katherine.
    ii. David.
   iii. Johanna, m. Hugo Dutton.

2. JOHN[K] DE ST. PIERRE died on the Thursday after the Feast of St. Lucy the Virgin 18
Edw. I (1289-1290).

  He married KATHERINE, who was living 21 Edw. I, and was perhaps the daughter of
Thomas Dutton [Ormerod, *Chester*, 2:598; *Vis. Shropshire 1623*, 424].

  He was granted one-half of the manor of Bunbury by Isabella Burnel, his cousin. He
also held most of Beeston, a fourth of Bikerton, and a moiety of Horton. His properties had
a yearly value of one hundred shillings.

  Children, listed by Ormerod:
   i. David[J], of record 5 Edw. I (1311-1312); ancestor of Roger Horton.
   ii. Urian, l. 12 Edw. I (1283-1284); m. Isolda, who was of record as a widow
    5 Edw. II (1311-1312) and 3 Edw. III (1329-1330).
* iii. Elen[na], m. (contract 9 Edw. II [1315-1316]) Philip[J] de Egerton.

§ § §

SAVAGE

The research on this line was based at first on George Ormerod's *History of Chester* [1:718, 2:711-718]. Clifton, the manor house of later generations of this line, was later called Rock-Savage. Ormerod described the house as a "sumptuous building" erected by Sir John Savage in 1565. John, Constable of Cheshire and Baron of Halton, gave Clifton to Galfrid or Geffrey[P] de Dutton of Dutton, younger son of Hugh Dutton, during the reign of King Henry II (1154-1189). Geffrey's posterity were known as the Lords of Chedle.

1. Sir JOHN[M] SAVAGE was of Stennesby, Derbyshire, according to an undated deed of about 1206 in the pedigree of Savage of Clifton in Rylands' edition of *The Visitation of Cheshire, 1580*, p. 203.

He married AVICE[M] WALKINGTON, daughter and heiress of that family, whose arms were *Gu. a chev. bet. 3 martlets Arg.*

Son and heir, from the pedigree:

    2.   i.   John[L], knight.

2. Sir JOHN[L] SAVAGE was next in the pedigree of Savage of Clifton.

Son and heir:

    3.   i.   Robert[K], knight.

3. Sir ROBERT[K] SAVAGE was next in the pedigree of Savage of Clifton.

Son and heir:

    4.   i.   John[J], d. 1386; m. about 1376, as her second husband, Margaret[J] Daniell (or Danyers).

4. Sir JOHN[J] SAVAGE was listed as the fourth generation in the pedigree of Savage of Clifton [Rylands' *Vis. Cheshire 1580*, 203]; he died in 1386.

He married about 1376, as her second husband, MARGARET[J] DANIELL*, who died 6 Hen. VI (1427-1428), daughter and heir of Sir Thomas Daniers, Lord of Bradley and Clifton. She had married first, in 1369, John Ratcliffe, who died leaving no issue. She married third, in Nov. 1388, Piers Legh of Maxfield, younger son of Robert[K] Legh of Adlington.

She inherited all her mother's lands. Having survived all her husbands, as a widow she gave the moiety of Gropenhall to her son Piers in 4 Hen. IV (1403). To her son John[I] Savage she gave the liberty to bear her arms, deeded to her by her father.

Children, by second husband, surnamed Savage:

    5.   i.   John[I] Savage, d. 1 Aug. 1450; m. (1) Maude[I] Swynnerton, m. (2) Elena (–) de Haryngton.

           ii.   Elizabeth.

           iii.   Blanch.

           vi.   Margaret, poss. dau., m. 1419 John Dutton (who d. 1445), second son of Sir Piers Dutton of Dutton; they were ancestors of President George H.W. Bush [Roberts' *Ancestors of American Presidents*].

Children, by third husband, surnamed Legh:

           v.   Piers, ancestor of the Leghs of Lime in Maxfield hundred.

           vi.   John, escheator of Cheshire 1435, ancestor of the Leghs of Ridge nigh Maxfield.

5. Sir JOHN[I] SAVAGE, of Clifton, Cheshire, died 1 Aug. 1450.

He married first, about July 1401 [Roskell, 3:480], MAUDE[I] SWYNNARTON*, widow of Humphrey de Peshale and William[H] de Ipstones [Weis, *MCS5*, 98A:9]. She brought him the manor of Barrow. This marriage caused a feud between the Savages and the Peshalls, involving suits over her estates as well as violence [Roskell, 4:480].

He married second, by 1428, Elena, widow of James de Haryngton.

He fought at Agincourt in 1415, and was knighted in 1416.

Children, listed by Ormerod, the last four not listed by Rylands [*Vis. Cheshire*]:

     i.   Parnell[H], m. Reynold Leigh of Blackbrooke.
     ii.   Anne, m. Charles Nowell.
     iii. Beatrix, m. Sir Hamnett Carrington, heir to Sir Thomas his brother.
     iv. Blanche, m. Sir Thomas Carrington; no issue.
     v.   Maude, m. Sir Thomas Booth of Barton in Lancashire.
     vi. Alice, m. Sir Henry Bold.
6.   vii. John, son and heir, d. 29 June 1463; m. Eleanor (or Elizabeth)[G] Brereton.
     viii. Ellin, m. Peter Warburton.
     ix. William.
     x.   Arnold, m. Elen, dau. of William, son of Sir Richard de la Lee juxtà Bacford.
     xi. George.
     xii. Roger.

6. JOHN[H] SAVAGE, Esquire, of Clifton, Cheshire, died 29 June 1463, aged 53.

His wife was not named in the Savage pedigree by Ormerod, but was identified by him in 3:89 as ELEANOR[G] (or Elizabeth) BRERETON* [Rylands' *Vis. Cheshire 1580*, 203].

Children, listed by Ormerod:

7.   i.   John[G], son and heir, m. Katharine[G] Stanley.
     ii.   Margery, m. (1) 1442 Edmund Legh of Baggiley in Cheshire [Ormerod, 1:551], m. (2) 1477 Thomas Leycester of Nether Tabley, Esq., as his second wife.
     iii. Margaret, m. (1) John Maxfield, m. (2) perhaps Randle Mainwaring of Carincham, third son of Randle Manwaring of Over Poever [however, Weis in *MCS5*, 98A:10, stated this second marriage needs proof; the pedigree of Savage of Clifton in Rylands' *Vis. Cheshire 1580* (203-204) lists Margaret as wife of Sir William Stanley of Hooton].
     iv. Jane, m. John Hanford [Honford?] of Hanford [Rylands, 203].

7. Sir JOHN[G] SAVAGE, Sr., K.G., of Clifton, Cheshire, born about 1423 (aged 40 in 1463 [Earwaker, 1:188]), died 22 Nov. 1495 [Weis, *AR7*, 57:37 and 233:37], aged "73," and was buried at Macclesfield.

He married KATHERINE[H] STANLEY*, sister of Thomas Stanley, 1st Earl of Derby, and heiress of the manor of Camden [Faris, *PA2*, 323].

He was knighted in 1477 and fought at Bosworth in 1485.

Children, listed by Ormerod, with additions from Rylands' *Vis. Cheshire 1580* [204]:

     i.   Sir John[F], K.G., son and heir, slain at Boulogne in 1492; m. Dorothy Vernon, dau. and heiress of Ralph Vernon of Shipbrook; he was in charge of the left wing at Bosworth Field as a supporter of Henry VII.
     ii.   Thomas, d. 1508, bur. York; Archbishop of York 1501.
     iii. Sir Humfrey.
     iv. Lawrence.
     v.   James.

vi. Sir Edmund (or Sir Edward), m. 1538 Mary Sparke, daughter and heir of William Sparke of Surrey, and widow of Roger Legh del Ridge nigh Maxfield; knighted at Leith, Scotland, 11 May 1544.

vii. Sir Christopher, d. 1513; m. Anne Stanley (dau. of Sir John Stanley of Elford), his cousin; lord of manors of Aston Subedge, Camden, Burlington and Westington, Gloucs. [Weis, *AR7*, 57:38].

viii. William.

ix. George.

x. Sir Richard.

xi. Ellen (or Elenor), d. 1492; m. 1467 Sir Peter (or Piers) Legh of Lyme, Cheshire, who became a priest and d. Lyme in Handley 11 Aug. 1527.

xii. Katharine, m. (lic. 4 Nov. [Weis, *AR7*, 233:38]) 1479 Thomas Legh, Esq., who d. Adlington, Cheshire, 8 Aug. 1519 [*MCS5*, 106:12].

* xiii. Margaret, m. (1) John[F] Honford of Honford, Cheshire, who d. c. 1485, m. (2) Sir Edmund Trafford of Trafford in Lancashire, who d. 1513 [Earwaker, *East Cheshire*, 1:63, 70].

xiv. Alice, m. Roger de Pilkington of Lancashire.

xv. Elizabeth, m. John Leeke (or Leake [Rylands, 204]), son of William Leeke of Langford, Derbyshire.

§ § §

DE SCALES

This family is not related to that of Hardwin de Scalers, or Deschalers, of Hertfordshire, Cambridgeshire and Yorkshire [*CP*, 11:496e].

The material below has been drawn from an article by Michael J. Hughes in Appendix J, "The Descent of Scales," in Cokayne [*CP*, 11:J:152-154] as well as the material on pages 496-503 of volume 11.

Sir ROGER[S] DE SCALES I died before 1198, when his son Robert was in possession of Wetherden, Suffolk. He married MURIEL[S], who may have been a daughter of Geoffrey de Lisewis [*CP*, 11:497f].

ROBERT[R] DE SCALES I may have been dead by Michaelmas 1201, when a Roger de Scales possessed Wetherden. He married ALICE[R], who may have been a sister of Margaret, wife of Will. de Wichenton, Sr. [*CP*, 11:498b].

Sir ROGER[Q] DE SCALES II died before 25 June 1215. He married first Margery de Beaufou [*CP*, 11:J:152], a coheir of Fulk de Beaufou. He married second Maud, who survived him and married second William de Beauchamp.

ROBERT[P] DE SCALES II died before 23 Jan. 1250. He married ALICE[P] DE ROUCESTRE, daughter of William and sister of William [*CP*, 11:J:153] and Piers de Roucestre of Newsells, Hertfordshire, and Rivenhall, Essex.

ROBERT[O] DE SCALES III, born in Newselles, Herefordshire, died before 20 Jan. 1267. He married CLEMENCE[O], who survived him. In 1267 she paid a fine to have the wardship of his land and heir, and license to marry as she wished. She married second Roger de Vaux.

Sir ROBERT[N] DE SCALES IV, 1st Lord Scales, born in Middleton, near Lynn, Norfolk, died before 4 Sept. 1305. He married ISABEL[N] DE BURNEL [*CP*, 11:500l], who died before 26 July 1333.

7. Sir ROBERT[M] DE SCALES, who was aged 26 or more at the time of his father's death in 1305, died on or before 10 Oct. 1335.

He married EGELINE[M] COURTENAY, who died on or before 10 Oct. 1335. She has been identified as a sister of Hugh de Courtenay, Earl of Devon, and daughter of Sir Hugh de Courtenay, of Okehampton in Devon, by Eleanor le Despenser (who was living in March 1314/5), daughter of Hugh le Despenser, lord le Despenser [CP, 11:501i; cf. BP, 1:833]. Sir Hugh de Courtenay was son and heir of John de Courtenay of Okehampton, who died 3 May 1274, by Isabel de Vere, who was living Feb. 1298/9, daughter of Hugh de Vere, Earl of Oxford. John de Courtenay of Okehampton was son and heir of Robert de Courtenay of Okehampton, who died 26 July 1242, by Mary de Reviers (or de Vernon), 5th Earl of Devon. Hugh de Courtenay, Earl of Devon, was born about 1275, died 23 Dec. 1340, and was buried at Cowick near Exeter 5 Feb. 1340/1, having married in 1292 Agnes St. John of Basing, Hampshire, who died 11 June 1345 and was buried at Cowick.

On 8 Oct. 1305 Edward I took his homage and commanded the escheator to give him seisin. He was summoned to Parliament from 3 Nov. 1306 to 14 March 1321/2. Knighted Westminster with Prince Edward on 22 May 1306, he was summoned on 18 Jan. 1307/8 to attend the Coronation of Edward II, and was summoned against Robert le Brus in 1308, and against the Scots from 1315 to 1323.

In 1314 he granted a well to the Friars Minors of Lynn. In 1319 he was a commissioner of oyer and terminer in Norfolk. In 1321 he was forbidden to attend the convention of peers at Doncaster.

Children [CP, 11:501-502; Weis, AR7, 222:34]:

    i.   Robert[L], b. c. 1311; d. 13 Aug. 1369; m. before 6 May 1335 Catherine de Ufford, dau. of Robert de Ufford, 1st Earl of Suffolk, by Margaret de Norwich, dau. of Walter de Norwich [CP, 14:572].

 * ii. Isabella, d. 6 Sept. 1361; m. John[L] de Sudeley, Lord Sudeley of Sudeley, Gloucs., who d. on or before 19 Feb. 1340.

§ § §

DE SEGRAVE

This pedigree was initially developed from Cokayne's *Complete Peerage* [11:596-605].

1. HEREWARD[N] OF SEGRAVE was of Leicestershire, England, before 1166.
Child, mentioned by Cokayne:

 2.   i.   Gilbert[M], prob. d. before Michaelmas 1201; m.

2. GILBERT[M] HEREWARD DE SEGRAVE died probably before Michaelmas of 1201.
His wife is unknown.

In 1166 he held a quarter of a knight's fee, perhaps in Brailes, Warwickshire, of William, Earl of Warwick (who held no part of Seagrave, Leics.). In 1187-1188 he accounted for the revenues of the Abbey of St. Mary, Leicester, with Robert the canon. In 1196 he was a justice in eyre for Lincolnshire with Henry de Whiston. In 1197 he held land in the town of Leicester of Alice de Duston, and in 1198-1199 he owed 400 marks for aid in the King's War.

Child, from Cokayne:

 3.   i.   Stephen[L], d. Leicester Abbey 1241; m. (1) Rohese[P] Despenser, sister of Hugh Despenser, m. (2) Ida (sister of Henry de Hastings), who m. (2) without license Hugh Peche, and d. shortly before 2 March 1288/9.

3. STEPHEN[L] DE SEGRAVE died in Leicester Abbey in 1241.

He married first ROHESE[P] DESPENSER[+], sister of Hugh Despenser and daughter of Thomas[Q] Dispensator [*CP*, 14:576], and had with her a virgate of land in Barrow on Soar in frank marriage [*CP*, 11:601f, which cited Nichols' *Hist. Leics.*, 2:1:App. p. 113].

He married second Ida de Hastings, sister of Henry de Hastings, according to Dugdale's *Baronage* [1:672, which cited the collection of Robert Glover, Somerset Herald].

Before 1200 he witnessed a grant to Chaucombe Priory, and in 1206 he and William Picot were *custos* of the pleas for the crown of Leicestershire. In 1208 he was attorney for the Prior of the Hospital of Jerusalem. He received many grants of land from 1215/6 to 1233/4, and from Jan. 1217/8 he was constantly engaged in judicial duties. In 1220 he was one of those advising King Henry III to come to an agreement with Queen Berengaria, the widow of King Richard I. He was given custody of counties and castles in the early 1220s, and in 1229 was Chief Justice. On 28 April 1230, when Hubert de Burgh, the justiciar, traveled to France with Henry III, the government was entrusted to the Bishop of Chichester as Chancellor and Stephen de Segrave. In 1230 he was Sheriff of the counties of Buckingham, Bedford, Worcester, Leicester and Northampton. In April 1231 he was one of those who heard a dispute between the king and the citizens of London. In 1231 and 1232 he was appointed to resolve problems concerning Llywelyn ab Iorwerth, and in 1232 he was made Justiciar upon the fall of Hubert de Burgh, who was ordered on 8 Aug. to hand over Dover and the Tower of London to Stephen. In 1233, with Piers Bishop of Winchester and Robert Passelewe, he was advising the king on all matters of state, but he soon fell out of favor and was forced to account for receipts and expenses. He was removed from the Council, and reconciled with the king after 2 Feb. 1234/5, on making a heavy payment. In May-June 1236 he was back in favor, and in 1239 he was recalled to the Council, becoming the king's Chief Advisor in spite of his advanced age.

Children, two mentioned by Cokayne, with the last two from Baker [*Northants.*, 1:589]:

  i. John[K], d. 1229; m. Emma de Cauz, dau. and heir of Roger de Cauz.

4. ii. Gilbert, d. Pons in Poitou before 8 Oct. 1254; m. before 30 Sept. 1231 Amabil[M] de Chaucombe, who m. (2) Roger[N] de Somery, and was bur. at Chaucombe Priory.

  iii. Stephen, of Brinklow in Warks.

  iv. Eleanor, m. Robert Hovell.

4. GILBERT[K] DE SEGRAVE died in Pons in Poitou before 8 Oct. 1254.

He married before 30 Sept. 1231 AMABIL[M] DE CHAUCOMBE, who died about 1278, daughter and heiress of Robert de Chaucombe (or Chalcombe [*CP*, 14:586]), whose daughter Millicent married Ralph Basset. Amabil married second Roger[N] de Somery; she was buried at Chaucombe Priory.

On 4 Sept. 1232 he was given custody of the castle and manor of Newcastle-under-Lyme; he served in Brittany before 16 March 1232/3. Often of record, he continued service to the point that by Easter term 1251 he was sitting as third judge in the King's Bench, and by 1253-1254 he was with the king in Gascony.

According to Matthew Paris he, the Earl of Warwick and other English nobles were returning to England from Gascony when they were imprisoned by the citizens of Pons, who ignored a safe conduct granted by the King of France.

Child, from Cokayne:

5. i. Nicholas[J], b. in 1238; d. before 12 Nov. 1295, bur. Chaucombe Priory; m. Maud.

5. Sir NICHOLAS[J] DE SEGRAVE, the first Lord Segrave, was aged 16 on 17 Dec. 1254, died before 12 Nov. 1295, and was buried at Chaucombe Priory.

He married MAUD, who was possibly a member of the Lucy family [*CP*, 11:605d].

On 28 March 1259 he was recorded as going on a pilgrimage to Pontigny, and on 28 Oct. 1259 he crossed with the king to France. On 16 Sept. 1261 he was at Windsor to swear he would never oppose the king, but in May 1262 he did so in Parliament. In July 1263 he joined the king in Worcester, where he was knighted on 1 Aug. before going with the king to Wales. He was at the siege of Rochester with the Earl of Gloucester, Henry de Hastings and others in April 1264, and commanded the Londoners at the battle of Lewes on 14 May 1264.

On 4 Aug. 1265 he was wounded and taken prisoner at the battle of Evesham, and on 25 Oct. his lands were granted to Edmund, the king's son, but on 28 April 1266 he was coming to the king's court to make peace. On 1 July 1267 he was pardoned, and on 12 May 1270 he was going to the Holy Land with the king and Prince Edward. He was summoned to serve in Wales in 1276, 1277, 1282 and 1283, and on 28 June 1283 was summoned to Shrewsbury to treat with Dafydd ap Gruffudd. He served on various commissions from 1290 to 1294, and was summoned to Parliament at Westminster on 24 June 1295.

Children, from the pedigree and Cokayne [11:605]:

      i.   John[1], b. c. 1256; d. before 4 Oct. 1325, bur. Chaucombe Priory; m. Christiane de Plessis (or Plessy); Lord Segrave.

*   ii.   Eleanor, m. Alan[1] la Zouche, who d. 1313/4 [Weis, *AR*7, 31:29].

§ § §

✓ SIBTON

This section is from the Hopton pedigree in *The Visitation of Shropshire, 1623* [255]. Sibdon (now Sibdon Carwood) is in Shropshire.

1. WILLIAM[M] SIBTON was son of Roger Sibton, according to the *Visitation*.

He bore arms of *Vert*, an eagle displayed or debruised by a *bend componée argent* and *gules*.

A William de Sibbeton was enrolled as lord of Wistanstow and Sibton prior to 1346 [Eyton, 11:271].

Child:

*   i.   Margaret[L], m. Lawrence[L] Hawberke, Justice in 1357.

§ § §

DE SODINGTON

This data was extracted from G.W. Watson's treatment of Blount in Cokayne [*CP*, 2:196].

1. RALPH[L] SODINGTON of Sodington, Worcestershire, was among the subtenants of Mortimer of Wigmore.

Children, the first three mentioned by Watson [*CP*, 2:196], and the last two by "B.B." ["Pedigrees from the Plea Rolls," *Collectanea Topographica et Genealogica*, 1 (1834), 146]:

      i.   Ralph[K], was succeeded by his brother William.

  ii. Sir William, heir of his brother Ralph, d. 1301 [Nash, *Worcestershire*, 2:162; *Coll. Top. et Gen.*, 1:146; Burke's *Commoners*, 3:164].

* iii. Joan, living 1331; m. before Feb. 1294 Sir Walter[K] le Blount.

  iv. Eustachia, m. W'o de Doverdal.

  v. Marta, m. Reginald le Porter.

§ § §

DE SOMERY

Not only are the origins of this family unknown, but there is no proven link with de Somery families elsewhere.

Sir JOHN[P] DE SOMERY, at some time of Little Crawley, Buckinghamshire, England, died during the reign of King Richard I of England (1189-1199) [Cokayne's *Complete Peerage*, 12:110e]. He married HAWISE[P] PAYNEL, who was dead by 1194.

RALPH[O] DE SOMERY, lord of Dudley, Worcestershire, England, died between Michaelmas 1210 and Michaelmas 1211. He married MARGARET[O] MARSHAL, who married, secondly, Maurice de Gant alias Berkeley, who died in Portsmouth 20 April 1230 [see Grazebrook, *Colls. Hist. Staffs.*, 9:13]; she was living in 1242-43.

ROGER[N] DE SOMERY, Lord Dudley of Dudley, Worcestershire, died on or before 26 Aug. 1273 [Weis, *AR7*, 81:29]. He married first Nichole d'Aubigny. He married second AMABIL[N] DE CHAUCOMBE, who died about 1278, daughter and coheir of Sir Robert[O] de Chaucombe of Chaucombe, Northamptonshire, and the widow of Sir Gilbert[K] de Segrave.

4. ROGER[M] DE SOMERY, Baron Dudley from 1290, born 24 June 1255, died on or shortly before 11 Oct. 1291.

He married AGNES, who died 23 Nov. 1308. She was summoned to attend the coronation of Edward II in Feb. 1308.

He held Dinas Powys in Wales. By a writ dated 25 March 1282 (10 Edw. I), he and others were directed to take the field against the Welsh at once. He was involved in the Welsh War in 1287 when he was summoned personally to attend the King at Gloucester three weeks from the Feast of St. John the Baptist (which was on 15 July).

Children, listed by Grazebrook:

  i. Sir John[L], successor, b. 1280; d. 29 Dec. 1321; m. Lucy; no children, left his two sisters as coheirs.

  ii. Roger, slain c. 1306 by Walter de Wynterton.

* iii. Margaret, b. 1290; d. 1384; m. Sir John[L] de Sutton, Lord of Dudley Castle.

  iv. Joan, b. 1292, m. John de Botetourt, who was d. by 1322.

§ § §

SPERNOR

This line as presented has been taken from an ancestor table by Mr. Marlyn Lewis. Research in Warwickshire sources should help.

1. Sir JOHN[N] DURVASSAL, of Coughton in Warwickshire, died after 1241/2. He was steward to the Earl of Warwick and Justice of Assize.

Child:

2. i. Roger[M], d. after 1244/5; m. Eva (–) de Ewenlode.

2. Sir ROGER[M] DURVASSAL, of Coughton in Warwickshire, died after 1244/5 [Watney, *Wallop Family*, 290].
He married EVA (—) DE EWENLODE.
Child:
   3.   i.   Philip[L], m. Felicia[L] Camville.

3. PHILIP[L] DURVASSAL was of Coughton in Warwickshire [see *Wallop Family*, 290].
He married FELICIA CAMVILLE, daughter of Robert de Camvill, Lord of Arrow [Watney, *Wallop Family*, 2:290].
Child:
   4.   i.   Thomas[K], d. after 1278/9; m. Margeria.

4. THOMAS[K] DURVASSAL of Coughton in Warwickshire, died after 1278/9 [Watney, 290].
He married MARGERIA.
Child:
   5.   i.   John[J], d. after 1330/1; m. Sibilla[J] Corbicon of Sudeley, Warks.

5. JOHN[J] DURVASSAL of Coughton in Warwickshire, died after 1330/1 [Watney, 625].
He married SIBILLA[J] CORBICON of Sudeley in Warwickshire.
He was probably the John Durvassal of Spernovere (Spernall) who sued Peter Corbuson of Stodleye for land in Stodleye, according to the *de Banco* rolls of Michaelmas 20 Edw. III [Wrottesley, *The Genealogist*, new series, 10 (1893-1894), 31].
Child:
   6.   i.   William[I] Spernor, alias Durvassal, m. by 1400, Alice[I] de Sulney.

6. WILLIAM[I] SPERNOR, alias Durvassal, died in 1401.
He married, as her third husband, by 1400, ALICE[I] DE SULNEY [*TGM*, 15:119].
Of Spernoll in Warwickshire and Frankley in Worcestershire, he was chief steward of the estates of Thomas Beauchamp, Earl of Warwick, and Knight of the Shire for Warwickshire and Worcestershire.
Child:
   *   i.   Joyce (or Jocosa)[H], d. before 1435; m. William[H] Swynfyn.

§ § §

DE STAFFORD OF STAFFORDSHIRE

The material below has been drawn from Cokayne's treatment of the Stafford family in the *Complete Peerage*. The ancestry of Robert[S] de Stafford, immediately below, is to be found in Cokayne's treatment of the Tony family, as well as under Toeni, below.
An Erdeswick pedigree from an unidentified volume of *Miscellanea Genealogica et Heraldica* varies in the early generations.
ROBERT[S] DE STAFFORD, a younger son of Roger[T] de Toeni I [Cokayne, *CP*, 12:F:13], probably died in 1088, and was no doubt buried at Evesham Abbey of Wrottesley and Loynton in Staffordshire. He is said to have married an Avice de Clare, but she has not been traced.
NICHOLAS[R] DE STAFFORD died in or after 1138 and was buried at Stone in Staffordshire. His wife, known as MAUDE MOOLTE, was said to have been a daughter of an Earl of Chester, but no such person can be documented. She was buried at Stone.

ROBERT^Q DE STAFFORD last appeared in the Pipe Rolls in 24 Hen. II (1177-1178) and probably died between then and 31 Hen. II (1184-1185). He was buried at Stone with his wife. He married Avice, who was buried with him. There may have been another marriage.

MILLICENT^P DE STAFFORD was dead in Jan. 1224/5, and was buried with her husband at Stone. She married, before 1193, HERVEY BAGOT, who assumed the name of de Stafford upon assuming the barony on his marriage to the heiress of the title. He died before 25 August 1214, his wife surviving him. He was certainly descended from Bagot, who in 1086 held Bramshall under Robert de Stafford.

HERVEY^O DE STAFFORD died before 12 May 1237, and was buried at Stone. He married, in or before 1214, PERNELL^P DE FERRIÈRES, who survived her husband, and was buried at Stone.

ROBERT^N DE STAFFORD died before 4 June 1261. He married, first, ALICE^N CORBET, daughter of coheir of Thomas^O Corbet, 5th Baron of Caus, Salop, and married, second, Joan, who survived him.

NICHOLAS^M DE STAFFORD died at the siege of Deresloyn or Droslan Castle in Wales, apparently as a result of being crushed by a falling wall, on or about 1 August 1287, and was buried at Stone. In 1272 a Staffordshire jury stated he had been given by the King in marriage to a daughter of Geoffrey "de Langeley," probably the de Langley who died in 1274; apparently his wife predeceased him.

8.   EDMUND^L DE STAFFORD, 1st Baron Stafford, born 15 July 1273, died before 12 August 1308, and was buried in the church of the Friars Minors of Stafford.

He married, in or before 1298, MARGARET^L BASSET*. Margaret survived her husband and married, secondly, Thomas de Pype. She died 17 March 1336/7, and was buried at Tysoe, Warwickshire.

On 20 August 1294 he had done homage and was to have his lands; on 4 July 1297 he was about to go beyond the seas with the King. He was summoned to service against the Scots in 1298, 1299, 1301, 1302 and 1308. From 6 Feb. 1298/9 to 26 August 1307 he was summoned to Parliament [*DNB*]. In 1300 his seal was appended to the Barons' letter to the Pope. On 18 Jan. 1307/8 he attended the coronation of King Edward II.

Children:
- 9.   i.   Sir Ralph^K, b. 24 Sept. 1301; d. 31 August 1372; m. (1) Katharine^K Hastang, m. (2) Margaret^K de Audley.
-      ii.   Sir Richard, d. 13 Aug. 1380; m. (1) before 16 March 1339 Isabel^K de Vernon, m. (2) before 6 Nov. 1371 Maud, who lived in Lichfield in 1381, and was l. 1386.

9. Sir RALPH^K DE STAFFORD, K.G., lord Stafford and 1st Earl of Stafford, born 24 Sept. 1301, died 31 August 1372 and was buried at Tonbridge with his second wife, Margaret, at the feet of her parents.

He married, first, about 1326-1327, KATHARINE^K HASTANG*.

Lord Stafford married, second, before 6 July 1336, MARGARET^K DE AUDLEY*, who died 16 Sept. 1348, and was buried at Tonbridge, Kent.

On 6 Dec. 1323 he had done homage and was to have his father's lands. On 16 April 1325 he was in the King's service with his mother and stepfather, Thomas de Pype, and his own brothers in the company of Ralph Basset, 2nd Lord Basset of Drayton, Constable of Dover Castle. On 6 April 1327 he was summoned to serve against the Scots, and on 21 March 1331/2 he was in the commission of the peace for Staffordshire. In 1332 he sailed from Barton-on-Humber with Edward, son of John de Balliol, to invade Scotland. From 29 Nov. 1336 to 25 Nov. 1350 he was summoned to Parliament.

On 6 July 1336 a commission was established to investigate a complaint by Hugh[L] de Audley, who was then soon to be created Earl of Gloucester, that Ralph de Stafford and others (most of them relatives), broke into his close in Thaxted, Essex, carried away his goods as well as his daughter and heiress, whom Ralph married against her will, when Margaret was about twelve years old.

King Edward III intervened to protect Ralph, who, after making his peace, was given with Margaret a large part of the Gloucester inheritance.

On 29 Nov. 1339 he returned with the King from France, and on 22 June 1340 he was at the battle of Sluys. By 10 Feb. 1340/1 he was Steward of the King's Household. In 1342 he sailed to Brittany, taking part in the siege of Vannes, where he was taken prisoner, to be exchanged for de Clichon in the truce of Malestroit on 19 Jan. 1342/3. He was appointed with others on 20 May 1343 to treat with the Pope; in the same year he was sent to help raise the siege of Lochmaben Castle in Scotland. The next year he was in Gascony with a small force, and on 13 Sept. 1344 he participated in the tournament at Hereford as a challenger of the nobles of the county. On 23 Feb. 1344/5 he was appointed Seneschal of Aquitaine or Gascony, continuing in office until 15 March 1345/6. During 1346 he successfully defended Alguillon against John, son of King Philip of France. In August 1346 he was fighting in Crécy, and on 10 Oct. he was again Seneschal of Aquitaine, but by 16 March 1346/7 he was with the King before Calais. On 25 Sept. 1347 he was one of those empowered to arrange a peace treaty with the envoys from Philip de Valois.

On 6 Feb. 1347/8 he was licensed to make castles of his dwellings at Stafford and Madeley. He was a founding Knight of the Garter on 23 April 1348. On 4 July 1348 he was promised £573 towards his charges in the King's service in foreign parts, and on 6 Sept. 1348 he was granted for life 600 marks annually for his continued service with the King with sixty men-at-arms. On 29 August 1350 he was present at the naval battle off Winchelsea. On 5 March 1350/1 he was created the 1st Earl of Stafford. While engaged in France he was attacked in his billet, 26 Nov. 1359, by a band of Frenchmen, but managed to fight them off. He was involved in treaty negotiations with France in 1360. He spent part of 1361 in Ireland and crossed to France again with the King in 1369.

Child, by first wife [Weis, *MCS*5, 28:6; *AR*7, lines 32, 55; one daughter, according to Faris, *PA*1, 6]:

*   i.   Joan[J], m. Sir Nicholas[K] Beke.

Children, by second wife, listed by Cokayne, Weis [*Ancestral Roots*] and/or Norr [10]:

      ii.   Ralph, d. 1347; m. Maud (daughter and coheir of Henry [of Grosmont], Duke of Lancaster), who m. (2) William V, Duke of Bavaria, but d. 10 April 1362, aged 23, without issue.

*   iii.   Elizabeth, d. 7 Aug. 1375; m. (1) Fulk le Strange, Lord Strange of Blackmere, who d. 1349, aged 18, m. (2) Sir John[K] Ferrers, m. (3) Sir Reynold de Cobham, Lord Cobham, as his first wife.

     iv.   Joan, d. before 1397; m. (1) John Cherleton, Lord Cherleton, who d. 13 July 1374, m. (2) 1379 Gilbert[J] Talbot (widower of Petronilla[J] [or Pernel] Botiller), who d. 24 April 1387.

      v.   Hugh, d. Rhodes (now in Greece) 16 (or 13 [*BP*, 2:2680]) Oct. 1386, bur. at Stone; m. before 1 March 1350/1 Philippe de Beauchamp, dau. of Thomas de Beauchamp, Earl of Warwick, by Katharine, dau. of Roger[K] de Mortimer, 1st Earl of March; she d. 1386, bur. at Stone.

*   vi.   Katherine, d. 1361; m. 25 Dec. 1357 Sir John[J] de Sutton.

     vii.   Beatrice, d. 14 April 1415 [Weis, *AR*7, 9:32; m. (1) 1350 Maurice Fitz Maurice, Earl of Desmond, who d. 1358, m. (2) (license of 1 Jan.

1358/9) Thomas[K] de Ros, m. (3) by 20 Aug. 1385 Sir Richard Burley, K.G., who d. 23 May 1387.

§ § §

DE STAFFORD OF STANDON

The relationship between this line and the main line of the Staffords has not been determined definitively.

Sir WILLIAM[N] DE STAFFORD died after 1251/2; according to Watney [*Wallop Family*, 715], he was a son of Hervey Bagot and Millicent de Stafford. He married ALDITHA[N] VERNON.

Sir WILLIAM[M] DE STAFFORD was mentioned in Watney's *Wallop Family* [715]. He married ERMENTRUDE[P] DE FERRERS.

Sir ROBERT[M] DE STAFFORD was mentioned in *Wallop Family* [715]. He married GUNDREDA, who died in 1308.

4. Sir WILLIAM[L] DE STAFFORD of Standon, Bramshall and Amblecote, Staffordshire, died after 1318. Watney [715] states he was a son of Sir William de Stafford and Ermentrude Fitz Walkelin, that his grandfather was Sir William de Stafford of Bramshall, who was of record about 1251-1252 (and married Alditha Vernon), son of Hervey Bagot.

He married his cousin ISABELLA[L] DE STAFFORD, daughter of Sir Robert[M] de Stafford, above. She died after 1309.

He was M.P. for Staffordshire in 1318 [Watney, 715].

Children:

*   i.   Emma[K], of Sandon Bramshall and Amblecote, Staffs., m. Robert[K] de Pipe.
       ii.   John, m. (2) Margaret de Stafford [Weis, *AR7*, 55:33].

§ § §

STANLEY

The following treatment was based on Ormerod's pedigree of "Stanley of Alderly" in *The History of the County Palatine and City of Chester* (Helmsby edition, 1882) [3:577-578], as was extended in J.P. Earwaker's pedigree of "Stanley of Alderly, &c" in his history of *East Cheshire*, with additional data from Weis' *Ancestral Roots* and sources cited within, as well as James Croston's *County Families of Lancashire and Cheshire* (London: John Heywood, 1887), and then completely revised to follow the line as presented by W. Ferguson Irvine in *Transactions of the Historic Society of Lancashire and Cheshire*, volume 105.

George Ormerod [*Chester*, 2:411, with editorial matter in brackets by Thomas Helsby] states, "The Stanleys...are well known to be a younger branch of the house of Audley, descended from Adam de Stanlegh, brother of Lydulph [or Lyulph,] de Audley, who assumed [or rather, according to the custom of the times, obtained from its bestowal by others, and by long user,] the local name of a township in Staffordshire, afterwards granted to his son William. Adam, son of this Lydulph de Audley, by deed without date [about 1200 according to Irvine, *Trans. Historic Soc. of Lancs. and Cheshire*, 105:45], grants to this William, son of Adam de Stanlegh his uncle, all Stanlegh and Balterley, (with a proviso, that, if they cannot be warranted, an equivalent shall be given) in exchange for

Thalc, [of Talk o' th' Hill,] and subject to the yearly rent of 12d. payable on the feast of St. Michael. Among the witnesses occur Adam and Thomas, brothers of William de Stanlegh.

"[Adam de Stanlegh, son of William, (the latter most probably identical with the above-named grantee of Adam de Audlegh,) occurs 23 Edw. I. and was most probably father of] William de Stanlegh, heir male of William son of [the first] Adam de Stanlegh before mentioned. [This William's presumed father, Adam, most likely] settled in Cheshire [temp. Edw. I. William de Stanlegh settled at Storeton] in the reign of Edw. II. on marrying [Joan, or] Jane, one of the daughters and coheirs of sir Philip Bamville, of Storeton, kt. forester of Wirral, by whom she had issue John Stanley son and heir, who inherited, in right of his mother, the bailywick of the forest of Wirrall, and a share of the manor of Storeton, whose son, William Stanley, proved his right to the same in a plea to a quo warranto before Jordan de Macclesfield, justice in eyre to the earl of Chester."

James Croston attributed the family name to Stanleigh, or Stoneleigh, "an insignificant hamlet" about five kilometers southwest of Leek, Staffordshire.

J. Horace Round's *Peerage and Pedigree* deals with early tall tales of Stanley descent from the Earl of Mercia [2:22-36], while Irvine [105:45] has pointed out that the editors of *The Complete Peerage* were unaware of the collection of Stanley of Hooton muniments in the John Rylands Library in Manchester.

1. ADAM^Q DE STANLEY, born say 1125, died perhaps about 1200, was of Staffordshire. Irvine suggests [105:50] he may have married about 1160.

According to Eyton, Adam de Audley granted half of the manor of Bagnall to Adam de Stanley, perhaps about 1180 according to Irvine. This manor was in the hands of Sir Walter^O de Stanley in 1282-1283, and adjoined Stanley on the south.

Son and heir, mentioned by Irvine:
2.   i.   William^P, of Staffs.

2. WILLIAM^P DE STANLEY, born say 1170, died perhaps 1230, was of Staffordshire. He may have married about 1230.

According to Irvine [105:50], it was the William of this generation who exchanged Thalk for Stonelegh with his cousin Adam de Audley (Aldithlegh in Ormerod [2:415], who had married Mabel, daughter and heir of William, vel Henry de Stonelegh. Thus according to Ormerod William^P's father was not William^Q, but rather Adam^Q de Aldithley, who had a brother Lyulph de Aldithlegh; their father was given as Adam de Aldithlegh, als. Audley, of Staffordshire in the time of King Henry I. However, as Ormerod's editor noted, four generations would cover two centuries).

A William de Stanley appeared as one of fifteen witnesses to a charter given by Ranulf de Blundeville, Earl of Chester, in the period 1210-1217 at Macclesfield.

Children, listed by Earwaker:
3.   i.   Sir Walter^O, d. c. 1285; m.
      ii.   John, d. 1288; took Holy orders, presented c. 1267 with the valuable living of Astbury, and became a *Magister*.

3. WALTER^O DE STANLEY, born say 1215, was dead in 1285. He probably married about 1240.

He first appeared in the records in 1256, and in 1272 he was a juryman at the Staffordshire Assizes. In 1283 he sued for disseisin concerning a wood appurtenant to his free tenement in Stanley.

Children, mentioned by Irvine:
4.   i.   William^N, d. c. 1322; m. Joan^N de Bamville.

ii.   Benedict, involved in land transactions in Congleton 1280-1285.

4. WILLIAM[N] DE STANLEY, Lord of Stanlegh, Staffordshire, born say 1250, died about 1322 [Irvine, 105:53], certainly before 20 Edw. II (1326-1327).

He married at Astbury Church, 27 Sept. 1282 [Ormerod, 2:415], JOAN[N] DE BAMVILLE*, then aged 20, eldest daughter and coheiress of Sir Philip de Bamville, Lord of Stourton, Cheshire. Joan was a widow 19-20 Edw. II (1325-1327) and was living in 1334.

As found in Irvine [105:52-53], the *Calendar of Inquisitions post mortem* [2:306] contains: "[4 March 1284] Cradoc de Greves sworn and examined says that William de Stanleghe contracted marriage with Joan [daugher of Philip de Baumvill] saying 'Joan I give thee my troth to have and to hold thee for my lawful wife to my life's end,' and the said Joan gave him her troth by like words; it was before the death of the said Philip, on Sunday after St. Matthew two years ago, before Adam de Hoton and Dawe de Coupeland, at the church of Asteburi; for the said Philip, his wife and family, were at a banquet (*convivium*) of Master John de Stanleghe, and Joan doubting that her father would marry her to a son of her stepmother, on that occasion accepted the same William as her husband. Robert de Bebington and many others agree; Adam de Hoton, Dawe de Coupeland and others agree, except as to the form of the words used...."

On 1285, on his father's death, he sued as William son of Walter de Stanley his neighbors the brothers Robert, Stephen and John de Bagenholt, as well as others for insulting, wounding and illtreating the plaintiff at Stanley near Leak, claiming damages of £40. The Bagenholt brothers were recorded in the gaol delivery in Staffordshire in 1293 as being involved in many robberies with several others, including two sons of Sir Geoffrey de Gresley. Upon their escape they became outlaws.

In 1287 William and Joan apparently borrowed money from Robert de Whitmore, a Staffordshire man who was a merchant in Chester; the loan was still being repaid in 1324. In June 1327 Joan was receiving payments from Richard de Mascy of Tatton.

He appeared at the Staffordshire Assizes in two cases on 7 Jan. 1293.

He held the manor and bailiwick of Wirrall Forest, Chester. This was really the beginning of the Stanley family fortunes. A grant of twenty marks per annum, in lieu of the forestership, as a result of deforestation, in 35 Edw. I (1306-1307) can be attributed to this generation.

Children, listed by Earwaker and Irvine:

5.   i.   John[M], m. Emma.
       ii.   Adam.
      iii.   daughter, listed only by Earwaker, perhaps m. Roger Carswell.

5. JOHN[M] STANLEY, born say 1285, was of Stourton in Wirrall in Chester.

It is said that he married Mabel Hausket, daughter of Sir James Hausket of Stourton Parva, Cheshire. Irvine [105:54] calls her Mabel Hawkset, and states that no such family or person is associated with Stourton Parva during this period. The story seems to have originated with John Seacome's *Memoirs of the House of Stanley* (Liverpool, 1741), which contains a vague reference to Heralds Office, Chester. However, W. Ferguson Irvine [105:54] states that a charter (in the John Rylands Library, Manchester) dated in Sefton, Lancashire, 13 Feb. 1310 proves that John's father endowed him with the manors of Stanlegh and Over Elkeston in Staffordshire, mentioning John and his wife EMMA, who may have been a daughter of Walter Molyneux or of Sir Robert Lathom.

He entered into a recognizance of £20 with a John le Blount of Chester in 1313-1314.

Child, from Irvine:

6.   i.   William[L], d. April 1360.

6. WILLIAM^L DE STANLEY, born no doubt not earlier than 1310 [Irvine, 105:56], died in April 1360.

He married about 1330; according to *The Complete Peerage* he married Alice de Massy of Timperley, Cheshire [Irvine, 105:58], but Ormerod assigns this wife to Sir William^K de Stanley, and no evidence has been found to support either conjecture.

Records of his dealings with lands and houses in Storeton begin in 1333, the year he began to build a dovecote on his hall. His dealing with trespasses as chief forester of Wirral are accounted for in *Transactions of the Historic Society of Lancashire and Cheshire*, vol. 101.

Children, listed by Earwaker and Irvine [105:57], with the last from *Burke's Peerage* (1999), [1:815]:

   i. Alice, m. (settlement dated 1340) Randle de Rotern of Kyngeslegh.
 7. ii. Sir William^K, b. 1337; d. June 1398.
 8. iii. Sir John, d. Ardee, Ireland, 6 Jan. 1413-14; m. c. 1385 Isabel^J de Lathom.
   iv. Ellen, m. 1359 John fitz Stephen de Merton.
   v. Henry.

7. Sir WILLIAM^K DE STANLEY, born in 1337 [Irvine, *Trans.*, 105:57], died about 18 June 1398 [Irvine, *Trans. Historic Soc.*, 105:59].

He was Lord of Stourton in Wirrall, in Cheshire, and Stanlegh in Staffordshire.

He was knighted 26 Edw. III (1352-1353). He probably built Storeton Hall in 1360. Wirral was disafforested in 1376.

He was aged 50 or more when he gave evidence in the Scrope-Grosvenor trial in Chester on 3 Sept. 1386.

Barry Coward [*The Stanleys*, 2-3] called him a "middling landowner" who could leave a younger son little more than, in the words of one Thomas Wilson, "that which the cat left on the malt-heap." As W. Ferguson Irvine puts it [*Trans.*, 105:59], "While his younger brother...was pursuing his almost incredibly meteoric career,... William had to content himself with a grant from the king of the advowries of Cheshire, the office of the keeper of the royal park of Shotwick, and later [a poor] annuity of twenty marks."

Children, listed by Ormerod, with no evidence for the last two:

 9. i. Sir William^J, m. Margaret^J de Hooton.
   iii. Matilda (or Maud).
   iv. Henry.

8. Sir JOHN^K DE STANLEY, K.G., Sovereign of the Isle of Man, born about 1340, died in Ardee, Ireland, 6 Jan. 1413/4 (18 Jan. 1414 in Roskell [4:455], and about 28 Jan. 1414 in Irvine [105:57]), and was buried in Burscough Priory [Ormerod, 2:416].

He married about 1385 ISABEL^J DE LATHOM*, who died 26 Oct. 1414, according to her *inquisition post mortem*.

As a boy he probably heard much about the battles of Crécy and Neville's Cross, had personal knowledge of the Black Death, which decimated the population of Wirral in the summer of 1349, and the social unrest and the Peasant Revolt which followed [Irvine, 105:57].

His father gave him a small estate in Newton, near Macclesfield, on the Cheshire-Staffordshire border. In 1369 he was found guilty of an attack on Thurstaston Hall with his brother William, Sir Ralph de Vernon and others. Nine years later he was convicted of murdering his second cousin by marriage, Thomas de Clotton, gaining a pardon from Richard II through the help of Sir Thomas Tryvet, whom John joined en route for Aquitaine. However, in France he apparently had a good military experience, which led to his appointment in Ireland [Coward, 3], which was made more important by the fact that Robert de Vere, Earl of Oxford and Lieutenant of Ireland, never visited that place.

He was Lord of Lathom and Knowsley, served King Richard II about 1385-1386 as Lord Deputy of Ireland, and in 1388 he was warden of the east march. In 1389 he returned to Ireland as Justiciar (where he received the manor of Blake Castle in 1389 [Brydges' Collins's Peerage, 3:52]), where his campaigns of 1389-1391 enjoyed such success that the Irish leaders submitted to Richard II in 1395.

In 1394 he was justice of Chester. He was appointed Sheriff of the county of Roxburgh, Scotland, in 1396 and served as Captain of Roxburgh Castle for ten years.

As the House of Lancaster (the Duke of Hereford, afterwards King Henry IV) gained power he submitted, and on the accession of Henry IV, 29 Sept. 1399, was returned to Ireland as Lord Lieutenant. He also served as constable of Rokesbergh, Scotland, and of Windsor Castle, and as steward of the King's household.

Royal service did not provide riches. Knighted by Edward III, he received a cash annuity of 100 marks annually from Richard II, and in 1397 he bought three estates in Cheshire (Bidston, Moreton and Saughall Massie) from John Lestrange. The bulk of his wealth was derived from his wife's inheritance, for at the death of a niece about 1388 she was heir of extensive Lathom estates in the Hundred of West Derby, Lancashire. He must have been acquainted intimately with the dissatisfaction of northerners over the reign of Richard II; while he apparently did not take sides over Bolingbroke's usurpation there was no break in his record of public service. Soon after 1399 he was granted the honor of Dungarvon to add to his profits, which enabled him to serve as Lieutenant in Ireland at a time when the Royal treasury paid its bills irregularly. Then in 1400 he was given the Cheshire estates of the Earl of Salisbury, who had been attainted, including Raby, Ledsham, Mollington, Torot, Chester, Claverton, Nether Bebington and Lee-by-Bretherton, and more in Flintshire.

According to Roskell [4:456], vituperative "attacks made...by contemporary Irish polemicists claimed that he had grown rich through venality and extortion." He did have ample income from official sources.

In 1403 he became steward of the household of the Prince of Wales, and from 1405 to 1412 he served as Steward of the King's Household, but it was not until 1408 that King Henry IV's position was assured, with the capture of the strongholds of Owain Glyndŵr. Stanley's support must have been valuable in suppressing the Percies and Lord Scrope as well [Coward, 4].

On 19 Oct. 1405 he was granted the Isle of Man for life, and on 6 April 1406 the grant from King Henry IV was made perpetual upon payment of two falcons to each king at his coronation. The family retained this power until the death of James Stanley in 1736 without male issue. Sir John built a fortified house in Liverpool to facilitate communications with Man, was created Knight of the Garter in 1413, and spent the final year of his life, after landing at Clantarf (near Dublin), 7 Oct. 1413, as Lieutenant of Ireland, where he "granted no protection to cleric or layman or to the poets of Ireland, for he plundered every one of its clerics and men of skill in every art on whom he laid hands and exposed them to cold and beggary. He plundered Niall son of Aed OhUicinn in Usnagh of Meath.... After this the Ui Uicinn made lampoons of John Stanley and he lived only five weeks till he died from the venom of the lampoons" [Coward, 4, cited Otway-Ruthven's Medieval Ireland, 347].

Children, listed by Ormerod:

10. i. Sir John[J], d. 1437; m. Isabel[l] de Harington.

ii. Henry, second son.

    iii.   Thomas, m. Matilda de Arderne, dau. and heir of Sir John de Arderne of Elford, Staffs. [Ormerod, 3:566], by Catherine Stafford [Brydges, 3:54], ancestor of the Stanleys of Pipe.

    iv.   Sir Ralph.

    v.   daughter, mentioned by Earwaker [2:602].

    vi.   daughter.

9. Sir WILLIAM^J DE STANLEY of Hooton, Cheshire, was Lord of Stanley and Storeton in Wirral, Cheshire, was aged 30 on 16 June 1398 and died 2 Feb. 1428 [Irvine, *Trans.*, 105:61].

He married as a child, about 1376, MARGARET^J (or Margery) DE HOOTON*, whose father died 14 Sept. 1396.

He succeeded to Hooton by right of his wife in 1396, and in 1397 received a grant of a life annuity of 100/- upon being retained for service for life. In Feb. 1399 he was commissioned to raise eighty archers and take them to Ireland in the king's train, but by 15 May 1399 he was the subject of an arrest warrant, probably as a suspected sympathizer to Henry of Lancaster. King Richard II surrendered at Flint Castle on 19 August 1399, and on Sept. 30 the reign of Henry IV began. By 28 Jan. 1400 William was of record as conservator of the peace in the Cheshire hundred of Wirral. By 22 Sept. 1401 he was recorded as a knight who had rendered homage.

He was in Ireland serving his brother as Lord Deputy in 1401, and helped build defences against the Welsh rebels of Owain Glyndŵr, and then in the summer of 1402 was engaged in a naval expedition at a wage of 2/- per day. However, he received a pardon for Percy's Rebellion 3 Nov. 5 Hen. IV (1403), having already been appointed a commissioner in Wirral on 11 Oct. His *inquisition post mortem* was dated 6 Hen. VI (1427-1428). He held the manor of Hooton in the Hundred of Wirral, as well as the manors of Great and Little Storeton, the bailiwick of the forest of Wirral [Ormerod, *Chester*, 2:447], and lands in Poulton-Lancelyn, Upton and Brumbrough.

Hooton was described as a township midway between Chester and Birkenhead, which occupied "a particularly beautiful view of the Forest Hills, the bend of the Mersey, and the opposite shore of Hale, and shaded with venerable oaks, which the Wirral breezes have elsewhere rarely afforded" [Ormerod, quoted by Croston, 5]. Sir William occupied Hooton when his father-in-law died in 1396.

Child, listed by Ormerod [2:416]:

11.   i.   Sir William^I, b. c. 1386; m. Blanche^I Arderne.

10. Sir JOHN^J STANLEY, K.G., first Baron Stanley, who was aged 28 in 2 Hen. V (1414-1415), died 27 Nov. [*BP*, 1:815] or early in Dec. 1437 [Roskell, 4:458]; the writ of *diem clausit extr.* was issued 14 Dec. 1437 [Hornyold-Strickland, 92].

He married by 1405 ISABEL (or Elizabeth)^J DE HARINGTON*, daughter of Sir Robert (or John) de Harington of Hornby, Lancashire, and sister of Sir William de Harington. This marriage to one of the leading Lancashire families indicated the family's rise in social status. By marriage he was allied with the Nevilles and Beauforts [Croston, 13].

He was Lord of Lathom and Knowsley, and Knight of the Shire for Lancaster in Parliament in May 1413 and Nov. 1414 [Roskell, 4:455], and was allowed by Henry V to retain his father's offices in Macclesfield, with their fees. He fought at Agincourt with a personal retinue of men-at-arms and archers, receiving his knighthood for his efforts. From 1416 he was increasingly in demand as an arbitrator [Roskell, 4:456]. He was constable of Caernarfon in 5 Hen. VI (1417-1418), and justice of Chester in 5 and 9 Hen. VI (1426-1427 and 1430-1431), constable of Caernarfon Castle in 1427, and Sheriff of Anglesey.

However, Coward stated that his royal service was confined to Henry V's French campaign in 1418, and that he spent much of his time after 1417 suppressing rebellions in the Isle of Man and codifying the laws there to solidify his sovereignty.

Hornyold-Strickland [93] states that a John Stanley, who died before 1485 (and was probable natural son of Sir John Stanley the brother of Sir Thomas Stanley, first Earl of Derby), married Elizabeth, daughter and coheiress of Sir John Harrington of Hornby (who was slain at Wakefield in 1460).

Children, listed by Ormerod:
12.   i.   Sir Thomas¹, d. 38 Hen. VI (1459-1460); m. Joan¹ Goushill.
       ii.   Richard, Archdeacon of Chester 1426-1432.
       iii. Edward, Archdeacon of Chester 1453-1461.
       iv.   Isabel (or Elizabeth [Brydges, 3:55]), m. (articles 10 March 1422 [Poynton deeds]) John de Warenne of Poynton.
       v.   Alice, m. Sir Thomas de Dutton, Lord of Dutton, Cheshire.

11. Sir WILLIAM¹ DE STANLEY, born about 1386, was living 4 Hen. VI, and died perhaps 6 Hen. VI (1427-1428), for his *inquisition post mortem* was dated that year.

He married BLANCHE¹ ARDERNE (daughter of Sir John Arderne of Aldford), who was of record as a widow 7 Hen. VI (1428-1429).

He was Lord of Stanley, Stourton and Hooton. He received a pardon for the Percy Rebellion on 3 Nov. 5 Hen. IV (1403), was a hero at the battle of Agincourt and knighted in 1415.

Children, listed by Ormerod:
       i.   Sir William^H, l. 1431; m. (1) Mary Savage, dau. of Sir John Savage of Clifton, m. (2) Alice de Houghton, dau. of Richard de Houghton of Houghton, Lancs.; Sheriff of Cheshire 2 Edw. IV, descendants shown in Bartrum's *Welsh Genealogies*, 1983 ed., vol. 10, Stanley charts.
       ii.   Elizabeth, m. by dispensation 1425 Thomas Poole of Poole, Esq.
       iii. Katherine, m. before 6 Hen. V (1418-1419) Ralph Arderne of Harden and Alvanley, Esq.
*   iv.   Isabel, m. by dispensation Robert^G Legh of Adlington.
       v.   Margery, m. Thomas Venables, Baron of Kinderton.
       vi.   George, possible son, l. 8-9 Hen. VI (1429-1431).

12. Sir THOMAS¹ STANLEY, Baron Stanley, K.G., of Lathom and Knowsley, died in Lent 38 Hen. VI (11 Feb. 1458/9 [Faris, *PA*2, 145], or 20 Feb. 1459 [Hornyold-Strickland, 95]). Writs of *diem cl. extr.* were issued 26 Feb. and 9 and 10 March following.

He married JOAN^H GOUSHILL*, daughter and heir of Sir Robert Goushill of Heveringham, Nottinghamshire, and widow of Thomas Mowbray, Duke of Norfolk. She was living in 1460.

In 1424 he was attacked by Sir Richard Molyneux in his father's tower at Liverpool; both were arrested after 3,000 men became involved, threatening to throw the Liverpool area into pandemonium.

He was knighted before 9 Hen. VI (1430-1431), when he was made Lord Lieutenant of Ireland for six years. He called a parliament in Ireland in 1432, and put down a rebellion against the English in 1435, when the English were engaged in France, taking Moyle O'Donel prisoner [Brydges, 3:55]. He was commissioned to arrest William and Thomas Poole, and John Hokes, for the rape of Isabel, widow of Sir John^H Botiller (of Butler of Bewsey), and to keep her safe. On 14 Dec. 1437 he was made constable of Chester Castle for life. By 1439 he was controller of the King's Household, and was benefitting from the generosity of Henry VI. He received annuities, land and local offices in Cheshire,

Lancashire and North Wales. In 26 Hen. VI (1447-1448) he was comptroller of the King's Household, and the next year he served as commissioner, helping to arrange a truce with the Scots, as well as the defence of Calais.

He was sent to Parliament for Lancashire from 16 Sept. 1627 to 30 June 1455, for a total of eight times, but was the target of growing opposition in the House of Commons, and in Oct. 1450 and April 1451 he was removed from the offices of justice and chamberlain of North Wales. Indeed Richard, Duke of York, had planned to imprison him while he was traveling through North Wales in Aug. 1450. When the Commons passed two Acts of Resumption in 1450 and 1451, he benefitted from one of the 186 exemptions to the first act, and suffered no worse than others from the second. By 1454 he had disassociated himself from the enemies of Richard, Duke of York, and by May and June of that year he was serving on York's protectorate council. Yet when the King recovered his position in 1455 Stanley was counted among his supporters, providing ten thousand men for the king at the battle of St. Albans on 22 May 1455.

Nonetheless he was elected to the Yorkist parliament the same year, and sat on a committee of the king's household appointed by Parliament. By August he was chamberlain of the royal household, and in Jan. 1456 he was exempted from another Act of Resumption. On 28 Jan. 1457 he was appointed to the council of Edward, Prince of Wales, and he attended the King's Council in 1457 and 1458.

On 20 Jan. 1455/6 he had been summoned to parliament as Lord Stanley [Brydges, 3:56]. He was Knight of the Garter in 1456.

Children, listed by Ormerod and Earwaker:

    i.   Sir Thomas[H], 2nd Baron Stanley and 1st Earl of Derby, aged 28 in 38 Hen. VI (1459-1460); d. Lathom 29 July 1504, bur. Burscough Priory in Lancashire; m. (1) after 10 May 1457 Eleanor Neville (sister of the Earl of Warwick [the King Maker] and dau. of Richard Neville, Earl of Salisbury), who was bur. St. James', Garlickhithe, London, m. (2), before Oct. 1473 [Faris, *PA*2, 361], as her fourth husband, Margaret Beaufort (dau. and heir of John Beaufort, Duke of Somerset, by Margaret Beauchamp [dau. of John Beauchamp, Lord Beauchamp of Bletsoe]), who had m. (1) before 18 Aug. 1450 John de la Pole (dissolved), m. (2) Edmund Tudor of Hadham, Earl of Richmond (by whom she was mother of King Henry VII of England), and m. (3) Sir Henry Stafford, son of Humphrey, 6th Earl of Stafford, and d. 29 June 1509, bur. Westminster Abbey; the victory over the Lancastrians at Towton in 1461 allowed him to survive, he betrayed Richard III at the battle of Bosworth in 1485, and she founded Christ's and St. John's Colleges, Cambridge.

    ii.   Sir William, K.G., of Holt Castle in Denbigh and Ridley, beheaded 16 Feb. 1494/5 on account of Perkin Warbeck's rebellion; m. Joyce Charleton, dau. of Edward Charleton, Lord Powys [Ormerod, 1:442 and 2:298], and the widow of Lord Tiptoft [Earwaker, 2:603]; "the richest subject for value in the kingdom" [Brydges, 3:57], instrumental in securing the crown for Henry VII at the battle of Bosworth, 22 Aug. 1485, had son William, whose dau. and heir Joan m. Sir Richard Brereton of Malpas [Brydges, 3:58].

    iii. Sir John, l. 1461 and 1476; d. before 1 Hen. VII (1485); m. Elizabeth de Wever, who d. Lent 1512, dau. and heir of Sir Thomas de Wever, Lord of Wever and Alderley, who m. (2) before 1 Hen. VII (before 22 Aug. 1485) Sir John Done of Utkinton.

iv.   James, d. c. 1485 [Croston, 38]; Archdeacon of Chester 1476, and Arch-
       deacon of Carlisle [Brydges, 3:56].
 v.   Elizabeth, m. (1) before 1432 Sir Richard Molyneux of Sefton, Lancs., who
       d. Blore Heath 23 Sept. 1459, m. (2) Thomas Strange.
*   vi.   Katherine, bur. Macclesfield Church, where there is a fine alter tomb for
       her and her husband; m. Sir John[G] Savage of Clifton and Macclesfield.
vii.   Margaret, d. c. 1481; m. (1) Sir William Troutbeck of Mobberly, Cheshire,
       who d. on the Lancastrian side at Blore Heath, 23 Sept. 1459, m. (2)
       Sir John Boteler of Bewsey, Lancs., Baron of Warrington, who d. 26
       Feb. 1463, m. (3) Henry Grey, Lord Grey of Codnor.

§ § §

LE STRANGE

ROLAND (or Roald)[Q] LESTRANGE (or Extraneus) was a tenant of Alan Fitz Fleald in 1122
when he witnessed, with other tenants, a charter of his lord to Castleacre Priory; he died
probably some time before 1158. He married MATILDA[Q] LE BRUN, daughter of Ralph[R] Fitz
Herlewin, alias Ralph de Hunstanton, and Helewisa[R] de Plaix, daughter of Hugh[S] de Plaix
of Bernham, Suffolk.

JOHN[P] LESTRANGE I, of Ness and Cheswardine, Shropshire, died before Michaelmas
1178. He married HAWISE.

JOHN[O] LESTRANGE II was dead by 20 Jan. 1233/4 [Eyton's Ant. Shropshire, 10:262; CP,
12:1:350], when his son gave homage. He married AMICIA.

JOHN[N] LESTRANGE III, Lord Strange of Knockyn in Shropshire, born say 1190, died in
Knockyn before 26 March 1269, when the king took homage from his son and heir, John.
He married LUCY[N] DE TREGOZ of Ewyas Harold, Herefordshire, who died in Knockyn after
1294.

ROBERT[M] LE STRANGE of Wrockwarden died perhaps in Litcham, Norfolk, on or before
10 Sept. [Eyton, Ant. Shropshire, 9:25] or 12 Oct. 1276 [CP, 12:1:341]. He married say
1250 ELEANOR[M] DE WHITCHURCH (or de Blancminster), of Blancminster, Norfolk, who died
about 1304, having married second Bogo de Knovill. Her father was William de
Blancminster.

6. FULK[L] LE STRANGE, 1st Lord Strange of Blackmere, was born about 1267 and was
dead by 23 Jan. 1323/4 [CP, 12:1:343].

He married ELEANOR[L] GIFFARD*, who died before her husband.

On 16 July 1289 it was ordered that he should have his brother's lands on the condition
of doing homage to the king when Edward I was next in England. In 1294 he was recorded
as going to Gascony, and from March 1298 until April 1323 he was summoned for service
against the Scots. In Feb. 1300/1 his seal was appended to the Barons' letter to the Pope.

He was summoned to Parliament from 4 March 1308/9 until 26 Dec. 1323. In 1312 he
adhered to Thomas Earl of Lancaster, and in 1315 he was pardoned some debts due from
his uncle Hamon for service in Gascony. He was appointed sénéschal of Aquitaine in 1322,
and the same year he was licensed to crenellate his dwelling in Whitchurch, Shropshire.
He was field commander of the forces of Edward I and Edward II in Scotland and France.

Children, listed by Weis [AR7, 29A:31], Cokayne [CP, 12:18], L'Estrange [Notes and
Queries, 199:98], as well as Le Strange Records [288]:

*   i.   Elizabeth[K], m. by March 1323 Sir Robert[J] Corbet of Moreton Corbet.

7.   ii.   John, 2nd Baron Blackmere, d. 21 July 1349; m. Ankaret^K Boteler, who d. 8 Oct. 1361.

      iii.   Maud, m. Bryan de Cornwall of Kynlet.

      iv.   Fulk, received Longnor from his father in 1322 [Eyton, 6:65], left infant daughters Joan (who m. John Careless or Carless), Eleanor (who m. Edward de Acton) [CP, 14:595-596] and Margaret, a nun of Lingbrooke.

      v.   Hamon, had Cheswardine in 1315 from John, and Betton from his brother Fulk.

7. JOHN^K LE STRANGE, 2nd Baron Strange of Blackmere, Shropshire, born about 1306, died 21 July 1349.

He married ANKARET^K BOTELER*, who died 8 Oct. 1361, having apparently married second Sir Thomas de Ferrers [CP, 12:1:343].

On 26 Feb. 1326/7 he had proved his age and done homage, and was to have seisin of his father's lands. He was summoned to Parliament from 23 Oct. 1330 to 10 March 1348/9. From 1332 he served in commissions at Salop, and in 1346 he was at Crécy and Calais.

Children [CP, 12:1:343-344, and Le Strange, 288]:

      i.   Fulk^J, b. c. 1330; d. of pestilence 30 Aug. or 2 Sept. 1349; m. c. 1346/7 Elizabeth^J Stafford (when she was under 13), who m. (2) Sir John^K Ferrers, who was slain in the battle of Nájera in Spain 3 April 1367 [Faris, PA2, 137], and m. (3) Sir Reynold de Cobham, Lord Cobham, as his first wife.

8.   ii.   John, b. 1322; d. 12 May 1361; m. Isabel^J Fitz Alan, who d. 29 Aug. 1396.

      iii.   Hamon, served at Crécy 1346, of record 1381.

      iv.   Eleanor (or Alianore), d. 20 April 1396; m. Reginald^K Grey, 2nd lord Grey de Ruthin.

8. JOHN^J LE STRANGE, 4th Baron Strange of Blackmere, born at Whitchurch 23 Jan. 1332 [Le Strange Records, 288 and 318], died 12 May 1361.

He married ISABEL (or Mary [CP, 12:1:344; Le Strange Records, 319])^J FITZ ALAN*, who died 29 Aug. 1396, having been known as the Lady of Corfham [Le Strange Records, 288].

He proved his aged in 1354, and on 30 Oct. of that year he was of record as having done homage. On 3 April 1360 he was summoned to Parliament.

Children:

      i.   John^I, b. 1353; d. 1375; m. Isabel^I de Beauchamp, who m. (2) William de Ufford, 2nd Earl of Suffolk.

*   ii.   Ankaret, heir of her brother's only dau. Elizabeth (who d. 23 Aug. 1383 [CP, 12:1:345]), b. 1361; d. Ascension Day 1 June 1413; m. (1) Sir Richard^I Talbot, m. (2) Thomas Nevill, Lord Furnivall.

§ § §

DE SUDELEY

This line was based on an ancestor table by Mr. Marlyn Lewis. Some of the sources given in Weis need to be noted, and consulted, including Atkins' Gloucestershire, 369; VCH Warwick, 5:70; Hist. Mon. St. Peter, Gloucs., 2:180; Publ. Pipe Roll Soc., n.s., 43, chart p.

lviii; Farrer's *Honours and Knights Fees*, 2:116; Parsons' *The Court and Household of Eleanor of Castile in 1290*, 48-50, and Salt, n.s., vol. 1945-46, 41-42.

This line should be studied in conjunction with de Beauchamp and de Ewyas.

RALPH[U] DE SUDELEY (son of Dreux, Count of Vexin, who died in 1035, and Godgifu, who died in 1055, daughter of Æthelred II, King of England, and Emma of Normandy), of Sudeley and Toddington, Gloucestershire, and Chilvers Coton, Warwickshire, died 21 Dec. 1057 [*CP*, 6:466, 9:128, 11:499-501, 11:D:109-110l, 12:1:411-414]. He married GETHA.

HAROLD[T] DE SUDELEY held his father's lands as well as Burton Dasset, Warwickshire.

JOHN[S] DE SUDELEY of Sudeley Castle and Toddington, Gloucestershire, appeared in the pipe roll of 1130. He married by 1130 GRACE DE TRACY, whose parentage is unknown [Weis, *AR*7, 222:27, cited Atkins, *Gloucestershire*, 369; *VCH Gloucs.*, 5:70; *Hist. Mon. St. Peter, Gloucs.*, 2:180, and Sanders, 85-86]. She was likely of the same generation as William de Tracy, bastard son of King Henry I [Weis, *AR*7, 222:27].

RALPH[R] DE SUDELEY was of age in 1135, and died in 1192. He married EMMA[P] DE BEAUCHAMP (Dugdale, *Baronage*, 1:428, assumed her father was William de Beauchamp of Elmley as Sir Bartholomew[O] de Sudeley held the manor of Fairfield in Belbroughton, Worcestershire, without service, it having been given in franc marriage to his ancestors [*CP*, 12:1:415p]).

RALPH[Q] DE SUDELEY died before 26 Feb. 1221/2. He married ISABEL[Q] DE STAFFORD, who was living 1242, and presumed to be the daughter of Maud de Stafford of Theddlethorpe, Lincolnshire [Weis, *AR*7, 222:29, cited Farrer, 2:116, which should be checked]. He is identical to that Ralph[N] de Sudeley who is found under de Ewyas as son of Ralph[O] de Sudeley and Emma[P] de Beauchamp.

RALPH[P] DE SUDELEY of Great Dassett, Warwickshire, later Burton Dasset, died on or before 19 March 1241/2. He married IMENIA, who was living in 1247, when she was said to be marriageable and "in the king's gift."

Sir BARTHOLOMEW[O] DE SUDELEY of Great Dassett and Chilvers Coton in Warwickshire, and Sudeley, Gloucestershire, died on or before 29 June 1280. He married JOAN, who was living in 1298.

JOHN[N] DE SUDELEY, Lord Sudeley, of Great Dassett, Warwickshire, and Sudeley, Gloucestershire, was aged 22 or 23 when his father died in 1280, and died on or before 18 April 1336. According to Cokayne, his wife is unknown [*CP*, 12:1:416].

9. BARTHOLOMEW[M] DE SUDELEY died before his wife, and in his father's lifetime.

He married MAUD[M] DE MONTFORT* of Beaudesert, Warwickshire, who died on or before 2 Oct. 1326. It has been suggested by Parsons' *The Court and Household of Eleanor of Castile in 1290*, 48-50, that she was descended from Alberic II, Count of Dammartin.

Child:

10.   i.   John[L], b. 1305; d. on or before 19 Feb. 1340; m. Isabella[L] de Scales.

10. JOHN[L] DE SUDELEY, Lord Sudeley of Sudeley, Gloucestershire, born in 1305, died on or before 19 Feb. 1339/40.

He married ISABELLA[L] DE SCALES*, who died 6 Sept. 1361.

In June 1326 his grandfather granted them the manor of Sudeley by fine; this was followed by a grant of the manor of La Grave in October.

Children, listed by W.L. Sheppard, Jr. ["Two Corrections for the New Complete Peerage," *Gen. Mag.*, 13:173-174], and *BP* [2:2758]:

*   i.   Joan[K], d. before 1367; m. (as his second wife) c. 1354 William[K] de Boteler, who d. Dec. 1361.

         ii.   John, only son and heir, d. 11 Aug. 1367.

iii.   Margery, b. c. 1337; d. by 14 May 1379; m. after 11 Aug. 1367 Sir Robert Massey; no issue.

§ § §

DE SUTTON

This line is based on the work of Jacobus and Weis, with additions from Cokayne's *Complete Peerage*, Ormerod's *Chester* and H. Sydney Grazebrook's "The Barons of Dudley."

HERVEY[Q] DE SUTTON was of Sutton-on-Trent.

ROWLAND[P] SUTTON was of Averam or Aram in Nottinghamshire, and married ALICE[P] DE LEXINGTON.

WILLIAM[O] SUTTON, born about 1215, died in 1268, seized of the manor of Worksop in Nottinghamshire. He married first Matilda, who was of record with her sister Alice in 1250. He married second Eva, who survived him and married second a Robert Paynell.

ROBERT[N] DE SUTTON, born about 1241, died 2 Edw. I (1273-74), seized of the manor and advowson of Worksop, Nottinghamshire, the manor of Sutton, Notts., and Aston le Walls and Byfield in Northamptonshire. Johanna was his widow.

5.   Sir RICHARD[M] DE SUTTON, born 29 Sept. 1266 [*BP*, 1:883], was living as late as 1346.

He married ISABEL[M] PATRIC* (widow of Philip Burnel, by whom she had no children), who was dead by 1318.

If Weis has been interpreted correctly, he stated that Sir Richard de Sutton was lord of Warsop, Sutton, Eakring and Cotham in Nottinghamshire, by right of his wife. However, Grazebrook differs. Sir Richard possessed Worksop and Aston le Walls, and brought Malpas, Shocklach and other lands in Cheshire to his descendants by his marriage.

In 1 Edw. II (1307-1308), Sir Richard de Sutton was permitted to settle the manor and advowson of Worksop, which was held of the king *in capite*, upon his son John de Sutton and Margaret de Somery, as it appeared that the manor of Aston le Walls would yield him about £20 yearly, and that his other lands guaranteed his ability to provide the feudal service due the crown.

Child:

6.   i.   Sir John[L], d. c. 1359; m. Margaret[L] de Somery.

6.   Sir JOHN[L] DE SUTTON, Lord of Dudley Castle, Staffordshire, England, from 1326, died about 1359.

He married MARGARET[L] DE SOMERY*, who died in 1384, the Baroness Dudley, sister and heir of John de Somery, who was born in 1278 and died 29 Dec. 1321.

From 10 to 13 Edw. II (1316-1320) he was engaged in wars in Scotland, and in 12 Edw. II (1318-1319) he was in the retinue of his brother-in-law, John de Somery.

He was accused of complicity in the rebellion of Thomas Earl of Lancaster against the king, and was extorted to give up all his right and interest in the castle and town of Dudley to Hugh le Despencer. In addition he gave up the manors of Sedgley, Swinford and Rowley-Somery, as well as other lands [H. Sydney Grazebrook, "The Barons of Dudley," 52], not obtaining restitution until Edward III became king.

He was knighted in 1326. In 20 Edw. II (1326-27), as Lord of Malpas, he acknowledged that he owed John de Charlton, Lord of Powys, £3000; his lands in Staffordshire stood as collateral.

Children:

   7.   i.   John^K, d. 1359; m. Isabel^K de Cherlton.

         ii.   Margaret, m. Sir Roger Hillary.

        iii.   Maud, possible dau., m. Ralph Jocelyn of Hyde Hall.

   7. JOHN^K DE SUTTON died on Friday before 23 Nov. 1359 [*CP*, 14:278]; the first *inquisition post mortem* was dated 1 Dec. 1359 [Grazebrook, 55].

   He married Lady ISABEL^K DE CHERLETON*, who died 10 April 1397, having married second Sir Richard Dudley, formerly Fisscher (or Fisher [*BP*, 1:883]), who became Baron Dudley in right of his wife and died before Easter 1382 [Montague-Smith, *TG*, 5:134].

   He was in the war against the Scots 7 Edw. III (1333-1334) and had letters of protection dated 8 April 1333 while he was in the retinue of Ralph Basset of Drayton.

   On 25 Feb. 16 Edw. III (1342/3) he was summoned to a council, which some have called a parliament [Cokayne, 4:479e].

   In 1350 he was a member of a force sent from England to relieve St. Jean d'Angely [Grazebrook, 54]. That year he was also summoned to Westminster to advise the king on defending England.

   When he died he held with his wife the vill of Dudley, the Castle of Dudley, the manors of Sedgley, King-Swinford, Rowley-Somery and Penn in Staffordshire, the manor of Aston in Northamptonshire, and other lands.

   Sir Richard Dudley and his wife Isabella sold the manors of Shocklach and Malpas about 1361.

Children, given by Grazebrook:

   8.   i.   John^J, b. c. 1338; m. (1) 25 Dec. 1357 Katherine^J Stafford, m. (2) Joan Clinton.

         ii.   Thomas, was with the Black Prince in France in 1369.

   8. Sir JOHN^J DE SUTTON, born about 1338, died probably in France about 1369.

   He married first, 25 Dec. 1357, KATHERINE^J STAFFORD*, who was born about 1340 and died by 25 Dec. 1361.

   He married second, after 1361, Joan Clinton (daughter of Sir John Clinton of Coleshill in Warwickshire), who was born about 1341 and had died by 1386, widow of Sir John de Montfort, who was of record 25 May 1361 [Faris, *PA2*, 122]. She married third, in 1370, Sir Henry ap Griffith of Wichnor in Staffordshire.

   In 43 Edw. III (1369-1370) he was on the roll of those at war in France.

Child, by first wife [Montague-Smith, *TG*, 5:131-139]:

   9.   i.   John^I, b. Coleshill, Warks., 6 Dec. 1361; d. c. 1396; m.

Child, by second wife:

         ii.   Joan, m. John de Cherleton, Lord of Powys, who d. 13 July 1374 [Weis, *MCS5*, 30:7].

   9. Sir JOHN^I DE SUTTON, of Dudley Castle, Staffordshire, born at Coleshill [Grazebrook, 61] in Arden in county Warwick, east of Birmingham, 6 Dec. 1361, died in 1395/6, according to an *inquisition post mortem* taken 10 March 1401 [Grazebrook, 62].

   Burke's Peerage (1999) [1:883] states that he married first ALICE, who died in 1392, a probable daughter of his guardian Philip le Despenser of Carlington.

   His wife, possibly a second one, has also been given as Joan, who was possibly daughter of John, Lord Arundel. The *inquisition post mortem* of wife Jane, who died on Monday in the fourth week of Lent, 1408, was taken in 1409.

He served in the King's Fleet under the Earl of Arundel when he came of age [Faris, *PA1*, 90].

An *inquisition post mortem*, taken in Cheshire 2 Hen. IV (1401), found he held the Castle of Malpas and half the castle of Shocklach, as well as other land [Ormerod, 2:601].

Son and heir:

   10.   i.   John^H, b. 1378/9; d. 1405/6; m. Constance^H Blount.

10. Sir JOHN^H DE SUTTON, of Dudley Castle, Staffordshire, born in Feb. or March 1379/80 [Faris, *PA2*, 122], died 28 Aug. 1406 [Faris, *PA2*, 123].

He married before 10 Dec. 1401 CONSTANCE^H BLOUNT* of Barton, Derbyshire, who died on Tuesday next before The Feast of St. Michael the Archangel in 11 Hen. VI (23 Sept. 1432). She was the childless widow of Hugh Hastings.

Children, listed by Grazebrook [64]:

   11.   i.   John^G, b. 25 Dec. 1400; d. 30 Sept. 1487; m. Elizabeth^G de Berkeley.
        ii.   Thomas.
       iii.   Humphrey, m. Eleanor Ross.

11. Sir JOHN^G DE SUTTON, alias DUDLEY, K.G., born 25 Dec. 1400, and baptized at Barton-under-Needwood, Derbyshire, died 30 Sept. 1487, having left a will dated 17 August 1487 [*P.C.C. 8 Miles*], and was buried in St. James' Priory, Dudley, while his monument was later moved to St. Edmund's, Dudley.

He married after 1422 ELIZABETH^G DE BERKELEY*, who died shortly before 8 Dec. 1478, and was buried in St. James' Priory, Dudley, widow of Sir Edward Cherleton, the last Lord Powys, who died 14 March 1420/1.

The first Lord Dudley, or Baron Sutton of Dudley, by 1423-24, he was a Knight of the Garter by 1459.

He carried the Standard at the funeral of King Henry V in 1422 (having served in France under him), and from 1428 to 1430 he was Lord Lieutenant of Ireland, succeeding Sir John de Grey. He made a savage attack on the O'Byrnes, who threatened the borders of the Irish Pale, and in 1429 presided over a parliament in Dublin; he resigned the following year. He was Constable of Clun Castle in 1435, member of parliament from 15 Feb. 1439/40 until his death in 1487 [*DNB*, 16:108; *CP*, 4:479], and Constable of Wigmore Castle, 20 May 1460. In 1440 he was appointed one of the Commissioners to attempt to negotiate a truce with the Duke of Burgundy.

In 1444 he was granted £100 annually to be paid out of the petty customs of the Port of London by King Henry VI. In 1447, as one of the Lords of the King's Council, he was an ambassador, with the Bishop of Chichester, to the Duke of Brittany in an effort to make peace. In 1449 he and others were appointed to settle issues with Burgundy, and negotiate trade issues with the Flemish.

The House of Commons petitioned for his removal, with others, from the King's councils in 1451, and that year he sided with the Lancastrians, was surprised at Gloucester on his return from Ireland by Richard Duke of York, and jailed in the Castle of Ludlow. On 23 May 1455 he was taken prisoner with the King at the battle of St. Albans, and was sent to the Tower with the king. However, there is extant a letter dated London, 22 Dec. 1456, written by Richard Duke of York to the King of France, naming *"le seigneur de Dudeley"* and Jehan Erneys, Esq., to deal with the issue of the marriage *"de Madame Magdalene avecques mon aisné filz Edward Comte de la Marche,"* who was afterwards King Edward IV. He returned to the service of King Henry VI and was wounded at Blore Heath on 23 Sept. 1459. On 23 Nov. 1459 he was awarded considerable income as a reward for his services.

On 26 Nov. 1460 he was of record as being about to set sail for France in the retinue of the Earl of Warwick.

As a favorite of King Edward IV he was awarded more revenues in 1466. He was Constable of the Tower from 1470 to 1483, and Chamberlain, with Richard (Fiennes), Lord Dacre, to Elizabeth, the Queen Consort. In 1477 he was on another diplomatic mission to the King of France with the Earl of Arundel. In 1483-84, and under King Henry VII, he was awarded more lands.

They were ancestors of President George Washington through their son Edmund by his first wife and of Capt. Mark Phillips by his second wife [*Genealogists' Magazine*, 17:503], of President Grover Cleveland through their daughter Jane, of President Herbert Clark Hoover through their son John Dudley, of President Gerald R. Ford, Jr., through their daughter Eleanor [Roberts' *Ancestors of American Presidents*].

Children, given in the Abell genealogy, Weis' *Ancestral Roots*, and Roberts, with additions from Grazebrook [71]:

*   i.   Jane (Joan)^F, m. Thomas^F Mainwaring of Ightfield, Cheshire, who d. 1508.

    ii.   Sir Edmund, d. after 6 July 1483; m. (1) Joyce Tiptoft, dau. of John Tiptoft (Lord Tibetot and Earl of Worcester) and Joyce Cherleton, m. (2) Matilda Clifford, dau. of Thomas de Clifford, 8th Lord Clifford, and Joan Dacre, and widow of Harington; ancestor of the historic Dudleys (including the Earls of Warwick and Queen Elizabeth's Earl of Leicester).

    iii.   Eleanor, m. (1) Sir Henry Beaumont of Wednesbury, Sheriff of Staffordshire, who d. 16 Nov. 1471 [1472 in Grazebrook], m. (2) George Stanley, of Hammerwich, Lichfield, Staffs., who d. 1508/9, bur. Lichfield Cathedral [Weis, *AR*7, 81A:37].

    iv.   John, of Hatherington, Sussex, d. 1501, bur. Arundel Castle (College Church); m. Elizabeth Bramshot; Sheriff of Surrey and Sussex in 2 Ric. III (1484-85); he was "the father of Edmund Dudley, the rapacious minister of King Henry VII., and the grandfather of the equally notorious John Duke of Northumberland" [Grazebrook, 72], ancestor of the Earls of Warwick and Leicester.

    v.   William, d. 29 Nov. 1483; Bishop of Durham, with a monument in Westminster Abbey.

    vi.   Oliver, slain in the battle of Edgecote, near Banbury, 25 July 1469; m. Katherine Nevill, who m. (2) Sir James Ratcliffe; she was dau. of George Nevill, Lord Latimer, and his wife Elizabeth Beauchamp, dau. and coheiress of Richard Beauchamp, Earl of Warwick, K.G.

    vii.   Margaret, m. Sir George Longueville of Little Billing, Northants.

    viii.   Katherine, possible dau., m. Lionel Loud.

§ § §

DE SWYNFEN

This line as presented has been taken from an ancestor table by Mr. Marlyn Lewis, and developed from other sources cited below.

1. HENRY^M DE SWYNFEN died after 1296.

He married SIBILLA^M DE AUST [Watney, *Wallop Family*, 796].

Child:
   2.   i.   Philip[L], d. after 1315.

2. PHILIP[L] DE AUST, Lord Swynfen, died after 1315 [Watney, 746].
Child:
   3.   i.   John[K], d. after 1330; m. Helena, who d. after 1347/8.

3. JOHN[K] DE AUST DE SWYNFEN died after 1330 [Watney, 746].
He married HELENA, who died after 1347/8.
Child:
   4.   i.   John[J], d. after 1375/6.

4. JOHN[J] DE SWYNFEN died after 1375/6 [*Wallop Family*, 746].
Child:
   5.   i.   Robert[I], l. 1409; m. Joan[I] de Pype.

5. ROBERT[J] DE SWYNFEN was lord of Le Wall, Staffordshire [*TGM*, 15:119-120], as late as 1409.
He married JOAN[I] DE PYPE, sister and heir of Robert Pype.
Child:
   6.   i.   William[H], "the Taverner," m. Joyce[H] Spernor, alias Durvassal, who d. before 1435.

6. WILLIAM[H] SWYNFEN, called "the Taverner," lived in Lichfield, Staffordshire.
He married JOYCE (or Jocosa)[H] SPERNOR*, alias Durvassal, who died before 1435.
Child:
   *   i.   Margaret[G], d. after 12 June 1471, bur. Tong, Shropshire; m. Sir William[G] Vernon of Haddon.

§ § §

SWYNNERTON

References given by Weis, *Ancestral Roots of Certain American Colonists*, 7th ed., include *CP* 6:530-531, *cf.* 530i; Banks' *Baronia Anglica Concentrata* 427; *Visit. Cheshire* (1580) (Glover for Flower), *Harl. Soc.* 93:203, and *VCH Lancs.* 3:141, and 6:303-304.

According to a pedigree by C.D.O. Bridgeman [originally in *Colls. Hist. Staffs.*, n.s., 13:214] and included in Chetwynd's "History of Pirehill Hundred," this line begins with Aslen[S] or Aelen, lord of Swinnerton in 1086, who had two sons. One of them married Elyna, daughter of Enisan de Walton. The other son was Robert[R] Fitz Aelen, lord of Swinnerton from 1122-1154. Robert Fitz Aelen had a son Robert[Q] Fitz Aelen II, whose first wife bore him Robert[P] de Swynnerton (died 1224), lord of Swynnerton, who married Mabel (who survived him), and had children Robert de Swynnerton, lord of Swynnerton about 1245, who died without issue, and Margery[O] de Swynnerton, who died 1244, and was the second wife of John[O] de Swynnerton, below.

By his second wife Robert[Q] Fitz Aelen II had two children of record. One was John[P] de Swinnerton, of record 1190-1215, and alias de Sugnall, and of Dorslow, or which he was lord by right of his wife Petronilla, of Little Sugnall and Dorslow. Robert[Q] Fitz Aelen II's other child was a daughter, the first wife of Robert de Sugnall. John[P] de Swinnerton was the father by his wife Petronilla de Sugnall of John[O] de Swynnerton, below.

1. JOHN[O] DE SWYNNERTON was a son of John de Swynnerton of Little Sugnall, according to the Rev. Charles Swynnerton in *Colls. Hist. Staffs.* [new series, vol. 3], which was cited by Cokayne [*CP*, 12:1:584c].

He married first, according to both Bridgeman and Charles Swynnerton, ELEANOR[O] DE PESHALE, daughter of Stephen de Peshale and sister and heir of Robert de Peshale in Eccleshall.

He married second Margery de Swynnerton, who was probably a sister and heir of Robert de Swynnerton, who in 1242-1243 held one knight's fee in Swinnerton in Staffordshire of Nicholas, Baron of Stafford, and took his father's place in a suit for land in Hatton. Cokayne called Robert[O] son and heir of Robert[P] de Swynnerton who died 20 Jan. 1224/5, having married Mabel, witnessed a charter of Hervey Bagot about 1185-1190, and served as knight *ad eligendum* for Staffordshire in 1212. Robert[P] was son and heir of Robert Fitz Eelen, who held one and one-third knights' fees of the Baron of Stafford in 1166 and was said to be either nephew or grandson and heir of Robert Fitz Aelen, who in 1122, 1125 and 1132 witnessed charters of Nicholas de Stafford to Kenilworth Priory. Robert Fitz Aelen's predecessor was Aslen, who held two hides in Swinnerton, Staffordshire, from Robert de Stafford.

In Oct. 1251 he and Margery were sued for debt. Apparently they were both dead in 1256-1257 when Roger de Swynnerton fined half a mark in gold to "have respite of his knighthood" [*CP*, 12:1:584].

He had lands in Parva Sugnall, Dorslow, Peshal, and, on his second marriage, Swynnerton.

Children, the first two mentioned by Cokayne, by first wife [Swynnerton, *Colls. Hist. Staffs.*, n.s., 3 (1900), 77-78]:

      i. Sir Roger[N] (called Robert by Swynnerton), d. in or before 1267-1268; m. Alice, who survived him [*cf. Colls. Hist. Staffs.* (1914), 2-3].

      ii. John de Suggenhall, m. Muriel, who sued for dower in 1284.

      iii. Richard de Peshall.

2.   iv. Stephen, of Isewall, d. on or before 8 Feb. 1297/8; m. Joan.

      v. Nicholas de Aspley, a monk, one of three executors of his step-mother's will.

      vi. Simon de Aspley, possible son.

2. STEPHEN[N] DE SWYNNERTON, of Isewall (Eyeswell, an estate by the town of Eccleswall in Staffordshire), was of record as the father of Roger[M], who was grandson of John[O].

In Oct. 1265 Stephen de Uireswell, John de Swynereston and Henry de Swynereston were impleaded by Odo de Hodenet for having entered Odo's manor of Hodnet during the disturbances and taking his goods and chattels. Before 1270 Stephen was called Stephen de Espley, de Espeleye or de Slyndon in charters. On 22 Aug. 1275 he served as a juror in Stafford, and on 17 May 1276 John de Swynnerton and Stephen de Uselewalle were jurors at the inquisition taken on the death of Henry de Audley, who had been killed by a fall from his horse [Swynnerton, *CHS*, n.s., 3:83-85].

Children:

3.   i. Roger[M], m. Joan.

     ii. John of Eccleshall, murdered before 4 Oct. 1315 [Swynnerton, 3:91-92].

3. ROGER[M] DE SWYNNERTON apparently died on or before 8 Feb. 1297/8.

He married JOAN, who survived him.

He inherited half of Great Sugnall and probably Isewall, but the latter went to his brother John [Swynnerton, 3:85].

In 1285 he was sued by Roger de Puleston and others for half the manor of Swinnerton, as heirs of John de Swynnerton. Apparently Roger had the case decided in his favor upon payment of a fine. In 1292-1293 he was a knight *ad eligendum* and coroner [*CP*, 12:1: 585].

Child:
4.   i.   Sir Roger[L], d. on or before 3 March 1337/8; m. Maud.

4. Sir ROGER[L] SWYNNERTON died on or before 3 March 1337/8.

He married MAUD, who presented to the church of Swinnerton in 1357/8.

Of record in 1305, he was pardoned for his part in the execution of Piers de Gavaston on 16 Oct. 1313. Recorded as lord of Swinnerton in 1316, he was appointed custodian of the town of Stafford on 2 Nov. 1317. In Feb. 1320/1 he was going overseas in the king's service, and on 30 Aug. 1321 he was Keeper of the Tower of London. He was involved in family feuds in Staffordshire in 1324 and later, and was a banneret in 1332. In 1333, after the battle of Halidon Hill, he was given a general pardon, and he served against the Scots in 1335 and 1337/8. He was summoned to Parliament 20 Dec. 1337.

Children [*CP*, 12:1:586-587]:
    i.   Roger[K], d. c. 1326; m. Maud, who was perhaps a Haughton.
    ii.   Robert, b. c. 1312; d. c. 1350; Dean of St. Mary's, Stafford, and rector of Barrow in Cheshire.
5.   iii.   Thomas, of Swynnerton, Staffs., d. 1361; m. Maud[K] de Holand.

5. Sir THOMAS[K] SWYNNERTON of Swynnerton, Staffordshire, was said to have died in Dec. 1361.

He married MAUD[K] DE HOLAND*, as was originally stated by Canon Bridgeman and then refuted by Cokayne [*CP*, 12:1:588c]. As summarized in Weis [*Ancestral Roots*, 7th ed., line 32], Maud was betrothed as a child to John de Mowbray [*CP*, 9:383c]. After the estates of John de Mowbray's father were confiscated, John (then about 12 years of age), his mother Aline, and Maud[K] de Holand, who was living with them, were taken on 26 Feb. 1321/2 to the Tower of London to be received by Roger[L] de Swynnerton, the Constable of the Tower and father of Thomas[K] [Weis cited *Cal. Pat. Rolls Edward II 1321-1324*, 75]. After the imprisonment of Maud's father, and the confiscation of his estates, control of the marriage of John was given to Henry, Earl of Lancaster, whose daughter Joan was then married to John de Mowbray, when he was 15. When John came of age he received a license to grant a life interest in two de Mowbray manors to Maud, who was then free to marry [*Cal. Pat. Rolls Edward III 1330-1334*, p. 368]. Donald Lines Jacobus' article, "Ancestry of Obadiah and Mary Bruen" [*TAG*, 26 (1950), 12-25, at p. 21], cited the Rev. Canon Bridgeman's "An Account of the Family of Swynnerton of Swynnerton and Elsewhere in the County of Stafford" [Wm. Salt Soc., vol. 7, part II], as having shown that Thomas de Swynnerton's widow was named Maud or Matilda, that there was formerly in Swynnerton church an "effigy of a woman over whom is written, 'Matildis de Swynnerton,' and a shield giving the arms of Holand.

In June 1338 he was preparing to go overseas with King Edward III, where he was serving in 1340. On 13 April 1341 he was exempted from holding any office against his will. However, on 18 Sept. 1341/2 he was Sheriff of Salop and Staffordshire, and soon after he held more offices. In 1345 his lands were taken into the king's hand, but in 1346 he served in the king's retinue from the passage to La Hogue and at the battle of Crécy, in Calais, and elsewhere. In 1347-1349 he was doorkeeper of the king's hall. On 14 Oct. 1357 Edward III gave £100 towards his ransom from the Scots. In 1358 he was the King's proxy in France and was apparently afterwards resident in the palace of the Savoy as a custodian of King John of France. He had another exemption from public service in 1360.

Richard[K] Done, who died about 1312, had married first Elen de Swynnerton, daughter of a Sir Thomas de Swynnerton of Staffordshire. Chetwynd [*Colls. Hist. Staffs.* (1914), 4] has created some confusion by calling Robert[J] de Swynnerton's wife Maud Beke.

Children, given by Chetwynd [*Colls. Hist. Staffs.* (1914), 4] and Roskell [3:480]:

6.   i.   Sir Robert[J], d. c. 1395; m. Elizabeth[J] Beke.

        ii.   Roger, pardoned June 1397 for the murder of Sir John[1] Ipstones in Feb. 1394.

6. Sir ROBERT[J] DE SWYNNERTON, of Swynnerton, Staffordshire, died before 12 Nov. 1396, according to Walter Chetwynd, by the "fall of a tower att Brest in Brittany, 19 Ric. II" (1395-1396) while attending John of Gaunt on his expedition to Spain [*Colls. Hist. Staffs.* (1914), 4].

He married first, in or before 1356, ELIZABETH[J] BEKE*, who died in or before 1373, daughter and heiress of Sir Nicholas Beke [*CP*, 12:1:588]. Apparently there was much litigation on the grounds that the marriage was within the prohibited degrees, although in 1364 (before Maude[1] was born) the couple obtained papal dispensation [*CP*, 12:1:588i].

He married second Joan, who as his widow had dower.

As lord of Swinnerton he obtained a pardon for outlawry in 1370. In Oct. 1374 he had protection for going overseas, and he was Knight of the Shire for Staffordshire in the Parliament summoned to meet at Gloucester 20 Oct. 1378. Barrow and Little Barrow were confirmed to Robert de Swynnerton 13 Dec. 2 Ric. II (1378).

While it has been suggested that he died in 1386 [*Colls. Hist. Staffs.*, 7:2:44], it would be strange for the case of his widow's dowry to come up ten years later [*CP*, 14:606].

Eventually the manor of Hopton, with a moiety of Tean, Caldon and one-third of Alstonfield came to her eldest son Ric. de Peshale, and were transmitted through him to the Blounts and Lacons. The other share of Tean and her rights in Barrow in Cheshire were passed to her son Sir John Savage.

Child, given by Cokayne: see p 214

*   i.   Maude[1], b. c. 1370; m. (1) Humphrey de Peshale [*cf. Colls. Hist. Staffs.*, n.s., 9:141], m. (2) William de Ipstones [Weis, *MCS5*, 98A:9] (who carried her off forcibly in 1391 [*Colls. Hist. Staffs.* (1914), 4]]), who d. 1399, m. (3) Sir John[1] Savage of Clifton, who d. 1 Aug. 1450.

Child, by second wife:

        ii.   Thomas, made persistent attempts to obtain the Swinnerton estates [*CP*, 12:1:588j], in a lawsuit which lasted 150 years [*Colls. Hist. Staffs.* (1914), 5].

§ § §

TALBOT

As this surname was based on a nickname it gives no clue to the origins of the families. The Talbot pedigree in *The Visitation of Shropshire, 1623* is quite inaccurate.

Further work on the children of Sir Gilbert[J] Talbot of Eccleswall is in order concerning Elizabeth Talbot who married before 3 Feb. 1379/80 Sir Henry[J] Grey of Wilton.

Joseph Morris's *Shropshire Genealogies* [1595] mentions a Philip[T] Talbot contemporary with Edward the Confessor, Richard[S] Talbot, who held lands of Walter Giffard, married a sister of Hugh de Gournay and had sons Geoffrey and Hugh, and Hugh[R] Talbot, who was governor of Plessy Castle in 1118, married Beatrice (daughter of William Mandeville), and had son Richard, William and Hugh.

RICHARD[Q] TALBOT, who was granted the manor of Linton in Herefordshire by King Henry II, died before Michaelmas 1175. Collins stated that he married a daughter of Stephen Bulmer of Appletreewick, Yorkshire, but Cokayne [*CP*, 12:1:607] was not satisfied with this identification.

Sir GILBERT[P] TALBOT died before 13 Feb. 1230/1.

RICHARD[O] TALBOT appears to have died before 13 April 1234 [*CP*, 12:1:608]. He married, between 1219 and 1224, ALINE[O] BASSET, who was widow of Drew de Montagu, who died in or before 1216, and sister of Gilbert Basset, justice of England [Brydges, 3:2-3], and daughter of Alan Basset of Wycombe, Buckinghamshire, by Aline, daughter and coheir of Philip de Gai.

GILBERT[N] TALBOT of Eccleswall, Herefordshire, died shortly before 8 Sept. 1274, and was buried at Wolmesley Priory in Herefordshire. He married GWENLLIAN[N] FERCH RHYS MECHYLL, Lord of Dynefor; she died in 1274. His marriage is discussed in Canon G.T.O. Bridgeman's *Princes of South Wales* [182-184, 186].

5. RICHARD[M] TALBOT, born in Longhope, Gloucestershire, about 1250, died shortly before 3 Sept. 1306.

He is said to have married after 7 Jan. 1268/9 SARAH[L] DE BEAUCHAMP[+] of Elmley, Worcestershire, who was living in July 1317. She was daughter of William[M] de Beauchamp of Elmley Castle, 5th Baron Beauchamp, and his wife Isabel[M] Mauduit.

On 26 July 1276 he had protection for going to Navarre with Edmund, the King's brother. On 30 March 1281 he was licensed to hunt and take with his own hands fox, cat, hare and wolf throughout the King's Forest of Dean. In 1297 and 1298 he was called three times to serve against the Scots, and on 14 July 1297 he was given custody of Cardiff in Wales. From Oct. 1299 to Oct. 1301 he served as Sheriff of Gloucester. His seal was attached to the Baron's letter to the Pope in 1301. That same year, on 12 May, he was directed to take 700 footmen of his selection to Berwick-on-Tweed; on 21 Nov. he was to take 500 to Linlithgow. On 1 March 1305/6 he was required to provide wheat and wine from Gloucestershire for the cause.

Children:

	i.	Katherine[L], b. c. 1274; m. Roger Chandos [Norr, 22].
6.	ii.	Sir Gilbert, b. 18 Oct. 1276; d. 24 Feb. 1345/6; said to have m. Anne[L] le Botiller of Wem.
7.	iii.	Richard, d. shortly before 10 Oct. 1328; m. Joan[L] de Mortimer, who b. 1291, d. shortly before 12 Jan. 1340/1.
	iv.	Wenllian, m. Sir Payne[M] de Turberville of Coyty, Glams., Wales, who d. c. 1315.
	v.	Thomas, priest [*CP*, 12:1:610d, 628b].
	vi.	Joan, m. (1) John Carew of Mulesford, m. (2) John de Dartmouth [Brydges, 3:3].

6. Sir GILBERT[L] TALBOT, 1st Lord Talbot, of Eccleswall, Herefordshire, born 18 Oct. 1276, died at Eccleswall 24 Feb. 1345/6.

It is said he married ANNE[L] LE BOTELER* of Wem, Shropshire.

Of record as a commissioner in 1311, he was among those pardoned in 1313 for having a share in the death of Piers de Gavaston. In each of the next two years he was summoned to serve against the Scots. As he was among those who took arms against the Despensers, he, his brother Richard Talbot of Richard's Castle, the Earl of Hereford and others were subjects of an order for arrest dated 15 Jan. 1321/2. The charges included attacking the King's subjects in Warwickshire and attacking and burning Bridgnorth. Therefore his lands were taken into the King's hands until further order. On 16 March 1321/2 he was captured in the battle of Boroughbridge, but was allowed to make a fine for his life and his lands. He was discharged from prison on 11 July, and pardoned 1 Nov. 1322.

On 28 Oct. 1322 he had been empowered to arrest malefactors in Gloucestershire, and in 1324 he was among the knights listed to attend the Great Council at Westminster. The next year he was summoned to service in Guienne as a condition of his pardon. On 13 Feb. 1326/7 his fines were cancelled by Edward III, and on 24 Nov. 1327 he was styled Banneret. In March 1327/8 he was the King's Chamberlain, and the next month he obtained grants to Eccleswall and Credenhill, as well as Longhope in Gloucestershire. He was Justice of South Wales on 23 Oct. 1330, and named his nephew, Rhys ap Gruffudd, as his Lieutenant [Brydges, 3:5]. He was summoned to Parliament from 27 Jan. 1331/2 to 20 April 1343. He also served as keeper of Bwlch-y-dinas and Blaenllyfni castles in Brecon, as well as Newcastle Emlyn and Carmarthen castles in Carmarthenshire. On 13 July 1337 he and Hugh le Despenser, as justices of South Wales, were appointed to be captains against the King's enemies.

Children:
8.   i.   Richard^K, b. c. 1305; d. Goderich Castle, Herefordshire, 23 Oct. 1356; m. 1326 Elizabeth^K Comyn, who d. 20 March 1372.

        ii. Philippa, m. Sir Philip de Clanvowe, who d. 1347 [Weis, AR7, 84B:31].

7. Sir RICHARD^L TALBOT of Richard's Castle, Herefordshire, born before 1288, died shortly before 10 Oct. 1328, and was buried with his grandfather Gilbert Talbot in Wormesley Priory, Herefordshire.

He married about 1317 (before 7 Aug. 1320) JOAN^L DE MORTIMER* of Burford (widow of Thomas de Bykenore, who died between 10 Oct. and 30 Dec. 1316, and whom she had married before 27 June 1305), who was born in 1291, and died shortly before 12 Jan. 1340/1, aged 49.

He was of record 16 April 1314 as going to Scotland with the King. He bore the arms of Hugh de Say of Richard's Castle, his wife's ancestor. He joined the Earl of Hereford and the barons against the Despensers, and participated in the burning of Bridgnorth and the battle of Boroughbridge. A warrant for his arrest was dated 15 Jan. 1321/2, but his lands and goods in Worcestershire were restored to him 14 Feb. 1321/2. On 27 Aug. 1324 he had protection to go to Aquitaine in the king's service, and was in Gascony in Nov. 1325. On 3 March 1327/8 he was keeper of the Honours of Peverel, Boulogne, Rayleigh and Haughley. He was never summoned to Parliament.

Children [CP, 12:1:629]:
     i.   Richard^K, d. 25 Nov. 1369; possessed a messuage and a virgate of land in La Lee, Gloucs., from 29 Sept. 1353, but his right of succession had been postponed 15 Feb. 1329/30 [CP, 12:1:629-630].

9.   ii. John, d. 20 Sept. 1355; m. Juliane^K de Grey of Ruthyn, who d. 1361.

        iii. Thomas, l. 15 Feb. 1329/30.

        iv. Richard, l. 15 Feb. 1329/30.

8. Sir RICHARD^K TALBOT, 2nd Lord Talbot, of Eccleswall in Linton, Herefordshire, was born about 1305, died in his primary residence at Goderich Castle in Herefordshire, 23 Oct. 1356, and was said to have been buried at Flanesford Priory.

He married between 24 July 1326 and 23 March 1326/7 ELIZABETH^K COMYN* of Badenach, Scotland, who died 20 March 1372, having married second, between 21 Feb.

1357/8 and 16 Feb. 1360/1 Sir John Bromwich, who died shortly before 20 Sept. 1388 [*CP*, 12:1:614].

Taken captive by the King Edward II's forces with his father at the battle of Borough-bridge on 16 March 1321/2, he was recorded as about to cross the sea with Edward III on 14 April 1329. He was summoned to Parliament from 27 Jan. 1331/2 to 20 Sept. 1355. As he claimed large holdings in Scotland by right of his wife, he joined Edward Balliol in his invasion of Scotland, contrary to orders from Edward III, in Aug. 1332. He was present at the victory over the Scots at Dupplin Moor on 12 August, and sat in Balliol's parliament at Edinburgh as lord de Mar on 10 Feb. 1333/4. However, when his advice was not taken he headed hastily towards England with a few friends and dependents in Sept. 1334, was surprised at Panmuir in Angus, captured by the Scots, imprisoned at Dumbarton, and forced to leave hostages for a ransom of £2000, which he paid [Brydges, 3:6].

He was keeper of Berwick-upon-Tweed in Dec. 1337, Banneret in 1338, keeper of Southampton in 1340, and served at the siege of Tournay in July 1340. He served as a captain in the English army under William de Bohun, Earl of Northampton, which defeated Charles of Blois at Morlaix 30 Sept. 1342 in the opening phase of the Hundred Years War. In May 1345 he was Steward of the King's Household, and he was with King Edward III at Crécy on 26 Aug. 1346 although he had been wounded. He remained active through the spring of 1349.

Children:

10.   i.   Gilbert^J, b. c. 1332; d. Roales, Spain, 24 April 1387; m. (1) before 8 Sept. 1352, Petronilla^J Butler, who was d. in 1368, m. (2) Joan de Stafford, dau. of Ralph de Stafford, Earl of Stafford.

        ii.   Catherine, m. Roger Chandos [Brydges, 3:8].

       iii.   Jane, m. Sir Nicholas Poynings [Brydges, 3:8].

9. Sir JOHN^K TALBOT of Richard's Castle, Herefordshire, born 29 Sept. 1317-1319, died 20 Sept. 1355 [*CP*, 12:1:630].

He married shortly before 14 Feb. 1329/30 JULIANE^K DE GREY* of Ruthyn, who died 29 Nov. or 1 Dec. 1361.

He fought in the 2nd division at the Battle of Crécy on 26 Aug. 1346, and was a knight in the retinue of the Earl of Lancaster during the siege of Calais in 1347. He was never summoned to Parliament.

Children:

11.   i.   John^J, d. 18 Feb. 1374/5; m. Catherine, who d. 1381, having m. (2) 1376 Sir John Seintclere.

        ii.   Sir Gilbert, b. c. 1346; d. 6 Feb. 1399; m. (1) by Nov. 1376 Margaret (widow of Sir John Blaumonster of Wighill, Yorks.), m. (2) by Oct. 1384 Joan (widow of John Wynow, Sir Nicholas Tamworth and Warin, 2nd Lord Lisle), m. (3) after Feb. 1396 Margaret Howard.

10. Sir GILBERT^J TALBOT, 3rd Baron Talbot, born about 1332, died of plague in Roales, Spain, 24 April 1387.

He married first, before 8 Sept. 1352, PETRONILLA (or Pernel)^J BUTLER*, granddaughter of King Edward I; she was of record 28 May 1365, but was dead in 1368.

He married second, before 16 Nov. 1379, Joan^J de Stafford, who was daughter of Ralph de Stafford, 1st Earl of Stafford [Brydges, *Collins' Peerage*, 8; *CP*, 12:1:615], and widow of John Cherleton, lord of Powys, who died 13 July 1374; she died before 1397.

He was in Gascony with the Prince of Wales and remained there, in the King's service, on 1 Feb. 1356/7. He was summoned to Parliament from 14 Aug. 1362 until 8 Aug. 1386.

On 6 June 1380 he was pardoned of outlawry for failing to appear to answer John Sewal, citizen and mercer of London, concerning a debt of £300. During the Peasants' Revolt in 1381 he fought the insurgents in Herefordshire. Joining Edmund of Langley, Earl of Cambridge, on his expedition to Portugal in 1381-1382, he participated in the capture of Higuera-la-Real in Badajoz. In April 1382 he was sent to Lisbon to demand payment of wages for the English and Gascon forces by the King of Portugal, but was received badly by Ferdinand because they had raided Estremadura against his orders.

He was summoned to be in Newcastle-on-Tyne on 14 July 1385 for service against the Scots, and served from July 1386 in John of Gaunt's unsuccessful expedition to Spain and Portugal; he was present for the capture of Vigo and the affair at Noya, and accompanied the Duchess Constance in visiting the King of Portugal at Oporto.

Children, by first wife [Faris, *PA2*, 349]:

12. i. Richard^I, b. c. 1361; d. London 7/9 Sept. 1396; m. before 23 Aug. 1383 Ankaret^I le Strange, who d. 1 June 1413.

  ii. Elizabeth, d. 10 Jan. 1401/2; m. before 3 Feb. 1379/80 Sir Henry Grey, who d. 22 April 1396.

11. JOHN^J TALBOT of Richard's Castle, Herefordshire, was baptized in the Church of St. Bartholomew there on 3 May 1337, and died 18 Feb. 1374/5, aged 37.

He married KATHERINE, who died shortly before 9 April 1381, having married second, between 29 Jan. And 12 May 1376, Sir John Seintclere.

His custody and marriage were granted to Isabel, daughter of Edward III, on 10 Dec. 1356. He was going beyond the seas with Lionel, Duke of Clarence, on 30 Nov. 1367, and on 5 Nov. 1373 was ordered to go to Ireland with the Earl of March. He was never summoned to Parliament.

Children [*CP*, 12:1:631]:

* i. Elizabeth^I, b. c. 1364; d. 3 Aug. 1407; m. Warine^J l'Archedekne.

  ii. Philippe, b. c. 1367; m. (1) Sir Robert de Assheton, who d. 9 Jan. 1383/4, m. (2) Sir Matthew de Gournay, who d. 24 Sept. 1406, aged 96, m. (3) as his first wife, before 24 Feb. 1407/8, John Tibetot (or Tiptoft).

  iii. Richard, b. c. 1369; d. 13/14 Sept. 1382; his custody and marriage had been granted also to Princess Isabel, then Countess of Bedford.

  iv. John, b. 25 Sept. 1374; d. July 1388.

12. Sir RICHARD^I TALBOT, 4th Baron Talbot and 1st Baron Talbot de Blackmere, born about 1361, died in London 7 [Brydges, 3:9] or 8 or 9 [*CP*] Sept. 1396, aged about 35.

He married before 23 Aug. 1383 ANKARET^I LE STRANGE*, who died 1 June 1413, aged about 52, having married second, between 8 March and 4 July 1401, Sir Thomas^I Neville, Lord Furnivall, as his second wife.

Knighted by Richard II at his Coronation on 16 July 1377, he was in Ireland with Edmund Mortimer, Earl of March, in Jan. 1380/1. He was summoned to Parliament from 3 March 1383/4 to 17 Dec. 1387 as Richard Talbot de Blackmere, the result of his marriage. After succeeding his father he continued to be summoned, no longer as of Blackmere, until 13 Nov. 1393. He summoned for duty against the Scots in 1385, and was involved in Ireland in 1389 and 1395.

Children [*CP*, 5:591, 11:698b; Brydges, 3:9, with the last from *BP*, 2:2604]:

  i. Sir Gilbert^H, K.G. 1407, of Goodrich and Whitchurch, b. 1383; d. siege of Rouen 19 Oct. 1418; m. (1) Joan Woodstock (dau. of Thomas of Woodstock, son of Edward III), m. (2) Beatrice, a Portuguese lady (perhaps of the family of Pinto [*CP*, 12:1:619]), who d. 25 Dec. 1447 (bur. East Sheffield, Berkshire), having m. (2) before 1423 Thomas Fettiplace of East Sheffield; had dau. Ankarette, who d. 13 Dec. 1421.

13.   ii.   John, b. 1384; d. battle of Castillon, France, 17 July 1453; m. (1) before 12 March 1406/7, Maude[H] de Neville, m. (2) Warwick Castle, 6 Sept. 1425, Margaret Beauchamp, who d. 1467.

       iii. Richard, d. 15 Aug. 1449, bur. St. Patrick's Cathedral, Dublin; Archbishop of Dublin from 20 Dec. 1417 until his death, Lord Chancellor of Ireland and privy counselor to Henry V and Henry VI.

       iv. Sir Thomas, of Wrockwardine, Salop, no issue.

        v. Sir William, killed by the servants of John Beauchamp, Lord Abergavenny; m. Eleanor Pearethe.

       vi. Anne, m. Hugh Courtenay, Earl of Devon.

      vii. Mary, d. 13 April 1433; m. (1) Sir Thomas Greene of Greene's Norton in Northampton, who d. 14 Dec. 1417 [*MCS5*, 34:9], m. (2) before 14 June 1420 John Notyngham [Faris, *PA2*, 158].

     viii. Alice, m. Sir Thomas Barre.

      ix. Elizabeth, m. Hugh de Cocksey of Worcestershire.

       x. Eleanor, m. Thomas de Sudeley.

13. Sir JOHN[H] TALBOT, K.G., 1st Earl of Shrewsbury, born in 1384, died in the battle of Castillon at Guienne on the Dordogne in France, 17 July 1453, and was buried at St. Alkmund's, Whitchurch in Shropshire, where there is a monumental inscription.

He married first, before 12 March 1406/7, MAUDE[H] DE NEVILLE*, who was aged 15 and more on 5 April 1407 [*CP*, 11:702d]. She died about 1423 and was buried in Worksop Priory in Nottinghamshire.

He married second at Warwick Castle, 6 Sept. 1425, Margaret Beauchamp, daughter of Richard Beauchamp, Earl of Warwick; she died 14 June 1467 and was buried in the Jesus Chapel of St. Paul's.

Known as Lord Talbot, Lord Furnivalle, Lord Talbot of Hallamshire, and Lord Strange of Blackmere, he acquired the great estates of the Furnivalle family in Hallamshire, including the seat at Sheffield Castle, which was held of the King in chief by homage and payment of a rent of two white greyhounds yearly at the Nativity of St. John the Baptist.

He was King's Esquire by 25 April 1407, when he was made keeper of the castle and lordship of Montgomery during the minority of Edmund, Earl of March. He witnessed, on 12 Sept. 1407, the agreement between Henry, Prince of Wales, and Rhys ap Llywelyn for the surrender of Aberystwyth.

He was summoned to Parliament from 26 Oct. 1409 to 26 Feb. 1420/1, at first as Lord Furnivall or de Halomshire, and later as a knight from 15 July 1413. He was committed to the Tower on 16 Nov. 1413, but on 11 Jan. 1413/4 was a commissioner charged to arrest and imprison Lollards. On 24 Feb. He was appointed King's Lieutenant of Ireland for six years with the power to appoint a deputy, and he was sworn in on 13 Nov. 1414. He attended the reception for Sigismund, King of the Romans (and later Emperor), at Dover in May 1416.

In May 1419 he took Donald MacMurrough prisoner, and transported that leading rebel to the Tower of London, leaving his brother Richard, Archbishop of Dublin, as his lord deputy. He also accompanied the king on his triumphant entry in Paris in 1420.

On 28 Sept. 1422 he was with King Henry VI at Windsor, and on 3 Oct. He was ordered to prevent riots on the Welsh marches. He was nominated Knight of the Garter 6 May 1424, and fought in the battle of Verneuil 17 Aug. 1424. He was Captain of Coutances and Pont de l'Arche 1 Jan. 1427/8, took Laval on 13 March 1427/8, was Captain of Falaise 8

Nov. 1428, and took part in the capture of Nogent-le-Roi and the siege of Orléans in 1428-1429. However, as a commander at the battle of Patay on 18 June 1429 he fought on foot with the archers and was taken prisoner by French forces under the command of Joan of Arc. Exchanged for Poton de Xaintrailles in July 1433, he joined the Duke of Burgundy; Patay was taken that month.

After a visit to England in 1434, he returned to France to command 800 men, captured Joigny on his way to Paris, took Beaumont-sur-Oise in May, and then Creil and Clermont; King Henry VI then created him Count of Clermont en Beauvoisis. He was at the siege of St. Denis in Sept. 1435, took the Pays de Caux in 1436, defeated la Hire at Ris, near Rouen, at the end of 1436, and captured Ivry and surprised Pontoise in Jan. and Feb. of 1436/7. He saved Le Crotoy from the Duke of Burgundy in 1437, and by 6 April 1437 was Marshal of France. In 1438 he captured Longueville and other castles in the Pays de Caux. He revictualled Meaux in 1439 and was Captain of the town of Harfleur in 1440.

Having been granted a pension of 300 gold salus per quarter on 3 Dec. 1440, he sacked Poissy in 1441, was lord of Graville-Sainte-Honorine before 1442 and besieged Dieppe in 1442. His eldest son, Sir John Talbot, served with him.

He was created the Earl of Salop in tail male on 20 May 1442, but was commonly known as the Earl of Shrewsbury. He was godfather to Elizabeth of York at Rouen on 22 March 1444/5, and received Louis de Bourbon, comte de Vendôme, and the other French ambassadors outside London on 16 July 1445. He was reappointed King's Lieutenant of Ireland for seven years on 12 March 1444/5, and was created Earl of Waterford on 17 July 1446, as well as Hereditary Steward of Ireland, for which service he was granted the City of Waterford and the barony of Dungarvan.

In Oct. 1449 he was one of the hostages for the surrender of Rouen, having defended it bravely, and on the surrender of Falaise he went to Rome, returning to England in Dec. 1450. Having been at Canterbury with the King on Candlemas Day, he was appointed as commander of the army on the sea with 4000 men [Brydges, 3:15] in March 1451/2, and Lieutenant of Aquitaine on 1 Sept. 1452. He recovered Bordeaux on 23 Oct. 1452, recovered most of the Bordelais, and then captured Fronsac in March 1452/3. However, while attempting to relieve Castillon on the Dordogne he attacked an entrenched French camp, and he, at age 80, and his fourth son John, Lord Lisle, were killed 17 [CP] or 20 or 7 [Brydges, 3:16] July 1453. According to Chartier's Chronique de Charles VII [ed. Vallet de Viriville, 3:6-7, cited by CP, 11:703], the little palfrey he had been riding on account of his age was killed by a cannon ball, and when he was thrown from the horse he was attacked by some archers and killed, according to Mathieu d'Escouchy, by the thrust of a dagger in the throat while wounded in the thighs and legs. His death is portrayed in one of the pictures in the Galerie des Batailles at Versailles. After he died the army was routed.

He was the hero of Shakespeare's Henry VI, part 1, in which the playwright called him "the great Alcides of the field."

Children, by first wife [CP, 11:704c-705]:

14. i.   Sir John[G], b. Shrewsbury, Shropshire c. 1413; d. battle of Northampton 10 July 1460; m. c. 1444 Elizabeth[G] Butler.

     ii. Thomas, b. Finglas, near Dublin, 19 June 1416; d. battle of Northampton 10 July 1460, bur. Church of Black Friars, Dublin.

     iii. Sir Christopher, also slain at battle of Northampton 10 July 1460.

Children, by second wife, listed in part by John Ashdown-Hill ["Seeking the Genes of Lady Eleanor Talbot," Genealogists' Magazine, 26 (Sept. 1998), 88]:

     iv. John, fourth son, Lord Lisle, b. c. 1426; killed in the battle of Castillon [BP, 2:2944] 17 July 1453; m. Joan Cheddar (who d. 15 July 1464

[*CP*, 8:57-58], dau. of Thomas Cheddar of Cheddar in Somerset),
widow of Richard Stafford, Esq.

v. Sir Humphrey [Brydges, 3:17], d. St. Catherine's on Mount Sinai in 1492;
m. Mary Champernoun; no issue; Marshall of Calais.

vi. Sir Lewis, d. 1492; seated at Penyard in Herefordshire [Brydges, 3:17].

vi. Eleanor, b. c. 1436; d. 30 June 1468; m. (1) Sir Thomas Butler, alleged
to have m. (2) Edward IV, King of England.

vii. Elizabeth, b. c. 1436; d. between 6 Nov. 1506 and 7 May 1507; m. by 27
Nov. 1448 John Mowbray, Duke of Norfolk, K.B., K.G., who d. 16/17
Jan. 1475/6 [*CP*, 9:609]; dau. Anne, b. 10 Dec. 1472, d. between 25
Jan. and 10 Nov. 1481, bur. Westminster Abbey, m. St. Stephen's
Chapel, Westminster, at age 5, 15 Jan. 1477/8, Richard, Duke of
York, who was murdered with his brother Edward V, in 1483.

viii. Joan, m. (1) 25 July 1457 James Berkeley, m. (2) 1487 Edmund Hunger-
ford, Esq.

14. Sir JOHN[G] TALBOT, K.B., K.G., 2nd Earl of Shrewsbury, born in Shrewsbury,
Shropshire, about 1413, died in the battle of Northampton for the Red Rose, 10 July 1460,
and was buried in Worksop Priory.

Although certainly affianced to Katherine Burnell, widow of Sir John Ratcliffe and
daughter of Sir Edward Burnel, apparently the marriage did not take place.

He married, about 1444, ELIZABETH[C] BUTLER*, who died 8 Sept. 1473 [Brydges, 3:19],
and was buried in Shrewsbury Abbey three days later [*CP*, 11:705].

He was knighted at Leicester 19 May 1426 [*CP*, 11:704], served in France in 1434 and
1442, and was King's Knight before 27 May 1443. He was Chancellor of Ireland on 12
Aug. 1446, and one of the lords who undertook to keep the sea for three years in April
1454. He raised money for the defense of Calais, 14 May 1455, and was summoned to
Parliament 26 May 1455 to 26 May 1458. He was Lord Treasurer of England from 5 Oct.
1456 until Oct. 1458, and was nominated Knight of the Garter before 13 May 1457. From
6 May 1458 he was Chief Butler for life. During the next two years he also served as Chief
Justice of Chester and Steward of Wakefield and of Ludlow.

He was slain, with his brother, Sir Christopher Talbot, while fighting on the Lancastrian
side at the Battle of Northampton, 10 July 1460, and was buried at Worksop Priory with his
mother.

Children, all by second wife, listed by Brydges:

i. John[F], 3rd Earl of Shrewsbury, d. Coventry 28 June 1473, aged 24; m.
Chapel of Maxstoke Castle, Warks., 36 Hen. VI (1457-1458) [*CP*,
14:580] Catherine Stafford (who d. 26 Dec. 1476), 5th dau. of Humphrey Stafford, 1st Duke of Buckingham.

ii. Sir James, d. 2 Sept. 1471 [*Burke's Peerage* (1970), 2434]; no issue.

* iii. Anne, d. 17 May 1494; m. 1467 Sir Henry[F] Vernon of Haddon, who d. 13
April 1515.

iv. Sir Gilbert, K.G. 1496, third son, b. 1452; d. of wounds suffered in the
battle of Bosworth 16 Aug. 1517, bur. Whitchurch in Shropshire; m.
(1) Elizabeth Greystoke, widow of Lord Scrope of Masham [Faris, *PA2*,
350], m. (2) as her third husband, Audrey (or Etheldreda) Cotton, dau.
of William Landwade Cotton of Landwade in county Cambridge, and
widow of Thomas Barton and Richard Gardiner, the latter a Lord
Mayor of London; of Grafton, Worcestershire; issue (*cf.* George[F]
Talbot).

v. Christopher, d. 19 Sept. 1516, bur. Whitchurch, Shropshire; Archdeacon of Chester [Brydges, 3:18], rector of Whitchurch.

vi. George, m. (1) Elizabeth Scrope of Bolton, m. (2) Etheldreda (or Audrey) Cotton of Landwade, Cambridgeshire, who d. 19 Sept. 1518 [BP, 2:2605], having m. (2) Thomas Barton, m. (3) Sir Richard Gardnier, Lord Mayor of London (cf. Sir Gilbert[F] Talbot).

vii. Margaret, m. Thomas Chaworth of Wyverton, Nottinghamshire, son of Sir William Chaworth.

§ § §

THORNTON of THORNTON

This line has been drawn from material in Ormerod's *History of Chester*, 2:14-17. The Township of Thornton in the Moors, or Thornton-le-Moors, is located in low, flat country about five miles northeast of Chester and one mile south of the River Mersey.

PETER[P] LE CLERC was secretary of Randle de Blundeville, Palatine Earl of Chester and Lord of Thorneton in Edisbury Hundred, Cheshire, England, in the time of Philip de Orreby, Justice of Chester, who was in office 10 John (1208-1209) to 13 Hen. III (1228-1229).

Sir RANULPH[O] (or Randle) LE ROTER, alias DE THORNETON, son and heir of Peter le Clerk, Lord of Thorneton, lived during the times of Philip de Orreby and Sir John de Grey, justices, and was dead by 28 Hen. III (1243-1244). He married AVICE[O] (or Amicia) DE KINGESLEY, daughter of Richard[P], Lord of Kingeslegh, and sister and coheir of Ranulph de Kingeslegh; she was living in 1279, and perhaps 2 Edw. II (1308-1309).

Sir PETER[N] LE ROTER, alias THORNETON, died 8 Edw. I. He married MATILDA[N] LE CLERK, daughter of Richard, son of William[O] le Clerk of Chester.

Sir RANDLE[M] LE ROTER died between 17 and 24 Edw. I (1288-1296). He married KATHERINE[M] DE ST. PIERRE (daughter of Sir Urian[N] de St. Pierre [or Sancto Pietro]), who married second Sir William[L] de Venables of Bradwall.

5. Sir PETER[L] (or Piers) DE THORNETON, knight, was son and heir, underage and ward of King Edward I, 24 Edw. I (1295-1296), was living in 1351 and died before 1358.

He married first LUCY[L] DE HELLESBY*, daughter and coheir of Sir William[M] de Hellesby.

He married second Philippa, by whom he had no children and who married second Sir Thomas de Dutton; her *inquisition post mortem* was held 13 Ric. II (1389-1390).

Apparently Sir William[M] de Hellesby transferred Hellesby and the lordship of Acton to Sir Peter in 17 Edw. II (1323-1324) and this was confirmed by Sir William's widow Hawise in 1332 [Ormerod, *Chester*, 2:120]. Sir Piers rendered services to the chief lord, the Abbot of Vale Royal.

He was one of the contributors to the magnificent feast given by the Abbot of Vale Royal at the consecration of his monastery on the Feast of the Assumption in 1330, his donation consisting of two cygnets and three porpoises, valued at 12s. He also gave estates to the support of the Cathedral of St. John, Chester, in which he was probably buried.

Children, listed by Ormerod:

* i. Ellen[K], eldest dau. and coheiress, d. before 38 Edw. III; m. Sir Thomas[K] de Dutton, knight.

ii. Margaret, m. (1) William de Golborne, m. (2) Henry[K] Done of Utkinton.

iii. Katherine, third dau., outlawed for felony.

iv. Emma, fourth dau., m. William de Weverham.

    v.   Maud, fifth dau., m. Henry de Beeston.
    vi. Elizabeth, sixth dau., m. Hamon Fitton of "Bolyn," Baron of Dunham Massey [Earwaker's *East Cheshire*, 1:50], who d. c. 1374.
    vii. Mary, seized of Hellesby; no issue.
    viii. Beatrix, m. Thomas de Seynesbury (or Sambury [*Vis. Cheshire 1580*, 111), who d. 1397, having survived her.

§ § §

DE TOENI

   This working outline of the family is based on Cokayne's *Complete Peerage*, 12:1:753-774, and appendix F.

HUGH[W] DE CALVACAMP was a Frenchman born about 890 [*CP*, 12:753]. His son, RALPH[V] DE TOENI I was said to have been the very powerful seigneur de Tosni in Eure, France.

RALPH[U] DE TOENI II, probably born before 970, was at the siege of Salerno in 1015-1016. Cokayne stated that it was possible that his wife was a collateral member of the ducal house, for, according to Orderic, Ralph's son Roger was descended from an alleged uncle of Rolf, the founder of Normandy.

4. ROGER[T] DE TOENI I, de Conches, was born probably about 990, died in battle in probably 1038 or 1039, and was buried in Conches, Seine-et-Marne, France 31 May.

It has been suggested that he married first Estephania de Barcelona, daughter of Raimund Borrel I, Count of Barcelona, Gerona and Osona (who died 25 Feb. 1018), and and Ermensinde de Carcassonne (who died 1 March 1057); they were married about 990. They were ancestors of the Berenguer family.

He married, possibly second, GODEHAUT, whose ancestry is unknown, and as his widow married Richard, 3rd Count of Evreux. She was a benefactor to Conches.

Children, of which Ralph and Robert were found in reliable sources:
        i.   Elbert[S].
        ii. Elinant.
5.   iii. Ralph III, b. c. 1025-1030; d. 24 March prob. 1101/2; m. Isabel (or Elizabeth) de Montfort.
*   iv. Robert de Stafford, prob. d. 1088 (for whom see Stafford); said to have m. Avice de Clare, who has not been identified.
        v.   Helbert.
        vi. Gazon.
        vii. Eliant.
        viii. Alice (or Adelise), bur. Lire Abbey, France; m. say 1051 William de Breteuil Fitz Osbern (son of Osbern, Steward of Normandy, and Emma of Ivry), who was said to have d. Flanders 20 Feb. 1070/1.
        ix   Robert.
        x.   son, m. Adela.

RALPH III[S] DE TOENI, de Conches, was born about 1025-1030, died 24 March probably in 1101/2, and was buried at Conches. He married ISABEL[S] (or Elizabeth) DE MONTFORT, daughter of Simon de Montfort, seigneur of Montfort l'Amauri; as a widow she took the veil at the priory of Haute-Bruyère. The names Isabel and Elizabeth were interchangeable at the time.

RALPH IV[M] DE TOENI, de Conches, Lord of Flamstead, Hertfordshire, died about 1126. He married in Hertfordshire, in 1103, ALICE[R] OF NORTHUMBERLAND.

ROGER III[Q] DE TOENI, Lord of Flamstead, Hertfordshire, born about 1104, died after Michaelmas 1157 and probably before 1162. He married IDA[Q] OF HAINAULT.

RALPH V[P] DE TOENI, de Conches, Lord of Flamstead, Hertfordshire, died in 1162. His wife, MARGARET[P], daughter of Robert, 2nd Earl OF LEICESTER; she was living in 1185, said then to be aged 60.

Sir ROGER IV[O] DE TOENI, de Conches, Lord of Flamstead, Hertfordshire, born say in 1160, died probably in Jan. 1208/9. He married by 1190 CONSTANCE[O] DE BEAUMONT-LE-VICOMTE, daughter of Richard I[P], Viscount of MAINE, who brought her husband the manor of South Tawton (or Ailrichescot), Devon, in free marriage; she was living overseas in 1126.

RALPH VI[N] DE TOENI, Lord of Flamstead, Hertfordshire, born say in 1189, died at sea about Michaelmas of 1239, while on a crusade. He married in 1232/3 PETRONILLA (or Pernel)[N] DE LACY, who was living in 1288, having married second, before 15 Oct. 1256, William St. Omer. She had the manor of Britford, Wiltshire, and Yarkhill, Herefordshire, in free marriage.

ROGER V[M] DE TOENI, Lord of Flamstead, Hertfordshire, born on Michaelmas of 1235, died before 12 May 1264. He was married first, about 1238, when a young child, to Alice de Bohun, who held the manors of Newton Tonay and East Coulston, Wiltshire. He married second, before 1255, ISABEL, whose marriage to the King's son, Edmund, was granted 12 May 1264. She was living in Feb. 1264/5.

12. RALPH VII[L] DE TOENI, Lord of Flamstead, Hertfordshire, born in 1255, died in France, presumably a prisoner, before 29 July 1295.

He married MARY (or Clarissa, who was living in 1283), who was probably Scottish.

He had protection, going to the Welsh Marches for King Edward I, on 18 Nov. 1276, and was summoned for service there in 1277, 1282, 1283 and 1287. He attended the Assembly of Shrewsbury in 1283. In 1285 he went overseas with the Earl of Hereford and Essex. In 1294 he was summoned to service in Gascony, and he was taken prisoner at Risonces on 31 Mar. 1295 and sent to Paris.

Children, from Cokayne and Weis:

      i.   Robert[K] de Toni (or Tony), b. Thornby, Scotland [sic, this compiler has not found a Thornby outside of Northants.], 4 April 1276; d. shortly before 28 Nov. 1309; m. Maud, who d. before 1348, dau. of Malise, 6th Earl of Strathearn; no issue; his barony became extinct.

  *   ii.   Alice, b. before 8 Jan. 1283; d. 1 Jan. 1324/5; m. (1) Thomas Leyburne, m. (2) before 28 Feb. 1309/10 Guy[K] de Beauchamp, who d. 12 Aug. 1315, m. (3) Sir William la Zouche de Mortimer, Lord Zouche of Mortimer.

§ § §

DE TOFT

Thomas Helsby, the editor of the second edition of George Ormerod's *History of Chester*, who cited Harleian Manuscripts 1244 [1:501] stated that the Toft family was probably descended from Arnold de Toft, father of Orme de Toft, who was father of Benedict, who was of record in 1242 and was probably an older brother of Walter[N] de Toft.

1. WALTER[N] DE TOFT lived in Cheshire during the reigns of Richard I and King John.

He assumed his surname from his place of residence.
Child:
    2.   i.   Roger^M, l. 1230.

2. Roger^M de Toft was living in 1230, when he acquired one-sixth of the township of Toft from Gervase, son of Hugh de Mobberley.

He also purchased several lands in Toft in Bucklow Hundred of Cheshire from Robert (son of Wentlyan), who had lands by right of his marriage to Alice, daughter of a Hugh de Toft.
Children:
        i.   Roger^L, m. c. 1272 Beatrix Venables, dau. of Hugh Venables of Kinderton.
   3. ii.   William, m. 1277 Joan^L de Lostock.
     iii.   Margaret, m. 1272 William Manwaring, son of Roger Manwaring.

3. William^L de Toft was born say 1250, and was dead in 1316.

He married 1277 Joan^L de Lostock, daughter of Richard^K de Lostock and sister of Richard de Lostock-Gralam; she was heir to her brothers Richard (who married Agnes Wilburham) and Thomas, both of whom had no issue. About 1316 she married second Thomas^L de Vernon of Shipbrook [Ormerod, *History*, 3:163-164], who died about 1336. She married third 1337 William de Hallam of Hallum in Newton juxtà Daresbury [Ormerod, 2nd ed., 3:163-164; Ormerod, 1st ed., 1:494]. The second edition of Ormerod's *History of Chester* [1:670] contains a pedigree chart stating that Richard^K de Lostock (who married Emme de Merton) was son of Gralam de Lostock and Letitia his wife (of the reign of Henry III), and that Gralam^L was in turn son of Gralamus^M, son of Ricardus^N de Runchamp, son of Hugh^O de Runchamp, lord of Lostock. The town of Lostock-Gralam was named after Gralamus^M, who gave the town of Lees to Lidulf of Twamlow about the reign of King John, and sold Hulme juxtà Nether Peover to Richard, son of Randle Grosvenor in 1234.

Ormerod [1:670] states that Joan married second, about 1316, Thomas Vernon, and had a son Richard Vernon, and then married third William Hallum of Hallum in Newton juxtà Daresbury, but this would have had to occur after about thirty-nine years of marriage to her first husband.
Children:
        i.   Roger^K de Holford, d. 1330; m. Margery le Dispenser; no issue.
  *   ii.   Agnes, m. (1?) William^K de Carrington, who d. before 26 Edw. I (1297-1298), m. (2?) Walter de Acton (alias Hapesford); two other husbands, of whom see more under Plumley [Ormerod's *Chester*, 1:502], but the entry on Plumley [1:669-673] revealed nothing.
     iii.   Henry, m. Margery; ancestor of Holford of Holford.

§ § §

DE TOLTHORPE

Thomas Blore's *History of Rutland* (1811) indicates that William^K, below, was called Robert, son of Thomas and brother of John. Thomas married Juliana de Freney, daughter of William de Freney; she received a virgate of land in Wythme (later South Witham in Lincolnshire) from her father in frank-marriage.

1. William^K de Tolthorpe of Tolthorpe in Rutland was mentioned as the father of the wife of Sir Giles^J Erdington by G.W. Watson in Cokayne [5:86-87].

He married ALICE[K] DE NORMANVILLE, daughter of Sir Ralph de Normanville of Eppingham in Rutland.

The manor of Knossington in Leicestershire was connected to the family.

Children, given in Cokayne [5:86-87] and Blore [213]:

      i.   Matilda[J], m. Nicholas de Burton, Burgess of Stanford, who was of record 22 Edw. I (1293-1294) and 20 Edw. II (1327), but was dead 1 Edw. III (1327-1328).

*   ii.   Elizabeth, m. Sir Giles[J] de Erdington, who was living 10 June 1359.

§ § §

DE VENABLES

Ormerod's *History of Cheshire* [3:198-199], presents the Venables family in a pedigree drawn by Sir Peter Leycester and corrected from *inquisitions post mortem*, plea and recognizance rolls, and the Venables chartulary, with more recent data from the family.

The Harleian MS 1424, fol. 141, pedigree of the family which was printed in the *Visitation of Cheshire 1580* varies somewhat from the line given below.

GILBERT[S] DE VENABLES, alias Venator, was living in 1086. The pedigree roll of Legh of Adlington, in Cheshire, makes the allegation that he was a younger brother of Stephen, Earl of Blois, and hence son of Eudo, Earl of Blois.

——[R] DE VENABLES was noted only as the father of GILBERT[Q] DE VENABLES, 1st Baron of Kinderton, who died during the reign of King Henry II (1154-1189), having married Margery, daughter of Walthew, or Waltheof, son of Wolfric, who was the Lord of Hatton according to the pedigree of Legh of Adlington.

Sir WILLIAM[P] DE VENABLES, who was the 2nd Baron of Kinderton in 1188, survived as late as 12 Hen. III (1227-1228).

HUGH[O] DE VENABLES was 3rd Baron of Kinderton at the time of Roger, Abbot of Chester, 1240-1249. This generation was called Hamon in Glover and Flower's *Visitation of Cheshire*, 227. He was divorced from his first wife, Wentlian. He married second, ALICE DE OXTON, daughter of Ranulph de Oxton.

Sir ROGER[N] DE VENABLES, 4th Baron of Kinderton, was heir about 1240 and died about 1261. He married about 1240 ALICE[N] DE PENINTON, daughter of Alan de Peninton of Peninton-hall, Lancashire [Corry, *Hist. Lancs.*, 1:422].

7. Sir WILLIAM[M] DE VENABLES, 5th Baron of Kinderton, was of record in 1251 [Glover and Flower, 227] and 1267 and was living 20 Edw. I (1291-1292) [Earwaker's *Hist. Sandbach*, 128], but was dead in 1293.

He married, apparently second, in 1253, MARGARET[M] DE DUTTON*, daughter of Thomas de Dutton, lord of Dutton, who was knighted 38 Hen. III (1253-1254); she was mentioned as a widow 21 Edw. I (1292-1293), and was called Margery by Corry [*Hist. Lancs.*, 2:663].

Child, perhaps by a first wife:

      i.   Cecily[L], m. Adam, the clerk of Allehulme, near Brereton.

Children, by second wife:

8.   ii.   Hugh, d. 4 Edw. 2 (1310-1311); m. 1295 Agatha[L] de Vernon.

*   iii.   Sir William, of Bradwell (for descendants see Legh of Adlington); m. (1) Agnes[M] de Legh, m. (2) Katherine de St. Pierre, widow of Sir Randle[M] le Roter of Thornton; she was l. 1313 [Ormerod, 3:113].

8. Sir HUGH[L] DE VENABLES, 6th Baron of Kinderton in 16 Edw. I (1287-1288) [Corry, 2:663], died 4 Edw. 2 (1310).

It is said that he married 23 Edw. I (1294-1295) Agatha[L] de Vernon, daughter of Sir Ralph de Vernon, Baron of Shipbrook. She married second, about 6 Edw. II (1332), David de Hulgreve, and survived her grandson William.

By a deed witnessed by Sir Ralph de Vernon, Sir Hamo de Masci, Sir William de Brereton, William de Baggeleigh, William de Venables and Richard de Fouleshurst (who was then in 1308 Sheriff of Cheshire), he granted his son Hugh the manor of Bradwell.

Children, the first nine listed by Ormerod, and the rest by Glover and Flower [230]:

    9.   i.   Hugh[K], m. (1) Elizabeth de Modburlegh (Mobberley), m. (2) Katherine[K] de Houghton.

          ii.   Reginald, of Hope in Bradwell; had issue.

         iii.   Roger, of record 1336.

         iv.   John, of record 1336.

          v.   William, no issue.

         vi.   Ellen, m. John[K] Arderne.

        vii.   Isabel, m. David[l] de Egerton.

  *   viii.   Anilla, m. Sir William[H] Brereton of Brereton.

  *   ix.   Elizabeth, m. Richard[L] Done of Utkinton, Cheshire.

          x.   Peter of Antrobus [Glover and Flower's *Visitation of Cheshire*, 227].

         xi.   Sir Richard of Bollin, m. c. 1375 Jane Fitton [Glover and Flower, 228], who m. (2) Nicholas de Vernon, who d. 20 April 1388 [Earwaker's *East Cheshire*, 1:51].

        xii.   Thomas, of Horton and Hartford.

9. Sir HUGH[K] DE VENABLES, Baron of Kinderton, died 41 Edw. 3 (1367-1368).

He married first Elizabeth[K] de Modburlegh (or Mobberley), daughter of William, and sister and coheiress of Sir Ralph de Modburlegh, Lord of Mobberley.

He married second KATHERINE[K] DE HOUGHTON*.

He was of record as a minor 4 Edw. II (1310-1311).

Children, by first wife:

          i.   William[J], d. before his father in 1350; m. (1) Agnes de Dutton of Warburton, m. (2) Maud de Vernon of Shipbrook; left Maude and Katherine, who died without issue during the life of their grandfather.

         ii.   John, d. before his father; m. Isabel[l] de Eggerton, dau. of Philip Eggerton; had son William.

Children, by second wife:

  10.   iii.   Hugh, m. (1) Ellen (de Huxlegh) de Brooke, m. (2) Margery de Cotton.

         iv.   Roger, m. Elizabeth (Golborne) le Roter, heiress of William Golborne.

          v.   Thomas, perhaps a monk of Vale Royal in 1344.

         vi.   Richard, m. Joane Fitton of Bollin, Cheshire, who m. (2) Nicholas de Vernon [Earwaker, 1:46].

  *   vii.   Joan, poss. m. Sir Thomas[L] de Lathom, Lord of Lathom, Lancs.

10. HUGH[J] DE VENABLES, 8th Baron of Kinderton, Cheshire, was dead in 6 Ric. II (1382-1383).

He married first Ellen de Huxlegh, daughter of Robert de Huxlegh and widow of a de Brooke. Her sons William and Richard died without issue.

He married second MARGERY DE COTON, only daughter of Hugh de Cotton and sister of Hugh de Coton of Rudhe[a]th [Ormerod, 1:539; Glover and Flower, 228, gave her father as Perkin Cotton]; she was of record as a widow in 11 Ric. II (1387-1388) and in 1398.

He was an adult when he succeeded his father, and was sheriff of Cheshire in 1378.

Children, by first wife:

    i.   William[I], no issue.

   ii.   Richard, no issue.

Children, by second wife, the last three listed only by Glover and Flower [228]:

  iii.   Richard, m. Isabel de Langton of Newton and of Walton, Lancs., dau. of Rawlin Langton [Glover and Flower, 228]; Baron of Kinderton at age of 18, sheriff of Cheshire 1386, taken prisoner at battle of Shrewsbury and beheaded at Walsingham 4 Hen. IV (1403).

  iv.   William, m. Blanche, widow of Sir Hugh Browe; constable of the Castle of Chester, was with Henry IV in South Wales during Owain Glyndŵr's uprising, granted Baron of Kynderton by Henry IV on his brother's attainder, but settled the barony on his nephew Hugh, son of Sir Richard.

   v.   Margery, d. 1448; m. (1) Richard Buckley of Chedill (Bulkelegh of Cheadle in Earwaker's *East Cheshire* [1:181]), Cheshire, who d. 1390, m. (2) 16 Ric. 2 (1392 [Ormerod] or before 1391 [Earwaker]) Randle[I] Mainwaring.

  vi.   Thomas, of Horton in Hartford, ancestor of Venables of Agden [Ormerod, 1:539].

  vii.   Ellin, m. Thomas Erdeswick.

 viii.   Æmilia, m. William Brereton [but note Anilla, two generations earlier].

  ix.   Isabell, m. David Egerton, son of Phillip Egerton [but note Isabel, two generations earlier].

§ § §

DE VERDUN

Vernon Norr has made the allegation that the ancestral line of Bertram[S] de Verdun may have been from Bertram de Verdun, born about 1024, who came to England with William the Conqueror and was a tenant at Farnham Royal in 1086, through Norman de Verdun, who was born about 1050 and had lands in 1133, Ives de Verdun, born about 1076 and for whom no relationship to Bertram de Verdun can be proved, and William de Verdun, who held a fee in 1166 and married Lacelina de Clynton, whose husband is not named in *Gen. Mag.*, new ser., 20:165.

However, the outline is so sketchy it is obvious it cannot be proved.

BERTRAM[S] DE VERDUN, son of Lascelyn de Clynton [*Gen. Mag.*, new ser., 20:165], was said to have died 21 Oct. 1271, when, according to the *Annals of Clonmacnoise* [Royal Soc. of Antiq. (I.), p. 251], he and thirteen knights were poisoned together in England. He married first, before 14 May 1244, MARGARET[M] DE LACY. He married second, before 1267, Eleanor, who was living 10 June 1278.

NICHOLAS[R] DE VERDUN was of Alton, Staffordshire. According to Cokayne [*CP*, 12:2:148], he died without issue.

ROHESE[Q] DE VERDUN was daughter, and perhaps heir of Nicholas. She married THEOBALD[O] LE BOTILLER (for whom see BUTLER* of Ireland), some of whose heirs, at least, assumed their mother's surname.

JOHN[P] DE VERDUN, born in 1233, died in 1274. He married first, 14 May 1244, MARGARET[M] DE LACY, Lady of Dulek [Weis, *MCS5*, 13:4], who died after 10 June 1276. He married second Alianore, who survived him [Banks, 445].

5. THEOBALD[O] DE VERDUN, 1st Lord Verdun, Lord of Dulek, of Weobley, born about 1248, died in Alton, Staffordshire, 24 Aug. 1309, and was buried 13 Oct. 1309 in Croxden Abbey in Staffordshire.

He married, by 6 Nov. 1276, MARGERY[O] (or Eleanor), heiress of a quarter hundred of Bisley, Gloucestershire.

He styled himself Constable of Ireland about 1282-1284 [*CP*, 12:2;249]. He was in Parliament 18 Edw. I (1290), and was among those granting aid for the marriage of the King's daughter. He was again summoned to Parliament from 1295 to 1309, was summoned for service against the Scots from 1291 to 1309 except in 1294, when he served in Gascony, and 1297 when he was excused because of ill-health and the recent death of his son John in spite of the King's displeasure with his "letter of excuse."

At Michaelmas 1291 his involvement in the quarrel between the Earls of Hereford and Gloucester led to his imprisonment and the confiscation of Ewyas Lacy, but he was released, with his lands restored to him on 8 June 1292, on payment of 500 marks. His seal as *Dominus de Webbele* was attached to the Barons' letter to the Pope in 1301.

Children, in part listed by Vernon S. Norr [128]:

      i.   John[N], d. Ireland 13 June 1297 [*CP*, 12:2:250].

6.   ii. Theobald, b. 8 Sept. 1278; d. Alton 27 July 1316; m. (1) Wigmore 29 July 1302 Maud[K] de Mortimer, m. (2) 4 Feb. 1315/6 Elizabeth de Clare.

     iii. Miles, b. c. 1280; bought lands in 1317.

     iv. Sir Nicholas, b. c. 1282; bought lands in 1317.

6. Sir THEOBALD[N] DE VERDUN, 2nd Lord Verdun and Lord of Weobley, born 8 Sept. 1278, died in Alton, Staffordshire, 27 July 1316, and was buried at Croxden Abbey.

He married first, in Wigmore in Herefordshire, 29 July 1302, MAUD[K] DE MORTIMER*, who died in Alton, Staffs., 17/18 Sept. 1312 after childbirth. She was buried in Croxden Abbey on 9 Oct. 1312.

He married second near Bristol, 4 Feb. 1315/6, against the King's will and without his license, Elizabeth (or Isabel)[L] de Clare (widow of John[K] de Burgh, Earl of Ulster, who died 1313), who died 4 Nov. 1360, aged 65, and was buried in the aisle of St. Mary's, Ware [mi], having married third Roger Damory, who died "in rebellion" at Tutbury Castle 13/14 March 1321/2. She endowed University Hall, Cambridge.

On the death of his brother John he was ordered by King Edward I on 14 July 1297, to serve overseas in John's place, and was summoned frequently against the Scots until 1316.

Knighted by Edward I in Northumberland, 24 June 1298, he fought in the second line at the battle of Falkirk, 22 July 1298. Summoned as a Member of Parliament from 1299 to 1314, he was Justiciar of Ireland from 30 April 1313 until Jan. 1314/5.

Children, listed by T.C. Banks [*Baronia*, 445], by first wife [*CP*, 12:2:251]:

  *   i.   Joane[M], b. Wootton, Stanton Lacy, Salop, 9/11 Aug. 1303, bapt. in Church of Onibury, Salop; d. Alton, Staffs., 2 Oct. 1334, bur. 7/8 Jan. 1334/5; m. (1) 21 Sept. 1316 John de Montagu, m. (2) 24 Feb. 1317/8 Thomas[K] de Furnivall, 2nd Lord Furnivall, who d. 5, 7 or 14 Oct. 1339.

*   ii.   Elizabeth, second dau., of Stoke-upon-Tern, Shropshire, d. 1 May 1360,
               bur. Grey Friars, London]; m. before 11 June 1320 Sir Bartholomew[M]
               de Burghersh, who d. 3 Aug. 1355.

*   iii.   Margery, b. and bapt. Alton, Staffs.; d. c. 1377 [Sanders, 96]; m. (1)
               before 20 Feb. 1326/7 William le Blount (who d. shortly before 3 Oct.
               1337), m. (2) before 18 Oct. 1339 Sir Mark Husee (or Hussey, who d.
               shortly before 10 Feb. 1345/6), m. (3) before 10 Sept. 1355 Sir John[L]
               de Crophull, of Bonnington, Nottinghamshire, who d. 3 July 1383.

Child, by second wife, born posthumously:

       iv.   Isabel, b. Amesbury, Wilts., 21 March 1316/7, bapt. Amesbury with
               Queen Isabel as her godmother; d. 25 July 1349, aged 32; m. before
               20 Feb. 1330/1 Henry[L] Ferrers, 2nd Baron Ferrers of Groby, who d. 15
               Sept. 1343.

§ § §

VERNON OF HADDON

Sir Richard[N] de Vernon, who died after 1252, having married Margaret[N] de Vipont, is
not accounted for herein, although the *Visitation of Shropshire* places him as father of Sir
Richard[M], below. According to the Grazebrook and Rylands edition of the *Visitation of
Shropshire* of 1623, the line commenced with Richard[O] Vernon of Haddon, Derbyshire,
armigerous, who married Isabella Gernous, daughter of Galfr'i Gernous, who was second
son of Sir William Gernous.

The presentation below is very different from the line shown in Sir Bernard Burke's
Genealogical and Heraldic History of the Peerage, Baronetage and Knightage, 97th ed.
(1939), 2467, but similar to *Burke's Peerage* (1999) [2:2884].

1. GILBERT[O] FRANCIS died in 1278.

He married HAWISE[O] VERNON, daughter of Robert[P] Vernon, and widow of Richard[O]
Vernon, who was apparently the son of William[P] Vernon, half brother of Robert[P] Vernon.

In 1225 William[P] Vernon, son of Richard Vernon of Haddon, Derbyshire, was holding
two-thirds of Pitchcott Manor, Buckinghamshire as Roger Pipard's tenant, but had the
whole fee in 1235 [*Victoria Co. Hist. Bucks.*, 4:89], apparently as guardian of Hawise,
daughter of his half-brother Robert[P] Vernon.

Son and heir:

       2.   i.   Richard[N], m. dau. of Michael de Hartcla.

2. RICHARD[N] FRANCIS ALIAS VERNON was the son and heir of Gilbert[O] Francis.

He married the daughter of Michael DE HARTCLA.

He took his mother's surname and gained seisin of Pitchcott Manor before 1302 [*VCH
Bucks.*, 4:90].

Son and heir:

       3.   i.   Richard[M], l. 1330; m. (1) Alianore de Frenes, m. (2) Juliane[M] de Vesci.

3. Sir RICHARD[M] DE VERNON, of Haddon and Baslow in Derbyshire, and Harlaston in
Staffordshire, was living in 1330 [Weis, 63A:33].

He married first Alianore de Frenes, daughter of Giles de Frenes (or Fenes) of Pitchcott
Manor, Buckinghamshire.

He married second, it has been alleged, JULIANA[M] DE VESCI*; the widow Juliane Vernon was assigned dower in 1378. However, she was identified as daughter of William de Vesci of Harlaston, Staffordshire, who died in Gascony shortly after 7 Oct. 1253, by his second wife Agnes de Ferrers, whom he was said to have married in 1244, about a century too early. When Sir Richard[M] died in 1376, his son Richard being a minor, the custody of Pitchcott Manor, Buckinghamshire, was granted to Thomas of Woodstock, son of King Edward III [*VCH Bucks.*, 4:90]. Juliana was called Felicia in the 1623 *Visitation of Shropshire*.

In 1323 he was sued by his son's widow, Maud, for a third of Fitchcock Manor in dower, but a grant of free warren was made to Sir Richard[M] in 1328.

Child, by second wife:

    4.   i.   Richard[L], d. 1323; m. (2) Maud[L] de Canville, who l. 1348.

4. Sir RICHARD[L] DE VERNON died shortly before 3 Feb. 1322/3.

The name of his first wife is not known.

He married second, after 1313, Maud de Camville, daughter of Sir William de Camville, K.B., by an unknown first wife, and heiress of Clifton Campville, Staffs., and Arrow and Bramcote in Warwickshire, and lands in Ireland; Maud was living in 1348, but was apparently dead in 1351, when her daughter and son-in-law appointed attorneys to represent them in Ireland.

He was of Haddon and Baslow in Derbyshire, and Pitchcott in Buckinghamshire. He was the heir apparent, but died before his father. His widow, Maud, claimed dower in Pitchcott in 1323 and 1331, and was coheir in 1338 with her four sisters. She was not the mother of Richard de Vernon's son William, as Maud's inheritance went entirely to her daughter Isabel to William's exclusion. In addition, Isabel's descendants quartered the Camville arms but not the Vernon arms, showing that Isabel was the heiress of her mother. Douglas Richardson of Salt Lake City, Utah, who contributed this revision, cited *VCH Bucks.* [4(1927):89-90], *Calendar of Patent Rolls, 1334-1338* [464], *1338-1340* [118], *1340-1343* [130, 393], *1343-1345* [561-562], *1345-1348* [448] and *1350-1354* [171], and *Feudal Aids* [1(1899):253, 261].

Children, mentioned by Weis [*AR7*, 63A:33] and Farrer as sons of Maud de Camville, at least William by an unknown first wife:

    5.   i.   William[K], b. 1313; d. by 1346; m.

        ii.   Sir Richard of Harlaston, m. Johanna ferch Sir Rhys Gruffudd.

Child, by second wife:

        iii.   Isabel, m. before 16 March 1339 Sir Richard de Stafford, K.B., of Pipe, Bushbury and Bridgeford (in Sleighford) in Staffordshire, and Chipping Campden (a gift of his uncle Ralph Basset) and other properties in Gloucestershire, and by right of his wife Clifton Campville in Staffs., and Arrow in Warks., who m. (2) Maud.

5. Sir WILLIAM[K] DE VERNON, of Haddon, Derbyshire, and Harlaston, Staffordshire, born in 1313, was dead by 1346 [Weis, 63A:34], when two-thirds of Pitchcott Manor, Bucks., was in the custody of the Earl of Northampton.

Although he was said to have married Margaret de Stockport, Douglas Richardson of Salt Lake City, Utah, has stated that his wife is unknown, citing as the correct reference *VCH Bucks.*, 4(1927):89-90. *Burke's Peerage* (1999) calls his wife Margaret, daughter of Robert de Stopford [2:2884].

He succeeded his grandfather early in 1331, "when Isabel widow of his grandfather and Maud widow of his father claimed dower in Pitchcott" [*VCH Bucks.*, 4:90].

Child:
6.   i.   Richard^J, d. 1376; m. Juliana^J de Pembrugge.

6. Sir RICHARD^J DE VERNON, of Haddon, Derbyshire, and Harlaston, Staffordshire, died 8 Sept. 1376 [Douglas Richardson of Salt Lake City, Utah, cited Roskell, 4(1992):44-46, 712-717, *VCH Bucks.*, 4(1927):89-90, *VCH Leics.*, 4(1958):414-416, *Cal. IPM*, 15(1970), 23-24, *Calendar of Patent Rolls, 1361-1364* (76, 184, 467), *1367-1370* (54, 61), *1374-1377* (494), Farnham's *Leics. Notes* [4:43-51 (not seen)], and *Feudal Aids*, 6(1920):592-594].

He married JULIANA^J DE PEMBRUGGE* (or Pembridge, of Carolingian descent), who was aged 60 in 1409, and died in 1410. In 1377 she made a vow of chastity before Robert, the Bishop of Coventry and Lichfield. On returning home with the king's license she was assaulted and wounded by William Bagot and others, and imprisoned first at Paulerspury in Northamptonshire and then Warwick Castle. In 1409 she was heir to her brother, Sir Fulk Pembridge, inheriting the castle and lordship of Tong in Shropshire and Aylestone in Leicestershire.

He was of Haddon, Appleby, Baslow, Harlaston and Pitchcott. In 1361 he was going to Gascony in the company of Richard de Stafford, husband of his aunt Isabel. In 1362 he was in England, and appointed John de Langton as his attorney in Ireland. In 1364 he was licensed to go on pilgrimage. In 1367 some people broke into the dwelling house of his manor at Meaburn Maulds in county Westmorland, and trespassed on his park, free warren and fisheries, and wounded some of his people at the manor of Newby in Morland in Westmorland.

Child:
7.   i.   Richard^I, b. 1370; d. 1400; m. Joan^I Griffith, ferch Rhys ap Gruffudd,

7. Sir RICHARD^I VERNON, of Haddon, Derbyshire, and Harlaston (or Harleston), Staffordshire, and of Appleby, Tong, Pitchcott and other properties, born about Feb. 1370 (aged 7½ on 8 Aug. 1377), died in 1400.

He married JOAN (or Jane)^I GRIFFITH (daughter of Sir Rhys ap Gruffudd of Wichnor in Staffordshire [*BP*, 2:2884], who died 1356, son of Gruffudd ap Hywel ap Gruffudd ab Ednyfed Fychan by Nest ferch Gwrwared ap Gwilym of Cemais), who died in 1380, a descendant of Charlemagne, of Llansadwrn and Abermarlais in Carmarthenshire, Wales, as well as Wichnor and Alrewas in Staffordshire, by his wife Isabel Stackpole, who was born about 1371, died in 1439, daughter and heiress of Richard Stackpole [Weis, *AR7*, 56A:35, and p. 62 note, but Richardson cited sources mentioned in the previous generation; see Bartrum's chart Marchudd 15]. In 1412 William Gamage attempted to expel her from Coety Castle in Glamorganshire. Eyton [2:226] also called her Joanna Griffith.

In 1400 Pitchcott Manor was granted by Edmund Earl of Stafford to Nicholas Bradshaw during the minority of Richard^H Vernon.

Children, listed by Eyton [*Ant. Shropshire*, 2:226]:
8.   i.   Richard^H, d. 24 Aug. 1451; m. 1410 Benedicta^H Ludlow, who l. 1427.
      ii.   Isabel, m. by 1410 William de Ludlow.
      iii. Joan, l. 1410.

8. Sir RICHARD^H VERNON, a minor in 1402/3, died 24 Aug. 1451, and was apparently entombed in Tong Church with his wife [Eyton, 2:225].

He was married by 25 Nov. 1410 to BENEDICTA^H LUDLOW*, who was living in 1427.

He was JP for Staffordshire in 1417 and for Derbyshire in 1422, as well as Sheriff of Staffordshire in 1416-1417 and of Derbyshire and Nottinghamshire in 1424. He served as M.P. for Staffordshire in 1419 and 1421, and for Derbyshire in 1422 and 1426 and later. He was Speaker of the Parliament at Leicester in 1426. He was steward of the Duchy of Lancaster estates from 1424 to 1444.

He served as Treasurer of Calais from 1445 to 1451 [*BP*, 2:2884]. In 1450 he granted Pitchcott Manor for life to his son Thomas subject to a rent charge during his own life to one Roger Palmer.

Child:

9.   i.   Sir William^G, third but oldest surviving son and heir, b. c. 1418; d. 31 July 1467; m. Margaret^G Swinfen.

       ii.   Thomas, m. Elizabeth; granted Pitchcott Manor for life in 1453 by Sir William^G Vernon.

9. Sir WILLIAM^G VERNON, of Haddon in Derbyshire, Harlaston and Kibblestone in Staffordshire, as well as Tong and Pitchcott, born about 1418, died 31 July (30 June?) 1467 [*cf. P.C.C. Godyn 9*] or 1461 [*cf. Chan. Inq. p.m. (ser. 2), xix, 129*].

He married about 1435 (or 1437) MARGARET^G SWYNFEN* (daughter of William Swynfen, and heiress of Sir Robert Pype), of Wall in Staffordshire, who died in 1490.

They were the ancestors of the Vernons of Tong and Haddon.

He was Knight of the Shire for Derbyshire (1442-1451 and 1467) and Staffordshire (1455-1456), and Treasurer of Calais [*VCH Buck.*, 4(1927):89-90, *VCH Staffs.*, 14(1990): 287, and 17(1976):15, *VCH Worcs.*, 3(1913):121, Wedgwood, 1(1936):907-908, Roskell, 4(1992):424-426, *Journal Derb. Arch. & Nat. Hist. Society*, 22:12 (not seen), J. Nichols, *Hist. and Antiq. of County of Leicester*, 3:2, and pedigree facing 982 (not seen), G. Griffiths' *History of Tong, Shropshire* (1894, p. 44), and Shaw's *Staffordshire*, 1:400-401, and 404 (not seen), were cited as references by Douglas Richardson], as well as Knight Constable of England [*BP*, 2:2884].

Children, among four sons and four daughters:

10.   i.   Sir Henry^F, b. 1445; d. 13 April 1515; m. 1467 Anne^F Talbot.

       ii.   Thomas, m. Anne Ludlow [*BP*, 2:2884].

10. Sir HENRY^F VERNON, born in 1445, died 13 April 1515 [*P.C.C. Holder 9*].

He married in 1467 ANNE^F TALBOT*, who died 17 May 1494.

He was of Haddon, Derbyshire, and built Haddon Hall. He served as Sheriff and Governor and Treasurer to Arthur, who was Prince of Wales and the eldest son of King Henry VII.

Children:

       i.   Richard^E, son and heir, d. 1518; m. Margaret Dymoke, son of Sir Richard Dymoke [*BP*, 2:2884]; had son Sir George Vernon, who d. 1566, who inherited Pitchcott Manor.

 *   ii.   Elizabeth, d. 29 March 1563, bur. Moreton Corbet; m. Sir Robert^E Corbet, who d. 11 April 1513, Sheriff of Shropshire.

§ § §

VERNON OF HATTON

The following was extracted from Ormerod's *History of Chester* [2:791-796].

1. Sir RALPH[L] DE VERNON of Shipbrook, knight 1307, was living in 1313 and had a release from John, son of Hugh de Hatton of Aldersey, of all his right to Hatton in Broxton Hundred in Cheshire, including 268 acres of land, 120 being in wood [Ormerod, 2:791]. Sir Ralph is not found in Ormerod's treatment of the Barony of Shipbrook [3:245-253]. The *Visitation of Cheshire, 1580* [232-234] offers no help either.

He married MATILDA[L] DE HATTON* (sole daughter and heiress of Hugh de Hatton), who was living 35 Edw. I (1307).

Children, from Ormerod's pedigree, surnamed Vernon:

    2.   i.   Robert[K], Lord of Hatton, m. Annabel de Oakes.

  *   ii.   Sir Thomas, Lord of Dutton (which see), m. Ellen[K] de Thorneton.

2. ROBERT[K] DE VERNON, Lord of Hatton, son and heir, died before 5 Edw. III (1332).

He married ANNABEL[K] DE OAKES, daughter and sole heiress of Geoffrey de Oakes; she was living in 1361.

Child, from Ormerod's pedigree, surnamed de Vernon:

    3.   i.   Ralph[J], Lord of Hatton, bur. Waverton; m. Margaret Brailsford.

3. RALPH[J] DE VERNON, Lord of Hatton, was buried under a marble stone in the choir of Waverton church.

He married MARGARET[J] BRAILSFORD, daughter and heiress of Ralph Brailsford.

Children, from Ormerod's pedigree, surnamed de Vernon:

    i.   Katherine[I], b. 1372; m. Hamon de Macsy of Podyngton.

    ii.   Eleanor, m. John de Malpas.

    iii.   Margaret.

    iv.   Elizabeth, b. 1384.

    v.   Isabell, b. 1389; m. — de Brasbridge.

  *   vi.   Petronilla, m. Hugh[I] Dutton; succeeded, perhaps by survivorship, to practically all the estates of the Hattons.

§ § §

VERNON OF SHIPBROOK

The following was constructed largely from Rylands' edition of the *Visitation of Cheshire*. However, the pedigrees vary widely. According to Harleian pedigrees 1424, folio 139b, and 1505, f. 143b, the line went from Warren[Q] le Vernon to Ralfe Vernon of Shipbrook to Sir Richard de Vernon to Sir Rafe Vernon to Sir Warren de Vernon.

This Sir Warren de Vernon married first Isabell, daughter and heir of William of Westley, Lord of Carthorpe [*Or, a bend azure*]. Sir Warren then married second Mabell, daughter and heiress of Sir John Henbury, widow of Sir Richard Thornborow of Thornborow; Mabell later married Sir Thomas Langton of Walton.

Sir Warren had by his wife Isabell son Warren of Westley, who left Isabell, daughter and heir. By his wife Mabell Sir Warren had son Sir Richard Vernon, who married Ellin, daughter of Sir Rafe Kirkland of Kirkland.

Sir Richard Vernon and Ellin Kirkland had son Sir Warren Vernon, Baron of Shipbrook, who married Ciceley, daughter of the Lord of Crew; they had two sons, Sir Ralfe[M] Vernon the Old, and Sir Richard (who married Avice, daughter and heir of Avenell of Haddon, son of John Mapresall of Haddon).

Ormerod's *History of Cheshire* has the line beginning with William, Lord of Vernon in Normandy, then Richard de Vernon, who was granted Shipbrook and fourteen other manors in Cheshire before Domesday (1086), then William de Vernon, Baron of Shipbrook, then Hugh de Vernon (if he was not son of Richard), then Warin de Vernon (a son, if not brother and heir of Hugh), and finally Richard, who was father of Warin[Q] de Vernon, next.

1. WARREN[Q] VERNON was Baron of Shipbrook, according to Harleian manuscript 1424, folio 139. In folio 139b it was stated he was made Baron by Hugh Lupus, who was Earl of Chester 1153-1181.

Children:
2.   i.   Richard de Osebrook[L], listed as second Baron in Harleian 1424, folio 139.
     ii. Ra[l]fe, listed as second Baron in Harleian 1424, folio 139b.
     iii. William.
     iv. Robert.

2. RICHARD[P] VERNON DE OSEBROOK was listed next in folio 139, living during the time of Richard I (1189-1199), according to Ormerod [3:252].

However in folio 139b the second generation was given as Ralfe, and the third generation as Sir Rafe.

Child, following the line in folio 139:
3.   i.   Warren[O], m. Auda Maulbank.

3. WARREN[O] DE VERNON was the third generation according to folio 139, and was living during the time of King John (1199-1216), according to Ormerod [3:245].

He married AUDA MAULBANK, daughter and heir of William Maulbank (or Malbank), Baron of Wich Malbank, and his wife the widow of Hugh Altaribus (*vulgo* Hawtrey), who was living 4 Hen. III (1219-1220). She had a son Hugo by her first marriage.

Children, listed by Ormerod [3:252]:
     i.   Warin[N], son and heir, m. Margaret de Audeville, dau. and heiress of Ralph de Audeville; had son Warin[M], among other children, living in 1240.
     ii. Ralph, a priest, rector of Hanwell who recovered a moiety of the barony from his nieces; according to Ormerod [*Chester*, 3:252] he married and had a legitimate dau. Eustatia, ancestress of the Whitmores of Thurstanston, and Sir Raulfe[M] de Vernon (below), who was illegitimate.
4.   iii. Mathew, only child shown in Harl. MS.
     iv. Nicholas, dead by 16 Edw. I (1287-1288); ancestor of Vernons of Whatcroft.
     v.   Richard, witness to Bostock's deed; perhaps l. 1270.

4. MATHEW[N] DE VERNON received Brickhull from his mother, who had it by inheritance by deed from Lord Bassett and Lady Philippa Malbank, his wife.

Child, mentioned in Harleian manuscripts [but given as son of Ralph[N] Vernon in Ormerod]:
5.   i.   Raulfe[M], m. (1) Maud de Ereby, m. (2) Mary Dacres.

5. Sir RAULFE[M] DE VERNON, y[e] Old, was said to have lived 150 years and was of record 16 Edw. I (1287-1288) and 19 Edw. II (1325-1326).

He married first Maud de Ereby, daughter of John Ereby and widow of John Hatton. She had a daughter Maud who married Sir Ralfe Vernon of Hanwell. Ormerod's *History of Cheshire* omitted this marriage [3:252].

He married second (or first) Mary Dacres, daughter of Lord Dacres.

He also had a paramour, Maud le Grosvenor, widow of John Hatton. Ormerod suggested [3:252] that they may have married eventually, and that she was probably of the family of Grosvenors of Holme in Allostock.

He was called Vernon of the Brand or Brent.

Children, by first wife, not mentioned by Ormerod:

 i. John[L].

 ii. Jane.

Children, by second wife:

 iii. Sir Ralfe, of Hanwell, m. Margret, according to folio 139, or Maud Hatton, according to the other folios (while Ormerod [3:252] stated that she was Margaret, dau. of Urien de St. Pierre, and a widow 13 Edw. II).

 iv. Richard, parson of Stockport 1306-1334, of Shipbrook.

 v. Thomas, of Lostock, m. Joane[L] de Lostock [Ormerod, 3:164], dau. of Richard de Lostok, lord of Lostok Gralam, widow of William de Toft (m. c. 1316), widow of Vernon 1336, remarried to William de Hallam, heir to her brothers; omitted in his father's settlement.

 vi. Nicholas, no issue [Ormerod, 3:252].

 vii. Hugh, no issue [Ormerod, 3:252].

Children, either by Mary Dacres [Harl. 1424:139b, 1505:143b, and Ormerod, 3:245 and 252] or Mary le Grosvenor [Harl. 1424, folio 139]:

 viii. Agatha, m. Jenkin Prescott [m. Sir Hugh[L] Venables in Ormerod, but note Avice, below].

 * ix. Rose, m. (1) Sir William[K] Brereton, m. (2) Sir Thomas Davenport.

 x. Avice, m. Sir H. Venables.

Children, by his paramour [Harleian 1424, folio 139]:

 xi. William, first named in a settlement to the remainder of the Grosvenor estate in 16 Edw. II (1323-1324), l. 8 Edw. III (1335-1336).

 6. xii. Richard, son of Mary Dacres, according to Harleian 1424:139b, 1505: 143b, 1424:140, and 1505:144.

 xiii. Robert, named following his brother Richard, son of Mary Dacres and parson of Stockport according to Augustine Vincent [Ormerod, 3:245].

 xiv. Maud, named after Robert in settlements, perhaps m. William[J] de Venables of Kinderton.

6. Sir RICHARD[L] VERNON was either the illegitimate son of Sir Raulfe[M] de Vernon, y[e] Old, or was his legitimate son by Mary Dacres, Sir Raulfe's second wife. Ormerod stated that he was illegitimate [3:252].

Children:

 7. i. Sir Ralfe[K], d. 1407; m. Margaret.

 ii. Sir Richard, captured at the battle of Shrewsbury and beheaded 1403; m. Elizabeth Dockensall [*cf.* Ormerod, 3:253]; had Richard who m. Isabel Malbank, dau. of Piers Malbank.

7. Sir RALFE[K] VERNON was Baron of Shipbrook from 1397 to 1407.

His widow Margaret was living 7 Hen. VI (1428-1429); her inquisition was dated the next year [Ormerod, 3:253].

His arms were *Or, a bend azure* [Rylands, *Vis. Cheshire*, 232]. He was a knight 39 Edw. III (1365-1366), and was said to be the heir of young Sir Ralfe.

Sole daughter and heiress, although there is a different listing altogether in Harl. 1424:139b and 1505:143b, and Ormerod mentioned a dau. listed by Leycester (but doubtful) named Ellen, wife of Sir John Savage of Clifton, on whom James Vernon settled the Barony of Shipbrook 5 Hen. VI (1426-1427):

Child, legitimate:

*   i.   Agnes[J], m. Sir William[J] Atherton.

Child, illegitimate:

    ii.   Thomas, d. 1419.

§ § §

DE VESCI OR DE VESEY

This name is commonly spelled de Vesci and de Vescy. Local histories of Staffordshire might be consulted. There is a discussion of the early descent of this family in Appendix B of Cokayne's *Complete Peerage*, vol. 12, part 2.

RANULF[T] THE MONEYER was dead in 1061.

RICHARD[S] FITZ RANULF was presumably dead in 1061 when his brother Waleran possessed the mill of Vains in Manche, Avranches.

JOHN[R] FITZ RICHARD was born presumably before 1056. About 1076 he claimed the mill of Vains suddenly, and seized it, but failed to prevail in the King's Court. John son of Richard gave the tithe of Saxlingham, Norfolk, to St. Peter's Abbey in Gloucester during the time of Abbot Serlon (1072-1103/4). In 1086 John *nepos* Waleran was tenant-in-chief in Norfolk (including Saxlingham) and of the single manor of Elsenham in Essex.

EUSTACE[Q] FITZ JOHN, born before 1100, was slain in North Wales in July 1157, when a part of the army of King Henry II of England was ambushed in the pass of Consyllt, near Basingwerk. He married first BEATRICE[Q] DE VESCY, only daughter and heir of Yves de Vescy, lord of Alnwick and Malton, allegedly by Alda Tyson, only daughter and heir of William Tyson, lord of Alnwick and Malton; Beatrice died in childbirth. He married second Agnes Fitz Neel, daughter of William Fitz Neel, baron of Halton in Cheshire and Constable of Chester. She was also elder sister and coheir of William Fitz Neel, who held the same offices as his father. She married second Robert Fitz Count, who was believed to be an illegitimate son of an earl of Chester; Robert became Constable of Chester *jure uxoris* and died in or before 1166.

WILLIAM[P] DE VESCY, having adopted his mother's name, died at Alnwick Abbey shortly before Michaelmas 1183, and was buried near the door of the chapter house there. He married before the period 1169-1171 BURGA[P] DE STUTEVILLE, daughter of Robert de Stuteville by his wife Helewise. Burga was living in 1185, but was buried with her husband near the door of the chapter house at Alnwick Abbey.

EUSTACE[O] DE VESCY, born about 1169-1171, was killed by an arrow through the head during a siege of Barnard Castle in August 1216 [*CP*, 12:2:276h] while marching from the north to do homage to Louis of France at Dover, England. He married at Roxburgh in 1193 MARGARET[O], daughter of William the Lion, King OF SCOTLAND. She was living on 13 Nov. 1218, and probably in 1226.

7. WILLIAM[N] DE VESCI (or de Vesey), of Harlaston, Staffordshire, died in Gascony shortly before 7 Oct. 1253, and was buried at Watton Priory in Yorkshire.

He married first, shortly after 16 May 1226, when he had livery of his inheritance, Isabel de Longespée, daughter of William[P] de Longespée, Earl of Salisbury, by Ela, only daughter and heir of William Fitz Patrick of Salisbury, Earl of Salisbury. She was buried in Alnwick Abbey.

He married second, before 1244, AGNES[N] DE FERRERS*, who married second Sir Robert[N] de Muscegros. She died 11 May 1290 and was buried in the Greyfriars at Scarborough [CP, 12:2:278].

In Jan. 1217/8 the custody of the entire Vescy fee with the heir and his marriage, was granted to William de Longespée, Earl of Salisbury, the King's uncle, to whom Margaret, the widow of Eustace, was ordered to deliver her son on 13 Nov. 1328. He was knighted about May 1329 and served King Henry III in Brittany in 1230. He was deputy to escort King Alexander and Queen Joan of Scotland to the English court in 1235 and 1237. He went with the king to Gascony in 1242, and in Dec. 1244 he was deputized with the abbots of Alnwick and Byland to receive the oath of Patrick and Walter Comyn, Scottish earls, to regularize their relationship with Henry III of England. In 1245 he served against the Welsh, and in 1253 in Gascony. He was the founder of the Carmelite Priory of Hulne in Northumberland.

Children, by second wife:

    i.   John[M], b. 18 July 1244; d. Montpellier, Gascony, prob. 10 Feb. 1288/9, bur. Alnwick Abbey; m. (1) Agnes, dau. of Manfred III, Marquess of Saluzzo, m. (2) by 26 Dec. 1280 Isabel de Beaumont (who d. shortly before 1 Nov. 1344, bur. in choir of Blackfriars at Scarborough), dau. of Louis de Brienne by Agnes de Beaumont.

    ii. William, b. 19 Sept. 1245; d. Malton 19 July 1297; m. after 25 July 1266 Isabel de Periton (who d. shortly before 5 Jan. 1314/5) [CP, 12:2:283], widow of Sir Robert[N] de Welle; no legitimate issue.

*   iii. Juliana, m. Sir Richard[M] de Vernon (?) as his second wife, *if this identification is not a century off*.

Child, hers by second husband, surnamed de Muscegros:

*   iv. Hawise, b. 21 Dec. 1276; d. between June 1340 and Dec. 1350; m. (1) William de Mortimer of Bridgewater, m. (2) before 1300 Sir John[M] Ferrers, who d. Gascony in Aug. 1312; m. (3) Sir John de Bures.

§ § §

DE WARENNE

This line as presented is based largely on Cokayne's entry for Surrey in CP, 12:1:491ff. The name was derived from the hamlet of Varenne on the river Varenne in dept. Seine-Inférieure in Normandy.

Not solved is the ancestry of Beatrice[Q] de Warenne, daughter of William of Wormegay, Norfolk, who married Doun[Q] Bardolf.

C.T. Clay's *Early Yorkshire Charters* [8:1-26, 40-129] is an exhaustive account of the family which formed the basis of Cokayne's presentation.

RODOLF[U] DE WARENNE, long alleged to have been filius Episcopi but of unknown parentage, was living in 1074. He married BEATRICE, who was living in 1053; she was likely a great-niece of Gunnor, the second wife of Robert I, Duke of Normandy. Stapleton [see *Archaeological Journal*, 3:6-12] and Eyton presented him as a son of Hugh, Bishop of Coutances, but Loyd disproved this theory [see *Yorkshire Archaeological Journal*, 31:102-103, cited in CP, 12:1:491g].

RODULF[T] DE WARENNE II was shown to be next in line by K.S.B. Keats-Rohan. He married EMMA[T].

WILLIAM[S] DE WARENNE I died at Lewes 24 June 1088 [*CP*, 12:1:495], apparently from a wound sustained at Pevensey, and was buried at Lewes beside his first wife. He married first GUNDRED[S], sister of Gerbod the Fleming, Earl of Chester, and Frederick, and possibly daughter of Gerbod, hereditary advocate of the abbey of St. Bertin at St. Omer [*CP*, 12:1:494]; she died in childbirth at Castle Acre, Norfolk, 27 May 1085, and was buried in the chapter house at Lewes. He married second a sister of Richard Guet, who was living in 1098.

WILLIAM[R] DE WARENNE II, 2nd Earl of Surrey, died probably 11 May 1138, and was buried at his father's feet at the chapter house at Lewes. He married in 1118, as her second husband, ISABEL[R] DE VERMANDOIS, Countess of Leicester, who died probably before July 1147. She had married first Sir Robert[S] de Beaumont, 1st Earl of Leicester, who died 5 June 1118.

WILLIAM[Q] DE WARENNE III, 3rd Earl of Surrey, was born probably in 1119, and died in the defiles of Laodicea, in the Holy Land, 19 Jan. 1147/8, slain in the rearguard of the army of the French King, which was cut to pieces. He married ELA[P] TALVAS, who was said to have died 4 Oct. 1174 [*CP*, 12:1:497], having married second, about 1152, Patrick de Salisbury, 1st Earl of Wiltshire or Salisbury, who died in 1168.

ISABEL[P] DE WARENNE, daughter of William de Warenne, Earl of Surrey, in her own right Countess of Surrey, died possibly 12 July 1203, and was buried in the Chapter House at Lewes. She married first William of Blois, son of King Stephen of England. She married second, probably in April 1164, HAMELIN[P] PLANTAGENET (illegitimate son of Geoffrey V Plantagenet, Count of Anjou and Duke of Normandy), who became Earl of Surrey and died 7 May 1202. He was buried in the Chapter House at Lewes.

WILLIAM[O] DE WARENNE, Earl of Surrey, died in London 27 May 1240, and was buried before the high alter in Lewes Priory. His first wife, Maud, was alleged to have been a daughter of the Earl of Arundel, to have died 6 Feb. 1215/6 and to have been buried in the Chapter House of Lewes Priory [*CP*, 12:1:502m]. He married second, before 13 Oct. 1225, as her second husband, MAUD[O] MARSHAL, daughter of Sir William Marshal, 3rd Earl of Pembroke, and Isabel de Clare, and widow of Hugh Bigod, Earl of Norfolk (who died in Feb. 1224/5); Maud died between 1 and 7 April 1248 [*CP*, 12:1:503].

JOHN[N] DE WARENNE, 7th Earl Warren and Earl of Surrey, of Warren, Sussex, born in or after Aug. 1231, died in Kennington, near London, about Michaelmas 1304, and was buried before the high alter at Lewes Priory in Lewes, Sussex. He married, in August 1247, ALICE[N] (or Alfais) DE LUSIGNAN (uterine half-sister of King Henry III), who died in Warren, Sussex, 2 Feb. 1255/6.

9.   WILLIAM[M] DE WARENNE, born in Warren, Sussex, in 1256, was killed in a tournament at Croydon, Surrey, in 15 Dec. 1286 [*CP*, 12:1:507], where he was ambushed by his rivals.

He married about June 1285 (by dispensation of Pope Clement V) JOAN[M] DE VERE[+] (daughter of Robert de Vere, 5th Earl of Oxford, and Alice de Sanford), who died on or before 23 Nov. 1293, and was buried before the high alter at Lewes Priory in Lewes, Sussex.

He was knighted at Winchester in 1285, and that year obtained quittance from the common summons in Essex, Buckinghamshire and Norfolk.

Children:

    i.   John[L], b. 30 June 1286; d. 29 June 1347; m. 25 May 1306 Joan of Bar, dau. of Henry III, comte de Bar, by Eleanor, daughter of King Edward I; no legitimate male issue.

*   ii.   Alice, of Arundel, Sussex, d. before 23 May 1338 [Weis, *AR*7, 60:31]; m. 1305 Sir Edmund[L] Fitz Alan, 8th Earl of Arundel, who was beheaded at Hereford 17 Nov. 1326.

§ § §

WARREN

This line needs amplification, as is shown at various points in the text. It is based on Rylands' *Visitation of Shropshire*, 348.

1.   JOHN[M] WARREN de Ightfield in Cheshire, was perhaps, according to Eyton's *Antiquities of Shropshire* [9:208-212], son of Griffin[N] de Warren, alias de Blancminster (Whitchurch) and de Ightfield.

He married AUDELIA[M] ALBANEY, daughter and heiress of Gruffith Albaney and his wife Audelia, daughter of Roger de Ightfield.

Son, from the pedigrees:
2.   i.   Gruffith[L], m. Wynifred de Broxton.

2.   GRUFFITH[L] WARREN de Ightfield, Cheshire, was listed next in the pedigree.

He married WYNIFRED[L] DE BROXTON, daughter and heiress of William de Broxton.

Son, from the pedigrees:
3.   i.   John[K], m. Elena Charleton.

3.   JOHN[J] WARREN married ELENA CHARLETON, daughter of John Charleton.

Son, from the pedigrees:
4.   i.   Gruffith[J], m. Matilda[J] le Strange.

4.   GRUFFITH[J] WARREN married MATILDA[J] LE STRANGE, daughter of a Lord Strange of Blackmere.

Son, from the pedigree:
5.   i.   Gruffith[I], m. Margaret[I] Corbet.

5.   GRUFFITH[I] WARREN married MARGARET[I] CORBET, daughter of Piers (or Peter) Corbet.

Son, from the pedigree:
6.   i.   John[H], m. Matilda[H] Cheyney.

6.   JOHN[H] WARREN was of Ightfield, Cheshire.

He married say 1420 MATILDA[H] CHEYNEY, daughter of Sir John Cheyney of Willaston, who married Maude de Capenhurst, and had two daughters and coheiresses, Maud (wife of William de Cholmondeley) and Margaret (wife of John Warren of Ightfield) [Ormerod, *Chester*, 3:491]. Ormerod believed he was an elder brother of Thomas Chanu, who died between 24 Hen. VI (1445-1446) and 23 Edw. IV (1483). A John Chanu of Wysterston (Cheyney of Willaston in Nantwich Hundred in Cheshire) was son and heir in 32 Hen. VI (1463-1464) of Thomas Chanu of Wysterston and Agnes his wife (who was living 23 Edw. IV [1483]); this John was of record in 1483 [Ormerod, *Chester*, 3:490]. The Cheyney mentions in *Notes and Queries*, seventh series, vol. 10, were not helpful, nor were the Harleian Society pedigrees or references to *The Genealogist* and other jounrals.

Children, listed by Grazebrook [*Visit. of Shropshire*, 348] and Cheshire pedigrees [from Harl MSS. 1535 & 1070, and from C.6. in the College of Arms, a MS. in Society of Genealogists, London, folio 294]:

    i.   Griffin (or Gruffith)^G.

    ii. Geffrey, of Ightfield.

*   iii. Margaret, m. William^G Mainwaring, who d. 6 March 14 Hen. VII (1499).

§ § §

DE WELLES

Cokayne's *Complete Peerage* refers the reader to W.O. Massingberd's material in *Lincolnshire Notes and Queries* [6:54-57]. Further references are made to Commander R.N. Smith [*Misc. Gen. et Her.*, 5th ser., 9:44-48], Rev. E.H.R. Tatham [Assoc. Arch. Soc., *Rep.*, 30:343-366]; Dudding's *History of Soleby with Thores-thorpe* [77-84]; Dudding's *History of Alford with Rigsby* [18-36]; "The Descent of the Manor of Ellington," *Arch. Aeliana* [4th ser., 5:1-12], and Canon C.W. Foster, *Aisthorpe and Thorpe in the Fallows* [27-32]. These sources have not been checked.

RAVEMER^S (or Rademer or Ragemer) died before 1115-1118, when he had been succeeded by his sons.

WALTER^R, son of Ragemar, was a tenant of Walter de Gant in the period 1115-1118.

WILLIAM^Q died before 1198. He married a daughter of Walter DE GANT by Maud, daughter of Stephen, Count of Brittany; she was a sister of Gilbert de Gant, Earl of Lincoln. In 1166 he was a tenant of Simon, Earl of Northampton for six and one-fifth knights' fees; he made gifts to the abbey of Louth Park and the priories of Sempringham and Greenfield, Lincolnshire.

ROBERT^P DE WELLE died before Michaelmas in 1206. He married MAUD, who survived him.

WILLIAM^O DE WELLE died in 1241-1242. He married in or before 1207 EMMA DE GRAINSBY (daughter and heir of William de Grainsby), who was living 30 Sept. 1226.

ROBERT^N DE WELLE, who was possibly escheator in Lindsey, Lincolnshire, in 1246, was granted free warren in his desmesne lands on 9 Sept. 1251. In April 1264 he had protection from King Henry III. He married ISABEL DE PERITON, second daughter and coheir of Adam de Periton of Ellington in Northumberland, Faxton in Northamptonshire, and Rampisham in Dorset, probably by Sarah. She married second, after 25 July 1266, and before 1269, William^M de Vesey (de Vesci), Lord Vesey, who died 19 July 1297 without legitimate heir. Isabel died shortly before 5 Jan. 1314/5 and was buried in Maldon Priory in Yorkshire.

7. ADAM^M DE WELLE, Baron Welles, died 1 Sept. 1311, and was buried in Greenfield Priory.

He married in or before 1296 JOAN^M D'ENGAINE (for whom see D'ENGAYNE*), the widow of Walter Fitz Robert, who died in 1293.

He was sued over the new market at Alford, Lincolnshire in Michaelmas term 1290. He joined Hugh le Despenser on his mission to the King of the Romans in June 1294, and was summoned for service beyond the seas in 1297, and against the Scots from 1299 to 1310. He fought in the King's Division at the battle of Falkirk on 22 July 1298. He served as Constable of Rockingham Castle and Keeper of the forest between Stamford and Oxford from 17 Jan. 1298/9 to August 1307, and was summoned to Parliament from 6 Feb. 1298/9 to 16 June 1311. He was at the siege of Caerlaverock in July 1300, joined in the Barons' Letter to the Pope of 12 Feb. 1300/1, and was summoned to the Coronation of Edward II, 18 Jan. 1307/8.

Children, mentioned by Cokayne [*CP*, 12:2:440e, 441c, 441d]:

    i.   Robert^L, b. Blatherwycke, in the great chamber by the hall in the manor of his grandfather, Sir John Engaine, 1 Jan. 1296/7, bapt. in the church of the Holy Trinity there; d. shortly before 29 Aug. 1320; m. 13 Nov. 1315 Maud^L de Clare, who d. 1 Feb. 1324/5; no issue; during his minority he had been a ward of Gilbert de Clare, Earl of Gloucester and Hertford.

8.   ii.   Adam, b. 22 July 1304; d. Feb. 1344/5; m. before 1334 Margaret^L Bardolph.

    iii.   Sir John.

    iv.   Margaret, nun of Greenfield.

    v.   Cecilia, nun of Greenfield.

8. ADAM^L DE WELLE, born 22 July 1304, died 24-28 Feb. 1344/5, and was buried with his wife.

He married before 1334 MARGARET^L BARDOLPH (for whom see BARDOLF*), who died before him and was buried in the Lady Chapel at Greenfield Priory.

He served on commissions of the peace and array in Lincolnshire during the period 1322-1344, and was summoned against the Scots 1333-1340, and to service in France and Brittany, 1342-1343. He was summoned to Parliament from 27 Jan. 1332 to 20 April 1344.

His will, dated 24 Feb. 1344/5, was proved in Lincoln Cathedral 4 April 1345.

Children, mentioned in will [*CP*, 12:2:441c]:

9.   i.   John^K, b. 1334; d. 1361; m. Maud^K de Ros, who d. 1388.

    ii.   Joan, m. de Cauntelo.

    iii.   Elizabeth, m. la Warre.

    iv.   Margaret, m. Deincourt.

9. JOHN^K DE WELLE, born in Bonthorpe, Lincolnshire, 23 Aug. 1334, bapt. the same day in the church of St. Helen, Willoughby, died 11 Oct. 1361.

He married MAUD^K DE ROS*, who was born about 1331 and died 9 Dec. 1388.

Given seizin of his lands on 27 Aug. 1355, he was summoned that year against the Scots, and was serving overseas in 1359-1360. He was summoned to Parliament from 15 Dec. 1357 to 20 Nov. 1360.

Child:

10.   i.   John^J, b. Conisholme, Lincs., 20 April 1352; d. Gowran, Ireland, 26 Aug. 1421; m. twice.

10. Sir JOHN^J DE WELLES, Lord Welles, was born at Conisholme, Lincolnshire, 20 April 1352, baptized that day in the Church of St. Peter there, and died 26 Aug. 1421.

According to *The Complete Peerage* [12:2:442-443], he married perhaps first, before May 1386 Eleanor (or Alianore) de Mowbray, daughter of John de Mowbray, 4th Baron Mowbray, and Elizabeth Segrave, daughter of John de Segrave, 4th Lord Segrave; she was born shortly before 25 March 1362 and may have been living in 1399.

He married, perhaps second, before 13 Aug. 1417, Margery, who died before 13 Aug. 1417. Maud[J] de Ros (or de Roos), daughter of William de Ros, has also been mentioned as a possible wife [see *TAG*, 37:114-115, 38:180].

His alleged first marriage was probably too late for the birth of Anne, who married in 1386.

Children:

    i.   Ives (or Eon)[I], son by first wife, m. Maud de Greystoke; had son Lionel.
*   ii. Anne, l. 1396; m. before 17 June 1386 James[I] Butler (or le Botiller), 3rd Earl of Ormond, who d. 6/7 Sept. 1405.

§ § §

WILLEY

This pedigree was developed initially from a mention by Eyton.

1. WARNER[O] DE WILILEIA, who was descended from Hugo de Wilileia, died in 1231. He married PETRONILLA[O] FITZ ODO.
Child, from the pedigree:
    2.   i.   Nicholas[N], m. before 1250 Burga[N] de Pichford.

2. NICHOLAS[N] DE WILILEG was the second generation given.
He married BURGA[N] DE PICHFORD, daughter of Ralph de Pichford [Eyton, *Antiquities of Shropshire*, 2:51].
Child, from the pedigree:
    3.   i.   Andrew[M] Fitz Nicholas, m. before 1250.

3. ANDREW[M] FITZ NICHOLAS lived in Willey.
He married, before 1250, a daughter of Walter de Hugford.
Child:
*   i.   Burga[L] of Willey, m. (1) Philip de Stapleton, m. (2) Richard[L] de Harley, who was dead in 1316.

§ § §

DE WOLVEY

Further research into the locality of Wolvey in Warwickshire is indicated.

1. Sir THOMAS[M] DE WOLVEY of Wolvey in Warwickshire was mentioned as the father of Joan, wife of Sir Henry[L] Erdington, by G.W. Watson in Cokayne [5:86].
His wife was named ALICE.
They were mentioned in the statutes and ordinances, dated 17 Oct. 1343, of the Collegiate Church of Astley, founded by their grandson, Sir Thomas de Asteley [*CP*, 5:86c].
Daughter, given in Cokayne [5:86]:
*   i.   Joan[L], m. before June 1315 Sir Henry[L] de Erdington.

§ § §

↳ YONG

Sibton is now Sibdon Carwood in Shropshire.

1. THOMAS[K] YONG was of Sibton in Shropshire.
He married ISOLD[K] HAWBERKE*.
He bore arms of *Argent*, three roses *gules* [*Vis. Shropshire*, 255].
Child:
*   i.   Joane[J], m. Sir Walter[J] Hopton.

§ § §

LA ZOUCHE

The following line has been treated in G.E. Cokayne's *Complete Peerage*, vol. 12, part 2, on pages 930-938.

According to Weis, this line is treated also in Père Anselme, 3:50-51; de la Borderie's *Histoire de Bretagne*, 3:614; du Paz' *Hist. Gén. de Plusiers Maison Illustré de Bretagne*, 20-21; P. Lerot's *Biographie Bretonne*, 2:646, and Brandenburg, ix:8, x:9, x:15, x:8, x:14a.

GEOFFREY[N], Vicomte of Porhoët, was son of Eudon I and Anne de León. He married HAWISE[N] OF BRITTANY.

ALAN CEOCHE[M], or la Coche, otherwise LA ZOUCHE, the younger brother of Eudon, or Eon, vicomte of Porhoët, was of record in England in 1172 and died in 1190. He married ALICE[M] DE BELMEIS, daughter and eventual heir of Philip de Belmeis of Tong, Salop, and Ashby, Leicestershire.

3. ROGER[L] LA ZOUCHE died shortly before 14 May 1238.
He married MARGARET, who was living in 1220, and probably also in 1232.

He paid £100 to have his brother William's lands in 1199. Those in England were seized in 1204, following a rebellion by the Bretons as a result of King John's apparent involvement in the assassination of Arthur, Earl of Brittany, at Rouen on 3 April 1203. This rebellion led to John's losing Normandy [Eyton, 2:212-213]. Roger la Zouche offered 100 marks to regain his English lands. He served in Poitou in 1204, 1205 and 1214, was in Ireland in 1210, and swore to support the Barons enforcing the Magna Carta in 1215. However, he joined the King in time to witness a royal charter on 11 June 1216, and was rewarded by both King John and his son and successor, King Henry III, with numerous grants of land.

On 6 Aug. 1220 he was licensed to go on a pilgrimage to Santiago de Compostella in Spain [Eyton, 2:216]. He was Sheriff of Devonshire from 10 Nov. 1228 to April of 1231, and served in Brittany in 1230. He witnessed the confirmation of the Magna Charta by King Henry III at Westminster on 28 Jan. 1236/7.

Children, from Cokayne and Sheppard:
4.   i.   Alan[K], d. 10 August 1270; m. Helen[K] de Quincy, who d. 1296.
    ii.   William, d. just before 3 Feb. [*BP*, 2:3100] 1271/2; m. shortly before 7 Jan. 1298/9; had dau. Joyce who was bur. 13 March 1289/90, having m. Roger de Mortimer of Richard's Castle, Hereford, who had sons Hugh (*d.s.p.m.* 1340, m. before 1290 Maud, niece of William le Marshall, two daus.) and William, Lord Zouche de Mortimer (d. 28 Feb. 1336/7).
5.   iii.   Eon (or Eudo), d. 1279; m. Millicent[K] de Cantelou.

   iv. Loretta, m. Gilbert de Sanford.

+   v. Alice, m. William^O de Harcourt, who m. (2) Hillary de Hastings [Weis, AR7, 56:29]; received Tong, Salop (she was called dau. of Alan^K in Eyton [2:222]).

4. ALAN^K DE LA ZOUCHE, 4th Baron Zouche, of Ashby la Zouche, Leicestershire, who died 10 August 1270, was of Molton, Devonshire.

He married before 1242 HELEN^K (or Elene) QUINCY$^+$, who was born in Winchester, Hampshire, about 1222, and died shortly before 20 Aug. 1296, third daughter and coheiress of Roger de Quincy, 2nd Earl of Winchester, and Helen of Galloway.

Eyton called him a jurist whose public career "was distinguished by steady loyalty, and a proportionate advancement of his house in riches and honor" [Eyton, 2:220].

In 1242-1243 he served in Gascony, and in 1250 he was Justice of Chester and the four cantrefs of North Wales. He served as Justiciar of Ireland from 1256 to 1258, Justice of the Forest South of Trent, Constable of Rockingham Castle and Sheriff of Northamptonshire in 1261-1264, and Warden of the City and Constable of the Tower of London in 1267-1268. He died of injuries inflicted by the 7th Earl of Surrey, with whom he was a party to a lawsuit [BP, 2:3100].

Children, the four younger sons not listed by name:

6. i. Sir Roger^J, d. 1285; m. Ela Longespee.

* ii. Margery, of Winchester, Hampshire, b. c. 1251; m. Roger^M Fitz Roger, 5th Baron Warkworth and Clavering, who d. Horsford, Norfolk, before 20 April 1310.

5. EON (or EUDO)^K LA ZOUCHE died between 28 April and 25 June 1279.

He married, before 13 Dec. 1273, MILLICENT^K DE CANTELOU$^+$ (or Cantilupe), who died shortly before 7 Jan. 1298/9, widow of John de Mohaut (or Monte Alto [F.N. Craig, "Lady Millicent's Cat and the Bullers Inheritance," TAG, 70 (1995), 100]), sister and coheir of George de Cauntelo, Lord of Abergavenny (who died without issue 18 Oct. 1273), and daughter of Sir William de Cauntelo, of Calne, Wiltshire, and Aston Cantlow, Warwickshire, by Eve, third daughter and coheir of William de Briouze (or more commonly de Braiose), Lord of Abergavenny. As a widow, Millicent obtained as her pourparty the manors of Harringworth and Bulwick in Northamptonshire, Totnes in Devonshire, and estates in Bedfordshire, Somersetshire and Wiltshire.

In July 1253 he had been granted the marriage of Agatha de Ferrers, sixth daughter of William, Earl of Derby; she was to be delivered to him 26 Feb. 1253/4. However, he transferred the marriage to Hugh Mortimer of Chelmarsh.

He brought the treasure of Ireland to the treasurer of the New Temple, London, in Sept. 1251. In 1254 he went with the Queen to the King in Gascony. He witnessed charters at Southwick and at Lambeth in 1257, and on 27 April 1261 was granted a pension of 30 marks (£20) a year. On 25 Dec. 1262 he was ordered to take over Prince Edward's castles of Chester, Beeston and Shotwick, holding them against Llywelyn ap Gruffudd until his brother Alan could arrive.

He was summoned to Windsor with horses and arms on 17 Oct. 1263 in support of the Crown in the Barons' War, 1264-65, and as a result was to be paid, 10 March 1266/7, 80 marks from Essex and Hertfordshire for expenses in subduing rebels in those counties. He was then of the King's household; he had livery of his wife's lands in England and Ireland, in 1273-75.

He was present at Parliament in Westminster, 19 May 1275, when he consented to customs payment on wool and hides exported through his Irish ports. He was also present in the Council at Westminster for the judgment against Llywelyn ap Gruffudd, Prince of Wales, on 12 Nov. 1276.

He served against the Welsh in 1277, and in Ireland in 1279.

Children, from Cokayne and Roberts:

    i.   Sir William^J, b. Harringworth, Northants., 18 or 21 Dec. 1276; d. March 1351/2 [*MCS*5, 74:5] m. Maud Lovel, dau. of John Lovel, 1st Lord Lovel (for whom see Weis, *AR*7, 215:29); Lord la Zouche.

*   ii.   Eve, b. c. 1281; d. 6 Dec. 1314 [*CP*, 14:87], bur. Portbury Church, Somerset; m. 1289 Maurice^J de Berkeley.

   iii.   Elizabeth [Roberts' *Ancestors of American Presidents*], m. 1287 Nicholas Poyntz, 2nd Lord Poyntz (for whom see Weis, *AR*7, 234A:32); they were ancestors of Pres. Rutherford B. Hayes.

   iv.   Eleanor [possible dau. of John de Montault, according to Sheppard in *TAG*, 49:4], m. c. 1286 (evidently as a child) Sir John de Harcourt [Weis, *AR*7, 38:30].

6. Sir ROGER^J LA ZOUCHE, Baron Zouche of Ashby, died just before 15 Oct. [*BP*, 2:3100] 1285.

According to Weis, who cited Old *CP*, 8:222, he married ELA LONGESPEE$^+$, who died by 19 July 1276 [*BP*, 2:3100].

Child, mentioned by Weis:

  7.   i.   Alan^I, b. 9 Oct. 1267; d. 1313/4; m. Eleanor^M de Segrave.

7. ALAN^I LA ZOUCHE, Baron Zouche of Ashby from 1299 to 1314, was born 9 Oct. [*BP*, 2:3100] 1267 and died in 1313/4.

He married ELEANOR^M DE SEGRAVE*.

He served in the military in Flanders, Gascony and Scotland, fighting the vanguard at the battle of Falkirk in King Edward I's victory over William Wallace in 1298. He was summoned to Parliament 6 Feb. 1298/9. Beginning in Feb. 1311/2 he served two years as Constable of Rockingham Castle and keeper of the forests between Oxford and Stamford bridges.

Children [*CP*, 14:386]:

    i.   Ellen (or Elena)^H, b. 1288; l. Oct. 1334; m. (1) April 1314 Nicholas de St. Maur (Seymour), who d. 8 Nov. 1316, m. (2) c. 1317 Alan de Charlton of Apley, Shropshire, who d. 2 Dec. 1360.

*   ii.   Maud, b. 1289; d. 31 May 1349; m. by 1309/10 Sir Robert^L de Holand, 1st Lord Holand, who was executed 7 Oct. 1328.

   iii.   Elizabeth, entered the nunnery of Brewood, Staffs. [see Maddicott, *EHR*, 86:458^1], by 1314 [*BP*, 2:3100].

§ § §

BIBLIOGRAPHY

The abbreviations used in this bibliography are explained on the last page of this section.

Abell, Horace A., and Lewis P. Abell. *The Abell Family in America; Robert Abell of Rehoboth, Mass., His English Ancestry and His Descendants.* Rutland, Vt.: The Tuttle Publishing Company, Inc., 1940.

"Abstracts of the Earliest Wills Upon Record in the County of Suffolk, Ms.," *NEHGR*, 2 (1848), 102-105, 180-186.

Altschul, Michael. *A Baronial Family in England: the Clares, 1217-1314.* Baltimore: The Johns Hopkins Press, 1965.

American and English Genealogies in the Library of Congress. Washington: Government Printing Office, 1919.

Anderson, Robert Charles. *The Great Migration Begins; Immigrants to New England 1620-1633*, vol. 1. Boston: New England Historic Genealogical Society, 1995.

Ashdown-Hill, John. "Seeking the Genes of Lady Eleanor Talbot," *Genealogists' Magazine*, 26 (Sept. 1998), 87-90.

Ashmole, Elias. *The Institution, Laws and Ceremonies of the Most Noble Order of the Garter.* Baltimore: Genealogical Publishing Co., Inc., 1971 [reprint of ed. of 1672].

B., B. "Pedigrees from the Plea Rolls, &c.," *Collectanea Topogaphica e Genealogica*, 1 (1834), 128-148.

B., W.H.B. "The Representation of the Barons of Dunham," *The Genealogist*, New Series, 16 (1899-1900), 16-23.

Baines, Edward. *History of the County Palatine and Duchy of Lancaster*, vols. 3-4. London: Fisher, Son & Co., 1836.

Baines, Edward. *History of the County Palatine and Duchy of Lancaster*, rev. ed., 2 vols. London: George Routledge and Sons, 1868.

Baines, Thomas, and William Fairbairn. *Lancashire and Cheshire, Past and Present*, 2 vols. in 4. London: William MacKenzie, n.d.

Baker, George. *The History and Antiquities of the County of Northampton*, 2 vols. London: John Bowyer Nichols and Son, 1822-1830 [Family History Center, West Los Angeles].

Banfield, Alan, and Neal Priestland. "The Family of Eleanor of Castile (died 1290)," *Omnibus*, 12 (1990), 101-107.

Banks, T.C. *The Dormant and Extinct Baronage of England*, 4 vols. London, 1807-1837.

Banks, Sir T.C. *Baronia Anglica Concentrata.* Ripon, 1844.

Barbier, Paul fils. *The Age of Owain Gwynedd, an Attempt at a Connected Account of the History of Wales from December, 1135, to November, 1170.* London: David Nutt, 1908.

Barlow, Lundie W. "The Ancestry of Saher de Quincy, Earl of Winchester," *NEHGR*, 112 (1958), 61-65.

Barrow, Geoffrey B. *The Genealogist's Guide.* London: The Research Publishing Co., 1977.

Bartrum, Peter C. *Welsh Genealogies, AD 300-1400*, 8 vols. University of Wales Press, 1974.

Bartrum, Peter C. *Welsh Genealogies, AD 1400-1500*, 16 vols. Aberystwyth: The National Library of Wales, 1983.

Bayne, Rev. Dom William W. "The Baronial Blounts and Some of Their Descendants," *English Genealogist*, 15/16 (1982), 414ff.

Beke, Charles T. "Observations on the Pedigree of the Family of Beke of Eresby, in the County of Lincoln," *Collectanea Topographica et Genealogica*, 4 (1837), 331-345.

Benalt, Thomas. *The Visitation of Lancashire and a Part of Cheshire Made in the Twenty-fourth Year of the Reign of King Henry the Eighth*, A.D. *1533*, ed. William Langton. The Chetham Society, 1876.

Bird, W.H.B. "Lostock and the Grosvenors," *The Ancestor*, No. 2 (July 1902), 148-155.

Blore, Thomas. *The History and Antiquities of the County of Rutland*. Stanford, 1811.

Bodine, Ronny O., and Brother Thomas W. Spaulding, Jr. *The Ancestry of Dorothea Poyntz*, preliminary ed., 1995.

Boothe, Ross Jr. "Pynchon Blood Royal," *TAG*, 39 (1963), 86-89.

Brabner, J.H.F. *The Comprehensive Gazetteer of England and Wales*, 2 vols. [A-Goathurst]. London: William MacKenzie, n.d.

Brainbridge, Miss H.A. "The Bulkeley Pedigree," *NEHGR*, 23 (1869), 299-304.

Brame, Arden H., Jr. II. "Proven Companions of the Conqueror at the Battle of Hastings, 14 October 1066," *Omnibus*, 12 (1990), 99-101.

Brereton, John. *Brereton, a Family History*. San Francisco, 1919.

Bridgeman, Rev. Canon. "An Account of the Family of Swynnerton, of Swynnerton and Elsewhere in the County of Stafford," *Collections for a History of Staffordshire*, ed. The William Salt Archaeological Society, 7 (1886), part II, 1-189 and i-xvii.

Bridgeman, Charles G.O. "The Devolution of the Manor of Edgmond in the Fourteenth and Following Centuries," *Transactions of the Shropshire Archæological and Natural History Society*, Fourth Series, 3 (1913), 57-108.

Brooke, Richard. "On Handford Old Hall, in Cheshire, Formerly the Residence of the Ancient Family of Brereton, with an Account of Cheadle Church, in That County, and of the Monuments of the Breretons in It," *Proceedings of the Historic Society of Lancashire and Cheshire*, 2 (1849), 41-54.

Brooke, Richard. *Visits to the Fields of Battle in England*. London: John Russell Smith, 1862.

Broughton, Sir Delves L. *Records of an Old Cheshire Family; A History of the Lords of the Manors of Delves near Uttoxeter in the County of Stafford & Doddington in the County of Chester*. London: Arnold Fairbairns & Company, Limited, 1908.

Brown, John C.J. "The Atherton Family in England," *NEHGR*, 35 (1881), 67-72.

Brydges, Sir Egerton. *Collins's Peerage of England*, 9 vols. London, 1812.

Brydges, Sir Egerton (Sa. Egerton de Bruges). *Stemmata Illustria; Præcipue Regia*. Paris: J. Smith, 1825 [Family History Center, West Los Angeles]

Burke, Arthur Meredith. *Key to the Ancient Parish Registers of England and Wales*. London: The Sackville Press, Ltd., 1908.

Burke, Sir Bernard. *Genealogical and Heraldic Dictionary of Great Britain and Ireland*, 4th ed., 2 vols. London: Harrison, Pall Mall, 1862.

Burke, Sir Bernard. *A Genealogical and Heraldic History of the Landed Gentry of Great Britain and Ireland*, 2 vols. London: Harrison, Pall Mall, 1879.

Burke, Sir Bernard. *A Genealogical History of the Dormant, Abeyant, Forfeited, and Extinct Peerages of the British Empire*. Baltimore: Genealogical Publishing Co., Inc., 1978.

Burke, Sir Bernard. *Burke's Genealogical and Heraldic History of the Peerage, Baronetage and Knightage*, 97th ed. London: Burke's Peerage Limited, 1939.

Burke, John. *A Genealogical and Heraldic History of the Commoners of Great Britain and Ireland*, 4 vols. London: Henry Colburn, 1835-1838.

Burke, John, and John Bernard Burke. *A Genealogical and Heraldic Dictionary of the Landed Gentry of Great Britain and Ireland*, 2 vols. London: Henry Colburn, 1846.

Burke, John, and John Bernard Burke. *A Genealogical and Heraldic History of the Extinct and Dormant Baronetcies of England, Ireland, and Scotland*, 2nd ed. London: John Russell Smith, 1844 [reprinted 1964].

Burke, John, and John Bernard Burke. *The Royal Families of England, Scotland, and Wales*, 2 vols. London: E. Churton, 1848-1851.

Burke's Genealogical and Heraldic Dictionary of the Landed Gentry, 15th ed., ed. By H. Pirie-Gordon. London: Shaw Publishing Co., Ltd., 1937.

Burke's Peerage & Baronetage, 106th ed., 2 vols. Crans: Burke's Peerage (Genealogical Books) Ltd, 1999.

Butler, Edward F. Sr. *The Descendants of Thomas Pincerna, Progenitor of the Butler Family*. Dallas, 1997.

Cabaniss, Allen. "Notes on Leuca and Robert de Mohaut," *The English Genealogist*, 4 (Sept. 1976), 94-95.

Cabaniss, Allen. "More on Leuca and Robert de Mohaut," *The English Genealogist*, No. 12 (1979), 264-265.

Cary Elwes, Dudley G. "De Braose Family," *The Genealogist*, 4 (1880), 133ff.

Cheshire Visitation Pedigrees 1663, by Arthur Adams. London: The Harleian Society, 1941.

Chetwynd, Walter of Ingestre (1679). "History of Pirehill Hundred," *CHS*, new series, 12 (1909), 7-273, and (1914), 1-183.

Clagett, Brice McAdoo. "The Ancestry of Capt. James Neale," *Maryland Genealogical Society Bulletin*, 31 (1990), 137-153.

Clark, George T. *The Land of Morgan: Being a Contribution Towards the History of Glamorgan*. London: Whiting & Co., Lim., 1883.

Clark, George T. *Limbus Patrum Morganiæ et Glamorganiæ, Being the Genealogies of the Older Families of the Lordships of Morgan and Glamorgan*. London: Wyman & Sons, 1886.

C[okayne], G.E. *The Complete Peerage*, 13 vols. London: The St Catherine Press, 1910-1940.

Collins, Arthur. *The Baronettage of England*, 2 vols. London, 1720.

Cook, Ross Keelye. "Zouche or la Zouche of Haryngworth," *TAG*, 43 (1967), 26.

Cooke, Robert. *The Visitation of Herefordshire*. Exeter, 1886.

Cope, Gilbert. *Genealogy of the Dutton Families of Pennsylvania*. West Chester, Pa., 1871.

[Corbet, Augusta Elizabeth.] *The Family of Corbet; Its Life and Times*, 2 vols. London: St. Catherine Press, 1914-1920.

Corry, J[ohn]. *The History of Lancashire*, 2 vols. London: Geo. B. Whittaker, 1825.

Coward, Barry. *The Stanleys, Lords Stanley and Earls of Darby 1385-1672; the Origins, Wealth and Power of a Landowning Family*. Manchester: The Chetham Society [ser. 3, vol. 30], 1983.

Craig, F.N. "Lady Millicent's Cat and the Bullers Inheritance: Colonial Immigrants, Feral Cats, and Medieval Genealogy," *TAG*, 70 (1995), 96-103.

Croston, James. *County Families of Lancashire and Cheshire*. London: John Heywood, 1887.

Curfman, Robert Joseph. "The Yale Descent from Braiose and Clare Through Pigott of Buckinghamshire," *TAG*, 56 (1980), 1-11.

Davenport, Robert Ralsey. *The Davenport Genealogy: History and Genealogy of the Ancestors and Descendants of the Rev. John Davenport, Founder of New Haven, Connecticut, and of Yale College*. [Cambridge, Mass., 1982].

Davies, John. *A History of Wales*. London: Allen Lane, The Penguin Press, 1993.

Delaborde, H.-François. *Jean de Joinville et les Seigneurs de Joinville suivi d'un Catalogue de Leurs Actes*. Paris; Imprimerie Nationale, 1894.

The Descent of George Washington from King John and Nine of the Twenty Five Baron Sureties of Magna Carta [printed chart on parchment].

"The Descent of Wattlesborough Through the Families of Corbet, Mawddwy, Burgh and Leighton," *Archæologica Cambrensis*, Fourth Series, 11 (1880), 6-8.

Dickinson, J.R. *The Lordship of Man Under the Stanleys, Government and Economy in the Isle of Man, 1580-1704*. Manchester: The Chetham Society [ser. 3, vol. 41], 1996.

Dictionary of National Biography, ed. Sidney Lee, vol. 54. London: Smith, Elder, & Co., 1898.

The Dictionary of National Biography, 22 vols. New York: The Macmillan Company, 1908.

The Dictionary of National Biography, 21 vols. Oxford: Oxford University Press, 1949-1950.

The Dictionary of Welsh Biography Down to 1940. London: The Honourable Society of Cymmrodorian, 1959.

Dugdale, William. *The Antiquities of Warwickshire*. London: Thomas Warren, 1656 [Rare Book Room, Los Angeles Public Library].

Dugdale, Sir William. *The Visitation of the County Palatine of Lancaster Made in the Year 1664-5*, ed. F.R. Raines. The Chetham Society, 1872.

Dwnn, Lewys. *Heraldic Visitations of Wales and Part of the Marches, Between the Years 1586 and 1613...*, Sir Samuel Rush Meyrick, ed., 2 vols. Llandovery: Welsh MSS. Society, 1846.

Dwnn, Lewis. *Pedigrees of Montgomeryshire Families Selected about the Year 1711-12 from Lewis Dwnn's Original Visitation, by the Celebrated Welsh Poet and Grammarian, John Rhydderch*. London: Whiting & Co., 1888.

Eales, Jacqueline. *Puritans and Roundheads, the Harleys of Brampton Bryan and the Outbreak of the English Civil War*. Cambridge: Cambridge University Press, 1990.

Earwaker, J.P. *East Cheshire: Past and Present; or a History of the Hundred of Macclesfield, in the County Palatine of Chester*, 2 vols. London, 1877-1880.

Earwaker, J.P. *The History of the Ancient Parish of Sandbach*. 1890.

Elliott, Dollye McAllister. "Brythonic & Cymric Celts," *English Genealogist*, 5-8 (1977), 173ff.

Encyclopædia Britannica.

The English Baronettage, 3 vols. London: Tho. Wotton, 1741.

Evans, Charles [F.H.] "Ancestor Table," *TG*, 4 (1983), 230-265.

Evans, Charles F.H. "Dammartin," *The Genealogists' Magazine*, 15 (1965-1967), 53-64.

Evans, Charles F.H. "Two Mortimer Notes," *NEHGR*, 116 (1962), 13-17.

"Extracts from the Plea Rolls: Pleas of the County of Chester Before Henry de Percy, Justice of Chester, on the Tuesday after Easter, 4 H. IV," *CHS*, 16 (1895), 40.

Eyton, Rev. R.W. *Antiquities of Shropshire*, 12 vols. London: John Russell Smith, 1854-1860.

Faris, David. *Plantagenet Ancestry of Seventeenth-Century Colonists*, 1st ed. Baltimore: Genealogical Publishing Co., Inc., 1996.

Faris, David. *Plantagenet Ancestry of Seventeenth-Century Colonists*, 2nd ed. Boston: New England Historic Genealogical Society, 1999.

Faris, David, and Douglas Richardson. "The Parents of Agatha, Wife of Edward the Exile," *NEHGR*, 152 (1998), 224-235.

Farrer, William, ed. *Final Concords of the County of Lancaster from the Original Chirographs, or Feet of Fines*. The Record Society for the Publication of Original Documents Relating to Lancashire and Cheshire, vols. 39 & 46. 1899-1903.

Farrer, William, and J. Brownbill, eds. *The Victoria History of the County of Lancaster*, 8 vols. London: Archibald Constable and Company Limited, 1906 plus.

Fletcher, W.G.D. "The Pedigree of Lingen," *Transactions of the Shropshire Archæological and Natural History Society*, 3rd series, 10 (1910), Miscellanea i-ii.

Forrest, H.E. "Some Old Shropshire Houses and Their Owners: Whitton," *Transactions of the Shropshire Archæological and Natural History Society*, 4th series, 5 (1915), 169ff.

Fosbroke, Thomas Dudley. *Berkeley Manuscripts: Abstracts Extracts of Smyth's Lives of the Berkeleys, Illustrative of Ancient Manne and the Constitution; Including all the Pedigrees in that Ancient Manuscript*. London: John Bowyer Nichols and Son, 1821.

Foster, Joseph. *Pedigrees of the County Families of England - Lancashire*. London, 1873.

The Four Visitations of Berkshire, ed. W. Harry Rylands. London: The Harleian Society, 1907.

Fowler, G. Herbert. "De St. Walery," *The Genealogist*, new series, 30 (1913-1914), 1-17.

Fraser, Antonia. *The Wives of Henry VIII*. New York: Alfred A. Knopf, 1993.

Gardner, David E., Derek Harland, and Frank Smith, compilers. *A Genealogical Atlas of England and Wales*. Salt Lake City: Deseret Book Company, 1960.

Glover, Robert, William Flower, William Fellows, Thomas Benolte and Thomas Chaloner. *The Visitation of Cheshire in the Year 1580, including those from the Visitation of Cheshire Made in the Year 1566, with an Appendix Containing the Visitation of a Part of Cheshire in the Year 1533, and a Fragment of the Visitation of the City of Chester in the Year 1591*, ed. John Paul Rylands. London: Harleian Society, 1882.

Gower, Granville Leveson. "The Pedygre of William Seylyard of Delaware in the parishe of Brasted in Kent, Esquire," *MGH*, Second Series, 1 (1886), 7-11.

Grimble, Ian. *The Harington Family*. New York: St. Martin's Press, n.d.

Guppy, Henry Brougham. *Homes of Family Names in Great Britain*. Baltimore: Genealogical Publishing Company, 1968.

Hall, Hamilton. "Note on the Family of Butler, Afterwards Earls of Ormonde," *The Genealogist*, new series, 15 (1909), 73-78.

Hansen, Col. Charles M. "The Barons of Wodhull with Observations on the Ancestry of George Elkinton, Emigrant to New Jersey," *TG*, 7-8 (1986-87), 4-127.

Hansen, Charles M. "The Descent of James[1] Claypoole of Philadelphia from Edward I," *TAG*, 67 (1992), 97-107.

Hansen, James L. "The Ancestry of Joan Legard, Grandmother of the Rev. William[1] Skepper/Skipper of Boston, Massachusetts," *TAG*, 69 (1994), 129-139.

Harvey, William Marsh. *The History and Antiquities of the Hundred of Willey in the County of Bedford*. London, 1872-1878.

Hey, David. *The Oxford Guide to Family History*. Oxford: Oxford University Press, 1993.

Hedley, W. Percy. *Northumberland Families*, 2 vols. The Society of Antiquaries of Newcastle Upon Tyne, 1968.

Historischer Atlas der Schweiz, herausgeben von Hektor Ammann und Karl Schib, 2nd ed. Aarau: Verlag H.R. Sauerländer & Co., 1958.

Hoff, Henry B. "*Plantagenet Ancestry of Seventeenth-Century Colonists...by David Faris*" [book review], *TAG*, 71 (1996), 187.

Holland, Bernard. *The Lancashire Hollands*. London: John Murray, 1917.

Hornyold-Strickland, Henry. *Biographical Sketches of the Members of Parliament of Lancashire (1290-1550)*. Chetham Society (vol. 93), 1935.

Horrest, H.E. "Some Old Shropshire Houses and Their Owners," *Transactions of the Shropshire Archæological and Natural History Society*, 4th ser., 7 (1918-1919), 131-158ff.

"The House of Scotsborough, Near Tenby," *Archæologia Cambrensis*, Sixth Series, 6 (1906), 84-86 [photocopies of these pages only].

Howard, Joseph Jackson, and Joseph Lemuel Chester, eds. *The Visitation of London, Anno Domini 1633, 1634, and 1635*. London: The Harleian Society [vol. 15], 1880.

Humphrey-Smith, Cecil R., ed. *The Phillimore Atlas and Index of Parish Registers.* Chichester, Sussex: Phillimore, 1984.

Humphrey-Smith, C[ecil] R. "The Robessart Tomb in Westminster Abbey," *Family History*, 2 (1964-1965), 143-149.

Hutchinson, Harold F. *Edward II, 1284-1327.* New York: Barnes & Noble Books, 1971.

Irvine, W. Ferguson. "The Early Stanleys," *Transactions of the Historic Society of Lancashire and Cheshire*, 105 (1963), 45-68.

Ives, E.W., ed. *Letters and Accounts of William Brereton of Malpas.* Record Society of Lancashire and Cheshire [vol. 116], 1976.

Jacobus, Donald Lines. "Ancestry of Obadiah and Mary Bruen," *TAG*, 26 (1950), 12-25.

Jenkins, R.T., ed. *The Dictionary of Welsh Biography Down to 1940*, Under the Auspices of the Honorable Society of Cymmrodorion. London, 1959.

Jetté, René. "Is the Mystery of the Origin of Agatha, Wife of Edward the *Exile*, Finally Solved?" *NEHGR*, 150 (1996), 417-432.

Jobe, Bill. "Murder in the Family Tree," *The Searcher*, 33 (1996), 200-202.

Jones, Frances. "The Dynasty of Powys," *The Transactions of the Honourable Society of Cymmrodorion* (1958), 23-32.

Jones, Francis. *The Princes and Principality of Wales.* Cardiff: University of Wales Press, 1969.

Jones, Gwyn. *A History of the Vikings*, rev. ed. Oxford: Oxford University Press, 1984.

Jones, Morris Charles. *The Feudal Barons of Powys.* London: J. Russell Smith, 1868.

Knights of Edward I, vol. 5. Harleian Society, 1932.

Lea, J. Henry. "The English Ancestry of the Families of Batt and Byley of Salisbury, Mass.: Batt Genealogy," *NEHGR*, 52 (1898), 46-51.

Leese, T. Anna. *Blood Royal: Issue of the Kings and Queens of Medieval England 1066-1399, the Normans and Plantagenets.* Bowie, Md.: Heritage Books, Inc., 1996.

Leighton, Stanley. "Wattlesborough Castle," *Transactions of the Shropshire Archæological and Natural History Society*, Fourth Series, 3 (1913), 283-290.

LeStrange, Hamon. *LeStrange Records, a Chronicle of the Early LeStranges of Norfolk and the March of Wales, A.D. 1100-1310, with the Lines of Knockin and Blackmere Continued to the Extinction.* London: Longmans, Green and Co., 1916.

L'Strange, J.K, "The Barony of Strange of Blackmere," *Notes and Queries*, 199 (1954), 98.

Lloyd, Rev. W.V. "Description of the Armorial Insignia of the Vaughans of Llwydiarth," *Collections Historical and Archaeological Relating to Montgomeryshire*, 14 (1881), 355-396.

Lofthouse, Jessica. *Lancashire's Old Families.* London: Robert Hale, 1972.

"The Lords of Stowheath Manor," *The Wolverhampton Antiquary*, 2 (1945), 103-107.

Maclagan, Michael. "The Ancestry of the English Beaumonts," *Studies in Genealogy and Family History in Tribute to Charles Evans on the Occasion of His Eightieth Birthday* (Salt Lake City: Association for the Promotion of Scholarship in Genealogy, Ltd., 1989), 190-196.

Maclean, Sir John. "Notice of Earthworks in the Parish of English Bicknor," *Transactions of the Bristol & Gloucestershire Archæological Society*, 4 (1879-1880), 313-319.

Maddicott, J.R. "Thomas of Lancaster and Sir Robert Holland: a Study in Noble Patronage," *The English Historical Review*, 340 (1971), 449-472.

Marshall, George W. *The Genealogist's Guide.* Baltimore: Genealogical Publishing Co., Inc., 1980.

Memorials of the Duttons of Dutton in Cheshire. London and Chester, 1901.

Meisel, Janet. *Barons of the Welsh Frontier: The Corbet, Pantulf, and Fitz Warin Families, 1066-1272.* Lincoln: University of Nebraska Press, 1980.

Messenger, Commander A.W.B. "The Arms of Mortimer," *Family History*, 1 (1962-1963), 140-149.

Metcalfe, Walter C., ed. *The Visitation of Northamptonshire Made in 1564 and 1618-19, with Northamptonshire Pedigrees*. London: Mitchell and Hughes, 1887.

Montague-Smith, Patrick W. "An Unrecorded Line of Descent from King Edward I of England with Some Early Settled American Descendants," *TG*, 5 (1984), 131-157.

Moor, C. *Knights of Edward I*, 5 vols. London: Harleian Society, 1929-1932.

Moorshead, Halver. "The Battle of Agincourt Honor Roll," *Family Chronicle* (March-April 1997), 27-35.

Morris, Joseph. *Shropshire Genealogies*, 10 vols. MS in Shrewsbury Public Library, Shropshire [FHC microfilm, West Los Angeles].

Mortimer, Richard. *Angevin England, 1154-1258*. Oxford: Blackwell, 1994.

Nash, T[readway Russell]. *Collections for the History of Worcestershire*, 2 vols. London: John Russell, 1781-1782 [Rare Book Room, Los Angeles Public Library].

National Geographic Atlas of the World, 6th ed. Washington, D.C.: National Geographic Society, 1990.

Newman, Roger Chatterton. *Brian Boru, King of Ireland*. Dublin: Anvil Books, 1983.

Newton, Lady E. *The House of Lyme*. New York: G.P. Putnam's Sons, 1917.

Nicholas, Thomas. *Annals and Antiquities of the Counties and County Families of Wales*, 2nd ed., 2 vols. Baltimore: Genealogical Publishing Co., 1991.

Nichols, John. *The History and Antiquites of the County of Leicestershire*, vol. 2, part 1. London, 1795 [Rare Book Room, Los Angeles Public Library].

Nicholls, John H. "The House of Rurik," *Omnibus*, 14 (1993), 19-20.

Nickerson, Herman, Jr. "Griffith Bowen of Wales and Massachusetts," *The Connecticut Nutmegger*, 19 (1986-1987), 588-596.

Norr, Vernon M. *Some Early English Pedigrees*. Arlington, Virginia, 1968.

O'Hart, John. *Irish Pedigrees; or, the Origin and Stem of the Irish Nation*, 5th ed., 2 vols. Baltimore: Genealogical Publishing Co., Inc., 1976.

Ordnance Survey Atlas of England and Wales, Quarter Inch to the Mile. Southampton: Ordnance Survey Office, [1929?].

Ormerod, George. *The History of the County Palatine and City of Chester*, 3 vols. London: Lackington, Hughes, Harding, Mavor, and Jones, 1819.

Ormerod, George. *The History of the County Palatine and City of Chester*, 2nd ed. rev. by Thomas Helsby, 3 vols. London: George Routledge and Sons, 1882.

Orpen, Goddard Henry. *Ireland under the Normans*, 4 vols. Oxford: Clarendon Press, 1911-1920.

Paget, Gerald. *The Lineage and Ancestry of H.R.H. Prince Charles, Prince of Wales*, 2 vols. Baltimore: Genealogical Publishing Co., Inc., 1977.

Paget, Guy, and Lionel Irvine. *Leicestershire*. London: Robert Hale Limited, 1950.

Parsons, John C. "Eleanor of Castile and the Countess of Ulster," *Genealogists' Magazine*, 20 (1980-1982), 335-339.

"Pedigree: Honford of Honford," *Proceedings of the Historic Society of Lancashire and Cheshire*, 2 (1849-1850), 54.

Pedigrees Made at the Visitation of Cheshire, 1613, taken by Richard St. George and Henry St. George, ed. Sir George J. Armytage and J. Paul Rylands. London: The Harleian Society, 1909.

Phillimore, W.P.W., ed. *The Visitation of the County of Worcester Made in the Year 1569*. London: The Harleian Society, 1888.

"Plea Rolls of the Reign of Edward I," *CHS*, pt. 1, 6 (1885), 57-211.

Pole, Ralph. [Charleton], *Notes and Queries*, 106 (Oct. 18, 1902), 317-318.

Pollard, William. *The Stanleys of Knowsley*. London: Frederick Warne and Co., 1869.

Poole, Keith B. *Historic Heraldic Families*. Newton Abbot, Devon: David & Charles, 1975.

Procter, Rev. W.G. "Notes on the Hesketh Pedigree," *Transactions of the Historic Society of Lancashire and Cheshire*, 62 [n.s. 26] (1910), 58-66.

Raines, F.R., ed. *The Visitation of the County Palatine of Lancaster Made in the Year 1567, by William Flower, Esq., Norroy King of Arms*. Lancaster: The Chetham Society [vol. 81], 1870.

Reade, Aleyn Lyell. *Audley Pedigrees*. 1929.

Reed, Paul C. "Another Look at Joan de Harley: Will Her Real Descendants Please Rise?" *TG*, 10 (1989 [1994]), 35-72.

Renaud, Frank. *Contributions Towards a History of the Ancient Parish of Prestbury, in Cheshire*. Manchester: Chetham Society (vol. 97), 1876.

Richardson, Douglas. "A Royal Ancestry for Mary (Cooke) Talcott of Hartford, Connecticut," *NEHGR*, 148 (1994), 255-258.

Roberts, Gary Boyd. *Ancestors of American Presidents*, First Authoritative Edition. Santa Clarita: Carl Boyer, 3rd, 1995.

Roberts, Gary Boyd. *The Royal Descents of 500 Immigrants to the of American Colonies or the United States*. Baltimore: Genealogical Publishing Co., Inc., 1993.

Robinson, Charles J. *A History of the Castles of Herefordshire and Their Lords*. London: Longmans & Co., 1869.

Robinson, Charles J. *A History of the Mansions and Manors of Herefordshire*. London: Longmans and Co., 1873.

Roskell, J.S., Linda Clark, and Carole Rawcliffe. *The History of Parliament: The House of Commons 1386-1421*, 4 vols. Stroud, Gloucestershire: Alan Sutton Publishing Ltd., 1993.

Round, J.H. "The Families of St. John and of Port," *The Genealogist*, new series, 16 (1899-1900), 1-13.

Round, J.H. "The Heirs of Richard de Lucy," *The Genealogist*, n.s., 15(1898-1899), 129-133.

Round, J. Horace. *The King's Sergeants and Officers of State with Their Coronation Services*. London: James Nisbet and Co., Ltd., 1911.

Round, J. Horace. *Peerage and Pedigree*, 2 vols. Baltimore: Genealogical Publishing Company, 1970.

Rubincam, Milton. "A Critique of Spanish Genealogy: The Ancestry of Sancha (de Ayala) Blount," *Studies in Genealogy and Family History in Tribute to Charles Evans on the Occasion of His Eightieth Birthday* (Salt Lake City: Association for the Promotion of Scholarship in Genealogy, Ltd., Occasional Publication No. 2, 1989), 263-271.

Rye, Walter. *Records and Record Searching*. London: George Allen, 1897.

Rylands, J. Paul. "A Vellum Pedigree-roll of the Family of Danyers, *alias* Danyell, of the County of Chester," *The Genealogist*, new series, 32 (1915-1916), 7-17.

Rylands, W. Harry, ed. *Staffordshire Pedigrees, Based on the Visitation...by William Dugdale...in the Year 1663-1664*. London: Harleian Society, 1912.

Sanders, I.J. *English Baronies, a Study of Their Origin and Descent 1086-1327*. Oxford: Clarendon Press, 1960.

The Scots Peerage, 9 vols., ed. James Balfour Paul. Edinburgh: David Douglas, 1904-1914.

Scott, Ronald McNair. *Robert the Bruce, King of Scots*. New York: Peter Bedrick Books, 1989.

Setzekorn, William D. "Queen Margaret's Chapel: a Personal Sanctuary for All Those by the Name of Margaret," *Omnibus*, 12 (1990), 141-142.

Shaw, William A[rthur]. *The Knights of England*, 2 vols. London: Sherratt and Hughes, 1906.

Sheppard, Walter Lee Jr. "Connections of Archbishop William la Zouche (†1352)," *TAG*, 49 (1973), 1-12.

Sheppard, Walter Lee Jr. "An Hitherto Unnoted Descent from King Henry I," *NEHGR*, 116 (1962), 278-280.

Sheppard, Walter Lee Jr. "Joan, Princess of Wales, Daughter of King John: Ancestress to Bulkeley, James, Mellowes, Welby, Whittingham, Haugh, and St. John-Whiting Families," *TAG*, 35 (1959), 29-33.

Sheppard, Walter L[ee] Jr. "Two Corrections for the New Complete Peerage," *The Genealogists' Magazine*, 13 (1959-1961), 173-175.

Sheppard, Walter Lee Jr. "Three Generations from Henry Fitz Roger, Note II — Holand," *NGSQ*, 60 (1972), 25-26.

Sorley, Merrow E. "William de Lichfield," *The Genealogists' Magazine*, 15 (1965-1968), 117-120.

Stames, R.G.F. "Sir Guy de Brian, K.G.," *The Devonshire Association for the Advancement of Science Literature and Art: Report and Transactions*, 92 (1960), 249.277.

Stargardt, J.A. *Europäische Stammtafeln*, neue folge, 13 vols. Marburg: J.A. Stargardt, 1978-1987.

Stuart, Roderick W. *Royalty for Commoners*, 2nd ed. Baltimore: Genealogical Publishing Co., Inc., 1992.

Swynnerton, Rev. Charles. "The Earlier Swynnertons of Eccleshall," *CHS*, new series, 3 (1903), 73-97.

Taylor, Nathaniel L., and Todd A. Farmerie, "Notes on the Ancestry of Sancha de Ayala," *NEHGR*, 152 (1998), 36-48.

Thompson, Neil D. "Abell - Cotton - Mainwaring: Maternal Ancestry of Robert Abell of Weymouth and Rehoboth, Mass.," *The Genealogist*, 5 (1984), 158-171.

Thoroton, Robert. *The Antiquities of Nottinghamshire*. London: Henry Mortlock, 1677 [Rare Book Room, Los Angeles Public Library].

Tildesley, M.L. "Sir Thomas Browne: His Skull, Portraits, and Ancestry," *Biometrika*, 15 (1923), 1-76ter.

Turton, W.H. "Notes and Queries: Early Ancestry of the Lords Grandison," *The Genealogist*, 30 (1913-1914), 144.

Tyerman, Christopher. *Who's Who In Early Medieval England (1066-1272)*. London: Shepheard-Walwyn, 1996.

The Victoria County History of Leicestershire, ed. William Page, W.G. Hoskins and R.B. Pugh, 5 vols. London, 1907-1914.

The Victoria History of the County of Buckingham, vol. 4, ed. William Page. London: The St. Catherine Press, 1927.

The Victoria History of the County of Lancaster, ed. William Farrer and J. Brownbill, 8 vols. London: James Street, 1906-1914.

The Victoria History of the County of Rutland, 2 vols. plus index. London: Archibald Constable and Company Limited, 1908; The St. Catherine Press, 1935, and Oxford University Press Humphrey Milford, 1936.

The Visitation of Cheshire [1533, 1566, 1580, 1591], ed. John Paul Rylands. London: Harleian Society, 1882.

The Visitation of the County of Buckingham Made in 1634 by John Philipot [et al.], ed. W. Harry Rylands. London: The Harleian Society, 1909.

The Visitation of the County of Leicester in the Year 1619, taken by William Camden, ed. John Fetherston. London: The Harleian Society, 1870.

The Visitation of London, Anno Domini 1633, 1634 and 1635, made by Sir Henry St. George, ed. Joseph Jackson Howard and Joseph Lemuel Chester, 2 vols. London: The Harleian Society, 1880-1883.

The Visitation of Shropshire Taken in the Year 1623 by Robert Tresswell...with Additions from...1569 and 1584, 2 vols., ed. George Grazebrook and John Paul Rylands. London: The Harleian Society, 1889.

The Visitation of the County of Worcester Made in the Year 1569, ed. W.P.W. Phillimore. London: The Harleian Society, 1888.

Wagner, Sir Anthony. *English Ancestry*. London: Oxford University Press, 1961.

Wagner, Sir Anthony. *Pedigree and Progress; Essays in the Genealogical Interpretation of History*. Phillimore & Co., Ltd., 1975.

Washington, George S.H.L. "Correspondence," *Genealogists' Magazine*, 17 (March 1974), 503.

Washington, S.H. Lee. "The Arms of the de Lancasters, Lords of Kendal," *NEHGR*, 96 (1942), 93-94.

Washington, S.H. Lee. "Genealogical Research in England: The Early History of the Stricklands of Sizergh, Ancestors of the Carletons of Massachusetts and the Washingtons of Virginia," *NEHGR*, 96 (1942), 99ff.

Watney, Vernon James. *The Wallop Family and Their Ancestry*, 4 vols. Oxford, 1928.

Watson, G.W. "Basset and Grey," *MGH*, fifth series, 8 (1932-1934), 202-206.

Watson, G.W. "The Bohuns of Midhurst," *The Genealogist*, new series, 28 (1911-1912), 1ff.

Watson, G.W. "Ormond and Kildare," *MGH*, fifth series, 8 (1932-1934), 229-231.

Wedgwood, Josiah C., M.P. *History of Parliament; Biographies of the Members of the Commons House, 1439-1509*. London: His Majesty's Stationery Office, 1936.

Weir, Janet D. *'Laugharneshire' Connections, a Family Memoir*. 1995.

Weis, Frederick Lewis. *Ancestral Roots of Certain American Colonists Who Came to America before 1700; The Lineage of Alfred the Great, Charlemagne, Malcolm of Scotland, Robert the Strong, and Some of Their Descendants*, 7th ed. with additions and corrections by Walter Lee Sheppard, Jr., assisted by David Faris. Baltimore: Genealogical Publishing Co., Inc., 1992.

Weis, Frederick Lewis. *Ancestral Roots of Sixty Colonists Who Came to New England Between 1623 and 1650; The Lineage of Alfred the Great, Charlemagne, Malcolm of Scotland, Robert the Strong, and Some of Their Descendants*, 6th ed. with additions and corrections by Walter Lee Sheppard, Jr., assisted by David Faris. Baltimore: Genealogical Publishing Co., Inc., 1988.

Weis, Frederick Lewis, with Walter Lee Sheppard, Jr. and David Faris. *The Magna Charta Sureties, 1215: The Barons Named in the Magna Charta, 1215 and Some of Their Descendants who Settled in America During the Early Colonial Years*, 5th ed. Baltimore: Genealogical Publishing Co., Inc., 1999.

Weyman, Henry T. "Shropshire Members of Parliament," *Transactions of the Shropshire Archæological and Natural History Society*, Fourth Series, 10 (1925-1926), 1ff.

White, Geoffrey N. "Financial Administration under Henry I," *Transactions of the Royal Historical Society*, 4th series, 8 (1925), 56-78.

White, Geoffrey N. "The First House of Bellême," *Transactions of the Royal Historical Society*, 4th series, 22 (1940), 67-99.

White, Robert. *Worksop, "The Dukery," and Sherwood Forest*. Worksop, 1875.

Whitmore, J.B. *A Genealogical Guide*. London: Walford Brothers, 1953.

Williams, Richard. *Montgomeryshire Worthies*, 2nd ed. Newtown, Wales [1894].

Wolfram, Herwig. *History of the Goths*, trans. Thomas J. Dunlap. Berkeley: University of California Press, 1988.

Wrottesley, George. "Extracts from the Plea Rolls of the Reign of Edward III," *CHS*, 12 (1891), 1-173.

Wrottesley, George. "Extracts from the Plea Rolls of the Reigns of Richard II. and Henry IV.," *CHS*, 15 (1894), 3-126.

Wrottesley, George. "Pedigrees from the Plea Rolls," *The Genealogist*, New Series, 8 (1891-1892), 33ff.

Wyatt, Stanley Charles. *Cheneys and Wyatts, a Brief History in Two Parts.* 1959.

§ § §

AL3	- Boyer's *Ancestral Lines*, 3rd ed.
AR7	- Weis' *Ancestral Roots*, 7th ed.
BP	- *Burke's Peerage* (1999)
CHS	- *Collections for a History of Staffordshire*
CP	- *The Complete Peerage*
EB	- *Encyclopædia Britannica*
EG	- *English Genealogist*
EHR	- *The English Historical Review*
GM	- *Genealogists' Magazine*
MCS5	- Weis' *Magna Charta Sureties*, 5th ed.
MGH	- *Miscellanea Genealogica et Heraldica*
NEHGR	- *The New England Historical and Genealogical Register*
PA1	- Faris' *Plantagenet Ancestry*, 1st ed.
PA2	- Faris' *Plantagenet Ancestry*, 2nd ed.
SP	- *Scots Peerage*
TAG	- *The American Genealogist*
TCN	- *The Connecticut Nutmegger*
TG	- *The Genealogist [New York and Salt Lake City]*

§ § §

PLACE INDEX

Most of the following place names are in England or France. Places were indexed under both local names, and counties and departments or provinces if appropriate. Many of the names are not spelled in accordance with modern usage, having been copied from a variety of sources.

§ § §

This index is alphabetized without regard to prefixes or titles. Many of the names have been copied from a variety of sources and are spelled inconsistently. Some Welsh names not significant to the ancestry of certain Americans are not indexed. Accent marks and letter combinations distinct in foreign languages have not been given special treatment herein.

INDEX OF NAMES 341

§ § §